Explaining Financial Crises

Hohenheimer Volkswirtschaftliche Schriften

Band 53

PETER LANG
Frankfurt am Main · Berlin · Bern · Bruxelles · New York · Oxford · Wien

Marc Peter Radke

Explaining Financial Crises

A Cyclical Approach

PETER LANG
Frankfurt am Main · Berlin · Bern · Bruxelles · New York · Oxford · Wien

Bibliographic Information published by Die Deutsche Bibliothek
Die Deutsche Bibliothek lists this publication in the Deutsche Nationalbibliografie; detailed bibliographic data is available in the internet at <http://dnb.ddb.de>.

Zugl.: Hohenheim, Univ., Diss., 2005

D 100
ISSN 0721-3085
ISBN 3-631-54350-6
US-ISBN 0-8204-7777-X

www.peterlang.de

To My Family
Barbara and Jan-Luca

All economic events, by their very nature, are motivated by crowd psychology ... Men think in herds; ... they go mad in herds, while they only recover their senses slowly, and one by one.

— Charles Mackay, Preface to the second edition of *Memoirs of Extraordinary Popular Delusions and the Madness of Crowds*, 1852, cited in Agénor (2004), p. 292.

Preface

After having completed my doctoral thesis which was approved by the Faculty of Business, Economics and Social Sciences at the University of Hohenheim in June 2005, I would like to express my gratitude to a number of persons and institutions without whose help this "novel" never could have been written.

Firstly, I would like to thank my wife Barbara Radke for her wonderful, heartfelt emotional support, for her patience, and for her understanding for all those late night and weekend working sessions throughout the creation of this book. Moreover, I am deeply indebted to our son Jan-Luca Radke who had to do lots of playground sessions without his father. A special thanks belongs to my parents Renate and Dietrich Radke who helped us a lot during one of the hardest parts of our life. Furthermore, I am grateful to Ela and Jens Friderichs who have given lectures to me and to my family, and hopefully will give us further lectures in the future on the mysteries of life and how to cope with them.

I would like to thank my supervisor Prof. Dr. Harald Hagemann for his professional support. He provided me a very friendly, liberal, and stimulating environment for research. Furthermore, I am deeply indebted to his personal support, and to his ever-human behaviour which motivated me in very difficult circumstances to finish my doctoral thesis. I am also very grateful to my second supervisor Prof. Dr. Hans-Michael Trautwein who supported my work with valuable suggestions and comments at our meetings in Hohenheim and Oldenburg. Moreover, I am deeply indebted to his personal assistance and to his loyalty. I am also indebted to Prof. Joaquim Pinto de Andrade for his encouraging comments and useful hints at our meetings in Hohenheim, Oldenburg and Brasília. Furthermore, I am very thankful to Prof. Dr. Heinz-Peter Spahn for assisting in the examination and administration procedure.

Many thanks go to my former and current colleagues for their emotional support and for the nice work atmosphere they provided at the Department of Economics at the University of Hohenheim. Particularly, I would like to thank (in alphabetical order) Dr. Tone Arnold, Andreja Benkovic, Isabell Benignus, Anand Chopra, Christine Eisenbraun, Andreas Findeis, PD Dr. Björn Frank, Oliver Frör, Dr. Daniel Hartmann, Michael Knittel, Oliver Kreh, Dr. Peter Kühnl, Ulrike Lehr, Dr. Jörg Naeve, Dr. Matthias Rösch, Ralf Rukwid, Oliver Schelling, Rosemarie Schlecht, Dr. Olaf Schneider, Deborah Schöller Markus Schreyer, Prof. Dr. Ulrich Schwalbe, Dr. Stephan Seiter, Sybille Sobczak, Dr. Udo Vullhorst, and Carsten Wander. Especially, I am indebted to my colleague and friend Dr. Karin Knottenbauer for her emotional and professional support.

I would like to thank the "Landesgraduiertenförderung des Landes Baden-Württemberg" for having been granted a generous scholarship for two and a half years.

I am also grateful to the "Stiftung Ausbildung, Fort- und Weiterbildung der Landesbank Baden-Württemberg" for having been granted a generous financial support for the publication of this book.

Mit Unterstützung der
Stiftung
Landesbank Baden-Württemberg
LB≡BW

Let me finally mention that this book has been typed with LaTeX 2ε. I would like to express my thanks to all those people who have created and continuously updated this nice and reliable software.

Marc Peter Radke
Stuttgart-Hohenheim, August 2005

Contents

List of Figures

List of Tables

Chapter 1

Introduction and Overview

1.1 History vs. Theory

Financial crises are nothing out of the ordinary. The history of financial crises, being at least as old as economic science, if not older, points out that financial crises, both in industrial and in developing countries, are a recurrent, or cyclical phenomenon.[1] Economic history has been characterized by a permanent change between tranquil periods with balanced economic development and smoothly functioning financial markets, and periods of severe disruptions in financial markets, having been accompanied by collapses of a large number of asset prices, sharp rises in interest rates, widespread bankruptcies among business firms and financial institutions, large drops in output, persistent low or even negative growth, high inflation, (debt-)deflation, financial disintermediation, high unemployment, rising income inequality, and political instability. It has to be emphasized however, that not all financial crises in the past were *systemic*, i.e. not all crises were associated with real economic downturns, widespread bankruptcies, and excess volatility in the general price level. Rather, there arose also so-called *spurious* financial crises which were characterized by collapses of asset prices in particular financial markets and isolated bankruptcies, but which did not cause real macroeconomic contractions. Though the following analysis contains an explicit distinction between spurious and systemic financial crises, the thematic focus lies primarily on the causes and consequences of systemic financial crises as they are associated with much larger reductions in economic welfare, having been only exceeded in the past by wars and natural disasters, than spurious financial crises.

Notwithstanding the fact that there have been permanent changes between tranquil and financial distress periods in the past, the frequency of systemic financial crises has been very irregular. For example, financial crises in the 20th century were clustered in four main periods. The first period from the late 1920s until the early 1930s was characterized by a worldwide international financial crisis both in industrialized countries (as e.g. in Austria, Finland, Germany, Japan, Norway, United Kingdom, United States) and in developing countries (as e.g. in Argentina, Brazil, Chile) which culminated in the Great Depression. The second wave of financial crises erupted in the early 1980s in the developing world after the breakdown of the Bretton Woods system, having been followed by the international debt crisis which led, especially in Latin America (as e.g. in Argentina, Chile, Mexico, Uruguay), to a state of depression in the Third World for almost one decade. The third

[1] For a detailed overview of the history of financial crises from 1618-1998, see e.g. Kindleberger (2000).

wave of financial crises in the mid-1980s and early 1990s emerged in the industrialized world (as e.g. in Finland 1990, Japan 1992, Norway 1987, Sweden 1992, U.S. 1984), having been accompanied by severe real economic downturns. The financial crisis in Japan in 1992, having been triggered by the stock market crash in 1990, is extraordinary as it has been followed by a still-lasting deep depression, deflationary spirals, and a liquidity trap situation, resembling very closely the macroeconomic situation of lots of countries during the Great Depression period in the 1930s. The fourth wave of financial crises in the mid-1990s and in the late-1990s erupted primarily in emerging market countries (Mexico 1994, Asia 1997/1998, Russia 1998, Brazil 1998) and was followed by long-lasting and deep recessions.

Howbeit the incidence of financial crises has been very irregular in the past, both historical case studies and long-term econometric studies with large country samples point out that systemic financial crises display similar characteristics regarding the behaviour of lots of economic variables before, during, and after the outbreak of a financial crisis. These stylized facts can be summarized in the following six propositions.

Firstly, financial crises are inseparably linked to business cycle fluctuations, where the outbreak of a financial crisis generally coincides with the peak of a business cycle. Business cycles which are associated with the occurrence of financial crises are generally subject to a much higher amplitude of all economic variables than tranquil time business cycles which are not associated with financial crises. As a result, financial crises are generally associated with excessive boom-bust cycles in goods and financial markets.

Secondly, the boom phase of a business cycle giving rise to a financial crisis generally begins with an improvement in national and international lending conditions (increasing credit supply, low nominal and real interest rates) being caused by a sudden rise in profit expectations. The stylized facts clearly point out that both the increased access to financial markets and the rise in profit expectations are positively correlated with the introduction of macroeconomic stabilization programmes, trade and financial liberalization policies, and with the emergence of new technology regimes. Furthermore, there is strong empirical evidence, especially in the post Bretton Woods era (1973 until today), that domestic and international financial liberalization policies are positively correlated with the occurrence of financial crises.

Thirdly, rising profit expectations and increasing access to financial markets induce a "cumulative upward process"[2] in goods and financial markets, being characterized by an investment boom, accelerating GDP growth, and rising stock market valuations. The investment boom is associated with a lending boom causing a general rise in indebtedness with business firms and financial institutions both in domestic and in foreign currency. On the supply side, the lending boom is driven by a general monetary expansion resulting from an increase in domestic bank lending which is facilitated by easy monetary conditions. Regarding developing and emerging market countries, domestic monetary expansions are mainly driven by large capital inflows which are intermediated by domestic banking systems, where domestic banks generally borrow in foreign currency, and lend

[2]Cumulative processes causing an economic upswing, i.e. an expansion in real economic activity, as well as relaxing financial market conditions, are labelled as cumulative "upward" processes in the following, whereas cumulative processes engendering an economic downturn, i.e. a contraction in real economic activity, as well as tightening financial market conditions, are labelled as cumulative "downward" processes.

to domestic agents in domestic currency. These capital inflow-induced lending booms are generally amplified by the existence of fixed exchange rate regimes, implying however an increase in financial instability as implicit or explicit exchange rate guarantees make most borrowers and lenders not to hedge against exchange rate risk. On the demand side, the lending boom is stimulated by profit expectations growing much faster than actual profits, implying that the growth in investment has to be increasingly financed by external debt due to a widening gap between earnings and expenditures. The overall rise in domestic and foreign indebtedness during the expansion phase is generally considered to be sustainable as profit expectations are self-fulfilling, i.e. a rise in expected profits induces a rise in investment, output and finally in actual profits, validating the initial increase in expectations, and inducing a further rise in profit expectations.

Fourthly, profit expectations generally tend to become increasingly unrealistic in the late boom phase due to self-reinforcing herding behaviour of investors, driving the economy into a state of "irrational exuberance", and giving rise to an asset bubble as expected asset returns increasingly deviate from actual returns. The growing divergence between expected and actual profits is mainly due to a switch from a rational, fundamental data-based expectation formation scheme, to a general market sentiment-based expectation formation scheme. Growing indebtedness based on unrealistic profit expectations leads to an overall rise in financial fragility as interest payments, as well as repayment of debt, grow faster than actual profits, implying a steady decline in liquidity and solvency positions of business firms and financial institutions. Moreover, profits, liquidity and solvency positions are reduced by rising interest rates due to an overproportional rise in demand for debt finance, and by rising domestic inflation leading to a deteriorating export performance via a real overvaluation of the domestic currency.

Fifthly, financial instability is revealed at the peak of the business cycle by beginning failures of highly-indebted business firms and financial institutions, giving rise to a burst of the stock market bubble, sharply rising interest rates due to increasing risk premia, a real macroeconomic contraction, and widespread bankruptcies among firms and banks due to large-scale domestic and foreign debt withdrawals, ending up in a severe domestic banking crisis. If the stock of foreign exchange reserves under fixed exchange rate regimes does not suffice to meet all capital outflows (foreign debt withdrawals and capital flight by domestic residents), both the domestic banking crisis and the real economic downturn are amplified, in case of the existence of a large foreign debt stock, by the occurrence of a currency crisis, ending up in a systemic "twin crisis" (being defined as the simultaneous occurrence of a banking and a currency crisis) due to a nominal and real appreciation of the foreign debt stock, and owing to high exchange rate stabilization-induced domestic interest rates.

Sixthly, the outbreak of a financial crisis induces a "cumulative downward process"[3] in goods and financial markets, being driven by collapsing profit expectations which very often undershoot due to self-reinforcing pessimistic herding behaviour. Sharply declining profit expectations induce a self-fulfilling and long-lasting real macroeconomic contraction as the expectations-led collapse of investment demand causes a fall in output, and finally in actual profits, validating the initial decline in expected profits, and inducing a further reduction in expected profits. In extreme cases, the cumulative downward process causes deflationary spirals, leading to a further macroeconomic contraction by a rise in real

[3]For this terminology, see footnote 2.

interest rates. Economies having been hit by a systemic financial crisis start to recover only when indebtedness, actual profits, expected profits, and liquidity and solvency positions have returned to "sustainable" levels, implying that in severe cases, the recovery phase can take several years.

It is very puzzling that economic science has not yet managed to eliminate the problem of systemic financial crises, though the analysis of the history of financial crises clearly points out that systemic financial distress is a cyclical and recurrent phenomenon with well-defined and hardly changing characteristics. Current standard theory of financial crises, which can be classified into two broad categories being outlined below, argues that the persistence of systemic financial crises throughout history is mainly due to the fact that systemic crises are caused by events which cannot be avoided or predicted, and whose adverse effects on real macroeconomic performance can be only alleviated imperfectly, or cannot be prevented at all by crisis management policies.

The first category of current standard theory, representing the "majority" in the financial crisis literature, argues that capitalist market economies are inherently stable, that agents' expectations are formed rationally, and that financial crises are caused by exogenous events, or "historical accidents". The view that crises are unpredictable and unavoidable is reflected in the fact that mainstream theory has developed four different classes, or "generations" of financial crisis models over the last 30 years which tried to explain each new wave of financial crises ex post, and which emphasize very different determinants of exogenously-caused financial distress.

The first class of models argues that financial crises are caused by inconsistent macroeconomic policies. Overly expansionary and overly contractionary monetary and fiscal policies finally lead to a collapse of asset prices, and to real macroeconomic contractions owing to a rise in actual and expected real interest rates, and due to an actual and expected depreciation of the home currency.

The second class of models, emphasizing the role of self-fulfilling expectations and the existence of multiple equilibria, argues that financial crises are the result of a random and exogenous shift in (rational) expectations regarding financial sector or exchange rate stability, from a "good" no-crisis-equilibrium to a "bad" crisis-equilibrium. The change in expectations is self-fulfilling, as the ex ante shift from optimistic towards pessimistic expectations induces bank runs and capital flight which lead to an actual breakdown of the financial and of the exchange rate system, and thereby to an ex post validation of pessimistic ex ante expectations. As the shift in expectations is generally assumed to be a random and exogenous event, self-fulfilling financial crises both cannot be predicted, and are not preceded by a deterioration of economic fundamentals.

The third class of models argues that financial crises are caused by a combination of moral hazard, exogenous shocks, and self-fulfilling expectations. Explicit or implicit government guarantees in the form of deposit insurance systems or fixed exchange rates make investors engage in much riskier and unhedged investment projects due to a rise in investments' expected values, since in case of default, losses are transferred to the tax payer. The increase in risk is assumed to be sustainable as long as losses are smaller than the exogenously given upper limit of government guarantees. However, if losses exceed the upper limit, the government is forced to suspend its guarantees, causing an actual default of the investor, and thereby a financial crisis. Regarding the trigger of financial crises, moral hazard models generally argue that crises are caused by exogenous shocks or self-fulfilling expectations, but deny an endogenous financial collapse. Respecting exogenous shock-driven models, financial crises are caused by large adverse random shocks to economic fundamentals, as e.g. by an exogenous rise in domestic or foreign interest rates, or by adverse terms of trade or technology shocks which lead to a suspension of government guarantees, to an actual default of the investor, and to a systemic financial crisis as losses exceed the upper limit of government guarantees. Concerning self-fulfilling expectations-driven models, financial crises are caused by a random shift from optimistic towards pessimistic expectations as to governments' ability to fulfill guarantees, triggering an actual default of the investor as losses exceed the guarantee's upper limit, and ending up as well in a full-fledged systemic financial crisis which validates pessimistic ex ante expectations ex post.

The fourth class of models argues that business firms and financial institutions are financially constrained by their balance sheet or net worth positions due to the existence of asymmetric information in financial markets. An increase in net worth implies an increase in lending and in expenditures, whereas a fall in net worth implies a reduction in lending and in expenditures. According to fourth-generation models, financial crises are caused either by adverse exogenous shocks to economic fundamentals, or by random and self-fulfilling shifts from optimistic towards pessimistic expectations as to firms or banks net worth position, leading to a collapse of asset prices and exchange rates, which induce large reductions in net worth, widespread bankruptcies, credit crunches and real macroeconomic contractions.

Unlike the first category of financial crisis models, representing the "mainstream approach" to financial crises, the second category of current standard theory, representing the "minority" in the financial crisis literature, argues that capitalist market economies are inherently unstable, and that financial crises are an endogenous, or "natural" outcome. Models of endogenous financial crises contend that there is a general endogenous build-up of financial fragility during the expansion phase of a business cycle by unrealistic expectations, overinvestment and overborrowing, leading finally to a financial collapse at the upper turning point when investors realize that expectations cannot be fulfilled. Collapsing asset prices and expectations lead to widespread bankruptcies, and to a deep and long lasting depression. Unlike mainstream models, endogenous financial crisis models generally do not provide an exact quantitative explanation of their basic hypotheses, firstly, as lots of endogenous financial crisis models are based on a qualitative-descriptive approach, and secondly, as most quantitative approaches concentrate on the mechanisms generating endogenous financial fragility and endogenous business cycles, but do not explain when endogenous financial fragility actually evolves into systemic financial crises.

"Testing" the validity of both categories of standard theory by confronting the model results with the stylized facts provides a mixed picture. That is, both categories are consistent with a series of empirical regularities, but also fail to explain important stylized facts. Regarding the common grounds of the mainstream approach to financial crises with the stylized facts, the models correctly demonstrate that financial distress is associated with high real domestic and foreign interest rates, real overvaluation of the domestic currency, pessimistic expectations, suspensions of government guarantees as e.g. the breakdown of fixed exchange rate regimes, credit and liquidity crunches, and real macroeconomic contractions. However, mainstream models do not consider the link between business cycle fluctuations and financial crises, as well as the irregular change between tranquil business cycle fluctuations and financial crisis cycles. Moreover, mainstream models deny an endogenous build-up of financial fragility due to overinvestment and overborrowing driven by unrealistic expectations which collapse at the upper turning point, and tend to undershoot during the bust phase.

Regarding the common grounds of the endogenous financial crisis approach with the history of financial crises, the models correctly reflect the empirical facts that financial crises are linked to business cycle fluctuations, that there is a general build-up of financial fragility during the boom phase by unrealistic expectations leading to overborrowing, and that the collapse of expectations leads to a severe and long-lasting downturn. However, the endogenous financial crisis approach fails to explain why there are also tranquil business cycle fluctuations indicating dynamic stability of capitalist systems, and why the occurrence of financial crisis cycles is irregular. Moreover, endogenous financial crisis models fail to provide a quantitative theory of the formation of expectations which is able to explain the growing divergence of fundamentals and expectations during the up- and the downswing, as well as the change of expectations at the business cycle turning points. Finally, endogenous financial crisis models fail to provide a general analytical explanation of the long-run dynamics of modern capitalist systems which are characterized by an irregular change between dynamic stability and instability.

Summing up, the comparison of both categories of standard theory with the stylized facts points out that there is no theoretical approach which provides a correct representation of systemic financial distress, firstly, because standard models concentrate too much on specific stylized features of financial crises, and secondly, because both the mainstream approach and the endogenous financial crisis approach are too polarized and deadlocked in their basic assumptions, preventing an objective representation of the "truth". Consequently, the persistence of financial crises throughout history could be, at least partly, attributed to the failure of economic theory of not having developed a "general" theoretical analysis of systemic financial crises which could be used to prevent crises, or to develop much better crisis management policies.

The present approach to be developed in this book, tries to overcome this "failure" of economic theory by providing an alternative and more general approach to financial crises which combines endogenous business cycle theory with current financial crisis theory. The main results of this "cyclical" approach to financial crises can be summarized in the following three propositions.

Firstly, if there are no exogenous shocks, capitalist systems tend to be cyclically stable in the long-run, as they converge to endogenous tranquil business cycles which are associated with financial tensions at the upper turning point, but which do not generate systemic financial distress. These tranquil long-run equilibrium cycles are mainly driven by an endogenous interaction between profit expectations, indebtedness of business firms, and lending behaviour of financial institutions.

Secondly, financial crisis cycles are caused by an exogenous positive shock to profit expectations, e.g. due to the emergence of a new technology regime, or owing to the implementation of liberalization and stabilization policies, giving rise to an enormous build-up of financial fragility by overly optimistic profit expectations, leading to overinvestment and overindebtedness. At the upper turning point of the financial crisis cycle, profit expectations collapse endogenously and induce a cumulative downward process, being associated with a stock market crash, a collapse of the domestic currency, widespread bankruptcies among firms and financial institutions, a general credit and liquidity crunch, and a long-lasting depression.

Thirdly, notwithstanding the fact that financial crisis cycles generate real sector and financial sector instability, economies tend to recover endogenously after the occurrence of a systemic financial crisis by converging back to tranquil equilibrium business cycle fluctuations.

This "cyclical" approach to financial crises is based on an innovative expectation formation scheme which combines the rational expectations hypothesis with Keynes' "Beauty Contest Theory", giving rise to an endogenous dynamic interaction between chartists, fundamentalists and rational investors, where the boom and the bust phase are dominated by chartist type behaviour, and the turning points by fundamentalist type and rational behaviour. The present approach differs from other chartist-fundamentalist approaches by the explicit consideration of the rational expectation hypothesis, implying that the behaviour of agents is not only determined by market sentiments and some fundamental economic variables of the model which can be observed, but additionally by (long-run) rational behaviour according to the rational expectations hypothesis. As a result, the present approach demonstrates that "irrational" herding behaviour and rational expectations are compatible with each other, and that especially this combination generates endogenous cycles in expectations, fitting the stylized facts both of tranquil business cycles, and of financial crisis cycles. Moreover, the present approach is founded on a sophisticated balance sheet approach with many assets, liquidity and net worth constraints, financial accelerator effects, and a rich set of transmission mechanisms (interest rate channel, exchange rate channel, asset price channel, credit channel, bank lending channel, balance sheet channel) being responsible for the transmission of financial sector shocks into the real sphere of an economy. As there are fundamental differences between financial crises in industrial and in emerging market economies regarding the financial structure, indebtedness, and exchange rate regimes, the present approach distinguishes explicitly between crises in industrialized and in emerging market economies, and derives different conclusions as to crisis prevention and crisis management policies.

1.2 Outline of the Book

Following the introduction, part I, consisting of chapters 2 and 3, develops both a theoretical and an empirical basis for the new "cyclical" approach to be developed in part II of the book. Chapter 2, elaborating theoretical principles of financial crises and financial stability, begins with a general definition of financial crises, describing financial distress as a multi-dimensional set of conditions and indicators in contrast to numerous, and largely differing definitions given by standard theory describing financial distress by very few and very specific conditions. Moreover, this general definition explicitly differentiates between systemic financial crises, i.e. crises leading to severe real macroeconomic contractions, and spurious financial crises being characterized by drops in asset prices, but having no effects on real macroeconomic activity. The distinction between systemic and spurious financial crises serves as a starting point for the following sections analyzing how financial market disturbances, i.e. asset price drops and surges in interest rates, are transmitted into the real sphere of economies, and how financial shocks can evolve into systemic financial crises. Furthermore, chapter 2 develops a new theoretical framework of the interaction of asset prices, financial constraints, financial market conditions, aggregate demand, real economic activity, and aggregate liquidity and solvency positions to illustrate the emergence of cumulative upward and downward processes during tranquil equilibrium business cycles and financial crisis cycles. After having studied the interactions between the real and the financial sphere of capitalist market economies, chapter 2 discusses various determinants of financial stability, i.e. factors determining whether a given set of financial market disturbances causes a full-fledged systemic financial crisis, or "only" a spurious financial crisis.

Chapter 3 elaborates the stylized facts of financial crises, having been already outlined briefly in the previous chapter, which serve as an empirical basis for the "cyclical" approach to be developed in part II. The analysis begins with a definition of currency, banking and twin crises from an empirical perspective, being employed to study both the frequency and the severity of financial crises during the last 120 years. The subsequent analysis discusses on the one hand the basic link between business cycles and financial crises, and on the other hand the link between financial liberalization, business cycle fluctuations, and the occurrence of systemic financial crises. Also, the financial liberalization process in the post Bretton Woods era, both in the industrialized and in the developing world, is going to be reviewed. The latter part of chapter 3 provides a detailed synopsis of numerous empirical studies analyzing the stylized behaviour of macroeconomic variables before, during, and after the occurrence of currency, banking, and twin crises in the post Bretton Woods era. Moreover, the analysis also compares the stylized behaviour of macroeconomic variables during periods of financial distress with the stylized behaviour during tranquil periods. All empirical and historical results are summarized in eight main propositions, or stylized facts which are used as a performance indicator for the empirical validity of financial crisis models. A comparison of the stylized facts with standard theory of financial crises points out, as aforementioned, that standard theory cannot explain important empirical regularities, being necessary to understand causes and consequences of systemic financial crises, as well as to develop methods to prevent, predict, and to manage crises efficiently.

The divergence between the stylized facts and standard theory is used as the starting point for a "new" cyclical theory of financial crises in part II of the book, consisting of chapters 4, 5, 6 and 7. Chapter 4 develops a theoretical open economy model of endogenous business cycle fluctuations and financial crises in industrial countries under flexible exchange rates. The static version of the model is based on a sophisticated balance sheet approach with a complex financial structure, many assets, and various transmission mechanisms. The real side of the model is characterized by the central role of business firms' profit rate being dependent on the financial structure of the economy. Moreover, aggregate economic activity is mainly driven by investment expenditures, where the investment function is described by a modified version of Tobin's q, implying that investment demand is dependent on stock prices, the actual price level, actual profits, expected profits, the real loan rate, the financial structure, and on the level of aggregate economic activity. The static version of the model is employed to describe various stages of a typical financial crisis cycle by a comparative-static analysis.

Subsequently, both the expected profit rate and the degree of indebtedness, being represented by firms' debt-asset ratio, are going to be endogenized to study the long-run dynamics of the system. The dynamic version of the model is based on a very uncommon and innovative kind of expectation formation scheme having not yet taken into consideration by standard approaches to financial crises, which combines the rational expectations hypothesis and Keynes' "Beauty Contest Theory", resulting in endogenous interactions between chartists, fundamentalists and rational investors. This synthetic expectation formation scheme allows for a theoretical explanation of endogenous cycles in profit expectations with irrational exuberance during the boom phase, "irrational undershooting" during the bust phase, and with rational and endogenous returns from unrealistic optimistic and unrealistic pessimistic expectations to real economic fundamentals at the turning points of business cycles. The dynamic analysis points out firstly, that capitalist market economies are cyclically stable and converge to tranquil business cycles, secondly, that financial crises are caused by large exogenous positive shocks to expectations, giving rise to an excessive business cycle ending up in a systemic financial crises, and thirdly, that after the occurrence of a financial crisis, economic systems recover endogenously, and return to tranquil business cycle fluctuations. The dynamic version of the model studies additionally the case when expectations are solely determined by market sentiments in a purely Keynesian fashion, and concludes that in this case, each business cycle can generate a systemic financial crisis. Finally, the model is compared both with standard models of financial crises and standard models of business cycle theory.

Chapter 5 develops a modified version of the industrial country model of chapter 4 for emerging market economies. The model differs substantially from the industrial country version with respect to the financial structure, as emerging market debt generally stems from international financial markets, and is denominated in foreign currency. Furthermore, the emerging market model assumes a fixed exchange rate regime allowing for a detailed analysis of real exchange rate misalignments over the business cycle, as well as for an investigation of the impact of a contractionary devaluation due to high foreign debt stocks in the case of twin crises. All other assumptions, as e.g. the expectations formation scheme, coincide with the industrial country model. Both the comparative-static and the dynamic version of the emerging market model demonstrate that in spite of fundamental differences in the model structure, financial crises in emerging markets are very similar to those in industrialized economies, and differ only with respect to two issues. Firstly, both tranquil and financial crisis cycles in emerging markets are driven by an endogenous interaction between international capital flows and profit expectations of domestic and international investors, whereas all cycles in industrial countries are driven by fluctuations in domestic bank debt and profit expectations of domestic investors. Secondly, in case of twin crises, the real macroeconomic contraction in emerging market is amplified by the outbreak of the currency crisis due to a nominal and real appreciation of the foreign debt stock (contractionary devaluation), whereas in industrial countries the contraction is dampened by the devaluation of the home currency (expansionary devaluation).

Chapter 6 develops a calibration model of financial crises in emerging markets on the basis of chapter 5 in order to enlarge the previous dynamic analysis which has been restricted to a qualitative phase diagram analysis of a nonlinear 2×2 system. Unlike the general function models in chapters 4 and 5, the calibration model is able to provide specific information on the transitional crisis dynamics of a large number of macroeconomic variables beyond the "cyclical steady state" during periods of financial distress. However, in order to remain analytically tractable, the dynamic nonlinear version of the emerging market model of chapter 5 has to be transformed into a dynamic linear model, implying that the transitional dynamics of typical financial crisis cycles have to be studied by a stepwise calibration procedure which differentiates between the boom phase, the overborrowing phase, and the bust phase. Apart from the calibration of financial crises as a cyclical phenomenon, chapter 6 additionally simulates the effects of an adverse foreign interest rate shock. Notwithstanding the fact that calibration techniques are subject to various limitations being discussed in detail, they constitute a precious complement to general function models. There is no explicit elaboration of an industrial country calibration model in chapter 6, as the emerging market model structure is richer and more complex than the industrial country case. Furthermore, the simulation results of the emerging market case can be simply applied to financial crises' periods in industrial countries.

Chapter 7 summarizes the main results of book and develops both new perspectives for economic theory and alternative policy recommendations for crisis prevention, crisis prediction, and crisis management.

Part I

Theoretical and Empirical Foundations

Chapter 2

Financial Crises and Financial Instability: Definitions and Principles

2.1 A General Definition of Financial Crises

There are almost as many definitions of financial crises in the economic literature as there are theories and historical episodes of financial distress. For example, monetarists define financial crises as banking panics leading to sharp contractions in the money supply and deep downswings in real economic activity (Friedman and Schwartz 1963). Advocates of the "financial fragility" approach, having a much broader view on financial distress, define financial crises as the occurrence of one or more events as e.g. sharp declines in asset prices, bankruptcies of large financial and nonfinancial firms, being possibly associated with real economic downturns and large drops in commodity prices (Fisher 1932, 1933, Minsky 1972, Eichengreen and Portes 1987, Kindleberger 2000). Proponents of the asymmetric information view on financial markets define financial crises by particular events as e.g. banking panics, and currency crises which are caused by adverse selection and/or moral hazard (Calomiris and Gorton 1991, McKinnon and Pill 1997, Krugman 1998). By way of contrast, supporters of credit constraint and balance sheet models define financial crises as an event which causes financial constraints to bind, leading to a drying up of liquidity in financial markets, and to real contractions (Mishkin 1991, Dornbusch 1999, Velasco 2001, Caballero and Krishnamurthy 2002).

These introductory examples, which are going to be discussed in more detail in the following chapters, are only an extract from many other definitions of financial crises which can be found in the economic literature. The reason for this large variety of definitions stems from the fact that no financial crisis one can observe in reality equals another one exactly, and, perhaps more importantly, that there is no consensus view on the causes and consequences of financial crises in economic theory. This contribution aims at overcoming this existing fragmentation by providing a more general or synthetic view on financial crises which can be used to explain different forms of financial distress by common theoretical concepts. Accordingly, the present approach does not define any longer financial crises by specific and singular events as described above, but by a general multi-dimensional set of conditions or indicators as follows:

*A **financial crisis** is a disturbance in financial markets being typically accompanied firstly, by a sudden, large, and widespread drop in financial asset prices (as e.g. declining stock and bond prices, decreasing market values of loans, or collapsing exchange rates), implying a large and sudden rise in interest rates on financial assets (as e.g. sharply increasing interest rates on bonds, loans, or money market instruments), and/or secondly, by a sudden, large, and widespread drop in real asset prices (as e.g. declining real estate prices, or dropping market prices for real capital).*

This widespread drop in asset prices is caused by an actual and/or expected decline in assets' rate of returns, which can be triggered firstly, by actual and/or expected negative real shocks (as e.g. adverse terms-of-trade shocks, large increases in input costs, or negative technology shocks), and/or secondly, by actual and/or expected negative financial shocks (as e.g. increasing real domestic or real foreign prime interest rates, exchange rate devaluations, increasing risk premia, or suspensions of government guarantees, as e.g. deposit insurance systems or bail-out guarantees).

Regarding their impact on real economic activity, financial crises can be subdivided into two categories, namely into systemic financial crises and spurious financial crises.

*A **systemic financial crisis** is defined as a situation in which asset price drops and rising interest rates cause firstly, a widespread disruption of financial markets' capacity to allocate financial funds into the most efficient production opportunities due to a general liquidity crunch and/or due to dysfunctions of the payment system, and secondly, real economic downturns, or even depressions and (debt-)deflation, by engendering widespread failures among financial and nonfinancial firms, and collapses in aggregate demand.*[1]

*By way of contrast, a **spurious** financial crisis is defined as a situation in which asset price drops and sharply rising interest rates firstly, do not interfere with financial markets' capacity to channel funds efficiently from savers to investors as disturbances are restricted to particular markets, sectors or agents, and secondly, do not cause real economic downturns as financial market disturbances are not transmitted into the real sector.*[2]

*In case domestic asset price disturbances spill over to foreign financial markets, as well as in case foreign financial market asset price disturbances induce domestic disturbances, they are labelled as **international financial crises**.*

[1]Financial market disturbances can also cause a failure of the government sector whose impact on the real sector differs however from widespread failures among financial and nonfinancial firms firstly, because the government sector cannot be liquidated, and secondly, as the government sector cannot be forced to give up its "production" activities. As a result, it is not clear whether a failure of the government sector can cause a systemic financial crisis. For that reason, a failure of the government sector was excluded from the general definition of systemic financial crises.

[2]Examples are stock market crashes, currency collapses, dropping real estate prices, or failures of financial or nonfinancial firms which do not lead to recessions, deflation, general liquidity crunches, or malfunctions of the payment system. Such events are examples of financial distress, yet they are no examples of systemic financial crises. Furthermore, spurious financial crises cannot cause a failure of the government sector.

If these internationally transmitted disturbances lead firstly, to a breakdown of financial markets' ability to allocate funds domestically and/or internationally, and cause secondly, domestic and/or international real economic downturns, they are called ***international systemic financial crises****. If, by way of contrast, there is no disruption of financial markets' ability to allocate funds domestically and/or internationally, as well as no domestic and/or international real economic downturns, they are labelled as* ***international spurious financial crises****.*

Despite the fact that this general definition of financial crises captures a great variety of possible forms of financial distress, it provides no concept explaining why some financial disturbances lead to systemic, and some to spurious financial crises. Consequently, there is no explanation of how financial market disturbances are transmitted into the real sector, and which "conditions" determine whether a given set of disturbances causes a systemic or a spurious financial crisis. Furthermore, the definition provides no explanation of the fundamental causes of real and/or financial shocks triggering financial crises, i.e. there is no explanation of whether financial crises are purely random events which are caused by exogenous shocks, or whether financial crises are endogenous phenomena resulting from inherent unstable interactions between the real and the financial sphere of modern capitalist economies.

To overcome these drawbacks, section 2.2 analyzes the interaction of asset price fluctuations and macroeconomic activity, whereas section 2.3 investigates factors determining the degree of "financial stability" or "systemic risk", i.e. overall macroeconomic conditions determining whether a given set of disturbances causes a systemic, or a spurious financial crisis. Section 2.4 sets out different theoretical views of the basic causes of financial crises, i.e. whether financial crises can be viewed as exogenous or endogenous events, or as a combination of both.

2.2 Asset Price Fluctuations and Aggregate Economic Activity

This section investigates the interaction of asset price changes and aggregate economic activity. There is broad empirical evidence that changes in asset prices generally tend to lead changes in real GDP growth. Yet, not all asset prices exhibit the characteristics of a leading indicator, depending predominantly on the depth of asset markets. Among a large number of assets, empirical studies singled out stock prices and government bond yield spreads, i.e. the difference between short-term and long-term returns on government bonds, as the best forward-looking indicators for future real output growth, whereas property and land prices were found to be more correlated with actual output growth.[3]

Notwithstanding the extensive empirical evidence on the leading indicator property of some asset prices, there is no general agreement on the causal linkages between asset prices and real economic activity in economic theory, stemming mainly from the fact that

[3]For empirical studies of the interaction of asset prices and output growth both in industrial and emerging market countries, see e.g. Asprem (1989), Fama (1990), International Monetary Fund (2000), chapter III, and Mauro (2000).

these linkages are complex and empirically difficult to determine. One class of theories claims that under rational expectations, asset prices are "only" leading indicators reflecting future changes in output by their forward-looking nature, i.e. there exists no causal relationship between changes in asset prices and output because asset prices only provide information about future developments in the real sector without having influence on output.[4] According to this view however, financial crises, as defined above, cannot arise. Spurious financial crises having no effect on the real sector, would only occur in case expectations about the future were wrong, which is ruled out under rational expectations.[5] Likewise, systemic financial crises could not arise per definition since there exists no transmission mechanism from asset prices to real economic activity.

By way of contrast, according to the more traditional theoretical view, asset price changes are assumed to influence real economic activity in two ways. Firstly, asset prices are assumed to induce alterations in aggregate demand via wealth and cost of capital effects. Secondly, asset prices are assumed to influence the degree of financial stability and the state of current financial distress by determining whether existing financial constraints (net worth and liquidity constraints) are fulfilled or not, influencing on the one hand potential output by deciding upon whether an economic entity is bankrupt or not, and on the other hand aggregate demand by determining the creditworthiness of borrowers, i.e. the availability of external funds, and therethrough the maximum amount of expenditures. Owing to this traditional view, both spurious and systemic financial crises, as defined above, are possible events to occur, firstly, due to the existence of various transmission mechanisms between the financial and the real sector, and secondly, due to the influence of asset prices on aggregate financial stability.

Summing up, according to the introductory general definition of financial crises in section 2.1, the present approach follows the more traditional view of the interaction of asset prices and output growth. Hence, after having discussed determinants of asset prices in section 2.2.1, section 2.2.2 analyzes how asset prices influence financial constraints and therethrough creditworthiness and the availability of external funds, whereas section 2.2.3 studies the influence of asset prices on aggregate demand. The results of sections 2.2.2 and 2.2.3 are employed to develop a qualitative approach in section 2.2.4 to the emergence of cumulative upward and downward processes, i.e. to economic dynamics which are characterized by self-sustaining or endogenous interdependencies between the real and the financial sector of an economy, leading either to steady increasing asset prices and increasing GDP growth, or to steady falling asset prices and steady declining, or even negative GDP growth, giving rise to systemic financial crises. The qualitative results of section 2.2.4, in combination with factors determining financial stability being discussed in section 2.3, serve as qualitative a basis for the quantitative approach in part II of the book.

[4]For this class of theories, see e.g. Morck, Schleifer and Vishny (1990).

[5]In case there are no shocks to the real sector leaving all "fundamentals" unchanged, which is the case during a spurious financial crisis, then, under the assumption of rational expectations, asset prices cannot change since there is no change in "fundamentals". Thus, a downward revision of expectations without a change in fundamentals indicates an expectation error which is excluded under the rational expectations hypothesis.

2.2.1 Determinants of Asset Prices

There are various theories and models of asset pricing in economics, as e.g. portfolio theory being based on the capital asset pricing model (CAPM), consumption based asset pricing theory being grounded on the consumption based capital asset pricing model (CCAMP), or production based asset pricing theory having evolved from stochastic growth and real business cycle theory. Albeit these theories differ with respect to assumptions, model structures, etc., they all have in common that the price of an asset is generally determined by the present value approach, stating that the price of an asset is determined by the sum of its discounted expected earnings or cash flows.

Expected cash flows are the asset's expected rents, cash or imputed, net of costs of operation, maintenance, taxes, etc. Interest costs, i.e. rates of return which the investor must pay to borrow funds to hold the asset, or opportunity costs, i.e. rates of return the investor must sacrifice by holding smaller amounts of other assets, are represented by the discount factor which is a risk-adjusted reference "interest" rate investors demand for holding the asset, being powerfully influenced by monetary policies, i.e. by short-term interest rates. It is important to note that interest or opportunity costs associated with the asset, are *not* subtracted from expected cash flows since expected cash flows represent the asset's "natural returns", which are independent of financing issues. Likewise, it must be emphasized that the discount factor is *not* a market interest rate on a specific kind of reference asset which investors could alternatively invest in, but a rate appropriate for the valuation of streams of future returns with the time patterns, uncertainties, and covariances of the asset's cash flows. That is, the discount factor can be interpreted as "mixed" rate, consisting of the return of a risk-free reference asset, *plus* an asset-specific risk premium reflecting all uncertainties and risks associated with the asset's cash flows.[6] Formally, the nominal market value, or the market price of an asset, P_A, being subject to an infinite income stream is given at time t in discrete form by

$$P_{A,t} = \sum_{s=t}^{\infty}(1+(i_{RF}+rp-\hat{p}^e))^{-(s-t)}\,CF_s^e = \sum_{s=t}^{\infty}(1+(i_{RF}+rp-\hat{p}^e))^{-(s-t)}\,CF_{r,s}^e\,P_s^e, \quad (2.1)$$

and in continuous form by

$$P_A(t) = \int_t^{\infty} e^{-(i_{RF}+rp-\hat{p}^e)(s-t)}\,CF^e(s)\;ds = \int_t^{\infty} e^{-(i_{RF}+rp-\hat{p}^e)(s-t)}\,CF_r^e(s)\,P^e(s)\;ds, \quad (2.2)$$

where CF_r^e denotes real expected cash flows or expected real earnings, P^e the expected price level, $CF^e = CF_r^e\,P^e$ nominal expected cash flows, i_{RF} the nominal risk-free interest rate of a risk-free reference asset (e.g. nominal interest rate on long-term government bonds being crucially dependent on monetary policies), rp the risk premium in nominal terms representing the asset's risk of default, $\hat{p}^e$ the price level's P expected growth rate being defined in discrete time as $\hat{p}_s^e = (P_{s+1}^e - P_s)/P_s$ and in continuous time as

[6] For example, regarding equities, the discount factor is *not* represented by the interest rate on long-term government bonds, or by the interest rate on long-term corporate bonds, but e.g. by the interest rate on long-term government bonds, representing the risk-free reference asset, plus an equity-specific risk premium reflecting all uncertainties and risks associated with the equity's cash flows.

$\hat{p}^e(s) = \dot{P}^e(s)/P(s)$, and $i_{RF} + rp - \hat{p}^e$ the risk-adjusted real expected reference interest rate.[7] In case the expected price level P^e and expected real earnings CF_r^e are constant over time, implying constant nominal earnings CF^e, the asset price at time t is given, both in discrete and in continuous form, by

$$P_A = \frac{CF^e}{i_{RF} + rp - \hat{p}^e} = \frac{CF_r^e \, P^e}{i_{RF} + rp - \hat{p}^e}. \tag{2.3}$$

According to the present value approach, asset prices decline/rise ceteris paribus, in case there is a fall/rise in expected real cash flows CF_r^e, a rise/fall in the nominal risk-free interest rate i_{RF}, a rise/fall in the risk premium in nominal terms rp, and a fall/rise in the expected price level P^e implying also a fall/rise in the price level's expected growth rate $\hat{p}^e$. Consequently, regarding financial crises, drops in asset prices can be caused by deteriorating "objective" fundamental data (fall in actual earnings[8], rise in current nominal risk-free interest rates), as well as by worsening "subjective" expectations as to future earnings, the expected price level and default risk.

Prominent applications of the present value approach are e.g. the "Gordon equation" (Gordon 1962), determining equity prices in a consumption based capital asset pricing model, Tobin's q theory of investment discussed in appendix A, and textbook illustrations of the determination of bond prices. Regarding the determination of exchange rates, it must be noted that the present value approach cannot be applied since exchange rates are no income generating assets whose return can be compared to another asset. Rather,

[7] Unlike most representations of nominal discounted present values which are generally stated in nominal terms, i.e. nominal expected cash flows are generally discounted by a nominal reference interest rate, equations 2.1 and 2.2 define *nominal* present values as a stream of future expected *nominal* earnings being discounted by an expected *real* reference interest rate since this kind of description allows for a better consideration of the impact of (expected) inflation. The definition of nominal discounted present values in equations 2.1 and 2.2 can be derived in four steps. Regarding the discrete time case in equation 2.1, the first step is to define the real market value, or the real discounted present value of an asset at time t, $P_{A_r,t}$, reading as $P_{A_r,t} = P_{A,t}/P_t = \sum_{s=t}^{\infty}(1+z_r)^{-(s-t)}\, CF_{r,s}^e$, where z_r denotes the real risk-adjusted reference interest rate. In the second step, real expected cash flows $CF_{r,s}^e$ are replaced by nominal expected cash flows CF_s^e which are deflated by the current price level P_t, leading to $P_{A_r,t} = P_{A,t}/P_t = \sum_{s=t}^{\infty}(1+z_r)^{-(s-t)}\,(CF_s^e/P_s^e)\,(P_s^e/P_t)$. In the third step, the real discounted present value is transformed into a nominal discounted present value via multiplication by the current price level at time t, P_t, resulting in $P_{A,t} = P_{A_r,t}\,P_t = \sum_{s=t}^{\infty}(1+z_r)^{-(s-t)}\,CF_s^e$. In the fourth step, the term $(1+z_r)^{-(s-t)}$ is replaced according to the multi-period Fisher relation, reading for $s \geq t$ as $(1+z_r)^{(s-t)} = (1+i_{RF}+rp)^{(s-t)}/(1+\hat{p}^e)^{(s-t)}$, which results in $P_{A,t} = P_{A_r,t}\,P_t = \sum_{s=t}^{\infty}(1+i_{RF}+rp)^{(s-t)}/(1+\hat{p}^e)^{(s-t)}\,CF_s^e$. Approximating the Fisher relation by the result that $z_r \approx i_{RF} + rp - \hat{p}^e$, the nominal discounted present value is given by $P_{A,t} = P_{A_r,t}\,P_t = \sum_{s=t}^{\infty}(1+(i_{RF}+rp-\hat{p}^e))^{-(s-t)}\,CF_s^e$, which corresponds exactly to equation 2.1. The derivation of the continuous case in equation 2.2 is described analogously to the discrete time case in four steps. Following step one above, the real market value of an asset at time t is given by $P_{A_r}(t) = P_A(t)/P(t) = \int_t^{\infty} e^{-z_r(s-t)}\,CF_r^e(s)\,ds$. According to step two, real expected cash flows are replaced by nominal expected cash flows, leading to $P_{A_r}(t) = P_A(t)/P(t) = \int_t^{\infty} e^{-z_r(s-t)}\,(CF^e(s)/P^e(s))\,(P^e(s)/P(t))\,ds$. Transforming the real discounted present value into the nominal discounted present value according to the step three via multiplication by the current price level $P(t)$ yields $P_A(t) = P_{A_r}(t)\,P(t) = \int_t^{\infty} e^{-z_r(s-t)}\,CF^e(s)\,ds$. As to step four, the multi-period Fisher relation, reading in continuous time for $s \geq t$ as $e^{z_r(s-t)} = e^{(i_{RF}+rp)(s-t)}/e^{\hat{p}^e(s-t)}$, or after having eliminated $(s-t)$ as $z_r = i_{RF} + rp - \hat{p}^e$, is used to replace z_r, which results in $P_A(t) = P_{A_r}(t)\,P(t) = \int_t^{\infty} e^{-(i_{RF}+rp-\hat{p}^e)(s-t)}\,CF^e(s)\,ds$, corresponding exactly to equation 2.2.

[8] Note that at time t, it holds that $CF_t^e = CF_t$ according to equation 2.1, and $CF^e(t) = CF(t)$ according to equation 2.2.

exchange rates' "market price" is determined by international transactions in services, goods and financial assets, which demands different approaches to price determination, as e.g. purchasing power theory (PPP), uncovered interest parity theory (UIP), or asset market approaches to the exchange rate.

2.2.2 Asset Prices and Financial Constraints

Asset prices have a decisive influence on real economic activity by their impact on financial constraints, determining a business unit's creditworthiness, the available amount of external finance and thereby the maximum amount of aggregate expenditures, as well as whether a business unit is bankrupt or not. As a result, the strength of the transmission from the financial into the real sphere of an economy, as well as the question of whether a financial crisis is spurious or systemic, depends on whether constraints are binding or not binding, and on whether constraints can be fulfilled at all.

There are two broad classes of financial constraints in economic theory whose explicit form depends on how financial markets are assumed to work. The theory of perfect capital markets, being outlined in section 2.2.2.1, is based on intertemporal Walrasian equilibrium theory and assumes that there are no frictions in financial markets, and that economic agents are only subject to an intertemporal solvency constraint. By way of contrast, the theory of imperfect capital markets, being reviewed in section 2.2.2.2, assumes that there are strong information asymmetries in financial markets leading to borrowing constraints which depend on agents' net worth. As there are strong differences between both perspectives, section 2.2.2.3 compares both theories with real world financial constraints and develops a synthetic view on the impact of financial constraints on real economic activity. This perspective is employed as a basis for section 2.2.4, analyzing the emergence of cumulative processes, and for the quantitative approach to financial crises being developed in part II of the book.

2.2.2.1 Perfect Capital Market Theory

The Existence of Intertemporal Solvency Constraints. Theoretical models as well as empirical studies of borrowing and lending have been often based on perfect capital market theory combined with general intertemporal Walrasian equilibrium theory.[9] As a result, financial constraints on borrowing and lending in perfect capital markets in a multi-period competitive environment are generally formulated as *intertemporal* conditions referring to the entire time span of the planning period, and not as static requirements which have to be fulfilled at a certain moment in time. As a thorough discussion of financial constraints under intertemporal decisions of agents would require a formal treatment, the following qualitative description is supplemented by a quantitative example in appendix B.

According to intertemporal maximization models, economic agents are generally subject to two financial constraints which determine whether an economic entity is bankrupt or not. The first condition to be fulfilled is the so-called no-Ponzi-game condition[10], being

[9] See e.g. Blanchard and Fischer (1989), and Obstfeld and Rogoff (1999).

[10] The no-Ponzi-game condition is named after Boston swindler C. Ponzi who promised very high returns to investors in the 1920s which he paid, at least for a certain time, by money from new investors. After

labelled in mathematical terms as the transversality condition. The no-Ponzi-game condition requires that the present value of debt/wealth of a representative agent at the end of the planning period has to be zero, i.e. the agent is not allowed to leave the scene without having repaid debt/without having consumed entire wealth. The second condition to be fulfilled is an intertemporal budget constraint, stating that the positive/negative present value of future net income, i.e. the positive/negative present value of output less private consumption (in a closed economy without investment and government expenditures), must not exceed the present value of initial debt plus interest payments/fall short of the present value of initial wealth, where debt/wealth has been generated by past consumption which has been higher/lower than income. In case the intertemporal budget constraint is not fulfilled, implying also a violation of the no-Ponzi-game condition, the economic unit is bankrupt or *intertemporally insolvent*, whereas in case the intertemporal budget constraint and the no-Ponzi-game condition are fulfilled, the economic unit is *intertemporally solvent.*

The Absence of Temporary Borrowing Constraints. The existence of the intertemporal solvency constraint combined with the no-Ponzi-game condition, guaranteeing the non-explosiveness of debt, implies that agents' spending can be temporarily higher than their income, and, much more importantly, that agents can borrow temporarily against future income *without any borrowing constraint.* Accordingly, as long as agents remain intertemporally solvent, there arises no bankruptcy at a specific moment in time since all due payment commitments can be met by borrowing temporarily without any restrictions.

The Irrelevance of the Financial Structure. The irrelevance of the financial structure for borrowing and lending in perfect capital markets has been highlighted by the Modigliani-Miller theorem (Modigliani and Miller 1958) whose results can be summarized in two propositions. Firstly, the capital structure, the debt-equity ratio, or corporate leverage is irrelevant for the present value of the firm, implying that optimal investment is independent of capital markets. This independence implies that the value of assets cannot be changed by altering the claims. It means that in perfect capital markets a firm cannot increase its market value simply by recombining debts against its assets and offering them in different forms. This result is based on the assumption that the value of a business firm depends solely on investment opportunities available to it, and that finance for investment is always available and not restricted by borrowing constraints. Secondly, as a consequence of the irrelevance of the capital structure, the cost of capital of a business firm is independent of the type of securities used to finance the project or the capital structure of the firm, i.e. there exist no differences between the costs of different financing instruments.

2.2.2.2 Imperfect Capital Market Theory

The Existence of Asymmetric Information and Credit Rationing. In sharp contrast to the theory of perfect capital markets, imperfect market capital theory, which has a long tradition in macroeconomics beginning with I. Fisher (1933) and J.M. Keynes

---

the flow of new money dried up, Ponzi could not longer pay investors and his fraud was revealed.

(1936) if not earlier authors[11], postulates that both the financial structure and capital markets in general have a decisive influence on aggregate economy activity by determining the strength of borrowing constraints and the costs of finance. The claim that goods and financial markets are mutually dependent is built on the basic assumption that capital markets are subject to asymmetric information, being an obstacle for a frictionless functioning of financial markets.

Asymmetric information in financial markets is defined as a situation in which one agent of a financial contract is much better informed than the other one. That is, borrowers who take loans have much better information about the prospective returns and risks associated with the investment project than lenders. This basic information asymmetry causes two forms of frictions in information flows, namely adverse selection and moral hazard, leading on the one hand to credit rationing and on the other hand to the existence of borrowing constraints.

Adverse selection occurs before a transaction has taken place and comes into being by the fact that the worst borrowers with highest credit risk have the most difficulties in receiving funds, and therefore are going to offer the highest interest rates since they are likely not to repay the loan. An adverse selection problem comes into being in case lenders grant loans only to those borrowers with highest interest rate offers, implying huge losses for lenders since borrowers with highest credit risk are most likely to be selected. Accordingly, since lenders cannot use the interest rate as a reliable indicator to distinguish "good" from "bad" borrowers, lenders may decide on granting no loans at all, even if there are good borrowers in the market. Thus, adverse selection may lead to *credit rationing* which is defined as a situation in which at a given interest rate, demand for credit is higher than credit supply.[12]

Moral hazard occurs after the transaction has taken place and comes into being in case the borrower earns profits in case the investment project succeeds, and bears no losses in case the project fails, since losses are paid by the lender or by the tax payer. This distortion in incentives leads to actions by the borrower which are immoral from the lender's point of view, as e.g. "overinvestment" in projects with very high risk, or an inefficient use of loans for personal (consumption) purposes of the borrower. In order to avoid such immoral actions by borrowers, lenders may engage in screening and monitoring, which however, can also cause credit rationing since lenders cannot assess whether a potential borrower is going to engage in immoral actions.

The Existence of Borrowing Constraints. Apart from credit rationing, adverse selection and moral hazard also lead to the emergence of *borrowing constraints* since potential losses for lenders can be reduced or avoided, either by imposing borrowing ceilings which prevent borrowers from borrowing an unlimited amount of credit, or by demanding risk-dependent interest rates, leading to an upward sloping supply schedule for credit.

Respecting the existence of borrowing ceilings, it is generally assumed that borrowers' assets are used as collateral, and that debt ceilings are formulated as a fraction of borrowers' net worth, where net worth is generally defined as the market, or discounted

[11] For an overview on the theory of imperfect capital markets, see Gertler (1988) and Trautwein (2000).

[12] For a detailed discussion on credit rationing in markets with asymmetric information, see Stiglitz and Weiss (1981, 1992), and Jaffee and Stiglitz (1990).

present value of assets less the market, or discounted present value of debt. All net worth concepts are grounded on the principle that the status of solvency or insolvency, as well as the influence of net worth on the availability of financial funds, and thereby on aggregate expenditures, are determined by the sign of net worth which can be positive, zero, or negative. In case net worth is negative, an economic unit is defined as being bankrupt or insolvent, and receives no financial funds. If, by way of contrast, net worth is equal to or greater than zero, an economic unit is defined as being solvent, where the amount of available finance, and thereby the amount of aggregate expenditure, is a positive function of borrowers' net worth, i.e. the higher net worth is, the more funds are available due to a lower credit risk, and the higher aggregate expenditures are.

Regarding the existence of risk-dependent interest rates, borrowing is constrained by the fact that "market" interest rates are assumed to consist of a risk-free rate and a risk premium, where the risk premium is either a convex function of agents' debt, or depends positively on agents' net worth serving as collateral. Thus, decreasing net worth, or increasing debt, lead to increasing financing costs which pose an upper limit on the amount of debt finance since the higher interest rate costs, the lower is the present value of an investment project.

The Existence of a "Financial Hierarchy". The existence of asymmetric information also causes a difference between costs of internal finance by retained earnings, and costs of external finance by debt or equity finance. Since internal finance, unlike external finance, requires no financial contract, there arise no information asymmetries, and thereby no "agency costs of lending", i.e. no external finance premium depending negatively on borrowers' net worth, or positively on borrowers' debt stock. Regarding external finance, there exists also a cost difference between debt and equity finance, where equity finance is more expensive than debt finance due to higher information asymmetries, because providing financial funds as a shareholder is associated with higher risk than as a traditional lender due to insecure earnings and a higher losses in case of default. Accordingly, a varying degree of information asymmetries depending on the form of the financial contract implies a *financial hierarchy* of finance costs, where internal finance by retained earnings is the cheapest finance form, followed by external debt finance bearing additionally an external finance premium, and external equity finance being the most expensive form of finance.[13]

The "Financial Accelerator" Effect. A further consequence of asymmetric information in financial markets is the emergence of the *financial accelerator* effect, stating that the financial sector of an economy accelerates both the upturn and the downturn of the business cycle. The financial accelerator effect arises from the fact that the costs of (investment) finance, and especially the external finance premium, are inversely related to borrowers' net worth position. As a result, aggregate investment is positively dependent on borrowers' net worth and negatively dependent on the the costs of capital. In case there is a sudden decrease in borrowers' net worth, which can be induced by a fall in asset prices, a reduction in cash flow and liquidity, a rise in foreign debt by devaluations, the

[13]For details on the theory of the financial hierarchy, see Townsend (1979), Myers (1984), Bernanke and Gertler (1989), and Greenwald and Stiglitz (1993). For empirical results regarding the existence of a financial hierarchy, see Gertler, Hubbard and Kashyap (1991), and Mayer (1991).

external finance premium rises inducing a reduction of investment expenditures. By way of contrast, in case there is a rise in borrowers' net worth, the external finance premium decreases and induces a rise in investment expenditures.[14]

The Existence of Banks and the Necessity of Financial Market Regulation. The dominant role of banks in the financial structure of capitalist economies can be explained as well by the existence of asymmetric information, since banks can be considered as producers of relevant information regarding the assessment of credit risk, which reduces existing asymmetries and allows for a much higher availability of funds. This argument can also be brought forward to explain the empirical fact that economic growth is positively correlated with the state of development of the domestic financial system. Furthermore, the existence of asymmetric information justifies the existence of financial market supervision and regulation by domestic and international regulation authorities to reduce existing asymmetries by screening and monitoring. In order to avoid financial distress, business firms and banks have to be obliged to disclose publicly relevant information about their financial liquidity and solvency status, as well as to adhere to common accounting standards. Accordingly, fast financial market liberalization being accompanied by lax supervision and regulation, limited screening and monitoring of financial institutions, weak accounting and disclosure rules, and by the absence of a security net for financial institutions, can lead very quickly to financial distress and financial crises due to an increase in information asymmetries.[15]

2.2.2.3 A Comparison with Real World Financial Constraints

Real World Financial Constraints. In reality, each economic unit is subject to a liquidity constraint and to a solvency constraint which are both employed to determine the status of bankruptcy, as well as the degree of creditworthiness, and thereby the amount of available debt finance and the amount of aggregate expenditures. Though bankruptcy law differs among countries, the real world status of bankruptcy is generally defined by two facts, namely by illiquidity and by insolvency. Regarding illiquidity, an economic unit is bankrupt in case due payment commitments cannot be fulfilled. This situation emerges in case current cash flow from "normal" operation is negative, and if there is no possibility to receive liquid funds, e.g. by new borrowing, or by selling assets to meet payment commitments, so that overall cash flow remains negative. Regarding insolvency, an economic unit is bankrupt in case its current net worth, i.e. the difference between assets and debts in its balance sheet, is negative. To become bankrupt, only one of the two conditions must be fulfilled, so not to be bankrupt requires both liquidity and solvency of an economic unit.

[14] For details on the financial accelerator effect, see Bernanke (1983), Greenwald, Stiglitz and Weiss (1984), Greenwald and Stiglitz (1993), Bernanke, Gertler and Gilchrist (1996, 1998), Kiyotaki and Moore (1997), and Miller and Stiglitz (1999).

[15] For further theoretical literature on credit rationing, borrowing constraints, the effects of balance sheet positions, the financial hierarchy, and the financial accelerator, see Bernanke (1983), Bernanke and Gertler (1989, 1990, 1994, 1995, 2000), Bernanke and Lown (1992), Gertler (1992), Gertler and Gilchrist (1993, 1994), and Bernanke, Gertler and Gilchrist (1998, 1999). For empirical studies of the effects of credit constraints on aggregate economic activity, see e.g. Bacchetta and Gerlach (1997) studying the impacts on consumption, and Fazzari, Hubbard and Petersen (1988) analyzing the impacts on investment.

Though there arise situations in which economic units are illiquid but solvent, or insolvent but liquid, in most cases the violation of one financial constraint induces the violation of the other one, since liquidity and solvency are interdependent. For example, in case one economic unit is illiquid and tries to fulfill due payment commitments by selling assets, the sale of assets can cause a large drop in asset prices thereby generating possibly insolvency. By way of contrast, in case an economic unit is insolvent, creditors may want to withdraw their funds quickly in order to reduce losses which may cause illiquidity of the debtor. Summing up, the real world bankruptcy status of an economic unit, and thereby its creditworthiness and the available amount of external finance, are determined by both the liquidity and the solvency status which are interdependent.

A Comparison with Perfect Capital Market Theory. Regarding the correspondences of perfect capital market theory with the stylized facts of real world financial constraints, there arises only one similarity, namely that bankruptcy is defined by cash flow positions. Regarding the differences, there are three issues to be mentioned. Firstly, regarding the definition of bankruptcy, perfect capital market theory neglects balance sheet positions, and refers to an intertemporal cash flow constraint. Secondly, according to perfect capital market theory, there are no temporary borrowing constraints, so that there is no influence of actual cash flow and net worth position on creditworthiness and real economic activity. Thirdly, due to the neglect of balance sheet effects, there arise no interdependencies between cash flow and balance sheet positions, i.e. between the liquidity and the solvency status.

A Comparison with Imperfect Capital Market Theory. Respecting the common grounds, imperfect capital market theory emphasizes in accordance with the stylized facts of real world financial constraints that net worth positions are a crucial determinant of creditworthiness and real economic activity due to the existence of borrowing ceilings and risk-dependent interest rates. Regarding the differences, imperfect capital market theory lacks a well-formulated theoretical link between the interaction of liquidity and balance sheet positions.

An Assessment. The comparison has shown that imperfect capital market theory provides useful tools to explain the stylized facts regarding the transmission of financial sector shocks into the real sphere of an economy. However, to be applicable to the explanation of financial crises, imperfect capital market theory has to be supplemented by three important elements. Firstly, according to bankruptcy law, liquidity and solvency have to be well-defined and distinguished from each other. Secondly, the interaction between solvency and liquidity constraints has to be elaborated, and thirdly, the connection between cash flows, profits, net worth and changes in the financial structure, i.e. changes in the composition of assets and debts, have to be clarified. These supplements are going to be taken into consideration in section 2.2.4, which, in combination with the ensuing section 2.2.3, provides a qualitative framework for the emergence of cumulative or endogenous processes, serving as a theoretical basis for the models being developed in part II of the book.

2.2.3 Asset Prices and Aggregate Demand

The influence of asset prices on aggregate demand is generally studied by the theory of monetary transmission mechanisms.[16] This section is not going to provide a general overview of monetary transmission mechanisms, but highlights the most important effects of asset price changes on aggregate demand, where stock prices and real property prices have been found empirically to be most influential.[17]

Asset Prices and Consumption. There are three effects according to which consumption is influenced by the level of asset prices. Firstly, consumption is generally assumed to depend at least partly on expected wage income. As increasing/decreasing asset prices affect such expectations by signalling faster/slower growth of future real income, there exists a positive correlation between the level of asset prices and current consumption.[18] Secondly, according to life cycle and/or permanent income models, consumption is positively dependent on households' lifetime financial resources, i.e. rising/falling asset prices increase/decrease lifetime resources and lead to an increase/decrease in current consumption.[19] Thirdly, as to imperfect capital market theory, information asymmetries prevent households from borrowing solely on the basis of future expected income to satisfy their consumption needs, as borrowing is constrained by households' net worth which is positively dependent on the level of asset prices. Accordingly, current consumption is a positive function of current disposable income and of the availability of external finance. In case there is a rise/fall in asset prices, households' net worth increases/decreases, leading to an increase/decrease in the available amount of borrowing and therethrough to an increase/decrease in current consumption.

Asset Prices and Investment. Asset prices influence investment via three main channels. Firstly, the credit channel of monetary policy, consisting of the bank lending and balance sheet channel, states that increasing/decreasing asset prices lead to increasing/decreasing net worth positions, as well as to increasing/decreasing cash flow positions, which increase/decrease the available amount external finance and lower/increase the agency cost of lending, thereby leading to an increase/decrease in aggregate investment. Secondly, according to the theory of the "flexible accelerator", investment is predominantly dependent on expected future output growth. Accordingly, rising/declining asset prices indicating faster/slower GDP growth in the future lead to an increase/decrease in aggregate investment.[20] Thirdly, Tobin's q theory of investment, being reviewed in appendix A, states that an increase/decrease in asset prices lowers/increases the cost of buying new capital goods relative to the costs of buying existing capital goods, e.g. at the stock exchange. Accordingly, if there is a rise/fall in Tobin's q, i.e. in the ratio of the

[16]For a review of monetary transmission mechanisms, see e.g. Hubbard (1995), and Mishkin (1995).

[17]For empirical studies of the impacts of asset prices on aggregate demand in industrialized countries, see e.g. Bank for International Settlements (1998).

[18]See e.g. Poterba and Samwick (1995).

[19]See e.g. Deaton (1992).

[20]See e.g. Jorgensen (1963). For empirical evidence on flexible accelerator models, see e.g. Mullins and Wadhwani (1989).

market valuation of existing capital goods to the costs of acquiring new capital, investment increases/decreases.[21]

The Influence of Exchange Rates. Though the exchange rate has not been classified as a typical financial asset, its impact on real economic activity has to be studied since revaluations or devaluations influence real economic activity via three main channels.

Firstly, according to standard textbook models, there exists a positive relationship between the real exchange rate and net exports, i.e. an increase/decrease in the real exchange rate by an appreciation/depreciation of the nominal exchange rate stimulates/dampens aggregate demand via increasing/decreasing net export. This mechanism is built on the assumption that the values of import and export elasticities fulfill the Robinson and/or the Marshall-Lerner-condition.In case these conditions are not fulfilled, net exports are a negative function of the real exchange rate giving rise e.g. to short-run J-curve effects.

Secondly, in case balance sheet positions are characterized by large unhedged positions in foreign currency, changes in nominal exchange rates alter net worth and cash flow positions, and thereby aggregate consumption and investment via changes in the available amount of finance, and in the agency cost of lending. For example, if balance sheets are characterized by large amounts of foreign debt denominated in foreign currency which are not hedged by foreign assets to the same amount, there exists an inverse relationship between the nominal exchange rate and consumption and investment expenditures since an increase/decrease in the exchange rate increases/decreases the nominal amount of debt in domestic currency, which reduces/increases net worth, causing a decrease/increase in the available amount of external funds and therethrough a decrease/increase in consumption and investment expenditures. By way of contrast, in case balance sheets are characterized by unhedged positions of foreign assets denominated in foreign currency, there is a positive relationship between the nominal exchange rate and consumption and investment.

Thirdly, there exists an inverse relationship between the nominal exchange rate and the costs of imported inputs having both an influence on aggregate demand and on aggregate supply. For example, if there is an increase in the nominal exchange rate, costs for imported inputs rise, implying on the one hand a negative supply shock shifting the aggregate supply schedule upwards, and on the other hand a reduction in investment demand via a reduction in profits leading to declines in asset prices. Fourthly, there exists an inverse relationship between the nominal exchange rate and consumption via price effects of imported consumption goods changing real wages. For example, if there is an increase in the nominal exchange rate, prices for imported consumption goods rise, causing a rise in the aggregate domestic price level which reduces real wages and therethrough consumption. Summing up, contrary to the standard assumption that there is a positive correlation between (nominal and real) exchange rates and aggregate demand via the net export effect, there are various factors which can reverse this relationship, being labelled in the economic literature as "contractionary devaluation", stating that a devaluation of the home currency does not lead to a domestic real expansion, but to a real macroeconomic contraction.[22]

---

[21] For empirical evidence on the impact of stock prices and Tobin's q on investment in the United States and Canada, see Barro (1990).

[22] For a detailed discussion of possible effects causing contractionary devaluations, see Krugman and Taylor (1978), Taylor (1983), and van Wijnbergen (1983a, 1983b).

2.2.4 Asset Prices, Liquidity, Solvency and the Emergence of Cumulative Processes

After having reviewed standard approaches to the influence of asset prices on real economic activity, this section develops a new framework regarding the interdependencies of financial sector disturbances and the real sphere of an economy by the introduction of a new concept in section 2.2.4.1 as to the interaction of the liquidity and the solvency status of economic units. This new concept allows for the determination of a wide range of causes for bankruptcy being analyzed in section 2.2.4.2, where the state of bankruptcy is defined, as opposed to standard models, according to real world bankruptcy law, having been already outlined in section 2.2.2.3. Furthermore, this basic framework of the determinants of bankruptcy, or of the determinants of systemic financial crises, is enlarged by the results of sections 2.2.1 to 2.2.3, resulting in an aggregate qualitative model of various transmission mechanisms being relevant for the propagation mechanisms of systemic financial crises. These various interdependencies of asset prices, liquidity, solvency, financial constraints, and real economic activity, having been neglected so far by standard approaches on financial crises, give rise to cumulative and self-sustaining upward and downward processes in macroeconomic activity, and in aggregate financial "health" via the influence of macroeconomic conditions on the (macroeconomic) determinants of bankruptcy and vice versa. This new framework discussed in section 2.2.4.3 implies, partly in accordance with the "financial accelerator" theory, that financial sector disturbances, no matter whether they are positive or negative, are generally amplified by various interdependencies between the financial and the real sector of an economy, and can lead either to long-lasting boom or bust periods, where macroeconomic contractions are associated with systemic financial crises. Though this section uses some formal expressions, the analysis is qualitative in nature, serving as a theoretical basis for the quantitative analysis in part II of the book.

2.2.4.1 Liquidity, Solvency, and Profits: Definitions and Interdependencies

To elaborate the interdependencies between liquidity, solvency, and profits, the analysis starts with a stylized balance sheet in figure 2.1 which is to portray the financial structure of a representative economic sector, as e.g. the firm or the banking sector. Figure 2.1 could be alternatively interpreted as a stylized balance sheet of a single economic unit. This microeconomic perspective however, is not able to study the sector-internal dynamics leading to self-sustaining expansions as well as contractions, because, for example, asset prices or risk-dependent interest rates cannot be influenced by a single economic unit's earnings, cash flows, or profits. By way of contrast, an entire economic sector as a whole determines its own market valuation by aggregate earnings, cash flows, and profits giving rise to endogenous expansions and contractions. Furthermore, a microeconomic perspective would neglect the fact that the analysis of (systemic) financial crises refers to widespread failures of a large fraction of business units in the firm and in the financial sector, and not to defaults of single economic entities.

All balance sheet positions in figure 2.1, being assumed to be function of time t, are priced at their current market or discounted present values. There are three types of assets. Asset type one are domestic productive assets being used as an input factor whose market value amounts to $P_A(t)\,A(t)$, where $A(t)$ denotes the real stock of domestic assets, and $P_A(t)$ the market price per real unit in domestic currency. The real stock of assets $A(t)$

Assets		*Debts*	
Domestic Assets	$P_A(t)\ A(t)$	Domestic Debt	$DB(t)$
Foreign Assets	$s(t)\ P^*_A(t)\ A^*(t)$	Foreign Debt	$s(t)\ DB^*(t)$
Liquid Monetary Assets	$LMA(t)$		
		Net Worth	$NW(t)$

Figure 2.1: Stylized Financial Structure of a Representative Economic Sector

priced at $P_A(t)$ can be interpreted as a weighted average of a large variety of domestic real and financial assets valued at their market prices. Asset type two are foreign productive assets, being also used as input factors, whose market value in domestic currency amount to $P_A^*(t)\, A^*(t)\, s(t)$, where $A^*(t)$ denotes the real stock of foreign assets, $P_A^*(t)$ the market price per real unit in foreign currency, and $s(t)$ the nominal exchange rate, expressing the price of one unit foreign currency in domestic currency. The real stock of foreign assets $A^*(t)$ valued at $P_A^*(t)$ can also be interpreted as a weighted average of a large variety of foreign real and financial assets valued at their market prices. Domestic and foreign productive assets $A(t)$ and $A^*(t)$ are assumed to be subject to depreciation. Asset type three are non-interest bearing liquid monetary assets $LMA(t)$ which are not used as an input factor, but to fulfill payment commitments; $LMA(t)$ can be interpreted e.g. as deposits with banks which can be liquidated instantly.

On the debt side, there are two types of liabilities. Firstly, (nominal) domestic debt $DB(t)$ in domestic currency, and secondly, foreign debt in domestic currency $s(t)\, DB^*(t)$, where $DB^*(t)$ denotes the nominal value of foreign debt in foreign currency. Net worth $NW(t)$ is the difference between assets and debts and can take a positive, zero, or negative sign. The debt-asset ratio, being defined as the ratio of the sum of debts to the sum of assets, i.e. $(DB(t) + s(t)\, DB^*(t))/(P_A(t)A(t) + s(t)P_A^*(t)A^*(t) + LMA(t))$, is an indirect indicator of the level of net worth as an increasing/decreasing debt-asset ratio indicates a decreasing/increasing level of net worth $NW(t)$. The net foreign position, being defined as foreign assets less foreign debt, i.e. formally as $P_A^*(t)A^*(t) - DB^*(t)$, provides information about the use of foreign debt on the asset side of the balance sheet, i.e. whether foreign debt is used to invest in domestic assets which are denominated in domestic currency, or in foreign assets which are denominated in foreign currency. In case foreign debt is used to invest in foreign assets, then the balance sheet exhibits a foreign neutral or a foreign net creditor position. In terms of the stylized balance sheet in figure 2.1, a foreign neutral or foreign net creditor position is characterized formally by $DB^*(t) \leq P_A^* A^*$, i.e. by foreign assets being equal or larger than foreign debt. If, by way of contrast, foreign debt is used partly or entirely to invest in domestic assets, then the balance sheet exhibits a foreign net debtor position which, in terms of figure 2.1 is characterized formally by $DB^*(t) > P_A^* A^*$, i.e. by foreign debt being larger than foreign assets.

In case figure 2.1 is interpreted as the stylized balance sheet of the business firm sector, the stock of domestic assets $A(t)$ valued at its market price $P_A(t)$ represents the capital stock valued at the stock exchange by aggregate equity prices, and other domestic financial assets, as e.g. domestic equities or bonds valued at their market prices. The nominal stock of foreign assets $P_A^*(t)A^*(t)$ can be interpreted as foreign direct investment in the form of real capital valued e.g. at replacement costs, and as foreign financial assets, as e.g. foreign bonds or equities valued at their market prices. Liquid monetary assets $LMA(t)$ represent deposits with banks. Domestic and foreign debt, i.e. $DB(t)$ and $DB^*(t)$, represent domestic and foreign bank loans. By way of contrast, if figure 2.1 is to represent the banking sector, the nominal stock of domestic assets $P_A(t)A(t)$ represents the stock of loans priced at its "quality", i.e. at its expected discounted present value, and other domestic financial assets valued at their market prices. The nominal stock of foreign assets $P_A^*(t)A^*(t)$ represents loans in foreign currency to foreigners, and other foreign financial assets valued at their market prices. Liquid monetary assets $LMA(t)$ represent central bank reserves which are a fraction of domestic and foreign deposits in foreign currency, being represented by $DB(t)$ and $DB^*(t)$, i.e it holds that $DB(t)+s(t)DB^*(t) = m\,LMA(t)$ where m denotes the money multiplier being the inverse of the required reserve ratio.

It has been assumed that the balance sheet in figure 2.1 consists only of *on-balance sheet* assets and debts though the use of *off-balance sheet* assets and debts, representing contingent assets and liabilities which are placed generally *below* the balance sheet, by financial and non-financial firms in industrial and in emerging market economies has increased steadily during the last two decades owing to the worldwide process of domestic and international financial market liberalization. Off-balance sheet positions can be subdivided in traditional ones, as e.g. guarantees, and in "newer" ones, as e.g. options, swaps, futures or forwards, being also called derivatives, or financial innovations. Contingent assets and claims can have adverse effects on aggregate financial stability as they are not used to hedge against risk, but to take risk deliberately. Furthermore, most financial innovations, so-called "Over The Counter" products, are not subject to common standards of financial market regulation as they are not traded at official future and option exchanges, facilitating excessive and uncontrolled risk taking. As a thorough discussion of the impacts of off-balance sheet positions on aggregate liquidity, solvency, and real economic activity would require a far larger and more detailed discussion than this contribution can manage, the potential impacts of off-balance sheet transactions on aggregate financial stability are described briefly in appendix C by a simple example, whereas the following discussion is going to be restricted to the analysis of on-balance sheet positions.

The *liquidity or cash flow status* of the representative economic sector is determined by money inflows less money outflows, stemming on the one hand from operating profits, and on the other hand from changes in asset and debt stocks. Operating profits $OP(t)$ are formally given by

$$OP(t) = EA(t) - i_{DB}(t)DB(t) - s(t)i_{DB}^*(t)DB^*(t), \tag{2.4}$$

where $EA(t)$ denotes nominal earnings in domestic currency, $i_{DB}(t)$ the interest rate on domestic debt, and $i_{DB}^*(t)$ the interest rate on foreign debt. Hence, operating profits are determined by nominal earnings $EA(t)$ less interest rate costs on domestic debt $i_{DB}(t)DB(t)$, and less interest rate costs on foreign debt, where nominal earnings $EA(t)$

are defined by

$$EA(t) = P(t)\,Y(\underset{+}{Y^d(t)}, \underset{+}{Y^s(t)}), \tag{2.5}$$

i.e. by the product of the domestic price level $P(t)$ and the sector's real aggregate output $Y(Y^d(t), Y^s(t))$, being positively dependent on demand conditions $Y^d(t)$ and supply conditions $Y^s(t)$ to be determined below.[23] Adding changes in asset and debt stocks to operating profits $OP(t)$ by equation 2.4 results in the cash flow or liquidity status at time t, $CF(t)$, which is formally given by

$$CF(t) = OP(t) - P_A(t)\dot{A}(t) - s(t)P_A^*(t)\dot{A}^*(t) - L\dot{M}A(t) + \dot{DB}(t) + s(t)\dot{DB}^*(t), \tag{2.6}$$

where $\dot{x}(t) = dx/dt$ denotes the time derivative of variable $x(t)$, i.e. the change of variable $x(t)$ at time t. Thus, the the cash flow position is determined by operating profits less changes in assets $-P_A(t)\dot{A}(t) - s(t)P_A^*(t)\dot{A}^*(t) - L\dot{M}A(t)$, plus changes in debt $\dot{DB}(t) + s(t)\dot{DB}^*(t)$.[24]

It has to be emphasized that cash flow position 2.6, resulting from normal operation and balance sheet transactions, may not be mixed up with actual or expected cash flows being used for asset price determination as outlined in equation 2.3, because cash flow by equation 2.6 refers to the overall liquidity status including financing costs and shifts in balance sheet items, whereas expected cash flows in equation 2.3 do only refer to net money inflows exclusive of interest rate or opportunity costs.

Nominal profits of the representative sector at time t, $PR(t)$, are determined by operating profits $OP(t)$, and by capital gains or losses resulting from changes in domestic asset prices $\dot{P}_A$, foreign asset prices $\dot{P}_A^*$, and in the exchange rate $\dot{s}(t)$. Formally, nominal profits $PR(t)$ are given by

$$PR(t) = OP(t) + \dot{P}_A(t)A(t) + \dot{s}(t)P_A^*(t)A^*(t) + s(t)\dot{P}_A^*(t)A^*(t) - \dot{s}(t)DB^*(t). \tag{2.7}$$

The *solvency status or net worth* at time t, $NW(t)$, is a backward looking variable[25], being determined by initial net worth at time $t = 0$, $NW(0)$, i.e. by the difference between the initial asset and debt stock at time $t = 0$, and by past accumulated and actual profits/losses. Formally, net worth is given by

$$NW(t) = NW(0) + \int_{s=0}^{t} PR(s)\,ds. \tag{2.8}$$

This definition of net worth excludes cash calls and/or write-downs which would cause changes in net worth by extraordinary alterations in assets and/or debts being not associated with "normal operation".[26]

[23] For reasons of simplicity, equation 2.5 assumes that there are no nominal earnings in foreign currency. However, this simplifying assumption is going to be given up later in section 2.2.4.3.

[24] Note that, for example, a sale of domestic asset A, i.e. $\dot{A}(t) < 0$, at price $P_A(t)$, leads to a money inflow to the amount of $-P_A(t)\dot{A}(t) > 0$, whereas a reduction of foreign debt DB^*, i.e. $\dot{DB}^*(t) < 0$, at the exchange rate $s(t)$, leads to a money outflow to the amount of $s(t)\dot{DB}^*(t) < 0$.

[25] For the distinction between backward and forward looking variables, as well as their influence on solutions of general dynamic rational expectations models, see appendix D.

[26] To illustrate the interdependencies between cash flows, profits, and net worth consider the following

2.2.4.2 Determinants of Bankruptcy

This paragraph analyzes possible causes of bankruptcy, where the state of bankruptcy is defined according to real world bankruptcy rules. Thus, an economic unit, or an economic sector, is defined to be bankrupt firstly, if it is illiquid, or secondly, if it is insolvent, or thirdly, if it is both illiquid and insolvent, where illiquidity is defined by a negative cash flow position according to equation 2.6, i.e. by $CF(t) < 0$, and insolvency by a negative net worth position according to equation 2.8, i.e. by $NW(t) < 0$. The following analysis provides only a short enumeration of possible determinants of illiquidity and insolvency, without considering explicitly both the interdependencies between different determinants and between illiquidity and insolvency, as these interdependencies give rise to cumulative processes which are going to be analyzed in the next paragraph.

Insolvency, or negative net worth $NW(t)$, can be caused according to equation 2.8 by past accumulated and/or actual losses which are greater than initial net worth.[27] Negative profits, or losses can be caused according to equations 2.4 and 2.7 ceteris paribus firstly, by a drop in nominal earnings $EA(t)$, which can be caused by a fall in the domestic price level $P(t)$, i.e. by (debt-) deflation, and/or by a drop in real output $Y(Y^d(t), Y^s(t))$ caused by deteriorating demand and supply conditions, secondly, by a rise in the domestic interest rate on debt $i_{DB}(t)$, thirdly, by a rise in the foreign interest rate on debt $i^*_{DB}(t)$, fourthly, by a drop in domestic asset prices $P_A(t)$, fifthly, by a drop in foreign asset prices $P^*_A(t)$, and sixthly, by a rise in the exchange rate $s(t)$ in case the nominal value of foreign assets is smaller than the nominal value of foreign debt, i.e. in case the sector is not hedged against currency risk. It has to be emphasized, that changes in asset and debt stocks are *not* responsible for a deterioration of the solvency status, since changes in asset and debt stocks are the result from past changes in profits.

Illiquidity, or a negative cash flow $CF(t)$, can be caused according to equations 2.4 and 2.6 ceteris paribus firstly, by a drop in nominal earnings $EA(t)$, which can stem from a drop in the domestic price level $P(t)$ and/or from a drop in output $Y(Y^d(t), Y^s(t))$, secondly, by a rise in the domestic interest rate on debt $i_{DB}(t)$, and thirdly, by a rise in the foreign interest rate on debt $i^*_{DB}(t)$. The same factors can lead to insolvency as they determine the state of operating profits by equation 2.4, being both an ingredient

---

example. The balance sheet positions according to figure 2.1 are assumed to have the following initial numerical values in $t = 0$: $P_A(0) = 1$, $A(0) = 5$, $P^*_A(0) = 0$, $A^*(0) = 0$, $LMA(0) = 3$, $DB(0) = 0$, $s(0) = 0$, $DB^*(0) = 0$ resulting in $NW(0) = 8$. Operating profit in $t = 1$ is $OP(1) = -4$, being assumed to be paid by a reduction in LMA. However, as the stock of LMA does not suffice to meet due payment obligations, the sector would become illiquid if there were no money inflows. Consider that the sector increases domestic debt by one unit, i.e. $\dot{DB}(1) = 1$, to obtain liquid financial means leading to increase in LMA by one unit, which is however spent immediately to meet the sector's payment obligations, i.e. the change in LMA amounts to $\dot{LMA}(1) = -3 + 1 - 1 = -3$. Accordingly, the operating loss of 4 units is financed by liquidating the initial stock of LMA by 3 units, and by taking a loan of 1 unit, generating a cash flow according to equation 2.6 in $t = 1$ to the amount of $CF(1) = OP(1) - \dot{LMA}(1) + \dot{DB}(1) = -4 - (-3) + 1 = 0$. Furthermore, consider that the price of domestic assets in $t = 1$ drops to $P_A(1) = 0.8$, i.e. $\dot{P}_A(1) = -0.2$, resulting in a total loss according to equation 2.7 of $PR(1) = OP(1) + \dot{P}_A(1)A(1) = -4 + (-0.2) \cdot 5 = -5$, as $A(1) = A(0) = 5$. Hence, net worth in $t = 1$, owing to equation 2.8, is given by $NW(1) = NW(0) + PR(1) = 8 - 5 = 3$, which can be alternatively obtained from new asset and debt stocks in $t = 1$ which amount to $P_A(1) = 0.8$, $A(1) = 5$, $P^*_A(1) = 0$, $A^*(1) = 0$, $LMA(1) = 0$, $DB(1) = 1$, $s(1) = 0$, $DB^*(1) = 0$, resulting in $NW(1) = 3$ as well.

[27] Insolvency implies a debt-asset ratio value of greater than one, indicating that the sum of debts is larger than the sum of assets.

of the liquidity status 2.6 and of nominal profits 2.7. Accordingly, liquidity and solvency are interdependent, i.e. illiquidity can cause insolvency and vice versa. Further causes for illiquidity according to equation 2.6 are changes in assets and debts leading to money outflows which overcompensate money inflows. Among various possibilities, there is one case which is of special empirical relevance, arising if demanded repayment of debt (money outflow) is larger than operating profits or losses plus returns from selling assets, i.e. if it holds that

$$\begin{aligned} -\dot{DB}(t) - s(t)\dot{DB}^*(t) \quad > \quad & EA(t) - i_{DB}(t)DB(t) - s(t)i^*_{DB}(t)DB^*(t) \\ & - P_A(t)\dot{A}(t) - s(t)P^*_A(t)\dot{A}^*(t) - \dot{LMA}(t), \end{aligned} \tag{2.9}$$

$$\text{where} \qquad \dot{DB}(t), \dot{DB}^*(t) < 0.$$

The banking sector, or single banks, are faced with condition 2.9 in case of a *bank run*, i.e. in case most domestic and/or foreign depositors withdraw their short-term funds $DB(t)$ and $s(t)DB^*(t)$. Banks however, never can meet an almost complete and sudden withdrawal of deposits as liquid monetary assets $LMA(t)$ (central bank reserves) are only a fraction of deposits, and operating profits $OP(t)$ are likely to be not able to cover all money outflows. Likewise, a liquidation of assets which would be necessary to prevent illiquidity is not possible firstly, as a considerable part of assets are long-term debt contracts, as e.g. mortgage loans or long-term business loans, which cannot be liquidated, and secondly, as a sudden and widespread withdrawal of short-term debt contracts, as e.g. roll-over business loans which could be theoretically liquidated instantly, is likely to cause illiquidity by firms according to condition 2.9, which increases the share of non-performing loans with banks and reduces banks' profits and net worth. As the banking sector cannot meet all payment commitments in case of a bank run, the only remaining possibility to prevent illiquidity is a massive lender of last resort intervention by the central bank, i.e. a large and extraordinary increase in liquid monetary assets $LMA(t)$ (central bank reserves) which are used to pay depositors. However, in case a large part of deposits are denominated in foreign currency, a central bank intervention cannot prevent illiquidity in case of a bank run; in that case, only a short-run liquidity support by international financial markets could avert bankruptcy by domestic banks, which is however an unrealistic scenario, as a bank run by foreigners indicates that domestic banks are faced with a *credit crunch* in international financial markets.

Illiquidity in the business firm sector according to condition 2.9 is, like a bank run, caused by a sudden and widespread withdrawal of short-term debt which can be induced, as aforementioned, by a bank run when banks try to meet payment commitments by calling roll-over loans. As business firms' operating profits in most cases do not suffice to meet a widespread liquidation of short-term debt, there arise two options to prevent illiquidity. Firstly, business firms can try to sell a widespread part of their assets, being labelled as a "fire-sale" of assets. However, in case an entire economic sector sells its assets, asset prices $P_A(t)$ and $P^*_A(t)$ are going to drop, reducing money inflows and causing additionally insolvency problems. Secondly, business firms can try to borrow new funds to repay existing debt. However, in case there is a widespread withdrawal of short-term business loans by banks, business firms are unlikely to receive new funds due to an overall credit crunch in domestic financial markets. As opposed to lender of last resort interventions which are able to prevent widespread illiquidity by banks, widespread illiquidity of business firms in most cases cannot be prevented by a "concerted action" of the banking sector due to coordination failures.

2.2.4.3 Cumulative Expansions and Contractions

Hitherto, the analysis concentrated on definitions as well as on interdependencies of liquidity, profits and solvency. However, to study the propagation mechanisms of systemic financial crises, the analysis has to be enlarged firstly, by the interdependencies of financial constraints, asset prices and real economic activity according to sections 2.2.1 to 2.2.3, and secondly, by the interdependencies of economic units' financial status and macroeconomic activity. Both kinds of interdependencies give rise to cumulative upward and downward processes, where macroeconomic contractions are associated with systemic financial crises. The following analysis distinguishes three main effects causing cumulative processes, where the first effect considers the emergence of demand-side cumulative processes, the second effect the emergence of financial-accelerator induced cumulative process, and the third effect the emergence of supply-side induced cumulative processes. As the following discussion refers to changes in aggregate economic activity, and not to changes in income of a certain sector, the definitions of liquidity, solvency, and profits according to section 2.2.4.1, refer in the following to the aggregate liquidity and solvency status, as well as to aggregate profits.

The Emergence of Demand-Side Cumulative Processes. Including the effects of varying real economic activity, or varying nominal earnings $P(t)\cdot Y(Y^d(t), Y^s(t))$ according to equation 2.5, requires that both the demand and the supply conditions $Y^d(t)$ and $Y^s(t)$ are endogenized. Demand conditions $Y^d(t)$ are assumed to be positively dependent on the market value of domestic and foreign assets according to the results of section 2.2.3, i.e. formally it holds that

$$Y^d(t) = Y^d(\underset{+}{P_A(t)A(t)}, \underset{+}{s(t)P_A^*(t)A^*(t)}). \tag{2.10}$$

By way of contrast, supply conditions $Y^s(t)$, i.e. potential output, are assumed to be positively dependent on the real stocks of domestic and foreign assets like output resulting from a production function. Formally it holds that

$$Y^s(t) = Y^s(\underset{+}{A(t)}, \underset{+}{A^*(t)}). \tag{2.11}$$

The influence of asset prices is included by assuming that domestic asset prices $P_A(t)$ are determined according to equation 2.3 by discounting nominal earnings $EA(t)$, where the discount factor is a weighted average of domestic and foreign interest rate costs as the stock of domestic assets $A(t)$ is financed both by domestic and by foreign debt. Formally, domestic asset prices are given by

$$P_A(t) = \frac{P(t)\,Y(Y^d(t), Y^s(t))}{\gamma i_{DB}(t) + (1-\gamma)(i^*_{DB}(t) + \hat{s}(t))}, \qquad 0 < \gamma < 1, \tag{2.12}$$

where $\hat{s}(t) = \dot{s}(t)/s(t)$ denotes the exchange rate's growth rate, $i^*_{DB}(t) + \hat{s}(t)$ foreign interest rate costs in domestic currency terms, and γ the weighting factor whose value depends on the percentage share of domestic debt finance of asset $A(t)$. For reasons of simplicity, foreign asset prices $P_A^*(t)$ are assumed to be negatively dependent on the foreign interest rate on debt $i_{DB}^*(t)$, i.e. formally it holds that

$$P_A^*(t) = P_A^*(\underset{-}{i_{DB}^*(t)}). \tag{2.13}$$

One important implication of endogenizing both asset prices and nominal earnings by equations 2.10 to 2.13, is the emergence of demand-side cumulative upward and downward processes by a self-sustaining interaction between domestic asset prices and real economic activity (nominal earnings). A drop/rise in nominal earnings according to equation 2.5 leads to a decline/rise in domestic asset prices according to equation 2.12, whereas the decline/rise in domestic asset prices causes a further drop/rise in nominal earnings by deteriorating/improving demand conditions according to equation 2.10, inducing a further decline/rise in domestic asset prices, and so on. Accordingly, once there is a decline/rise in asset prices or in real economic activity, an endogenous process is going to cause a further decline/rise in asset prices and real economic activity. Furthermore, an endogenous decline/rise in asset prices and real economic activity causes a self-sustaining decline/rise in cash flows, profits, and net worth according to equations 2.6, 2.7, and 2.8.

It must be emphasized however, that these demand-side cumulative upward and downward processes cannot start by themselves, but have to be "triggered" by an exogenous event. The main triggers according to equation 2.12, are changes in domestic and foreign interest rates $i_{DB}(t)$ and $i_{DB}^*(t)$, and changes in the exchange rate $s(t)$. For example, a rise in the domestic interest rate on debt causes a fall in asset prices and in aggregate earnings via deteriorating demand conditions, leading to reductions in cash flow, profits, net worth, whereas the drop in nominal earnings causes a further decline in asset prices, cash flow, profits, net worth, leading to a further decline in demand conditions, nominal earnings, asset prices, cash flow, profits, net worth, and so on. By way of contrast a drop in the domestic interest rate on debt causes a cumulative improvement in cash flow, profits, net worth, and asset prices, and engenders an overall macroeconomic expansion.

Though not explicitly considered by the model equations above, terms-of-trade shocks and technology shocks can also give rise to demand-side cumulative processes as both shocks lead to a change in nominal earnings. A rise/drop in the real exchange rate, caused either by exchange rate or inflation alterations, leads to a rise/fall in net exports and thereby in nominal earnings, causing an upward/downward cumulative process being associated with increasing/decreasing asset prices, nominal earnings, liquidity, profits, and net worth. Though technology shocks develop from the supply-side, they can give rise to demand-side cumulative processes as a positive/negative technology shock leads to improving/deteriorating supply conditions according to equation 2.11 by an increase/decrease in potential output at given stocks of real domestic and foreign assets, leading to a rise/fall in nominal earnings, asset prices, liquidity, profits, and net worth.[28]

[28]Technology shocks could be taken into consideration formally by the introduction of a technological efficiency parameter $J(t)$ in the supply conditions equation 2.11, reading in its modified form as

$$Y^s(t) = Y^s(\underset{+}{A(t)}, \underset{+}{A^*(t)}, \underset{+}{J(t)}),$$

and stating that potential output is positively dependent on the efficiency of production technology $J(t)$. A positive/negative technology shock leads to an increase/decrease in production efficiency, i.e. to

The Emergence of Financial-Accelerator Induced Cumulative Processes. Hitherto, cumulative upward and downward processes have been explained solely by the demand-side interaction of asset prices and real economic activity, where the influence of financial constraints, i.e. the influence of liquidity constraint $CF(t) \geq 0$, derived from equation 2.6, and the solvency constraint $NW(t) \geq 0$, derived from equation 2.8, have been neglected so far. However, the liquidity and the solvency constraint have an "accelerating" effect on the cumulative upward and downward process via alterations in financing conditions according to the "financial accelerator principle" which has been outlined in section 2.2.2.2. Including financial-accelerator induced cumulative processes in the model requires that financing conditions, i.e. the domestic and the foreign interest rate on debt $i_{DB}(t)$ and i^*_{DB}, as well as the available amount of debt finance $DB(t)$ and $DB^*(t)$, have to be endogenized. Following imperfect capital market theory, both the domestic and the foreign interest rate on debt $i_{DB}(t)$ and i^*_{DB} are assumed to be negatively dependent both on the cash flow $CF(t)$ and the net worth position $NW(t)$, i.e. formally it holds that

$$i_{DB}(t) = i_{DB}(\underset{-}{CF(t)}, \underset{-}{NW(t)}) \tag{2.14}$$

$$i^*_{DB}(t) = i^*_{DB}(\underset{-}{CF(t)}, \underset{-}{NW(t)}), \tag{2.15}$$

stating that an increase/decrease in cash flow and/or net worth reduces/increases default risk leading to relaxing/tightening financing conditions by declining/rising interest rates. Regarding the availability of debt finance, it is assumed that the stocks of available domestic and foreign debt, $DB(t)$ and $DB^*(t)$, are positively dependent on the cash flow and the net worth position, i.e. formally it holds that

$$DB(t) = DB(\underset{+}{CF(t)}, \underset{+}{NW(t)}) \tag{2.16}$$

$$DB^*(t) = DB^*(\underset{+}{CF(t)}, \underset{+}{NW(t)}), \tag{2.17}$$

stating that declining/rising default risk by increasing/decreasing cash flow and/or net worth leads to relaxing/tightening financing conditions by increasing/decreasing the amount of available debt.[29]

The impact of the financial accelerator effect on the exchange rate $s(t)$ in case of flexible exchange rate systems, and on foreign exchange reserves $Z(t)$ in case of fixed exchange rate systems, depends on whether changes in the foreign debt stock $DB^*(t)$ cause transactions in the foreign exchange market or not. Generally, the existence of transactions in the foreign exchange market is determined by the cash flow position in foreign currency $CF^*(t)$, being formally defined, following the balance sheet structure in figure 2.1, and equations 2.4 and 2.6, as

$$CF^*(t) = EA^*(t) - i^*(t)DB^*(t) - P^*_A(t)\dot{A}^*(t) + \dot{DB}^*(t), \tag{2.18}$$

that is, by nominal earnings in foreign currency $EA^*(t)$, which have been neglected so far for reasons of simplicity, less foreign interest costs, less changes in foreign assets

rise/fall in $J(t)$, and thereby to an increase/decrease in potential output $Y^s(t)$.

[29] It has to emphasized that the solvency status in equations 2.14 to 2.17, i.e. the net worth position $NW(t)$, could have been alternatively represented by the inverse of the debt-asset ratio.

$P_A^*(t)\dot{A}^*(t)$, plus changes in the foreign debt stock $\dot{DB}^*(t)$. If the foreign cash flow position is zero, i.e. if it holds that $CF^*(t) = 0$, there arise no transactions in the foreign exchange market, as money outflows in foreign currency can be "paid" completely by money inflows in foreign currency, implying that there is no need to exchange cash flows in domestic currency into foreign currency. By way of contrast, in case the foreign cash flow position is positive or negative, i.e. if it holds that $CF^*(t) \neq 0$, there arise transactions in the foreign exchange market as excess/lacking cash flow in foreign currency is sold/bought at the foreign exchange market, leading to an increase/decrease in the cash flow position in domestic currency $CF^D(t)$, being formally defined, following also the balance sheet structure in figure 2.1, by

$$CF^D(t) = EA(t) - i(t)DB(t) - P_A(t)\dot{A}(t) - L\dot{M}A(t) + \dot{DB}(t), \tag{2.19}$$

that is, by nominal earnings in domestic currency $EA(t)$, less interest payments on domestic debt $i(t)DB(t)$, less changes in domestic assets $P_A(t)\dot{A}(t)$ and in liquid monetary assets $L\dot{M}A(t)$, plus changes in domestic debt $\dot{DB}(t)$.[30]

Consequently, if there are variations in the foreign debt stock, i.e. if it holds that $\dot{DB}^*(t) \neq 0$, there arise no changes in the exchange rate $s(t)$, and in foreign exchange reserves $Z(t)$, if the foreign cash flow position remains zero, implying that changes in foreign debt are compensated by other components in the foreign cash flow position 2.18. For example, if an increase in foreign debt is used to finance an increase in foreign assets to the same amount, i.e. if it holds that $\dot{DB}^*(t) = -P_A^*(t)\dot{A}^*(t)$ where $\dot{A}^*(t) > 0$, there arise no transactions in the foreign exchange market, leaving the exchange rate and foreign exchange reserves unchanged. By way of contrast, there arise changes in the exchange rate and in foreign exchange reserves, in case variations in the debt stock are not completely compensated by other components of the foreign cash flow position 2.18, leading to changes in the domestic cash flow position 2.19.

Empirical evidence on episodes of financial crises shows firstly, that countries with large amounts of foreign debt, i.e. emerging market countries (as e.g. Thailand, Mexico, Argentina) but also industrial countries (as e.g. Norway, Sweden, Finland), are subject to large variations in the foreign debt stock, and secondly, that these variations cause either large swings in exchange rates or in foreign exchange reserves, implying that the foreign cash flow position is generally different from zero. The most important reason for a nonzero foreign cash flow position in case of variations in the foreign debt stock is the empirical fact that foreign debt is generally used for investment in domestic assets, generating income streams predominantly in domestic currency. Summing up, it is reasonable to assume that changes in the foreign debt stock $DB^*(t)$ generally lead to transactions in the foreign exchange market which lead to variations in the exchange rate $s(t)$ and in foreign exchange reserves $Z(t)$.

Consequently, in case of flexible exchange rate systems, a reduction/increase in foreign debt $DB^*(t)$ by foreign lenders leads to an increasing demand for/supply of foreign currency by domestic agents, causing a rise/fall of the exchange rate $s(t)$, as paying back/receiving foreign debt requires that domestic/foreign currency has to be exchanged

[30]The sum of the domestic cash flow position 2.19 and the foreign cash flow position 2.18 expressed in domestic currency, i.e. multiplied by the exchange rate $s(t)$, equals the overall cash flow position defined in equation 2.6 plus nominal earnings in foreign currency in domestic currency $s(t)EA^*(t)$ which have been neglected for reasons of simplicity in the previous analysis.

into foreign/domestic currency. Thus, it holds formally that

$$s(t) = s(\underset{-}{DB^*(t)}), \tag{2.20}$$

stating that a decrease/increase in foreign debt causes an increased demand/supply for foreign currency leading to a rise/fall of the exchange rate. Accordingly, capital outflows/inflows generally lead to a depreciation/appreciation of the home currency.

In case of fixed exchange rate systems, it seems reasonable to assume that a reduction/increase in foreign debt $DB^*(t)$ by foreign lenders leads to an increasing demand for/supply of foreign currency by domestic agents, causing a reduction/increase in foreign exchange reserves $Z(t)$. Ergo, the stock of foreign exchange reserves $Z(t)$ is formally given by

$$Z(t) = Z(\underset{+}{DB^*(t)}), \tag{2.21}$$

stating that a decrease/increase in foreign debt causes an increased demand/supply for foreign currency leading to a reduction/increase in the stock of foreign reserves. Consequently, capital outflows/inflows generally lead to a decline/rise of foreign exchange reserves. Foreign exchange reserves $Z(t)$ generally have an inverse effect on domestic interest rates $i(t)$ as a rising/declining stock of foreign exchange reserves increases/decreases the amount of high powered money, leading to a decrease/increase in domestic interest rates, i.e. formally it holds that

$$i(t) = i(\underset{-}{Z(t)}). \tag{2.22}$$

The inclusion of the influence of financial constraints on asset prices, real economic activity, liquidity, profits, and solvency generates cumulative upward and downward processes which are much larger in amplitude than demand-side cumulative processes, as they are reinforced by the financial accelerator effect via improving or deteriorating cash flow and net worth positions. A drop/rise in nominal earnings giving rise to a demand-side cumulative downward/upward process, being associated with declining/rising asset prices, cash flows, profits, net worth and deteriorating/improving demand conditions, is amplified firstly, by an increase/decrease in the domestic and in the foreign interest rates on debt $i_{DB}(t)$ and $i^*_{DB}(t)$ by equations 2.14 and 2.15, secondly, by a reduction/increase of available domestic and foreign debt finance $DB(t)$ and $DB^*(t)$ by equations 2.16 and 2.17, thirdly, in case of flexible exchange rate systems by a rise/fall in the exchange rate by equation 2.20, and fourthly, in case of fixed exchange rate systems, by a decrease/increase in the stock of foreign exchange reserves by equation 2.21 inducing an additional rise/fall in domestic interest rates by equation 2.22, leading to a further drop/rise in asset prices, to a further deterioration/improvement in demand conditions, to a further macroeconomic contraction/expansion, to further deteriorations/improvements in cash flow, profits and net worth, to further interest rate increases/decreases, to further revaluations/devaluations of the exchange rate, and to a further decrease/increase in the stock of foreign exchange reserves.

It is important to note that the inclusion of financial constraint effects does not longer require that cumulative processes are triggered by exogenous events, because interest rates and exchange rates (and foreign exchange reserves) are endogenous variables as well. Accordingly, there arises the possibility that cumulative processes are *purely endogenous* in nature, implying that macroeconomic expansions as well as contractions, which are possibly associated with systemic financial crises, are an inherent characteristic of modern economies, being discussed in detail in part II of the book.

The Emergence of Supply-Side Induced Cumulative Processes. A further effect, which has been neglected so far, but giving rise to further accelerations of demand-side and financial-accelerator induced cumulative processes, is the impact of supply-side induced cumulative processes through changes in supply conditions $Y^s(t)$, being induced by alterations in domestic and real asset stocks, $A(t)$ and $A^*(t)$, according to equation 2.11. It is reasonable to assume that the stocks of domestic and foreign assets $A(t)$ and $A^*(t)$, and thereby supply conditions $Y^s(t)$, are positively dependent on financing conditions, and on the availability of debt finance, since the acquisition of assets generally requires external funds. Hence, formally it holds that

$$A(t) = A(\underset{-}{i_{DB}(t)}, \underset{-}{i^*_{DB}(t)}, \underset{+}{DB(t)}, \underset{+}{DB^*(t)}) \tag{2.23}$$

$$A^*(t) = A^*(\underset{-}{i_{DB}(t)}, \underset{-}{i^*_{DB}(t)}, \underset{+}{DB(t)}, \underset{+}{DB^*(t)}), \tag{2.24}$$

stating that investment in domestic and foreign assets is negatively dependent on domestic and foreign interest rates, and positively dependent on the availability of domestic and foreign debt. Equations 2.23 and 2.24 imply that an overall macroeconomic contraction/expansion, being associated with falling/rising asset prices, nominal earnings, cash flow, profits, net worth, domestic and foreign debt stocks, and increasing/decreasing domestic interest rates, foreign interest rates, and exchange rates, is further dampened/accelerated by a decrease/increase in potential output, leading to a further reduction/increase in nominal earnings according to equation 2.5, and thereby to a further acceleration of the cumulative downward/upward process.

Changing supply conditions, i.e. changing asset stocks, have an additional accelerating effect on cumulative upward and downward processes by influencing asset prices. This effect is not captured by equations 2.12 and 2.13 as they do not determine asset prices by supply and demand conditions. However, during macroeconomic contractions/expansions, decreasing/increasing asset stocks lead to an additional decrease/increase in domestic and foreign asset prices by an increasing supply/demand of domestic and foreign assets. One important effect arises especially in times of financial distress, being labelled as *distress selling* or *fire-sale of assets*, when a large number of economic units is forced to sell large amounts of their asset stocks at the same time to meet payment obligations, as it has been for example described by condition 2.9, resulting in a collapse of asset prices causing further solvency and liquidity problems.

An Assessment. Summing up, there exist various transmission mechanisms causing endogenous upward and downward processes in overall macroeconomic activity, where expansions are associated with "financial health", and contractions with "financial distress". Furthermore, it has been emphasized that contractions, as well as expansions can be purely endogenous phenomena which are not caused by exogenous shocks. However, notwithstanding the fact, that the analysis can provide a deep understanding of cumulative processes, it does not provide an explanation why a process is expansionary or contractionary, i.e. there is no explanation why an expansionary process, being associated with strong liquidity and solvency positions, can suddenly turn into a systemic financial crisis which leads to a deep depression. Furthermore, the analysis also assumes that *all* liquidity and solvency disturbances are transmitted into the real sector, which would imply that any little disturbance in the liquidity and solvency status would lead either to a dynamically unstable never-ending expansion, or to a dynamically unstable never-ending contraction being associated with systemic financial crises; that is, regarding the analysis of financial crises, the framework does not distinguish between systemic and spurious financial crises. These drawbacks are going to be considered in the following section which studies the determinants of financial stability and allows for a distinction between spurious and systemic financial crises, or why some disturbances lead to the above mentioned cumulative processes and others not. Both the analysis of cumulative processes and financial stability are the necessary ingredients for the theoretical models in part II of the book.

2.3 Determinants of Financial Instability

After having discussed the interdependencies of asset prices, bankruptcy, and real economic activity, giving rise to systemic financial crises in case of adverse financial market disturbances, this section analyzes factors determining whether a given set of financial market disturbances causes either a spurious, or a systemic financial crisis, depending on the overall state of financial instability. Section 2.3.1 starts with a general definition of financial instability, being followed by the analysis of four important determinants of financial instability, where section 2.3.2 discusses the distribution of robust and fragile cash flow positions within an economy, section 2.3.3 the adequacy of refinancing positions, section 2.3.4 the volatility of asset prices and their use in the financial system, and section 2.3.5 the influence of monetary instability.

2.3.1 A General Definition of Financial Instability

Following the general definition of financial crises in section 2.1, spurious and systemic financial crises are subject to the same adverse shocks and drops in asset prices, but differ significantly with respect to their impact on real economic activity. In case of systemic financial crises, asset price drops cause, according to the results of section 2.2.4, widespread illiquidity and insolvency among agents, liquidity crunches, dysfunctions of the payment system, and collapses in aggregate economic activity. By way of contrast, spurious financial crises are characterized by the absence of widespread disruptions in financial market activity, as well as by the absence of collapses in real economic activity. Ergo, whether a given set of adverse disturbances in financial markets causes a disruption of financial markets' capacity to allocate funds efficiently and induces a strong contractive transmission into the real sector or not, is dependent firstly, on factors determining the robustness of aggregate cash flow and solvency positions to remain positive, secondly, on factors determining the robustness of real economic activity and financial market activity not to develop into a cumulative downward spiral. To put it differently, whether a given set of financial market disturbances causes a spurious or a systemic financial crisis depends on factors determining the degree of aggregate financial instability[31], being defined as follows:

> *The degree of aggregate* ***financial instability*** *of an economy is the level of probability that a given set of asset price disturbances, being triggered by actual and/or expected real and/or financial shocks, causes widespread illiquidity and insolvency among economic units, as well as a collapse of real economic activity. If, for a given set of disturbances, the probability of widespread failures and real economic downturns is high, then the economy is designated as being financially unstable. If, for the same given set of disturbances, the probability of widespread failures and drops in real economic activity is low, then the economy is called financially stable.*

This general definition implies that in case of financially unstable economies, even very small shocks and financial market disturbances suffice to cause a systemic financial crisis, whereas in case of financially stable economies, only huge shocks associated with very large drops in asset prices give rise to systemic financial crises.

2.3.2 Cash Flow Positions and Present Values

The first determinant of financial instability is the aggregate proneness to illiquidity and insolvency in case of adverse real and/or financial shocks. Determining the aggregate level of proneness to bankruptcy requires that the economy is disaggregated into single economic units, or into groups or sectors with similar determinants of the liquidity and solvency status in order to obtain a distribution of crisis-prone and financially robust economic entities which allows for the determination of the aggregate level of financial instability.

Assessing the overall financial stability of an economy according to the distribution of robust and fragile cash flow positions goes back on H. P. Minsky's analysis of financial fragility which is going to be set out in sections 2.3.2.1 and 2.3.2.2.[32] As Minsky's original concept is restricted to the analysis of financial fragility in closed economies, sections 2.3.2.3 and 2.3.2.4 enlarge Minsky's theory of financial stability to open economies.

2.3.2.1 Hedge, Speculative and Ponzi-Finance

In order to get a measure of potential aggregate illiquidity and insolvency in case of adverse shocks, the first step is to classify economic units on a microeconomic level according to their risk to become illiquid and insolvent, where Minsky defines three different states of risk, namely *hedge, speculative* and *"Ponzi" finance.* To distinguish between these different types of economic units, some definitions and theoretical concepts have to be introduced firstly.

[31]In the economic literature, financial instability is often labelled synonymously as financial fragility, financial vulnerability, or systemic risk.

[32]Sections 2.3.2.1 and 2.3.2.2 are based on Minsky (1972, 1975, 1977, 1978, 1980a, 1980b, 1982a, 1982b, 1986).

Basic Concepts. Consider a single business unit existing for some periods $t = 1, \ldots, n$, which faces a series of contractual cash payment commitments on debts PC_t, and a series of expected quasi rents, or expected gross nominal profits GPR_t^e, where both expected gross profits and payment commitments are separated into an income (interest) and into a return of principal components, like in a fully amortized contract. Accordingly, today's payment commitments PC_t, resulting from the current liability structure are defined as

$$PC_t = PC_t(y) + PC_t(a), \tag{2.25}$$

that is, by interest (income) payments on current debt $PC_t(y)$, plus repayment of the principal $PC_t(a)$. Expected gross nominal profits GPR_t^e are defined as

$$GPR_t^e = GPR_t^e(y) + GPR_t^e(a), \tag{2.26}$$

that is, as the expected net income part of cash flow $GPR_t^e(y)$ representing the "yield" of investment over replacement or acquisition costs, plus wastage or consumption of capital $GPR_t^e(a)$.

For a business unit to be viable, it is necessary that it holds that

$$\sum_{t=1}^{n} GPR_t^e > 0 \tag{2.27}$$

$$\sum_{t=1}^{n} GPR_t^e > \sum_{t=1}^{n} PC_t, \tag{2.28}$$

that is, that the sum of expected gross profits has to be greater than zero, and that the sum of expected gross profits has to be greater than the sum of payment commitments over the entire economic lifetime.[33]

The value, or capitalized net worth of a business unit, E, is defined by the discounted present value of expected gross profits less payment commitments, formally as

$$E = \sum_{t=1}^{n} k_t(GPR_t^e - PC_t), \tag{2.29}$$

where k_t represents the discount factor, reflecting financial market conditions which depend on market interest rates, and on general general risk conditions.[34] A tighten-

[33]This condition is also valid for the viability of a single investment project, where viability is defined, according to conditions 2.27 and 2.28, by the economic lifetime of investment. Note that there is a difference between the economic and the physical lifetime (point in time when the investment good becomes obsolete in a physical sense) of an investment project being analyzed by the vintage approach, discussing the influence of technological progress on inhomogeneous capital stocks. For literature on the vintage approach, see Johansen (1959), Solow (1962), Phelps (1963), and Solow et al. (1966).

[34]It is important to note that the capitalized net worth position E of a business unit according to Minsky differs from the standard definition of a firm's value according to perfect capital market theory with respect to the consideration of interest costs, and with respect to the consideration of the financial structure. Following perfect capital market theory, a firm's value is simply determined by discounting expected gross profits. That is, interest costs are *not* subtracted from expected gross profits, because interest costs are only considered by the discount factor, which implies, in accordance with the Modigliani-Miller theorem, that the financial structure is neglected as a determinant of the value of a firm. By way of contrast, Minsky's concept of the capitalized net worth of a business unit E explicitly considers interest costs, and thereby the financial structure by subtracting payment commitments PC_t from expected gross profits GPR_t^e.

ing/relaxation in financial market conditions is reflected by a fall/rise in k_t, indicating an increase/fall in market interest rates and in risk premia.

Hedge Finance. A hedge finance unit is characterized by the condition

$$GPR_t^e > PC_t \tag{2.30}$$

for all periods $t = 1, \ldots, n$, stating that in every period t, expected gross profits exceed payment commitments. According to equation 2.29, the present value, or the net worth of a hedge-finance unit E is independent of financial market conditions, i.e. a change in interest rates or in overall risk conditions, being reflected in a change of k_t, does not lead to changes in E. Thus, a tightening in financial markets cannot lead to bankruptcy, i.e. to a negative present value E, or to illiquidity by a sudden increase in PC_t. Hedge financing is only possibly in case the balance sheet's debt side contains only equities or long-term debt with maturity date $t = n$, and with fixed interest rates. However, negative net worth or illiquidity can arise in case actual cash flows fall short of anticipated cash flows and of the amount of payment commitments, which can be caused e.g. by unexpected increases in labour and material costs, or by unexpected drops in aggregate demand. To avoid such adverse events, hedge-finance units generally are going to hold money and marketable (short-term) financial assets which are not needed for normal operation and which serve only as an insurance against illiquidity and insolvency. Summing up, a hedge-finance unit is not dependent on the "normal" functioning of financial market, but on the "normal" functioning of product and factor markets.

Given that expectations are fulfilled and realized gross profits GPR_t exceed payment commitments in each period, i.e. if it holds that $GPR_t^e = GPR_t > PC_t$ for all t, a hedge finance unit receives net money inflows in each period. Furthermore, if the income portion of realized gross profits exceeds the income portion of payment commitments (interest rate costs), i.e. if $GPR_t(y) > PC_t(y)$, then net worth is going to increase in each period. The increase in net worth and in money holdings can be used to finance the acquisition of capital assets without changing the debt-asset ratio, or, in case capital assets are additionally financed by an increase in external debt, financing conditions are not going to deteriorate. Likewise, if net worth consists of equity shares, the fulfillment of expectations of hedge-finance units leads to an increase in share prices and to an increase in the wealth of stock holders.

Speculative Finance. For a speculative finance unit, it holds that

$$GPR_t^e < PC_t \qquad (t = 1, \ldots, m, \quad m \text{ small}) \tag{2.31}$$

$$GPR_t^e > PC_t \qquad (t = m+1, \ldots, n), \tag{2.32}$$

stating that near-term payment commitments (periods 1 to m) exceed near term expected gross profits, but that in the longer run (periods $m+1$ to n), expected gross profits exceed payment commitments. Furthermore, for a speculative finance unit, it holds that

$$\sum_{t=1}^{m} GPR_t^e(y) > \sum_{t=1}^{m} PC_t(y), \tag{2.33}$$

that is, though total payment commitments exceed total expected gross profits over the first m periods, the net income part of cash flow $GPR_t^e(y)$ exceeds interest rate costs $PC_t(y)$ in periods 1 to m. Hence, a speculative finance unit has a share of its principal on debt which falls due in the near term, but whose repayment exceeds the near term debt-repayment funds the unit's assets generate. To meet near-term payment obligations the speculative unit can either run down its money or liquid assets, or, if liquid assets do not suffice, the unit needs to place new debt or to roll over debt, i.e. speculative financing involves a short-term financing of long-term positions.[35] Thus, a prerequisite for speculative finance is that borrowers as well as lenders believe that there exists a market in which cash, being used to bridge liquidity gaps in early periods, can be obtained frictionlessly at required dates. Moreover, liquidity to fulfill payment commitments in early periods is assumed to be available at "normal" financing terms which do not detrimentally affect the probability that future obligations can be fulfilled.

A speculative finance unit's expected net worth or solvency position E depends crucially on the level of market interest rates and risk premia, determining the level of the discount rate k_t. For a set of "low" interest rates and risk premia, implying a "high" value of k_t, the expected discounted present value E is positive. By way of contrast, a tightening in financial market conditions, being associated with "high" market interest rates and risk premia, connoting a "low" value of k_t, can possibly cause a present value reversal, i.e. $E < 0$, implying insolvency of the business unit. Furthermore, in case the speculative finance unit operates under floating debt interest rates, a present value reversal is accelerated by an increase in payment commitments PC_t in case of financial market tightening. Accordingly, speculative finance is built on the assumption that interest rates will not move outside some acceptable range. Furthermore, a speculative finance unit can become insolvent, as a hedge finance unit, in case actual gross profits fall short of expected gross profits and of the amount of payment commitments. Summing up, a speculative finance unit is dependent on the "normal" functioning of product and factor markets like a hedge finance unit, but is additionally dependent on the "normal" functioning of financial markets. Thus, a speculative finance unit is exposed to higher risk of illiquidity and insolvency than a hedge finance unit.

Despite the fact that a speculative finance unit has to increase its stock of short-term debt and to decrease its liquid assets in early periods to bridge liquidity gaps, a speculative unit is able to decrease its short-term debt and to increase liquidity in the long-run, and thereby to increase its equity relative to its liabilities in case profit expectations are fulfilled, i.e. if $GPR_t^e = GPR_t$, as the income portion of gross profits exceeds the income portion of payment commitments (interest payments) in every period, i.e. because it holds that $GPR_t(y) > PC_t(y)$ for all t. Consequently, it is possible to increase net worth for speculative units even if debt is refinanced. However, in case the business unit is financed at least partly by equities, this statement is only valid if payment commitments include conventional payments of dividends, because in this case, the business unit has positive retained earnings. If, on the contrary, dividends are not included in payment commitments, it is possible that the income portion of payment commitments exceeds the income portion of gross profits, i.e. it is possible that $GPR_t(y) < PC_t(y)$, implying

[35] A third possibility is the fire-sale of assets if liquid assets do not suffice, and placing new debt or rolling over debt is not possible. However, this credit or liquidity crunch scenario emerges only if a financial crisis is already in place and is therefore neglected in the further analysis.

that dividends are paid out of current cash flow which reduces the future earning capacity of a business unit and increases the speculative nature of the unit. This kind of dividend policy can mirror unjustifiable optimistic expectations, as well as measures to preserve or to increase the market value of equities.

Banks, other financial institutions, treasuries with floating debt, and business firms rolling-over bank debt or commercial paper, are typical speculative finance units firstly, as they borrow short-term and invest in long-term projects, and secondly, as they deal very often with floating debt, making them vulnerable to interest rate changes since a business unit that borrows at floating interest rates is engaged in a form of speculative finance even though at current interest rates the unit is classified as a hedge finance unit.

"Ponzi" Finance. For a Ponzi finance unit, it holds that

$$GPR_t^e < PC_t \qquad (t = 1, \dots, n-1) \tag{2.34}$$
$$GPR_t^e \gg PC_t \qquad (t = n) \tag{2.35}$$

and

$$GPR_t^e(y) < PC_t(y) \qquad (t = 1, \dots, n-1) \tag{2.36}$$
$$GPR_t^e(y) \gg PC_t(y) \qquad (t = n), \tag{2.37}$$

stating that in all periods, except in the final period $t = n$, expected gross profits are lower than payment commitments, and interest rate costs exceed the net income part of cash flows. Consequently, in order to meet payment commitments in periods $t = 1$ to $t = n - 1$, a Ponzi finance unit has to increase its debt stock and to decrease liquidity steadily. Hence, a Ponzi financing scheme is, as a speculative financing scheme, built on the assumption of a "normal" functioning of financial markets, i.e. that debt to meet payment commitments can be placed frictionlessly at required dates and at "normal" financing conditions.

The expected present value E of Ponzi units is much more sensitive to interest rate and risk premia changes, as well as to disruptions in product and labour markets, than the present value of speculative finance units, implying that present value reversals can happen very fast if there are only slight interest rate and/or risk premia increases, or only small deteriorations in product and factor markets. Moreover, Ponzi units are vulnerable to changes in market sentiment regarding expected gross profits in the final period $t = n$, since the viability of a Ponzi unit depends on positive expectations regarding to an event far in the future. Only slight reassessments towards a more pessimistic outcome can lead to refusals to obtain liquidity by placing new debt, leading very quickly to bankruptcy and to a stop of the investment project. In contrast to speculative finance units, Ponzi finance units cannot increase their net worth and liquidity in the long run even if gross profit expectations are validated, i.e. even if it holds that $GPR_t^e = GPR_t$, as interest rate costs always exceed the net income part of cash flow except in the final period, implying that a Ponzi finance unit is subject to a steady decrease of net worth. Consequently, a Ponzi finance unit is exposed to much greater risk of illiquidity and insolvency than hedge and speculative finance units. In case of default, debt restructuring including refinancing and recapitalization is often used as an instrument to transform Ponzi units into speculative units and speculative units into hedge units.

Though Ponzi-investment projects can be tinged with fraud, there are lots of legal Ponzi finance schemes, generally emerging in case of investment projects with long construction periods, as e.g. investments in real estate or in high technology production. During the construction period, investors generally receive almost no cash income and have to finance current labour, material and interest rate costs by placing new debt. Furthermore, there is uncertainty about the development of costs, as well as about whether the completed investment project can be sold at a reasonable price or whether the project validates gross profit expectations. Thus, the investment project is only profitable if costs do not rise over expected levels, and if the sum of expected gross profits is higher than the sum of payment commitments. Likewise, Ponzi schemes also emerge in case of risky investments in real or financial assets when the costs of holding assets are higher than their general net income (dividends or returns), implying that overall returns are only positive in case asset prices appreciate substantially in the future to expected levels.[36]

Adverse Shocks and Financial Posture "Downgrading". It has to be emphasized that the classification of hedge, speculative and Ponzi finance units does not only depend on the cash flow position of business units, but also on the size, and on the type of adverse shocks. Thus, adverse shocks are able to transform e.g. a hedge finance unit into a Ponzi finance unit, implying a "downgrading" of liquidity and solvency positions.

Hedge finance units can be only downgraded to speculative and to Ponzi finance units in case of large adverse shocks in product or factor markets, but not by adverse shocks in financial markets. The trigger for the downgrading of a hedge finance unit has to take place somewhere else in the economy and is not caused by the behaviour of hedge finance units. However, this statement is only valid if hedge finance units' activities were not based upon unrealistic, euphoric expectations with respect to input costs and market development over time. Accordingly, the fragility of a hedge unit, measured as the probability to become a speculative or a Ponzi unit, can also stem from euphoric expectations with respect to factor and product markets. Speculative units can be downgraded to Ponzi finance units both by adverse shocks in the real and in the financial sector, i.e. by increases in factor costs, increases in interest rates and in risk premia. Ponzi finance units can be only downgraded to bankrupt finance units by both adverse real and financial sector shocks. Generally, the size of shocks being necessary to downgrade a business unit to the next lower financial posture decreases due to an increasing probability to become illiquid and insolvent for a given set of shocks.

[36]Investments in "New Economy" shares during the late 1990s are a typical example of Ponzi financing schemes. During the stock market hype in the late 1990s, high market prices of "New Economy" shares could not be justified by their performance, as cash flows were low or even negative for the near-term periods, and dividends were often not paid, so that holding the asset was not profitable in the near-term. However, investors expected an appreciation of "New Economy" share prices in the future which would have made an investment profitable. But when "New Economy" firms failed to validate investor expectations by actual cash flows and profits, profit expectations collapsed, and led to a worldwide stock market crash and to widespread bankruptcies among "New Economy" firms. A further example is the boom-bust cycle in stock markets during the 1920s having led to the Great Depression, which is a very nice equivalent to the incidents in the late 1990s.

2.3.2.2 Financial Instability in Closed Economies

The Weight of Hedge Finance Units in the Financial Structure of an Economy. Following the analysis of hedge, speculative and Ponzi finance units, a financial system is stable if adverse disturbances in product and factor markets, as well as increases in interest rates and risk premia, implying a decline in capitalization rates k_i, do not appreciably affect the ability of economic entities to fulfill their financial obligations. By way of contrast, in an unstable or fragile financial system, the same disturbances in financial, product and factor markets can affect adversely the ability of business units to fulfill their payment commitments. Ergo, the overall instability of financial systems increases if the ratio of speculative and Ponzi to hedge finance units increases. Furthermore, if there is an increase in the ratio of Ponzi finance to speculative finance and hedge finance units, the already prevailing fragility of the financial structure deteriorates further and is in danger to evolve into a cumulative downward spiral being associated with debt deflation processes.

Industry Structure and Economic Development as a Determinant of the Weight of Hedge Finance Units in the Financial Structure. The weight of hedge finance units in relation to speculative and Ponzi finance units is not only dependent on profit-maximizing decisions of agents with regard to the optimal liability structure, but also on the kind of industry structure and economic development.

Labour-intensive industry structures without high-tech machinery, being prevalent in low developed countries, are characterized by simple and cheap capital assets whose gestation period is short. A large fraction of external financing relates to financing of goods in commerce. In such systems debt repayment is closely linked to the income generation process because there are no sophisticated long-living investment goods with long construction periods which have to be financed by short-term debt. Hence, in such systems the fraction of speculative and Ponzi units in relation to hedge units is very small.

On the contrary, both in highly industrialized and in emerging market countries, the industry structure is characterized by capital-intensive production with high-tech machinery, implying that capital assets are long-living, complicated and expensive, and that gestation periods of investment goods are very long. In such systems, short-period cash flows yield a gross profit which is only very small in relation to the value of the capital assets. Unless financing is organized in long-term contracts, such economies are not able to generate sufficient cash flow to fulfill payment obligations in early periods of production without the use of short-term debt. As a result, the "normal" way of finance is to combine income cash flows from general operation with portfolio transactions by placing new short-term debt, or by rolling over debt. Thus, high developed or emerging market economies, using highly sophisticated capital assets, generally tend to have a higher fraction of speculative and Ponzi finance units than less industrialized countries, which can be seen by the fact that the size of the financial system is much smaller in less developed countries than in high developed or emerging market countries. Thus, high developed and emerging countries have a much more unstable financial structure than low developed countries.

These results have two important implications for economic development policies. Firstly, economic development or growth requires a strong development of the domestic financial sector to transform the industry structure from labour-intensive production with low productivity to capital-intensive production with high productivity. This result implies that domestic and/or international financial market liberalization is a favourable method to boost productivity and to reduce poverty in low developed countries. Secondly, the transition process towards capital-intensive production with a strong domestic financial sector is associated with an increase in financial instability making transition economies more vulnerable to financial crises. Consequently, financial market liberalization leads to an increase in financial instability and in the frequency of financial crises, which can be validated by the stylized facts being outlined in chapter 3. Summing up, financial liberalization is necessary for economic development but requires strong financial market regulation to prevent the overall financial structure from becoming too fragile.

The Size of Different Economic Sectors as a Determinant of the Weight of Hedge Finance Units in the Financial Structure. A further determinant of the weight of hedge finance units in relation to speculative and Ponzi finance units is the size of different economic sectors, as e.g. the firm, the household or the banking sector, in the total financial structure, as well as the composition of their income streams and payment commitments.

Financial intermediaries are generally, as aforementioned, speculative finance units as they transform by their very nature short-term debt (deposits) in long-term assets (loans), implying that the ability to fulfill near-term payment obligations (e.g. deposit withdrawals) requires a "normal" functioning of financial markets in order to place new debt, or to roll over debt at "normal" financing conditions. Moreover, as financial intermediaries' gross profits predominantly depend on the liquidity and the solvency status of business firms and households, financial intermediaries also depend on a frictionless functioning of product and factor markets.

Business firms can take all three financial postures, where the fraction of speculative and Ponzi finance units increases with the capital/labour ratio, so that the firm sector in industrialized, as well as in emerging market countries is dominated by speculative and Ponzi finance units. Hence, business firms depend on the frictionless functioning of product and factor markets to generate sufficient income streams, as well as on the "normal" functioning of financial markets to prevent an increase in financing costs.

Households' financial posture can be subdivided in two broad categories, namely in households' financial posture of consumption, and in households' financial posture of asset ownership. Households' financial posture of consumption, referring to households' consumption expenditures (housing included), is dominated by hedge finance units as debt contracts for consumption and mortgage finance are generally designed as fully amortized contracts, i.e. as series of (constant) payment commitments which are defined over the entire term of the debt contract, excluding a final extra repayment of a remaining part of the principal.[37] Ergo, as households' income streams mainly consist of wage income, households can only become speculative or Ponzi finance units if actual wage income falls short of expected wage income and other sources of disposable income, like e.g. unemployment insurance. Regarding mortgage debt, households can additionally get into liquidity and solvency problems in case the market value of the hypothecated asset falls short of the face value of outstanding debt as already discussed in section 2.2.4. However,

[37] A partially amortized contract includes a final payment at the end of the contract's lifetime which contains a part of the principal. An unamortized contract involves repayment of the entire principal at the end of the contract's lifetime. For this classification, see Minsky (1982b), p. 30.

a "downgrading" of households, or even a failure of households, can only occur if there has taken place a substantial decline in income and employment, i.e. consumer debt can amplify an economic downturn and a route to financial crises, as outlined in section 2.2.4.3, but it does not generate financial instability. Furthermore, financial market tightening by increasing interest rates and risk premia has no influence on financial stability of households' consumption financial posture.

By way of contrast, households' financial posture of asset ownership, referring to households' investment activities into financial assets, can generate financial instability as it is dominated by speculative and Ponzi finance. Households often engage, and especially during speculative boom phases, in debt finance of securities, as e.g. equities, options, or bonds. As income streams consist mainly of dividends or interest payments, which in most cases do not suffice to meet due payment commitments of debt contracts, and as the profitability of investment projects depends heavily on selling out the position at an appreciated price, households' portfolio is speculative if the interest rate on debt is lower than the portfolio's internal rate of return (e.g. the dividend/price ratio), and Ponzi, if the interest rate on debt is higher than than the portfolio's internal rate. Consequently, as income streams and payment commitments of households' asset ownership depend mainly on financial market conditions, increases in interest rates, as well as in risk premia can lead very quickly to a move from speculative to Ponzi finance or even to bankruptcy. However, since asset prices are also determined by income streams from product and factor markets, households can be downgraded additionally by adverse disturbances in the real sphere of the economy.

Governments are very often speculative finance units as income streams generally consist of tax revenues and new borrowing, i.e. government expenditures depend crucially on the ability to roll over short-term debt. As long as the sum of expected income streams exceeds the sum of future payment commitments on debts outstanding, there arise no liquidity and solvency problems for governments. However, if expected tax revenues fall short of payment commitments, e.g. due to an economic downturn, or if current running expenses increase, e.g. owing to a general interest rate increase, governments can become very quickly Ponzi units or even bankrupt since rolling over debt can become impossible. Generally, governments' incentives to engage in speculative or Ponzi finance are not aimed at generating financial instability wilfully. However, there are often distorting incentives which lead governments to engage in "unsound" fiscal policies by increasing short-term debt. Especially governments engaging in large floating short-term debt run the risk of becoming Ponzi or even bankrupt.

Summing up, financial instability increases in case of growing financial intermediation, in case of a growing government sector and increasing government expenditures, in case of a growing capital/labour ratio, and in case of growing investments of households in financial assets. Accordingly, financial stability depends heavily on the relative size of households' financial posture of consumption.

2.3.2.3 Foreign Hedge, Foreign Speculative, and Foreign Ponzi Finance

Minsky's original concept of hedge, speculative and Ponzi finance can be only applied to closed economies as it refers solely to money flows in domestic currency, as well as solely to domestic product, factor and financial market conditions. Financial crises in the 1990s however demonstrated, that systemic financial crises, both in emerging market and in industrialized countries, were influenced by asset and debt positions in foreign currency. Consequently, in order to get a correct measure of overall financial instability in open economies, cash flow positions resulting from transactions in foreign currency have to be considered explicitly. In order to be consistent with the degree of internal financial fragility, having been discussed in the two previous sections, this section enlarges Minsky's original concept by explicitly considering cash flow positions in foreign currency.

However, the classification of business units in hedge, speculative, and Ponzi units by taking into account cash flows in foreign currency is not as easy as Minsky's original concept for closed economies. For example, cash flow positions in domestic currency can be used to compensate cash flow positions in foreign currency and vice versa, making it very difficult to assess a business unit's financial posture. Moreover, cash flow positions in foreign currency can involve payment commitments in foreign currency, but income streams in domestic currency which have to be exchanged in the foreign exchange market to pay debt, exposing the business unit additionally to currency risk. Accordingly, to get a useful measure for financial instability, internal fragility, stemming from cash flow positions in domestic currency, i.e. from the distribution of hedge, speculative and Ponzi finance as defined in section 2.3.2.1, has to be separated from external fragility stemming from cash flow positions in foreign currency. To distinguish internal from external financial instability, external cash flow positions are labelled analogously to Minsky's original terminology as foreign hedge, foreign speculative, and foreign Ponzi finance. After having discussed the determinants of external financial fragility, section 2.3.2.4 is going to combine internal and external financial fragility to determine the overall degree of financial fragility of single units and of an entire economies.

Basic Concepts. The analysis of external cash flow positions follows the terminology and the basic concepts of section 2.3.2.1. The first step to determine the external cash flow position from the overall cash flow position of a business unit is to separate total payment commitments into "external" payment commitments in foreign currency, and into payment commitments in domestic currency. The second step is to single out "external" expected gross profits which are used to fulfill external payment commitments in foreign currency from total expected gross profits; it has to be emphasized, that external expected gross profits being used to pay foreign debt can be denominated both in domestic and in foreign currency. Then, in the third and last step, external expected gross profits, which are used to fulfill external payment commitments in foreign currency, and external payment obligations in foreign currency have to be compared, determining the external cash flow position.

In order to account for foreign exchange risk, evolving in case external expected gross profits are denominated partly, or entirely in domestic currency, the external cash flow position has to be separated further in external cash flow positions containing only money flows in foreign currency, and in external cash flow positions containing money flows in domestic currency as well which have to be exchanged in the foreign exchange market to fulfill external payment commitments.

In case all expected gross profits are denominated in foreign currency, and assuming that in this case income streams only result from transactions with foreigners, the external cash flow position consists only of money flows in foreign currency, implying that only foreign product, factor and financial market conditions are relevant for possible changes in the external financial posture. Accordingly, the external expected present value of a business unit E^* in foreign currency, being formally defined as

$$E^* = \sum_{t=1}^{n} k_t^*(GPR_t^{*e} - PC_t^*), \tag{2.38}$$

is determined by discounting external expected gross profits GPR_t^{*e} less external payment commitments PC_t^*, where the external discount factor k_t^* only consists of foreign interest rates and risk premia as financing costs need not to be "earned" in domestic currency.

By way of contrast, in case external expected gross profits contain at least partly income streams which are denominated in domestic currency, and assuming that these income streams only stem from transactions with domestic residents, the external cash flow position is additionally exposed to currency risk, implying that foreign product, factor, and financial market conditions, as well as domestic product and factor market conditions[38] are relevant for possible changes in the business unit's financial posture. Thus, in this case, the external discount rate k_t^* consists of foreign interest rates and risk premia, as well as of the expected rate of change of the exchange rate, as financing costs have to be "earned" in domestic currency, being subject to foreign exchange risk.

Foreign Hedge Finance. A prerequisite for a business unit to be classified as a foreign hedge finance unit, is that the external cash flow position has to be denominated in foreign currency in each period, i.e. external expected gross profits have to be denominated completely in foreign currency, implying that there arises no currency risk. Given that all net money flows are denominated in foreign currency, a foreign hedge finance unit's external expected gross profits exceed in all periods external payment commitments. Accordingly, a foreign hedge finance unit can be only downgraded, and external present value reversals can only happen in case of adverse shocks in foreign product and factor markets, as e.g. a decline in foreign GDP, or an adverse terms of trade shocks reducing domestic net exports. Foreign financial market disturbances cannot lead to downgrading or to external present value reversals.

On the contrary, a unit whose external expected gross profits exceed external payment commitments for all periods, but whose external expected gross profits are partly or entirely denominated in domestic currency, *cannot* be classified as a foreign hedge finance unit. Rather, such a unit engages in a form of speculative, or even Ponzi finance, due to considerable exchange rate risk, as devaluations of the home currency can lead very quickly to an external present value reversal, even in case of fixed exchange rates, since exchange rates are not invariable in the long-run.

[38]Business units are assumed not to depend on domestic financial market conditions because changes in domestic interest rates, as well as in domestic risk premia do not change payment commitments in foreign currency. It has to be emphasized however, that domestic financial market conditions do have an influence on a business unit's net worth via the impact on the external discount factor k_t^* in case external expected gross profits are partly or entirely denominated in domestic currency, and in case these gross profits are "earned" at home. In this case, the external discount factor should be weighted average of domestic and foreign financial market conditions including currency risk, where the weighting factor of domestic financial conditions should be determined by the proportion of external expected gross profits in domestic currency to total payment commitments in foreign currency. Yet, for reasons of simplicity, the influence of domestic financial market conditions on the external discount factor is neglected in the following.

Foreign Speculative and Foreign Super Speculative Finance. A *foreign speculative finance unit* is defined by four characteristics. Firstly, cash flow positions in all periods are denominated in foreign currency, implying that there arises no currency risk. Secondly, external payment commitments in early periods exceed external expected gross profits. Thirdly, in later periods, external expected gross profits exceed external payment commitments. Fourthly, in early periods interest payments on foreign debt are smaller than the net income part of external cash flow. Accordingly, a foreign speculative finance unit is dependent on the "normal" functioning of foreign financial markets in order to place foreign short-term debt, or to roll-over foreign debt at "normal" foreign financing conditions. Such a unit is vulnerable to adverse shocks in foreign product, factor and financial markets.

A *foreign super speculative finance unit* is defined by the same characteristics as a foreign speculative finance unit except for the fact that external expected gross profits are partly or entirely denominated in domestic currency, exposing the unit additionally to currency risk, and to adverse disturbances in domestic product and factor markets.

Foreign Ponzi and Foreign Super Ponzi Finance. A *foreign Ponzi finance unit* is defined by the following four characteristics. Firstly, cash flow positions in all periods are denominated in foreign currency. Secondly, in all periods except for the final period, external expected gross profits fall short of external payment commitments. Thirdly, only in the final period external expected gross profits exceed external payment commitments. Fourthly, in all periods except for the final period, interest rate costs on foreign debt exceed the net income part of external cash flow. As a result, a foreign Ponzi finance unit has to increase its foreign debt stock steadily and is dependent on a normal functioning of foreign financial markets to place steadily new foreign short-term debt, and to roll-over debt at "normal" foreign financing conditions. A foreign Ponzi finance unit is vulnerable to adverse disturbances in foreign product, factor, and financial markets.

A *foreign super Ponzi finance* is defined by the same characteristics as a foreign Ponzi finance except for the fact, that external expected gross profits are partly or entirely denominated in domestic currency, making the business unit additionally vulnerable to devaluations of the home currency and to adverse disturbances in domestic product and factor markets.

2.3.2.4 Financial Instability in Open Economies

This section studies in a first step determinants of external financial fragility according to the classification of the previous chapter, and enlarges in a second step the concept of internal financial fragility to an open economy context in order to combine finally both results to derive determinants of overall financial instability in open economies.

Determinants of External Financial Instability. Like internal financial instability, external financial instability increases if the ratio of foreign hedge finance units to all other external financial postures decreases, where the weight of foreign hedge finance units in the aggregate external position depends heavily on the stage of development of an economy.

Low developed countries with a low capital/labour ratio, low productivity, and an underdeveloped and often financially repressed[39] domestic financial system, tend to have almost no foreign debt as well as no income streams in foreign currency due to three reasons. Firstly domestic financial market regulation often prohibits to get into foreign debt. Secondly, foreign investors are not willing to invest in countries and industries with low productivity and low yields, and thirdly, low productivity implies low export performance and thereby low income streams in foreign currency. Consequently, as there arise almost no transactions in foreign currency, external financial instability in low developed countries is low.

High developed countries, being characterized by a high capital/labour ratio, average productivity, and well-developed domestic financial systems, tends to exhibit generally also a low degree of external financial instability, as the aggregate external cash flow position is dominated by foreign hedge finance units. An overall foreign hedge finance position develops from a low share of foreign debt in total debt, and from external income streams which are mostly denominated in domestic currency, or in foreign currencies with low exchange rate risk.[40]

Emerging market or transition economies are generally subject to a high degree of external financial fragility as the aggregate external cash flow position is dominated by foreign (super) speculative and foreign (super) Ponzi finance units. Emerging market or transition economies are subject to a very fast increasing capital/labour ratio, and to huge productivity increases. Yet, the increase in highly sophisticated capital assets with long gestation periods cannot be financed entirely by the domestic financial system, firstly as domestic savings are very often too low, and secondly, as emerging market and transition economies cannot issue domestic debt due to the "original sin" hypothesis[41], stating that due to past misbehaviour there is no possibility to borrow in domestic currency, leading to high share of debt denominated in foreign currency. Accordingly, emerging market and transition economies very often engage in heavy short-term foreign borrowing, where income streams are very often earned at home in domestic currency making them extremely vulnerable to foreign exchange risk.

A further determinant of the weight of foreign hedge finance units in the aggregate external finance position is the relative size of different economic sectors, as already outlined in section 2.3.2.2 for the case of internal financial instability. As external financial instability appears predominantly in emerging market and transition economies, the following description concentrates exclusively on external financial postures of different sectors in emerging market and transition economies.

---

[39]Accoring to McKinnon (1973), Shaw (1973), and Williamson and Mahar (1998), a financially repressed system is defined as a system in which government regulations determine the amount, the price, and the distribution of credit. These regulations are often reinforced by state-owned banks, by licensing and regulating private financial institutions with respect to their general management, and by controlling international capital movements.

[40]It has to be emphasized that there are exceptions, especially in the case of small high developed countries with a high degree of openness. For example, Norway, Sweden, and Finland borrowed heavily in foreign currency after domestic financial sector liberalization in the late 1980s, which caused high external financial instability and evolved into systemic financial crises in all three countries at the beginning of the 1990s.

[41]See e.g. Eichengreen and Hausmann (1999), and Velasco (2001).

Banks and financial intermediaries in emerging market and transition economies play a dominant role for domestic finance as information asymmetries do not allow business firms or households to take foreign debt directly abroad, implying that foreign funds are generally allocated via the domestic financial sector. Hence, financial intermediaries in emerging market and transition economies are generally foreign super speculative, or even foreign super Ponzi units (as well as domestic speculative finance units), as they transform domestic short-term debt (deposits in domestic currency) and foreign short-term debt (deposits or short-term loans in foreign currency) with floating interest rates, in long-term assets which are denominated in domestic currency (long-term domestic loans). This financial posture implies that the financial sector in emerging and transition economies is subject to high financial instability as it is vulnerable to disturbances in domestic and foreign product, factor and financial markets, as well as to disturbances in foreign exchange markets.

Business firms in emerging market and transition economies are generally subject to low external financial fragility as they are not able to borrow in foreign currency as mentioned above. It must be noted however, that very large business firms, or even conglomerates with international creditworthiness can take foreign debt, and very often engage in foreign short-term borrowing to finance domestic long-term assets generating predominantly income streams in domestic currency. Accordingly, if the industry structure is dominated by such conglomerates, the business firm sector contributes considerably to the emergence of external financial stability, as the external finance position is dominated by foreign super speculative and foreign super Ponzi units.

Households in emerging market and transition economies exhibit in general no external financial instability as they cannot engage in foreign debt finance, firstly, due to lacking creditworthiness, and secondly, due to lacking wealth.

Governments in emerging market and transition economies very often engage in heavy foreign short-term borrowing at flexible interest rates to finance domestic government expenditures as domestic tax revenues are not sufficient. As tax revenues are denominated in domestic currency, governments in emerging market and transition economies are in most cases foreign super speculative, or even foreign super Ponzi units. Accordingly, governments are highly vulnerable to disturbances in domestic and foreign product, factor, and financial markets, as well as to disturbances in foreign exchange markets.[42] It has to be emphasized however, that "unsound" external fiscal policies, which prevailed in the late 1970s and 1980s, have reduced enormously as international financial market liberalization has imposed fiscal discipline on governments.[43]

Summing up, external financial fragility in emerging market and transition economies increases with growing capital inflows which are allocated by the domestic financial system, as well as with increasing government expenditures which are financed by increasing short-term foreign debt.

[42]For example, Argentina's latest government debt default, as well as the international debt crisis in the 1980s were predominantly caused by external financial fragility which stemmed from heavy foreign short-term borrowing at flexible interest rates, having led to bankruptcy after international interest rates rose considerably and tax revenues dropped due to domestic recessions.

[43]For example, government policies in East Asia before the Asian crisis in 1997/1998 were sound and not subject to large amounts of short-term foreign debt.

Internal Financial Instability Revisited. To assess the overall degree of financial instability in open economies, the degree of internal financial stability, having been discussed in section 2.3.2.2, has to be modified to fit into an open economy context, as the degree of internal financial stability does not depend solely on domestic disturbances due to current account and capital account transactions. Regarding current account transactions, an initially internal financially stable economy with no external financial instability can be downgraded, e.g. by a drop in foreign GDP, or by a terms of trade shock reducing domestic net exports and thereby domestic expected gross profits which are used to pay back domestic debt. Regarding capital account transactions, in fully liberalized domestic and international capital markets interest parity can be assumed to hold, implying that an economy with no external financial instability, but with a low share of domestic hedge finance units, can be downgraded by a foreign interest rate increase, or by an expected devaluation of the home currency leading to rising domestic payment commitments.

Summing up, in case an economy is characterized by internal financial stability, and exhibits no external financial instability, disturbances in foreign product and factor markets can induce an increase in internal financial fragility, whereas foreign financial market disturbances do not have any considerable effects. In case an economy is characterized by no external, but by internal financial instability, disturbances in foreign product and factor markets, as well as disturbances in foreign financial markets can induce an increase in internal financial fragility.

Overall Financial Instability in Open Economies. Financial instability in open economies increases if internal financial instability increases and/or if external financial fragility increases. That is, overall financial instability increases if the ratio of hedge finance units to speculative and Ponzi finance units decreases, and/or if the ratio of foreign hedge finance units to foreign (super) speculative and foreign (super) Ponzi units decreases. Consequently, emerging market and transition economies are much more fragile than industrial or low developed economies, in case their domestic financial system as well as the capital account are liberalized, as they are additionally subject to high external fragility.

2.3.3 Adequacy of Refinancing Possibilities

This section refers to the analysis of internal and external cash flow positions of the previous section, and discusses how a systemic financial crisis can be prevented in case an economy is hit by large adverse domestic and/or foreign shocks, normally causing widespread bankruptcies and real economic downturns. The following analysis distinguishes among refinancing possibilities in domestic and in foreign currency, where domestic currency refinancing possibilities determine the degree of internal financial instability, and foreign currency refinancing possibilities determine the degree of external financial fragility.[44]

The Adequacy of Refinancing Possibilities in Domestic Currency. Large adverse disturbances in domestic and/or foreign product, factor and financial markets normally cause systemic financial crises by inducing an enormous downgrading of hedge finance units, and widespread bankruptcies among speculative and Ponzi finance units, as

[44]The analysis of domestic refinancing possibilities is based on Minsky (1972) and (1986), chapter 3.

payment commitments cannot be fulfilled any longer. However, large adverse shocks need not induce systemic financial crises if there exist possibilities for troubled business units to receive sufficient "emergency" liquidity to bridge short-run liquidity gaps. Thus, financial stability also depends crucially on the availability of refinancing resources providing sufficient short-term liquidity.

A troubled business unit whose income streams from normal operation do not suffice to fulfill payment obligations, generally has three possibilities to obtain short-term liquidity in order to prevent bankruptcy. Firstly, placing new debt or rolling over debt, secondly, running down liquid monetary assets, and thirdly, a fire-sale of financial and/or real assets.

The ability of households, business firms and governments to *place new debt* and/or to *run down liquid monetary assets* (as e.g. deposits) generally depends on the liquidity status of the financial sector. However, a liquidity crunch among households, firms and the government generally passes to a liquidity crisis of the financial sector due to large deposit withdrawals, and due to a maximum degree of lending, e.g. by an exhaustion of credit lines up to the maximum. That is, a private and government sector liquidity crisis evolving into a financial sector liquidity crisis as defined by condition 2.9 in section 2.2.4.2, passing over definitely into a systemic financial crisis, can be only prevented by an extraordinary provision of central bank credit.[45] Hence, financial instability decreases in case there are effective lender-of-last-resort interventions by central banks.

A widespread *fire-sale of assets* only generates sufficient liquidity by sales revenues in case the relevant *secondary* asset markets are independent of system behaviour. Otherwise, a widespread fire-sale of financial or real assets by households, firms, and banks causes an enormous drop in assets' market prices, causing insolvency and deteriorating liquidity problems as sales revenues drop sharply. Consequently, financial instability increases if the ratio of the value of those assets whose market value is independent of system behaviour to the value of assets which reflect system behaviour decreases. For an asset to be independent of system behaviour, the secondary market for the asset firstly, has to be pegged or rather protected, secondly, has to be very large and deep in order not to result in large price fluctuation if demand and supply conditions change rapidly, and thirdly, must not depend on overall financial conditions. For a secondary market to work effectively and to contribute to financial stability, an asset has to be transformed at any time into cash without a loss of its market value, which requires a set of position takers who buy significant amounts of assets for their own account, and who sell large amounts of assets out of their stock. Position takers in secondary markets in general finance their transactions by borrowing from financial intermediaries, which however does not prevent the occurrence of a systemic liquidity crisis as described above; in case of a widespread fire-sale, the position taker has to increase its bank debt to sell a large amount of assets he generally does not own. Consequently, a position taker contributing to financial stability must have additional sources of emergency or standby liquidity. However, the only source of finance which is truly independent of system behaviour is liquidity support by the central bank. Therefore, financial stability can be considerably increased in case position takers have unlimited access to central bank credit. Furthermore, financial stability can be increased if the central bank takes over the position taker function by itself to

[45] If central banks are not independent, a liquidity crisis of the government sector need not lead to a liquidity crisis of the financial sector. In this case, the government uses central bank reserves directly to pay outstanding debt which can lead to inflation and, in extreme cases, to hyperinflation.

stabilize assets' market prices, as e.g. the market price for Treasury bills, in case of large fluctuations in demand and supply conditions.

The Adequacy of Refinancing Possibilities in Foreign Currency. Troubled business units which cannot fulfill payment commitments in foreign currency, generally have three options to prevent bankruptcy. Firstly, a unit can engage in all activities described above to obtain liquidity in domestic currency and to sale revenues in the foreign exchange market. However, this strategy is subject to foreign exchange risk, as a large and sudden increase in demand for foreign currency leads either to a sharp devaluation of the home currency in case of flexible exchange rates, or to a large depletion of central bank foreign reserves in case of a fixed exchange rate system which can possibly lead to a suspension of the peg (and to a devaluation of the home currency) in case foreign reserves are not sufficient. Consequently, external financial instability is negatively dependent on the stock of central bank foreign reserves, and increases in case the foreign exchange market is highly volatile in case of sudden changes in demand and supply conditions.

Secondly, in case the business unit possesses foreign assets, the unit can sell these assets in a fire-sale action in foreign financial markets. This action is not subject to exchange rate risk, but depends on the liquidity of foreign financial markets. Consequently, external financial instability increases if the share of the market value of foreign assets which are independent of foreign system behaviour decreases.

Thirdly, the business unit can increase foreign debt, depending on the liquidity status of foreign financial intermediaries. That is, external financial instability decreases if there are effective lender-of-last-resort interventions by foreign central banks.

2.3.4 Excess Volatility in Asset Prices

This section studies the impact of asset price fluctuations on financial stability by asset prices' influence on long-run debt-asset ratios, as well as on long-run cash flow positions. Furthermore, this section analyzes the impact of asset price and debt-asset ratio swings on real economic activity, causing excessive and expectations-led boom-bust cycles in goods and in financial markets, and possibly giving rise to systemic financial crises during the bust phase.

A General Definition of Excess Volatility. Asset prices are subject to fluctuations if there is a change in asset prices' determinants. Using a simplified version of equation 2.3, an asset's market price P_A is given formally by

$$P_A = \frac{CF^e}{i_r} = \frac{CF_r^e\, P^e}{i - \hat{p}^e}, \tag{2.39}$$

that is, by expected nominal cash flows CF^e which are discounted by a real risk-adjusted interest rate i_r representing real finance costs. Expected nominal cash flows are defined as expected real cash flows CF_r^e valued at the expected price level P^e, i.e. as $CF^e = CF_r^e\, P^e$, whereas the real interest rate is defined as the difference between the risk-adjusted nominal interest rate i and the price level's P expected growth rate $\hat{p}^e = \dot{P}^e/P$, i.e. as $i_r = i - \hat{p}^e$.

In order to distinguish asset price volatility stemming from (expected or unexpected) price level effects, which are going to be discussed in section 2.3.5, from asset price volatility stemming from changes in expected real cash flows and from changes in nominal interest rates, it is assumed in the following, that there is no change in the actual and in the expected price level, implying that P, P^e and $\hat{p}^e$ remain constant. Accordingly, volatility in asset prices can be caused only by changes in expected real flows CF_r^e, and by changes in the nominal risk-adjusted interest rate i.

If expectations are formed according to the rational expectations hypothesis, i.e. if it holds that expected real cash flows are equal to actual real cash flows CF_r in case exogenous shocks are absent, formally if $CF_r^e = CF_r$, then a change in asset prices simply reflects changes in economic fundamentals.[46] This kind of asset price volatility, being consistent with actual changes in economic fundamentals, is labelled as *"normal"* or *"correct" asset price volatility*, as asset price changes indicate correctly fluctuations in economic fundamentals.

By way of contrast, *excess volatility in asset prices* emerges if expectations, and thereby asset prices, fluctuate with a much higher amplitude than changes in economic fundamentals, implying that expectations do mostly not coincide with actual economic fundamentals. By equation 2.39, excess volatility emerges in case changes in expected real cash flows are larger than changes in actual real cash flows in absolute terms, i.e. if it holds that $|dCF_r^e| > |dCF_r|$, implying that expected real cash flows are usually not equal to actual real cash flows, i.e. formally it usually holds that $CF_r^e \neq CF_r$. Consequently, excess volatility in asset prices does not indicate changes in fundamentals correctly, but reflects expected changes in fundamentals which are much larger than actual changes in fundamentals.

Excess Volatility and Extensive Boom-Bust Cycles in Financial and Goods Markets. The existence of excess volatility implies that in boom phases, asset prices generally reflect overly optimistic, or even euphoric expectations as to future growth of real cash flows, though actual growth of real cash flows is much lower. Formally, excess volatility in boom phases is defined by $dCF_r^e > dCF_r$ and $CF_r^e > CF_r$, implying the existence of an *asset price bubble* as an asset's actual market price, i.e. $P_A = CF^e/i_r = (CF_r^e P^e)/(i - \hat{p}^e)$, is much higher than its fundamental value $P_A^F = CF/i_r = CF_r P/(i - \hat{p}^e)$. Accordingly, an asset price bubble grows with an increasing difference between market prices and fundamental values, i.e. with a growing difference $P_A - P_A^F = ((CF_r^e P^e) - (CF_r P))/(i - \hat{p}^e)$.

Asset price bubbles generally cause a large acceleration in economic growth, being caused by demand-side, financial accelerator-induced and supply-side induced cumulative upward processes as described in section 2.2.4.3. Largely rising expenditures during excessive boom phases are financed by an increase in indebtedness leading to a significant rise in debt-asset ratios and to fall in net worth, as the actual growth in profits and cash flows is smaller than the growth in expenditures which are based on expected profits and cash flows. If domestic financial markets' capacity does not suffice to meet the increasing demand for credit, economies generally start to take foreign debt. Especially emerging market or transition economies, having very often an underdeveloped domestic financial system as outlined in section 2.3.2.4, depend on foreign financial markets' supply of credit in case of a domestic macroeconomic expansion. But also small industrialized countries,

[46] For a general description of the rational expectations hypothesis and its impact on formal solutions to general dynamic economic models, see appendix D.

whose domestic financial system cannot meet rising demand for credit often engage in foreign debt finance (as e.g. Norway, Sweden, and Finland in the late 1980s). As costs of taking foreign debt measured in domestic currency terms, as well as default risk, depend crucially on exchange rate risk, the build-up of foreign debt tends to be much higher in fixed and credible exchange rate systems than in flexible ones.

An increasing indebtedness both in domestic and in foreign currency, generally induces a build-up of aggregate financial instability, being outlined in more detail below, because future domestic and/or foreign interest payments, as well as repayment of domestic and/or foreign debt, can be only met in case future actual cash flows or income streams, both in domestic and in foreign currency, rise to expected levels. Consequently, there is a general increase in the risk of becoming illiquid or insolvent, as business units' future liquidity and solvency status depends increasingly on the validation of euphoric expectations by actual cash flows. If actual cash flows do not grow to expected levels, many business units are going to become illiquid or insolvent in the future.

Financial instability passes over into actual financial distress when agents realize that expectations were too optimistic, i.e. when actual income streams fall short of expected levels and of payment commitments, causing widespread illiquidity and insolvency. Business failures of especially highly leveraged business units act as triggering events for a sharp downward revision of expectations inducing a "burst" of the asset price bubble. Formally, the burst of an asset's market price P_A is induced, according to equation 2.39, by a sharp decline in expected real cash flows CF_r^e (and by an increase in the risk-adjusted nominal interest rate i due to increased default risk), as agents realize that actual real cash flows cannot grow up to expected levels in the future, i.e. agents realize that $CF_r \ll CF_r^e$.

The burst of asset price bubbles and beginning failures of highly leveraged business units are generally accompanied by a large increase in real domestic and/or foreign interest rates on debt, as well as by large domestic and/or foreign debt withdrawals due to a sharp increase in overall default risk. In case business units are highly indebted in foreign currency, large debt withdrawals cause, in case of fixed exchange rate systems, a large reduction in foreign exchange reserves according to results of section 2.2.4.3, which very often causes to a currency crisis, i.e. a large devaluation of the home currency, as foreign exchange reserves do not suffice to meet capital outflows. After a devaluation has taken place, the remaining stock of foreign debt is subject to a large increase domestic currency terms, deteriorating further the liquidity and solvency position of business units. In case of flexible exchange rate systems, large debt withdrawals lead to a devaluation of the home currency, also inducing a rise in the foreign debt stock in domestic currency terms.

Collapsing asset prices, rising interest rates, and increasing failures among business units induce a cumulative downward process according to the mechanisms described in section 2.2.4.3. Bust periods are also subject to excess volatility when asset prices reflect overly pessimistic expectations as to future declines in real cash flows, i.e. if expected declines in real cash flows are larger than actual declines. Formally, excess volatility in bust periods is characterized by $-dCF_r^e < -dCF_r$, and $CF_r^e < CF_r$. This "undershooting" of expectations aggravates the downswing more than necessary, as lenders expect default risk to be much higher than actual default risk, leading to higher real interest rates, to much larger drops in asset prices, to much stronger withdrawals of debt, and to much larger devaluations of the home currency, or to much larger declines in foreign exchange reserves, inducing more bankruptcies and a much deeper downswing. Excessive bust periods come to an end when agents realize that expectations had been too pessimistic, and when debt-asset ratios in balance sheets have declined to "sound" levels.

Excess Volatility, Self-Fulfilling Expectations, and Expectations-Led Cumulative Upward and Downward Processes. Excessive boom-bust cycles, leading to a build-up of financial instability by "overindebtedness", and possibly causing systemic financial crises, have their roots in *irreducible* uncertainty about the future. If uncertainty is not irreducible, as it is assumed in standard economic theory, rational expectations provide a powerful tool to forecast the future development without error in case exogenous shocks are absent, implying, as aforementioned, that excess volatility cannot arise. In a real-world environment however, uncertainty is not completely irreducible, connoting that expectations cannot be formed solely according to the rational expectations hypothesis. Rather, to assess future developments which are subject to irreducible uncertainty, expectations tend to be formed by reassessing the actual or past development into the future, implying an adaptive or even extrapolative expectation formation scheme which is compatible with excess volatility, as an increasing reliance can lead to a widening gap of expectations and fundamentals. As a result, real-world expectations tend to be subject to a mixed expectation formation scheme which varies over the business cycle, as boom and bust phases, giving rise to excess volatility, tend to be dominated by adaptive and extrapolative expectations, whereas at the turning points, when agents realize that past expectations have been unrealistic, the expectation formation scheme switches quickly from adaptive and extrapolative to a rational expectation formation scheme, i.e. back to economic fundamentals. Hence, the emergence of excess volatility, financial instability, and systemic financial crises depends crucially on different and varying expectation formation schemes over the business cycle. The degree of financial instability and the severity of the subsequent financial crises is determined firstly, by the strength of adaptive and extrapolative expectations during the upswing and the downswing relative to the influence of rational expectations, determining also the length of the expansion and the contraction phase, and secondly, by the velocity with which "unrealistic" adaptive and extrapolative expectations are transformed into a rational expectation formation scheme, determining the amplitude of asset price swings at the turning points.

The existence of excess volatility implies that the upswing and the downswing of extensive boom-bust cycles are mainly driven by cumulative processes in expectations, giving rise to *expectations-led cumulative upward and downward processes* in goods and financial markets, which are much larger in amplitude than standard cumulative processes described in section 2.2.4.3. Expectations-led cumulative upward/downward processes are characterized by a self-reinforcing expectation formation scheme, as a past increase/decrease in expected values leads to a further increase/decrease in expectations. However, expectations-led cumulative upward/downward processes may not be misunderstood in the sense that they are completely detached from the actual development of economic fundamentals. Rather, cumulative upward/downward processes induced by adaptive and extrapolative expectations are generally associated with an actual improvement/deterioration of fundamentals up to a certain boundary, justifying a further rise/fall in expectations. As a result, expectations during upswings and downswings are *self-fulfilling* up to a certain boundary, i.e. optimistic/pessimistic expectations about the future development generate an actual boom/contraction up to a certain limit by cumulative demand-side and financial accelerator-induced upward/downward processes.

Demand-side cumulative processes, as outlined in section 2.2.4.3, are accelerated by self-fulfilling expectations, as an increase/decrease in expectations causes a rise/drop in asset prices, leading to an improvement/deterioration of demand conditions and to an actual increase/decrease in nominal earnings, cash flows, and net worth, justifying ex post the initial increase/decrease in expectations. If this process was able to be continued, then this cumulative upward/downward process would be *no* example of excess volatility, but an example of *rational behaviour*, because in this case expectations would simply reflect correctly, and rationally ex ante the actual behaviour of fundamentals in the future, which would validate expectations ex post, and which would justify a further ex ante increase/decrease in expectations. However, the self-fulfilling character of expectations has a "natural limit" both in boom and in bust periods, which is going to be discussed in the following paragraph, implying that from a certain point on, expectations do not longer "predict" correctly future actual developments, but simply become unrealistic as expectations are not longer formed rationally; thus, expectations become increasingly adaptive and extrapolative, implying a widening gap between actual and expected values, i.e. expectations become overly optimistic in boom periods, and overly pessimistic in bust periods.

Financial-accelerator induced cumulative processes, as outlined in section 2.2.4.3, are amplified by self-fulfilling expectations, as self-fulfilling demand-side cumulative upward/downward processes induce an improvment/deterioration of the aggregate cash flow and solvency position, which justifies an increase/decrease in domestic and foreign indebtedness as well as a decrease/increase in domestic and foreign interest rates on debt, leading to a further improvement in cash flows and net worth, and justifying a further increase in indebtedness. A general rise in indebtedness in boom phases would be *no* example of an increase in financial instability caused by excess volatility, but also an example of rational behaviour, if actual income streams would rise to expected levels, because in this case, future cash flows would suffice to meet future interest payments and repayment of debt. The build-up of financial instability is about to begin if rising indebtedness is increasingly based on unrealistic adaptive and extrapolative expectations about future income streams, resulting in widespread bankruptcies in the future, as future payment commitments cannot be met. Likewise, debt withdrawals and increases in interest rates on debt during bust periods would be *no* example of "expectation undershooting" in case default risk was assessed by actual cash flow and net worth positions, and not by expected ones which are overly pessimistic.

Summing up, if there emerges large excess volatility in asset prices, business cycles tend to have a much larger amplitude than business cycles without serious excess volatility. Furthermore, excess volatility and excessive boom-bust cycles are generally associated with a large build-up of financial instability which very often induces systemic financial crises, whereas "tranquil" business cycles without heavy excess volatility tend to exhibit no, or only a slight build-up of financial instability which does not pass over into systemic financial crises. These boom-bust cycles driven by excessive volatility in expectations, and their interaction with the financial accelerator, are going to be discussed and modelled formally in detail in part II of the book, as they are one of the most important determinants of systemic financial crises.

"Natural" Limits of Self-Fulfilling Expectations and Expectations-Led Cumulative Processes. It has been argued that both boom and bust phases are not subject to excess volatility in case expectations are self-fulfilling, i.e. if an increase/decrease in expectations leads to an actual macroeconomic expansion/contraction. If there was no limit to the self-fulfilling nature of expectations, positive economic growth based on rational behaviour could be sustained forever without any increase in financial instability if there were no negative exogenous shocks. However, self-fulfilling expectations are subject to "natural" limits in the real and in the financial sphere of modern capitalist economies which prevent never-ending expansions/contractions by disappointing overly optimistic/pessimistic expectations through an actual deterioration/improvement in cash flow and solvency positions, inducing a downward/upward revision of expectations to actual fundamentals.

In the real sphere of modern capitalist economies there are three main factors preventing a never-ending boom/bust driven by self-fulfilling expectations. Firstly, regarding boom periods, aggregate demand cannot increase unboundedly, as it is limited by maximum production capacity and subject to saturation effects. Respecting bust periods, aggregate demand cannot fall to zero, as there exists a minimum of demand. Secondly, in boom periods, aggregate supply cannot increase limitless due to an upper bound of capacity utilization in a static environment. In a dynamic environment, an increase in production capacity is subject to long gestation periods, implying that output cannot grow as fast as expected output. Regarding bust phases, aggregate supply cannot fall to zero, as there is a minimum of aggregate demand which has to be satisfied, and as a reduction in production capacity is also subject to a long time horizon in comparison with fluctuations in expected output. Thirdly, in boom phases, output cannot be expanded at expected costs as there arise labour and material shortages, connoting an increase in input costs and a deterioration of cash flow and net worth positions. In open economies with fixed exchange rates, rising input costs lead to a deterioration of international competitiveness and to real revaluation of the home currency. In bust phases, a reduction in output leads to lower input costs and to an improvement in international competitiveness, implying an improvement in cash flow and net worth positions.

In the financial sphere of modern capitalist economies there are three factors preventing unbounded expansions/contractions. Firstly, regarding boom periods, rising input costs imply rising actual and/or expected inflation, leading to monetary tightening by central banks. A general increase in interest rates connotes a deterioration of cash flows and net worth positions due to rising payment commitments. In bust periods, lowering input costs causing disinflation lead to monetary expansions and to an improvement in cash flow and net worth positions. Secondly, in boom periods, which are subject to rising debt-asset ratios and rising interest rates, it is possible that there arises a sudden change in overall risk perception by market participants, assessing current indebtedness and cash flow positions as not sustainable. This increase in overall risk perception leads to rising domestic and foreign interest rates on debt due to rising risk premia independently of monetary tightening, to a general tightening of liquidity conditions in domestic and international financial markets, and to rising foreign exchange reserve outflows (especially in the case of fixed exchange rate systems) implying higher domestic interest rates. In bust periods, being subject to falling debt-asset ratios and lowering interest rates, it is possible that there is a relaxation in overall risk perception by market participants, assessing current indebtedness and cash flow positions as sustainable. This relaxation in overall risk perception leads to a fall in risk premia, to a decrease in domestic and foreign interest rates on debt independently of monetary policy, to a relaxation in the overall liquidity condition in domestic and international financial markets, and to increasing foreign exchange reserves inflows (especially in case of fixed exchange rate systems) implying lower domestic interest rates. Thirdly, in boom periods, deteriorating cash flow and net worth positions of financial institutions, as well as rising foreign exchange reserves outflows, can cause government authorities to suspend government guarantees in the form of deposit insurance, and bail-out guarantees of troubled banks, as well as to give up a fixed exchange rate regime, as future losses are unavoidable and would lead to an increase in government indebtedness which is not sustainable, e.g. due to rising domestic inflation. A suspension of government guarantees, as well as a suspension of a fixed exchange rate system causes contingent losses to become actual losses leading to a rise in risk premia, to an increase in interest rates, and to a deterioration of financial markets' liquidity. In bust periods, the existence of government guarantees, as well as the stability of a fixed exchange rate regime can induce an increase in credibility, leading to lower risk premia, lower interest rates and to a relaxation of liquidity conditions in financial markets.

Hitherto, the discussion referred only to factors leading to an actual boundedness of cumulative processes driven by self-fulfilling expectations. However, expectations as to the factors mentioned above can have the same effect due to their self-fulfilling nature. For example, an increase in expected inflation due to expected rising factor costs leads to an expected increase in interest rates, which can lead to an actual interest rate increase in case expected inflation leads to an actual increase in factor costs. Consequently, self-fulfilling expansions and contractions are limited by *actual and expected* bounds.

Summing up, excess volatility in expectations and in asset prices is caused by agents not considering natural bounds of expectations-led cumulative processes, leading to an adaptive or extrapolative expectation formation scheme, and to a widening gap of expectations and fundamentals. Despite the fact that the limits mentioned above represent no new information for economic agents, as they are prevalent during each business cycle, overly optimistic expectations during boom phases generally abstract from the boundaries of expansion, predominantly due to the belief that "natural" limits of past business cycles have disappeared, e.g. by the introduction of new technology regimes (as e.g. the introduction of new continuous process technologies after World War I having contributed to the stock market bubble in the late 1920s, or the introduction of information and communication technologies having given rise to the "New Economy" bubble during the late 1990s), or by fundamental changes in the order of domestic and international financial markets (as e.g. large-scale financial liberalization policies in the post Bretton Woods era). By way of contrast, in bust periods agents generally tend to expectation undershooting as overly pessimistic expectations are stronger than the belief in a natural lower limit.

Excess Volatility and Financial Instability. It has been argued that financial instability is generally built up during boom phases by excessively rising asset prices and sharply increasing debt-asset ratios. However, as rising asset prices and increasing debt-asset ratios are a common stylized fact of business cycles' boom periods[47] which do not all cause financial fragility and financial crises, an increase in financial instability cannot be simply detected by a rising debt-asset ratio. Rather, whether an increase in the debt-asset ratio indicates a rise in financial instability or not, depends on the question whether the initial increase in indebtedness is sustainable or not.

Generally, an increase in debt-finance is *sustainable* if there is no long-run drop in the aggregate liquidity and in the aggregate solvency position of an economy. Consequently, a sustainable increase in debt finance is accompanied by a constant or increasing long-run cash flow position, by a constant or decreasing long-run debt-asset ratio, implying a constant or increasing long-run net worth position. For an increase in debt-finance to be sustainable, the rise in the sum of long-run profits has to be equal or larger than the increase in indebtedness, which can be seen formally by equations 2.6 and 2.8. It has to be emphasized that a sustainable debt increase can be subject to a decrease in the net worth and in the cash flow position, but only in the *short-run*, stemming e.g. from long gestation periods. Consequently, a sustainable increase in indebtedness requires that expectations as to future income streams, on which the initial increase in debt-finance is based, are going to be validated by the actual development of future income streams, i.e. that the formation of expectations has been rational or realistic.

By way of contrast, an *unsustainable* increase in indebtedness is characterized by a long-run deterioration of the aggregate liquidity and solvency status of an economy, implying possibly widespread illiquidity and insolvency in the long-run. Accordingly, an unsustainable increase in indebtedness is accompanied by a decreasing long-run cash flow position, by an increasing long-run debt-asset ratio, reflecting a decline in the long-run net worth position. For an increase in the debt-asset ratio to be unsustainable, the initial increase in indebtedness has to be larger than the sum of long run profits by equations 2.6 and 2.8. If the sum of long-run profits is negative, there is a further rise in the long-run debt-asset ratio. Furthermore, an unsustainable increase in indebtedness has to be based on unrealistic euphoric expectations as to future income streams which cannot be validated, implying either that the initial increase in indebtedness can be repaid only with deteriorating liquidity and solvency positions, or that the debt increase cannot be repaid as income streams fall short of payment commitments, leading to systemic financial crises.

Summing up, a growing positive divergence between expected and actual real cash flows causes steadily increasing asset prices which reflect a growing divergence between expected and actual economic fundamentals. This growing positive divergence between expected and actual fundamentals induces an increasing degree of financial instability *if* the steadily rising overall debt-asset ratio is increasingly based on irrational or unrealistic expectations about the future, implying that the increasing debt stock both in domestic and in foreign currency becomes more and more unsustainable. On the contrary, in case expectations are formed rationally, there is *no* increase in financial instability, as increasing short-run indebtedness is sustainable owing to realistic and rational expectations. However, if expectations become more and more irrational, i.e. more and more overly optimistic, a growing degree of financial instability causes an increasing drop in asset prices when agents realize that actual income streams fall short of payment commitments. The larger the drop in asset prices, and the larger the impact of widespread bankruptcies on

[47] For an overview of the stylized time patterns of major economic indicators of empirical business cycle analysis, see Moore (1983), chapter 6, and Zarnowitz (1992), pp. 23-28.

real economic activity, the higher is the probability that expectations tend to undershoot, i.e. to be overly pessimistic, which induces a much longer bust period than necessary by high real interest rates, by excessive debt withdrawals, and by collapsing exchange rates, leading to further bankruptcies and to a further decline in real economic activity.

Empirical studies of excess volatility and its impact on financial instability and aggregate economic activity[48] conclude that especially stock and real property prices tend to be subject to excess volatility, giving rise to a build-up of financial instability by a significant increase in debt-asset ratios of business firms, households and financial intermediaries. Though bond markets are generally subject to much less volatility than stock and real property prices, bond prices too can exhibit excess volatility if actual or expected changes in macroeconomic fundamentals cause investors to change abruptly their expectations for inflation and real interest rates. Excess volatility in bond prices and in real interest rates can adversely affect real economic activity via the interest rate channel as the volume of investment financed by bonds (and by long-term borrowing) is typically much larger than the volume financed by equities (Crockett 1997).

2.3.5 Monetary Instability and Debt Deflation

This section studies the impact of price level fluctuations on financial instability by their influence on asset prices and real economic activity via volatility in real interest rates, real borrowing costs, and real debt burdens.

Price Level Instability, Excess Volatility, Extensive Boom-Bust Cycles and Financial Instability. According to the "Schwartz" hypothesis, named after A. Schwartz (1981, 1986, 1995, 1997), and according to I. Fisher's (1932, 1933) business cycle theory, price level instability can aggravate, or even cause financial instability by inducing uncertainties and unrealistic expectations of borrowers and lenders about potential real returns of investment projects. The Schwartz hypothesis, as well as I. Fisher's business cycles theory are very similar to the asset price excess volatility hypothesis, having been outlined in the previous section 2.3.4, as they also claim that financial instability and subsequent financial crises are caused by unrealistic and highly volatile expectations of agents inducing excessive boom-bust cycles in goods and financial markets. Both theories differ however with respect to the "driving" variable of the system, as they claim that excessive boom-bust cycles, financial instability and excess volatility in asset prices are not mainly caused by unrealistic expectations as to real cash flows, but by unrealistic expectations as to the price level's growth rate, resulting in unrealistic expectations concerning real interest rates, real borrowing costs, and real returns.[49]

The emergence of excess volatility in asset prices by excess volatility in the expected price level and in the price level's expected growth rate can be formally outlined by a modified version of equation 2.3, which corresponds to equation 2.39, determining an

[48]For studies of the nexus between excess volatility and financial instability, see e.g. Bank for International Settlements (1998), International Monetary Fund (2000, 2003a, 2003b) Bordo and Jeanne (2002), Borio and Lowe (2002). For the empirical nexus of financial stability and economic growth, see e.g. Levine (1997).

[49]For empirical tests, as well as for a review of the literature on the link between price stability and financial stability, see e.g. Bordo and Wheelock (1998), Bordo, Dueker and Wheelock (2000, 2001a).

asset's market price P_A as

$$P_A = \frac{CF_r^e P^e}{i - \hat{p}^e}, \tag{2.40}$$

that is, as the discounted present value of expected nominal cash flows, where P^e denotes the expected price level, CF_r^e expected real cash flows, $CF^e = CF_r^e P^e$ expected nominal cash flows, i the nominal risk-adjusted interest rate, $\hat{p}^e = \dot{P}^e/P$ the price level's expected growth rate, and $i - \hat{p}^e$ the expected risk-adjusted real interest rate.

In order to study the emergence of excess volatility in asset prices due to excess volatility in expected future prices, it is assumed in the following that expected real cash flows CF_r^e are constant, implying that volatility in asset prices is caused by fluctuations in the expected price level, in the price level's expected growth rate, and in the nominal interest rate. Consequently, excess volatility emerges in case price expectations are subject to larger fluctuations than the actual price level, implying that price expectations are not formed rationally. Formally, excess volatility emerges if $|dP^e| > |dP|$ and $|d\hat{p}^e| > |d\hat{p}|$, implying that it usually holds that $P^e \neq P$.

The existence of excess volatility in expectations regarding the future price level implies that boom phases, which are generally associated with inflationary pressures, lead to overly optimistic expectations of real returns and asset prices by overly optimistic expectations as to real interest rates and nominal cash flows via actually rising inflation, and via an expected accelerating inflation rate for the future. These overly optimistic expectations give rise to the emergence of an asset price bubble, as expected cash flows are much higher than actual, and as expected real interest rates are much lower than actual. Formally, excess volatility in asset prices due to expected inflation being much higher than actual inflation is defined, according to equation 2.40, as $dP^e > dP$ and $d\hat{p}^e > d\hat{p}^e$, implying $P^e > P$.

The asset price bubble induces a cumulative upward process in goods and financial markets via expectations-led demand-side and financial accelerator-induced processes as described in sections 2.2.4.3 and 2.3.4. A growing difference between the expected and the actual inflation rate by an increasing reliance on adaptive and extrapolative expectation formation schemes, induces a build-up of financial instability by increasing debt-asset ratios, as the future liquidity and solvency status depend increasingly on the validation of euphoric inflation expectations. If the actual inflation rate does not rise to expected levels due to disinflation or even deflation, asset prices are going to collapse inducing widespread failures among firms and financial institutions.

As outlined in section 2.3.4, the boom phase comes to a halt and passes over into actual financial distress, when agents realize that inflation expectations had been unrealistic due to an actual deterioration of cash flow and liquidity positions, being induced generally by *disinflation* or even *deflation*, resulting from tightening monetary policy, from an overall increase in the assessment of risk, and from a reduction in growth. Deflation, disinflation and rising nominal interest rates lead to an increase in actual and expected real interest rates, causing failures of especially highly leveraged business units and triggering the asset price bubble's burst. Formally, according to equation 2.40, the collapse of asset prices P_A can be induced by a rise in the nominal interest rate i, by a fall in the expected price level P^e, and by a fall in the price level's expected growth rate $\hat{p}^e$.

The burst of the asset price bubble, as well as failures of business firms and financial institutions induce an expectations-led cumulative downward process which tends to exhibit excess volatility if expected future changes of the price level are smaller than the actual change of the price level, and if the price level's expected future growth rate is smaller than the price level's actual growth rate.[50] Formally, according to equation 2.40, excess volatility in bust phases is characterized by $dP^e < dP$ and $d\hat{p}^e < d\hat{p}$ implying $P^e < P$. This "expectation undershooting" comes to an end when agents realize that expectations had been too pessimistic, and that cash flow and solvency positions, as well as debt-asset ratios have returned to sustainable levels.

Summing up, financial instability increases/decreases with increasing/decreasing monetary instability, implying that financial instability is reduced by monetary policy aiming at a stabilization of the price level's actual and expected growth rate, and increases if monetary authorities cause unexpected changes in the price level's growth rate by unexpected and discretionary shifts in monetary policy leading to excess volatility in price expectations.

Monetary Instability and Real Debt Burdens - Debt Inflation and Debt Deflation. Hitherto, the discussion referred mainly to the impact of price level instability on real interest rates, real borrowing costs and asset prices, and neglected the impact of changing real debt burdens via debt inflation and debt deflation on financial instability, having been originally emphasized by I. Fisher (1932, 1933). Debt inflation and debt deflation are commonly defined by the real value of net debt, which is defined as the real value of the sum of debts less the real value of the sum of assets.[51] Applying this definition to the stylized balance sheet in figure 2.1, the real value of net debt, NDB_r, is given as

$$NDB_r = \frac{NDB}{P} = \frac{DB + s\,DB^* - (P_A A + sP_A^* A^* + LMA)}{P}, \tag{2.41}$$

where NDB denotes the nominal value of net debt, and P the general price level. It has to be emphasized that the real value of net debt can be only used to define debt inflation and debt inflation by identifying their determinants, but cannot be applied to "measure" changes in the real debt burden via changing values in NDB_r which has a negative sign in case of solvency, and a positive sign in case of insolvency. For example, in case of solvency, a fall in P_A and P_A^*, both engendering debt deflation being outlined below, cause a rise of NDB_r, whereas a fall in P, also causing debt deflation, leads to a fall in NDB_r.

The term "debt inflation", designating a fall in the real debt burden, and the term "debt deflation", labelling a rise in the real debt burden, are not uniformly defined in the economic literature. While some authors associate debt inflation/debt deflation with a rise/fall in the aggregate price level, other authors have emphasized asset price inflation/deflation. Common to all definitions is the neglect of open-economy effects, as e.g. the influence of a changing external value of a currency, or the influence of foreign asset prices. In order to overcome existing inconsistencies and to enlarge existing definitions, the present contribution defines debt inflation/debt deflation following equation 2.41, firstly, as a rise/fall in prices of domestic and foreign assets P_A and P_A^*, secondly, as a rise/fall in the general price level P, thirdly, as a fall/rise in the exchange rate s in case the balance sheet exhibits a foreign net debtor position ($DB^* > P_A^* A^*$), and as a

[50] Note that this statements is valid both in the case of deflation and in the case of disinflation.

[51] For the definition of the real value of net debt, as well as for an overview of the literature on the influence of changing real debt burdens on financial stability, see e.g. Eichengreen and Grossman (1997).

rise/fall in the exchange rate s in case the balance sheet exhibits a foreign net creditor position ($DB^* < P_A^* A^*$). Among debt inflation/debt deflation, the real debt burden decreases/increases in case of a fall/rise in domestic debt and/or foreign debt DB and DB^*, as well as in case of a rise/fall in domestic and/or foreign asset stocks LMA, A and A^*, implying a fall/rise in the debt-asset ratio.

Financial instability increases/decreases if there is debt deflation/debt inflation, as the amount of debt repayment in real terms increases/decreases. Combining the results of the previous paragraph and of section 2.3.4, boom phases driven by excess volatility are able to lower financial instability due to debt inflation, being caused by a rise in domestic, and possibly foreign asset prices P_A and P_A^*, by a rise in the domestic price level P, and in case of flexible exchange rates combined with a foreign net debtor position by a fall in the exchange rate s. It has to emphasized however, that the fall in the real debt burden is dampened, or can be even overcompensated by an increase in the debt-asset ratio. Consequently, in case there is excessive overborrowing during boom phases which overcompensates the reduction in the real debt burden via inflation, rising asset prices and declining exchange rates, being characteristic of the period just before the upper turning point, financial instability increases.

Bust periods are generally associated with an increase in financial instability due to debt deflation, causing a rise in the real debt burden via declining domestic, and possibly foreign asset prices, deflation, and via an increase in the exchange rate in case of a foreign net debtor position. It has to be emphasized as well, that the rise in the real debt burden can be dampened, or even overcompensated by a general decrease in the debt-asset ratio during the late bust phase. As a result, in case of large reductions in the debt-asset ratio which overcompensate the rise in the real debt burden by deflation, declining asset prices, and rising exchange rates, being characteristic of the period just before the lower turning point, financial instability decreases.

2.4 Exogenous and Endogenous Financial Crises

This section discusses briefly different theoretical views of the fundamental causes of financial crises by applying the present analysis of financial instability and financial crises of sections 2.1 to 2.3 to current approaches to financial crises, which are discussed in much more detail in sections 4.5 and 5.5. Standard theory of financial crises, which is going to be discussed in detail in sections 3.5, 4.5, and 5.5, can be classified into two broad categories, namely in theories of endogenously caused financial crises, and in theories of exogenously caused financial crises, as already outlined briefly in section 1.1. The largest part of the existing literature on the causes of financial distress is dominated by standard or mainstream economic theory, assuming that modern capitalist economies are inherently stable and that financial crises can be only caused by adverse exogenous shocks to economic fundamentals, or by an exogenous shift from optimistic towards pessimistic (rational) expectations which become self-fulfilling. By way of contrast, models stressing the endogenous character of financial instability and financial crises, representing the minority in the financial crises literature, assume that modern capitalist economies are inherently unstable, as there are interactions between the real and the financial sphere of modern economies which cause an endogenous build-up of financial instability, leading finally to financial crises.

The following discussion analyzes the propagation mechanisms of exogenous shock-driven and endogenous financial crises, being followed by a short description of mixed approaches. The sections ends with an outlook on an alternative mixed perspective on financial crises which is going to be developed formally in part II of the book.

Exogenous Shock-Driven Financial Crises. Models of exogenous shock-driven financial crises generally abstract from financial instability as defined in section 2.3, as they assume that modern capitalist economies are inherently stable and that agents are subject to rational behaviour. Consequently, financial instability cannot arise as excess volatility in asset prices and in the price level, leading to overindebtedness according to unrealistic expectations, are not possible. Thus, the only possibility for financial crises to occur are large random exogenous shocks to economic fundamentals, or random exogenous shifts in (rational) expectations which become self-fulfilling. Moreover, exogenous-shock driven models are not characterized by extensive boom-bust cycles, but describe only the contractionary effect on real economic activity in case of large exogenous shocks, as the build-up of financial instability during expansionary phases is excluded by the existence of rational expectations.

Following the general definition of financial crises in section 2.3.1, the logic of financial crises driven by exogenous shocks to economic fundamentals runs from random exogenous real sector shocks, as e.g. adverse terms of trade or technology shocks, and/or random exogenous financial sector shocks, as e.g. domestic or foreign interest rate increases, to collapses in asset prices whose effects on general financial market conditions and real economic activity depend on the size of the initial exogenous shock, determining whether a crisis is systemic or spurious. Consequently, large/small adverse exogenous real and/or financial shocks lead to large/small drops in asset prices causing a systemic/spurious financial crises.

Respecting the propagation mechanism of financial crises driven by random shifts in (rational) expectations, the logic runs from an exogenous deterioration of ex ante expectations regarding real sector or financial sector variables, to actions by agents which lead to an actual deterioration of real sector of financial variables and to a collapse of asset prices, so that expectations are validated ex post, i.e. expectations are self-fulfilling. For example, an expected depreciation of the home currency, and an expected rise in domestic interest rates being associated with an expected drop in asset prices, leads to actual large capital outflows, an actual rise in domestic interest rates, an actual collapse of asset prices and, if foreign exchange reserves do not suffice, to an actual devaluation of the home currency. The size of the asset price drop, as well as the impact on real economic activity and financial market conditions, depends on the size of the shift in expectations. Accordingly, a small/large deterioration of expectations leads to an actual small/large drop in asset prices inducing a spurious/systemic financial crisis.

Endogenous Financial Crises. Models of endogenous financial crises contend that financial distress is caused by an *endogenous* build-up of financial instability as described in section 2.3 in boom phases, passing over finally into financial crises, and real economic contractions due to expectations-led overindebtedness. Accordingly, models of endogenous financial crises assume that modern capitalist economies are inherently unstable due to unrealistic and irrational expectations giving rise to extensive boom-bust cycles, and that financial crises are a "normal" outcome of economic development.

Following the general definition of financial crises according to section 2.1, and the financial instability analysis owing to section 2.3, the logic of endogenous financial crisis models runs from an endogenous increase in indebtedness, asset prices, inflation, and real economic activity to an unavoidable deterioration of real and financial market activity as described in section 2.3.4 due to the existence of natural limits. Consequently, the endogenous increase in financial instability causes *endogenous* deteriorations in the real and/or in the financial sector, as e.g. rising input costs, a terms of trade deterioration, domestic and foreign interest rate increases, increases in overall risk perception, etc., which lead endogenously to a drop in asset prices and to systemic financial crises as financial instability is high. In contrast to exogenous-shock driven models, even very small "shocks", i.e. small endogenous deteriorations in the real and/or in the financial sector, suffice to cause systemic financial crises. Consequently, according to the theory of endogenous financial crises, spurious financial crises are a very rare event.

Mixed Approaches. There are only few models of financial crises arguing that financial distress is caused by the combination of exogenous and endogenous factors. Regarding standard theory of financial crises, only asymmetric information models stressing the importance of moral hazard driven financial distress provide a mixed approach. According to these models, moral hazard induces a large endogenous build-up of financial instability by an immoral increase in indebtedness due to distorted risk perceptions resulting from government guarantees. For example, if there is a general government guarantee to bail-out troubled banks, investment decisions by bankers are more risky than without the existence of these guarantees, as the government takes over losses in case of default. Notwithstanding the fact that moral hazard driven financial crisis models explain the build-up of financial instability by endogenous mechanisms, they argue that financial crises only occur in case of exogenous shocks. Consequently, the endogenous build-up of financial instability is sustainable as long as there are no exogenous shocks. Moreover, the reason for an endogenous build-up of financial fragility is the existence of exogenously given government guarantees. Thus, if there were no government guarantees, there would be no endogenous build-up of financial fragility at all.

An Outlook on a Synthetic View of Financial Crises. A detailed analysis of the stylized facts of financial crises, which is going to be set out in the following chapter, shows that financial crises are neither purely exogenous nor purely endogenous events, and that it is unrealistic to assume that a large endogenous build-up of financial instability evolves into a systemic financial crisis only if there arise exogenous shocks. Hence, as the next chapter is going to point out, current approaches to financial crises are too polarized to provide a full understanding of the propagation mechanisms of financial crises.

The present approach, formally outlined in part II of the book, tries to overcome the existing polarization by developing a synthetic view of financial crises which argues, based on stylized facts of business cycles and financial crises, that modern capitalist economies are generally subject to cyclical fluctuations in goods and financial markets, being driven by *endogenous* fluctuations in expectations and indebtedness. These endogenous business cycles are characterized by cumulative upward and downward processes which are inherently stable in the absence of exogenous shocks. Hence, a "normal" functioning implies an endogenous build-up of a low degree of financial instability during the boom phase, which however does not cause a systemic financial crisis but only a mild recession giving rise to the next business cycle. By way of contrast, systemic financial crises can be caused only by positive exogenous shocks to expectations leading to an unsustainable increase in financial instability and to extensive boom-bust cycles, or by exogenous adverse real or financial sector shocks resulting in a large contraction.

Chapter 3

Stylized Facts and Standard Theory of Financial Crises

3.1 Defining and Identifying Financial Crises

Hitherto, financial crises have been defined and categorized, according to the general definition set out in section 2.1, by asset price drops and by the strength of the transmission mechanism of financial sector disturbances into the real sphere of an economy. Notwithstanding the fact that this general definition provides deep theoretical insights into the explanation of financial crises and financial instability, it cannot be applied to identify and to "measure" financial crises empirically due to a limited capacity to observe and to process relevant variables. If financial crises were identified and measured according to the general definition set out in section 2.1, an empirical study would have to observe asset price and interest rate behaviour of a large number of different financial and real assets, as well as a huge number of microeconomic cash flow and balance sheet data of a large number of financial and nonfinancial firms, being not feasible from an empirical perspective.

In order to bridge the gap between the necessity of a multidimensional approach to identify and to measure financial crises, and a limited capacity and number of well-observable macroeconomic variables and indicators, the empirical literature generally distinguishes among three types of financial crises, namely, currency crises, banking crises and twin crises (being defined as the simultaneous occurrence of currency and banking crises within a certain time period), whose identification and measurement is not trivial, but feasible from an empirical perspective. The following three subsections 3.1.1 to 3.1.3 are going to describe both the empirical definition as well the identification of currency, banking and twin crises, serving as a basis for the following sections of this chapter.

3.1.1 Currency Crises

Following the empirical literature on financial crises, currency crises are generally defined as follows:

> *A currency crisis is a situation in which a speculative attack on the exchange value of a currency causes a devaluation, or a sharp depreciation of the currency, or forces authorities (central banks or governments) to defend the cur-*

rency by raising sharply short-term interest rates, or by selling large volumes of foreign exchange reserves.

This definition reflects the empirical fact that currency crises can be observed under all kinds of exchange rate regimes, and need not result in a devaluation or depreciation of the currency in case authorities successfully defended a speculative attack. Furthermore, the definition states that a crisis situation only arises in case of the emergence of speculative pressure on a currency by the private sector, implying that not each devaluation or depreciation can be labelled as a currency crisis, like e.g. regular devaluations directed by officials (realignments), an official widening of fluctuation bands, or "normal" depreciations of flexible exchange rates.

Empirically, currency crises are identified by an *index of speculative pressure* (ISP), which is generally calculated, following the definition above, as a weighted average of nominal exchange rate changes, short-term interest rate changes and foreign exchange reserve changes, where all variables are measured relative to a reference country, being characterized by a stable and credible currency.[1] Formally, a general index of speculative pressure on country x's currency at time t, $ISP_{x,t}$, could take the following form,

$$ISP_{x,t} = \frac{1}{\sigma_s}\left(\frac{\Delta s_{x,t}}{s_{x,t-1}}\right) + \frac{1}{\sigma_i}\Delta(i_{x,t} - i_{ref,t}) - \frac{1}{\sigma_Z}\left(\frac{\Delta Z_{x,t}}{Z_{x,t-1}} - \frac{\Delta Z_{ref,t}}{Z_{ref,t-1}}\right),$$

where $s_{x,t}$ denotes the price of one unit of the reference country's currency in x's currency at time t, $i_{x,t}$ the short-term interest rate in country x at time t, $i_{ref,t}$ the short-term interest rate in the reference country at time t, $Z_{x,t}$ foreign exchange reserves of country x at time t, and $Z_{ref,t}$ foreign exchange reserves of the reference country at time t, and Δy_j the change of variable y in country j between time t and $t-1$, i.e. it holds that $\Delta y_j = y_{j,t} - y_{j,t-1}$. Since the volatility of exchange rates, interest rate differentials and foreign exchange reserves differentials is very different, the three components are generally weighted by the inverse of their standard deviation to equalize the volatilities of the three components, thereby preventing any one of them dominating the index, where σ_s denotes the standard deviation of the rate of change of the nominal exchange rate s_x, σ_i the standard deviation of the change of the short-term interest rate differential, and σ_Z the standard deviation of the difference of the rate of change of foreign exchange reserves in the reference country and in country x.[2]

Currency crises are defined as "extreme" values of the speculative pressure index, where extreme values are distinguished from "normal" values by exceptional deviations

[1]For a theoretical foundation of the speculative pressure index's components, see Girton and Roper (1977).

[2]For this type of speculative pressure index based on the general definition of currency crises as aforementioned, see e.g. Eichengreen, Rose and Wyplosz (1995, 1996), International Monetary Fund (1998a), chapter IV, Goldstein et al. (2000), and Bordo et al. (2001b). Though most empirical studies use speculative pressure indexes as represented above, there are also studies, as e.g. Kaminsky and Reinhart (1999), which neglect short-term interest rate changes due to the existence of interest rate controls in some sample countries. Other studies, as e.g. Goldfajn and Valdés (1997a), use real exchange rate changes instead of nominal exchange rate changes to distinguish changes in nominal exchange rates caused by inflation differentials from changes which affect the purchasing power of a currency. According to these studies, nominal depreciations that solely keep up with inflation differentials leaving the real exchange rate unchanged, are not considered as currency crises, implying that large devaluations stemming from hyperinflation are not classified as currency crises.

from average deviations. Formally, currency crises are identified in most cases by ISP-values which are 2 standard deviations or more above the sample mean, i.e. currency crises are defined by an $ISP_{x,t}$ value, satisfying

$$ISP_{x,t} > \mu_{ISP} + 2\ \sigma_{ISP},$$

where μ_{ISP} denotes the sample mean, σ_{ISP} the standard deviation of the ISP-index.[3]

3.1.2 Banking Crises

In contrast to currency crises, the empirical literature provides no general definition of banking crises which could serve as a basis for their empirical identification. Rather, empirical studies mainly refer to a mixed set of empirically observable indicators which are used to "define" banking crises. In order to establish a uniform basis for the empirical analysis of banking distress in the following, banking crises are defined, according to the results of section 2.2.4, as follows:

> *A banking crisis is a situation in which the banking sector is faced with sharply deteriorating liquidity and/or solvency positions, causing bankruptcy by illiquidity and/or insolvency, or inducing interventions by central banks and governments in the form of liquidity and capital support (bail-out programmes) to prevent bankruptcies.*

Empirically, banking crises are identified predominantly by a qualitative approach stressing "events" due to the lack of quantitative high-frequency data.[4] The first group of events indicating a banking crisis are bank runs which lead to a closure, or to a merger of one of more financial institutions, or which cause a takeover of one of more banks by the public sector. Bank runs, having been defined formally by condition 2.9 in section 2.2.4.2, are generally identified by changes in bank deposits, and thereby indicate bankruptcy in the form of illiquidity, stemming from the debt side of banks' balance sheets.

However, though data on bank deposits are readily available for almost all countries, detecting banking crises by bank runs can be a very poor measure for banking distress if there are effective lender of last resort interventions by central banks, or if there exist efficient deposit insurance systems, preventing bank runs in spite of severe distress in the banking sector. Furthermore, in most cases, bank runs are the result rather than the cause of banking sector distress, because illiquidity and insolvency in recent years were predominantly caused by a deterioration of banks' asset quality, having been induced e.g. by collapses in real estate or stock prices, or by increasing bankruptcies in the nonfinancial sector having led to a rise in the share of nonperforming loans. This suggests that large fluctuations in real estate and stock prices, the share of nonperforming loans in banks' portfolios and indicators of business failures could serve as much better indicators for banking distress than bank runs. However, data for these variables are readily not available or are incomplete due to banks' desire to hire liquidity and solvency problems as long as possible. Hence, given these data limitations, banking crises which are not associated

---

[3] Some studies, as e.g. Eichengreen, Rose and Wyplosz (1996), use a smaller range, defining currency crises by ISP-values which are 1.5 standard deviations or more above the sample mean.

[4] For this type of approach to identify banking crises, see e.g. Sundararajan and Baliño (1991), Lindgren et al. (1996), and Kaminsky and Reinhart (1998, 1999).

with bank runs, are generally identified by a second group of events which concentrates on closures, mergers, takeovers, or massive central bank or government assistance to one ore more financial institutions.

3.1.3 Twin Crises

The empirical literature provides a controversial perspective respecting both the definition and the identification of twin crises. For example, Kaminsky and Reinhart's (1998, 1999) definition of twin crises reads as follows:

> *A twin crisis is a situation in which a banking crisis is followed by a currency crisis.*

According to this definition, implying that currency crises which are followed by banking crises are not considered as twin crises, episodes of twin crises are identified as instances in which the beginning of a banking crisis is followed by a currency crisis within 48 months, where currency crises and banking crises are identified as aforementioned. By way of contrast, according to Glick and Hutchinson (1999), twin crises' definition is less restrictive as it allows for both directions of causality, reading as follows:

> *A twin crisis is a situation in which a banking crises is associated with a currency crises, or vice versa.*

Following this definition, twin crises are identified as instances in which a banking crisis is accompanied by a currency crisis in either the previous, current, or following year. Summing up, as there exists no consensus view on both the definition and the identification method of twin crises, the following description of the stylized facts of twin crises is going to adopt all definitions and identification methods of each empirical study cited.

3.2 Frequency and Severity of Financial Crises

This section is based on the empirical studies by Bordo et al. (2001b) and Eichengreen and Bordo (2002). These two studies are exceptional in comparison to other studies, as e.g. Kaminsky and Reinhart (1998, 1999) and International Monetary Fund (1998a, chapter IV), as they investigate the incidence and costs of financial crises over the last 120 years, distinguishing the gold standard period (1880-1913), the interwar period (1919-1939), the Bretton Woods period (1945-1971), and the post Bretton Woods period (1973-1997), whereas other studies only refer to the post Bretton Woods era. A historical perspective over 120 years, taking into consideration very different monetary, financial and exchange rate regimes with distinct degrees of financial market liberalization and openness of capital accounts, allows for a much better, and more objective analysis of the questions whether the crisis problem has grown more frequent and more severe in the recent decade, and whether domestic and international financial liberalization generally cause a higher degree of financial instability.

The sample consists of 21 countries containing both industrial and emerging market nations for the entire 120-year period. To ease the comparison with other studies referring solely to the post Bretton Woods era, as e.g. Kaminsky and Reinhart (1998, 1999) and

International Monetary Fund (1998a, chapter IV), the study additionally contains a 56-country sample for the 1973-1997 period. Crises dates are identified by the methods outlined in section 3.1. For further details regarding the country sample or crises dates, see the Web Appendix of Bordo et al. (2001b), and section 3.3.

The incidence of financial crises is quantified by the crisis frequency, being calculated by dividing the number of crises by the number of country-year observations in each sub-period, representing the annual probability of a financial crisis in per cent. Furthermore, crisis frequency in each sub-period is determined separately for currency crises, banking crises, twin crises, and for the sum of all crises. The severity of financial crises is measured by the average recovery time and by the output loss. To quantify both numbers, a trend rate of GDP growth is calculated for the five years preceding a financial crisis. Then, average recovery time, being equivalent to crisis duration, is computed as the number of years until actual GDP growth has returned to the GDP growth trend. Subsequently, output loss is computed as the cumulated difference, over the average recovery time, between actual GDP growth and trend GDP growth.

The following description of the empirical data by Bordo et al. (2001b) and Eichengreen and Bordo (2002) does not coincide completely with the authors' interpretation, but departs partly, especially with respect to the effects of financial liberalization.

3.2.1 Incidence of Financial Crises

All Crises. Table 3.1 summarizes the frequency of financial crises in each sub-period for all sample countries, where the last column portrays the crisis frequency for the sum of currency, banking and twin crises. It shows that the overall frequency of financial crises has grown since 1973 and is high by historical standards. Only the interwar period, being dominated by financial distress caused by the Great Depression, is subject to a slightly higher crisis frequency. A frequency of 12.2% for the 56-country sample during the 1973-1997 period indicates that there was a probability of one eights that countries suffered a currency, banking, or twin crisis in a given year. Comparing the post Bretton Woods era with the gold standard era indicates that financial instability need not be solely caused by globalization of goods and financial markets.

Currency Crises. Table 3.1 indicates that the high overall crisis frequency in the post Bretton Woods era is mainly caused by the high frequency of currency crises (7.5%), being highest by historical standards. Only the Bretton Woods era is characterized by nearly the same frequency of currency crises. There is an observable trend towards an increasing frequency of currency crises from 1880 until 1997, indicating that instability in foreign exchange markets does not only depend on the degree of capital mobility, but also on the credibility of currency pegs even in times of stiff financial market regulations and capital controls, as e.g. during the Bretton Woods era.

Banking and Twin Crises. Highest frequency of banking and twin crises can be observed during the interwar period, having been caused mainly by the Great Depression. However, crisis frequency during the post Bretton Woods era closely follows the financially unstable interwar period. By way of contrast, tight regulations of domestic and international financial markets during the Bretton Woods era led to an almost complete absence of banking and twin crises, despite a high currency crisis frequency indicating that capital controls were not as successful as banking regulation. Comparing the goldstandard era with the post Bretton Woods era shows a similar degree of financial instability, implying that especially the occurrence of banking and twin crises, being subject to highest costs as described below, is positively correlated with the degree of financial liberalization.

Table 3.1: Frequency of Financial Crises (annual % probability), 1880-1997

Period	Banking Crises	Currency Crises	Twin Crises	All Crises
1880-1913	2.3	1.2	1.4	4.9
1919-1939	4.8	4.3	4.0	13.2
1945-1971	0.0	6.9	0.2	7.0
1973-1997 (21 countries)	2.0	5.2	2.5	9.7
1973-1997 (56 countries)	2.3	7.5	2.4	12.2

Source: Eichengreen and Bordo (2002), p. 40.

Crisis Frequency in Industrial and Emerging Market Countries. Table 3.2 summarizes the frequency of financial crises separately for industrial and emerging market countries from 1880 until 1997, where the 56-country sample for the post Bretton Woods era has been neglected. It indicates that financial crises during the goldstandard and during the post Bretton Woods era were mainly centered in emerging market countries, whereas financial crises during the interwar era occurred predominantly in industrial countries. This result validates the findings by de Cecco (1974), Bernanke and James (1991), and Triffin (1998), stating that the financial stability of the center countries (industrial nations) and the financial instability of the periphery (emerging market nations) during the goldstandard era reversed during the interwar period which has been characterized by a financially unstable center and a financially stable periphery.

In order to study the question of whether financial crises have become more frequent within the post Bretton Woods era, Bordo et al. divided the period 1973-1997 in two periods, where 1988 was taken as the borderline when huge portfolio flows from industrial countries to emerging markets started. Regarding currency crises, the first period 1973-1987 was subject to a higher frequency (8.8% annual probability for all countries) than the second period 1988-1997 (5.6% annual probability for all countries), whereas the frequency of banking and twin crises has risen sharply during the second period. The authors calculated that the frequency of banking and twin crises in the second period doubled in the 21-country sample, and increased by 50% in the 56-country sample, indicating that the frequency of financial crises, especially in emerging market countries as aforementioned, has sharply risen during the second half of the post Bretton Woods era.[5]

[5]For similar results regarding crisis frequency within the post Bretton Woods era, see International Monetary Fund (1998a), chapter IV, and Kaminsky and Reinhart (1999).

An Assessment. Summing up, the comparison of the frequency of financial crises over the last 120 years indicates that financial crises have become more frequent in the post Bretton Woods era, and are subject to almost the same crisis frequency as in the inter-war years. Particular impressive is the increase in the frequency of twin crises, both in industrial and especially in emerging market countries, during the second half of the post Bretton Woods era, being only slightly surpassed by twin crises' frequency during the Great Depression period.

Table 3.2: Frequency of Financial Crises in Industrial and Emerging Market Countries (annual % probability), 1880-1997

Period	Banking Crises	Currency Crises	Twin Crises	All Crises
Industrial Countries				
1880-1913	2.0	1.0	0.5	3.5
1919-1939	3.7	4.3	4.0	12.0
1945-1971	0.0	5.4	0.0	5.4
1973-1997	2.5	8.1	1.7	12.2
Emerging Market Countries				
1880-1913	2.6	1.4	1.9	6.0
1919-1939	5.8	2.5	2.5	10.8
1945-1971	0.0	10.3	0.6	10.9
1973-1997	2.4	9.8	14.6	26.8

Source: Bordo et al. (2001b), Web Appendix, Table 1.

3.2.2 Duration and Costs of Financial Crises

Average Recovery Time. Table 3.3 summarizes the duration patterns of financial crises over the last 120 years. As for currency crises, the average recovery time in the post Bretton Woods era, especially for industrial countries, has fallen in comparison with the goldstandard era, though the frequency of currency crises was much higher in the post Bretton Woods era. Furthermore, average recovery time of currency crises in the 1913-1997 period has fallen significantly, especially for industrial countries as well, in comparison with the goldstandard period, whereas there are no further signs of changing time patterns during the 1913-1997 period. By way of contrast, comparing the average recovery time from twin crises of the goldstandard era with the post Bretton Woods period indicates a significant rise over time, again most remarkably in industrial countries, whereas there is no significant change in emerging market countries. Regarding the average recovery time from twin crises for all countries, there is a significant rise over the last 120 years which is only interrupted by the Bretton Woods period. Concerning the average recovery time from banking crises, there is no significant change in time patterns. Summing up all time trends for all countries and all crises, there is no significant change in the average recovery time during the last 120 years.

Table 3.3: Duration of Financial Crises in Industrial and Emerging Market Countries (average recovery time in years), 1880-1997

	1880-1913	1919-1939	1945-1971	1973-1997 (21 countries)	1973-1997 (56 countries)
Currency Crises					
All Countries	2.6	1.9	1.8	1.9	2.1
Industrial Countries	3.0	1.9	1.7	1.8	2.0
Emerging Countries	2.5	2.0	2.1	2.0	2.1
Banking Crises					
All Countries	2.3	2.4	†	3.1	2.6
Industrial Countries	3.0	2.5	†	3.4	3.1
Emerging Countries	2.0	2.1	†	1.0	2.4
Twin Crises					
All Countries	2.2	2.7	1.0	3.7	3.8
Industrial Countries	1.0	2.3	†	5.4	5.0
Emerging Countries	2.4	4.3	1.0	2.3	3.4
All Crises					
All Countries	2.4	2.4	1.8	2.6	2.5
Industrial Countries	2.7	2.3	1.6	2.8	2.7
Emerging Countries	2.3	2.6	2.0	2.1	2.4

†: no crisis
Source: Bordo et al. (2001b), Web Appendix, Table 3.

Output Losses. Table 3.4 represents a summary of the costs of financial crises in the form of cumulated GDP growth loss. Comparing the two globalization periods 1880-1913 and 1973-1997 indicates that output losses of currency and banking crises declined in the 1973-1997 period, whereas the costs of twin crises increased. Highest output losses for all types of crises during the last 120 years are centered in the interwar period. Most striking are the high output costs of currency and twin crises in comparison with the other periods, especially in emerging market countries, despite the fact that industrial countries were subject to higher crisis frequency in interwar period. Respecting banking crises, output losses in 1919-1939 period were highest as well, but with a smaller difference to the other periods. Comparing the Bretton Woods period with the post Bretton Woods era indicates that, notwithstanding the fact that output loss from each type of crisis remains constant, output loss in the 1973-1997 period for all crises is larger than in the 1945-1971 period, being mainly caused by an increasing incidence of banking and twin crises in the post Bretton Woods era.

Table 3.4: Output Loss in Industrial and Emerging Market Countries (cumulated GDP growth loss in per cent), 1880-1997

	1880-1913	1919-1939	1945-1971	1973-1997 (21 countries)	1973-1997 (56 countries)
Currency Crises					
All Countries	8.3	14.2	5.2	4.0	5.5
Industrial Countries	3.7	11.4	2.4	3.0	3.8
Emerging Countries	9.8	26.5	9.0	8.5	6.4
Banking Crises					
All Countries	8.3	10.5	†	7.0	6.2
Industrial Countries	11.6	11.5	†	7.9	7.0
Emerging Countries	7.2	8.9	†	0.0	5.8
Twin Crises					
All Countries	14.5	15.8	1.7	15.7	18.6
Industrial Countries	0.0	13.8	†	17.5	15.6
Emerging Countries	16.3	24.0	1.7	14.1	19.5
All Crises					
All Countries	9.8	13.4	5.2	7.8	8.3
Industrial Countries	7.7	12.3	2.4	6.7	6.3
Emerging Countries	10.4	16.5	8.6	10.8	9.2

†: no crisis
Source: Bordo et al. (2001b), Web Appendix, Table 3.

Financial Crises With Output Losses. Table 3.5 illustrates that not each financial crisis was associated with output losses. In the post Bretton Woods era, approximately 75-80% of all financial crises led to a drop in economic growth, where twin crises represent an exception, because each twin crisis causes a recession. The time patterns for other periods are similar, but also exhibit slight variations, as e.g. the fact that financial crises in the goldstandard era were generally subject to larger output losses than financial crises during the interwar, or during the Bretton Woods era.

An Assessment. Summing up, both the time patterns of average recovery time and of output losses indicate that financial crises have not become more severe. The depth of financial crises in the two globalization eras 1880-1913 and 1973-1997 are similar high, being only surpassed by the interwar period. The depth of financial crises in the Bretton Woods period, having been subject to stiff domestic and international financial market regulations, is exceptional low due to the absence of banking crises. However, though the crisis problem has not grown more severe regarding the average effect of currency, banking, and twin crises on the real sector, the crisis problem *on the aggregate* has grown

Table 3.5: Financial Crises with Output Losses of Total Financial Crises (in per cent), 1880-1997

	1880-1913	1919-1939	1945-1971	1973-1997 (21 countries)	1973-1997 (56 countries)
Currency Crises					
All Countries	75.00	56.25	72.97	78.26	72.94
Industrial Countries	100.00	53.85	57.14	84.21	82.14
Emerging Countries	66.67	66.67	93.75	50.00	68.42
Banking Crises					
All Countries	86.67	72.22	†	66.67	73.08
Industrial Countries	100.00	72.23	†	75.00	66.67
Emerging Countries	81.82	71.43	†	0.00	76.47
Twin Crises					
All Countries	77.78	87.50	100.00	100.00	100.00
Industrial Countries	0.00	83.33	†	100.00	100.00
Emerging Countries	87.50	100.00	100.00	100.00	100.00
All Crises					
All Countries	80.65	70.83	72.97	80.95	77.94
Industrial Countries	85.71	68.57	55.00	83.87	80.95
Emerging Countries	79.17	76.92	94.12	72.73	76.60

†: no crisis
Source: Bordo et al. (2001b), Web Appendix, Table 6.

during the post Bretton Woods era due to an increasing crisis frequency, especially of twin crises whose adverse effects on output have also grown over time.

3.3 Business Cycles, Financial Liberalization, and Financial Crises

3.3.1 Basic Links

Tables 3.6 to 3.10, being based on Bordo et al. (2001b) and Eichengreen and Bordo (2002), portray business cycle turning points and financial crises dates over the last 120 years, distinguishing the goldstandard period 1880-1913 (table 3.6), the interwar period 1919-1939 (table 3.7), the Bretton Woods period 1940-1971, and the post Bretton Woods period 1972-1998 (tables 3.9 and 3.10). The country sample for the 1880-1998 period consists of twelve selected countries (Argentina, Brazil, Canada, Chile, Finland, France, Germany, Japan, Norway, Sweden, UK, US), where the post Bretton Woods period has been enlarged by eleven further countries (Denmark, Indonesia, Israel, Korea, Malaysia,

Mexico, Philippines, Spain, Thailand, Turkey, Uruguay), as well as by the dates of the beginning of financial liberalization in the aftermath of the breakdown of the Bretton Woods system, which are taken from Williamson and Mahar (1998) who define financial liberalization by six dimensions, namely by the elimination of credit controls, the deregulation of interest rates, free entry into the banking and into the financial services industry, bank autonomy, private ownership of banks, and by the liberalization of international capital flows.[6] Regarding financial crises dates, tables 3.6 to 3.10 illustrate the occurrence of banking and currency crises and waive an extra specification of twin crises, since they are indicated, as outlined in section 3.1.3, by a banking crisis which is accompanied by a currency crises in the previous, current, or following year.

The analysis of the empirical data with respect to the link between business cycles, financial liberalization and financial crises depicted in tables 3.6 to 3.10 can be summarized in five empirical regularities which hold for the entire 120 year period, thereby providing important insights into the causes and propagation mechanisms of financial crises which serve as a basis for the theoretical analysis in part II of the book.

Firstly, in periods of highly regulated financial systems, as e.g. in the Bretton Woods era and in the beginning of the post Bretton Woods period, there is no apparent link between banking and currency crises, indicating that the frequency of twin crises is low or even absent, as already stated in the previous section. By way of contrast, in periods of liberalized domestic and international financial markets, as e.g. in the goldstandard era, in the interwar period, and in the second half of the post Bretton Woods period, banking and currency crises become closely intertwined, implying that the frequency of twin crises is positively correlated with the degree of financial liberalization. Respecting the post Bretton Woods era, there exists a very close link between financial liberalization and the occurrence of twin crises.[7]

Secondly, financial crises are inseparably associated with business cycles fluctuations. Currency, banking and twin crises generally occur shortly after economies have passed business cycle peaks and enter a recession, or the downswing period. Recessions following financial crises are more severe in terms of GDP losses than recessions without the occurrence of a financial crisis, i.e. crises make recessions worse.[8]

Thirdly, twin crises are subject to a characteristic time pattern regarding the order of banking and currency crises. In most cases, a twin crisis starts with banking sector problems after the economy has entered a recession leading to a currency crisis. The currency crash deepens further the banking crisis and aggravates the recession by high domestic interest rates which have been increased to defend the exchange rate peg, or to support risky exposures of domestic residents in foreign currency, engendering a vicious spiral. Accordingly, the direction of causality between currency and banking crises is not unidirectional. The empirical picture indicates that there are also cases in which twin crises are initiated by currency crises, being however subject to a much lower incidence.

Fourthly, notwithstanding the fact that financial crises occur recurrently over time and are an inseparable part of business cycles, not each business cycle is associated with finan-

[6]The causes and elements of large-scale financial sector liberalization in the post Bretton Woods era, both in industrial and in emerging market countries, are briefly discussed in the following section.

[7]For this result, see also Kaminsky and Reinhart (1999).

[8]For this result, see also Mitchel (1941), Cagan (1965), Zarnovitz (1992), pp. 105-109, Milesi-Ferretti and Razin (1998), Honohan and Klingebiel (2000), and International Monetary Fund (2002), chapter III.

cial crises. Rather, there are periods with "tranquil" business cycles being characterized by stable financial and goods market conditions, which are interrupted by business cycles being associated with financial crises. As the following section is going to show, cycles associated with financial crises are subject to a much higher amplitude of macroeconomic variables than tranquil business cycles. That is, business cycles generating financial crises are characterized by an extensive expansion phase, being driven by domestic credit booms and large volumes of capital inflows which lead to asset price bubbles and overindebtedness, and finally to severe and systemic financial crises being followed by recessions, or even depressions and debt-deflation.[9]

Fifthly, after the occurrence of financial crises associated with deep downswings in macroeconomic activity, economies generally tend to recover and return to tranquil business cycle fluctuations, though the recovery period can be very long. This result suggests that economies tend to be cyclically stable in the long-run, i.e. economies tend to return endogenously after a "financial crisis cycle" to tranquil business cycle fluctuations. Furthermore, this observation suggests also that financial crises are not a "natural" or endogenous outcome of capitalist systems, but can be considered as the result of some exogenous events giving rise to extensive boom-bust cycles which lead to financial crises.

A further important empirical regularity, which however cannot be derived from tables 3.6 to 3.10, is the stylized fact, that both tranquil and financial crisis business cycles in emerging markets are subject to much higher amplitudes, i.e. to much higher fluctuations in real and financial sector variables, than tranquil and financial crisis cycles in industrial countries.[10] There are three main explanations for higher amplitudes of business cycles in emerging markets. Firstly, emerging market are more vulnerable to commodity price and terms of trade shocks as they export highly specialized products, and as they are more dependent on commodity imports, as e.g. oil. Secondly, financial systems in emerging market countries are less developed and less regulated than financial systems in industrial countries, implying less possibilities to diversify risk (credit risk, exchange rate risk, etc.), a higher degree of systemic risk due to larger information asymmetries, and larger fluctuations in domestic credit and capital flows. Thirdly, macroeconomic policies in emerging markets tend to be procyclical owing to weak institutions and larger external shocks requiring larger compensating macroeconomic policies.[11]

3.3.2 Financial Liberalization in the Post Bretton Woods Era

It has been argued in the previous section that there exists a close empirical link between financial sector liberalization and the occurrence of extensive boom-bust cycles giving rise to twin crises, being very marked in the post Bretton Woods era. In order to get a deeper understanding of financial liberalization policies in the post Bretton Woods era,

[9]Theoretical and empirical research on the macroeconomic effects of credit booms, as e.g. by Gavin and Hausmann (1996), suggest that the more rapid growth is during the expansion phase, the deeper and the sharper is the drop in growth during the downswing.

[10]For this general result, see e.g. International Monetary Fund (2002), chapter III. For results on industrial countries see e.g. Blanchard and Simon (2001), and for results on emerging market countries e.g. De Ferranti et al. (2000).

[11]For reasons for higher macroeconomic volatility in emerging market countries, see e.g. Caballero (2000), Eichengreen and Moody (2000), International Monetary Fund (2002), chapter III, and Cashin and McDermott (2002).

this section is going to provide background information on the causes for widespread liberalization policies, both in industrial and in emerging market countries, and discusses furthermore theoretical arguments, expected benefits and empirical evidence on financial liberalization.

Causes for Liberalization Policies in Industrial Countries. Widespread liberalization policies in industrial countries in the 1980s originated from a neoclassical counter-revolution in economic theory and policy which was initiated by conservative governments in the U.S., Canada, Britain and West Germany in the late 1970s. The causes for liberalization stemmed from a bad economic macroeconomic performance during the 1970s especially in the U.S., which was characterized by stagflation and low productivity growth.

The poor macroeconomic record was predominantly explained by an ineffective demand-side policy mix that increased aggregate demand with easy money while restricting output with high taxes, by the two oil price shocks in 1973 and 1979, and by a breakdown of the Phillips-Curve due to the existence of rational expectations having resulted in the inefficiency of monetary policy as a demand management tool. Furthermore, stagflation and low productivity growth were also explained by inefficient government regulation of network industries, as e.g. in the telecommunications and aviation sectors, and by heavy domestic and international financial market regulations in the form of interest rate controls, capital controls, etc., having led to an inefficient allocation of savings into investment opportunities, to low GDP growth, and to low productivity growth. Strong financial market regulations at the beginning of the early 1970s originated from the Bretton Woods system and were imposed, as a consequence of the Great Depression, to prevent future systemic financial crises.

In order to improve macroeconomic performance, the Reagan administration in the U.S. officially abandoned conventional demand management policies, and implemented supply-side economics in order to expand output by lowering the after-tax cost of labour and capital which was supported in the beginning by tight monetary policy to restrain inflation. Supply-side economics is based on the neoclassical view that relative prices determine macroeconomic performance as they govern economic agents' decision how to allocate income between consumption and saving, and how to allocate time between leisure and work. Regarding economic policy, supply-side economics generally claims that fiscal policy can be only stimulative by lowering the marginal tax rate, leading to an increase in the discounted income stream, to a rise in the price for current consumption and thereby to higher savings, to a rise in the price for leisure and thereby to an increasing labour supply, which increases investment and promotes growth. By way of contrast, fiscal policy is not believed to be stimulative by increasing disposable income, for example by raising government expenditures. Monetary policy as a demand management tool is believed to ineffective due to the existence of rational expectations. Respecting the origin of business cycle fluctuations, supply-side economics generally assumes that business cycles, following "real business cycle theory", are mainly driven by exogenous shocks to technology and preferences, and by the incentives and disincentives of tax policy, but not by monetary phenomena as Keynesians and monetarists would claim.[12]

For supply-side policy to work efficiently, distortions in the price mechanism have to be absent which requires that markets are fully competitive. As a result, the belief that

[12]For a formal treatment of supply-side economics, see e.g. Lucas (1990).

markets are only efficient in case they are fully liberalized led to widespread liberalization policies in all regulated sectors and fields, as e.g. in aviation, telecommunications, financial services, international trade, international capital movements, etc.[13]

Causes for Liberalization Policies in Emerging Markets. Product, factor and financial markets in emerging market countries were heavily regulated at the beginning of the post Bretton Woods period, predominantly as a consequence of the "International Dependence Revolution" underdevelopment theory of the 1960s. Dependence theory argues that Third World underdevelopment is predominantly caused by predatory activities of the First World. To end predation, the Third World has to protect itself by heavy government interventions from the First World by limiting international trade with the First World to become autarkic, and by outright expropriation of privately owned assets, as public asset ownership and control is believed to be more effective to reduce poverty, income inequality, and unemployment. A widespread implementation of dependence theory in emerging market countries led to the evolution of socialist societies, very often by violent overthrows of existing elites, to industrial nationalization and to financial repression.

A financially repressed economy is subject to heavy government regulations determining the price, the amount and the distribution of credit. Furthermore, financially repressed systems are characterized by administered interest rates at levels below market-clearing interest rates. These artificial interest rates generally cause credit rationing which represses investment finance due to a shortage of savings. Administered interest rates below market-clearing levels are predominantly set to finance budget deficits by the issuance of low-interest bonds to private financial institutions, having led very often to negative real interest rates by high fiscal deficit-induced inflation. Another way to finance budget deficits in financially repressed economies is to tax the banking system by high required reserve ratios (up to 50%) if income taxes are low, if domestic markets for the issuance of government debt are absent, and if there exists no access to international credit markets.[14]

The neoclassical counterrevolution in industrial countries in the late 1970s led to a fundamental change in the theoretical view about economic development in emerging market countries. As opposed to dependence theorist, proponents of the neoclassical counterrevolution argue that underdevelopment in emerging markets results predominantly from poor resource allocation caused by incorrect pricing and heavy government interventions. To end underdevelopment, economic growth and productivity have to be boosted by widespread liberalization of factor, product, and financial markets, by privatizing state-owned enterprises, and by promoting free trade. As past macroeconomic records under heavy government interventions were poor, there was a quick switch to market fundamentalism in emerging market countries at the end of the 1970s and at the beginning of the 1980s.

The first wave of extensive liberalization of product, factor, and especially of financial markets, mainly in Latin America (Brazil, Mexico, and in the Southern Cone countries Chile, Argentina and Uruguay[15]) and in Africa, gave rise to extensive boom phases which

---

[13]For further details on liberalization policies and supply-side economics in industrial countries, see e.g. Krugman (1994) and Roberts (2003).

[14]For details on financial repression, see McKinnon (1973), Shaw (1973), and McKinnon and Matthieson (1981).

[15]For details on the liberalization process in the Southern Cone countries having been followed by

were mainly driven by foreign capital inflows from European and US-American banks, and which led to heavy overborrowing. The boom phases came to an end at the beginning of the 1980s due to four reasons. Firstly, overly optimistic expectations with regard to revenues from future exports were disappointed due to dropping market prices for international non-oil tradables and recessions in industrial countries which led to an enormous deterioration of the terms of trade and of the current account. Secondly, capital inflows were predominantly used to finance private consumption and government expenditures which led to a large increase in fiscal deficits, imports, real overvaluations of domestic currencies by high inflation and fixed exchange rates, and to large current account deficits, having caused an enormous deterioration of the international liquidity and solvency position to service due foreign debt. Thirdly, the two oil price shocks in 1973 and 1979 led also to an enormous deterioration of the current account of non-oil exporting emerging market countries. Fourthly, the imposition of supply-side economics in the US led to sharply increasing interest rates and to a further deterioration of emerging market countries' liquidity and solvency position as most foreign debt was short-term and subject to floating interest rates. These four factors led to the international debt crisis, which was initiated by international illiquidity of Mexico in 1982, having been followed by most Latin American countries and later by a large number of other emerging market countries. International bankruptcy of emerging market countries led to systemic twin crises by sudden and large capital outflows. These systemic financial crises caused severe and long-lasting recessions especially in Latin America, being often referred to as the "lost decade", which is illustrated in tables 3.9 and 3.10 (see especially Argentina, Brazil, Chile, Mexico and Uruguay).[16]

The international debt crisis during the 1980s led to a drying up of international liquidity for emerging market countries as access to international capital market was denied. However, in the early 1990s the second wave of liberalization policies in emerging market countries started, having been initiated by the establishment of the "Washington Consensus" by J. Williamson as the lowest common denominator of policy advice by the World Bank and the International Monetary Fund to Latin American countries in 1989 to overcome the adverse impacts of international debt crisis. Following Williamson (1990, 2000), the Washington Consensus can be summarized in ten propositions, namely, fiscal discipline, redirection of government expenditures in fields with high prospective future returns to improve income distribution as e.g. health care, tax reform by lowering marginal tax rates (as proposed by supply-side economics), interest rate liberalization, competitive exchange rates, trade liberalization, liberalization of inflows of foreign direct investment, privatization, deregulation to abandon barriers of entry and exit, and the establishment of secure property rights. The Washington Consensus led to large-scale liberalization policies, especially in financial sectors, which attracted a new wave of large capital inflows to emerging market countries having caused extensive booms and overborrowing which ended, as the international debt crisis, in severe financial crises in Mexico (1994), Asia (1997-1998), Argentina (1995 and 2000), and in Brazil and Russia (1998) which led almost to a collapse of the U.S. banking system (LTCM affair). Furthermore, large-scale financial liberalization in the 1990s led also to severe financial crises in the Nordic countries Finland,

severe twin crises, see e.g. Diaz-Alejandro (1985) and Velasco (1987).

[16]For details on the international debt crisis, see e.g. Bank for International Settlements (1983), Sachs and Larrain (1993), and Lamfallusy (2000).

Norway and Sweden which are comparable to the emerging market crises in Mexico (1994) and in Asia (1997-1998).[17]

Theoretical Arguments for the Efficiency of Liberalization. The general argument that liberalization policies, and especially financial liberalization which is going to be referred to in the following, improve economic efficiency originates from the combination of the first part of the fundamental theorem on welfare economics with the efficient (capital) market hypothesis (Eatwell 1996). The first part of the fundamental theorem on welfare economics states that each equilibrium in competitive markets is Pareto-optimal, implying that only liberalized financial markets can be efficient.[18]

The efficient (capital) market hypothesis can be interpreted as an application of the rational expectations hypothesis to the pricing of securities whose results can be summarized in three fundamental statements. Firstly, financial markets are assumed to be efficient with respect to the collection and the processing of information, implying that prices of securities are set so that the optimal forecast of a security's return corresponds to the security's equilibrium return which equals, under rational expectations, the security's expected return. Secondly, in an efficient market which is fully competitive, all unexploited profit opportunities will be eliminated, which implies that in efficient capital markets, all prices of securities always reflect market fundamentals.[19] Thirdly, government interventions can only increase the efficiency of financial markets in case government officials have a better understanding and more information regarding the pricing of securities.

Summing up, the first part of the fundamental theorem on welfare economics states that highest economic efficiency in the real economy can be only reached if goods markets are fully liberalized and competitive, whereas the efficient (capital) market hypothesis states that prices of securities can only reflect correctly the "true" fundamentals of the real sector if financial markets are fully liberalized and competitive, so that information can be collected and processed optimally. As a result, if both goods and financial markets are fully liberalized and competitive, goods markets generate Pareto-efficient equilibria which are reflected correctly in financial asset prices, permitting agents trading assets in fully competitive financial markets to make Pareto-efficient decisions.

Expected Benefits and Empirical Evidence on the Impact of Financial Liberalization. Financial liberalization is generally expected to engender three main benefits. Firstly, liberalized domestic and international capital markets are expected to allocate savings into the most productive investment opportunities. Secondly, savings and thereby investment are expected to increase, inducing higher long-run growth. Thirdly,

[17] According to Williamson (2000), the need for liberalization was misinterpreted as a swing to the opposite extreme of market fundamentalism and for a minimalist role of the government. For more detailed discussions of the entire set of policies following the Washington Consensus and their consequences for emerging market countries, see Berg and Taylor (2000), Taylor (2000), Gore (2000), and Stretton (2000).

[18] The second part of the fundamental theorem on welfare economics states that any Pareto-optimum has to be a competitive equilibrium, or alternatively, that any allocation on the contract curve can be sustained as a competitive equilibrium. The third part states that there is no logically inerrant way to aggregate preferences of individuals, implying that the problem of distribution cannot be solved and is therefore neglected.

[19] Consequently, excess volatility, as described in section 2.3.4, is not possible according to the efficient (capital) market hypothesis.

capital is expected to flow from capital-rich (industrial) countries into capital-poor but opportunity-rich (emerging market) countries leading to a long-run convergence in economic development.[20]

Empirical evidence however shows, that despite a more efficient allocation of savings into investment opportunities, financial liberalization has not led to higher savings, higher investment and higher growth in the past. Rather, there is strong empirical evidence that financial liberalization generates financial crises with adverse repercussions on growth. Furthermore, though international gross capital flows have been large, net capital flows have been very small and were predominantly allocated in developed countries, particularly in the U.S. There is no empirical evidence that there are convergence-inducing capital flows from capital-rich industrial countries to opportunity-rich emerging markets nations, as capital flows to emerging markets are highly volatile, dominated by short-term portfolio investments, and lead in most cases to systemic financial crises when capital inflows come to a sudden stop, or turn into quick capital outflows. In the post Bretton Woods period, there were two main boom-bust cycles in capital flows to emerging market countries. The first boom-bust cycle of capital flows to emerging market countries began in the late 1970s with the first large-scale financial liberalization period which ended up in the international debt crisis in the early 1980s. Until the mid-1990s emerging markets' access to international capital markets was denied so that net capital flows on the average were almost zero from 1982 until 1992. The second boom-bust cycle was initiated by Washington Consensus-induced financial liberalization processes which ended up in the Mexican crisis in 1994, and in the Asian crisis 1997-1998.[21]

3.4 Stylized Behaviour of Macroeconomic Variables During Episodes of Financial Crises

This section studies the stylized behaviour of a large number of macroeconomic variables before, during, and after the occurrence of currency, banking, and twin crises, where the analysis is restricted to the post Bretton Woods era (1973-1997) due to the lack of appropriate empirical data for earlier periods. The empirical literature on financial crises provides three different classes of studies which can be used to describe the stylized behaviour of macrovariables during periods of financial distress. The first class of studies[22] analyzes the average behaviour of macrovariables before, during and after the occurrence of financial crises by comparison with "tranquil" periods which are characterized by the

[20]For more details on expected benefits of financial liberalization, see Eatwell (1996), pp. 9-10, Eichengreen et al. (1998), pp. 12-17, Stiglitz (2000), pp. 1076-1079, and Ishii and Habermeier (2002), chapter 2, pp. 5-14.

[21]For more empirical details on the impact of financial liberalization, see Rodrik (1998), Williamson and Mahar (1998), Stiglitz (2000), Bakker and Chapple (2002), Kaminsky and Schmukler (2003), and Prasad et al. (2003). For empirical data on capital flows to emerging countries in the post Bretton Woods era, see Goldstein (1995), Calvo, Leiderman and Reinhart (1996), Agénor and Montiel (1999), chapter 15, Montiel and Reinhart (1999), U.S. Council of Economic Advisors (1999), chapter 6, Akyüz and Cornford (2000), and International Monetary Fund (2003a), chapter IV.

[22]See, for example, studies by Eichengreen, Rose and Wyplosz (1995), Eichengreen and Rose (1998), International Monetary Fund (1998a, chapter IV), Kamin (1999), and Kaminsky and Reinhart (1999).

absence of financial distress. These studies generally use large country samples consisting of both industrial and emerging market countries.

The second class of studies[23] analyzes the stylized behaviour of macrovariables of single countries, or of small country groups in case studies. In contrast to the first class of studies, the second class generally does not compare the behaviour of variables during periods of financial distress with the behaviour during tranquil periods. Furthermore, second class studies referring to country groups use either pure industrial country samples or pure emerging market country studies, and do not consider mixed country samples.

The third class of studies[24], focusing on the analysis of business cycle characteristics of balance sheet data (liquidity and solvency indicators), is neglected by most standard empirical and theoretical approaches to financial crises as they are considered not to have an explanatory power with respect to the causes of financial crises. However, the introductory analysis on financial crises in chapter 2, as well as the description of empirical regularities in section 3.3 have shown that periods of financial distress are inseparably linked to business cycle fluctuations and variations in liquidity and solvency positions of economic units, providing a justification to declare the stylized business cycle characteristics of balance sheet data as stylized facts of financial crises. Moreover, studies of the third class generally refer to the stylized behaviour of balance sheet data over long time horizons including periods of financial crises. In contrast to studies of the first and of the second class, studies of the third class are only available for industrial countries, firstly, because standard approaches to financial crises generally neglect balance sheet data, and secondly, because the availability of balance sheet data in emerging market economies is limited.

The following description of the stylized behaviour of macroeconomic variables during episodes of financial distress refers predominantly to studies of the first and of the third class and analyzes the evolution of 35 macroeconomic variables before, during, and after the outbreak of currency, banking and twin crises, where variables are classified into financial market, current account, capital account, real sector and balance sheet variables. The description of the evolution of excess real M1 balances, the ratio of M2 to foreign exchange reserves, the M2 multiplier, the ratio of domestic credit to GDP, real commercial bank deposits, the real interest rate on deposits, the ratio of lending rates to deposit rates, equity prices, real estate prices, the real exchange rate, the terms of trade, foreign exchange reserves, the domestic-foreign real interest rate differential on deposits, the ratio of short-term capital inflow to GDP, and output is based on Kaminsky and Reinhart (1999), whereas the description of the time patters of nominal M2 growth, the change in the M2 to M1 ratio, the current account balance, the ratio of private capital net inflow to GDP, inflation, and the ratio of investment to GDP is based on International Monetary Fund (1998a, chapter IV). The behaviour of world interest rates, the ratio of interest payments to GDP, the ratio of short-term foreign debt to total foreign debt, the ratio of interest payments to GDP, and the ratio of total debt to GDP is based on Eichengreen and Rose

[23]See, for example, studies by Dornbusch, Goldfajn and Valdés (1995), Rojas-Suarez and Weisbrod (1995), Sachs, Tornell and Velasco (1996), Garcia-Herrero (1997), Drees and Pazarbasioglu (1998), Eichengreen et al. (1998), International Monetary Fund (1998b), chapter IV, Kaminsky and Reinhart (1998), Frydl and Alexander (1999), Palma (2000), Nakaso (2001), Bordo and Jeanne (2002), Gosh et al. (2002), Ishii and Habermeier (2002), and Werner (2003).

[24]See, for example, studies by Bordo and Jeanne (2002), International Monetary Fund (2002), chapter III, and International Monetary Fund (2003b), chapter II.

(1998), whereas the evolution of the real lending rate is taken from Palma (2000). The description of the evolution of the interest coverage of the corporate and the banking sector, gross and net profits of the corporate sector, net profits of the banking sector, the ratio of short-term domestic debt to total domestic debt, the market valuation of firms (Tobin's q), the debt-asset ratio of firms and banks, and the ratio of debt to market value of equity of firms is based on International Monetary Fund (2003b, chapter II).

Descriptions of the stylized behaviour of macroeconomic variables which are based on studies by Eichengreen and Rose (1998), International Monetary Fund (1998a, chapter IV), and Kaminsky and Reinhart (1999), compare the pre- and post-crisis behaviour of a variable relative to its tranquil period mean. An above-average/below-average value of a variable indicates that the value of the variables lies above/below its tranquil period mean. If there is no explicit differentiation between a variable's behaviour during episodes of currency, banking, and twin crises, the statement is valid for all three types of crises. Descriptions of the stylized behaviour of variables which are based on International Monetary Fund (2003b, chapter II) refer to the average behaviour of variables before and after the burst of stock market and real estate bubbles, and do not explicitly consider additionally the date of the outbreak of currency, banking, and twin crises. However, as the following analysis is going to show, the outbreak of currency, banking and twin crises, is generally preceded by the burst of stock market and real estate bubbles, implying that the pre-bubble period generally refers to the pre-crisis period, and that the post-bubble period refers both to the (short) period before the outbreak of the crisis and to the entire post-crisis period. In case there arise significant differences between the behaviour after the burst of the bubble and the behaviour during the post-crisis period, the description considers all three periods (pre-bubble period, post-bubble-pre-crisis period, and post-crisis period).

3.4.1 Financial Market Variables

3.4.1.1 Monetary Aggregates and Foreign Exchange Reserves

Excess Real M1 Balances.[25] Excess real M1 balances increase above-average before the crisis and peak at the outbreak, indicating either lax monetary policy, or fiscal deficit financing by central banks. In the post-crisis period, excess real M1 balances decrease, but remain higher than in tranquil periods.

Nominal M2 Growth. There is an above-average monetary expansion in the pre-crisis period which peaks before the outbreak. From its peak, nominal M2 growth falls steadily until the outbreak of the crisis, but remains higher than in tranquil periods. After the crisis, nominal M2 growth increases slightly and remains at levels above the average.

Ratio of M2 to M1. There is an above-average increase before the crisis which peaks before the outbreak. After the peak, there is a fall at first, which turns into a sharp increase just before the outbreak of the crisis indicating possibly liquidity supports to troubled financial institutions by central banks. After the crisis, there is a further increase being higher than in tranquil times.

[25]Excess real M1 balances are defined and calculated as actual less estimated money demand.

Ratio of M2 to Foreign Exchange Reserves. Prior to the crisis, the ratio increases above-average, where the increase is caused by a large rise in nominal M2 growth and by a sharp decline in foreign exchange reserves indicating increasing financial vulnerability due to a decreasing backing of foreign liabilities by international reserves. After the outbreak of the crisis, the ratio falls steadily and reaches below-average levels.

M2 Multiplier. The M2 multiplier rises steadily above-average before the crisis and peaks before the outbreak, which is mainly due to drastic reductions in required reserve ratios which generally accompany financial liberalization policies. After its peak, the multiplier decreases steadily and reaches lower levels than in tranquil times.

3.4.1.2 Deposits and Domestic Credit

Ratio of Domestic Credit to GDP. The time pattern of the domestic credit/GDP ratio exhibits the characteristics of typical boom-bust cycle in domestic credit markets and in real economic activity. Before the crisis, there is an above-average increase in the ratio owing to an overproportional rise in domestic credit as the economy is still in an expansion phase with rapid GDP growth (see below). The domestic credit/GDP ratio reaches its peak at the outbreak of the crisis when the (over-)leveraging of the private sector becomes evident by deteriorating liquidity and solvency positions due to a fall in GDP which begins shortly before the outbreak of the crisis and passes into a recession. The domestic credit/GDP ratio falls sharply to slightly below-average levels in the post-crisis period due to an overproportional decline in domestic credit, indicating a credit-crunch induced recession.

Real Commercial Bank Deposits. Real bank deposits remain at average levels in the pre-crisis period. After the outbreak of the crisis, real bank deposits decrease sharply to lower levels than in tranquil times, indicating possibly capital flight or bank runs.

3.4.1.3 Interest Rates

Real Interest Rate on Deposits. The real interest rate on deposits exhibits a different behaviour for currency, banking and twin crises. For currency crises, the real deposit rate remains at below-average levels before, during and after the crisis, indicating either lax monetary policy, or administered interest rates as most currency crises occurred in the 1973-1987 period when financial markets were still highly regulated. For banking and twin crises, the real deposit rate remains at above-average levels before, during and after the crisis. Above-average rates before the occurrence of banking and twin crisis, whose frequency increased markedly in the 1987-1998 period, can be due to interest rate liberalization, high risk taking by banks, or tight monetary policy to defend the currency peg, whereas above-average rates after the occurrence of banking and twin crises possibly reflect banks' response to the risk of increasing deposit withdrawals.

Real Lending Rate. The real lending rate declines sharply before the crisis, reflecting the boom phase in private credit markets, but starts to increase shortly before the crisis when financial difficulties in the private sector are revealed, and credit market conditions start to tighten. After the crisis, there is a further sharp increase in the real lending rate, indicating a credit crunch which aggravates the downturn in real economic activity (see below).

Ratio of Lending to Deposit Rate. Before the crisis, the ratio remains at an average level, but starts to increase just before the outbreak of the crisis, indicating an increase in credit risk. After the crisis, the ratio remains higher than in tranquil times, indicating the unwillingness to lend.

3.4.1.4 Equity and Real Estate Prices

Equity Prices. Before the crisis, there is an above-average increase in stock prices which very often passes into a stock market bubble. The upward trend reverses just before the outbreak of the crisis, when the stock market bubble bursts and stock prices fall sharply to below-average values due to deteriorating liquidity and solvency positions which are mainly caused by rising domestic and foreign lending rates, and real overvaluations of the domestic currency (see below). After the burst of the stock market bubble, stock prices decrease further and reach their lowest levels at the peak of the crisis. In the post-crisis period, stock prices remain lower than in tranquil periods.

Real Estate Prices. Real estate prices are subject to the same stylized behaviour as stock prices.

3.4.2 Current Account Variables

Real Exchange Rate.[26] In the pre-crisis period, the real exchange rate is lower relative to its average level during tranquil times, and declines further until the outbreak of the crisis, indicating a large real overvaluation of the domestic currency. At the outbreak of the crisis, the real exchange rate reverses sharply and rises to above-average levels, where the increase at the onset of the crisis is more pronounced during episodes of currency and twin crises due to large nominal devaluations of the domestic currency. Especially exchange-rate-based inflation stabilization programmes very often lead to large real overvaluations of the domestic currency and undermine international competitiveness, as domestic inflation fails to reduce to foreign levels. In the post-crisis phase, the real exchange rate appreciates substantially and remains at higher levels than in tranquil times.

Terms of Trade.[27] The terms of trade are lower than in tranquil periods and deteriorate further until the outbreak of the crisis. After the crisis, the terms of trade improve and rise to average levels.

Current Account Balance. In the pre-crisis period, there is a large above-average current account deficit which deepens steadily just before the outbreak of the crisis. Increasing

[26]The real exchange rate is defined as the ratio of the price of foreign goods (in domestic currency) to the price of domestic goods, i.e. formally, the real exchange rate s_r is given by $s_r = s\,P^*/P$, where s denotes the nominal exchange rate (the price of one unit of foreign currency in domestic currency), P^* the foreign price level, and P the domestic price level. The real exchange rate is measured by its deviation from trend relative to tranquil periods, indicating the degree of misalignment.

[27]The terms of trade are defined as the ratio of the unit value of exports to the unit value of imports.

current account deficits are generally caused by poor export performance and rising boom-induced imports, where the growth of imports of consumer goods is overproportionally high. In the post-crisis period, the current account reverses quickly and passes into a current account surplus which is larger than in tranquil times. Current account reversals are generally caused by a large drop in imports due to a considerable decline in GDP, and by an improving export performance mainly due to a large nominal devaluation of the domestic currency.

3.4.3 Capital Account Variables

Foreign Exchange Reserves. Prior to the crisis, central banks lose foreign exchange reserves at an above-average rate which accelerates just before the outbreak. The loss in reserves peaks at the outbreak of the crisis. The discontinuous decline in foreign exchange reserves indicates that central banks try to "lean against the wind" by fighting reserve losses with contractionary monetary policy (see the behaviour of interest rates) before the currency collapse. After the crisis, i.e. after the devaluation or floatation, there is a rise in foreign exchange reserves to tranquil time levels.

Real Interest Rate Differential Between Domestic and Foreign Deposits. There are different time patterns for currency, banking and twin crises. Regarding currency crises, the real interest differential is lower than in tranquil times before, during, and after the crisis, indicating that there arise no devaluation expectations in the pre-crisis period. Respecting banking and twin crises, the differential increases markedly relative to tranquil times in the run-up to the crisis indicating devaluation expectations, and returns to average levels in the post-crisis period.

World Interest Rates.[28] In the pre-crisis period, world interest rates are higher than during tranquil times and rise steadily up to their peak at the outbreak of the crisis. After the outbreak, world interest rates remain firstly at the crisis level and decline afterwards to tranquil time levels. The increase in world interest rates in the pre-crisis period may either reflect an exogenous shock, or increasing risk premia on foreign debt when financial difficulties in the private sector are revealed. The decline in the post-crisis period may reflect decreasing credit risk.

Ratio of Private Capital Net Inflow to GDP. The ratio increases in the pre-crisis period at an above-average rate and peaks just before the outbreak of the crisis. After its peak, the ratio declines and reaches its lowest point at the outbreak of the crisis but still at above-average levels. In the post-crisis period the ratio remains constant at slightly above-average values. It has to be emphasized that the private capital net inflow/GDP ratio consists of both FDI and portfolio flows, where FDI flows are always positive and prevent the private capital net inflow/GDP ratio from becoming negative. By way of contrast, portfolio flows sharply increase in the run-up to the crisis, indicating an increasing leverage in foreign currency, and come to a "sudden stop" just before the outbreak, being followed by large net portfolio outflows during the crisis and in the post-crisis period.

[28] World interest rates are determined as a weighted average of short-term "Northern" interest rates for the United States, Germany, Japan, France, the United Kingdom and Switzerland.

Ratio of Short-Term Capital Inflow to GDP. This ratio, consisting mainly of short-term portfolio flows, is characterized by the same boom-bust cycle pattern as the domestic credit/GDP ratio. The ratio increases sharply in the pre-crisis period at an above-average rate and comes to a "sudden stop" just before the outbreak of the crisis. After its peak, the ratio declines sharply to below-average levels due to large net capital outflows, and reaches its lowest level at the outbreak of the crisis. In the post-crisis period the ratio slightly increases but remains at lower levels than in tranquil times.

3.4.4 Real Sector Variables

Output. The time pattern of output exhibits the characteristics of a typical extensive boom-bust cycle. In the pre-crisis period, there is an above-average increase in GDP indicating a boom in the real sector. The boom comes to a halt in the run-up to the crisis, and turns into a recession just before the outbreak, being mainly caused by rising domestic and foreign interest rates, and by the real overvaluation of the domestic currency. The recession, being characterized by large below-average GDP values, deepens due to the outbreak of the crisis, and reaches its lowest level in the post-crisis period. Afterwards, output recovers and returns to tranquil time levels. As aforementioned in section 3.2.2, recessions accompanied by banking and twin crises are much deeper than recessions accompanied by currency crises.

Inflation. The inflation rate is characterized by above-average levels during the entire pre-crisis period, and decreases slightly in the run-up to the crisis until the outbreak. The decline in the inflation rate in the pre-crisis period may be caused by attempts to reduce the real overvaluation of the domestic currency and to curb the overheating of the economy. After the outbreak of the crisis, there is a large above-average rise in inflation, being mainly caused by the nominal devaluation of the domestic currency which is reflected in increasing domestic prices. After its post-crisis-peak, inflation starts to reduce slightly, but is still higher than during tranquil times.

Ratio of Investment to GDP. The boom-bust cycle in real output is largely driven by an extensive boom-bust cycle in investment which is induced by the boom-bust cycle in domestic credit and in net capital flows. Prior to the crisis, there is an above-average increase in the investment/GDP ratio, where investment is increasingly financed by domestic and foreign debt.[29] The investment boom peaks just before the outbreak of the crisis like the domestic credit/GDP ratio, the private net capital inflow/GDP ratio and the short-term capital inflow/GDP ratio. After its peak, the investment/GDP ratio declines steadily. The outbreak of the crisis leads to a further deterioration of the investment/GDP ratio which reaches lower levels than during tranquil times in the post-crisis period.

Ratio of Fiscal Deficit to GDP. Though lots of crises in the early post Bretton Woods period, especially in emerging market countries, were predominantly driven by unsound

[29]Investment booms have been very often subject to an overproportional rise in real estate investment by comparison with investment in machinery, infrastructure and business construction, having induced a bubble in real estate prices, as e.g. in Japan in the late 1980s (Werner 2003, p. 100) or in Mexico in the early 1990s (Palma 2000, p. 21).

fiscal and monetary policies, there is only a slight rise in the fiscal deficit/GDP ratio in the pre-crisis period relative to tranquil times, indicating that fiscal deficits have played a less regular role in past financial crises. The increase in the fiscal deficit/GDP ratio may be caused either by higher government spending, or by a recession-induced shortfall in revenues. The fiscal/deficit ratio improves in the post-crisis period.

3.4.5 Balance Sheet Variables

3.4.5.1 Liquidity and Profit Variables

Interest Coverage of the Corporate and the Banking Sector.[30] In the pre-crisis period, interest coverage firstly increases steadily and peaks some time before the burst of the asset price bubble and before the outbreak of the crisis. The pre-crisis rise in interest coverage is caused by a large output-induced rise in earnings, which overcompensates increasing interest expenses. The overall rise in interest expenses is due to a percentage increase in total debt being larger than the decrease in interest rates. From its peak, interest coverage declines sharply until the outbreak of the crisis. The fall in interest coverage is caused by a output-induced drop in nominal earnings and by rising interest expenses. The rise in interest expenses is due to rising domestic and foreign interest rates and due to percentage reductions in debt which are smaller than the increase in interest rates. Furthermore, interest expenses in foreign currency increase sharply during episodes of currency and twin crises by nominal devaluations of the domestic currency. In the post-crisis period, there is a further decline in the interest coverage which recovers later on. A similar measure to assess the influence of interest expenses on the overall liquidity position is the ratio of interest payments to GDP, as e.g. used in Eichengreen and Rose (1998), which is subject to a steady increase before, during, and after the occurrence of the crisis, indicating also a deteriorating liquidity position over the entire boom-bust cycle.

Gross and Net Profits of the Corporate Sector. In the pre-crisis period, gross profits of the corporate sector, which are defined as earnings before interest, taxes, and depreciation, increase steadily until the burst of the asset price bubble and collapse afterwards during the entire post-crisis period. By way of contrast, net profits, which are defined as earnings less interest expenses before taxes and depreciation, increase in the pre-crisis period, but peak before the asset bubble's burst and decline steadily afterwards during the entire post-crisis period.

Ratio of Investment to Retained Earnings. Prior to the crisis, there is a large rise in the ratio of investment to retained earnings, implying an increasing debt-asset ratio (see below) because the increase in investment is larger than retained earnings. The ratio peaks at the outbreak of the crisis and is subject to a large decline in the post-crisis period due to a large drop in investment.

Net Profits of the Banking Sector. Net profits of the banking sector are subject to the same time pattern as net profits of the corporate sector, where net profits are additionally

[30] Interest coverage of the corporate and the banking sector is defined as the ratio of earnings before interest, taxes, and depreciation to interest expenses.

decreased after their peak by increasing non-performing loans when the economy starts to enter the recession period just before the asset price bubble's burst.

Ratio of Short-Term Domestic Debt to Total Debt. There is a considerable rise in the ratio of domestic short-term debt to total debt in the pre-crisis period, indicating rising liquidity risk as firms and banks become increasingly dependent on financial markets' capacity to roll-over short-term debt. The ratio peaks at the asset price bubble's burst and is subject to a slow fall during the entire post-crisis period. This time pattern indicates that the willingness to lend does not consider the drop in net profits before the bubble's burst as an indicator for increasing liquidity risk.

Ratio of Short-Term Foreign Debt to Total Debt. The ratio of short-term foreign debt to total debt follows the same time pattern as the ratio of short-term domestic debt to total domestic debt, being also consistent with the behaviour of the ratio of short-term capital inflows to GDP. Consequently, there is a further rise in liquidity risk during the boom phase, as firms and banks additionally depend on foreign financial markets' capacity to roll-over short-term debt in foreign currency.

3.4.5.2 Market Valuation and Solvency Variables

Market Valuation of Firms - Tobin's q. Market valuation of firms, or Tobin's q[31], being measured by the ratio of market to book value of equity (as a proxy for Tobin's q), increases steadily and peaks when the asset bubble bursts. Afterwards, there is a steady decline during the entire post-crisis period.

Debt-Asset Ratio of Firms and Banks.[32] There is a considerable rise in the debt-asset ratio in the period before the burst of the asset price bubble, being predominantly caused by the large increase in short-term domestic and foreign debt. After the burst of the asset price bubble, there is a further, but smaller rise in the debt-asset ratio, peaking during the post-crisis period. The rise in the debt-asset ratio in the post-bubble period is caused firstly, by an increase in domestic and foreign interest rates, secondly, by a transformation of short-term debt and short-term interest payment obligations which both cannot be met into long-term debt contracts, and thirdly, by nominal devaluations of the domestic currency which lead to an increase in the stock of foreign debt valued in domestic currency. After its peak, the debt-asset ratio starts to decline only slightly in the late post-crisis period as the protracted process of deleveraging in the bust period is generally impeded by low net profits due to low nominal earnings and high interest expenses.

Ratio of Total Debt to GDP. A similar indicator for the degree of indebtedness both in domestic and in foreign currency, as well as for an economy's potential to repay the

[31]For details on Tobin's q, see appendix A.

[32]The debt-asset ratio is defined as the ratio of the sum of domestic and foreign debt to the sum of domestic and foreign assets.

debt burden, is the ratio of total debt to GDP which increases before, during, and after the outbreak of the crisis indicating increasing liquidity and solvency difficulties.

Ratio of Debt to Market Value of Equity of Firms. There is only a slight increase in the ratio of debt to market value of equity in the period before the burst of the asset price bubble as rising leverage is masked by an overcompensating increase in the market value of firms. After the burst of the asset price bubble, there is a sharp increase in the ratio due to a sharp decrease in the market valuation of firms revealing high corporate leverage. There is a further increase in the ratio during the post-crisis period due to a further decline in the market valuation of firms and due to a further rise in indebtedness. The debt to market value value of equity ratio peaks in the late post-crisis period and starts to decline afterwards.

3.4.6 An Assessment

The stylized behaviour of the 35 macroeconomic variables during episodes of financial crises can be summarized in the following eight propositions.

Firstly, business cycles being associated with financial crises are subject to much larger fluctuations in *all* macroeconomic variables than business cycles during tranquil times. Accordingly, financial crises are generally linked to extensive, and very often to excessive boom-bust cycles in goods and financial markets.

Secondly, the boom phase of business cycles giving rise financial crises often begins with a large exogenous *positive* shock to financial institutions (as e.g. financial liberalization, or increasing access to international financial markets) extending the access to domestic and international financing. Another source of excessive boom-bust cycles inducing financial crises, which has not been considered in the previous empirical analysis, is the emergence of new technology regimes which also lead to an increasing access to domestic and international financing due to actual and expected increases in productivity and profits.[33]

Thirdly, increasing access to domestic and international financing, as well as the introduction of new technology regimes, induce a rise in expected profits by lower actual, and lower expected interest rates, and by an expected rise in productivity. Both factors cause an investment boom, an acceleration of GDP growth, sharply rising stock market valuations of corporations and banks reflecting the expected rise in future profits, an increase in actual gross and net profits, cash flows, and net worth positions, giving rise to a further expansion in real economic activity. As a result, the boom phase is characterized by a cumulative upward process driven by, as outlined in section 2.2.4.3, demand-side, financial-accelerator induced, and supply-side induced cumulative processes.

Fourthly, the boom phase causes an increase in the overall debt-asset ratio, both by an increase in domestic and in foreign debt. On the supply side, the lending boom is fueled

[33]For example, the extensive boom phases of the business cycles having been associated with the Great Depression were not only driven by easy monetary and financing conditions, but also by the emergence of new information and communication technologies like radio, and by new mass production processes, as e.g. the introduction of assembly-line production in the automobile industry (Eichengreen and Mitchener 2003). In a similar way, the New Economy bubble of the late 1990s, having peaked in 2000, was also driven by the introduction of new information and communication technologies, as e.g. the internet, which were expected to generate an enormous rise in overall productivity and in profits.

by a general monetary expansion due to an increase in domestic bank lending being facilitated by easy monetary conditions, and due to large volumes of capital inflows. On the demand side, the lending boom is driven by profit expectations growing faster than actual profits (or retained earnings), so that investment growth has to be increasingly financed by external domestic and/or foreign debt. As short-term interest rates tend to be lower than long-term interest rates during the boom phase, there is an overproportional increase in short-term debt finance. Increasing debt-asset ratios are considered to be sustainable because profits are expected to rise to future levels which allow to repay debt, being reflected in a constant ratio of debt to market value of equity due to a compensating rise in stock market valuations. Accordingly, the longer the boom phase lasts, the more expectations rely on overall market sentiment, rather than on a rational observation of fundamentals, giving rise to an increasing stock market bubble.

Fifthly, there is a large and endogenous rise in financial instability during the upswing due to overborrowing and overinvestment, which are induced by cumulative demand-side and financial accelerator processes. Following the results of section 2.3, financial fragility increases owing to a decrease in the ratio of hedge finance units to speculative and Ponzi finance units, and owing to a decrease in the ratio of foreign hedge finance units to foreign (super) speculative and foreign (super) Ponzi finance units, being reflected in an overproportional rise in short-term domestic and foreign borrowing. Furthermore, financial instability increases due to excess volatility in asset prices, as GDP and investment growth are based on increasingly optimistic profit expectations which are much larger than actual values, giving rise to an unsustainable increase in the overall debt-asset ratio. Excess volatility due to rising inflation expectations is also possible, but not as significant as excess volatility due to overly optimistic profit expectations. The increase in financial instability due to unrealistic profit expectations, driving the economy into a state of "irrational exuberance", is predominantly reflected in a steady increase in indebtedness and rising stock market valuations of firms and banks in the late boom phase, though overall net profits start to fall, signalling upcoming liquidity and solvency problems.

Sixthly, financial instability is revealed by large firms and/or banks becoming illiquid or insolvent due to a slow down in earnings, caused by an slow down in GDP growth, and due to rising interest rates. Both the slow down in GDP growth and rising interest rates, leading to a decline in net profits, are caused by a mixture of endogenous and exogenous mechanisms. Regarding endogenous mechanisms, net profits are reduced by rising input costs when the economy reaches the frontier of capacity utilization, inducing a rising real overvaluation of the domestic currency. Furthermore, net profits are reduced by endogenously rising debt costs due to an unsustainable increase in the debt-asset ratio leading to a rise in risk premia. Regarding exogenous mechanisms, central banks very often start to tighten monetary policy in the late boom phase to dampen the economy's overheating, leading also to rising domestic interest rates, to a reduction in GDP growth, and to a decline in net profits; however, domestic contractionary monetary policy during the upswing can also be interpreted as an endogenous policy response to an endogenous debt-led, and expectations-led overheating of the economy. By way of contrast, foreign contractionary monetary policy, which leads to declining domestic net profits and large capital outflows owing to large foreign debt stocks, represents a purely exogenous event. Beginning failures of large corporations and/or banks generally trigger the burst of the asset price bubble and induce the downswing by demand-side, financial-accelerator induced, and supply-side induced cumulative processes. Dropping stock market valuations, rising risk premia, increasing domestic and foreign interest rates, a real overvaluation of the domestic currency, large withdrawals of domestic and foreign debt, and a decline in real economic activity cause widespread bankruptcies among firms and financial institutions, ending up in a severe banking crises. In case foreign exchange reserves do not suffice to meet net capital outflows, a currency crisis follows which deepens the banking crises by high domestic interest rates, and by nominal appreciations of the foreign debt stock because of large nominal devaluations of the home currency.

Seventhly, the financial crisis is followed by a long-lasting recession, or even by a depression with deflationary spirals (see e.g. Japan in the late 1990s), as the process of deleveraging, i.e. the reduction in the overall debt-asset ratio, during bust phases of business cycles being associated with financial crises requires much more time than the deleveraging process during the downswing of tranquil time business cycles because of a much higher build-up of debt during the upswing.

Eighthly, financial crises are typically preceded by a large number of weak and worsening economic fundamentals. Financial crises where economic fundamentals were sound are very rare. Banking, currency and twin crises have common origins, where for twin crises economic fundamentals and financial instability tend to be worse, and lead, as aforementioned, to more severe recessions.

These eight propositions are going to be discussed in more detail in sections 4.3.2 and 5.3.2 in part II of the book by a theoretical description of different stages of a stylized business cycle giving rise to financial crises, where section 4.3.2 refers to financial crises in industrialized countries, and section 5.3.2 to financial crises in emerging market countries.

3.5 Standard Theory of Financial Crises and its Correspondence with the Stylized Facts

Standard theory of financial crises provides five main explanations for the causes of financial distress, being reflected in five classes of financial crisis models. Four classes of financial crisis models, which are labelled in the following as inconsistent macroeconomic policy models (section 3.5.1), self-fulfilling expectations models (section 3.5.2), asymmetric information models (section 3.5.3), credit constraint and balance sheet models (section 3.5.4), represent the mainstream approach to financial crises, arguing, as outlined in sections 1.1 and 2.4, that capitalist market economies are inherently stable and that financial crises can be only caused by large exogenous shocks to economic fundamentals, or by random exogenous shifts from optimistic towards pessimistic (rational) expectations which become self-fulfilling. The fifth class of models, being labelled in the following as endogenous financial crisis approach (section 3.5.5), and representing the minority of the financial crises literature, is often neglected in discussions on the causes of financial crises, mainly because endogenous financial crisis models argue that capitalist market economies are inherently unstable, and that financial crises are a "natural" outcome if there is no interventionist monetary and fiscal policy to prevent crises, or to dampen their adverse effects on the real economy. However, this model class is the only one which argues that financial crises are generally linked to business cycle fluctuations, and is therefore explicitly taken into consideration.

The following discussion provides a short overview of each class of models in sections 3.5.1 to 3.5.5, and compares the model results with the stylized facts having been elaborated in the previous sections. Section 3.5.6 summarizes the results and is going to show that no model class can provide a detailed explanation of the stylized facts, as already argued in the introductory section 1.1. The analysis is set out without references as sections 4.5 and 5.5 provide a much more detailed discussion of numerous approaches of each model class.[34]

3.5.1 Inconsistent Macroeconomic Policy Models

This class of models argues that financial crises are predominantly caused by overly expansionary monetary or fiscal policies, or by excessive contractionary monetary policies. Regarding banking crises, expansionary monetary policy, or money-financed fiscal deficits lead to rising actual and expected inflation which are reflected in rising interest rates, causing a fall in the nominal value of banks' assets side of the balance sheet which consists of bonds. As banks' debt side of the balance sheet only consists of non-interest bearing deposits which do not change in value in case of interest rate changes, excessive monetary policy ultimately lead to banks' insolvency. Another source of banking crises is overly contractionary monetary policy leading to deflation. In this case, banks' insolvency stems also from a fall in the nominal value of banks' asset side consisting of bonds, as there is a steady increase in bankruptcies of debtors due to debt deflation and rising real interest rates. Furthermore, banks' debt side, consisting mainly of deposits, is also subject to an enormous rise in real terms leading ultimately to widespread failures of banks.

Currency crises are caused by excessive expansionary monetary policies, or by money-financed fiscal deficits, leading to falling domestic interest rates, and thereby to large capital outflows which are "financed" by a depletion of foreign exchange reserves to stabilize the fixed exchange rate. However, when the stock of foreign exchange reserves is used up, or has fallen to a certain minimum threshold value, a speculative attack on the currency is unavoidable, leading to a sharp devaluation of the home currency.

Twin crises are also explained by overly expansionary monetary policies, or by large money-financed fiscal deficits which lead to a collapse of the fixed exchange rate system, and thereby to a domestic banking crisis, as banks' debt side is characterized by large amounts of foreign debt which are subject to a substantial rise by the devaluation of the home currency.

A comparison of the model results with the stylized facts shows that there are both common grounds and differences. Concerning the common grounds, there arise two similarities. Firstly, inconsistent macroeconomic policy models show that rising domestic interest rates, as well as deflation lead to a substantial increase financial fragility by deteriorating solvency positions which can cause domestic banking crises. Secondly, this

[34] Apart from standard theory, there are also empirical approaches to the causes of financial crises, as e.g. empirical work by Meltzer (1995), Caprio and Klingebiel (1996), Goldstein and Turner (1996), Hausmann and Rojas-Suaréz (1996), Lindgren et al. (1996), Sachs et al. (1996), Sheng (1996), Blejer, Feldman and Feltenstein (1997), Demirgüç-Kunt and Detragiache (1997), Garcia-Herrero and Baliño (1997), Kaminsky, Lizondo and Reinhart (1997), Eichengreen and Rose (1999), Hardy and Pazarbaşioğlu (1999), and Summers (2000), which are however based on standard models of financial crises. Hence, these empirical approaches generally identify similar factors causing financial distress like standard theory, and therefore are not going to be reviewed in the book.

model class is consistent with the fact that collapses of fixed exchange rate regimes are preceded by large capital outflows causing a devaluation of the home currency, which either engenders, or deteriorates a domestic banking crisis in case banks' stock of foreign debt is comparatively high before the outbreak of the crisis.

Respecting the differences, there are three issues to be mentioned. Firstly, inconsistent macroeconomic policy models do not consider the link between business cycles and financial crises. Secondly, there is no explanation of the endogenous build-up of financial fragility during the boom phase by largely rising domestic and foreign debt stocks. Thirdly, this model class does not consider fluctuations in expectations of private agents driving asset prices and real economic activity during a financial crisis cycle.

3.5.2 Self-Fulfilling Expectations Models

This model class argues that financial crises are caused by random shifts in expectations of private agents, inducing a switch from a "no-crisis-equilibrium", being characterized by a solvent financial sector and a stable fixed exchange rate regime, to a "crisis-equilibrium", being characterized by insolvent banks and a breakdown of the fixed exchange rate regime. Expectations are self-fulfilling as optimistic ex ante expectations regarding financial sector and exchange rate stability do not induce bank runs or capital flight, and thereby lead to actual financial stability which validates optimistic expectations ex post. By way of contrast, arising pessimistic ex ante expectations regarding financial sector solvency and exchange rate stability induce bank runs and capital flight, and cause thereby banking, currency and twin crises which validate pessimistic expectations ex post. As the switch in expectations from the no-crisis to the crisis-equilibrium is generally assumed to be a random event being independent of the state of economic fundamentals, financial crises cannot be predicted as they are not preceded by deteriorating fundamentals.

Respecting the common grounds with the stylized facts of financial crises, there arise two similarities. Firstly, self-fulfilling expectations models validate the empirical fact that financial crises are associated with depreciation expectations of the home currency, and pessimistic expectations as to solvency positions of the financial sector, where tranquil times are associated with optimistic expectations. Secondly, this model class is consistent with the fact that expectations are a crucial determinant of financial stability and real economic activity, as expectations are at least partly self-fulfilling and induce cumulative processes. That is, boom phases are typically preceded by optimistic expectations being reflected in rising asset prices, whereas a financial crisis is preceded by collapsing expectations which are reflected in asset price busts before the outbreak of banking, currency, or twin crises.

Regarding the differences, there are three issues to be mentioned. Firstly, empirical data unequivocally indicate that financial crises are typically preceded by deteriorating fundamentals and a considerable rise in financial fragility, which is denied by self-fulfilling expectations models as they argue that financial crises are caused by sudden and random events which cannot be predicted. Secondly, this model class does not consider the link between business cycles and financial crises. Thirdly, though self-fulfilling expectations models explain financial crises by a switch from "good" to "bad" expectations, they do not explain the endogenous boom-bust cycle in expectations, as well as the boom-bust cycle in domestic and foreign indebtedness.

3.5.3 Asymmetric Information Models

This model class explains financial crises predominantly as a consequence of moral hazard, originating from implicit or explicit government guarantees to bail out both domestic, and foreign investors in case of default. The existence of government guarantees, e.g. to bail out troubled banks, or to defend a fixed exchange rate level, induces a rise in the expected return of insecure, risky investment projects, as losses are taken over by the government, and indirectly by the tax payer. This distortion in agents' risk perception causes agents to engage in much riskier, and in much more investment projects than they would do in case guarantees were absent. Accordingly, implicit or explicit government guarantees lead to excessive risk taking, overinvestment, and to overborrowing both in domestic, and in foreign currency.

For financial crises to occur, there has to be an exogenous upper limit of government support which cannot be exceeded. For example, governments are going to suspend their guarantee to bail out troubled banks if the budget deficit reaches unsustainable levels causing e.g. high inflation, or high domestic interest rates. Moreover, governments' guarantee to defend an exchange rate peg is going to be suspended in case the stock of foreign exchange reserves has declined to zero. Accordingly, in case losses are higher than the exogenously given upper bound of government guarantees, the government is going to suspend its guarantees, leading to banking, currency, and twin crises.

Respecting the triggering events of financial crises, moral hazard driven models argue that crises are caused either by exogenous shocks to fundamentals, or by self-fulfilling expectations, but deny an endogenous financial collapse in spite of an endogenous build-up of financial fragility, which is however due to exogenously given government guarantees. Concerning exogenous shock-driven moral hazard models, financial distress is caused by an adverse exogenous shock to fundamentals, as e.g. a decline in productivity, or a rise in interest rates, leading to a "bad" realized return of investment projects, and causing losses to firms and banks which induce a suspension of government guarantees, and thereby systemic financial crises. Regarding self-fulfilling expectations-driven moral hazard models, financial crises are explained by a shift from optimistic ex ante expectations regarding governments' ability to fulfill guarantees, to pessimistic ex ante expectations, which induce bank runs and capital flight as the government is expected to suspend guarantees in the future. Actual failures of banks and declining foreign exchange reserves cause an actual suspension of government guarantees, leading to banking, currency and twin crises, and validating investors' pessimistic ex ante expectations ex post. The switch from the "good" to the "bad" equilibrium is assumed to be a random event which cannot be explained, implying that financial crises are an unpredictable event.

Respecting the common grounds of asymmetric information models with the stylized facts, there arise four similarities. Firstly, financial crises are preceded by a boom phase, leading to overinvestment and overborrowing both in domestic and in foreign currency due to distorted, and overly optimistic expectations which do not correspond to actual fundamentals. Secondly, financial crises are associated both with a deterioration of fundamentals, and with collapsing expectations. Thirdly, especially self-fulfilling expectations-driven moral hazard models show that expectations are a crucial determinant of financial stability and real economic activity, as optimistic expectations lead to a prosperous macroeconomic environment, whereas the shift towards pessimistic expectations induces recessions, and in severe cases, systemic financial crises. Fourthly, especially exogenous-shock driven models argue that financial crises are triggered by exogenous shocks, like e.g. rising foreign interest rates, or terms of trade shocks.

Concerning the differences, there are four issues to be mentioned. Firstly, according to moral hazard models, the build-up of financial fragility during the boom phase is only due to exogenously given government guarantees, while the stylized facts show at least partly an (endogenous) build-up of financial fragility, being independent of government guarantees owing to three reasons. The first reason concerns the empirical fact that other historical episodes of financial crises, as e.g. the Great Depression period during the interwar era (1913-1939), have shown that there is a build-up of financial fragility driven by overly optimistic expectations even in case government guarantees, as e.g. deposit insurance systems and effective lender of last resort interventions, are absent. The second reason refers to the stylized fact that tranquil and financial crisis business cycles take turns even in periods which are characterized by the existence of government guarantees which do not change over time significantly, as e.g. in the post Bretton Woods era. Accordingly, financial fragility and financial crises cycles cannot be solely induced by the existence of government guarantees. The third reason concerns the stylized fact that there is a very strong positive correlation between financial liberalization and financial crises, indicating that government guarantees are not the sole reason for a build-up of financial fragility, and that overly optimistic profit expectations are not solely driven by the existence of government guarantees. Secondly, moral hazard models argue that financial crises can be only triggered by an actual or expected suspension of government guarantees, whereas the stylized facts show that financial crises are triggered at least partly by an endogenous process of deteriorating fundamentals, being independent of an actual or expected suspension of government guarantees for two reasons. The first reason concerns, as aforementioned, the stylized fact that there were historical episodes of financial crises which occurred without any government guarantees, as e.g. in the Great Depression period. The second reason refers to the fact that there were crises which occurred in an environment with stable and credible government guarantees (as e.g. the Japanese banking crisis in the early 1990s, the Savings and Loan crisis in the U.S. in the early 1980s, or the Nordic banking crisis in the early 1990s) which were not abandoned despite enormous costs. Thirdly, especially self-fulfilling expectations-driven moral hazard models predict that financial crises are an unpredictable event, whereas the stylized facts indicate that crises are typically preceded by deteriorating fundamentals. Fourthly, moral hazard models assume that the build-up of financial fragility is sustainable as long as there arise no exogenous shocks or pessimistic self-fulfilling expectations, whereas the stylized facts show that there are at least partly endogenous mechanisms triggering financial crises due to an unsustainable build-up of financial fragility.

3.5.4 Credit Constraint and Balance Sheet Models

This model class argues that financial crises are caused by financial constraints becoming binding due to sharp drops in firms' net worth positions which lead to credit and liquidity crunches, and thereby to a collapse of investment and output. Credit constraint and balance sheet models are based on the theory of imperfect capital markets[35], and argue that external investment finance is constrained by borrowing ceilings which depend positively

[35] For details, see section 2.2.2.2.

on firms' net worth position. Regarding models of financial crises in industrial countries, net worth is assumed to be predominantly influenced by the asset side of firms' balance sheet, i.e. net worth is assumed to depend positively on the level of asset prices. By way of contrast, models of financial crises in emerging market countries assume that net worth is predominantly influenced by the debt side of firms' balance sheet which is characterized by large stocks of foreign debt, i.e. net worth is assumed to depend negatively on the level of foreign debt, and negatively on the level of the exchange rate, as an increase in the nominal exchange rate, i.e. a nominal devaluation of the home currency, leads to an increase in the nominal value of foreign debt in domestic currency terms. Consequently, rising asset prices and decreasing exchange rate levels cause an increase in firms' net worth and a rise in the credit supply, inducing an increase in investment and output. On the contrary, a collapse of asset prices, or of the home currency causes a drop in firms' net worth and a credit or liquidity crunch, inducing a decline in investment and output.

According to credit constraint and balance sheet models, financial crises can be caused either by adverse exogenous shocks to economic fundamentals, or by a shift towards self-fulfilling pessimistic expectations. Exogenous shock-driven models argue that adverse exogenous shocks, as e.g. negative productivity or technology shocks, a deterioration of the terms of trade, or an increase in domestic or foreign interest rates, lead to a collapse of asset prices and to devaluations of the home currency, inducing a decline in firms' net worth and a credit crunch, which finally lead to banking, currency, and twin crises. By way of contrast, self-fulfilling expectations models argue that a shift from optimistic towards pessimistic (profit) expectations induces a collapse of asset prices and devaluations of the home currency, leading to banking, currency, and twin crisis, and validating ex post investors' pessimistic expectations. The shift in expectations is assumed, as in other self-fulfilling expectations models, to be a random and unpredictable event which cannot be explained by the model.

Regarding the common grounds of credit constraint and balance sheet models with the stylized facts of financial crises, there arise three similarities. Firstly, financial crises and subsequent recessions are associated with sharp reductions in the available amount of domestic and foreign credit, leading to widespread illiquidity and insolvency. Secondly, financial crises are preceded by deteriorating fundamentals, as e.g. rising interest rates, or deteriorating terms of trade as claimed by exogenous shock-driven models. Thirdly, expectations are a crucial determinant of financial stability and macroeconomic activity, as financial stability and macroeconomic expansions are generally associated with optimistic (profit) expectations, whereas financial crises and recessions are accompanied by pessimistic expectations.

Respecting the differences, there are five issues to be mentioned. Firstly, credit constraint and balance sheet models do not consider the link between business cycle fluctuations and financial crises. Secondly, credit constraint and balance sheet models do not explain the boom-bust cycle in profit expectations and domestic and foreign indebtedness. Thirdly, according to credit constraint and balance sheet models, financial instability and financial crises are not caused by an endogenous build-up of financial fragility during the boom phase, but by exogenous shocks or self-fulfilling expectations, contradicting the stylized facts. Fourthly, according to self-fulfilling expectations models, financial crises are an unpredictable event, being not associated with a deterioration of fundamentals which cannot be validated by the stylized facts. Fifthly, exogenous shock-driven models argue that economic fundamentals can only deteriorate due to adverse shocks, whereas the stylized facts indicate at least partly an endogenous deterioration of fundamentals.

3.5.5 Endogenous Financial Crisis Models

This model class, representing the minority in the financial crises literature, argues that capitalist economies are inherently unstable, and that financial crises are an unavoidable and endogenous event, being inseparably linked to business cycle fluctuations. Endogenous financial crisis models, referring predominantly to closed economies and thereby to banking crises, argue that there is an unsustainable and endogenous build-up of financial fragility by overinvestment and overborrowing during the boom phase of a business cycle, driven by overly optimistic profit expectations. Financial crises are triggered endogenously at the upper turning point of the business cycle by rising interest rates and declining profits, stemming from an inelastic credit supply and rising labour and material costs. Collapsing asset prices and widespread illiquidity and insolvency reveal that expectations have been overly optimistic and induce an undershooting process by overly pessimistic expectations, leading to a severe depression accompanied by deflation and by a liquidity trap situation. There are no endogenous mechanisms which lead to a recovery of the economy. Thus, only expansionary fiscal policies can induce a macroeconomic expansion which possibly leads to a new systemic financial crisis.

Regarding the common grounds of endogenous financial crisis models with the stylized facts, there arise three similarities. Firstly, endogenous financial crisis models are consistent with the stylized fact that financial crises are inseparably linked to business cycle fluctuations. Secondly, endogenous financial crisis models argue that there is an endogenous build-up of financial fragility leading to an endogenous outbreak of financial crises by endogenously deteriorating fundamentals. Thirdly, financial crises are followed by severe recessions and collapsing expectations.

Respecting the differences, there are two issued to be mentioned. Firstly, endogenous financial crisis models argue that every business cycle leads to systemic financial crises and that economies are inherently unstable, contradicting the stylized fact that there are also tranquil business cycle fluctuations. Secondly, endogenous financial crisis models argue that there is a purely endogenous build-up of financial fragility during financial crises business cycles by overly optimistic expectations, whereas the stylized facts indicate that unsustainable financial fragility during financial crises business cycles is initially caused by an exogenous positive shock to expectations.

3.5.6 An Assessment

The discussion of the model results and their correspondence with the stylized facts demonstrates that standard approaches to financial crises are consistent with a series of empirical regularities, but also fail to explain important stylized facts which are necessary for understanding the propagation mechanisms of financial crises, and which could be used to predict and to prevent future crises. Summing up, there are four stylized facts which are not explained by standard theory. Firstly, financial crises are inseparably linked to business cycle fluctuations, where financial crisis cycles are induced by positive exogenous shocks, as e.g. financial liberalization shocks. In case of the absence of exogenous shocks, economies tend to be cyclically stable, and exhibit tranquil business cycle fluctuations. Tranquil business cycles are also associated with an endogenous build-up of financial fragility during the boom phase, which however cannot induce systemic financial crises, but gives rise to "normal" economic downturns. Secondly, the emergence of financial crises cycles is a multi-period and long-run phenomenon which is interrupted by tranquil business cycles. Thirdly, both tranquil and financial crises business cycles are driven by endogenous changes in domestic and foreign indebtedness and by endogenous fluctuations in expectations, giving rise to endogenous fluctuations in macroeconomic activity and in financial stability. Fourthly, the rational expectations hypothesis does not hold in the short-run, as expectations tend to be additionally driven by market sentiments during the boom and bust phase of each business cycle. However, the change of expectations at the turning points, both during tranquil and financial crises business cycles, suggests the view that the rational expectations hypothesis holds at least in the long-run.

The aim of this work is both to overcome these deficiencies of standard theory, and to develop a synthetic approach to financial crises in part II of the book, combining the results of exogenous-shock driven mainstream models and of endogenous financial crisis models. Chapter 4 develops a nonlinear dynamic model of endogenous business cycle fluctuations and exogenous shock-driven financial crises in industrial countries under flexible exchange rates. The model uses an innovative expectation formation scheme which combines the rational expectations hypothesis with (Keynesian) market sentiment-driven expectation formation schemes, giving rise to dynamic interactions between chartists, fundamentalists and rational investors. Furthermore, the model develops endogenous debt and expectation dynamics, engendering endogenous fluctuations in macroeconomic activity and in financial stability, which, in case of positive exogenous shocks to expectations, can induce a typical financial crisis cycle leading to a systemic twin crisis. Chapter 5 develops a similar model of endogenous business cycles and financial crises in emerging market countries and considers explicitly the role of fluctuations in foreign debt, and the role of fixed exchange rate systems in the propagation mechanism of systemic financial crises. Chapter 6 develops a dynamic calibration model of financial crises in emerging markets in order to highlight the transitional dynamics of a large number of macroeconomic variables during financial crises business cycles which cannot be studied by the general function models in chapters 4 and 5. There is no explicit development of a dynamic calibration model of financial crises in industrial countries as the results of the emerging market case in chapter 6 can be easily applied to financial crises in industrial countries.

Table 3.6: Financial Crises Dates and Business Cycle Turning Points During the Gold-standard Era (1880-1913)

Date	Argentina	Brazil	Canada	Chile	Finland	France	Germany	Japan	Norway	Sweden	UK	US
1883												
1884		T			P							BC
1885	CC				T		P			P	P	T
1886									T			
1887	T		T	CC		T	T					
1888		P		T		CC	P			T		P
1889	P	BC,CC			P	P,BC		T			T	
1890	BC,CC	BC	P						P	P	BC	CC
1891	BC		CC	P								P,CC
1892	T						T	P			P	T
1893			CC		T	T	CC			T		P,BC, CC
1894	P						P		T			
1895							T					T
1896				T	P			T		P		
1897		BC	T								T	
1898	T	T,CC		BC,CC		P	P					
1899												
1900	P	BC		P	BC			P,CC			P	
1901		BC	P			T	T,BC	BC	P			P
1902	T	P						T				
1903					T					T		
1904			T			P		P,CC				T
1905				T	P		P		T	P		
1906			P			T						
1907				BC		BC	CC	T,BC		BC		P,BC
1908	CC	T	CC			P		CC	P			
1909						T		P				T
1909			T						T			
1910					T		T			T		
1911			P			P		T				P
1912	P	P		P			P			P	T	
1913						T				T		

BC: Banking Crises, CC: Currency Crises, P: Business Cycle Peaks, T: Business Cycle Troughs.

Source: Bordo et al. (2001b), Web Appendix.

Table 3.7: Financial Crises Dates and Business Cycle Turning Points During the Interwar Period (1919-1939)

Date	Argentina	Brazil	Canada	Chile	Finland	France	Germany	Japan	Norway	Sweden	UK	US
1913						T				T		
1914								P				
1915			T	T	P				P	P		T
1916	T	T										
1917								T			P	
1918			P	P	T							P
1919		P								T		
1920	P		T							P		
1921	T	T	CC	T	P,BC CC			P,CC	P,BC		T	T
1922						T			T,BC			
1923	P	BC	BC		T	CC			BC	T		
1924		P	P	P	P	P			P		P	P
1925			T	BC	T							
1926	T	T		T		CC	T				T	T
1927								T,BC	T			
1928		P			P							
1929	P,CC		P,CC	P			P		P	P	P	P
1930	CC	CC				BC		P				BC
1931	BC,CC	CC	CC	CC	T,BC CC	BC	BC,CC	CC	BC,CC	BC,CC BC,CC	CC	BC
1932	T,CC	T		T		BC	T	CC				BC
1933			T					T	T	T		T,BC CC
1934	BC	CC					CC					
1935	P			P			P					
1936		P	P			T,CC	T					P
1937		CC	CC		P	CC			P		T	
1938	T									P		
1939					BC			P	T			T

BC: Banking Crises, CC: Currency Crises, P: Business Cycle Peaks, T: Business Cycle Troughs. Missing entries for business cycle turning points during World War I reflect absence of GDP data.

Source: Bordo et al. (2001b), Web Appendix.

Table 3.8: Financial Crises Dates and Business Cycle Turning Points During the Bretton Woods Period (1940-1971)

Date	Argentina	Brazil	Canada	Chile	Finland	France	Germany	Japan	Norway	Sweden	UK	US
1940	P				T							
1941								T				
1942											P	
1943		T	P	T				P		T		P
1944	T			P	P			T				
1945											T	
1946									T		CC	
1947		P	T							P		
1948	P				T	CC					CC	T
1949		T		T	CC		CC		P,CC	CC	P	
1950	CC	P	CC									
1951			P				P	T	T	T		
1952	T	T										P
1953		P		P,CC			T			P	T	
1954			T			T		P				T
1955		T		T			P		P		P	P
1956	P	P			P	P						
1957			P	P		CC						
1958					T		T			T	T	
1959	CC	CC						T	T			T
1960				T		T						
1961			T		P		P		P		P,CC	CC
1962	CC	T,CC	CC	P,CC								
1963	T	BC,CC					T	P			T	
1964				T		P	P		T	P	CC	
1965		P,CC									P,CC	
1966	P								P	T	CC	
1967	CC		P	P	T	T	T		P		T,CC	P
1968	T			CC		CC		T				
1969				T							P	
1970	CC		T								T	T
1971		T			CC			P	CC	CC		CC

BC: Banking Crises, CC: Currency Crises, P: Business Cycle Peaks, T: Business Cycle Troughs.

Source: Bordo et al. (2001b), Web Appendix.

Table 3.9: Financial Crises Dates, Business Cycle Turning Points and Beginning of Financial Liberalization During the Post Bretton Woods Era (1972-1998), Part I

Date	Argentina	Brazil	Canada	Chile	Denmark	Finland	France	Germany	Indonesia	Israel	Japan	Korea
1972	P			P			P	P				
1973			P		T							
1974				FL	P	P						
1975		FL,P	T	CC					CC			
1976	CC			T,BC	T,CC		T	T	T		T	
1977	FL,T	T		CC		T		BC		BC,CC		
1978					P		P		CC	T		P
1979	P		P					P			FL	
1980	BC	P	FL	P	FL			FL	P	P	P	CC
1981			CC	BC		P						
1982	CC			CC	T	FL						
1983	T	T	T						FL,CC			FL
1984	CC			T,CC						T		P
1985	BC			P,CC						FL	T	
1986			CC		P	T,CC	T		CC			
1987	FL,P CC	P,CC			BC				T	P		
1988				P				T				
1989	BC,CC		P		T	P						P
1990	T	BC, CC		T T	P P	BC, CC	P P			T T	P P	
1991	CC			P				P	P			
1992		T	T	T	CC		CC		BC		BC	
1993	P			P	T,CC	T,CC			T			T
1994		BC					T,BC					
1995	BC,CC	P		T				T				
1996					P				P	P		P
1997	T			P					BC, CC			BC, CC
1998	P	CC							BC, CC			BC CC

BC: Banking Crises, CC: Currency Crises, P: Business Cycle Peaks, T: Business Cycle Troughs, FL: Beginning of Financial Liberalization.

Note: The financial systems of Canada, Germany and the UK were largely liberalized during the entire post Bretton Woods era; the dates of financial liberalization in these countries indicate only the liberalization of the remaining parts of their financial systems.

Source: Bordo et al. (2001b), Web Appendix, and Williamson and Mahar (1998), Tables 4 and 5.

Table 3.10: Financial Crises Dates, Business Cycle Turning Points and Beginning of Financial Liberalization During the Post Bretton Woods Era (1972-1998), Part II

Date	Malaysia	Mexico	Norway	Philippines	Spain	Sweden	Thailand	Turkey	UK	Uruguay	US
1972											
1973					FL				P		
1974		FL			P						P
1975	CC		T	P		P	T			CC	
1976	T	CC		T	CC			FL	T,CC	FL	T
1977					BC	T		P,CC			
1978	FL	T							P		
1979	P						P	CC		CC	P
1980			P,FL	FL		FL,P			P	P	
1981		P,BC		BC				T		BC	
1982		CC		P,CC	CC	T		BC	T,CC	CC	FL,T
1983	P	CC	T	CC			BC			CC	
1984								CC		T	BC,CC
1985	BC	CC			T		FL				
1986			P,CC	T,CC				P		CC	
1987	T		BC								
1988		T								P	P
1989				P					P		
1990	P	CC	T	CC	P	P		T		T	
1991		FL				BC		BC,CC			
1992		P			CC	CC		P	T,CC		T
1993	T			T		T				P	
1994		BC,CC			T			BC,CC			
1995		CC			CC		P	T,CC			
1996	P	T		P		P			P		
1997	CC			CC			BC,CC	P		T	
1998	BC, CC	P	P	BC		T	BC,CC			P	P

BC: Banking Crises, CC: Currency Crises, P: Business Cycle Peaks, T: Business Cycle Troughs, FL: Beginning of Financial Liberalization.

Note: The financial system of the U.S. was largely liberalized during the entire post Bretton Woods era; the date of financial liberalization indicates the liberalization of the remaining parts of the U.S.'s financial systems.

Source: Bordo et al. (2001b), Web Appendix, and Williamson and Mahar (1998), Tables 4 and 5.

Part II

A Cyclical Theory of Financial Crises

Chapter 4

A Model of Financial Crises and Endogenous Fluctuations in Industrial Countries

4.1 The Real Side

Consider a large and fully industrialized country whose currency floats freely against other industrial countries, and is used as a nominal anchor, or as an international reserve currency by emerging market and transition economies.

Output is assumed to be determined by the demand side of the economy. The resulting goods market equilibrium condition is formally given by

$$PY = PY^d(\underset{+}{C}, \underset{+}{I}, \underset{+}{G}, \underset{+}{NX}),$$

stating that nominal output PY, where P denotes the domestic price level and Y real output, is determined positively by real consumption demand C, by real investment demand I, by real government expenditure G and by real net exports NX. The nominal capital stock PK, where K denotes the real capital stock, being equal to replacement costs or to the supply price of capital, is used as the numéraire of the model. Dividing both sides of the goods market equilibrium by the numéraire PK, and assuming an additive aggregate demand function yields

$$u = \frac{Y}{K} = \frac{C}{K} + \frac{I}{K} + \frac{G}{K} + \frac{NX}{K},$$

where output is transformed into the output/capital ratio or capacity utilization $u = Y/K$, and real demand components are expressed in terms of the real capital stock. For reasons of simplicity, real consumption demand is excluded from the model, i.e. $C/K = 0$. The second demand component I/K representing the real growth rate of the capital stock $\hat{K}$ ($I/K = \dot{K}/K = \hat{K}$) is assumed to be positively determined by Tobin's q, being derived in detail below and explained in appendix A, resulting in the "desired" growth rate of the capital stock

$$\frac{I}{K} = \hat{K} = \eta(\underset{+}{q}).$$

Government expenditure is assumed to be determined inversely by the real value of public debt being financed by the issuance of government bonds, and by real interest payments on debt. Accordingly, real government expenditure adjusted for the capital stock $g = G/K$ is assumed to be negatively dependent on the real interest rate on government bonds $i - \hat{p}$, where i denotes the nominal interest rate on bonds, and $\hat{p} = \dot{P}/P$ the growth rate of the domestic price level, formally

$$\frac{G}{K} = g = g(\underset{-}{i - \hat{p}}).$$

Real net exports adjusted for the capital stock $nx = NX/K$ are assumed to depend positively on the growth rate of the real exchange rate $\hat{s} + \hat{p}^* - \hat{p}$, where $\hat{s} = \dot{s}/s$ denotes the growth rate of the nominal exchange rate s expressing the price of one unit of foreign currency in domestic currency, and $\hat{p}^* = \dot{P}^*/P^*$ the foreign price level's growth rate which is assumed to be constant at zero, i.e. it holds that $\hat{p}^* = 0$; as a result, real net exports are given by

$$\frac{NX}{K} = nx = nx(\underset{+}{\hat{s} - \hat{p}}).$$

Furthermore, it is assumed that the Robinson-condition is fulfilled according to reactions of the current account to real exchange rate movements, ruling out abnormal reactions, i.e. a real appreciation of the exchange rate (real depreciation of the home currency) leads to an increase in nx, and a real depreciation of the exchange rate (real appreciation of the home currency) leads to a decrease in nx. The negative dependence of nx on capacity utilization u by import demand is neglected for reasons of simplicity and does not change the model results significantly. Summing up, goods market equilibrium is given by

$$u = \eta(\underset{+}{q}) + g(\underset{-}{i - \hat{p}}) + nx(\underset{+}{\hat{s} - \hat{p}}). \tag{4.1}$$

Though the impact of q, i and $\hat{s}$ on u is unequivocal in equation 4.1, the influence of $\hat{p}$ on u is not clear. On the one hand, an increase in $\hat{p}$ leads to an increase in government expenditure by the reduction of the real interest rate on bonds $i - \hat{p}$, whereas on the other hand, an increase in $\hat{p}$ leads to a deterioration of the current account, i.e. nx decreases. Though a neutral, positive, as well as, negative influence of $\hat{p}$ on u can be justified, it is assumed in the present model that the overall impact of the growth rate of the price level on capacity utilization being denoted as $\partial u/\partial \hat{p}_a$ is positive, where $\partial \hat{p}_a$ reflects both the influence of $\hat{p}$ on $nx(\cdot)$ and the effect of $\hat{p}$ on $g(\cdot)$. As a result, inflation leads to an expansion in output, and deflation to a contraction since the influence of net exports is assumed to be smaller than the influence of government expenditure. Formally, it holds that

$$\frac{\partial u}{\partial \hat{p}_a} = \frac{\partial g}{\partial (i - \hat{p})} \frac{\partial (i - \hat{p})}{\partial \hat{p}} + \frac{\partial nx}{\partial (\hat{s} - \hat{p})} \frac{\partial (\hat{s} - \hat{p})}{\partial \hat{p}} = -\frac{\partial g}{\partial (i - \hat{p})} - \frac{\partial nx}{\partial (\hat{s} - \hat{p})} > 0.$$

Firms' profits and their influence on investment and expectations play a central role in the model. Gross nominal profits Q_g are given formally as

$$Q_g = PY - wN - \delta PK,$$

that is, by earnings PY less labour costs wN, where w denotes the nominal wage rate and N labour input, and less depreciation on the capital stock δPK, where δ denotes the depreciation rate. Net profits Q, or just profits, are determined by gross profits less external financing costs, i.e. less interest rate costs on the stock of loans jL, where j denotes the nominal interest rate on bank loans and L the nominal stock of loans. Formally, net profits are determined as

$$Q = PY - wN - \delta PK - jL.$$

The gross and the net profit rate on capital are derived by dividing gross, as well as net profits by the numéraire PK. The gross profit rate r_g is given by

$$r_g = \frac{PY}{PK} - \frac{wN}{PK} - \frac{\delta PK}{PK} = u(1-v) - \delta,$$

where $v = wN/(PY)$ denotes the wage share with respect to gross nominal product[1] which is treated as a parameter in the model which increases e.g. if nominal wages rise, or in case of a negative shock to labour productivity Y/N. Furthermore, imperfect competition in goods markets is assumed, i.e. firms possess market power, implying that the wage share is less than gross nominal product; formally, it holds that $v < 1$. The net profit rate r, or just *the* profit rate, is given by

$$r = \frac{PY}{PK} - \frac{wN}{PK} - \frac{\delta PK}{PK} - \frac{jL}{PK} = u(1-v) - \delta - j\lambda, \tag{4.2}$$

where $\lambda = L/(PK)$ is the debt-asset ratio relating the stock of loans outstanding to the capital stock valued at replacement costs.

The supply side of the model is represented by a simplified Phillips curve given by

$$\hat{p} = \psi(\underset{+}{u - u^*}), \tag{4.3}$$

stating that capacity utilization which exceeds the "natural full employment level" of capacity utilization, being defined as $u^* > 0$, causes inflation, and a situation $u < u^*$ deflation. This definition of the price level's growth rate neglects inflation or deflation expectations since they are incorporated in the expected profit rate on capital being derived in detail below. Furthermore, the direct influence of the exchange rate's growth rate $\hat{s}$ on $\hat{p}$ is neglected. This assumption can be justified by the fact that industrial countries like the U.S. or the Euro area can be considered as rather closed economies, and that the influence of exchange rate variations via imported inputs can be neglected. However, an indirect influence of $\hat{s}$ on $\hat{p}$ is incorporated in the model by the fact that an increase in $\hat{s}$ leads, according to equation 4.1, to an increase in net exports and therefore, to an increase in capacity utilization increasing $\hat{p}$ according to equation 4.3.

4.2 The Financial Side

4.2.1 A Stylized Financial Structure

A simplified and stylized financial structure of an industrialized economy can be described by the economy-wide balance sheets in figure 4.1. There are six types of agents in the

[1]Note that $\frac{wN}{PK}\frac{PY}{PY} = \frac{wN}{PY}\frac{PY}{PK} = vu.$

economy: households, firms, government, banks, the central bank and foreign agents. Though there has been a substantial movement towards disintermediation in the last decade, banks still dominate the financial system of industrialized countries regarding the allocation of capital between savers and investors by bank loans.[2]

Households

Deposits	D	Net Worth	NW_{HH}
Domestic Government Bonds	$P_{BD} B_{DH}$		
Foreign Government Bonds	$s\, P_{BF} B_{FH}$		
Equities	$P_E E_H$		

Banks

Deposits at Central Bank *(Required Reserves)*	$D_{BA}(=\tau D)$	Deposits	D
Loans to Firms	L		
Equities	$P_E E_B$		
Domestic Government Bonds	$P_{BD} B_{DB}$	Net Worth	NW_{BA}

Firms

Capital Stock *(Valued at Demand Price of Capital)*	$P_K K$	Loans from Banks	L
		Equities	$P_E(E_H+E_B)$

Central Bank

Domestic Credit Component	H	Deposits of Commercial Banks *(Required Reserves, Interest-Free Bank Reserves)*	D_{BA}
			$=M$ *(High-Powered Money)*

Government

Net Worth *(Negative)*	NW_{Gov}	Domestic Government Bonds	$P_{BD}(B_{DB}+B_{DH})$

Figure 4.1: Stylized Financial Structure in Industrial Countries

There are seven sorts of assets being held by economic agents. The first sort are deposits conventionally held by households with banks. The second sort are domestic government bonds which are held by domestic households and banks. Foreign government bonds which constitute asset sort three are held only by households. Domestic and foreign government bonds are imperfect substitutes since domestic bonds are assumed to bear a risk premium reflecting the country's risk of default. Firms' capital stock, constituting asset type four, is partly financed by the issuance of equities, being asset sort five, which are held by households and banks. Commercial paper and corporate bond markets are neglected for reasons of simplicity, implying that credit is solely supplied by bank loans to firms, constituting asset type six, in order to finance the remaining part of the capital stock. Asset type seven is high powered money issued by the central bank, and held by commercial banks in the form of required reserves; in order to simplify the model, excess reserves held by banks are neglected. The central bank does not hold foreign reserves due to the flexible exchange rate system.

Assets and debts are priced at their current market or discounted present values, i.e. there is no distinction between book and market values. The real stock of bonds is

[2]For empirical data, see Mishkin (2000), p. 391.

denoted as B_{xx}, where the first subscript denotes whether bonds are Domestic or Foreign, and the second one denotes whether they are held by Households or by Banks. The real stock of equities is denoted as E_x, where the subscript denotes whether equities are held by Households or by Banks. The entire real stocks of equities and domestic government bonds are given as $E = E_H + E_B$ and $B = B_{DH} + B_{DB}$. Since bonds and equities are traded in official markets, they are quoted at their market prices P_{xx} denoting the price of one real unit of bonds or equities in domestic or foreign currency, where the first subscript describes whether it concerns the price of Bonds or Equities; the second subscript distinguishes between Domestic or Foreign bond prices. Bond prices are inversely related to their interest rates. Nominal market values of equity and bond holdings are $P_E E_x$ and $P_{Bx} B_{xx}$. Foreign bonds are denoted in foreign currency, and stocks are multiplied by the exchange rate s.

Households hold their nominal net worth NW_{HH} in the form of deposits D, domestic government bonds $P_{DB} B_{DH}$, foreign government bonds $sP_{FB} B_{FH}$ and equities $P_E E_H$.

Firms finance the capital stock by issuing equities E and taking loans L from banks. It is assumed firstly, that equities cannot be traded internationally due to information asymmetries, and secondly, that the stock of equities E does not vary in the short run, implying that new investment is financed internally by retained earnings, and predominantly externally by taking new loans which is highly compatible with the "credit view" of macroeconomic activity. The market value of the capital stock $P_K K$, where P_K denotes the demand price of capital[3], is evaluated via the equity market and the amount of bank loans. As a result, the demand price of capital can be simply derived from firms' balance sheet identity as

$$P_K = \frac{L + P_E E}{K}.$$

This definition assumes a zero net worth of firms, i.e. the equity price adjusts to bring the stock market into equilibrium.[4]

Banks act as intermediaries between investors and savers. They create deposits as a multiple of the domestic credit component H, being equal to high powered money M (monetary base), and supply loans to firms. Since cash is excluded from the model, demand for high powered money by commercial banks, being held as deposits at the central bank D_{BA}, stems from a required reserve ratio τ controlled by monetary authorities, being reflected in the money multiplier $m = 1/\tau$, where it holds that $D_{BA} = H = \frac{1}{m} D$.[5] In an environment of financial liberalization and deregulation of domestic and international

[3]For a definition of the demand price of capital, see appendix A.

[4]This assumption can be found, for example, in Taylor (1985) and in Franke and Semmler (1994), whereas Taylor and O'Connell (1985) explicitly assume nonzero net worth because they argue that large outstanding levels of corporate net worth appear to be characteristic of modern capitalism. Allowing for net worth of firms would call for the introduction of an additional asset market equation, one determining P_K and the other one P_E. After having determined the demand price and the equity price, net worth could be determined by the balance sheet identity. However, allowing for firms' net worth in the model would not change the basic results, and is therefore neglected.

[5]A more sophisticated model which attaches greater weight on the money supply process should endogenize the money multiplier m by the introduction of excess reserves, as for example in Bernanke and Blinder (1988). However, endogenizing m does not change the model results significantly, and is neglected for reasons of simplicity.

capital markets, banks are also assumed to be allowed to hold corporate equities[6] and government bonds. Though banks are allowed to engage in active asset management, empirical data show that banks' business is dominated by creating deposits and loans.[7] Banks are assumed not to take loans in foreign currency.[8] Banks' adding-up constraint

$$(1-\tau)D + NW_{Ba} - P_E E_B - P_{DB} B_{DB} = L, \qquad \text{where} \qquad \tau D = D_{BA} = H,$$

shows that banks' inputs consist of deposits adjusted for required reserves, plus banks' net worth NW_{Ba}, less equity and bond holdings, which are used for the creation of loans.

The domestic and the foreign government issue bonds, held by households and banks, to finance their budget deficits. The market value of domestic bonds amounts to $P_{DB}B$, and the market value of foreign bonds, denoted in foreign currency, $sP_{BF}B_{FH}$. The stocks of domestic and foreign government bonds are treated as exogenous in the model. The domestic government does not own any assets, resulting in a negative net worth, i.e. $NW_{Gov} < 0$.

Monetary policy takes the form of controlling the domestic credit component H and the required reserve ratio τ. The central bank does not use the exchange rate as a policy tool, i.e. there are no interventions in the foreign exchange market.

Private domestic wealth W_P (central bank and government excluded), which is determined by consolidating the balance sheets of households, firms and banks in figure 4.1, is given by

$$W_P = NW_{HH} + NW_{BA} = P_{DB}B + sP_{FB}B_{FH} + H + P_K K,$$

that is, by the sum of households' and banks' net worth, consisting of domestic government bonds, foreign government bonds, base money and the nominal value of the capital stock since inside debt (loans and deposits) cancels out. Overall domestic wealth W, i.e. the sum of households', government's and banks' net worth, being determined by consolidating all entries in figure 4.1, is formally given by

$$W = NW_{HH} + NW_{BA} + NW_{Gov} = sP_{FB}B_{FH} + H + P_K K,$$

i.e. by the sum of foreign government bonds, base money, and the nominal value of the capital stock.

4.2.2 Financial Market Equilibria

Economic models emphasizing the influence of balance sheet positions on aggregate economic activity generally use a standardized portfolio technique to determine asset prices and their influence on real sector variables. According to this standardized portfolio approach along the lines of Tobin and Brainard (1968), Tobin (1969), Tobin and Buiter

[6]For example, Japanese banks' portfolios contain large fractions of equities, making them very vulnerable to stock market volatility.

[7]Empirical data for the U.S. banking system can be found e.g. in Mishkin (2000), p. 422, or in various issues of the Federal Reserve Bulletin.

[8]Generally, in the wake of global financial deregulation and liberalization, banking sectors of reserve currency countries grant loans in domestic currency to emerging market and transition economies. Problems evolving from foreign debt in emerging market and transition economies are discussed in chapter 5.

(1980), Taylor (1983, 1991), Franke and Semmler (1994, 1999), Frankel (1995), and Semmler (2003), private wealth, which is only held by households, is determined in a first step by consolidating balance sheets of all sectors except for the government and the central bank in order to eliminate inside debt, as e.g. bank loans or deposits. In a second step, households' asset excess demand functions are specified as a function of households' net worth and asset returns; all asset excess demand functions add up to households' net worth. Finally, in a third step, asset market equilibria, which determine asset returns and the behaviour of real sector variables, are specified by households' asset excess demand functions, and by asset supply stocks which are often assumed to be exogenous.

Though this standardized portfolio approach is a highly sophisticated tool to model the complex financial sphere of an economy, an application to the present financial model structure given in figure 4.1, which is predominantly designed to explain the evolution of financial crises, would be inappropriate for two reasons. Firstly, standardized portfolio approaches, as described above, assume that wealth is entirely held by households. Financial crises however, are characterized in most cases by net worth deficiencies and illiquidity of sectors other than households, which requires to consider not only households' net worth. If one follows the standard theoretical, as well as empirical literature on financial crises, especially net worth positions of the firm and the banking sector are important for the explanation of financial distress which do not exist by definition in a standardized portfolio approach. Secondly, standard approaches do not consider explicitly debt structures of different sectors, as e.g. firms' and banks' debt-asset ratio, since inside debt generally cancels out by consolidating private sector's balance sheets. Accordingly, as to standardized portfolio techniques, an economy's debt structure is assumed to be determined predominantly from households' portfolio decisions and not by the interaction of the firm and the financial sector. Yet, empirical data have shown that especially the debt-structure and the liquidity status of firms and banks, resulting on the one hand from firms' investment decisions, and on the other hand from financial intermediaries' risk perceptions as to the expansion of credit, play a dominant role in the propagation of financial crises. In order to overcome these drawbacks of standard portfolio techniques, the financial structure given in figure 4.1 is transformed into four financial market equilibria equations, containing all seven sorts of assets, as in an extended IS-LM model, where banks' and firms' liquidity and solvency status is explicitly considered. As opposed to standard portfolio techniques, the resulting financial market equilibria equations do not correspond exactly to the financial structure given in figure 4.1, but represent a realistic approximation with special emphasis on liquidity and net worth positions.

The equilibrium condition in the market for deposits normalized by the numéraire PK reads as

$$m\,h = d(\underset{+}{u}, \underset{-}{\hat{p}}, \underset{-}{i - \hat{p}}, \underset{-}{r + \rho}), \tag{4.4}$$

where the left hand side denotes deposit supply by banks, and the right hand side deposit demand by households. Deposit supply by banks is a multiple of normalized base money $h = H/(PK)$, where $m = 1/\tau$ denotes the money multiplier. The term $1/h = PK/H$ is the "velocity" of base money with respect to the nominal value of the capital stock. Normalized deposit demand $d(\cdot) = D(\cdot)/PK$ by households is assumed to arise from two main sources. Firstly, since cash is excluded from the model, deposit demand stems from transaction purposes depending positively on capacity utilization u. Secondly, according to the financial structure given in figure 4.1, deposits are a part of households' net worth

NW_{HH} which can be split among deposits, equities, domestic and foreign government bonds. Accordingly, as to portfolio considerations, deposit demand varies positively with its own return, and negatively with the returns of other assets. Since deposits are assumed to bear no interest, the real return of holding deposits is negatively dependent on the price level's growth rate $\hat{p}$. Hence, ceteris paribus, households flee from deposits in case of inflation and increase deposit demand in case of deflation. The negative dependence of deposit demand $d(\cdot)$ on the real interest rate on domestic government bonds $i - \hat{p}$, where i denotes the nominal interest rate on domestic government bonds which is determined by the nominal interest rate on foreign government bonds i^* according to a risk adjusted interest rate parity condition being anaylized below, can be interpreted as the traditional "speculative" demand for money or deposits, respectively. The negative dependence of $d(\cdot)$ on the expected profit rate $r^e = r + \rho$ on capital, being equivalent to the expected return of holding equities, where ρ denotes the "state of confidence" representing the difference between the expected and the actual profit rate, states that households shift their portfolios from deposits into equities in case the expected profit rate increases.

The formation of profit expectations is assumed to cover the entire time horizon of capital goods' life cycle. Consequently, the state of confidence parameter ρ represents the state of long-term profit expectations which can be interpreted as an expected average value over a longer time horizon reflecting investors' "animal spirits" which can vary substantially over the business cycle.[9] In case the state of confidence is positive, i.e. $\rho > 0$, agents expect a higher profit rate in the future than today's actual profit rate, i.e. it holds that $r^e > r$. In case the state of confidence is negative, i.e. $\rho < 0$, agents expect a lower profit rate in the future than today's actual profit rate, i.e. it holds that $r^e < r$. In case the state of confidence is zero, i.e. $\rho = 0$, agents expect the actual profit rate to prevail in the future, i.e. it holds that $r^e = r$.[10] This long-term view on profit expectations explicitly takes into consideration that capital goods are long living and often irreversible, implying that investment is not only exposed to "normal" risk which can be captured by some objective or subjective probability distributions, but is additionally exposed to some "real" risk which cannot be foreseen and which is also very volatile over the business cycle. This kind of uncertainty as to the formation of expectations in the present model implies the invalidity of the rational expectations hypothesis in its strict form at least in the short-run, since the application of the rational expectations in the present case would not allow profit expectations to differ from the actual profit rate except for the case of random, exogenous shocks. However, in order to describe business cycles, as well as financial crises as expectations-driven events, business confidence has to vary

[9]Explaining business cycle fluctuations predominantly by variations of expectations and business confidence has a long tradition in economic theory. The asymmetry of the upswing and the downswing, i.e. steady improving real and financial variables during the upturn, and sudden reversals first in financial, and then in real variables at the beginning of the downturn, is generally explained by the instability of business confidence as emphasized e.g. by Hawtrey ((1926) 1950), Keynes (1936), Lavington (1921) and Minsky (1972, 1975, 1977, 1978, 1980b, 1982a, 1982b, 1986). For this overview see also Flaschel, Franke and Semmler (1997), p. 421. For a more general overview of the role of business confidence during different stages of the business cycles, see Boyd and Blatt (1988).

[10]For the use of the state of confidence as one of the driving forces of the business cycle and financial crises in economic theory, see e.g. Keynes (1936), p. 158, Minsky (1978), Semmler and Franke (1994), Flaschel, Franke and Semmler (1997), chapter 12, Taylor and O'Connell (1985), Taylor (1991), chapters 5 and 6.

considerably over the business cycle, since otherwise, business cycles and financial crises would be modelled as events induced by random exogenous shocks and not by endogenous mechanisms.[11] In the following analysis, the state of confidence ρ is going to be one of the main driving forces of business cycles and financial crises, being treated as a parameter in the comparative-static analysis, and as an endogenous variable in the dynamic version of the model.

Though households are assumed to adjust deposit demand $d(\cdot)$ inversely to variations in the price level's growth rate $\hat{p}$ due to the direct negative influence of the real return on deposits, the overall impact on deposit demand is not clear due to an indirect, but counteracting force by the real interest rate on domestic government bonds $i - \hat{p}$. For example, in case of inflation, households reduce on the one hand deposit demand owing to the direct effect of $\hat{p}$ on $d(\cdot)$, but at the same time increase deposit demand due to the indirect but positive effect of a decreasing real interest rate on government bonds $i-\hat{p}$ on $d(\cdot)$. Though the theoretical as well as the empirical literature is not very clear about the overall influence of the price level's growth rate on deposit demand, denoted as $\partial d/\partial \hat{p}_a$ in the model, it is assumed that the overall impact of $\hat{p}$ on u is positive, i.e. households reduce their money holdings in case of deflation and increase money holdings in case of inflation. Formally, it holds that

$$\frac{\partial d}{\partial \hat{p}_a} = \frac{\partial d}{\partial \hat{p}} + \frac{\partial d}{\partial (i-\hat{p})}\frac{\partial (i-\hat{p})}{\partial \hat{p}} = \frac{\partial d}{\partial \hat{p}} - \frac{\partial d}{\partial (i-\hat{p})} > 0,$$

stating that the indirect influence of $i - \hat{p}$ on $d(\cdot)$ is larger than the direct influence of $\hat{p}$ on $d(\cdot)$.

The international market for government bonds is characterized by imperfect capital mobility due to the existence of a risk premium rp on domestic government bonds, implying a divergence from uncovered interest parity (UIP). Assuming the absence of capital controls and instantaneous portfolio adjustments, equilibrium in the international market for government bonds is given by risk adjusted UIP, formally

$$i = i^* + \hat{s}^e + rp,$$

stating that the nominal domestic government bond rate i equals the nominal foreign government bond rate i^*, adjusted for expected exchange rate changes $\hat{s}^e = \dot{s}^e/s$, and for the risk premium rp. The risk premium rp is assumed to reflect on the one hand domestic government bonds' risk of default, but, on the other hand, also a general country risk premium since financial distress in the private sector, caused by real or financial disruptions, leads to financial problems (illiquidity or even insolvency) in the government sector. For example, private sector induced financial distress in the government sector can be caused by extraordinary expenditures resulting from bailing out troubled financial intermediaries by capital injections, or from compensating depositors being covered by deposit insurance systems. Furthermore, in case of private sector financial distress, tax revenues are subject to sharp declines leading very quickly to liquidity problems of the government.

[11] A critical assessment of the model results in comparison with standard business cycle and financial crises theories with special emphasis on the controversy over their exogenous or endogenous nature is outlined in chapters 4.5 and 4.6.

Regarding the determinants of exchange rate expectations and risk premia, standard macroeconomic models often assume them to be exogenous variables or parameters. Yet, financial crises are characterized by sudden and large changes both in the exchange rate's expected growth rate and in the risk premium, being caused by a sudden revelation of aggregate financial distress stemming from adverse real or financial sector problems. Thus, as opposed to standard models, the explanation of financial crises has to consider both $\hat{s}^e$ and rp as endogenous variables depending on real and/or financial sector variables. Owing to the existence of imperfect foresight in the present model, exchange rate expectations and risk assessments are subject to the same uncertainty as profit expectations, since future exchange rate movements or changes in country risk are determined by future real and financial sector developments which cannot be foreseen perfectly. As a result, the formation of exchange rate expectations and risk assessments cannot be modelled according to the rational expectations hypothesis, but have to rely on other determinants. Since rational expectations cannot be applied in the present case, and the theoretical as well as the empirical literature is not very clear about the factors determining exchange rates and risk premia, the model assumes that changes in $\hat{s}^e$, as well as in rp are determined by the state of confidence parameter ρ representing a "catch all" variable, providing information for the "strength" or "weakness" of the domestic economy's financial status. Modelling $\hat{s}^e$ and rp as dependent variables of ρ implies that domestic and foreign investors have the same interpretation of ρ. If $\rho > 0$, domestic and foreign investors believe in the "strength" of the domestic economy, leading on the one hand to a reduction in the risk premium due to expected improvements in the overall liquidity and solvency status of the private and the government sector, and on the other hand to depreciation expectations of the exchange rate in the long-run due to increasing credibility in the domestic currency, being based on the belief that a high performance country yields either future current account surpluses due to high profitability (which can compensate current current account deficits), or enjoys large capital inflows leading to a future capital account surplus. If on the other hand, $\rho < 0$, domestic and foreign investors are very pessimistic about the performance of the domestic economy, leading to an increase in the risk premium and to devaluation expectations due to lacking credibility in the domestic currency, based on the belief that low profitability leads to future current account deficits and to capital account deficits caused by capital outflows. As a result, risk adjusted UIP can be formulated as

$$i = i^* + \beta(\underset{-}{\rho}), \tag{4.5}$$

stating that in case $\rho > 0$, implying $\beta(\rho) < 0$ (lower or even negative risk premium and depreciation expectations of the exchange rate), it holds that $i < i^*$, in case $\rho < 0$, implying $\beta(\rho) > 0$ (higher positive risk premium and appreciation expectations of the exchange rate), it holds that $i > i^*$, and in case $\rho = 0$, implying $\beta(\rho) = 0$, it holds that $i = i^*$.

Equity market equilibrium determining share prices P_E can be formally described by the condition

$$P_E E = E^d(\underset{-}{u}, \underset{+}{\hat{p}}, \underset{-}{i - \hat{p}}, \underset{+}{r + \rho}),$$

where the right hand side represents the nominal demand for equities $E^d(\cdot)$, and the left hand side the supply or the market value of equities, where the nominal stock of equities E is assumed to be constant. Nominal demand for equities E^d can be assumed to be predominantly influenced by households' portfolio choices, i.e. by the same determinants as households' demand for deposits in equation 4.4. As a result, nominal demand for equities can be modelled as being negatively dependent on capacity utilization, positively dependent on the inflation rate, negatively dependent on the real interest rate on bonds, and positively dependent on the expected profit rate. The level of share prices P_E is of special importance in the model since aggregate investment is assumed to depend on general stock market conditions according to Tobin's q theory of investment[12]. Tobin's q in its original version is defined as the ratio of the market value of existing capital goods valued at the demand price of capital P_K to reproduction costs of new capital goods valued at the supply price of capital being equivalent to the general price level P, i.e. it holds that $q = P_K/P$. General stock market conditions, i.e. the level of share prices P_E, and the level of Tobin's q are linked by firms' balance sheet identity according to figure 4.1, defining the demand price of capital as $P_K = (L + P_E E)/K$ under the assumption of zero net worth of firms. According to this definition, the demand price of capital P_K is determined by the stock of loans L, by the nominal stock of equities E, by the equity price P_E, and by the real value of the capital stock K. However, since the nominal stock of equities E and the real capital stock K are assumed to be constant, and the nominal stock of loans L is treated as a parameter, the equity price P_E can be implicitly determined by the the demand price of capital P_K. Consequently, equity market market equilibrium and share prices P_E can be subsumed under the equilibrium condition in the market for real capital determining the demand price of capital P_K.[13] Formally, the equilibrium condition in the market for real capital can be stated as

$$P_K K = K^d(\underset{-}{u}, \underset{+}{\hat{p}}, \underset{-}{i - \hat{p}}, \underset{+}{r + \rho}),$$

where the left hand side represents the capital stock valued at the demand price of capital implying thereby a certain market value of equities, and the right hand side the nominal demand for the real capital stock $K^d(\cdot)$ implicitly containing the demand for equities. Since the demand for equities corresponds to the demand for real capital, nominal demand for real capital $K^d(\cdot)$ depends on the same variables as equity demand $E^d(\cdot)$. Dividing both sides of the real capital market equilibrium by the numéraire PK yields a modified equation determining Tobin's q as

$$q = \frac{P_K}{P} = \frac{1}{PK} K^d(\underset{-}{u}, \underset{-}{\hat{p}}, \underset{-}{i - \hat{p}}, \underset{+}{r + \rho}).$$

This version of Tobin's q however, is only of limited applicability to the present model owing to additional partial derivatives whose magnitudes in relation to other partial derivatives can be only specified by restrictive assumptions. In contrast to the equilibrium condition in the market for real capital, Tobin's q can be determined alternatively in a much simpler way along the lines of Tobin's original version (see appendix A) as the ratio

[12]See appendix A for a detailed discussion on Tobin's q-theory of investment.

[13]This procedure, as e.g. applied by Tobin (1969), has been chosen for reasons of simplicity since the explicit consideration of both the market for equities and the market for real capital would have called for an additional asset market equation, and for the explicit consideration of firms' net worth. For an explicit consideration of the equity market equilibrium, see Taylor and O'Connell (1985), Semmler and Franke (1994), and Flaschel, Franke and Semmler (1997).

of the gross profit rate on capital to a risk adjusted real interest rate investors demand for holding capital assets. In the present model, the "gross" version of Tobin's q_g could be expressed as

$$q_g = \frac{r_g + \rho}{j - \hat{p}},$$

stating that q_g is the ratio of the expected gross profit rate to the real interest rate on bank loans (to be determined below) which constitutes the risk adjusted interest rate banks demand for granting loans being invested in capital assets by firms. The correct version of Tobin's q would call for the use of the expected real interest rate on bank loans, which would require the introduction of inflation expectations. Still, it can be shown in the dynamic analysis that expectations regarding the change of the price level are already incorporated in the state of confidence parameter ρ. The gross version of Tobin's q however, is only of limited interest for the present model since it does not consider firms' debt-asset structure by neglecting external finance costs, i.e. the liquidity as well as solvency position of firms are assumed not to have any influence on the market valuation of the capital stock. Thus, taking explicitly into consideration firms' financial structure containing interest payments on debt requires the use of the expected *net* profit rate $r + \rho$, transforming the original "gross" version of Tobin's q into a "net" version being expressed as

$$q = \frac{r + \rho}{j - \hat{p}}.$$

For reasons of analytical tractability, this net version of Tobin's q can be restated in a much simpler linearized form[14], being used in the present model as

$$q = r + \rho - (j - \hat{p}). \tag{4.6}$$

This net version of Tobin's q is both an indicator for the liquidity position and for the solvency position of business firms. The liquidity status of the firm sector is measured via the influence of r on q. Illiquidity in the present model would mean that earnings fall short of expenses, causing r to become negative and causing q to decrease, or even to become negative as well. Liquidity problems can emanate both from negative real sector shocks and from financial market disruptions. Negative real sector shocks, as e.g. a large drop in capacity utilization u caused by a sudden drop in aggregate demand, lead to a large drop in earnings and in r, causing Tobin's q to fall. By way of contrast, negative financial market shocks, indicated by a sharp increase in the loan rate j, lead on the one hand to an indirect reduction in q via a reduction in r due to rising debt costs, and on the other hand, to a direct reduction in q via an increase in j. The solvency status is directly measured by the level of Tobin's q, i.e. by the level of the demand price of capital P_K at a given price level P. Solvency difficulties arise from a decreasing demand price of capital P_K (for a given P), i.e. from decreasing equity prices. In case the capital stock valued at the demand price of capital falls short of the nominal value of loans L the firm sector is bankrupt.[15] Tobin's q also shows that solvency problems, i.e. a fall in q, can arise from liquidity problems, i.e. from a drop in r, from sharp drops

[14] For the use of a linearized version of Tobin's q, see e.g. Taylor and O'Connell (1985), and Taylor (1991), chapters 5 and 6.

[15] According to the financial structure given in figure 4.1, this definition of bankruptcy, i.e. negative net worth, corresponds to a theoretical situation with negative equity prices being not possible in reality.

in long-term expectations ρ, and from declines in $\hat{p}$ (especially in deflationary periods), all factors causing q to fall. Liquidity problems stemming from solvency problems cannot be directly derived from the definition of Tobin's q and require an explicit consideration of the transmission mechanisms between the real and financial sphere of the economy. For example, a sudden drop in the state of confidence ρ leading quickly to solvency problems, i.e. to a fall in q, lead with a time lag to a fall in aggregate demand via a reduction in investment demand according to equation 4.1, causing liquidity problems by reduced earnings and a declining profit rate r, deteriorating solvency problems by a further reduction in q. As a result, once solvency and liquidity problems come into being, they tend to reinforce themselves by a cumulative downward process. By way of contrast, improving solvency and liquidity positions lead to a cumulative upward trend with steady increasing stock market valuations and ameliorating liquidity positions. Summing up, liquidity and solvency problems indicated by a drop of Tobin's q can be caused by a fall in r, a fall in ρ, an increase in j or by a fall in $\hat{p}$. Since changes in r, ρ, j and $\hat{p}$ alter the liquidity and the solvency status of the firm sector, Tobin's q also has a deep influence on credit market conditions. According to the theory of imperfect capital markets, business firms' access to credit market depends crucially on the collateral value measured by the capital stock valued at the demand price of capital, and on their general liquidity position. Consequently, Tobin's q is also an important indicator for relaxing or tightening credit market conditions.

Apart from being an indicator for liquidity, solvency, and credit market conditions, Tobin's q, in its form as the sole determinant of the investment function by equation 4.1, also captures the fact that investment decisions in the model both have a medium-run and a long-run perspective. The medium-run perspective may relate e.g. to a time period of up to three years in reality, whereas the long-run perspective refers to the entire lifetime of capital. In the medium-run, investment demand is assumed to be mainly determined by overall goods market demand, because firms attempt to have a "normal" capacity utilization. A positive dependence of investment on capacity utilization calls for an accelerator type investment function which is reflected in the model by the indirect positive effect of capacity utilization on Tobin's q via a positive effect on the profit rate. That is, higher capacity utilization u leads to an increase in the profit rate r by equation 4.2, inducing a rise in Tobin's q by equation 4.6, and a further rise in capacity utilization u via an increase in investment demand $\eta(q)$ according to equation 4.1. As a result, this medium-run perspective on the investment function also reflects the fact that the model is subject to self-reinforcing upward and downward processes in the real and in the financial sector. The long-run perspective on investment demand is represented by a positive dependence of investment demand on the "state of confidence" parameter ρ via Tobin's q, reflecting long-run profit expectations which are going to be endogenized in the dynamic version of the model, and leading to endogenous business cycles due to accelerations and

However, in practice, economic units are often defined as bankrupt in case net worth falls below some positive lower limit which corresponds to positive or zero equity prices being a realistic scenario. In terms of the model, there is no exact definition of bankruptcy in terms of equity prices since the equity market has been subsumed under the market for real capital. One possible definition of bankruptcy which is used in the following, corresponding to negative net worth in reality, is a negative value of the linearized version of Tobin's q according to equation 4.6 in case the expected profit rate falls short of the real loan rate, i.e. in case it holds that $r + \rho < j - \hat{p}$, implying $q < 0$.

decelerations of the inherent cumulative processes during different stages of the business cycle.[16]

The explicit consideration of the loan market is consistent with "credit view" of macroeconomic activity. In its strict version, the credit view assumes that monetary policy is able to influence the availability of bank loans directly and instantaneously. Nevertheless, loans are generally designed as medium-term or even long-term contracts which cannot be adjusted instantly.[17] Taking into consideration that the entire stock of loans can be adjusted only with some time lags, it is assumed that the stock of loans L, or in terms of the numéraire, the debt-asset ratio $\lambda = L/(PK)$, is predetermined in the short run. As a result, banks are assumed to satisfy, at least in the short-run, completely loan demand by firms L^d which is equivalent to the current stock of loans L, i.e. it holds that $L^d = L$. In terms of the numéraire, firms' "warranted" or demanded debt-asset ratio λ^d is equivalent to the actual debt-asset ratio λ which is satisfied by banks, i.e. it holds that $\lambda^d = \lambda$. In terms of the model, the fact that the stock of loans is predetermined in the short-run and can be only adjusted with some time lags, is considered by treating the debt-asset ratio λ as a parameter in the comparative-static version of the model, whereas the long-run dynamic analysis allows for changes in the debt-asset ratio by endogenizing λ, where banks have a strong influence on the stock of loans.

The fact that banks are assumed to satisfy entire demand for loans of firms at least in the short-run does not imply that banks' loan supply L^s is only dependent on firms' loan demand. By way of contrast, banks' supply of loans L^s, or in terms of the numéraire, banks' "warranted" supply of the debt-asset ratio λ^s, depends on various determinants in the model which are going to be analyzed below. Consequently, the equilibrium condition in the loan market in terms of nominal loan values reads as

$$L = L^s,$$

where the left hand side denotes the current stock of loans L, being equivalent to firms' loan demand L^d, and the right hand side the warranted supply of loans by banks L^s. Dividing both sides of the equilibrium condition by the numéraire PK, and considering explicitly loan supply determinants, yields the loan market equilibrium in terms of the debt-asset ratio as

$$\lambda = \lambda^s(\underset{+}{mh}, \underset{+}{j - \hat{p}}, \underset{+}{q}, \underset{-}{\alpha}), \tag{4.7}$$

where $\lambda^s(\cdot) = L^s(\cdot)/(PK)$ is the "warranted supply of the debt-asset ratio" by banks, and λ the actual or demanded debt-asset ratio by firms. According to equilibrium condition 4.7, banks' warranted supply of the debt-asset ratio $\lambda^s(\cdot)$ is assumed to depend on four determinants. Firstly, according to money multiplier theory, $\lambda^s(\cdot)$ is positively dependent on the the amount of normalized deposits mh.[18] Secondly, normalized loan supply $\lambda^s(\cdot)$ is positively dependent on the real interest rate on bank loans $j - \hat{p}$ because a higher loan rate on an existing level of loans increases banks' profits. Thirdly, normalized loan

[16]For a similar type of investment function, see Flaschel, Franke and Semmler (1997), chapter 12.

[17]Even credit lines which can be adjusted each day as stipulated, can be viewed as a, at least, medium-term financial agreement.

[18]The influence of the deposit amount on the loan amount, as well as its theoretical foundation can be found in almost every textbook on monetary macroeconomics. See e.g. Bofinger, Reichle, Schächter (1996), or Jarchow (1998), chapters III.2 and III.3.

supply depends positively on Tobin's q, reflecting firms' liquidity and collateral position and being an indicator for firms' risk of default. Furthermore, Tobin's q is also used as an indicator for banks' solvency and liquidity position which are important determinants for overall loan supply according to national and international regulation standards, as e.g. the Basel II agreement which requires each bank to assess the risk of each individual debt and asset contract, obliging it to provide sufficient collateral in the form of net worth depending on the degree of risk. Thus, deteriorating liquidity and solvency positions among firms require a higher net worth of banks which, in times of recessions, can be only achieved by withdrawing risky loans, leading very often to illiquidity and insolvency of debtors, and further deteriorating the aggregate liquidity and solvency status. As a result, the liquidity and solvency dependent availability of credit tends to accelerate upswings as well as downswings by a procyclical variation in the amount of credit, being designated as the financial accelerator mechanism which has been described in section 2.2.2.2. Approximating banks' liquidity and solvency position by firms' Tobin's q can be justified by the fact that the liquidity and solvency position of firms, which is heavily influenced by the interest rate on loans j, determine the amount of non-performing loans, and thereby banks' profits, liquidity and solvency. Furthermore, since banks are allowed, in the wake of global financial liberalization, to hold more risky assets like e.g. equities, gains and losses in the market for real capital influencing banks' net worth can be captured by Tobin's q. Summing up, a rising Tobin's q coincides with rising net worth and liquidity positions of banks, leading to an increase in the supply of loans. Fourthly, the intensity of financial market regulation (interest rate caps or quotas on the loan supply, etc.) determines the amount of loans supply which is captured by a negative dependence of $\lambda^s(\cdot)$ on parameter α, i.e. deeper financial market regulation is indicated by an increase in α lowering normalized loan supply λ^s.

Loan market equilibrium is assumed to be achieved by variations in the nominal loan rate j. For example, a larger amount of deposits mh caused by expansionary monetary policy, an increase in q caused by an increase in the state of confidence ρ, or a decrease in the regulation parameter α cause an excess supply of loans leading to a decrease in the price of loans j, and thereby to a reduction in the supply of loans until the market is in equilibrium again.

4.3 Short-Run Comparative-Static Analysis

4.3.1 General Results

The macromodel consists of equations 4.1 to 4.7, containing seven endogenous variables $\hat{s}, q, j, \hat{p}, r, u, i$ and eight parameters $\lambda, \rho, m, h, v, \delta, \alpha, i^*$. Finding the partial derivatives of all endogenous variables with respect to all parameters requires the transformation of the set of simultaneous equations into the following form

$$F^1(\hat{s}, q, j, \hat{p}, r, u, i; \lambda, \rho, m, h, v, \delta, \alpha, i^*) = 0$$
$$F^2(\hat{s}, q, j, \hat{p}, r, u, i; \lambda, \rho, m, h, v, \delta, \alpha, i^*) = 0$$
$$\dots\dots\dots\dots\dots\dots\dots\dots\dots\dots\dots\dots$$
$$F^7(\hat{s}, q, j, \hat{p}, r, u, i; \lambda, \rho, m, h, v, \delta, \alpha, i^*) = 0.$$

Transforming equations 4.1 to 4.7 into the required form yields the new system

$$F^1 = u - \eta(q) - g(i - \hat{p}) - nx(\hat{s} - \hat{p}) = 0 \quad (4.8)$$
$$F^2 = r - u(1 - v) + \delta + j\lambda = 0 \quad (4.9)$$
$$F^3 = \hat{p} - \psi(u - u^*) = 0 \quad (4.10)$$
$$F^4 = m\,h - d(u, \hat{p}, i - \hat{p}, r + \rho) = 0 \quad (4.11)$$
$$F^5 = i - i^* - \beta(\rho) = 0 \quad (4.12)$$
$$F^6 = q - r - \rho + j - \hat{p} = 0 \quad (4.13)$$
$$F^7 = \lambda - \lambda^s(m\,h, j - \hat{p}, q, \alpha) = 0 \quad (4.14)$$

Since not all functions are explicitly defined, one has to show firstly that the model can be solved in principle for all endogenous variables by using the implicit-function theorem. It can be shown that the system consisting of equations 4.8 to 4.14 satisfies the conditions of the implicit-function theorem, because (1) $F^1, \cdots, F^7$ have continuous derivatives (since all the component functions have continuous derivatives by assumptions) with respect to all endogenous variables and with respect to all parameters, and (2) the determinant of the Jacobian matrix with respect to all endogenous variables when evaluated at the initial equilibrium (which is assumed to exist), as well as elsewhere is nonzero, which is going to be examined below.

After having shown that the system can be solved in principle for all endogenous variables, even if it may be not possible to obtain the solution in an explicit form, the partial derivatives of system 4.8 to 4.14 can be found by solving the following system of simultaneous equations

$$\mathbf{J} \cdot \mathbf{v} = \mathbf{z}$$

for $\mathbf{v}$, where $\mathbf{J}$ denotes the Jacobian matrix of the system 4.8 to 4.14 with respect to all endogenous variables, $\mathbf{v}$ the vector of differentials of all endogenous variables, and $\mathbf{z}$ the vector of differentials with respect to all parameters. Explicitly defined, the system reads as

$$
\begin{bmatrix}
-nx_{\hat{s}-\hat{p}} & -\eta_q & 0 & -u_{\hat{p}_a} & 0 & 1 & -g_{i-\hat{p}} \\
0 & 0 & \lambda & 0 & 1 & v-1 & 0 \\
0 & 0 & 0 & 1 & 0 & -\psi_u & 0 \\
0 & 0 & 0 & -d_{\hat{p}_a} & -d_{r+\rho} & -d_u & -d_{i-\hat{p}} \\
0 & 0 & 0 & 0 & 0 & 0 & 1 \\
0 & 1 & 1 & -1 & -1 & 0 & 0 \\
0 & -\lambda^s_q & -\lambda^s_{j-\hat{p}} & \lambda^s_{j-\hat{p}} & 0 & 0 & 0
\end{bmatrix}
\cdot
\begin{bmatrix}
d\hat{s} \\ dq \\ dj \\ d\hat{p} \\ dr \\ du \\ di
\end{bmatrix}
=
\begin{bmatrix}
0 \\
-dv\, u - d\delta - d\lambda\, j \\
0 \\
-dm\, h - dh\, m + d\rho\, d_{r+\rho} \\
di^* + d\rho\, \beta_\rho \\
d\rho \\
-d\lambda + dm\, h\, \lambda^s_{mh} + dh\, m\, \lambda^s_{mh} + d\alpha\, \lambda^s_\alpha
\end{bmatrix}
\tag{4.15}
$$

where partial derivatives are denoted as $x_i = \partial x / \partial i$; for example, $\lambda^s_{j-\hat{p}} = \partial \lambda^s / \partial (j - \hat{p})$ denotes the partial derivative of λ^s with respect to $j - \hat{p}$.

The determinant of the Jacobian matrix of system 4.15 is given by

$$|\mathbf{J}| = -nx_{\hat{s}-\hat{p}}(d_{r+\rho}(\lambda^s_{j-\hat{p}} - \lambda^s_q)(-1 + v + \lambda\psi_u) - (\lambda^s_{j-\hat{p}} - (1+\lambda)\lambda^s_q)(d_u + d_{\hat{p}_a}\psi_u)).$$

The sign of the determinant can be shown to be positive under the following four assumptions. Firstly, banks' reaction on variations of the real interest rate on loans $j - \hat{p}$ with respect to loan supply is much larger than their reaction on variations of Tobin's q, formally $\lambda^s_{j-\hat{p}} \gg \lambda^s_q$. Taking into consideration firms' balance sheet identity having been normalized by the numéraire, and reading as

$$\frac{P_K K}{PK} = \frac{L + P_E E}{PK}$$
$$q = \lambda + \frac{P_E E}{PK},$$

it can be argued that an increase in the normalized collateral value q by a definite amount x, being e.g. caused by an increase in the equity price P_E, induces banks to increase the asset-debt ratio maximally by the same amount x implying that a value of $\lambda^s_q = 1$ is a realistic assumption, stating that loan supply can only be increased to that amount to which collateral increases. However, it is reasonable to assume that e.g. an increase in the real interest rate on bank loans of one percentage point increases banks' supply of loans more than one percent, i.e. a realistic value is $\lambda^s_{j-\hat{p}} \gg 1$. Secondly, a realistic value for the asset-debt ratio is $0 < \lambda < 1$. Values of $\lambda < 0$ are not possible because in that case firms own claims against the banking sector, whereas values of $\lambda > 1$ are possible, which are however ruled out since they correspond to bankruptcy of the entire firm sector which is a very unrealistic scenario. Thirdly, the reaction of inflation with respect to changes in capacity utilization is assumed to be a very small number $\psi_u \ll 1$ because an increase of one percent in capacity utilization leads only to a very small increase in inflation, being much lower than one percentage point. Fourthly, economic agents' reaction of money demand with respect to capacity utilization is assumed to be larger in absolute terms than their money demand reaction with respect to the expected profit rate, i.e. $|d_u| > |d_{r+\rho}|$. Using these assumptions and taking into consideration that $v < 1$, the signs of the different parts of the determinant of the Jacobian matrix are as follows

$$\lambda^s_{j-\hat{p}} - \lambda^s_q > 0, \quad \lambda^s_{j-\hat{p}} - (1+\lambda)\lambda^s_q > 0, \quad (-1+v+\lambda\psi_u) < 0, \quad (d_u + d_{\hat{p}_a}\psi_u) > 0,$$

resulting in

$$|(d_{r+\rho}(\lambda^s_{j-\hat{p}} - \lambda^s_q)(-1+v+\lambda\psi_u))| < |(\lambda^s_{j-\hat{p}} - (1+\lambda)\lambda^s_q)(d_u + d_{\hat{p}_a}\psi_u)|,$$

and thereby leading to a positive sign of the determinant of the Jacobian, i.e. it holds that

$$|\mathbf{J}| > 0.$$

The partial derivatives of all endogenous variables with respect to all parameters can be found by using Cramer's rule, or by finding the inverse matrix. Table 4.1 represents a synopsis of the signs of all partial derivatives. All partial derivatives are explicitly given in section 4.7.

Table 4.1: Signs of Qualitative Impact Effects on Temporary Variables

Response in	u	r	$\hat{p}$	q	j	i	$\hat{s}$
λ	-	-	-	-	+	0	$-^{\S}$
ρ	+	+	+	+	-	-	$+^{\S}$
h	+	+	+	+	-	0	$+^{\S}$
m	+	+	+	+	-	0	$+^{\S}$
α	-	-	-	-	+	0	-
i^*	+	+	+	+	-	+	$+^{\S}$
v	-	-	-	-	+	0	-
δ	-	-	-	-	+	0	-

§: Explicit sign ambiguous, i.e. $\gtreqless 0$ (see section 4.7). Signs in table chosen by assumption.

Though most of the partial derivatives have got an unequivocal sign there are various counteracting forces and different interdependencies behind each partial derivative owing to the complex model structure. Therefore, the following qualitative description of an exogenous increase in each parameter highlights only the most important and most influential transmission channel within the model for each case, and is definitely not complete.

A rise in indebtedness λ lowers according to equation 4.2 the profit rate on capital r, leading to a decline in Tobin's q according to equation 4.6. A decrease in q lowers the growth rate of the capital stock $\eta(q)$ and capacity utilization u according to equation 4.1 which leads to a further decline in r and in q according to equations 4.2 and 4.6. A decline in q lowers firms' net worth and banks' profits which induces banks to demand a higher loan rate j as a compensation for a higher credit risk according to equation 4.7, which leads to a further decline in r and u. Decreasing capacity utilization leads according to equation 4.3 to lower inflation $\hat{p}$, or even to deflation. This decreasing inflation or deflation effect has an additional dampening effect on capacity utilization via an increase in the real interest rate on government bonds $i - \hat{p}$, which induces a reduction in government spending $g(i - \hat{p})$. Yet, a lowering value of $\hat{p}$ has also a stimulating effect on u via an increasing real exchange rate $\hat{s} - \hat{p}$, stimulating net exports nx which could increase u, r, q and lower j. In equilibrium however, the initial stimulation of nx is going to be completely compensated by a depreciation of the exchange rate, or equivalently by an appreciation of the home currency, i.e. by a decrease in $\hat{s}$. The reason for the exchange rate compensating the initial price effect stems from the fact that the capital account is zero in equilibrium due to the UIP assumption according to equation 4.5, requiring the current account also to take a zero value in equilibrium. A balanced current account in the present model can only be reached in case the exchange rate offsets the initial price effect because there is no dependence of nx on u like in the standard Mundell-Fleming model. In the case considered above, a decreasing value of $\hat{p}$ increases net exports leading to an excess supply of foreign currency which causes the exchange rate to depreciate as long as external equilibrium is restored. As it is indicated in table 4.1, especially the signs of the exchange rate's rate of change cannot be determined unequivocally (see section 4.7). However, since the signs of the price level's rate of change $\hat{p}$ are unambiguous, the sign of the exchange rate's rate of change must be the same like for $\hat{p}$ due to the fact that the current account must be balanced in equilibrium. Summing up, the overall effect of an increasing value of λ is a decrease in $u, \hat{p}, r, q, \hat{s}$ and an increase in j. The overall impact of λ on the domestic interest rate on government bonds is zero because, according to equation 4.5, i only depends on parameters i^* and ρ in the model. Thus, i only reacts on changes in i^* and ρ and otherwise not.

A rise in the state of confidence parameter ρ acts directly in the opposite way as an increase in indebtedness λ with respect to $u, r, q, \hat{p}$ and j. An increase in ρ raises Tobin's q according to equation 4.6, thereby stimulating the growth rate of investment demand $\eta(q)$ and capacity utilization u according to equation 4.1 which leads to an increase in the profit rate r according to equation 4.2. As to credit market conditions, a rising q increases firms' collateral and banks profits, resulting in a decline in the interest rate on bank loans j inducing a further rise in r, q and u. According to equation 4.3, the rise in u leads to an increase in the growth rate of the price level $\hat{p}$. Since the expected growth rate of the exchange rate depends negatively on ρ, a rise in ρ causes an appreciation expectation of the home currency, i.e. $\hat{s}^e < 0$, which firstly leads temporarily to capital inflows and to an actual appreciation of the home currency. According to equation 4.5, expected appreciation of the home currency and capital inflows very quickly lead to a lower domestic interest rate on government bonds i in order to restore UIP. Inflation and appreciation of the home currency reduce net exports nx temporarily but in order to restore a balanced current account in final equilibrium, the domestic currency has to devalue, i.e. $\hat{s} > 0$, since the temporary current account deficit leads to an excess supply of home currency, and therefore to a devaluation of the home currency in the final equilibrium.

An increase in normalized high-powered money h, as well as an increase in the money multiplier m induced by a reduction in the required reserve ratio τ, can be analyzed together simply as expansionary monetary policy.[19] A monetary expansion leads, via a lower interest rate on bank loans j stemming from an increasing stock of deposits according to equation 4.7, to an increase in the profit rate r according to equation 4.2, thereby leading to a rising Tobin's q according to equation 4.6, to a higher growth rate of the capital stock $\eta(q)$, and to an increase in capacity utilization u according to equation 4.1. Expansion of domestic activity by monetary policy leads to the conventional result of an increase in the growth rate of the price level $\hat{p}$ according to equation 4.3 which is compensated by a depreciation of the home currency, i.e. $\hat{s}$ rises.[20] The effect on the domestic interest rate on government bonds i in equilibrium is, as already explained above, zero.

A rise in α meaning stronger financial regulation with respect to the supply of loans leads according to equation 4.7 to a higher interest rate on loans j, thereby reducing $r, q, \eta(q), u, \hat{p}$ and $\hat{s}$ according to equations 4.1 to 4.3 and 4.6. The effect on i is zero as already mentioned.

An increase in the foreign interest rate i^* leads to an increase in the nominal domestic interest rate on government bonds i to the same amount according to equation 4.5, and to an appreciation of the exchange rate $\hat{s}$ because of an excess demand for foreign currency stimulating net exports temporarily. In equilibrium net exports are again zero by the compensating effect of a rising $\hat{p}$. Though net exports are zero in equilibrium, and a rising nominal interest rate on government bonds i reduces government spending, capacity utilization increases. The reason for this result is the fact that inflation increases much faster than the nominal domestic interest rate on bonds which, as a net effect, reduces the real interest rate on government bonds, leading to much higher government spending, and thereby increasing u according to equation 4.1. Higher domestic activity leads to increases in r and q according to equations 4.2 and 4.6, stimulating a further expansion in u. A higher collateral value reduces the nominal interest rate on loans j according to 4.7.

The effects of a higher wage share v, caused e.g. by an increase in the nominal wage w or by a fall in labour productivity Y/N, and an increase in the depreciation rate δ, caused e.g. by a negative technology shock, lead to the same aggregate results.[21] Both negative shocks lead to a reduction in the profit rate r, as well as in Tobin's q according to equations 4.2 and 4.6. A lower collateral value and decreasing bank profits induce banks to demand a higher loan rate j according to equation 4.7 which in turn leads to a further decline in r and q. A lower value of q leads to a shrinking value of capacity utilization u caused by a drop in the growth rate of the capital stock $\eta(q)$, which leads to a decline in the growth rate of the price level $\hat{p}$, stimulating net exports temporarily and leading the domestic currency to revalue in equilibrium, i.e. $\hat{s}$ decreases. The impact on i is zero as explained above.

[19]For each kind of shock, partial derivatives are almost identical, and only differ with respect to variables h and m. See section 4.7 for a formal derivation of these results.

[20]The model also verifies the standard Mundell-Fleming result stating that monetary policy under flexible exchange rates causes temporarily a lower domestic interest rate (which rises again very quickly to its original level if UIP holds), thereby leading to capital outflows, and to an appreciation of the exchange rate stimulating net exports and output.

[21]All partial derivatives with respect to changes in v and δ are almost identical and differ only by partial derivatives with respect to v, containing additionally the variable u in a multiplicative way. See section 4.7 for further details.

4.3.2 A Comparative-Static View of Financial Crises

Recent empirical research on financial crises has identified the following nine empirical regularities, outlined in chapter 3, which a consistent theory of financial crises should be able to explain. Firstly, banking, currency and twin crises both in industrial and in emerging market countries are in most cases linked to extensive boom-bust cycles in goods and financial markets. Secondly, though financial crises have a cyclical, recurrent character over time, not each business cycle generates financial crises, i.e. there are "tranquil" business cycles with stable financial and goods market conditions, which are sometimes interrupted by extensive cycles generating financial crises. Thirdly, the boom phase of extensive business cycles generating financial crises is often marked by a large exogenous positive shock as e.g. financial liberalization, or the emergence of a new technology regime. Fourthly, during the boom phase of a financial crisis cycle, financial fragility increases in the form of rising debt-asset ratios, a rising share of short-term debt to total debt, and rising external financing costs. Fifthly, financial crises happen after the economy has entered a recession being accompanied by an overvalued currency, increases in domestic and international interest rates, etc. Sixthly, the bust phase and financial crises are commonly preceded by a large domestic and external worsening of economic fundamentals, i.e. panic-driven financial crises caused by a random sudden shift in market sentiment at sound fundamentals are very rare. Seventhly, the recovery phase after the occurrence of a financial crisis is characterized by an improvement in economic fundamentals, and by a reduction in financial fragility due to a reduction in aggregate indebtedness. Eighthly, the time patterns of most macroeconomic variables during extensive boom-bust cycles generating financial crises in industrial countries, are very similar to those in emerging market countries except for the fact that emerging market countries' debt is denominated in foreign currency whereas industrial countries' debt is mostly denominated in domestic currency. Ninthly, though crises in industrial and emerging market countries are similar regarding the time patterns of macroeconomic variables, crisis frequency in emerging markets, especially in the post Bretton Woods era, is higher, i.e. there are less "tranquil" cycles in emerging market countries than in industrial countries.

These empirical regularities are used in the following for a theoretical construction of a highly stylized extensive boom-bust cycle engendering financial crises. This stylized theoretical financial crisis cycle is described in a first step by the comparative-static results of the model according to table 4.1 which provide a much deeper understanding of financial and goods markets' behaviour during different stages of business cycles than an investigation of empirical results could do. It must be noted however, that the formal explanation of the stylized facts by the signs of partial derivatives according to table 4.1 is only a qualitative description, since there is no possibility to determine explicitly the net effects on all endogenous variables if two or more counteracting parameters are varied due to the absence of a function describing in which relation different parameters are varied during different stages of the business cycle. Especially the debt-asset ratio λ, and the state of confidence ρ, being the two core driving variables of a financial crisis cycle, move in almost all stages of the cycle in the same direction, implying an ambiguous effect on aggregate economic activity according to table 4.1, since the net effect depends firstly, on the relative growth of the two parameters, and secondly, on the relative strength of influence on all endogenous variables, which both cannot be specified quantitatively by the comparative-static version of the model. As a result, the comparative-static description of a typical financial crisis cycle is a theoretically based qualitative approach analyzing, among other important determinants as e.g. monetary policy, which of the two counteracting effects of λ and ρ dominates in each phase of the cycle as a theoretical base for the dynamic version of the model in chapter 4.4, which is able to verify the comparative-static results by endogenizing λ and ρ.

The Boom Phase. The boom phase starts with growing expectations of higher future profits, or equivalently with a rise in the "state of confidence" after an initial positive shock in one or more sectors in the economy (technology shock, domestic and international financial liberalization, etc.), inducing firms to increase investment which is financed by rising leverage. If monetary conditions are favourable, the initial boom in one sector of the economy spreads over to other sectors by various goods market and financial market linkages. Rising aggregate demand leads to higher cash flows and profits causing asset prices to rise (Tobin's q increases). Higher stock market valuations increase net worth and collateral, making corporate balance sheets look sounder and reduce corporate risk. Due to higher collateral values, borrowing costs drop and lead to higher borrowing and investment. The debt structure becomes more short-term, since short-term rates tend to be much lower than long-term rates in boom phases. Summing up, during a boom corporate liquidity, profitability and solvency increase, leading to a higher valuation of firms in financial markets though the debt-to-asset ratio increases, whereas the debt-to-market capitalization ratio remains almost unchanged.

In terms of the model, a positive technology shock expressed by a fall in δ, and/or a financial liberalization shock being indicated by a fall in α or by a rise in m caused by a reduction of the required reserve ratio τ, both lead to an economic expansion which is amplified by a simultaneous increase in the state of confidence parameter ρ. Favourable monetary conditions are represented by an increase in h, and perhaps by a further increase in m. Rising leverage for increasing investment finance is indicated by an increase in the debt-asset ratio λ. Though an increase in indebtedness λ has a contractionary effect on overall macroeconomic activity, the net effect is expansionary, since the changes in α, δ, ρ, h and m, all causing a macroeconomic expansion, overcompensate the debt-led contraction. Summing up, the boom phase is characterized by an increase in capacity utilization u, caused by larger investment demand $\eta(q)$ through an increase in Tobin's q, an increase in the profit rate r, an increase in inflation $\hat{p}$, a decrease in the loan rate j, a decrease in the interest rate on government bonds i, and by a depreciation of the home currency, i.e. by a rise in $\hat{s}$ caused by inflation.

The Overborrowing Symptom. During the boom phase of a financial crisis cycle, firms start to engage in excessive "overborrowing", being defined as a situation with largely growing debt-asset ratios caused by a rapid expansion of investment and declining or stagnating internal cash flows, requiring an increasing stock of external finance in the form of taking new loans or issuing new equities. Whether an economy tends to increase more equity or more bank loan financing depends on the nature of the financial system, that is whether the system is more bank-based or more market-based.[22] The following

[22]European and Japanese financial systems are bank-based, whereas North-American financial systems are more market-based.

description of overborrowing processes refers to a bank-based system, i.e. external finance is only provided in the form of bank loans.

The rapid growth of investment and indebtedness is based on very fast growing profit expectations increasing faster than actual gross profits (profits before external financing costs) though net profits (profits minus external financing costs) stagnate, i.e. additional gross profits caused by an expansion of sales do not lead to an increase in net profits due to an increase in external financing costs of approximately the same size. In order to differentiate the overborrowing phase from a state of "irrational exuberance" (which is going to be explained in the following paragraph), both being parts of the upswing, the overborrowing process is defined by a constant positive net profit rate, whereas a state of irrational exuberance[23] is defined by a shrinking positive net profit rate with a minimum at zero, since a negative net profit rate corresponds to a situation of illiquidity which does not allow for a further expansion process due to a downward revision of expectations.

The extent and the velocity of a debt-led investment boom depends on the one hand on firms' warranted expansion of investment, but on the other hand, also on financial markets' willingness to expand credit. Consequently, a large capacity of an economy's financial system to place new debt as well as favourable monetary conditions are necessary prerequisites for an overborrowing process. High profitability, favourable liquidity conditions and increasing net worth among financial intermediaries, caused by increasing interest income and less non-performing loans during the boom phase, attract additional financial means (e.g. by an increase in deposits, or new issues of debentures) which allow for the expansion of loans, being predominantly driven by rising profit expectations of banks since financial intermediaries live in the same expectational climate as firms. Favourable monetary conditions, i.e. a comparatively low aggregate interest rate level, caused by low inflation and low growth during the expansion phase of a business cycle, support the expansion of indebtedness among firms. The overborrowing process among firms is also accompanied by a lagged overborrowing process among financial intermediaries since they are also subject to stagnating cash flows due to increasing external debt costs, requiring to finance further expansions of credit by an increase in their debt-asset ratio. Furthermore, an ongoing expansion of credit, both in the firm and in the financial sector, leads at some point to rising refinancing costs even at unchanged favourable monetary conditions due to the existence of a natural maximum amount of credit, determined by the level of the discount rate and by the required reserve ratio. Rising external financing costs lead to a further amplification of the overborrowing effect due to a widening gap between stagnating available internal cash flows and rising expenses which are financed by increasing debt-asset ratios.

The overborrowing process both in the firm and in the financial sector causes a rising vulnerability of an economy to volatility in goods and in financial markets. The financial sector depends increasingly on the ability of the corporate sector to fulfill its debt payment commitments which can be realized only if there is a further actual expansion in aggregate demand. The corporate sector depends more and more on the willingness of financial markets to roll-over or to place new debt, which in turn depends on general monetary conditions and on financial markets' expectations on future profitability of firms. Accordingly, in an "overborrowing" environment, general financial fragility, i.e.

[23]For the "irrational exuberance" phenomenon in connection with the "New Economy" stock market bubble, see e.g. Shiller (2000).

the probability that only little negative shocks in either goods or in financial markets can lead to widespread failures of firms and financial intermediaries, increases intensely.

In terms of the model, the overborrowing process is described by an increase in the debt-asset ratio λ and in the state of confidence ρ, the expansionary effect of ρ being larger than the contractionary effect of λ. The overall expansionary net effect leads to further increase in capacity utilization u, inflation $\hat{p}$, Tobin's q, and in the exchange rate's growth rate $\hat{s}$, and to a decrease in the loan rate j and in the domestic bond rate i, whereas the profit rate r remains constant.

The Upper Turning Point and "Irrational Exuberance". The time path to the upper turning point of the business cycle is characterized by a further deterioration of cash flows and by a shrinking net profit rate since interest rate costs, caused by further excessive overborrowing, increase by a larger amount than earnings which cannot be increased as expected. Accordingly, the path to the upper turning point is characterized by a tremendous increase in financial fragility. However, though net profits are actually decreasing, asset prices and leverage tend to increase still further because profit expectations tend to follow a cumulative upward trend, mainly driven by a self-reinforcing cycle without any consideration of a deterioration of fundamental data driving the economy in a state of a "bubble economy" and "irrational exuberance".[24] The bubble in financial markets is generally accompanied by an overheating in the real sector leading to rising inflation due to an excess demand at almost full capacity utilization. After a period of steady goods market inflation and asset price inflation, monetary authorities start to tighten monetary conditions, leading to a general tightening in financial markets and to a further decline in corporate and bank profits. Although monetary tightening serves to convince economic agents that expectations are exaggerated and should lead to a downward revision of expectations, contractionary monetary policy need not be the trigger for the burst of an asset price bubble. There are situations possible (see e.g. the "New Economy Hype" in year 2000 in the U.S.) in which asset prices and leverage keep on increasing despite monetary tightening, being caused by an extraordinary and further rise in profit expectations.

In terms of the model, the time path to the upper turning point of the business cycle is characterized by a reduction in m and h due to monetary contraction, and by further and more extensive overborrowing, i.e. by an increase in λ and ρ. As opposed to the overborrowing phase, the negative influence of an increasing λ on the profit rate r is larger than the positive influence of an increasing ρ on r, i.e. r declines with a lower bound of zero as outlined above. Intuitively, these developments would be generally assumed to cause an overall macroeconomic contraction. However, the overall net effect is expansionary mainly driven by a rising value of Tobin's q. Though Tobin's q declines ceteris paribus by the fall in r, there is a rise due to an overcompensating increase in the state of confidence ρ representing an "irrational" increase in profit expectations and asset prices. Summing up, the path to the upper turning point is characterized by an increase in capacity utilization u, inflation $\hat{p}$, Tobin's q, in the exchange rate's growth rate $\hat{s}$, and by a decrease in the bond rate i and in the loan rate j in spite of a declining profit rate r.

[24]The term "bubble economy" refers to a situation in which actual movements of economic variables, e.g. rising stock prices and excessive bank lending, cannot be justified by actual fundamental data, and are solely based on "irrational" positive expectations.

The Burst of the Bubble. The end of the excessive expansionary process in goods and financial markets is generally marked by a sudden stop in the expansion of credit and by a collapse of asset prices, leading to an aggregate deterioration of net worth positions and to sharp interest rate increases reflecting the magnified risk of default. These macroeconomic effects are caused by a sharp downward revision of profit expectations when investors realize that past expectations have been unrealistic, that the economy is financially fragile, and that "mania" expectations cannot be fulfilled by actual developments. The triggering event, or "wake-up call", for an asset bubble's burst can be either an *endogenous* failure of an important bank or corporation caused by past excessive overborrowing, or contractionary monetary policy. According to the conventional view on financial crises, monetary tightening is often viewed as an exogenous shock being the sole triggering event of an asset bubble's burst which could have been avoided if there had been no monetary contraction. It must be noted however firstly, that monetary tightening can be also viewed as an *endogenous* phenomenon to constrain rising inflation which has been caused by an endogenous debt-led investment boom, and secondly, that a monetary contraction *can* be the trigger for an asset bubble's, but can also merely aggravate the collapse of expectations which occurred before monetary tightening. The reason why contractionary monetary policy is often viewed as the sole exogenous triggering event of an asset bubble's burst stems from the fact that monetary tightening often marks the beginning of the asset price decline, and that a monetary contraction aggravates the downward revision of expectations leading to a further decline in asset prices.

In terms of the model, the collapse of profit expectations is represented by a large and sudden drop in the state of confidence ρ, leading to a large decline in Tobin's q, and to a large and sudden rise in the loan rate j, and in the bond rate i. The *sudden stop* in the expansion of credit is represented by a sharp fall in the growth rate of the debt asset ratio λ to zero.

The Bust Cycle, Financial Crisis, Liquidity Trap and Debt Deflation. Whether an economy enters a severe financial crisis including a recession or even a depression depends firstly, on the extent of the drop in asset prices, and secondly on the vulnerability of firms' and financial intermediaries' liquidity and solvency positions in case of a large asset price drop. Consequently, if there is low vulnerability or only a small drop in asset prices, a burst of a bubble does not cause severe disruptions in financial and goods markets and serves more as an event to readjust expectations to their fundamentals. By way of contrast, if firms and banks are highly leveraged, and collateral and liquidity positions react very sensitively to changes in asset prices, a severe financial crises (twin crisis) involving an austere recession, or even a depression is likely going to occur.

Regarding the emergence of a full-fledged financial crisis, the initial fall in profit expectations having given rise to the asset price bubble's burst causes widespread insolvency and illiquidity among firms. As to insolvency, the downward revision of expectations and falling asset prices have caused shrinking net worth positions, leading to a further drop in expectations due to an increased risk of default. Liquidity positions deteriorate on the one hand by rising interest rates caused by increased default risk, and on the other hand by a sharp reduction in sales due to a fall in aggregate demand induced mainly by firms cutting investment expenditures to fulfill due payment commitments. Furthermore, the cumulative process of collapsing expectations and asset prices, as well as the self-reinforcing deterioration of firms' liquidity and solvency is often magnified additionally by rating agencies grading down a huge part of the corporate sector.

Regarding the availability of credit, financial intermediaries not only increase loan rates, but also start to cut credit lines and roll-over loans causing a severe credit crunch and further illiquidity among firms. There is no possibility to receive new liquid funds at financial markets by placing new debt, even at very high rates, since financial markets liquidity has dried up due to an overall increase in risk and uncertainty. As a result, firms are forced to start a "fire-sale" of their assets since there is no possibility to serve due loans out of current cash flow. However, a widespread "fire-sale" of assets leads to further drops in asset prices, collateral, net worth and liquidity and causes further illiquidity and bankruptcy among firms. Financial intermediaries incur severe losses due to sharp drops in interest rate income and rapid increases in non-performing loans, leading also to illiquidity, "fire-sale" of assets, and to widespread insolvency among banks. Accordingly, financial intermediaries are not able to protect themselves against losses by calling loans or by increasing interest rates, since these actions cause further losses in the corporate and, as a result, in the financial sector.

In the pre-World War II era, failures of financial intermediaries additionally triggered severe banking panics which led to a money supply collapse, massive deflation and financial disintermediation due to the absence of an effective lender of last resort and deposit insurance systems. In the post-World War II era, however, banking panics and their negative repercussions on goods and financial markets have been prevented through effective lender of last resort actions and deposit insurance systems. Though monetary policy has become effective in stabilizing the money supply and liquidity of banks, banking insolvency caused by drops in asset prices and losses through high shares of non-performing loans can still lead to severe banking crises nowadays. Furthermore, if there is a very sharp contraction in asset prices and in banks' and business firms' net worth, deflationary spirals increasing real interest rates, real interest payments, and the real stock of debt, leading to a further depression in output, cannot be prevented by expansionary monetary policy. In extreme cases, a "liquidity trap" situation can emerge which does not necessarily require that the interest rate remains constant at a minimum level (or even at zero) when the money supply is increased like in standard textbook IS-LM analysis. The impotence of monetary policy can even happen when the central banks' discount rate is positive and continues to fall as the money supply is increased. The reason for the ineffectiveness of monetary policy, even if the discount rate is above the zero level, stems from the fact that pessimistic expectations, drops in output, which reduce the actual profit rate, and deflation, lead to an enormous decline in Tobin's q and in the marginal efficiency of capital reducing investment demand and output. Even if the central bank lowers the discount rate to zero, there is no mechanism leading to a recovering value of the marginal efficiency of capital and Tobin's q which would stimulate aggregate investment and output.

The domestic financial crisis being subject to a severe banking crisis, widespread corporate failures, deflation and "liquidity trap" situations, can be accompanied by a speculative attack on the domestic currency causing a twin crisis, and possibly very high domestic interest rates due to increased country risk and large devaluation expectations of the home currency. The currency crisis exacerbates temporarily the recession because substantial depreciations are typically associated with sharp current account reversals, requiring the economy to quickly adjust the balance between domestic saving and investment by reducing output. However, if there are no debt contracts denominated in foreign currency, a devaluation of the home currency has, in the medium and in the long-run, an expansionary effect on output via stimulating net exports facilitating the recovery phase.

In terms of the model, a financial crisis engendering a severe recession, or even a depression, is caused by a further large decline in the state of confidence ρ, leading to a decrease in capacity utilization u, in the price level's growth rate $\hat{p}$ (where $\hat{p} < 0$ is a realistic scenario), in the profit rate r, in Tobin's q, and to a sharp increase in the loan rate j and in the interest rate on government bonds i. In the short run, the exchange rate appreciates sharply, i.e. $\hat{s} > 0$, due to rising capital outflows caused by devaluation expectations and a rising country risk premium. In severe cases, there arises the possibility of a currency crisis (inducing a twin crisis), i.e. a large rise in $\hat{s}$. In the long-run however, the sharp reduction in ρ leads to an appreciation of the home currency, i.e. to $\hat{s} < 0$, due to a large macroeconomic contraction, causing the domestic price level's growth rate $\hat{p}$ and the exchange rate's growth rate $\hat{s}$ to fall. Despite expansionary lender of last resort actions and compensations by deposit insurance systems, being represented by increasing values of m and h, there is an overall macroeconomic contraction owing to overcompensating negative effect of a drop in the state of confidence ρ being typical of a "liquidity trap" situation, i.e. expansionary monetary policy via a reduction in j cannot increase Tobin's q due to very low levels of $r, u, \hat{p}$ and ρ. In the same way, a reduction in the debt-asset ratio λ, caused by financial intermediaries reducing the available stock of debt, cannot "turn" the economy into recovery due to the dominance of the contractionary ρ-effect.

The Recovery Phase. During the bust cycle period, firms and financial intermediaries start adjusting their external finance position by reducing the overall debt stock, and by cutting investment spending. The period of deleveraging is going to impede investment as long as firms' and financial intermediaries' debt levels are seen as abnormally high, and liquidity positions are seen as too weak. A new phase of expansion will begin only if debt and liquidity of the corporate as well of the financial sector are viewed as sustainable.

In terms of the model, the economy only begins to recover if a decrease in the debt-asset ratio λ leads to an increase in the state of confidence ρ, inducing an economic expansion with an increase in capacity utilization u, in the profit rate r, in the price level's growth rate $\hat{p}$, in Tobin's q, in the exchange rate's growth rate $\hat{s}$, and a decrease in the loan rate j and in the domestic bond rate i.

4.4 Long-Run Dynamic Analysis

4.4.1 Finance, Investment and Long-Run Profit Expectations

Though lots of parameters have been varied in the comparative-static description of financial crises, the two "driving" forces for the emergence of boom-bust cycles including financial crises are the "state of confidence" parameter ρ and the debt-asset ratio λ. The technique of comparative statics however, is very unsatisfactory because it only allows a description of real world phenomena by varying exogenous parameters in a certain range; there is no explanation in a static model why expectations suddenly change and why credit constraints are binding from a certain point on. In order to overcome these shortcomings of comparative-statics, the dynamic version of the model is going to endogenize the state of confidence parameter ρ and the debt-asset ratio λ in order to show firstly, that financial fragility is an *endogenous* phenomenon of each business cycle, secondly that market economies tend to be dynamically and cyclically stable by the emergence of endogenous business cycles without financial crises, and thirdly, that excessive boom-bust cycles generating financial crises are caused by exogenous *positive* shocks to expectations catapulting an initially, cyclically stable economy to an unstable and highly financially fragile cycle, which however converges, after the occurrence of a financial crisis, to its cyclical and dynamically stable steady state.

The Dynamic Behaviour of Long-Run Profit Expectations. Empirical studies, as well as the comparative-static description of financial crises in industrial countries according to section 4.3.2, have shown that the dynamic behaviour of profit expectations (and asset prices) can be described by a cumulative upward and downward processes in the boom and in the bust phase without any counteracting or equilibrating forces, whereas at the upper and lower turning point of the business cycle, cumulative processes are reversed by some "new" kind of information, resulting in a change of the direction of movement in expectations. An early economic treatment of this sort of behaviour of expectations can be found in Keynes' theory of "the state of long-term expectations".[25] According to Keynes, it is not possible to form expectations of the future on the basis of the *"most probable forecast"* (Keynes 1936, p. 148) having the same time horizon as an investment in real capital goods; in most cases *"there is no scientific basis on which to form any calculable probability whatever"* (Keynes 1937, p. 114). In order to deal with this kind of uncertainty which cannot be reduced, Keynes identifies three principles according to which expectations are formed in reality:

> *(1) We assume that the present is a much more serviceable guide to the future than a candid examination of past experiences would show it to have been hitherto. In other words we largely ignore the prospect of future changes about the actual character of which we know nothing.*
>
> *(2) We assume that the* ***existing*** *state of opinion as expressed in prices and the character of existing output is based on a* ***correct*** *summing up of future prospects, so that we can accept it as such unless and until something new and relevant comes into the picture.*
>
> *(3) Knowing that our own individual judgement is worthless, we endeavor to fall back on the judgment of the the rest of the world which is perhaps better informed. That is, we endeavor to conform with the behaviour of the majority or the average. The psychology of a society of individuals each of whom is endeavoring to copy the others leads to what we may strictly term a conventional judgment (Keynes 1937, p. 114, Keynes' emphasis).*[26]

Point (1) states that expectations are based on the current or present state without any effort to predict future events by extrapolation of past events. Point (2) states that expectations only change if new events can be foreseen; otherwise expectations are based on the present state. Point (3) states that individual expectations are not only based

[25]See e.g. chapter 12, "The State of Long-Term Expectations" in the General Theory (Keynes 1936).
[26]See also Flaschel, Franke and Semmler (1997), p. 344.

on "objective" factors but also on the average opinion of the market which is very well explained by Keynes' example of the "newspaper beauty contest" where the readers

> *... have to pick out the six prettiest faces from a hundred photographs, the prize being awarded to the competitor whose choice most nearly corresponds to the average preferences of the competitors as a whole; so that each competitor has to pick, not those faces which he himself finds prettiest, but those which he thinks likeliest to catch the fancy of the other competitors, all of whom are looking at the problem from the same point of view (Keynes 1936, p. 156).*[27]

Transferring the "beauty contest theory" to investment decisions, the market valuation of investment goods, i.e. the valuation of the demand price of capital, is not based on "objective" or "real" facts. On the contrary, under the influence of mass psychology, market valuations are based on anticipation what average opinion expects the average opinion to be[28], i.e. investors base their decisions on general conventions which are formed by the market. This behaviour is rational both for persons without any special knowledge and for persons with special knowledge because expecting what the market expects will result in higher returns than expecting what individual interpretations of "objective fundamentals" would say. As a result, investment decisions will be heavily influenced by bulls and bears of stock markets and not primarily by individual assessments which is described by Keynes as

> *[t]he entrepreneurs, who are directly responsible, will find it financially advantageous, and often unavoidable, to fall in with the ideas of the market, even though they themselves are better instructed (Keynes 1936, p. 316).*[29]

Applying Keynes' theory of the formation of (profit) expectations to the present model results in the change of the state of confidence ρ depending positively on the actual state of expectations. Consequently, the state of confidence is going to increase further if the actual state of confidence is positive, and is going to decrease further in case the actual state of confidence is negative. Formally, this formation of expectations scheme can be described by

$$\dot{\rho} = \underset{+}{f(\rho)},$$

stating that the time derivative of the state of confidence $\dot{\rho} = \partial\rho/\partial t$ is positively dependent on the actual state of confidence ρ. This general differential equation allows for unstable exploding upward and downward movements depending on the initial state. From a business cycle perspective, this positive feedback loop mechanism allows for the emergence of cumulative boom and bust periods. However, this theoretical expectation formation scheme is incomplete since it does not explain a reversal of cumulative processes, i.e. it contains no counteracting forces slowing down the cumulative processes, and turning them back into the reverse direction at the turning points of the business cycle. Reversals of cumulative upward and downward processes in goods and financial markets are usually caused by the emergence of "new" information revealing that the current level of asset

[27]Other authors, like e.g. Flaschel, Franke and Semmler (1997), p. 344, and Eatwell and Taylor (2000), pp. 12 and 15, also refer to Keynes' theory of the formation of expectations.

[28]See Keynes (1936), p. 156, and Eatwell and Taylor (2000), p. 12.

[29]See also Flaschel, Franke and Semmler (1997), p. 422.

and goods prices does not correspond to actual fundamental data, causing sudden and large changes in asset and goods prices. Thus, the formal adjustment equation of the state of confidence has to be additionally dependent on "objective" factors representing a norm in the form of "economic fundamentals". These objective factors have to be able to reinforce, to slow down, and even to reverse cumulative processes. Though there are numerous economic fundamentals which could be taken as an "objective" basis for expectations, the present model refers on two core fundamentals which are also used in real world assessments of current expectations, namely current profitability and the degree of indebtedness.

An obvious indicator for current profitability in the model is the actual profit rate r. However, using r provides no information whether current profitability is "high" or "low", or whether an investment in real capital is risky or riskless. As a result, current profitability can be only assessed by comparing the profit rate r to a riskless reference yield. The real interest rate on government bonds $i-\hat{p}$ serves as a good riskless reference interest rate which investors can realize by shifting their portfolios from equities into government bonds with comparable low risk. Thus, the difference between the two rates σ, formally given as

$$\sigma = r - (i - \hat{p}),$$

serves as a much better indicator. The difference σ can be interpreted as the risk premium firms have to pay to investors for holding capital assets because the profit rate r is, as outlined above, a good indicator for liquidity and solvency risk. Regarding the influence of σ on the formation of profit expectations, it holds that a shrinking value of σ, caused by a fall in r and $\hat{p}$, or by an increase in i, indicates that investment in capital assets becomes more risky in comparison to government bonds, and will cause a reduction in the change of the "state of confidence" parameter $\dot{\rho}$. By way of contrast, an increasing σ lowers the risk of capital assets, and thereby leads to an increasing value of $\dot{\rho}$.

The level of indebtedness, serving as the second economic fundamental in the model, and providing information about the financial fragility of business firms' balance sheet structure, is measured by the debt-asset ratio λ being an indicator for liquidity and solvency risk. A high level of λ indicates high liquidity risk since a large part of current cash flow has to be employed for interest rate costs and repayment of the principal, i.e. only small shocks, as e.g. a drop in earnings or only small interest rate increases, can lead to illiquidity. Regarding solvency risk, the higher the debt-asset ratio λ, the quicker insolvency emerges from a given drop in asset prices. By way of contrast, a low debt-asset ratio indicates low liquidity and low solvency risk. Respecting the influence of the debt-asset ratio λ on profit expectations, it holds that a high level of λ leads to a drop in profit expectations, whereas a low level of λ causes profit expectations to rise, i.e. it holds that a higher λ causes $\dot{\rho}$ to shrink, whereas a lower λ causes $\dot{\rho}$ to rise.

Summing up, a formal representation of the change of the state of confidence parameter could read as

$$\dot{\rho} = f(\underset{+}{\rho}, \underset{+}{\sigma}, \underset{-}{\lambda}),$$

stating that the change of the state of confidence is a positive function of the actual state of confidence, a positive function of the risk premium and a negative function of the debt-asset ratio.[30] This kind of expectation formation scheme is able to explain cumulative movements in expectations during the boom and the bust phase, as well as changes of past cumulative processes into the reverse direction at the turning points. During the boom and the bust phase, the positive influence of ρ on $\dot{\rho}$ will dominate. However, at the turning points, the influence of σ and λ will dominate and "turn" the past development into the reverse direction. For example, as the comparative-static description of financial crises has shown, during the boom phase, the level of indebtedness is going to increase which reduces net profits, leading to a slow down of the boom and to a reversal into a bust cycle. During the bust cycle, the debt-asset ratio decreases and net profits are going to increase after some time, leading to a slow down of the cumulative downward trend and to a reversal for a new upswing.

This formal expectation formation scheme can be explained alternatively by business cycle phase dependent behaviour of two different kinds of investors.[31] Type one investors are feedback investors, noise traders[32], or chartists. They have no expert knowledge and generally follow market sentiments by extrapolating past time trends into the future, i.e. in the boom phase, they speculate on increasing asset prices, and in the bust phase, they speculate on decreasing asset prices. Type two investors, so-called fundamentalists, are better informed, use more sophisticated forecasts, and rely more on fundamental data. Standard theory of financial markets would state that noise traders cannot survive forever in financial markets because changes in market sentiments are compensated by counter-acting rational arbitrageurs, so that less informed and less competitive investors are either going to be driven out of the market, or improve their performance by learning from past losses. As a result, according to standard theory, financial markets tend to be efficient due to the dominance of rational investors. Reality however, shows that this development does not take place as predicted by standard theory. For example, there arise situations especially in the boom and bust phase of business cycles in which fundamentalists follow general market sentiments though "objective" fundamental data would indicate a speculation against the trend. This phenomenon can be explained by the dominance of chartist behaviour in boom and bust phases, so that fundamentalists following chartist behaviour may earn higher yields than fundamentalists basing their expectations on a rational assessment of fundamental data. Thus, in boom and bust phases it seems useful for fundamentalists to follow general market opinion though they are more sensitive to new available data than feedback investors by observing more closely the evolution of fundamental variables which possibly could indicate a reversal of the ongoing cumulative process. As a result, the longer a boom or a bust phase is under way, and the more market prices differ from their fundamental value, the more fundamentalists attach increasing weight to fundamental factors by beginning to speculate against the market which, in the end, leads to a reversal of the past cumulative process. Summing up, during the boom and the bust phase of the business cycle, chartist behaviour, which is also adopted by a great number of fundamentalists, dominates general trading strategies, whereas at the turning points, the weight of fundamentalist behaviour dominates general

[30]For a similar time derivative of the "state of confidence" parameter, see Flaschel, Franke and Semmler (1997), p. 346.

[31]For this example, see Flaschel, Franke and Semmler (1997), p. 346.

[32]See Shleifer and Summers (1990) for an overview on noise trader theory.

market behaviour, overcompensating chartist strategies and causing the past cumulative process, i.e. past general market sentiment, to reverse.[33]

The chartist-fundamentalist, or Keynesian theory of the formation of expectations has been criticized as being old-fashioned and not applicable to economic models by the rational expectations school due to the absence of intertemporal optimizing agents and efficient forecasts of variables based on the current status of available information. As to the rational expectations hypothesis, modelling expectations as being driven by general market opinion and by some economic fundamentals whose development can be only observed and not explained is unrealistic, since agents are generally rational in the sense that optimizing agents develop a correct model of the real world on which expectations are based. As a result, expectations and actual values of variables can only differ in case of unforeseen, exogenous shocks; otherwise, expected values are going to be realized since the real world is assumed to behave exactly according to the theoretical model developed by agents. In spite of the fact that the rational expectations hypothesis provides a powerful tool to analyze macroeconomic phenomena, its application is limited by agents' degree of available information about the future. Even Lucas (1977a) has argued that the rational expectations hypothesis does not hold under complete and irreducible uncertainty which has been assumed to prevail in the present model. Rather, in an environment with uncertainty, the formation of expectations according to the rational expectations hypothesis can also be characterized as "extrapolating expectations" by which proxies for future values of variables are obtained.[34] As a result, the rational expectations hypothesis' criticism of the chartist-fundamentalist theory of the formation of expectations does not hold in the present model, though it seems reasonable to assume that agents possess at least a limited form rationality even in a world with irreducible uncertainty, since there are efforts to base expectations on theoretical models in the real world. Standard macroeconomic theory however, has not provided yet an approach combining both schemes to describe

[33]The chartist-fundamentalist theory of the formation of (profit) expectations has been also tested by numerical simulations of non-linear dynamic models (chaos theory models) by Arthur et al. (1997) who mimicked markets made up of heterogenous traders (rational investors vs. feedback or noise traders), where rational investors were modelled, in contrast to the original chartist-fundamentalist theory, as forming their expectations according to the rational expectations hypothesis, and not according to a number of fundamentals. Arthur et al.'s experiment consisted of varying the relative weight of rational investors and feedback traders in order to test different trading strategies which were applied to the Santa Fe's computerized artificial stock market. Arthur et al. derived two important results from their numerical simulations. Firstly, when agents were modelled as adapting very slowly their forecasts to new observations of the market's behaviour, i.e. when agents were modelled predominantly as fundamentalists relying more on objective factors of an underlying model than on conventional wisdom of the market (rational expectations hypothesis), the market converged to a rational expectations regime. In such a regime "mutant" expectations could not yield extraordinary high profits, trading volume remained low and the theory of efficient financial markets could be validated. Secondly, when agents were modelled as adapting to new market observations at a more realistic (and faster) rate, heterogenous beliefs persisted and the market organized itself into a complex regime. A rich market psychology, i.e. a rich set of expectations became observable. Technical trading, i.e. chartists' strategy, emerged as a profitable activity and bubbles and crashes emerged from time to time. Trading volume varied over time with periods of very intensive market activity and periods with quiet market activity. Time series on prices showed persistence in volatility and in trading volume and individual behaviour of agents evolved over time, i.e. behaviour was path-dependent, and did not settle down like in a rational expectations equilibrium model.

[34]See Lucas (1977a), p. 7, Nerlove (1984), and Flaschel, Franke and Semmler (1997), p. 347.

the formation of expectations under real world conditions being subject to irreducible uncertainty since standard theory considers both approaches as not being compatible.

In contrast to standard macroeconomic theory, the present model is designed to provide an expectation formation scheme under irreducible uncertainty which contains at least some long-run rationality of investors, i.e. it combines the chartist-fundamentalist approach with a modified form of the rational expectations hypothesis. Thus far, it has been assumed that the change of the confidence parameter depends positively on the actual state of confidence, i.e. it has been argued that $\partial\dot{\rho}/\partial\rho > 0$. This assumption however, is not consistent with rational behaviour according to the rational expectations hypothesis, since it neglects agents' knowledge of a theoretical model describing the real world as given by equations 4.1 to 4.7, which would imply the expectations rule $r^e = r$ (expected profit rate equals actual profit rate), i.e. $\rho = 0$ for all t. Furthermore, the assumption $\partial\dot{\rho}/\partial\rho > 0$ implies that investors' expectations never converge to actual equilibrium values, but "undershoot" or "overshoot" infinitely the actual equilibrium values which is an unrealistic scenario from an empirical viewpoint. The only kind of "rationality" built in the model preventing expectations to implode or to explode is the increasing reliance at the turning points on "objective" or fundamental data which, however, can be only *observed* but *not explained* by investors. In other words, investors' expectations are adjusted back to fundamentals by a "wake-up call" scenario, implying that there is no knowledge of how fundamentals are determined and how these fundamentals can be explained by an economic model. According to the chartist-fundamentalist expectation formation scheme, investors are modelled as "naive and simple" behaving agents to follow general market conventions without any knowledge of economic nexus' who only change their economic "direction of thinking" in case they get surprised by a "big-bang" event. Moreover, investors are also denied to learn from past experience since there is no mechanism inducing them to develop an economic model which is able to explain the recurrent discrepancy between fundamentals and expectations during each business cycle, and which can be used to base expectations on.

These and other drawbacks of the chartist-fundamentalist expectation formation scheme led rational expectations theorists to believe that economic agents are able to learn from past experience inducing them to develop a "correct" economic model of the real world on which expectations are going to be based. Yet, as outlined above, a pure application of the rational expectations hypothesis is also problematic as to its empirical evidence, since it cannot explain herding behaviour and cumulative processes in the absence of exogenous shocks[35], which can be much better explained by the chartist-fundamentalist theory. Furthermore, the rational expectations hypothesis loses its validity in case of real world irreducible uncertainty, which is assumed to be existent in the model.

Summarizing, both schools of thought have their drawbacks but also contain important insights to describe real world phenomena. Accordingly, for the formation of (profit) expectations under irreducible uncertainty, it seems reasonable to use both the chartist-

[35]It is possible to generate cyclical fluctuations in macromodels being subject to rational expectations which however, requires the assumption of exogenous shocks following well-defined stochastic processes. In such an environment, rational expectations are self-fulfilling, generating boom-bust cycles in goods and financial markets. By way of contrast, there is no possibility to generate endogenous cycles in rational expectations models if there are no exogenous shocks. These topics are going to be discussed in further detail in section 4.6, comparing the present theory of endogenous business cycles with alternative business cycle theories.

fundamentalist theory stating that investors tend to cumulative expectation processes which can be slowed down by investors realizing that expectations have been too pessimistic or optimistic in comparison to fundamental data, and the rational expectations theory stating that investors are rational in the sense that they have knowledge of fundamental economic processes inducing them to form an economic model on which expectations can be based. In terms of the model, rational behaviour is introduced by the assumption of *long-run rationality* of economic agents which means that they believe in the long-run rational expectations equilibrium $r^e = r$, implying a long-run steady state value of the state of confidence $\rho_E = 0$. By way of contrast, the model excludes *short-run rationality*, i.e. the rational expectations hypothesis in its original form, i.e. $r^e = r$ and $\rho_E = 0$ do not necessarily hold for all t. Accordingly, though agents believe in the long-run rational expectations equilibrium $\rho_E = 0$, the current state of confidence ρ is allowed to differ substantially from its steady state level ρ_E in the short-run, but is assumed to converge to its steady state level in the long-run by agents adjusting their current expectations to the steady state level in case the difference $\rho - \rho_E$ is too large or too small. This definition of long-run rationality implies that there exists, independently of the actual state of economic fundamentals (σ and λ) and chartist forecasts, a *"corridor"* or a *"normal range"* around the long-run rational expectations equilibrium $\rho_E = 0$, in which the current state of confidence ρ can move, but which cannot be left by ρ due to counteracting forces in case ρ reaches the "boundaries" of the corridor. The size of this corridor can be very large in reality and is subject to variations between different business cycles since large positive shocks, as e.g. the "New Economy" shock in the late 1990s, cause the corridor to increase, whereas a "normal" business cycle without any large shocks, causes the corridor to shrink.

The combination of long-run rationality and chartist-fundamentalist behaviour calls for a modified function for the change of the confidence parameter with respect to the state of confidence, formally given as

$$\dot{\rho} = f(\underset{-,0,+}{\rho}, \underset{+}{\sigma}, \underset{-}{\lambda}), \tag{4.16}$$

where it holds that $\partial\dot{\rho}/\partial\rho \gtreqless 0$. This function assumes that over some "normal" range of the confidence parameter $\rho_l < \rho < \rho_u$, where ρ_l denotes the negative lower limit ($\rho_l < 0$) and ρ_u the positive upper limit ($\rho_u > 0$) of the corridor, it holds that $\partial\dot{\rho}/\partial\rho > 0$, stating that investors follow general market sentiments, because speculating against the market trend would result in losses, i.e. ρ is expected to continue its past rise/fall in case the current value of ρ is positive/negative. Yet, the closer the current value of ρ moves to the upper and the lower limit of the normal range, the more investors start to doubt of its consistency with the long-run steady state level $\rho_E = 0$. Formally, the derivative $\partial\dot{\rho}/\partial\rho > 0$ is decreasing both in range $0 < \rho < \rho_u$ for increasing values of ρ, and in range $0 > \rho > \rho_l$ for decreasing values of ρ. At the upper and the lower bounds ρ_u and ρ_l, agents stop to believe that ρ is going to continue its past trend, i.e. at the corner points ρ reaches its maximum/minimum, which can be justified rationally, or which is still consistent with its long-run equilibrium value $\rho_E = 0$, respectively. Formally, at the corner points ρ_u and ρ_u, it holds that $\partial\dot{\rho}/\partial\rho = 0$. If the state of confidence exceeds, or falls short of the normal range, i.e. in regions $\rho < \rho_l$ and $\rho > \rho_u$, investors start to "break" the past trend into the reverse direction by speculating against past general market sentiments since agents realize that the current change of expectations $\dot{\rho}$ and the current level of expectations ρ cannot be "rational", i.e. "irrational exuberance" or "irrational understatement" are regarded as being actually irrational, or as not being consistent with the long-run equilibrium level $\rho_E = 0$. Formally, in regions $\rho < \rho_l$ and $\rho > \rho_u$, it holds that $\partial\dot{\rho}/\partial\rho < 0$. Though long-run rationality guarantees that profit expectations converge back into the normal range $\rho_u > 0 > \rho_l$ in case the normal range has been left irrespective of the actual level of fundamental data, there exists some probability that regions $\rho < \rho_l$ and $\rho > \rho_u$ are never reached in reality and that, as a result, the reversal of expectations at the turning points of the business cycle is driven both by a switch from chartist-driven expectations to fundamentals-driven expectations, and by rational investors slowing down the growth of profit expectations.

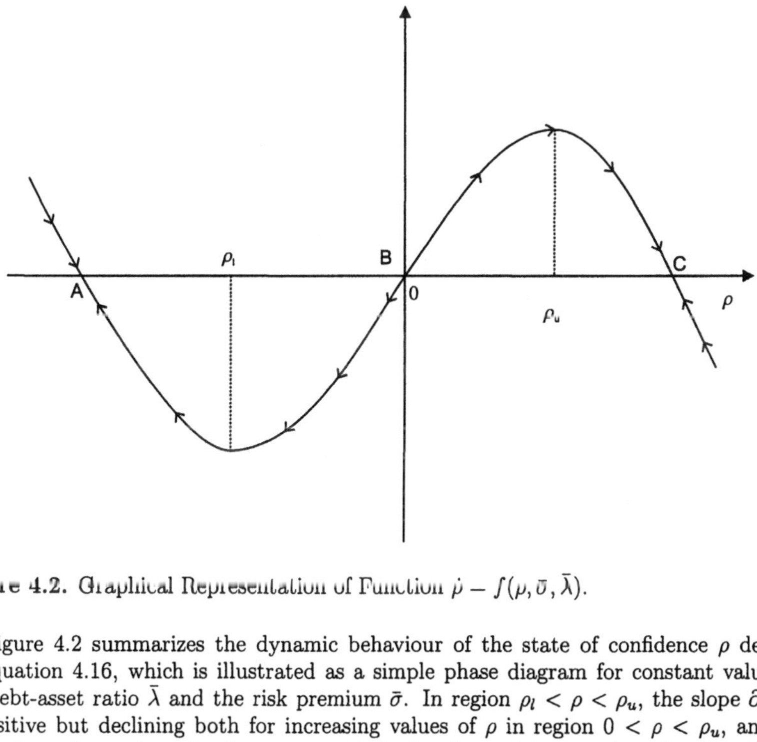

Figure 4.2. Graphical Representation of Function $\dot{\rho} = f(\rho, \bar{\sigma}, \bar{\lambda})$.

Figure 4.2 summarizes the dynamic behaviour of the state of confidence ρ defined by equation 4.16, which is illustrated as a simple phase diagram for constant values of the debt-asset ratio $\bar{\lambda}$ and the risk premium $\bar{\sigma}$. In region $\rho_l < \rho < \rho_u$, the slope $\partial\dot{\rho}/\partial\rho$ is positive but declining both for increasing values of ρ in region $0 < \rho < \rho_u$, and for decreasing values ρ in region $0 > \rho > \rho_l$. At the turning points ρ_u and ρ_l, the slope $\partial\dot{\rho}/\partial\rho$ is zero. In regions $\rho < \rho_l$ and $\rho > \rho_u$, the slope $\partial\dot{\rho}/\partial\rho$ is negative. There arise three dynamic equilibria A, B and C, where B represents the rational expectations equilibrium $\rho_E = 0$ being dynamically unstable, and A and B "irrational" long-run equilibria being dynamically stable. Equilibria A and C are denoted as "irrational" equilibria since they correspond to a stable long-run situation being characterized firstly, by investors steadily over- or underestimating the actual profit rate, and secondly, by the expected profit rate lying outside the normal range, a situation which cannot be validated by the stylized facts. This result is a first hint that the economic system tends to instability if investors follow general market sentiments, and to stability in case investors speculate against "mass psychology" due to the belief in the long-run rational expectations equilibrium $\rho_E = 0$, leading however to "irrational" and stable long-run multiple equilibria.

The Dynamic Behaviour of the Debt-Asset Ratio. The present model assumes that the firm sector has two sources of finance for (net) investment: retained earnings and (net) borrowing from banks. Issuance of new shares is neglected but would not change the general results of the model.[36] Formally, the nominal financing condition for new investment can be stated as

$$P\,I = \eta(q)\,K\,P = s_r\,r\,P\,K + \dot{L}, \tag{4.17}$$

where s_r denotes the retention ratio or the "saving rate" out of profits, $s_r\,r\,P\,K$ retained earnings, and $\dot{L}$ the new amount of loans. This perspective treats loans as a residual, implying that firms are not directly quantity constrained as to the amount of loans. However, since financial intermediaries live in the same expectational climate like private investors, a kind of credit rationing takes places via the influence of Tobin's q on the amount of new investment. If, for example, the state of confidence deteriorates suddenly, the result in the model is a quick reduction in investment; the same reduction in investment can be also explained by banks cutting their supply of new borrowing due to the deterioration of expectations. As a result, though there is no explicit credit rationing owing to the assumption of bank loans serving as a residual in the financing process, some kind of implicit credit rationing is incorporated via Tobin's q. Dividing both sides of equation 4.17 by the numéraire PK, and taking into consideration that it holds that $1/PK = \lambda/L$, the nominal financing condition in terms of growth rates can be restated as

$$\eta(q) = s_r\,r + \frac{\dot{L}}{L}\lambda.$$

The dynamic behaviour of the debt-asset ratio in differential equation form is derived firstly, by solving the growth rate of the debt asset ratio, formally given as

$$\frac{\dot{\lambda}}{\lambda} = \frac{\dot{L}}{L} - \frac{\dot{P}}{P} - \frac{\dot{K}}{K} = \frac{\dot{L}}{L} - \hat{p} - \eta(q),$$

for $\dot{\lambda}$, reading as

$$\dot{\lambda} = \frac{\dot{L}}{L}\lambda - \hat{p}\,\lambda - \eta(q)\,\lambda,$$

secondly, by solving the modified nominal financing condition for $(\dot{L}/L)\lambda$ reading as

$$\frac{\dot{L}}{L}\lambda = \eta(q) - s_r\,r,$$

[36]Neglecting the issuance of new equities as another possible form of external finance can be justified, according to the theory of imperfect capital markets and according to empirical data, by the fact that retained earnings and loans are the cheapest and thereby the most important sources of finance.

and thirdly, by inserting the expression $(\dot{L}/L)\lambda$ into the above given equation for $\dot{\lambda}$, resulting after some further algebra in the change of the debt-asset ratio, formally given by

$$\dot{\lambda} = (1-\lambda)\,\eta(q) - s_r\, r - \hat{p}\,\lambda. \tag{4.18}$$

Hence, an increase in indebtedness, i.e. a rise in $\dot{\lambda}$ for a given λ, results ceteris paribus from an increase in the capital stock's growth rate $\eta(q)$, from a fall in the retention ratio s_r, from a fall in the profit rate r, and from a fall in the price level's growth rate $\hat{p}$ reflecting Fisher's debt deflation process in disinflationary or deflationary periods.

4.4.2 The Local Dynamics of the System

Equations 4.16 and 4.18 constitute a nonlinear differential equation system in the two variables λ and ρ, formally given by

$$\dot{\lambda} = F_1(\lambda,\rho) = (1-\lambda)\,\eta(q) - s_r\, r - \hat{p}\,\lambda \tag{4.19}$$

$$\dot{\rho} = F_2(\lambda,\rho) = f(\rho,\sigma,\lambda). \tag{4.20}$$

To study the local dynamics of the system, the nonlinear system has to be linearized around the local intertemporal equilibrium point λ_E, ρ_E by a linear Taylor expansion, formally described by

$$\begin{bmatrix}\dot{\lambda}\\ \dot{\rho}\end{bmatrix} = \begin{bmatrix}\frac{\partial F_1}{\partial \lambda} & \frac{\partial F_1}{\partial \rho}\\ \frac{\partial F_2}{\partial \lambda} & \frac{\partial F_2}{\partial \rho}\end{bmatrix}_{(\lambda_E,\rho_E)} \cdot \begin{bmatrix}\lambda-\lambda_E\\ \rho-\rho_E\end{bmatrix} = \mathbf{J_E}\cdot\begin{bmatrix}\lambda-\lambda_E\\ \rho-\rho_E\end{bmatrix},$$

where $\mathbf{J_E}$ denotes the Jacobian matrix evaluated at the local intertemporal equilibrium λ_E, ρ_E. The signs of the partial derivatives of the Jacobian matrix $\mathbf{J_E}$ are evaluated by making use of the partial derivatives' signs of the comparative static analysis given explicitly in section 4.7. The partial derivative of function F_1 with respect to λ is given as

$$\frac{\partial F_1}{\partial \lambda} = (-\eta(q) - \hat{p}) + (1-\lambda)\frac{d\eta}{dq}\frac{\partial q}{\partial \lambda} + (-s_r)\frac{\partial r}{\partial \lambda} + (-\lambda)\frac{\partial \hat{p}}{\partial \lambda} \qquad < 0,$$

which is assumed to be negative because s_r and $\partial\hat{p}/\partial\lambda$ are comparatively small in relation to other terms. The partial derivative of function F_1 with respect to ρ reads as

$$\frac{\partial F_1}{\partial \rho} = (1-\lambda)\frac{d\eta}{dq}\frac{\partial q}{\partial \rho} + (-s_r)\frac{\partial r}{\partial \rho} + (-\lambda)\frac{\partial \hat{p}}{\partial \rho} \qquad > 0,$$

which is assumed to have a positive sign because, like in the case above, s_r and $\partial\hat{p}/\partial\rho$ are comparatively small in relation to the other terms. The partial derivative of F_2 with respect to λ is given by

$$\frac{\partial F_2}{\partial \lambda} = \frac{\partial f}{\partial \lambda} + \frac{\partial f}{\partial \sigma}\frac{\partial \sigma}{\partial \lambda} \qquad < 0,$$

being negative, where it holds that

$$\frac{\partial \sigma}{\partial \lambda} = \frac{\partial \sigma}{\partial r}\frac{\partial r}{\partial \lambda} + \frac{\partial \sigma}{\partial \hat{p}}\frac{\partial \hat{p}}{\partial \lambda} \qquad < 0.$$

The partial derivative of function F_2 with respect to ρ, determining whether investors follow or speculate against general market conventions depending on the actual levels of the state of confidence and economic fundamentals, is the core variable determining stability or instability of the system which is formally given by

$$\frac{\partial F_2}{\partial \rho} = \frac{\partial f}{\partial \rho} + \frac{\partial f}{\partial \sigma}\frac{\partial \sigma}{\partial \rho} \quad \gtreqless 0,$$

where it holds that

$$\frac{\partial f}{\partial \rho} \gtreqless 0, \quad \frac{\partial \sigma}{\partial \rho} = \frac{\partial r}{\partial \rho} + \frac{\partial \sigma}{\partial i}\frac{\partial i}{\partial \rho} + \frac{\partial \sigma}{\partial \hat{p}}\frac{\partial \hat{p}}{\partial \rho} > 0 \quad \text{and} \quad \frac{\partial f}{\partial \sigma}\frac{\partial \sigma}{\partial \rho} > 0.$$

Ergo, the sign of $\partial F_2/\partial \rho$ is ambiguous, depending on the sign of $\partial f/\partial \rho$, i.e. on the actual position of the state of confidence ρ within the normal range $\rho_l < 0 < \rho_u$ having been discussed before. Summing up, the Jacobian matrix can take the following signs

$$\mathbf{J} = \begin{bmatrix} \frac{\partial F_1}{\partial \lambda} & \frac{\partial F_1}{\partial \rho} \\ \frac{\partial F_2}{\partial \lambda} & \frac{\partial F_2}{\partial \rho} \end{bmatrix} = \begin{bmatrix} - & + \\ - & -,0,+ \end{bmatrix},$$

where local asymptotic stability or instability depends on the signs of $\partial F_2/\partial \rho$ and $\partial f/\partial \rho$, i.e. on investors' willingness to follow general market conventions irrespective of the current state of fundamentals.

Regarding local dynamic stability of potential intertemporal equilibria, which are going to be discussed in the following section, there arise three possible stability patterns. *Case 1* comprises three subcases, where subcase 1 refers to a situation in which the state of confidence at the fixed point ρ_E lies inside the normal range $\rho_l < 0 < \rho_u$ but is located nearly to the corner points, i.e. when investors willingness to keep on following general market sentiments declines rapidly; formally, subcase 1 corresponds to an only slightly positive sign of derivative $\partial f/\partial \rho$. Subcase 2 refers to the situation when the state of confidence at the fixed point ρ_E coincides with the two corner points ρ_l and ρ_u, i.e. when investors stop to follow the past trend of general market sentiment since the minimum/maximum value of ρ has been reached which is still compatible with the long-run rational expectations equilibrium $\rho_E = 0$; formally, this situation corresponds to a zero value of derivative $\partial f/\partial \rho$. Subcase 3 refers to the situation when the state of confidence at the fixed point ρ_E lies outside the normal range in regions $\rho < \rho_l$ and $\rho > \rho_u$, i.e. when investors speculate against the past market trend since the actual level of ρ is viewed as being irrationally underestimated/exaggerated and not compatible with the long-run rational expectations equilibrium $\rho_E = 0$; formally, subcase 3 corresponds to a negative sign of derivative $\partial f/\partial \rho$. Summing up, case 1 is formally characterized by the condition

$$\frac{\partial f}{\partial \rho} \leqslant 0 \quad \text{or} \quad \frac{\partial f}{\partial \rho} > 0 \quad \text{but very small},$$

leading to a negative, zero or a slightly positive (in comparison to cases 2 and 3) sign of derivative $\partial F_2/\partial \rho$, since

$$\frac{\partial F_2}{\partial \rho} = \underbrace{\frac{\partial f}{\partial \rho}}_{-,0,+\text{small}} + \underbrace{\frac{\partial f}{\partial \sigma}}_{+}\underbrace{\frac{\partial \sigma}{\partial \rho}}_{+},$$

resulting in

$$\frac{\partial F_2}{\partial \rho} \leqslant 0 \quad \text{or} \quad \frac{\partial F_2}{\partial \rho} > 0 \quad \text{but very small.}$$

A local fixed point being subject to formal conditions of case 1 exhibits local asymptotic stability due to a negative sign of the trace and a positive sign of the determinant of the Jacobian evaluated at the intertemporal equilibrium, i.e. the local fixed point is either a stable node or a stable focus. Formally, it holds that

$$tr\,\mathbf{J_E} = \underset{-}{\frac{\partial F_1}{\partial \lambda}} + \underset{-,0,+\,\text{small}}{\frac{\partial F_2}{\partial \rho}} < 0$$

and

$$|\mathbf{J_E}| = \underset{-}{\frac{\partial F_1}{\partial \lambda}} \underset{-,0,+\,\text{small}}{\frac{\partial F_2}{\partial \rho}} - \underset{+}{\frac{\partial F_1}{\partial \rho}} \underset{-}{\frac{\partial F_2}{\partial \lambda}} > 0.$$

Case 2 and case 3 both refer to a situation when the state of confidence at the fixed point ρ_E lies close to the rational expectations equilibrium $\rho_E = 0$ inside the normal range $\rho_l < 0 < \rho_u$, i.e. when investors' willingness to follow general market sentiments by extrapolating past realizations of ρ into the future is has reached its maximum. However, investors' willingness to follow general market sentiments can be subdivided on the one hand into a case being characterized by "hypersensitively" reacting investors constituting case 2, and on the other hand into with "normally" reacting investors constituting case 3 giving rise to different dynamic stability patters.

Case 2 relating to hypersensitively reacting investors, refers to a situation when expectations within the normal range near to the rational expectations equilibrium react very sensitively to general market sentiments, leading to a large value of $\dot{\rho}$ in absolute terms at a given fixed point. Formally, case 2 is characterized by the condition

$$\frac{\partial f}{\partial \rho} \gg 0,$$

leading to a large positive sign of derivative $\partial F_2/\partial \rho$ since it holds that

$$\frac{\partial F_2}{\partial \rho} = \underset{+\text{large}}{\frac{\partial f}{\partial \rho}} + \underset{+}{\frac{\partial f}{\partial \sigma}} \underset{+}{\frac{\partial \sigma}{\partial \rho}} \gg 0.$$

A local fixed point being subject to the characteristics of hypersensitively reacting investors exhibits saddle point behaviour, i.e. the local fixed point is dynamically unstable since the determinant of the Jacobian matrix is negative which constitutes a necessary and sufficient condition for a saddle point equilibrium independently of the sign of the trace. Formally, the trace and the determinant of the Jacobian evaluated at the local fixed point are given by

$$tr\,\mathbf{J_E} = \underset{-}{\frac{\partial F_1}{\partial \lambda}} + \underset{+\,\text{large}}{\frac{\partial F_2}{\partial \rho}} \gg 0$$

and

$$|\mathbf{J_E}| = \underset{-}{\frac{\partial F_1}{\partial \lambda}} \underset{+\,\text{large}}{\frac{\partial F_2}{\partial \rho}} - \underset{+}{\frac{\partial F_1}{\partial \rho}} \underset{-}{\frac{\partial F_2}{\partial \lambda}} < 0.$$

Case 3 refers to a situation when expectations within the normal range near to the rational expectations equilibrium follow general market sentiments in a "normal" way, i.e. when the same fixed point near the rational expectations equilibrium as in case 2 leads to a much smaller value of $\dot{\rho}$ in absolute terms. Formally, normally reacting investors in case 3 are described by the condition

$$\frac{\partial f}{\partial \rho} > 0,$$

where the positive sign is smaller than in case 2, but larger than in case 1. As a result, derivative $\partial F_2/\partial \rho$ has also a "normal" positive sign since

$$\frac{\partial F_2}{\partial \rho} = \underset{+}{\frac{\partial f}{\partial \rho}} + \underset{+}{\frac{\partial f}{\partial \sigma}} \underset{+}{\frac{\partial \sigma}{\partial \rho}} > 0,$$

which is however smaller than in case 2. A local fixed point being subject to formal conditions of case 3 is subject to local asymptotic instability, because both the trace and the determinant have a positive sign, i.e. the local fixed point exhibits either the characteristics of an unstable node or an unstable focus. Formally, the trace is given by

$$tr\, \mathbf{J_E} = \underset{-}{\frac{\partial F_1}{\partial \lambda}} + \underset{+}{\frac{\partial F_2}{\partial \rho}} > 0,$$

having a positive sign since it holds that $|\partial F_1/\partial \lambda| < |\partial F_2/\partial \rho|$ which is consistent with the assumptions made in cases 1 and 2. The determinant is given by

$$|\mathbf{J_E}| = \underset{-}{\frac{\partial F_1}{\partial \lambda}} \underset{+}{\frac{\partial F_2}{\partial \rho}} - \underset{+}{\frac{\partial F_1}{\partial \rho}} \underset{-}{\frac{\partial F_2}{\partial \lambda}} > 0,$$

however, having a positive sign only if condition

$$|\underset{-}{\frac{\partial F_1}{\partial \lambda}} \underset{+}{\frac{\partial F_2}{\partial \rho}}| < |\underset{+}{\frac{\partial F_1}{\partial \rho}} \underset{-}{\frac{\partial F_2}{\partial \lambda}}|$$

is fulfilled which is going to be proved in the following phase diagram analysis.

4.4.3 Phase Diagram Analysis

The slope of demarcation curve $\dot{\lambda} = F_1(\lambda, \rho) = 0$, being denoted as $(d\lambda/d\rho)_{F_1}$ and derived from equation 4.19, is positive over the entire range because

$$\left(\frac{d\lambda}{d\rho}\right)_{F_1} = -\frac{\frac{\partial F_1}{\partial \rho}}{\frac{\partial F_1}{\partial \lambda}} > 0.$$

The slope of demarcation curve $\dot{\rho} = F_2(\lambda, \rho) = 0$, being denoted as $(d\lambda/d\rho)_{F_2}$ and derived from equation 4.20, varies with ρ since it depends on the slope of function $\partial F_2/\partial \rho$ which is determined by the slope of function $\dot{\rho} = f(\rho, \sigma, \lambda)$ depicted in figure 4.2 for constant values $\bar{\sigma}$ and $\bar{\lambda}$. Formally, the slope of the demarcation curve $\dot{\rho} = F_2(\lambda, \rho) = 0$ is given by

$$\left(\frac{d\lambda}{d\rho}\right)_{F_2} = -\frac{\overset{-,0,+}{\frac{\partial F_2}{\partial \rho}}}{\underset{-}{\frac{\partial F_2}{\partial \lambda}}} \lesseqgtr 0.$$

Since $\partial F_2/\partial\lambda$ is negative, a negative sign of $\partial F_2/\partial\rho$ caused by a negative value of $\partial f/\partial\rho$ for which it holds that $|\partial f/\partial\rho| > |(\partial f/\partial\sigma)(\partial\sigma/d\rho)|$, leads to a negative slope of demarcation curve $\dot{\rho} = 0$, i.e. to $(\partial\lambda/\partial\rho)_{F_2} < 0$. A negative value of $\partial f/\partial\rho$ which amounts to $\partial f/\partial\rho = (-\partial f/\partial\sigma)(\partial\sigma/d\rho)$ leads to a zero value of $\partial F_2/\partial\rho$, and therefore to a zero slope of demarcation curve $\dot{\rho} = F_2(\lambda, \rho) = 0$, i.e. to $(\partial\lambda/\partial\rho)_{F_2} = 0$. A negative value of $\partial f/\partial\rho$ for which it holds that $|\partial f/\partial\rho| < |(\partial f/\partial\sigma)(\partial\sigma/d\rho)|$, a zero value of $\partial f/\partial\rho$, and all positive values of $\partial f/\partial\rho$ lead to a positive sign of $\partial F_2/\partial\rho$, and therefore to a positive slope of demarcation curve $\dot{\rho} = F_2(\lambda, \rho) = 0$, i.e. to $(\partial\lambda/\partial\rho)_{F_2} > 0$. Though the points with zero slope of demarcation curve $\dot{\rho} = F_2(\lambda, \rho) = 0$ do not equal exactly the outer bounds of the normal range ρ_l and ρ_u but only approximately, the shape of demarcation curve $\dot{\rho} = F_2(\lambda, \rho) = 0$ can be explained analogously to the course of function $\dot{\rho} = f(\rho, \sigma, \lambda)$. As a result, demarcation curve $\dot{\rho} = F_2(\lambda, \rho) = 0$ exhibits a positive slope in case ρ is located within the area of the normal range, a shrinking positive slope reducing to zero in case ρ reaches the area of the two corner points ρ_l and ρ_u, and a negative slope in case ρ reaches the area outside the normal range.

Despite the fact that each demarcation curve $\dot{\rho} = F_2(\lambda, \rho) = 0$ exhibits the same basic cubic shape as function $\dot{\rho} = f(\rho, \sigma, \lambda)$, demarcation curves can differ with respect to their steepness within and outside the normal range depending on the strength of the influence of the current state of confidence ρ on investors' change in profit expectations $\partial f/\partial\rho$. As outlined in the local stability analysis in section 4.4.2, two relevant cases of investors' behaviour giving rise to different local dynamics have to be distinguished, i.e. the case of "normally", and the case of "hypersensitively" reacting investors within the normal range of ρ, having been discussed as cases 2 and 3 of local stability analysis. As a result, phase diagram analysis has to consider as well both possible forms of investors' behaviour being reflected in two different classes of demarcation curve $\dot{\rho} = F_2(\lambda, \rho) = 0$. Figure 4.3 depicts two possible demarcation curves $\dot{\rho} = F_2(\lambda, \rho) = 0$, where the solid line corresponds to case 3 of local stability analysis assuming "normally" reacting investors within the normal range, i.e. it holds that $\partial f/\partial\rho > 0$ within the normal range, whereas the dotted line corresponds to case 2 of local stability analysis assuming "hypersensitively" reacting investors within the normal range, i.e. here it holds that $\partial f/\partial\rho \gg 0$ within the normal range. As a result, the more sensitively investors react to changes in ρ within the normal range, the steeper the demarcation curve $\dot{\rho} = 0$ in the normal range becomes. It must be noted that no explicit distinction has been made between normal and hypersensitive investors' behaviour outside the normal range since it does not influence significantly the dynamic patterns of the model. As a result, though the slope of the dotted demarcation curve in figure 4.3 outside the normal range is assumed to be steeper than the slope of the solid demarcation curve, it is also possible that the slope of the dotted lined outside the normal range is flatter than the slope of the solid line.

The distinction among hypersensitively and normally reacting investors, resulting in different shapes of demarcation curve $\dot{\rho} = F_2(\lambda, \rho) = 0$ and in different phase diagrams

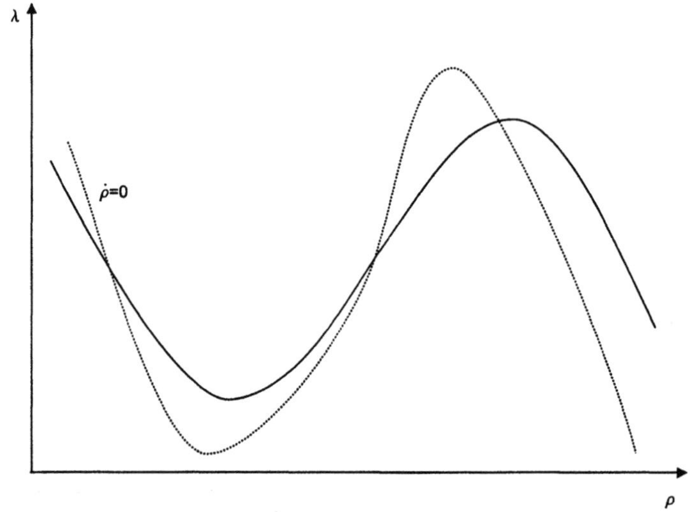

Figure 4.3: Possible Demarcation Curves $\dot{\rho} = 0$ Depending on Investors' Sensitivity as to Changes in ρ

being illustrated in figures 4.4 and 4.5, is not only of crucial importance for the local dynamics of the system, but also for the number of possible intertemporal equilibria, determining the global dynamics of the system. Figure 4.4 refers to the case when investors react very sensitively as to changes in the state of confidence ρ, being represented by a comparatively steep demarcation curve $\dot{\rho} = F_2(\lambda, \rho) = 0$ in the normal range. As phase diagram analysis in figure 4.4 indicates, there arise three fixed points A, B and C with different stability patterns. Points A and C are local asymptotically stable because of a local negatively sloped demarcation curve $\dot{\rho} = F_2(\lambda, \rho) = 0$ (since $\partial f/\partial \rho < 0$ and $\partial F_2/\partial \rho$ at A and C), and a positively sloped demarcation curve $\dot{\lambda} = F_1(\lambda, \rho) = 0$, i.e. formally it holds that

$$\underset{+}{\left(\frac{\partial \lambda}{\partial \rho}\right)_{F_1}} > \underset{-}{\left(\frac{\partial \lambda}{\partial \rho}\right)_{F_2}}$$

$$-\frac{\frac{\partial F_1}{\partial \rho}}{\frac{\partial F_1}{\partial \lambda}} > -\frac{\frac{\partial F_2}{\partial \rho}}{\frac{\partial F_2}{\partial \lambda}},$$

which, after rearranging terms, can be transformed into the Jacobian's determinant at the fixed points A and C, being denoted as $|\mathbf{J}|_{(A,C)}$, which exhibits a positive sign since it holds that

$$|\mathbf{J}|_{(A,C)} = \underset{-}{\frac{\partial F_1}{\partial \lambda}} \underset{-}{\frac{\partial F_2}{\partial \rho}} - \underset{+}{\frac{\partial F_1}{\partial \rho}} \underset{-}{\frac{\partial F_2}{\partial \lambda}} > 0.$$

The trace of the Jacobian matrix at fixed points A and C, being denoted as $tr\mathbf{J}_{(A,C)}$, exhibits a negative sign because

$$tr\mathbf{J}_{(A,C)} = \underset{-}{\frac{\partial F_1}{\partial \lambda}} + \underset{-}{\frac{\partial F_2}{\partial \rho}} < 0,$$

causing local asymptotic stability of points A and C according to case 1 of local stability analysis.

Equilibrium point B is subject to saddle point behaviour since both demarcation curves exhibit a positive slope, where demarcation curve $\dot{\rho} = F_2(\lambda, \rho) = 0$, being subject to $\partial f/\partial \rho \gg 0$ and $\partial F_2/\partial \rho \gg 0$, is steeper than demarcation curve $\dot{\lambda} = F_1(\lambda, \rho) = 0$, i.e. formally it holds that

$$\underset{+}{\left(\frac{\partial \lambda}{\partial \rho}\right)_{F_1}} < \underset{+}{\left(\frac{\partial \lambda}{\partial \rho}\right)_{F_2}}$$

$$-\frac{\frac{\partial F_1}{\partial \rho}}{\frac{\partial F_1}{\partial \lambda}} < -\frac{\frac{\partial F_2}{\partial \rho}}{\frac{\partial F_2}{\partial \lambda}},$$

which can be transformed by rearranging terms into the Jacobian's determinant at point B, being denoted as $|\mathbf{J}_{(B)}|$, having a negative sign because

$$|\mathbf{J}_{(B)}| = \underset{-}{\frac{\partial F_1}{\partial \lambda}} \underset{+\text{large}}{\frac{\partial F_2}{\partial \rho}} - \underset{+}{\frac{\partial F_1}{\partial \rho}} \underset{-}{\frac{\partial F_2}{\partial \lambda}} < 0.$$

The trace of the Jacobian matrix at point B, being denoted as $tr\mathbf{J}_{(B)}$, exhibits a positive sign because

$$tr\mathbf{J}_{(B)} = \underset{-}{\frac{\partial F_1}{\partial \lambda}} + \underset{+\text{large}}{\frac{\partial F_2}{\partial \rho}} > 0,$$

giving rise to saddle point behaviour corresponding to case 2 of local stability analysis in section 4.4.2.

Though the case of multiple equilibria depicted in figure 4.4 is a possible theoretical solution, it has no empirical relevance since settling down in stable fixed points A or C would mean that economic agents persistently under- or overestimate the actual profit rate due to $\rho_E \neq 0$ in A and C lying near the corner points of the normal range of ρ. Consequently, hypersensitively reacting investors do not behave rationally even in the long-run, which has been assumed explicitly to hold according to the expectation formation scheme $\dot{\rho} = f(\rho, \sigma, \lambda)$. Moreover, the dynamic system is subject to path dependent behaviour, i.e. whether the system comes to a halt in the "good" (golden-age) boom equilibrium C, or settles down in the "bad" depression equilibrium A, is a matter of chance since the long-run steady-state is dependent on the initial starting position which can be located everywhere in the (λ, ρ)-space. Guaranteeing a unique long-run stable solution at point B by assuming, like in rational expectations models, that rational investors can always "jump" on the stable branches of the saddle point is not possible in the present case since the state of confidence ρ does not exhibit the characteristics of a pure forward looking or jump variable, firstly, owing to its dependence on the two backward looking

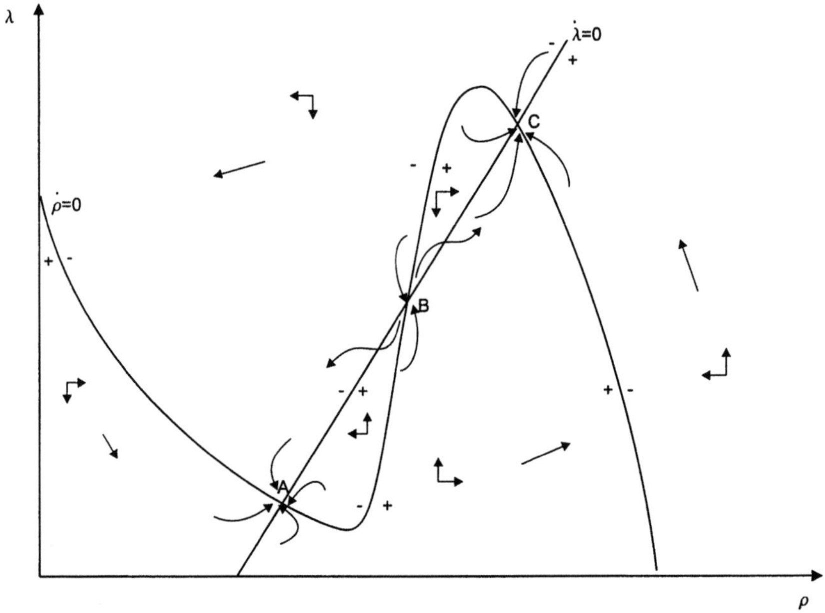

Figure 4.4: Phase Diagram in Case of Hypersensitively Reacting Investors Within the Normal Range of ρ

variables σ and λ, and secondly due to the assumption that investors are not subject to (short-run) rational behaviour according to the rational expectations hypothesis.[37]

It has to be emphasized however, that there exists the possibility of jumps in ρ independently of the current state of economic fundamentals σ and λ, in case the economy is hit by direct exogenous shocks having only an influence on the current state of ρ. By way of contrast, direct exogenous shocks to fundamentals σ and λ, as well as indirect exogenous shocks to σ and λ via shocks to other variables influencing σ and λ, do not lead to a jump in ρ. For example, the introduction of a new technology regime or beginning financial liberalization can cause a sudden upward "jump" in ρ due to a discontinuous rise in profit expectations though there is no change in fundamentals σ and λ, as well as no exogenous shock to other variables influencing σ and λ. Despite the fact that direct shocks to ρ lead to a discontinuous change of the ρ-coordinate within the (λ, ρ)-space, they do not cause a change of the two demarcation curves, as well as no alteration of the vector field, i.e. there is no change of trajectories. As a result, direct exogenous shocks to the state of confidence ρ interrupt past dynamic behaviour by jumping to another new initial condition setting up a new dynamic process in the (λ, ρ)-space. In the same way, a direct exogenous shock to the debt-asset ratio λ causes a change of the λ-coordinate within the (λ, ρ)-space without changing demarcation curves and trajectories. By way of

[37] For the distinction between forward and backward looking variables, and their influence on general solutions to rational expectations models, see appendix D.

contrast, a direct exogenous shock to σ, as well as any exogenous shock to other variables influencing σ cause firstly, a change both in the position and in the slope of the two demarcation curves, and secondly, a change in the slope of the current trajectory though the system rests at the current (λ, ρ)-coordinate at the moment of the shock, i.e. there arise no jumps within the (λ, ρ)-space but changes in the vector field.[38]

Despite the fact that there are possible jumps in the state of confidence ρ, there is no mechanism as in rational expectations models guaranteeing that the jump in ρ catapults the dynamic system to the stable branches of the saddle point, thereby leading to a unique and asymptotically stable intertemporal equilibrium. As a result, the dynamic system under hypersensitively reacting investors is most likely to settle down either in stable fixed point point A or in stable fixed point C, since the probability of reaching the stable branches of the saddle point B is very low. However, settling down in A or C means that investors are subject to long-run expectations errors, which is on the one hand a very unrealistic scenario from an empirical point of view, and on the other hand not consistent with the model assumption of long-run rational behaviour. Thus, it seems reasonable to assume that, in case the system has settled down either in A or C, investors are going to readjust their profit expectations after having realized that expectations cannot be fulfilled by the actual development of the profit rate, leading to a change in the expectation formation scheme until the actual profit rate corresponds to its expectation value, i.e. until the system comes to a halt in the long-run rational expectations equilibrium $\rho_E = 0$. Formally, the assumption of readjusting expectations as long as they are fulfilled by actual data means that settling down either in A or C leads to a shift in the expectation formation function $\dot{\rho} = f(\rho, \sigma, \lambda)$ and, as a result, in demarcation curve $\dot{\rho} = F_2(\lambda, \rho) = 0$ until the long-run rational expectations equilibrium $\rho_E = 0$ is realized.

Accordingly, it seems reasonable to assume that the long-run steady state value of the state of confidence ρ is the long-run rational expectations equilibrium $\rho_E = 0$ since each constellation $r^e \neq r$ leads to a readjustment of functions $\dot{\rho} = f(\rho, \sigma, \lambda)$ and $\dot{\rho} = F_2(\lambda, \rho) = 0$ until $\rho_E = 0$ is realized. Moreover, it seems also reasonable to assume that there exists only one fixed point (λ_E, ρ_E) for which it holds that $\rho_E = 0$ and $\lambda_E > 0$[39], since a unique value for ρ_E implies a unique value for λ_E due to the fact that demarcation curve $\dot{\lambda} = F_1(\lambda, \rho) = 0$ is a strictly monotone increasing function in the (λ, ρ)-space. However, these two assumptions, which are necessary conditions for a meaningful empirical result, require that investors react "normally" within the normal range for ρ, i.e. the dynamic system has to fulfill the condition $\partial f / \partial \rho > 0$ and $\partial F_2 / \partial \rho > 0$ within the normal range, implying a much less steeper demarcation curve $\dot{\rho} = F_2(\lambda, \rho) = 0$, and giving rise to a single fixed point as depicted in figure 4.5.

---

[38]The impact of different kinds of exogenous shocks on the (λ, ρ)-phase plane can be studied by analyzing the impact on the two demarcation curves, as well as on the integral curves which are formally given by

$$\frac{d\lambda}{d\rho} = \frac{F_1(\lambda, \rho)}{F_2(\lambda, \rho)} = \frac{(1-\lambda)\,\eta(q) - s_r\, r - \hat{p}\,\lambda}{f(\rho, \sigma, \lambda)},$$

having been derived by eliminating dt from system 4.19 and 4.20. For a formal treatment of integral curves, see Gandolfo (1997), chapter 21.3.2.1.

[39]Negative values for λ, which would imply that the firm sector owns financial claims towards the banking system, are excluded by assumption.

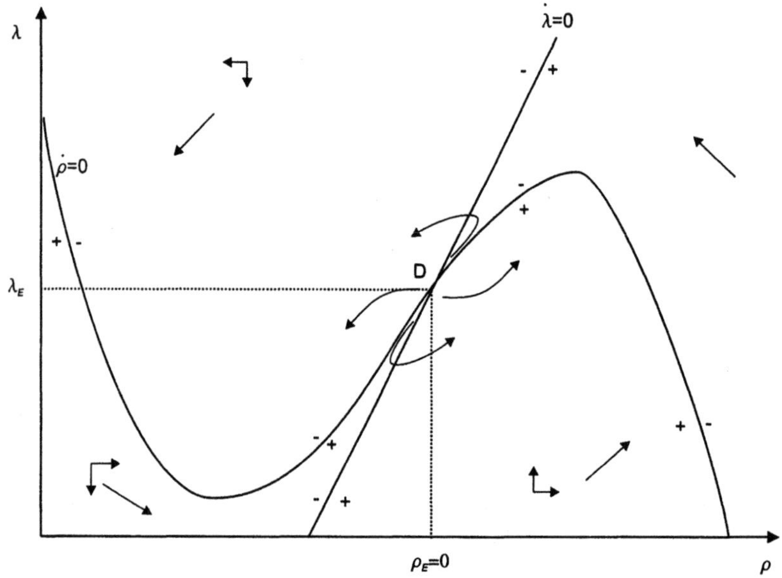

Figure 4.5: Phase Diagram in Case of Normally Reacting Investors Within the Normal Range of ρ

The dynamic system under normally reacting investors in figure 4.5 is characterized by a single fixed point D for which it holds that $\rho_E = 0$ and $\lambda_E > 0$. Equilibrium point D is asymptotically unstable since both demarcation curves have a positive slope, whereas the slope of demarcation curve $\dot{\lambda} = F_1(\lambda, \rho) = 0$ is steeper than demarcation curve $\dot{\rho} = F_2(\lambda, \rho) = 0$ at point D because $\partial f / \partial \rho > 0$ and $\partial F_2 / \partial \rho > 0$, i.e. formally it holds that

$$\underset{+}{\left(\frac{\partial \lambda}{\partial \rho}\right)_{F_1}} > \underset{+}{\left(\frac{\partial \lambda}{\partial \rho}\right)_{F_2}}$$

$$-\frac{\frac{\partial F_1}{\partial \rho}}{\frac{\partial F_1}{\partial \lambda}} > -\frac{\frac{\partial F_2}{\partial \rho}}{\frac{\partial F_2}{\partial \lambda}}.$$

This inequality yields, after rearranging terms, the determinant of the Jacobian at fixed point D, being denoted as $|\mathbf{J}_{(D)}|$, having a positive sign since

$$|\mathbf{J}_{(D)}| = \underset{-}{\frac{\partial F_1}{\partial \lambda}} \underset{+\text{normal}}{\frac{\partial F_2}{\partial \rho}} - \underset{+}{\frac{\partial F_1}{\partial \rho}} \underset{-}{\frac{\partial F_2}{\partial \lambda}} > 0.$$

The trace of the Jacobian matrix at fixed point D, which is denoted as $tr\mathbf{J}_{(D)}$, has also a positive sign since

$$tr\mathbf{J}_{(D)} = \underset{-}{\frac{\partial F_1}{\partial \lambda}} + \underset{+\text{normal}}{\frac{\partial F_2}{\partial \rho}} > 0,$$

giving rise to an unstable local fixed point (unstable node or unstable focus) according to case 3 of local stability analysis in section 4.4.2. One important dynamic property of the phase diagram in figure 4.5 is the fact that the non-linear system causes counterclockwise cyclical motions which cannot converge to the unstable fixed point D, giving rise to the question of global dynamic stability being analyzed in the following section.

4.4.4 The Global Dynamics of the System

The Emergence of a Globally Stable Closed Orbit. Phase diagram analysis has concluded that the case of normally reacting investors depicted in figure 4.5 can be considered as a good approximation to the formation of expectations under irreducible uncertainty since it allows for a single fixed point at the long-run rational expectations equilibrium $\rho_E = 0$. However, a first ad-hoc interpretation of the global dynamics in figure 4.5 causes doubts regarding global dynamic stability in the sense that the system actually converges to $\rho_E = 0$ for two reasons. Firstly, though the long-run rational expectations equilibrium $\rho_E = 0$ exists, the system cannot settle down in unstable fixed point D unless the system starts in point D. Secondly, it is not clear whether the system is going to explode by outward spiraling counterclockwise motions, or whether the system comes to a cyclical halt, i.e. whether the system converges to a closed curve so that there exists at least a cyclical tendency to reach the long-run rational expectations equilibrium $\rho_E = 0$. That is, there arises the question whether the model economy is subject to increasing instability in the sense that boom-bust cycles and financial crises tend to become more and more pronounced, or whether there exists a "cyclical" equilibrium to which the system converges, being characterized by stable boom-bust cycles with constant amplitudes which are possibly subject to financial distress.

In mathematical terms, the main question reads whether there arise closed orbits in figure 4.5 which are attractors. If a closed orbit is an attractor, it will be defined as a *limit cycle* in the following. The existence of limit cycles can be proved by the *Poincaré-Bendixon theorem* providing sufficient conditions for the existence of closed orbits in particular sub-areas of the plane[40] which reads as:

Theorem 4.1 (The Poincaré-Bendixon Theorem) *A non-empty compact limit set of a C^1 dynamical system in $\mathbb{R}^2$, which contains no fixed point, is a closed orbit.*

The proof of the existence of closed orbits in the present case by applying the Poincaré-Bendixon theorem is outlined by geometrical considerations of figure 4.6 which is an extended version of figure 4.5. The first prerequisite for the emergence of closed orbits is the existence of an invariant or compact set $\mathcal{D}$. In geometrical terms, an invariant set $\mathcal{D}$ is a set whose vector field on the boundary points inwards everywhere, so that all trajectories once having entered the set will stay within the compact set for all t. The definition of an invariant set $\mathcal{D}$ in the (λ, ρ)-space requires to impose global boundedness on variables λ and ρ. Regarding the debt-asset ratio λ, values smaller than zero, i.e. $\lambda < 0$, are not possible by definition since a negative debt-asset ratio would imply that business firms own claims on the banking sector. Thus, it seems reasonable to assume

[40]Detailed discussions of the Poincaré-Bendixon theorem can be found in Mas-Collel (1986), pp. 64-67, Hirsch and Smale (1974), chapter 11, Lorenz (1993), chapter 2, Guckenheimer and Holmes (1986), p. 44 and Gandolfo (1997), chapter 24.3.

$\lambda = 0$ as a lower bound which cannot be fallen short of. Respecting the upper bound of λ, a value smaller than one, i.e. $\lambda < 1$, could serve as a realistic reference value. However, in case of systemic financial crises, a value greater than one, i.e. $\lambda > 1$ implying bankruptcy of the entire firm sector, has to be regarded, though being an event with low probability from an empirical viewpoint, as a possible scenario as well. As a result, it seems reasonable to assume an upper bound $\lambda > 1$ to exist, which however cannot increase to infinity, since in case of bankruptcy of the entire firm sector debt relief or debt restructuring supported by the domestic government is likely to occur preventing λ to exceed a certain positive threshold. Summing up, the debt-asset ratio λ is assumed to have a lower bound $\lambda = 0$, and an upper positive bound $\lambda > 1$. Regarding global boundedness of the state of confidence, ρ is allowed to take possible negative and positive values largely lying outside the normal range $\rho_l < 0 < \rho_u$, which are however bounded since it seems unrealistic to assume infinite positive as well as infinite negative values of ρ. Summing up, the model assumes that there exists a negative lower and a positive upper bound for ρ whose range exceeds the normal range $\rho_l < 0 < \rho_u$.

The global bounds imposed on λ and ρ within the (λ, ρ)-space allow for the construction of an invariant set in figure 4.6 which is given by the simply connected set[41] $\mathcal{D}$ being described by rectangle $EFGH$. As the vector field on the boundaries of compact set $\mathcal{D}$ in figure 4.6 indicates, there arise situations in which trajectories may hit the boundaries, but cannot leave due to global boundedness assumptions on λ and ρ to guarantee that a trajectory once having entered the compact set $\mathcal{D}$ cannot leave it any more. For example, the trajectory starting in point Z hits the boundary of $\mathcal{D}$ in Z' and would naturally leave compact set $\mathcal{D}$ in northwest direction unless it has been assumed that there exists an upper bound for λ. As a result, once the trajectory starting in Z has reached point Z', the trajectory is going to move along the vertical boundary from Z' to Q, and then back into the interior of set $\mathcal{D}$. In case the boundaries' modification along the passages GQ, HS and EO was neglected by giving up the strict boundedness assumptions on λ and ρ, an alternative invariant set could be set up by area $OFPQRST$ which reduces the feasible global range of λ and ρ but arises naturally. Despite the fact that compact set $OFPQRST$ requires less restrictive assumptions respecting global boundedness, the following analysis refers to compact set $\mathcal{D}$ described by area $EFGH$ since the global boundedness assumptions made above on λ and ρ cover a broader class of possible realizations within the (λ, ρ)-space both from a theoretical and from an empirical viewpoint.

After having shown that the first prerequisite for the emergence of closed orbits is met, i.e. that a trajectory, once having entered the invariant set $\mathcal{D}$, stays within the set for all t, there arises the question how a trajectory may move after it has entered the set, i.e. whether the system converges to a closed orbit within compact set $\mathcal{D}$, or whether the system is subject to different dynamic patterns excluding the existence of closed orbits. In mathematical terms, the question reads whether the invariant set $\mathcal{D}$ contains limit sets. In $\mathbb{R}^2$ there exist three possible forms of limit sets, namely fixed point attractors, limit cycles and saddle loops (or separatrices), differing firstly with respect to the number of fixed points, and secondly with respect to the local stability properties of these fixed points. In case the invariant set $\mathcal{D} \subset \mathbb{R}^2$ contains limit sets, all three types of limit sets are possible among which the Poincarée-Bendixon theorem distinguishes. A fixed point attractor as

[41] For the difference between "simply connected sets" and "connected sets" see Arrowsmith and Place (1990), p. 111 and Debreu (1959), p. 15.

one possible form of limit sets in $\mathbb{R}^2$ does not give rise to a closed orbit according to the Poincaré-Bendixon theorem since it requires the limit set to contain no fixed point, i.e. to contain only *one* fixed point being locally *unstable*, so that trajectories starting near the fixed point are going to be repelled from it. Consequently, as trajectories in continuous-time dynamical systems cannot cross, the only possible remaining limit sets emerging in the compact set $\mathcal{D}$ are limit cycles or saddle loops if the fixed point is unstable. As saddle loops imply at least one further fixed point being subject to saddle point behaviour, this possibility is excluded from the Poincaré-Bendixon theorem. As a result, if there is no possibility for trajectories to leave the compact set $\mathcal{D}$ once they have entered the set, and if there is no possibility for trajectories to reach the single unstable fixed point, and if there is no possibility for trajectories at first to spiral inwards to the fixed point and afterwards to spiral outwards to the boundaries of $\mathcal{D}$ and vice versa since trajectories cannot cross, it follows that all initial points in the compact set $\mathcal{D}$ must converge to a closed curve, i.e. to a limit cycle for $t \rightarrow \infty$.

Despite the fact that the Poincaré-Bendixon theorem excludes the fixed point from the limit set giving rise to a closed orbit, a closed orbit in $\mathbb{R}^2$ always encloses a fixed point according to the following theorem:

Theorem 4.2 *A closed trajectory of a continuously differentiable dynamical system in* $\mathbb{R}^2$*, given by the two-dimensional differential equation system*

$$\dot{x}_1 = f(x_1, x_2)$$
$$\dot{x}_2 = g(x_1, x_2),$$

must necessarily enclose a fixed point with $\dot{x}_1 = \dot{x}_2 = 0$.[42]

Summing up, the existence of a closed orbit in $\mathbb{R}^2$ for a given dynamic system according to the Poincarée-Bendixon theorem can be proved by the following procedure. At first, locate a fixed point of the dynamic system and explore its stability characteristics. Then, in case the fixed point is unstable, search for a compact set $\mathcal{D}$ enclosing the unstable fixed point. In case a closed orbit does not coincide with the boundaries of invariant set $\mathcal{D}$, the vector field of the dynamic system must point into the interior of set $\mathcal{D}$ giving rise to closed orbits and to at least one limit cycle.

In terms of figure 4.6, the Poincaré-Bendixon theorem is fulfilled since firstly, the fixed point D is unstable, and secondly, everywhere on the boundary of the compact set $\mathcal{D}$ the vector field points inwards implying the existence of a globally stable closed orbit, i.e. a limit cycle, which is drawn as a thick circle moving in counterclockwise direction. The convergence of all initial points in $\mathcal{D}$ towards the limit cycle is shown by two sample trajectories, one starting in point I spiraling inwards and converging to the limit cycle, and the other one starting in point J spiraling outwards and converging to the limit cycle.

One drawback of the Poincaré-Bendixon theorem is the fact that the theorem only provides sufficient conditions for the existence of closed orbits in an invariant set $\mathcal{D}$, but does not make any statement about the number of closed orbits. Thus, it is possible that, as e.g. in figure 4.6, there arise several closed orbits. Accordingly, the Poincaré-Bendixon theorem only provides sufficient conditions for the existence of *at least* one limit cycle, i.e. a closed orbit being dynamically stable. It is obvious that in case there are more closed

[42]See Boyce and DiPrima (1977), p. 445, Hirsch and Smale (1974), p. 252, and Lorenz (1993), p. 41.

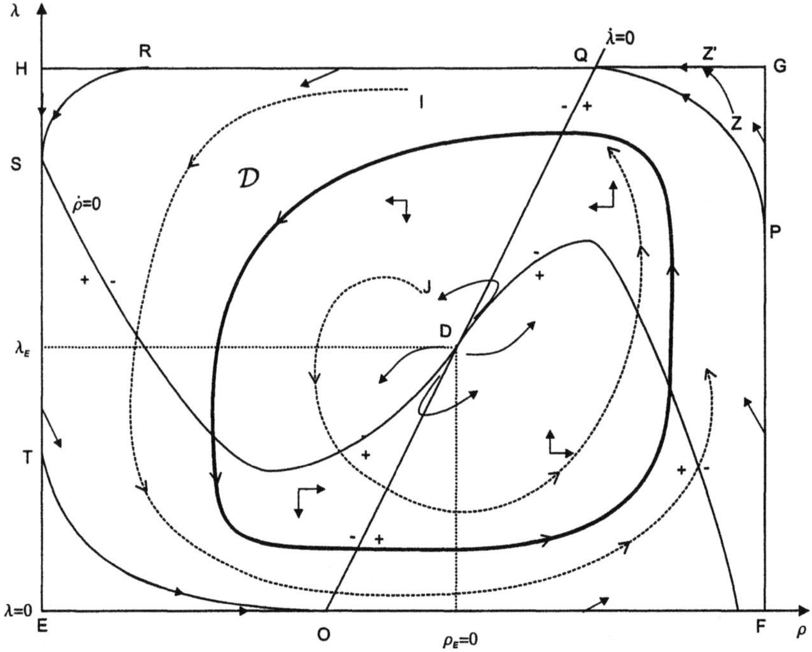

Figure 4.6: The Emergence of a Limit Cycle

orbits, not all of them can be attracting, i.e. not all closed orbits can be limit cycles. It holds that in case the fixed point is unstable, the innermost cycle in the compact set $\mathcal{D}$ is stable, that is, that the innermost closed orbit in $\mathcal{D}$ is a limit cycle. Additional closed orbits with increasing amplitude are alternately unstable and stable implying that the innermost and the outermost closed orbits are limit cycles. Ergo, if there exists only one closed orbit, this closed orbit is a limit cycle.

The question of how many closed orbits arise in a dynamical system is highly important since the choice of the initial condition in case of multiple cycles determines the long-run amplitude. Especially in business cycle models, the number of cycles determines whether it is possible to reduce the amplitude by "choosing the most convenient initial condition" or not. In the present case, the number of cycles is of special importance since in the case of multiple limit cycles there arise some equilibrium cycles near the unstable fixed point D being subject to low long-run amplitudes and financial stability, whereas there exist other long-run equilibrium cycles having a much larger radius with high amplitudes and much longer duration, giving rise to permanent and recurrent financial crises. Which kind of cycle is going to be realized in the long-run is dependent on the initial condition which is predominantly influenced by exogenous shocks. As a result, the existence of multiple limit cycles in the present case implies general dynamic instability of the model economy since exogenous events are able to catapult a long-run financially stable economy with low business cycle amplitudes into a long-run financially unstable economy with high business cycle amplitudes and vice versa. Furthermore, the existence of multiple limit cycles excludes the existence of endogenous mechanisms which guarantee a return to a cyclically equilibrium situation with low amplitudes and financial stability after the model economy has been hit by an adverse exogenous shock.

This result justifies permanent market interventions of a social planner in order to guarantee a long-run financially stable equilibrium situation with low business cycle amplitudes. Mathematically, interventions by a social planner in case of multiple limit cycles would mean to "choose" a "better" initial condition after the occurrence of a shock in order to guarantee a long-run convergence to a limit cycle with low business cycle amplitudes and financial stability. Yet, despite the existence of multiple cycles, it is often not possible to set up a new dynamic process by jumping instantaneously to a new and "better" initial condition after the occurrence of an adverse exogenous shock due to the backward looking characteristics of λ and ρ, as well as due to the inability of the social planner to cause a sudden change in profit expectations.

It has to be emphasized however, that the debt-asset ratio can be controlled by the social planner via financial market regulation in order to prevent a shift from a financially stable into a financially unstable situation in the case of an exogenous shock. For example, imposing an upper bound on the level of indebtedness by credit ceilings reduces the risk of widespread illiquidity and insolvency in case of an adverse shock. However, in a financially liberalized system there is no possibility for a social planner to guarantee financial stability by imposing global bounds on λ. Furthermore, though it has been argued above that there are no possibilities for a social planner to induce jumps in the (λ, ρ)-space after an adverse shocks, there exists the possibility to change the debt-asset ratio via debt relief or debt restructuring negotiations, initiating a new dynamic process by jumping to a new initial condition. Still, in most cases, debt relief or debt restructuring negotiations only take place a long time after an economy has experienced a systemic financial crises which has been followed by a long depression period. Thus, though it is possible for a social planner to change the debt-asset ratio, there is no possibility to catapult λ to a favourable initial condition shortly after the occurrence of an adverse shock in order to neutralize negative repercussions immediately.

Consequently, the existence of multiple limit cycles implies firstly, that capitalist systems are inherently unstable, secondly, that long-run stability or long-run instability are determined by random events, thirdly, that an economy being subject to a "vicious" equilibrium cycle with high amplitudes experiences recurrent financial crises, and fourthly, that vicious cycles can be only left by exogenous events. However, stylized facts of financial crises have shown firstly, that economies tend to be stable in the long-run, secondly. that financial crises are not predominantly a consequence of exogenous shocks but also an endogenous phenomenon, thirdly, that not each business cycle generates financial crises, and fourthly, that in spite of very long recovery periods, economies generally tend to return to an equilibrium situation being characterized by low business cycle amplitudes and financial stability. Consequently, the case of multiple limit cycles seems not to be applicable to real world phenomena. By way of contrast, in case the dynamic system is subject to only one closed orbit, which could serve as an reference equilibrium business cycle with moderate amplitudes and financial stability representing "tranquil times", there are endogenous mechanisms guaranteeing a return to the equilibrium cycle in case the economy has been hit by an exogenous shock having induced an excessive boom-bust cycle and a financial crisis. Furthermore, a single limit cycle with long-run endogenous financial stability would make permanent interventions by a social planner superfluous. As a result, the model's potential to be applicable to real world phenomena depends on the number of closed orbits arising from system 4.19 and 4.20.

There are only few methods of determining the uniqueness of limit cycles which are not generally applicable to all dynamic systems due to their complexity. One of the few non-linear dynamical systems for which sufficient conditions for the uniqueness of limit cycles can be established is the so-called generalized Liénard-equation having been developed from the van der Pol equation which describes relaxation phenomena in physics.[43] Hence, in order to prove the uniqueness of a limit cycle in economic systems, the original non-linear system has to be transformed, if it is possible at all, into a generalized Liénard-equation which requires very restrictive assumptions regarding the differential equation system.[44] The technique of the generalized Liéneard-van-der-Pol equation is not going to be applied in the present case firstly, in order not to lose the general validity of the model, and secondly, due to arising complexity which would not provide more relevant insights. A more convenient method to prove the existence and uniqueness of closed orbits, which does not require a transformation of the original dynamic system into a specific functional form, is the application of the *Hopf Bifurcation Theorem* named after E. Hopf (1942) being used in the present case and outlined in detail below.

The Emergence of a Supercritical Hopf Bifurcation. The local stability properties of non-linear systems are generally examined in a two step procedure, where the first step involves a transformation of the non-linear system into a linear one, and the second step an analysis of the Jacobian's trace and determinant at the local fixed points. In case the real parts of the latent roots of the linearly approximated dynamical system are negative/positive, the original non-linear system is locally stable/unstable. However, if the real parts of the linearly approximated system are zero, giving rise to cyclical behaviour, it is not possible any more to examine the local behaviour of the non-linear system by its linear approximation since the *Hartman-Grobman Theorem*[45] is only valid for nonzero real roots. This is exactly the case where the Hopf bifurcation theorem comes into help to study the local dynamics of the non-linear system.

Bifurcation theory in general studies the question whether the qualitative characteristics of a dynamic system change when one or more (exogenous) parameters are changed. The value of the parameter at which the dynamic patterns change is called bifurcation value. The Hopf bifurcation theorem, requiring at least a 2×2 system to appear, is of special interest since it shows how a system with a stable fixed point can lose its stability, giving rise to a (possibly) stable closed orbit when an important parameter on which

[43]For an analytical treatment regarding the uniqueness of limit cycles by applying the Liénard-equation, see e.g. Yan-Qian (1986), Gandolfo (1997), pp. 439-441, and Lorenz (1993), chapters 2.3 and 2.5.

[44]For the transformation of Kaldor's (1940) non-linear business cycle model into a relaxation oscillation type model by modifying assumptions see e.g. Gandolfo (1997), pp. 445-447 and Lorenz (1993), pp. 57-60.

[45]The *Hartman-Grobman Theorem* states that the local properties of a linearized (non-linear) dynamical system can be carried over to the original non-linear system if the linear system's Jacobian matrix has no root with zero real part (zero real root or pure imaginary root). For details, see Guckenheimer and Holmes (1986), p. 13.

the system depends, is changed. It has been outlined many times in the present model that both the local, as well as the global dynamics of system 4.19 and 4.20 are predominantly determined by the strength of the influence of the current state of confidence ρ on investors' change in profit expectations $\dot{\rho}$, so that derivative $\partial f/\partial \rho$ can be used as the relevant parameter μ to study the nature of bifurcation that takes place when investors' sensitivity changes.

The Hopf bifurcation theorem consists of two parts. The *existence part* provides sufficient conditions for the emergence of closed orbits in a neighborhood of a fixed point under certain conditions, whereas the *stability part* provides sufficient conditions for orbital stability of the cycle.[46] To study the nature of the Hopf bifurcation, consider the continuous-time system

$$\dot{\mathbf{x}} = \mathbf{f}(\mathbf{x}, \mu), \quad \mathbf{x} \in \mathbb{R}^n, \quad \mu \in \mathbb{R},$$

where μ is the bifurcation parameter. Assume that the system possesses an unique equilibrium point $\mathbf{x}_0^*$ at the value μ_0 of the parameter μ, i.e. assume that for each value of μ the system has an isolated equilibrium point $\mathbf{x}_0^*$ which can be obtain by solving the system

$$\dot{\mathbf{x}} = \mathbf{0} = \mathbf{f}(\mathbf{x}_0^*, \mu_0).$$

Likewise, assume that the determinant of the Jacobian matrix $\mathbf{J}$ of the basic system differs from zero for all possible fixed points $(\mathbf{x}, \mu)$. Then, by applying the implicit function theorem it can be shown that there exists a smooth function $\mathbf{x}^* = \mathbf{x}^*(\mu)$, that is, for every parameter value μ (in a certain neighborhood) there exists a unique fixed point $\mathbf{x}^*$.

In order to derive the formal conditions of the existence part of the Hopf bifurcation theorem, assume that this fixed point is stable for small values of μ, i.e. that the system has a stable fixed point for values $\mu < \mu_0$.[47] The existence part itself provides sufficient conditions for the existence of closed orbits in a neighborhood of a fixed point for appropriate values of the parameter μ, reading as[48]:

Theorem 4.3 (Hopf Bifurcation - Existence Part) *Suppose that the dynamic system*

$$\dot{\mathbf{x}} = \mathbf{f}(\mathbf{x}, \mu), \quad \mathbf{x} \in \mathbb{R}^n, \quad \mu \in \mathbb{R}$$

has a fixed point $(\mathbf{x}_0^*, \mu_0)$ *at which the following properties are satisfied:*

H.1 The Jacobian matrix of the dynamical system, evalued at $(\mathbf{x}_0^*, \mu_0)$*, has a pair of pure imaginary eigenvalues and no other eigenvalues with zero real parts.*

This implies that there is a smooth curve of fixed points $(\mathbf{x}^*(\mu), \mu)$ *with* $\mathbf{x}^*(\mu_0) = \mathbf{x}_0^*$. *The complex conjugate eigenvalues* $\theta(\mu), \bar{\theta}(\mu)$ *of the Jacobian which are purely imaginary at* $\mu = \mu_0$ *vary smoothly with* μ. *If moreover*

[46] For formal treatments of the Hopf bifurcation theorem, see e.g. Gandolfo (1997), pp. 475-479, Guckenheimer and Holmes (1986) pp. 150-154 , Lorenz (1993), pp. 95-101, and Wiggins (1990), chapter 3, pp. 253-386.

[47] Alternatively, it is possible as well to assume that there exists an unstable fixed point for values $\mu < \mu_0$. In that case, all statements which are going to be made above in the form of $\mu \gtrless \mu_0$ have to be reversed.

[48] See Gandolfo (1997), p. 477 and Lorenz , pp. 95-96.

H.2 $\left.\frac{d\,Re\,\theta(\mu)}{d\mu}\right|_{\mu=\mu_0} > 0,$

then the system has a family of periodic solutions where the critical value μ_0 is called the Hopf bifurcation point of the system.

The theorem states firstly, that in case parameter μ is increased from $\mu < \mu_0$ to $\mu > \mu_0$ the unique fixed point changes its stability properties from local stability into local instability as the real parts $Re\,\theta$ become positive, and secondly, that there arise closed orbits for $\mu \geq \mu_0$.

Consequently, in order to show the emergence of closed orbits in the present case the first step, according to condition *H.1* of the existence part, is to show the emergence of pure imaginary roots at the critical value $\mu = \mu_0$ where it holds that $\mu = \partial f/\partial \rho = \partial \dot{\rho}/\partial \rho$. The characteristic equation of the system 4.19 and 4.20, being determined from the Jacobian matrix, reads as

$$\theta^2 + \underbrace{\left(-\frac{\partial F_1}{\partial \lambda} - \frac{\partial F_2}{\partial \rho}\right)}_{a_1=-tr\mathbf{J}} \theta + \underbrace{\left(\frac{\partial F_1}{\partial \lambda}\frac{\partial F_2}{\partial \rho} - \frac{\partial F_1}{\partial \rho}\frac{\partial F_2}{\partial \lambda}\right)}_{a_2=|\mathbf{J}|} = 0,$$

giving the roots as

$$\theta_{1,2} = \underbrace{\frac{-a_1}{2}}_{Re\,\theta} \pm \frac{\sqrt{4a_2 - a_1^2}}{2}\, i.$$

A pair of pure imaginary roots emerges only in case the following two conditions are fulfilled. Firstly, the determinant of the Jacobian $|\mathbf{J}| = a_2$ has to have a positive sign, i.e. formally it must hold that

$$|\mathbf{J}| = a_2 > 0,$$

and secondly, the real part of the roots has to become zero which implies a zero value of the Jacobian's trace $tr\mathbf{J} = -a_1$, i.e. formally it must hold that

$$Re\,\theta = \frac{-a_1}{2} = 0 \quad \text{implying} \quad a_1 = -tr\mathbf{J} = 0.$$

The first condition $a_2 = |\mathbf{J}| > 0$ is met since the positive slope of demarcation curve $\dot{\lambda} = F_1(\lambda, \rho) = 0$ is larger than the positive slope of demarcation curve $\dot{\rho} = F_2(\lambda, \rho) = 0$, a condition which has been imposed in order to guarantee the unique long-run rational expectations equilibrium in figures 4.5 and 4.6. Generally, the system has a positive determinant firstly, in case $\partial f/\partial \rho$ has a negative or zero value, i.e. in case $\mu = \partial f/\partial \rho \leq 0$, and secondly in case $\partial f/\partial \rho$ is "normally" positive, i.e. in case $\mu = \partial f/\partial \rho > 0$, implying "normally" reacting investors within the normal range; these two cases correspond to cases 1 and 3 of the local stability analysis. However, condition $a_2 > 0$ is not met in case investors behave hypersensitively, i.e in case it holds that $\mu = \partial f/\partial \rho \gg 0$, corresponding to case 2 of local stability analysis which has been ruled out. Summing up, condition $a_2 > 0$ is fulfilled for all possible values of function 4.20.

The second condition $a_1 = 0$ determines the critical value of the parameter μ, or the Hopf bifurcation point, when the real part becomes zero giving rise to the emergence of closed orbits. Using the fact that $\partial F_2/\partial\rho = \partial f/\partial\rho + (\partial f/\partial\sigma)(\partial\sigma/\partial\rho)$, the Hopf bifurcation point $\mu_0 = (\partial f/\partial\rho)_0$ is given as

$$\mu_0 = \left(\frac{\partial f}{\partial\rho}\right)_0 = -\frac{\partial F_1}{\partial\lambda} - \frac{\partial f}{\partial\sigma}\frac{\partial\sigma}{\partial\rho},$$

stating that at μ_0, the real parts of the roots $Re\,\theta$, and a_1 become zero. To answer the question which nature the real parts of the roots possess for values $\mu > \mu_0$ and $\mu < \mu_0$, one can show that if

$$Re\,\theta = \frac{-a_1}{2} \lesseqgtr 0,$$

implying

$$a_1 \gtreqless 0,$$

then it holds that

$$-\frac{\partial F_1}{\partial\lambda} - \frac{\partial f}{\partial\sigma}\frac{\partial\sigma}{\partial\rho} \gtreqless \frac{\partial f}{\partial\rho},$$

or

$$\mu_0 \gtreqless \mu,$$

respectively. Summing up, it holds that

$$Re\,\theta \lesseqgtr 0 \quad \Leftrightarrow \quad a_1 \gtreqless 0 \quad \Leftrightarrow \quad \mu \lesseqgtr \mu_0.$$

Using words, this condition implies that for values $\mu < \mu_0$, there arise no closed orbits and that there exists a stable fixed point because of $a_1 > 0$ implying $Re\,\theta < 0$. For values $\mu > \mu_0$, there arise closed orbits and the fixed point is unstable because of $a_1 < 0$ implying $Re\,\theta > 0$. At the bifurcation point it holds that $\mu = \mu_0$, implying $a_1 = 0$ and $Re\,\theta = 0$, i.e. there arise closed orbits since the real parts of the roots vanish, and the fixed point is locally unstable. Summing up, condition *H.1* is fulfilled, i.e. at μ_0 the Jacobian has a pair of pure imaginary roots $\theta = \pm\sqrt{a_2}\,i$ causing cyclical behaviour of the system. The roots remain conjugate complex for $\mu > \mu_0$ sufficiently near to μ_0.

As to condition *H.2* of the Hopf bifurcation theorem, it is easy to check that

$$\left.\frac{d\,Re\,\theta(\mu)}{d\,\mu}\right|_{\mu=\mu_0} = \left.\frac{d(-\frac{1}{2}\,a_1)}{d\left(\frac{\partial f}{\partial\rho}\right)}\right|_{\mu=\mu_0} = -\frac{1}{2}\left(-\frac{\partial F_1}{\partial\lambda} - \left(\frac{\partial f}{\partial\rho} + \frac{\partial f}{\partial\sigma}\frac{\partial\sigma}{\partial\rho}\right)\right) = \frac{1}{2} \quad > 0,$$

i.e. condition *H.2* is fulfilled as well. Consequently, the existence of a closed orbit in the present model according to theorem 4.3 is proved.

Despite the fact that the existence part of the Hopf bifurcation theorem 4.3 provides sufficient conditions for the emergence of closed orbits it cannot make any statement on stability properties of emerging cycles. Generally, checking the stability of closed orbits by calculating the normal form of a dynamical system is very complex and does, in lots of cases, not give any results for general function models unless the models are going to be parameterized which means referring to a special subcase and losing the general validity of the results.[49] This drawback gives rise to the conclusion that bifurcation theory in

[49] For a formal treatment and applications of the normal form technique, see Guckenheimer and Holmes (1986), pp. 152-156, 160-165, Lorenz (1993), pp. 99-107, Lux (1992), pp. 188-190, Marsden and McCracken (1976), Wiggins (1990), chapter 2.2, pp. 211-229 and chapter 3.1B, pp. 270-278.

comparison with the Poincaré-Bendixon theorem cannot provide any new insights and is in a certain sense "inferior" because the Poincaré-Bendixon theorem can prove, among the emergence of closed orbits, the existence of at least one limit cycle. However, if the stability properties of a Hopf bifurcation can be determined, bifurcation theory can provide useful insights as to the uniqueness of limit cycles which cannot be investigated by the Poincaré-Bendixon theorem, but only by generalized Liénard equations which are difficult to use. Still, in many cases, checking the stability of the closed orbits emerging from Hopf bifurcations is as laborious as applying the generalized Liénard equation, so that the determination of the number of limit cycles remains a difficult, if not impossible task.

There are special cases however, being characterized by specific functional forms of demarcation curves, as e.g. quadratic or cubic functions, giving rise to so-called sub- or supercritical Hopf bifurcations which allow for the determination of the number and the stability of closed orbits. In the present case, it can be shown that the situation in figure 4.6 engenders only *one stable limit cycle* since the Hopf bifurcation is *supercritical.*[50] The *supercritical Hopf bifurcation* is characterized by the fact that for parameter values $\mu < \mu_0$, the local fixed point is stable and there are no closed orbits, whereas for parameter values $\mu > \mu_0$ the fixed point is unstable and there are closed orbits which are attractors, i.e. limit cycles appear. Generally, there arises a supercritical Hopf bifurcation in $\mathbb{R}^2$, if firstly, one of the two demarcation curves can be described by a polynomial of the type

$$\lambda(\rho) = -b_0\rho^3 + b_1\rho^2 \pm b_2\rho \pm b_3, \qquad b_i > 0,$$

where b_1 has to be chosen sufficiently small, giving rise to a cubic function of the type shown in figure 4.6, and secondly, if the second demarcation curve is steeper at the fixed point than the non-linear demarcation curve.[51] In the present case in figure 4.6, these two conditions are fulfilled, since firstly, demarcation curve $\dot{\rho} = F_1(\lambda, \rho) = 0$ can be described by the cubic polynomial cited above, and secondly, because demarcation curve $\dot{\lambda} = F_2(\lambda, \rho) = 0$ is steeper in fixed point D than demarcation curve $\dot{\rho} = F_1(\lambda, \rho) = 0$.

Summing up, the Hopf bifurcation in the present case is supercritical which implies that for each parameter value there is only one cyclically stable closed orbit. This implies in terms of figure 4.6, which is drawn for a special parameter value $\mu > \mu_0$, that there exists *only one limit cycle*, i.e. all trajectories starting in the invariant set $\mathcal{D}$ converge to this limit cycle. In this case, the local information of the Hopf bifurcation serves to specify the global information of the Poincaré-Bendixon theorem.

4.4.5 A Dynamic View of Financial Crises and Macroeconomic Fluctuations

Empirical data and the comparative static version of the model have shown that the two core variables λ and ρ are mainly responsible for the emergence of boom-bust cycles

[50] Generally, the subcritical case, which is not going to be discussed in the following, and the supercritical case of the Hopf bifurcation are the most important cases whereas lots of other possibilities can emerge. For a full discussion and graphical representations of different cases, see Wiggins (1990), chapter 3.1B pp. 270-278. For a graphical representation and comparison of the subcritical and the supercritical case, see Lorenz (1993), pp. 97-101.

[51] For a formal treatment of these conditions, see Wiggins (1990) chapter 3.1B, pp. 270-278, Lux (1992), p. 189, and Flaschel, Franke and Semmler (1997), chapter 3, pp. 33-60.

involving systemic financial crises. Other variables, like e.g. monetary policy variables m and h, have an influence as well, but chiefly *react* on changes in λ and ρ, i.e. changes in m and h can be interpreted as an endogenous reaction on the current state of λ and ρ, and not as exogenous events irrespective of the actual level of λ and ρ. One main drawback of comparative static analysis has been its descriptive-static character, so that stylized facts of financial crises could be explained only qualitatively by the use of static partial derivatives which were not in a position to determine quantitatively the overall net effect on endogenous variables in case the two counteracting forces λ and ρ have moved into the same direction. The dynamic version of the model however, bridges this theoretical gap by deriving explicit time paths for λ and ρ, giving rise to an *endogenous* explanation of business cycles and financial fragility inducing financial crises. As financial crises are generally linked to business cycles, but not each business cycle generates a financial crisis, the following analysis is going to distinguish between so-called "equilibrium business cycles" generating no financial crisis and serving as a reference position, and cycles involving systemic financial crises.

4.4.5.1 The Emergence of Endogenous Long-Run Equilibrium Business Cycles

The long-run dynamic analysis has shown that the model economy, after it has been hit by an exogenous shock catapulting the system away from the limit cycle into the interior of compact set $\mathcal{D}$, converges in the long-run to a cyclically stable closed orbit with constant amplitudes by counterclockwise cyclical motions. As the two sample trajectories in figure 4.6 indicate, there are two possible forms of converging to the limit cycle. Initial conditions within compact set $\mathcal{D}$ but outside the limit cycle, as e.g. point I in figure 4.6, generate several cycles with shrinking amplitudes as they converge to the limit cycle; however, all converging cycles are subject to larger amplitudes than the closed orbit. By way of contrast, initial conditions within invariant set $\mathcal{D}$ but inside the limit cycle, as e.g. point J in figure 4.6, create several cycles with growing amplitudes where all cycles are subject to smaller amplitudes than the limit cycle. Once a trajectory has fully converged to the limit cycle, subsequent cycles (which can be theoretically infinite) exhibit a constant amplitude. Summing up, there exist three theoretical forms of long-run dynamic behaviour, i.e. a movement on the limit cycle, convergence from the outer region to the limit cycle, and convergence from the inner region to the limit cycle.

After having determined possible theoretical forms of long-run behaviour, there arises the question whether the dynamic patterns of the model fit the stylized facts of financial crises, or whether the model predicts outcomes which are theoretically possible, but never come up in reality. In graphical terms, there arises the question of whether the entire compact set $\mathcal{D}$ represents a feasible set for arising time paths, or whether some regions of invariant set $\mathcal{D}$ have to be excluded because they represent empirically irrelevant cases. The empirical analysis has identified the following four stylized facts regarding the long-run dynamics of financial crises and business cycles which are going to be compared with the theoretical long-run behaviour predicted by the model. Firstly, systemic financial crises are part of extensive boom-bust cycles in goods and financial markets being reflected in much larger amplitudes of key macroeconomic variables than in "tranquil times", i.e. during business cycles without the occurrence of financial crisis. Secondly, not each business cycle generates a financial crises. Thirdly, boom-bust cycles generating financial crises are often preceded by a large exogenous shock, as e.g. the introduction of a new technology regime or liberalization of financial and goods markets, having a positive effect on expected future productivity and profits. Fourthly, after the occurrence of financial crises, economies generally tend to converge back to tranquil business cycle fluctuations though recovery periods can be very long (see e.g. the long recovery period following the Great Depression in the 1930s and 1940s, or the Japanese recovery path during the last decade without having recovered yet).

A comparison of long-run stylized facts with the dynamic patterns of the model, being illustrated in figure 4.7 which is a slightly modified version of figure 4.6, leads to the conclusion that the single limit cycle, being defined by points A, B, C, D and E, represents an equilibrium business cycle to which economies converge in the long-run being characterized by modest and constant amplitudes and by the absence of financial crises. It has to be pointed out however, that even equilibrium business cycles in tranquil times generate scattered financial distress on the upper turning point of the business cycle leading to illiquidity and insolvency of business and financial firms. Still, this kind of financial distress is not in a position to cause a widespread system financial crises since only a small fraction of firms and banks are financially fragile. The inner area of the limit cycle in figure 4.7 represents an empirical irrelevant region since there are no disequilibrium cycles in reality with growing amplitudes converging to a stable long-run cycle, being subject to larger fluctuations and a higher degree of financial fragility on the upper turning point than all cycles during the convergence process. By way of contrast, the region between the boundaries of compact set $\mathcal{D}$ and the outer bounds of the limit cycle gives rise firstly, to business cycles having a much larger amplitude than the equilibrium business cycle, and secondly, to cycles whose amplitude is shrinking during the convergence process. These cycles are subject to much larger fluctuations in the debt-asset ratio and in profit expectations giving rise to a build-up of widespread financial fragility during the upswing and possibly to systemic financial crises during the downswing. Consequently, it seems reasonable to assume that the feasible region for real world business cycles has to be restricted to the invariant set $\mathcal{D}$ without the inner area of the limit cycle. Summing up, empirical evidence gives rise to the supposition that, in terms of the model, there are periods in which trajectories do move outside the limit cycle generating high amplitudes and financial crises, whereas there are also periods in which trajectories move in the neighbourhood of, or on the limit cycle engendering modest boom-bust periods being characterized by a normal functioning of goods and financial markets. If there are no exogenous shocks, economies tend to converge to the limit cycle over time with shrinking amplitudes and declining financial fragility, i.e. economies tend to be cyclically and financially stable in the long-run. Consequently, systemic financial crises can be only induced by large exogenous shocks catapulting the system away from the limit cycle into the outer region.

In order to study the difference between periods of modest business cycles and extensive boom-bust periods involving systemic financial crises, the following description starts with a stylized *endogenous* equilibrium business cycle, being located on the limit cycle serving as a reference time path. The boom phase starts in point A after the last business cycle has ended when agents realize that economic fundamentals, both λ and σ, have returned to sound levels giving rise to a quick and comparatively large increase in profit expectations. This increase in ρ leads to a rise in investment demand which is financed

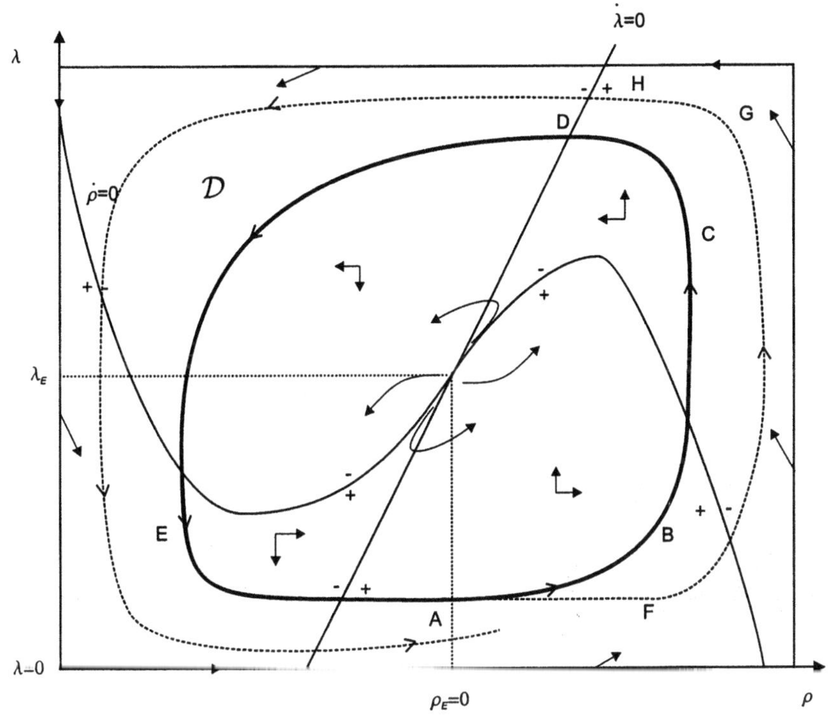

Figure 4.7: A Dynamic Description of Financial Crises in Industrial Countries

mainly by profits and not by a pronounced increase in indebtedness though λ starts to rise slowly. As the state of confidence ρ increases much faster than the debt asset ratio λ, there is an overall macroeconomic expansion which is characterized, according to the comparative static results given in table 4.1, by an increase in $u, r, \hat{p}, q$ and $\hat{s}$ and by a decline in $\jmath$ and $\imath$. Though the expectation formation scheme is dominated by fundamentalist behaviour at the beginning of the boom phase, being indicated by time path from A to B, there is a rising reliance on general market sentiments, i.e. chartist type behaviour increases overproportionally.

The overborrowing process starts in point B, which is characterized by much lower debt-asset ratios than an overborrowing process of an extensive boom-bust cycle that generates financial crises. As a result, though an equilibrium cycle cannot cause a financial crisis, there arises a small degree of financial fragility by overborrowing. During the overborrowing phase, the level of λ increases sharply because profit expectations rise much faster than actual profits, so that the large rise in investment demand is going to be mainly financed by increasing external indebtedness, leading to lower growth, or even to stagnation of actual profits due to rising debt costs. Despite the fact that there is a deterioration of profits, the state of confidence ρ is subject to a further significant rise, firstly, due to the dominance of chartist type behaviour, and secondly, because fundamentals provide a neutral picture where both λ and σ rise.[52] The significant rise in the state of confidence ρ, dominating the increase in the debt-asset ratio λ with respect to the overall macroeconomic performance, causes a further macroeconomic expansion being characterized by an additional rise in $u, \hat{p}, q$ and $\hat{s}$, and a further decline in j and i, where r remains constant.

The time path to the upper turning point C is subject to an increasing overborrowing process driving the economy into a state of exuberance, which is however less pronounced than during cycles that generate financial crises. Though there is a large increase in the debt-asset ratio λ leading to a decline in the profit rate r and in the risk premium σ, profit expectations and investment demand are subject to a further rise since the dominance of chartist type behaviour has reached its maximum. There is a further macroeconomic expansion due to the dominance of ρ over λ though the growth rate of ρ is declining, leading to a further increase in $u, \hat{p}, q$ and $\hat{s}$, and to a further decline in j and i, where r deteriorates with a minimum lower bound of zero.

At the upper turning point C, the growth in ρ ends, firstly because agents realize that expectations cannot be validated by current profits being zero or even negative, and secondly because the current state of ρ is located near, or outside the boundaries of the normal range of ρ. As a result, there is a sudden switch in the formation of expectations at point C from chartist type behaviour to fundamentalist type behaviour, leading to a sharp decline in ρ. In reality, this sudden change in expectations can be caused by very small, but *endogenous* events, as e.g. overborrowing-induced illiquidity or insolvency of some business firms or banks. This pessimistic shift in expectations causes a general tightening of financial market conditions being characterized by declining asset prices, i.e. by a drop in Tobin's q, and by rising interest rates j and i due to deteriorating collateral and net worth positions. Though there is a general tightening of financial market conditions, the debt-asset ratio λ is subject to a further rise on the path from point C to D, since potential illiquidity (due to $r < 0$) is avoided by an increase in short-term debt according to equation 4.19. In case financial markets are not willing to bridge the liquidity gap, some firms and banks may become illiquid or even insolvent. However, even if there arises a total liquidity and credit crunch, a financial crisis is not going to occur since overall financial fragility is very low.

The bust phase starts in point D which is characterized by a reduction in the debt-asset ratio λ due to a deleveraging process, being financed by cutting investment expenditures to a large extent in order to pay back outstanding loans. Furthermore, expectations start to be dominated again by chartist type behaviour, leading to an accelerating pessimism among investors. Despite the fact that there is a positive impulse on macroeconomic performance by a reduction in λ, the negative effect of a quickly declining ρ dominates, so that there is an overall macroeconomic contraction being characterized by a reduction in $u, r, \hat{p}, q$ and $\hat{s}$, and by a rise in j and i. The length of the downswing depends predominantly on how fast balance sheets are deleveraged, i.e. on the effect of the debt-asset ratio λ on the state of confidence ρ.

The recovery phase starts in point E when investors realize that actual profits have been underestimated, i.e. it holds that $r^e < r$. The expectation formation scheme then

[52]Though the actual profit rate r declines, there is a rise in the risk premium σ due to a rise in $\hat{p}$ and a decline in i.

again switches from pessimistic chartist type behaviour to more or less optimistic fundamentalist type behaviour, firstly, because improved macroeconomic fundamentals σ and λ do not justify any longer a decline in ρ, and secondly, because ρ has moved to the lower, or outside the lower bound of the normal range. The recovery path from point E to A is subject to an almost constant debt-asset ratio λ, and to an increasing state of confidence ρ leading to an overall macroeconomic recovery. This recovery process is characterized by an increase in $u, r, \hat{p}, q$ and $\hat{s}$, and by a decline in j and i, giving rise to a new equilibrium business cycle with the same dynamic patterns as the cycle described above.

4.4.5.2 The Emergence of Financial Crises

Extensive boom-bust cycles involving financial crises typically begin after the recovery phase of an equilibrium business cycle by the occurrence of a large positive exogenous shock to profit expectations which, in terms of figure 4.7, catapults the economy from point A to point F. Exogenous shocks to the state of confidence ρ can take e.g. the form of positive technology shocks which, in the view of economic agents, revolutionize an economy's entire productivity scheme of past decades, causing a large rise in expected productivity and profitability. An alternative source of rising profit expectations can be a switch to another economic school of thought, as for example a change from an interventional economic system to a more liberal scheme, involving widespread liberalization of goods and financial markets which are believed to increase overall efficiency, productivity, and profitability.

The boom phase starting in point F exhibits the same features as the boom period on the equilibrium business cycle but to a much larger extent. Investment demand, and thereby actual profits, increase substantially, causing only a modest increase in the debt-asset ratio λ since most of investment is financed by internal profits. Favourable fundamentals, i.e. a large σ due to a large r and a low λ, and large profits validating the initial increase in profit expectations, lead very quickly to a shift of the expectation formation scheme from fundamentalist to chartist behaviour. There is a huge macroeconomic expansion being subject to an increase in $u, r, \hat{p}, q$ and $\hat{s}$, and a decline in j and i reflecting favourable financial market conditions.

The overborrowing process begins much earlier, and is characterized by a much larger increase in the debt-asset ratio λ than the overborrowing phase during tranquil times. Though there is a much larger increase in the actual profit rate than during tranquil times, the debt-asset ratio λ increases as profit expectations and investment demand rise much faster than actual profits. The formation of expectations is predominantly driven by chartist type behaviour causing the state of confidence ρ to rise much faster than the debt-asset ratio λ. Consequently, there is a further expansion in macroeconomic activity being indicated by a further rise in $u, r, \hat{p}, q$ and $\hat{s}$, and a further decline in j and i, where the positive growth in r declines rapidly due to rising debt costs.

The path to the upper turning point is characterized by "mania" expectations, driving the economy during the latter phase of the overborrowing process into a state of "irrational exuberance" giving rise to a large asset price bubble. Though the actual profit rate r declines owing to an overproportional rise in the debt-asset ratio, the state of confidence ρ and investment demand are subject to a further rise due to the dominance of chartist type behaviour which neglects very poor levels of fundamentals, i.e. a very high λ and a very low σ, induced by a very low profit rate r. As the "irrational" increase in ρ

(despite a declining r) dominates the increase in the debt-asset ratio λ, there is a further macroeconomic expansion being subject to an increase in $u, \hat{p}, q$ and $\hat{s}$, and a further decline in j and i, where r shrinks rapidly up to a lower bound of zero.

The overborrowing process comes to a halt at upper turning point at point G when agents suddenly realize that profit expectations cannot be validated any more by actual profits. Profit expectations collapse due to an abrupt switch from chartist type to fundamentalist type behaviour which is induced on the one hand, by a historical poor record of fundamentals λ and σ, and on the other hand, by an actual value of ρ which lies on the upper, or outside the upper bound of the normal range. The breakdown of profit expectations can be triggered either by very small *endogenous* shocks, as e.g. the failure of an important bank or business firm[53], which would be not in a position to cause an aggregate downward shift in expectations in case financial fragility was low, or by contractionary monetary policy. According to the standard view on financial crises, monetary tightening is often viewed as an exogenous shock inducing a financial crisis which would not have happened in case there had been no monetary contraction. However, according to the present view on financial crises, monetary tightening in the form of an exogenous shock would never be able to cause a financial crises by itself if there had been no massive build-up of financial fragility during the boom and the overborrowing phase. Consequently, even if a monetary contraction takes the form of an exogenous event, it only accelerates the *endogenous* collapse of expectations which would have occurred also without monetary tightening. By way of contrast, monetary tightening on the upper turning of the business cycle can be also interpreted as an *endogenous* reaction on the overborrowing process to stop a further increase in asset and goods prices. The fall in ρ causes the asset price bubble to burst, being indicated by a rapid fall in q, and by a sharp rise in interest rates j and i. Deteriorating net worth positions, rising debt costs, and a drying-up of liquidity cause a sudden stop in the debt-asset ratio's growth rate, which leads to widespread illiquidity and insolvency among firms and financial institutions. In terms of figure 4.7, the sudden stop at the upper turning point G is indicated by an almost constant value of λ on path GH which, in contrast to the equilibrium business cycle, does not allow an increase in λ after the asset price bubble's burst. Consequently, during tranquil times, a downward shift in expectations allows for a continuous financing or rolling over of due payment obligations, whereas during excessive cycles the breakdown of ρ leads to an interruption of credit chains and to a severe domestic banking crisis due to a largely rising amount of nonperforming loans.

Point H marks the beginning of the bust phase, being characterized initially by a period of constant high debt levels which is followed by large debt reducing and debt restructuring efforts, and by a further collapse of profit expectations being mainly driven by pessimistic chartist type behaviour. The abrupt reduction in λ causes further illiquidity and insolvency, as well as a sharp reduction in investment expenditures. Notwithstanding the expansionary macroeconomic effect of deleveraging, there is a severe macroeconomic contraction due to the sharp decline in ρ, being characterized by large drops in $u, \hat{p}$ and q, and a further rise in j and i, where r becomes negative. The fall in ρ can possibly induce

[53]Such failures are often accompanied by the unveiling of criminal accounting practices which were used to hush up severe liquidity and/or solvency problems. One recent example is the Enron debacle in the U.S. For details, see Crafts (2000), and International Monetary Fund (2000, chapter II, p.5).

a currency crisis and thereby a twin crisis in case largely rising devaluation expectations lead to a sharp drop in $\hat{s}$.

Lender of last resort interventions by monetary authorities, indicated by an increase in h and m, are able to reduce at least partly widespread illiquidity and possibly insolvency among financial institutions by providing large amounts of liquidity to stop a further fire-sale of assets and interruptions of credit chains. However, central banks cannot reduce the aggregate debt stock among firms and banks, i.e. monetary policy can only avoid illiquidity and insolvency but cannot reduce λ. In graphical terms, there is no possibility to jump downward at point H to a trajectory being located between the limit cycle and the current cycle by increasing h and m. The only effect of an increase in h and m is a change of the slope of the current trajectory in point H from almost zero to a positive value, as well as a slight change of both demarcation curves, so that the reduction in λ takes possibly less time than without monetary intervention. As a result, even if there is an effective lender of last resort intervention, monetary policy cannot prevent a large macroeconomic contraction because the process of deleveraging requires to reduce investment expenditures, which leads to a further fall in $u, \hat{p}, q$ and r, and to a further rise in j and i. In case short-run lender of last resort actions do not lead to a quick restructuring of banks' balance sheets, a liquidity trap situation accompanied by deflationary spirals, and a long lasting depression period can emerge, since short-run liquidity supports do not prevent banks from insolvency. Consequently, the duration of the bust phase depends on an economy's capacity to restructure poor balance sheets.[54]

The recovery phase begins when fundamentals λ and σ have returned to sound levels, and when investors realize that profits have been steadily underestimated owing to pessimistic chartist behaviour, having led to an actual value of ρ being located at the lower, or outside the lower bound of the normal range. The expectation formation scheme then switches back from chartist type behaviour to fundamentalist type behaviour giving rise to a macroeconomic expansion, being subject to a rise in $u, \hat{p}, q, r$ and $\hat{s}$, and a decline in j and i. In case there are no further exogenous shocks, the next cycle following the financial crisis cycle has a much lower amplitude and is going to converge to the tranquil time equilibrium business cycle.

It must be noted that such systemic crises cycles as described above are very rare because huge positive shocks to expectations in the form of new technology regimes or liberalization efforts are rare events as well. Typical examples of systemic crises in industrial countries are the two "New Economy" hypes in the 1920s and in the 1990s, and the developments in Japan from the late 1980s up to now. However, in reality there arise intermediate cases which cause boom-bust cycles involving financial distress as well, but to a far smaller extent than the systemic crises mentioned above.

[54] This result could explain the Japanese depression since lots of banks are potentially bankrupt and can only survive by massive government interventions in the form of liquidity supports. However, these poor bank balance sheets do not allow for a new expansion of credit giving rise to a new upswing. Consequently, the Japanese economy is possibly going to turn into recovery only when bank balance sheets have been restructured. By way of contrast, liquidity supports of U.S. Federal Reserve could prevent a systemic banking crisis after the failure of the LTCM hedge fund in 1998 since a large fraction of the U.S. banking system was subject to sound balance sheet positions.

4.4.6 A Keynesian Perspective on Global Dynamics

Hitherto, the formation of expectations has been modelled as a synthesis between the chartist-fundamentalist or Keynesian approach, and the rational expectations school. It has been assumed that investors' expectations are influenced by general market sentiments as well as by fundamentals, but also rely on long-run rationality guaranteeing a reversal of profit expectations irrespective of the current state of fundamentals in case the normal corridor has been left. By way of contrast, this section is going to abstract from long-run rationality by investors, so that expectations are formed according to a pure chartist-fundamentalist approach giving rise to the important question whether a Keynesian expectation formation scheme is subject to different dynamic patterns in comparison with a world involving long-run rationality.

Formally, a pure chartist-fundamentalist approach requires to relinquish the "normal range" assumption, i.e. the assumption $\partial f/\partial \rho \leq 0$ on the outer bounds ρ_l and ρ_u, as well as the existence of ρ_l and ρ_u are going to be abandoned. This modified expectation formation scheme gives rise to a modified non-linear differential equation in the state of confidence ρ, which is given by

$$\dot{\rho} = F_2(\lambda, \rho) = f(\underset{+}{\rho}, \underset{+}{\sigma}, \underset{-}{\lambda}), \tag{4.21}$$

stating that the change of the state of confidence $\dot{\rho}$ is positively dependent on the actual state of confidence ρ, positively dependent on σ, and negatively dependent on λ. Though it holds that $\partial f/\partial \rho$ is positive over the entire range of ρ, it is assumed that $\partial f/\partial \rho$ becomes less positive in case ρ departs from the intertemporal equilibrium $\rho_E = 0$, whose existence, even in a pure chartist-fundamentalist world, is going to be proved below. These assumptions result in an S-shaped demarcation curve $\dot{\rho} = 0$, implying that investors believe in an infinitely increasing or decreasing state of confidence ρ, whose change $\dot{\rho}$ however declines the more ρ departs from $\rho_E = 0$. The dynamic behaviour of the debt-asset ratio follows equation 4.19 as before.

The new dynamic system consisting of equations 4.19 and 4.21 generates, as well as the model involving long-run rationality, two different forms of long-run dynamics depending on investors' sensitivity $\partial f/\partial \rho$ near the intertemporal equilibrium $\rho_E = 0$. The first case, being illustrated in figure 4.8, refers to hypersensitively reacting investors near the intertemporal equilibrium $\rho_E = 0$, i.e. it holds that $\partial f/\partial \rho \gg 0$ near $\rho_E = 0$, giving rise to multiple equilibria. According to the local stability analysis in section 4.4.2, points A and C are locally unstable whereas point B exhibits the characteristics of a saddle point. Regarding the global dynamics of the system, rectangle $OPQR$ describes an invariant or compact set $\mathcal{D}$, where the boundaries have been determined in the same way as in section 4.4.4. An application of the Poincaré-Bendixon theorem shows that invariant set $\mathcal{D}$ contains a limit set in the form of a saddle loop (a homoclinic orbit or also known as separatrices) consisting of the two loops surrounding the unstable fixed points A and C and the saddle point B itself.[55] All initial points within invariant set $\mathcal{D}$ which do not lie on the saddle loop give rise to trajectories converging to the saddle loop. Thus, trajectories starting near points A and C spiral outwards to the saddle loop whereas trajectories

[55]For details, see Guckenheimer and Holmes (1986), pp. 46-48 and 290-295, and Lorenz (1993), pp. 39-43.

starting outside the saddle loop spiral inwards and converge to the saddle loop. Once a trajectory has reached the saddle loop, the system converges to fixed point B.

Though the case of hypersensitively reacting investors represents one possible form of global dynamic behaviour, it does not fit the stylized facts. Trajectories starting inside the saddle loop would either produce only boom cycles with increasing amplitudes if the initial point lies near fixed point C, or only bust cycles with increasing amplitudes in case the initial point lies near fixed point A. In the long-run, both types of cycles converge to the saddle loop for $t \rightarrow \infty$, causing the system to settle down in fixed point B. If, on the other hand, trajectories start outside the saddle loop, there emerge boom-bust patterns around the equilibrium in B which are however dampened around point B, i.e. each traverse from boom to bust, and vice versa, is going to be soothed. In the long-run, these dampened cycles converge to the saddle loop for $t \rightarrow \infty$ as well, coming to a halt in fixed point B. If the system starts on the saddle loop (except in point B), there arises only one boom or only one bust cycle, coming to a halt in fixed point B. Summing up,

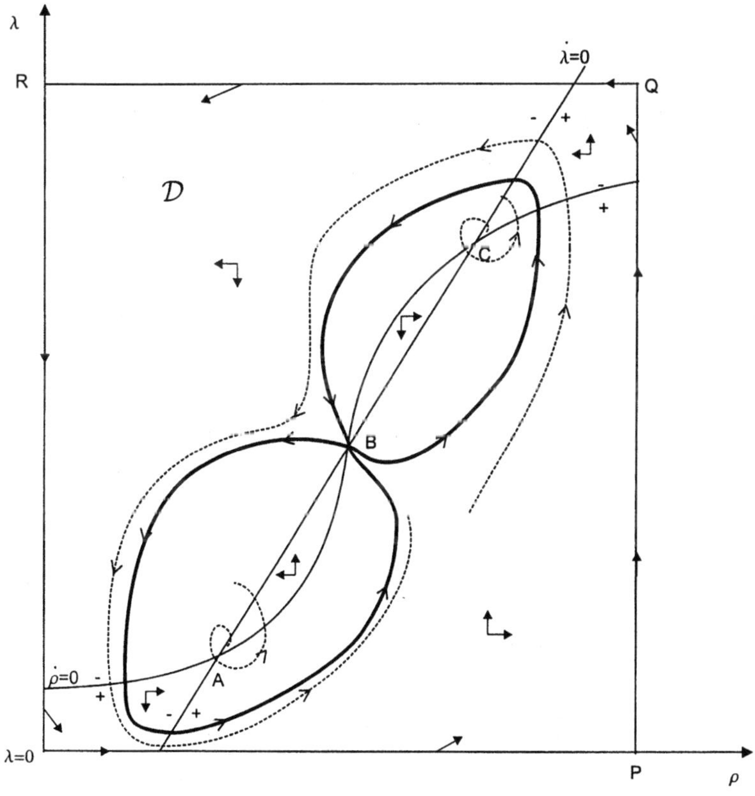

Figure 4.8: Global Keynesian Dynamics with Hypersensitively Reacting Investors

there is no time pattern emerging from the hypersensitive case which corresponds to the stylized facts due to the emergence of multiple equilibria.

Hence, in order to rule out multiple equilibria it seems reasonable to assume "normally" reacting investors around the intertemporal equilibrium $\rho_E = 0$, i.e. it holds that $\partial f / \partial \rho > 0$ near $\rho_E = 0$, giving rise to a single fixed point which is illustrated in figure 4.9. The assumption that the intertemporal equilibrium value of the state of confidence in a pure chartist-fundamentalist world corresponds to the long-run rational expectations equilibrium $\rho_E = 0$ seems to be an arbitrary assumption at first sight. However, in case the system settles down at an equilibrium value $\rho_E \neq 0$, implying $r \neq r^e$ in the long-run, it is likely that agents are going to readjust their profit expectations resulting in a shift in function $\dot{\rho} = f(\rho, \lambda, \sigma)$ and in demarcation curve $\dot{\rho} = 0$ until profit expectations correspond to the actual level of profits in the long-run. Consequently, it is reasonable to assume the existence of a long-run equilibrium value $\rho_E = 0$, implying $r = r^e$, even in a pure chartist-fundamentalist world.

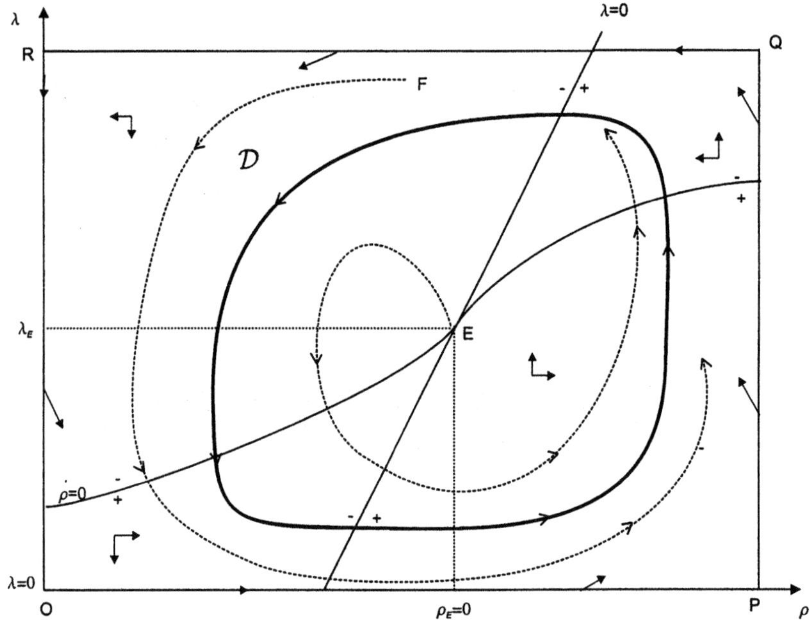

Figure 4.9: Global Keynesian Dynamics with Normally Reacting Investors

The global dynamics under normally reacting investors depicted in figure 4.9 lead to the emergence of closed orbits according to the Poincaré-Bendixon theorem since the fixed point E is locally unstable, and rectangle $OPQR$ represents an invariant set $\mathcal{D}$ whose boundaries have been determined by the procedure outlined in section 4.4.4. It is not possible however, to ensure that there exists only one closed orbit, i.e. it is open whether there arises a supercritical Hopf bifurcation. In case there arise multiple closed orbits and limit cycles, the economy is subject to cyclical instability since there exist equilibrium cycles near the fixed point E with low amplitudes, being comparable to the equilibrium cycle under long-run rationality, as well as equilibrium cycles which lie near the boundaries of compact set $\mathcal{D}$ implying possibly financial crises on each business cycle. Thus, financial stability, as well as equilibrium fluctuations depend on the initial condition, i.e. exogenous shocks are in a position to catapult an initially cyclically stable economy into an "equilibrium" situation with huge fluctuations in goods and financial markets resulting possibly in financial crises.

Despite the fact that there is no possibility to determine the number of cycles, there arise also important differences to the long-run rationality case if there exists only one limit cycle as drawn in figure 4.9, which corresponds much better to the stylized facts since there exists only one stable equilibrium cycle to which economies converge in the long-run. Firstly, the equilibrium business cycle under a pure chartist-fundamentalist expectation formation scheme is subject to larger equilibrium fluctuations as an equilibrium cycle under long-run rational behaviour due to the absence of the counteracting force $\partial f/\partial \rho < 0$ outside the normal range. Secondly, financial distress on the upper turning point of the equilibrium cycle is much larger than under long-run rational behaviour since there is a longer and deeper build-up of financial fragility during the boom and the overborrowing phase. Thus, there arises the possibility that each equilibrium cycle is subject to a financial crisis. Thirdly, in case the equilibrium cycle is not subject to financial crises on the upper turning point, economies tend to be cyclically stable in the long-run implying that financial crises can be only induced by large positive shocks to expectations as in the long-run rationality case. However, in case a positive shock to ρ has induced an extensive boom-bust cycle, the subsequent financial crisis is much deeper and lasts much longer than under long-run rationality since there is no dampening effect $\partial f/\partial \rho < 0$ outside the normal range.

Summing up, the comparison between the Keynesian and the long-run rationality approach gives rise to the supposition that the assumption of long-run rationality leads to model results which correspond much better to the stylized facts than a pure chartist-fundamentalist regime. By way of contrast, a pure rational expectations approach is not in a position to explain endogenous equilibrium fluctuations and endogenous financial fragility in a world without exogenous shocks. Consequently, only the combination of both approaches is able to provide better insights into business cycles and their link to financial crises.

4.5 A Comparison with Standard Theory of Financial Crises

The present "cyclical" approach to financial crises differs substantially from standard models which have been briefly set out and compared to the stylized facts of financial crises in section 3.5. In order to highlight these differences, as well as the advantages of the present approach over existing models, sections 4.5.1 to 4.5.5 review the most important standard models of financial crises, which have been classified according to section 3.5 into inconsistent macroeconomic policy models, self-fulfilling expectations models, asymmetric information models, credit constraint and balance sheet models, and endogenous financial crisis models, and elaborate the basic mechanisms triggering financial crises in terms of the comparative-static version of the industrial country model, being also an evidence for the universal validity of the model. This procedure could have been performed alternatively by means of a dynamic framework, which however would not have provided more insights than a comparative-static framework. It is self-evident that the present model structure cannot exactly fit all standard models which are going to be discussed in the following, and therefore refers sometimes, if necessary, to other variables or parameters than in the original models, which however can catch the basic logic of the standard models. Section 4.5.6 discusses briefly both the common grounds and differences of the industrial country model in comparison with standard approaches to financial crises, and highlights the new elements of the present approach that distinguish it from standard models.

The following analysis refers exclusively to standard models which can be applied to industrial countries with flexible exchange rates. Standard models of financial crises in emerging market countries, emphasizing both the role of large foreign debt stocks and the role of fixed exchange rates in the propagation mechanisms of financial crises, are discussed in section 5.5.

4.5.1 Inconsistent Macroeconomic Policy Models

Predictable Bank Runs Due to Deflationary Monetary Policies. Flood and Garber (1981b) discuss the effects of deflationary monetary policies on banking liquidity and solvency in a perfect foresight model. Their model, which refers closely to I. Fisher's (1911) theory of bank defaults caused by deflation, was mainly motivated by the occurrence of multiple banking crises in the U.S. during the Great Depression period from 1929 until 1933. They argue that the main cause of widespread bank runs following the stock market crash in 1929 and the first banking crises in 1930 was the Federal Reserve's refusal to provide liquidity supports to troubled banks which experienced liquidity shortages caused by large-scale deposit withdrawals. The large number of bank runs caused a massive reduction in the money supply which led to an extensive credit crunch followed by an output collapse and deflation. According to Flood and Garber, the fall in the price level triggered further bank runs since deflation reduced banks' asset values whereas banks' debts, i.e. commitments to pay one unit high-powered money for one unit of deposits, remained constant, having led to a steady deterioration of banks' net worth, and in case bank debts were not longer covered by bank assets, to bank runs.

In their model, banks transform deposits D into reserves R and long-term bonds $P_B\,B$, where P_B denotes the market price of bonds, and B the real stock of bonds held by banks; the entire real stock of bonds in the model economy is denoted as $\bar{B}$, i.e. $B/\bar{B}$ represents banks' real share of bonds in the model economy. Banks have committed themselves to pay on demand one unit of high-powered money for each unit of deposits. Furthermore, it is assumed that there is no deposit insurance system and that deposits do not earn interest. Owing to the absence of a deposit insurance system, banks remain liquid and solvent and suffer no bank runs as long as debts are fully covered by banks' assets, i.e. as long as it holds that $R + P_B B = D$; for reasons of simplicity, bank capital is assumed to be zero. The firm sector of the model economy finances itself by issuing bonds to banks and other creditors, and receives nominal earnings from selling output to the amount of $P\bar{Y}$, where P denotes the nominal price level, and $\bar{Y}$ real output, the product of labour and capital, which is assumed as fixed. Nominal earnings of the firm sector are distributed among bond holders and the labour force. Bond holders earn a fraction $\theta P \bar{Y}$ of nominal earnings, whereas labour receives $(1-\theta) P \bar{Y}$. Bonds' market price P_B is positively dependent on nominal earnings $P\bar{Y}$, i.e. positively dependent on variations of the price level.

In case of deflation which is caused by the central bank reducing steadily high powered money, banks suffer asset losses on the one hand from a reduction in nominal earnings, and on the other hand from a reduction in the bond price. In order to maintain the nominal value of their assets, banks have to purchase new bonds to offset losses. Banks are willing to purchase additional bonds as long as their earnings from asset holding exceed the sum of portfolio managing costs and capital losses, i.e. as long as it holds that $\theta P_B \bar{Y} (B/\bar{B}) + \dot{P}_B B > T B$ where T denotes the cost per bond of managing banks' portfolio. Persistent deflation however, leads to a suspension of full asset backing, i.e. to $R + P_B B < D$, since earnings of holding bonds eventually fall short of costs, i.e. steady deflation leads to $\theta P_B \bar{Y} (B/\bar{B}) + \dot{P}_B B < T B$. At the moment when it is not longer profitable to maintain full asset backing, depositors run the bank in the absence of an effective deposit insurance system in order to minimize their losses because agents foresee a further reduction in the price level due to perfect foresight.

Translating Flood and Garber's model into the present industrial country model structure in which banks' assets consist only of loans to firms, the central bank's refuse to provide liquidity supports to troubled banks is indicated, like in the original Flood and Garber model, by a steady fall in high-powered money h which leads to reductions in u, r, and $\hat{p}$, and to an increase in the loan rate j caused by a credit crunch due to shrinking deposits $m\,h$. The exchange rate depreciates because of the initial gain in competitiveness caused by deflation. All effects lead to a shrinking net worth of business firms being indicated by a fall in Tobin's q, giving rise to a fall in banks' net worth due to an increase in non-performing loans and losses on the stock exchange, being also indicated by a shrinking value of q. This process of economic contraction lasts until banks' net worth reaches a zero value. At that moment, depositors run the bank because a further decline in $\hat{p}$ which can be foreseen, and which would cause losses to holders of deposits. A bank run involves generally a sudden switch from deposits into cash or high-powered money, leading to a sharp drop in the money multiplier caused by a sudden increases in the currency/deposit ratio, and in the reserve/deposit ratio due to banks' increasing need for high-powered money. Since cash was excluded from the model, a run could be modelled by a sudden increase in the demand for bonds or equities, indicated by an increase in derivatives $d_{r+\rho}$ and $d_{i-\hat{p}}$. However, comparative-static analysis has not considered these shocks. In order to follow Flood and Garber, cash can simply be introduced in the model by assuming that in case of a run the reserve/deposit ratio increases to $\tau = 1$, reducing the money multiplier suddenly also to a value of 1 indicating that banks must hold one unit of high-powered money for each unit of deposits. In terms of the model, a sharp fall in the money multiplier m to a value of $m = 1$ causes a further decrease in $u, r, \hat{p}, q, \hat{s}$, and a further increase in j deteriorating the initial fall in the money supply. Since banks have to liquidate loans in order to receive high-powered money from the central bank, a credit crunch is going to follow, being indicated by a sharp fall in λ which reduces the negative effects of m and h partly. But, as shown in the dynamic version of the model, business firms' investment activity is indirectly constrained by available credit, i.e. investment demand is going to collapse leading to a further deterioration because of accelerating deflation. Since economic activity is mainly determined by expectations, bank runs and a widespread contraction will lead additionally to a sharp drop in ρ, leading to further bank runs, contraction and deflation.

It is important to note that Flood and Garber explicitly assume the absence of an effective deposit insurance system. However, the model keeps its general validity also in case of an effective deposit insurance system. In this case, depositors do not provoke a bank run, but banks simply go bankrupt by deflation which leads not to such a dramatic reduction in the money multiplier like in the bank run scenario, but also to a drastic contraction in bank lending due to disintermediation effects. Furthermore, in case there is a widespread failure of banks, the existence of a deposit insurance system is no guarantee for the absence of a bank run. It seems possible that in extreme cases guarantees lose their credibility because losses have reached such a high dimension that a bail-out seems to be unrealistic triggering a bank run.

Predictable Bank Runs Due to Inflationary Monetary Policies. The idea that the existence of a deposit insurance system does not prevent depositors from a bank run in case government guarantees are no longer credible due to high capital losses among banks, has been discussed in Flood and Garber's second paper (1981a) which had been stimulated by the Savings and Loan (S & L) crises in the U.S. from 1981 until 1991. This model, in contrast to the preceding one, shows how an inflationary environment can induce a bank run.

In Flood and Garber's model, the S & L's asset side consists of long-term bonds representing fixed-interest mortgages, whereas the debt side contains only deposits and net worth. They assume that the central bank pursues an inflationary policy by a steady increase in high powered money. As they abstract from real sector responses by assuming that output is constant, an increase in the money supply is completely transmitted into an increase in the price level or in the inflation rate. Assuming the Fisher equation to hold with a constant real interest rate, increasing inflation results in a steady rising nominal interest rate which reduces the market value of bonds leading to a shrinking net worth, because deposits do not change in nominal terms. Flood and Garber assume that though there is a deposit insurance system, losses of S & L institutions are only financed partly by the lender of last resort. If losses, being indicated by negative net worth, exceed a certain value guaranteed by the government, then the run occurs.

In terms of the industrial country model, inflationary monetary policy is represented, as in the Flood and Garber model, by an increase in high powered money h leading to an expansion in the real sector being indicated by increases in u, r, q and a reduction in j; an increase in the money supply leads to inflation causing an appreciation of the exchange rate $\hat{s}$. However, since the model does not consider explicitly inflation expectations and does not assume the validity of the Fisher equation, inflation caused by an increase in h does not lead automatically to higher nominal interest rates. Still, it has been argued at the outset that inflation expectations are already incorporated in the state of confidence parameter ρ. An increase in inflation then leads to an expectation of higher nominal interest rates in the future, reducing expected profits and thereby inducing a declining value of ρ. In an accelerating inflationary environment, the resulting drop in the state of confidence can provoke a banking crisis and an adjacent bank run by reducing u, r

and increasing j and i, causing a drop in business firms' and banks' net worth which is indicated by a falling q; moreover, accelerating inflation leads to a devaluation of the home currency, indicating the outbreak of a currency, and of a twin crisis if, according to the index of speculative pressure (section 3.1.1), certain threshold values of $\hat{s}, i$ and j are exceeded. If banks' negative net worth falls short of a certain negative value having been guaranteed by the lender of last resort, depositors run the bank. All events following the bank run coincide with the above mentioned case of deflationary monetary policy.

First-Generation Currency Crises Due to Inconsistent Expansionary Monetary Policy. Krugman's (1979), and Flood and Garber's (1984a) first generation currency crises models and their extensions[56] abstract from the existence of a banking sector and refer exclusively to the breakdown of fixed exchange rate regimes caused by excessive expansionary monetary policies, which are predominantly induced by money-financed fiscal deficits. According to first-generation currency crises models, a steady increase in high-powered money leads to a steady fall in foreign exchange reserves to the same amount due to capital outflows, being induced by a steady downward pressure on domestic interest rates. The speculative attack on the domestic currency, which is followed by a flexible exchange rate regime, occurs when the flexible shadow exchange rate has increased to the level of the fixed exchange rate, i.e. when speculators can earn profits by buying the central bank's remaining stock of foreign exchange reserves at the fixed exchange rate, and selling them later at an appreciated post-crisis flexible exchange rate.[57] As most of first-generation models assume a constant value of output, first-generation currency crises models cannot explain the occurrence of systemic financial crises.[58]

In terms of the industrial country model, a first generation currency crisis, which, in the present case, occurs under a flexible exchange rate regime leading to a large devaluation of the (flexible) home currency, is caused by an increase in high-powered money h, leading to a rise in $\hat{s}$, and being accompanied by a real sector expansion which is represented by an increase in $u, r, q, \hat{p}$, and by a reduction in j.

Latest models of the explanation of twin crises caused by inconsistent expansionary monetary policies, as e.g. the model by Buch and Heinrich (1999), cannot be applied to the industrial country model, since they refer to emerging market economies with large foreign debt stocks. These models are going to be discussed in chapter 5.5.1.

4.5.2 Self-Fulfilling Expectations Models

Unpredictable Bank Runs Due to "Random Withdrawals". The closed-economy bank run model by Diamond and Dybvig (1983) studies the effects of a sudden shift in expectations due to external shocks on banking liquidity and solvency. The Diamond-Dybvig model is based on the assumption that there is an asymmetry between investment projects to mature and the time horizon of investors. Investors are modelled as short-sighted agents since they need short-run resources for consumption, or want to possess

[56]For an overview of first generation currency crises models and their extensions, see e.g. Agénor, Bhandari and Flood (1992), and Flood and Marion (1998).

[57]For a detailed discussion of Krugman's (1979), and Flood and Garber's (1984a) models, see Radke (2000a).

[58]One exception considering explicitly output effects in a first-generation model is Willman (1988).

liquid assets to invest in other investment projects in the short-run. In contrast to investors' short-run time horizon, investment projects need time to mature, i.e. short-run interruptions are not profitable. In order to overcome this tradeoff, Diamond and Dybvig introduce banks and explain their existence by their function of transforming maturities. Banks try to maximize profits by offering short-term assets (deposits) to investors, and by investing these proceeds in production (granting loans) which needs time to mature. In other words, banks transform their illiquid assets into liquid ones. This transformation by banks enables the economy to raise more funds for long-term investment, but also engenders the possibility of bank runs.

Diamond and Dybvig show that there exist two kinds of equilibria, a "superior" and an "inferior" one. The "superior" equilibrium is characterized by a situation in which banks offer a positive return on deposits, and allow early withdrawals which can be met by banks' reserves because only a small fraction of depositors wants to withdraw deposits in the short-run. Banks are able to invest most of deposits into the long-term high-yield technology which allows a prosperous economic development. This equilibrium to prevail requires that each depositor has to trust in other depositors also not to withdraw their funds in the short-run, and that all depositors believe in banks' ability to satisfy short-term withdrawals. If however, depositors lose confidence in the banking system by the believe that banks are unsafe, and additionally believe that all other depositors share the same view, a bank run, the "inferior" equilibrium, occurs with all depositors withdrawing in the short-run. Banks are forced to liquidate long-run investments which causes great harm to the real sector in order to meet cash withdrawals. Since the liquidation value of long-term assets is less than the amount of deposits, banks fail in case of a bank run. According to Calomiris and Gorton (1991), depositors' hurriedness to withdraw in case of a bank-run results form the first-come-first-served rule of deposit withdrawals. Depositors withdrawing too late receive nothing, which causes them to compete for being the first to withdraw. Which equilibrium prevails depends, according to Diamond and Dybvig, on random factors and cannot be foreseen. The event which triggers the move from the "no-run-equilibrium" to the "run-equilibrium" may depend on commonly observed random variables like bad earnings, an observed run at another bank, but it is also possible that expectations shift without any negative shock to banks' fundamentals, implying that if depositors expect a bank run to occur, the bank run is going to occur. In order to prevent bank runs, Diamond and Dybvig recommend establishing deposit insurance systems, so that a switch from "good" to "bad" expectations is no longer possible, as depositors are guaranteed to obtain their funds at any time.

In terms of the industrial country model, the Diamond-Dybvig story can be set out simply by shifts in the state of confidence parameter. If all economic agents believe in the healthiness of the banking system, which depends on business firms and general financial market conditions, the state of confidence parameter is positive, indicating further future profits. The economy is financially stable, being represented by "low" values of i and j, and is subject to real sector growth indicated by "large" values of u, r and q. There is inflation and a steady devaluation of the home currency. The "bank-run" equilibrium is caused by a sudden downward shift in the state of confidence, where it holds that $\rho < 0$, causing a collapse of the real economy indicated by "low" values of u, r, q, and inducing a financial crisis being represented by "high" interest rates i and j; furthermore, the economy can tip into deflation, leading to an appreciation of the home currency.

Second-Generation Currency Crises Due to Self-Fulfilling Expectations. Self-fulfilling currency crises models by Obstfeld (1986, 1994, 1997) are discussed in chapter 5.5.2, as these models refer to fixed exchange rate regimes and policy rules which contradict in some situations, thereby forcing authorities to devalue.

"Random Withdrawal" Bank Runs in the Open Economy. There are various approaches, as for example by Garber and Grilli (1989), Goldfajn and Valdés (1997b), and Chang and Velasco (1998a, 1998b, 1998c, 1999) which extend the closed-economy Diamond and Dybvig model to the open economy. In contrast to the closed-economy Diamond and Dybvig model, the debt side of banks' balance sheets additionally contains deposits in foreign currency, while the asset side still consists of long-term domestic assets denominated in domestic currency. As the book value of banks' long-term assets in the short-run, i.e. their short-run liquidation value, is smaller than the book value of deposits, financial intermediaries are susceptible to bank runs which cause a bank's failure due to illiquidity and insolvency. Since banks' debt side contains a considerable stock of foreign deposits, banks are not only subject to the risk of a bank run by domestic depositors, but additionally to the risk of a bank run by foreign depositors, being followed by a currency crisis due to large capital outflows. Bank runs are caused, as in the original Diamond-Dybvig model, by a self-fulfilling shift in expectations induced by an exogenous shock. Since most of the models refer to twin crises in emerging market economies by emphasizing the interaction of large foreign debt stocks with domestic banks and fixed exchange rate regimes, they are discussed in chapter 5.5.2.

One exception however, is the approach by Chang and Velasco (1998a, 1998b, 1998c, 1999), considering explicitly the case of a bank run being caused solely by domestic residents. As there are no deposit withdrawals by foreign depositors, there arises no currency crisis. Chang and Velasco assume that in case of a bank run by domestic depositors, banks can always repay foreign debt even if there arise liquidity problems because of the possibility to roll-over foreign debt. As in the Diamond-Dybvig case, there are two possible equilibria. The "good" one is characterized by only some depositors withdrawing deposits in the short-run; these withdrawals can be financed completely by borrowing from abroad and there is no need to liquidate long-term assets. The "bank run" equilibrium is characterized by a situation in which all domestic agents want to withdraw their deposits because of the widespread believe that everyone else is going to withdraw deposits. If there is no deposit insurance system providing short-run liquidity supports, banks are going to fail in case of a bank run.

In terms of the industrial country model, Chang and Velasco's approach can be also set out by sudden shifts in the state of confidence parameter ρ, leading to the same results like the application of the Diamond-Dybvig case. A special feature however, is the effect on the exchange rate in case of the bank-run, i.e. if it holds that $\rho < 0$, as the contraction in the real sector causing deflationary pressures possibly leads to a currency crisis which is, in contrast to the general case of currency crises, characterized by a sharp appreciation of the domestic currency, and not by a depreciation.[59]

[59]This special case of currency crises has been also emphasized by Grilli (1986) in terms of a modified first-generation currency crisis model by Flood and Garber (1984a).

4.5.3 Asymmetric Information Models

Unpredictable Bank Runs Due to Asymmetric Information and Exogenous Shocks. Models of bank runs caused by asymmetric information and exogenous shocks, as e.g. by Gorton (1985), Chari and Jagannathan (1988), Calomiris and Gorton (1991), and Calomiris and Kahn (1991), also emphasize the role of multiple equilibria like Diamond and Dybvig, but explain the move from the "no-run-equilibrium" to the "run-equilibrium" by an exogenous triggering event which provides "new" information for depositors about the quality of banks' assets.

As a large fraction of banks' assets are nonmarketable, depositors cannot monitor perfectly asset quality. Besides, depositors cannot distinguish "good" banks from "bad" banks, i.e. they do not know which banks are most affected by a negative shock. As a result, in case of a large negative exogenous shock, depositors decide to run all banks. After the run, banks suspend convertibility and sort out "bad" failed banks due to their information advantage. From this perspective, bank runs can solve the information asymmetry between depositors and banks, and can help depositors to monitor banks more efficiently. If, on the contrary, there are no adverse shocks, there will be no bank runs, since depositors believe in the healthiness of the banking system. Consequently, widespread bank runs can be only triggered by an exogenous shock, and not by a pure shift of self-fulfilling expectations as in the Diamond-Dybvig (1983) model. Since the probability of shocks cannot be determined in these models, bank runs remain an unpredictable event.

In terms of the industrial country model, the change from the "good" to the "bad" equilibrium can be explained by a change from a positive ρ value to a negative ρ value which is caused by some "news". For example, a sudden change in the banking regulation scheme (e.g. the introduction of the Basel II capital accord) limiting banks' credit supply, being represented by a sharp increase in α, reduces banks' net worth and could trigger a run; in the same way, an adverse productivity shock, being indicated by a sudden increase in the wage share v, or by a sudden increase in the depreciation rate δ lowering firms' profits and banks' net worth, could be a triggering event for a bank run.

Moral Hazard, Overinvestment and Overborrowing Due to Exogenous Shocks or Owing to Self-Fulfilling Expectations - Third-Generation Models. The literature on moral hazard driven financial crises, being labelled as the third-generation approach to financial crises, emphasizes that implicit or explicit government guarantees on the liabilities of banks, on foreign investors' claims, on the stability of exchange rates, or investment subsidies raise the private return on assets, making creditors and debtors engage in riskier investment projects than they would do if there were no guarantees, as in case of default, losses are transferred to the tax payer. Moral hazard driven booms being subject to overinvestment, overborrowing, and asset price bubbles can generate financial crises if one additionally assumes the existence of an exogenous limit on the cumulative financial costs of government support policies. In case the financial government support has reached its maximum, and is going to, or expected to be suspended in the future, expected asset returns collapse, leading to widespread bankruptcies among firms and banks, and in severe cases, to full-fledged financial crises. In the case of deposit insurance systems or guarantees to bail-out troubled banks, governments are going to abandon guarantees if the budget deficit reaches undesirable levels which would cause high inflation. In case of fixed exchange rate systems, central banks' reserves limit the credibility of guarantees;

if there are huge outflows reducing reserves to zero, and if there is no possibility to get reserves from international capital markets, the fixed parity has to be abandoned.

Regarding the suspensions' causes, being the triggering events of financial crises, the literature on third-generation models differentiates among exogenous shocks and self-fulfilling expectations. In case a huge shock, like e.g. an interest rate or negative productivity shock, exhausts governments capacity to bail out the banking system, or to guarantee a fixed exchange rate for financial claims of international investors, there will be a suspension of government guarantees leading to a bank run, to a currency, or to a twin crisis. However, governments' capacity to fulfill guarantees can be likewise exhausted by a simple shift in expectations. If agents start to believe, without any fundamental reason, that government guarantees will be removed in the future, agents are going to run on banks or currencies, making the government provide financial support due to its obligation to bail out banks, or to support the exchange rate. When governments' resources to bail out banks or to stabilize exchange rates are used up, a banking, currency crisis or twin crisis is going to follow, validating ex post investors' pessimistic ex ante expectations. If, on the other hand, investors believe in the stability of future government guarantees, there will be no financial crisis, validating investors' optimistic ex ante expectations.

Apart from the distinction between self-fulfilling and exogenous shock driven financial crises, third generation approaches can be classified into closed economy models which concentrate on government guarantees to bail-out the banking system, like e.g. Krugman (1998), and into open economy models, as e.g. Diaz-Alejandro (1985), Velasco (1987), McKinnon (1993), Dooley (1997), McKinnon and Pill (1997, 1998, 1999), Burnside, Eichenbaum and Rebelo (1998), and Corsetti, Pesenti and Roubini (1998), focusing additionally, next to bail-out promises, on government guarantees to maintain a fixed exchange rate regime. Since the industrial country financial crisis model operates under a flexible exchange rate system and does not consider foreign debt, this paragraph refers to closed economy approaches emphasizing the role of government guarantees to bail-out troubled banks, whereas open economy approaches generating twin crises are discussed in section 5.5.3.

The Diamond-Dybvig (1983) literature recommended the establishment of deposit insurance systems to prevent future bank runs, but did not take into account that deposit guarantees can cause banks to grant much riskier loans than in the absence of guarantees, since in the case of banks' default, e.g. due to large fraction of non-performing loans, losses which would have normally to be borne by depositors, are taken over by the government, and indirectly by the tax payer. This argument was brought forward by Krugman (1998) in connection to the Asian crisis. In his model, only banks allocate funds to investment projects which are assumed to be protected against losses by government guarantees. Banks face two different investment projects; one secure investment with a known yield, and one risky investment whose yield is not known at the beginning, but for which probabilities for different outcomes ("good" or "bad") are available. A risk neutral investor will calculate the expected profit rate of the risky investment and compares it to the known profit rate of the secure investment. In case the expected value is lower than the known secure value, the risky investment will not be carried out. However, in case the government establishes guarantees, the probability of default of the risky investment can be neglected since losses are borne by the government. As a result, the expected profit rate of the risky investment project is going to increase to its so-called "Pangloss" value, causing risk-neutral banks to engage in the risky investment project in case its expected yield is higher than the yield of the secure investment project. In case the risky investment project turns out to be the more profitable one, banks are going to invest all funds into the risky investment project and will extend investment to an amount which is larger than under the absence of government guarantees, i.e. moral hazard leads to overinvestment. Since investment has to be financed mainly externally, the increase in banks' debt is also larger than under the lack of guarantees, i.e. overinvestment leads to overborrowing, making the market price of the risky investment good, in case of an perfectly inelastic supply (as e.g. in case of land or housing), increase significantly. Accordingly, overinvestment and overborrowing lead to the emergence of asset price bubbles. This bubble effect however, amplifies banks' losses in case of default, because there arise not only lower yields, but additionally larger capital losses since banks are more indebted than it would be optimal due to the distortion in expected yields.

According to Krugman (1998), there are two possible triggers for a full-fledged financial crisis. Firstly, an exogenous shock causes a bad return of the risky investment, generating huge losses with banks which exceed the government's capacity to bail-out all troubled banks, and therefore leading to a guarantee suspension and to a banking crises. Secondly, self-fulfilling expectations, making the end of the guarantee regime endogenous, can cause a financial crisis, which validates ex post the initial shift towards pessimistic expectations. If banks' are believed to incur huge losses leading to abolishment of guarantees, there will be a plunge in asset prices, and depositors who expect that there is no bail-out are going to run on banks, inducing a severe financial crisis. If however, there is the widespread believe that there arise no losses, there is also no believe that the guarantee system will be abandoned which prevents a financial crises. Yet, the switch from the "no-crisis" to the "crisis-equilibrium" is assumed to be random and not explained by the model.

In terms of the industrial country model, moral hazard driven overinvestment can be represented by the government explicitly guaranteeing to subsidize firms in case firms incur losses due to unfavourable outcomes of a risky investment project. This explicit guarantee on firms also implies an implicit guarantee to bail out banks because losses in the firm sector, which would lead to non-performing loans in the banking sector, are taken over by the government. Assume that there are two different technologies in which firms can invest. Technology 1 is assumed to be secure whose return or profit rate is $r_1 = E(r_1) = 0.09$, implying a state of confidence value of $\rho = 0$. Technology 2 is assumed to be risky in the sense that there exist two possible outcomes of the profit rate, one realization value being negative $-r_{2n} = -0.08$, and the other one being positive $r_{2p} = 0.2$, both with equal probability 0.5. As a result, the expected value of the profit rate of the risky investment project amounts to $E(r_2) = 0.5 \cdot (-0.08) + 0.5 \cdot 0.2 = 0.06$, being smaller than the expected value of the secure investment in case of the absence of government guarantees, i.e. it holds that $E(r_2) = 0.06 < E(r_1) = 0.09$. Accordingly, without government guarantees, firms are going to invest solely in the secure technology 1, implying a state of confidence value of $\rho = 0$.

Introducing government guarantees however, changes the expected value of the risky investment project. Since in case of default, losses are taken over by the government, i.e. in case of an unfavourable outcome the government pays $r_g = 0.08$ to firms, resulting in an actual profit rate of $r_{2d} = r_{2n} + r_g = -0.08 + 0.08 = 0$, the risky investment project has an expected value of $E(r_2) = 0.5 \cdot 0 + 0.5 \cdot 0.2 = 0.1$ (its "Pangloss" value), implying a state of confidence value of $\rho = 0.1$. Comparing expected values of both investment projects in case of the existence of government guarantees makes firms invest into the risky investment project since it holds that $E(r_1) = 0.09 < E(r_2) = 0.1$. As a result, since the state of confidence ρ increases from 0 to 0.1 by investing in technology 2 and not in technology 1 due to the existence of government guarantees, there is a large macroeconomic expansion induced by overinvestment, i.e. $r, q, u, \hat{p}, \hat{s}$ increase and j and i decrease. Overinvestment leads to overborrowing by firms, being represented by an significant increase in the debt-asset ratio λ, dampening but not offsetting the macroeconomic expansion induced by the rise in ρ.

A financial crisis in this state of overborrowing and overinvestment can emanate either from an exogenous shock or from self-fulfilling expections. As to the shock scenario, consider a negative productivity shock (increase in v or δ), validating the expected negative realization value $-r_{2n} = -0.08$. This drop in the actual profit rate leads to declines in $q, u, \hat{p}, \hat{s}$ and increases in j and i, causing bankruptcies in the firm and in the banking sector since losses exceed government guarantees inducing depositors to run on banks. All events following the bank run are identical with those described in the Diamond-Dybvig model. If, by way of contrast, there is no negative shock and an actual value of $r_{2p} = 0.2$ can be realized, no crisis is going to happen. Regarding self-fulfilling expectations as a triggering event, assume that agents expect government guarantees not to be continued in the future, making expected profits drop to $E(r) = 0.5 \cdot (-0.08) + 0.5 \cdot 0.2 < 0.06$, implying a fall in ρ, leading to a decline in $r, q, u, \hat{p}, \hat{s}$, and to a rise in j and i, forcing the government to subsidize firms in case profits are negative. If guarantees are actually suspended, since losses exceed the government's financial resources, agents' initial shift towards pessimistic expectations is going to be validated ex post by the occurrence of a banking crisis. If, on the other hand, agents believe in the continuation of government guarantees, there is no drop in ρ, and therefore no macroeconomic contraction followed by a financial crisis, also validating ex post agents' optimistic expectations.

4.5.4 Credit Constraint and Balance Sheet Models

Borrowing Constraints, Financial Crises and Output Collapses Due to Exogenous Shocks and Self-Fulfilling Expectations - Fourth-Generation Models. Credit constraint and balance sheet models of financial crises, being labelled as the fourth-generation approach to financial crises[60], are based on the theory of imperfect capital markets having been outlined in detail in section 2.2.2.2.[61] The theory of imperfect capital markets generally assumes that the existence of information asymmetries in financial markets leads to credit rationing and gives rise to the financial accelerator effect. The rationale for considering explicitly balance sheet and net worth positions in theoretical models of financial crises resulted from the stylized fact that financial crises in the 1990s, both in industrial and emerging market countries, were accompanied by large collapses in investment and output owing to credit crunches, having been induced by large drops in net worth positions of business firms and banks due to collapses in asset prices and exchange rates. Though credit constraint and balance sheet financial crisis models are built upon the nature of asymmetric information, they are not classified as asymmetric

[60] For this terminology, see Krugman (2001).

[61] For references, see also section 2.2.2.2.

information models according to section 4.5.3, since the causes of financial crises do not have their roots in distorted incentives of agents, but in borrowing constraints, becoming binding conditional on an increase in asymmetric information.

In terms of fourth-generation models, a financial crisis is defined as a situation in which there is a sudden increase in credit constraints, as e.g. cuts in credit lines or refusals to roll-over debt and/or an impetuous increase in interest rates on debt due to a rise in risk premiums, leading to a sharp drying-up of liquidity in credit markets (credit crunch), and to collapses in output since investment finance is assumed to hinge largely upon external finance according to the existence of a financial hierarchy. In severe cases, financial markets stop working and do not provide any longer necessary information to overcome existing asymmetries. This sharp contraction in the available amount of credit and output is assumed either to stem from exogenous shocks which increase asymmetric information, aggravating the difficulty for financial intermediaries to distinguish between "good" and "bad" risks, or due to self-fulfilling expectations. Both forms of financial crises are going to be discussed in the following paragraphs.

Financial Crises Due to Exogenous Shocks. A very prominent example of the asymmetric information view of financial crises both in industrial and in emerging market countries, being triggered by exogenous shocks and leading to binding credit and balance sheet constraints, is given by Mishkin (1991, 1996, 1997, 1998a, 1998b, 1999a, 1999b). He analyzes different kinds of exogenous shocks like unexpected variations in the inflation rate, interest rate changes, exchange rate changes, stock market crashes, etc. In all cases, exogenous shocks to the financial system interfere with information flows, leading to a contraction in credit supply. For example, a stock market crash, or a sharp interest rate increase reduce net worth of financial and business firms, leading to a reduction in available credit, investment and output; in severe cases, a drying-up in lending can cause a severe financial crises. Other examples which mainly refer to (international) credit constraints of emerging market countries owing to borrowing in foreign currency, which become binding and/or are going to be cut back in case of exogenous shocks, are given by Dornbusch (1998a, 1998b, 1999, 2001), Céspedes, Chang and Velasco (2001a, 2001b), Velasco (2001, 2002), and Caballero and Krishnamurthy (2002), being discussed in chapter 5.5.4.

Translating these ideas into the industrial country model can be done by various kinds of shocks. Productivity shocks for example, being represented by increasing values in v and δ, lead to an economic contraction via a reduction in the "borrowing constraint" being represented by Tobin's q. A collapse of Tobin's q, indicating large drops in liquidity and net worth positions, lead to a decline in $u, r, q, \hat{p}, \hat{s}$, and to an increase in j, causing in severe cases a full-fledged banking crisis and to lots of bankruptcies among firms. Shocks like the sudden bankruptcy of an important business or financial firm can cause a sharp decline in the "state of confidence" ρ and in Tobin's q, generating the same adverse macroeconomic effects like increases in v and δ.

Financial Crises Due to Self-Fulfilling Expectations. Fourth-generation financial crisis models driven by self-fulfilling expectations go back predominantly to Aghion, Bacchetta and Banerjee (2000, 2001, 2003) using an optimization approach, and to Krugman (1999a, 1999b, 2001) using a modified Mundell-Fleming approach. Following Krugman's fourth-generation approach, financial crises are caused by a sudden shift from optimistic towards pessimistic (profit) expectations, which can be induced by small shocks, or simply without any reason. Collapsing expectations lead to sharp declines in asset prices and exchange rates, inducing systemic financial crises due to large drops in business firms' net worth, either by falling asset values, or by increasing foreign debt stocks valued in domestic currency due to nominal depreciations of the home currency. The collapse of asset prices and exchange rates, as well as the outbreak of financial crises validates ex post investors' ex ante shift towards pessimistic expectations.

Krugman develops two different fourth-generation models, one on emerging market crises (Krugman 1999a, 1999b), relating to the influence of exchange rate variations on business firms' net worth in case of large foreign debt stocks to be discussed in chapter 5.5.2, and a second one on financial crises in industrial countries (Krugman 2001), which is going to be analyzed in the following, relating to the influence of changing asset prices on business firms' net worth positions.

In Krugman's (2001) closed economy model, business firms' investment activities are constrained by their net worth which depends on the level of asset prices. Asset prices, which are represented by Tobin's q, depend positively on output and negatively on interest rates. There arise two possible simultaneous asset and goods market equilibria. The "no-crisis" equilibrium is characterized by a strong confidence in the economy, high asset prices, strong net worth and high output. The "crisis" equilibrium, on the other hand, is characterized by low confidence in the economy, low asset prices, weak net worth and low output. Furthermore, the "crisis" equilibrium is characterized by a "liquidity trap" situation, as nominal interest rate cuts by the central bank to a minimum level of zero do not induce a recovery of the economy owing to the maintenance of pessimistic profit expectations. By way of contrast, both expansionary and contractionary monetary policy in the "no-crisis" equilibrium remain effective. Accordingly, there is no endogenous mechanism leading to a reversal of expectations and to a recovery of the economy. Financial crises, i.e. a switch from the "no-crisis" to the "crisis" equilibrium, are triggered by a sudden shift from optimistic towards pessimistic expectations as to the economy's profitability, causing a large decline in asset prices, net worth, investment, and in output, thereby validating the initial shift towards pessimistic expectations. Factors causing a shift in expectations are assumed to be purely random, and are not going to be explained by the model, as in all other self-fulfilling expectations models.

Translating the mechanisms of the Krugman model into the present model can be done easily by referring to the Diamond-Dybvig story which has been explained by exogenous shifts in the state of confidence parameter ρ. The "no-crisis" equilibrium is characterized by all agents having a strong confidence into the economy, indicated by a comparatively "high" level of ρ, causing comparatively "low" interest rate levels of i and j, and "high" levels of u, r and q. The shift from the "no-crisis" to the "crisis-equilibrium" is caused by a sudden downward shift in ρ, causing comparatively "high" interest rates j and i, and "low" values in u, r and q. As Krugman argues, in "normal" times, the low confidence equilibrium could be left by the central bank cutting interest rates, being represented by a large increase in high-powered money h, reducing j and stimulating u, r and q. If however, the confidence parameter ρ is at very low levels, a sharp increase in h can only reduce the loan rate j to zero, but has no influence on u, r and q. Furthermore, since the economy is in depression, a shrinking value of u causes deflation $\hat{p} < 0$, increasing the real interest rate on loans $j - \hat{p}$ at a constant nominal rate $j = 0$, and therethrough leading to a further decline in q, r and u.

4.5.5 Endogenous Financial Crisis Models

The Financial Instability Hypothesis by H. P. Minsky. Minsky's (1972, 1975, 1977, 1978, 1980a, 1980b, 1982a, 1982b, 1986) financial instability hypothesis[62] differs from all models reviewed so far as to four important aspects. Firstly, Minsky's theory, which is restricted to closed industrialized economies, argues that market economies are inherently unstable, and that systemic financial crises, driven by an endogenous build-up of financial fragility, are an unavoidable and endogenous outcome of modern capitalist systems if there are no government or central bank interventions to prevent financial crises, or to dampen their adverse effects on goods and financial markets. Secondly, Minsky claims that financial crises are inseparably linked to business cycle fluctuations, where financial instability is built up endogenously during the upswing and evolves into a systemic financial crises when the economy enters the downswing period. Thirdly, Minsky's approach is built on a balance sheet approach considering explicitly liquidity and net worth positions. Fourthly, notwithstanding the fact that the financial instability hypothesis is dynamic in nature, Minsky's theory is formulated as a qualitative-descriptive and comparative-static approach.[63]

Minsky's financial instability hypothesis consists of five theoretical components. The first component, Minsky's theory of financial stability, which has been discussed in detail in sections 2.3.2.1 and 2.3.2.2, distinguishes financially fragile from financially stable economies by the ratio of hedge finance to speculative finance and Ponzi finance units. If the ratio is comparatively high, the economy's financial structure is stable, whereas a low ratio indicates a fragile financial structure. The second component, Minsky's theory of the determinants of aggregate profits, is based on M. Kalecki's (1971) theory of profits which is outlined in more detail in appendix E. According to Kalecki's approach, the amount of investment determines the amount of profits, i.e. rising/declining investment expenditures generate higher/lower profits. The third component, Minsky's theory of investment, is largely based on Keynes' (1936, 1937) theory of investment, stating, in a very simplified way, that the aggregate level of investment is positively dependent on the ratio of the expected profit rate to the debt interest rate.[64] Accordingly, investment increases/decreases if there is a rise/fall in the expected profit rate, and/or if the there is a fall/rise in the debt interest rate. The fourth component, Minsky's view of the formation

[62] Minsky's financial instability hypothesis has been applied by C. Kindleberger (2000) to explain various historical episodes of financial crises and is therefore often designated as the Minsky-Kindleberger approach to financial crises.

[63] Some formal treatments of Minsky's financial instability hypothesis can be found in Taylor and O'Connell (1985), Palley (1996), chapter 12, and Nasica (2000).

[64] Minsky's, or Keynes' investment function is an early version of Tobin's q theory of investment, since investment is assumed to be positively dependent on the difference between the demand price of capital (price of existing capital goods), being largely dependent on expected profits, and the supply price of capital (reproduction costs of investment goods). Moreover, as capital markets are assumed to be imperfect due to asymmetric information, investment is assumed to be determined additionally by subjective assessments of borrower's and lender's risk which are both dependent on aggregate actual and expected profits. For further details on Minsky's theory of investment, see especially Minsky (1975), chapters IV and V.

of profit expectations, has not been explicitly considered by Minsky, but relies largely on Keynes' beauty contest theory, i.e. profit expectations are determined according to a chartist-type behaviour of agents. The fifth component, Minsky's theory of the financial structure, states that the degree of indebtedness is determined by the relation of profits to investment. Hence, if actual profits exceed/fall short of investment expenditures, there is a fall/rise in overall indebtedness. Furthermore, a given degree of indebtedness can be only be maintained in case actual profits are viewed to be sufficient to repay debt in the future.

The second, third, and fourth component give rise to the emergence of cumulative upward and downward processes in goods and financial markets which are driven by the interaction of actual profits, expected profits, and investment. A rise/fall in investment causes a rise/fall in actual profits, leading to a rise/fall in expected profits generating a further increase/decrease in investment, and so on. The fifth component determines how long a cumulative upward or downward process is sustainable. If the expansionary process is characterized by a faster increase in expected profits and investment than in actual profits, the increase in indebtedness is maintained as long as actual profits are expected to rise to future levels which enable debt to be repaid; otherwise the expansionary process is reversed into a contractionary cumulative downward process with decreasing indebtedness which comes to a halt if investors realize that actual profits have fallen less than expected.

A typical Minsky cycle begins with the recovery phase of the last business cycle when indebtedness has returned to sustainable levels, i.e. when the ratio of hedge finance units to speculative finance and Ponzi finance units has increased. Such a financially robust structure is characterized by short-term interest rates being lower than long-term rates, and by the expected profit rate being higher than long-term interest rates. The fact that short-term interest rates are lower than long-term interest rates during the recovery phase of the last business cycles, i.e. during tranquil times, can be explained either by expectations theory of the term structure of interest rates, or by the liquidity premium theory. Moreover, since debt restructuring after the last financial crisis is generally characterized by transforming short term debt into long-term debt, the financial structure is characterized by a large fraction of liquid assets, by a low share of short-term debt, and by a much higher share of long-term debt (due to rising hedge finance arrangements), giving rise to very low short-term interest rates. The fact that the expected profit rate is larger than the long-term interest rate can be explained by very low aggregate investment and profits due to the last financial crisis. Consequently, only a small rise in investment expenditures leads very quickly to an increase in actual profits.

According to Minsky, this relation between short-term rates, long-term rates, and the expected profit rate induces an *endogenous* build-up of financial fragility, as profits can be made by increasing investment expenditures which are financed by "cheap" short-term debt. That is, profit opportunities which stem from a robust financial structure cause an endogenous shift from financial stability to financial instability. Accordingly, the recovery phase of the last business cycle is followed by a boom phase which is driven by a cumulative upward process, stemming from the interaction of actual profits, investment, and expected profits, which leads to a significant fall in the ratio of hedge finance units to speculative finance and Ponzi finance units due to a significant rise in speculative and Ponzi finance units. Furthermore, as expectations are driven by chartist-type behaviour, there is a large rise in overall indebtedness as profit expectations and investment expenditures grow faster than actual profits.

The boom phase comes to an end at the upper turning point due to an endogenous, and general rise in interest rates which is caused by a steadily rising demand for financing, and by a limited supply of financing. The positive growth in actual profits is dampened or even reversed by rising wages and factor costs as capacity utilization reaches its maximum. Furthermore, rising wages and factor costs lead to contractionary monetary policies by central banks to fight inflationary pressures. Rising interest rates and declining profits lead, according to sections 2.3.2.1 and 2.3.2.2, to present value reversals and to financial posture downgrading, which cause a sharp decline in asset prices and a large rise in bankruptcies among firms and banks, evolving into a deep systemic banking crisis which is accompanied by a liquidity trap situation and deflationary pressures as emphasized by Fisher (1933, 1932), if there are no effective lender of last resort interventions by the central bank. In case monetary authorities do not prevent a full-fledged systemic financial crisis, the depression phase can be only left in case there is large rise in the government budget deficit which leads to a rise in aggregate profits (see appendix E for details) and to a decline in overall indebtedness, as there are no endogenous mechanisms which induce a recovery.

In terms of the present model, Minsky's financial instability hypothesis can be illustrated by the dynamic Keynesian version depicted in figure 4.9, and characterized by a pure chartist-type behaviour of agents. As mentioned in section 4.4.6, under pure chartist-type behaviour, there arises the possibility that each business cycle gives rise to financial crises, corresponding exactly to Minsky's results.

Other Approaches. There are similar approaches, as e.g. works of George (1879), Robbins (1934), Galbraith (1972), Borio, Furfine and Lowe (2001), Villa (2001), and Borio and Lowe (2002), which explain systemic financial crises as an outcome of excessive debt-led, and expectations-led business cycle fluctuations. However, most of these approaches are formulated as qualitative descriptions, or as empirical studies of historical episodes of financial crises and do not provide a comparable theoretical foundation as Minsky. Furthermore, as these approaches mainly rely on specific historical episodes, it is not clear whether financial crises are considered as an endogenous outcome, or as an event having been caused by exogenous shocks.

4.5.6 An Assessment

After having set out the most important standard approaches to financial crises, this section compares standard theory of financial crises with the industrial country model by elaborating the differences and common grounds, and by highlighting new elements of the present approach which have been neglected so far by standard models of financial crises.

A Comparison with Inconsistent Macroeconomic Policy Models. Respecting the common grounds of the present approach with inconsistent macroeconomic policy models, there are four similarities to be mentioned. Firstly, both approaches show that rising nominal interest rates, dropping asset prices and debt deflation, being associated with rising real interest rates, cause a substantial rise in financial fragility by deteriorating solvency and liquidity positions. Secondly, both types of models argue that both currency and twin crises are preceded by large capital outflows and depreciation expectations of the home currency. Thirdly, both approaches claim that, in case of twin crises, the banking crisis precedes the currency crisis which deepens the banking crisis. Fourthly, both types of models assume that financial crises are caused by exogenous factors, where inconsistent macroeconomic policy models stress excessive expansionary monetary and fiscal policies, and the present approach an exogenous positive shock to expectations.

Regarding the differences, there are four issues to be named. Firstly, inconsistent macroeconomic policy models do not consider the link between endogenous business cycle fluctuations and the occurrence of financial crises. Secondly, inconsistent macroeconomic policy models do not consider endogenous fluctuations in the debt-asset ratio and in profit expectations as the driving forces of tranquil and financial crises business cycles. Thirdly, inconsistent macroeconomic policy models only consider exogenous policy factors causing financial crises, and abstract from mechanisms inducing an endogenous build-up of financial fragility leading unavoidably to the occurrence of financial crises. Fourthly, inconsistent macroeconomic policy models generally assume the rational expectations hypothesis to hold, and abstract from market sentiment-driven expectations giving rise to cumulative processes.

A Comparison with Self-Fulfilling Expectations Models. As regards the common grounds, there are three similarities to be mentioned. Firstly, both approaches show that expectations are a crucial determinant of real economic activity and financial stability, as expectations are self-fulling and induce cumulative processes. Secondly, both types of models illustrate that stable financial conditions are associated with optimistic expectations as to real and financial sector variables, whereas financial instability is associated with pessimistic expectations. Thirdly, in both approaches, financial crises are induced by exogenous shocks to expectations.

As to the differences, there are five issues to be named. Firstly, self-fulfilling expectations models do not consider the link between business cycle fluctuations and financial crises as the present approach. Secondly, the approach of self-fulfilling expectations does not explain the endogenous build-up of financial fragility by endogenous interactions of expectations and overindebtedness, as both (rational) expectations and the degree of indebtedness are treated as exogenous variables, and do only change in case of random shocks. Thirdly, though both approaches claim that financial crises are caused by exogenous shocks to expectations, self-fulfilling expectations models argue that crises are caused by a shift from optimistic towards pessimistic expectations, whereas the industrial country model argues that financial distress is caused by a shift from pessimistic towards optimistic expectations. Fourthly, according to self-fulfilling expectations models, financial crises are unpredictable, random events which are not preceded by a deterioration of fundamentals, whereas the industrial country model shows that financial crises are preceded by a deterioration of almost all economic fundamentals, and that financial crises are the consequence of a past build-up of financial fragility. Fifthly, self-fulfilling expectations models assume the rational expectations hypothesis to hold, and do not consider chartist-type expectations which induce cumulative processes.

A Comparison with Asymmetric Information Models. As regards the common grounds of the industrial country model with asymmetric information models, there are four issues to be mentioned. Firstly, both approaches argue that financial crises are preceded by a boom phase which is driven by overly optimistic expectations, leading to overinvestment, overborrowing and to a considerable build-up of financial fragility. Secondly, both approaches show that financial crises are associated with both deteriorating fundamentals and collapsing expectations. Thirdly, especially self-fulfilling expectations-driven moral hazard models show, like the present approach, that stable financial market conditions are associated with optimistic expectations, whereas financial crises are associated with pessimistic expectations. Fourthly, both approaches argue that financial crises are induced by exogenous shocks.

Respecting the differences, there are six issues to be named. Firstly, moral hazard models do not consider the link between tranquil business cycle fluctuations and financial crises cycles. Secondly, moral hazard models do not explain the build-up of financial fragility by endogenous mechanisms, but by exogenously given government guarantees. Thirdly, moral hazard models assume that financial crises can be only triggered by exogenous shocks to fundamentals, or by self-fulfilling expectations with regard to the maintenance of government guarantees, and exclude the possibility of endogenously caused financial distress despite a considerable build-up of financial fragility during the boom phase. Fourthly, though both approaches argue that financial crises are caused by exogenous shocks to expectations (especially self-fulfilling expectations-driven moral hazard models), moral hazard models assume that financial crises are driven by a switch from optimistic to pessimistic expectations, whereas the industrial country model argues that crises are driven by a switch from pessimistic to optimistic expectations. Fifthly, following self-fulfilling expectations-driven moral hazard models, financial crises are an unpredictable event which are not preceded by deteriorating fundamentals, whereas the industrial country model is characterized by an endogenous deterioration of all fundamentals before the outbreak of the crisis. Sixthly, moral hazard models generally assume the rational expectations hypothesis to hold, and abstract from market sentiment-driven expectation formation schemes.

A Comparison with Credit Constraint and Balance Sheet Models. As regards the common grounds, there are three similarities to be mentioned. Firstly, both approaches argue that financial crises and subsequent recessions are caused by a considerable reduction in domestic and foreign debt finance, i.e. by financial constraints which become binding. Secondly, both approaches argue that financial crises are accompanied by both deteriorating fundamentals and collapsing profit expectations. Thirdly, both approaches argue that financial crises are caused by exogenous shocks. Fourthly, especially self-fulfilling expectations-driven credit constraint models show, as the industrial country model, that both financial stability and a macroeconomic activity depend crucially on the state of profit expectations.

Respecting the differences, there are six issued to be named. Firstly, credit constraint and balance sheet models do not consider the link between business cycle fluctuations and financial crises. Secondly, credit constraint and balance sheet models are not subject to endogenous fluctuations in expectations and in indebtedness. Thirdly, credit constraint and balance sheet models do not explain the build-up of financial fragility by endogenous processes, but by exogenous shocks to fundamentals and by shifts towards self-fulfilling pessimistic expectations. Fourthly, especially self-fulfilling expectations-driven credit constraint models argue that financial crises are caused by a shift from optimistic towards pessimistic expectations, whereas the present approach emphasizes the shift from pessimistic towards optimistic expectations as the triggering event. Fifthly, especially self-fulfilling expectations-driven credit constraint models argue that financial crises are an unpredictable event, while the industrial country model is subject to an endogenous deterioration of all fundamentals before the outbreak of the crisis. Sixthly, credit constraint and balance sheet models assume the rational expectations hypothesis to hold and do not consider market sentiment-driven expectations giving rise to cumulative upward and downward processes.

A Comparison with Endogenous Financial Crisis Models. Regarding the common grounds, there are two similarities. Firstly, both approaches show that financial crises and business cycles are inseparably linked to each other. Secondly, financial crises are caused by endogenous debt and expectation dynamics.

As for the differences, there are four issues to be mentioned. Firstly, endogenous financial crisis models argue that every business cycle can lead to financial crises, i.e. that capitalist economies are inherently unstable, whereas the industrial country model indicates that capitalist economies are inherently cyclically stable, and that financial crises are an exogenous event. Secondly, endogenous financial crisis models argue that expectations are solely driven by market sentiments and neglect a long-run rational behaviour of agents. Thirdly, endogenous financial crisis models argue that there are no endogenous mechanisms inducing a recovery of an economy which has been hit by a financial crisis, whereas the industrial country model points out that even in case of a financial crisis, market economies are stable as there exists an endogenous recovery mechanism which however, can take a very long time. Fourthly, in contrast to endogenous financial crisis models, the present approach provides a sophisticated theoretical foundation and distinguishes explicitly between a "normal" degree of financial fragility being associated with tranquil business cycles, and "excess" financial fragility causing systemic financial distress.

New Elements. The comparison of standard models of financial crises with the industrial country models has shown that the present "cyclical" approach to financial crises provides important extensions for further research on financial crises both from a methodological-theoretical, and from an empirical perspective.

Regarding the methodological-theoretical perspective, the present approach offers six innovations. Firstly, the model contains a strict dynamic framework for an open economy, being not restricted to few periods, or to a closed economy. Secondly, the model is based on a sophisticated financial structure being developed from balance sheets with many assets, and contains a banking sector being the most important institution for the allocation of credit. Furthermore, the model emphasizes the important role of net worth and collateral both for business cycle fluctuations and for financial crises, being often neglected by standard models. Thirdly, the model structure considers explicitly, in contrast to standard models, various important transmission mechanisms (interest rate channel, exchange rate channel, asset price channel, bank lending channel, balance sheet channel) between the real and the financial sphere in an open economy, allowing for an illustration how financial disturbances can generate real sector or systemic financial crises. Fourthly, the model provides a synthesis between the rational expectations school and the Keynesian view of the formation of expectations, fitting much better the stylized facts of the behaviour of expectations than each theory on its own. Fifthly, the model provides a theoretical link between business cycle fluctuations and financial crises which has been generally omitted by standard approaches except for Minsky's theory, which however, provides no quantitative foundation, and assumes that each business cycle is accompanied by a financial crisis. Sixthly, the present approach provides a theoretical synthesis with respect to the financial stability of capitalist market economies, and with respect to the nature of triggers of financial crises. The industrial country model illustrates that capitalist economies are cyclically stable, though each business cycle is accompanied by a weak form of endogenous financial fragility, and that financial crises are caused by exogenous positive shocks to expectations which induce an endogenous process of above-average financial fragility and financial crises. By way of contrast, standard theory offers only two polar views. Standard theory of exogenous financial crises argues that capitalist economies are inherently stable without any appearance of financial fragility, and that financial crises can be only triggered by adverse shocks to fundamentals and expectations, whereas standard theory of endogenous financial crises argues that capitalist economies are inherently unstable, and that financial crises occur purely endogenously.

Regarding the empirical perspective, the present approach to financial crises offers two innovations. Firstly, in contrast to all other financial crisis models, the present approach contains most of the major indicators as variables which are used by empirical research to describe the influence of financial distress on various macroeconomic variables, and to develop early warning systems, as e.g. the debt-asset ratio, business firms' and banks' profit rate, net cash flows, Tobin's q, loan rates, bond and stock prices, etc. Secondly, the model's predictions of the behaviour of macroeconomic variables before, during, and after financial crises fits very closely the stylized facts of financial crises, whereas predictions by standard approaches very often only refer to the post-crisis period, and are restricted to a limited number of variables. Furthermore, predictions made by standard model in some cases do not fit the stylized facts, as e.g. the prediction by self-fulfilling expectations models that financial crises are not preceded by a deterioration of fundamentals.

4.6 A Comparison with Standard Business Cycle Theory

The dynamic version of the present model provides both a dynamic theory of financial crises and a theory of endogenous fluctuations in aggregate economic activity. After having assessed the differences, as well as the common grounds of the present approach with standard theory of financial crises, this section compares the model's mechanisms giving rise to fluctuations in real and financial markets with recent work on business cycle theory. The theoretical literature on business cycles can be classified in two broad categories, namely theories explaining cyclical fluctuations by endogenous mechanisms, and theories interpreting the business cycle as a cyclical response to exogenous financial or real disturbances. As opposed to the analysis of standard theory of financial crisis, the following description does not contain a detailed description, as well as a comparative-static examination of various business cycles theories, but only a short comparative analysis of the "main driving forces" of cyclical fluctuations in aggregate economic activity.

4.6.1 Theories of Endogenous Business Cycles

Fluctuations in Bank Credit as the Main Source of Aggregate Volatility. Early theories on business cycles explain the cumulative processes of inflationary expansions and deflationary contractions by money and bank credit fluctuations giving rise to fluctuations in investment, and thereby in aggregate economic activity. Wicksell ((1898) 1936) explains fluctuations in bank credit by discrepancies between the "natural interest rate", being equivalent to the expected marginal profit rate on new investment which determines aggregate investment, and the "market rate", being equivalent to the interest rate on bank loans which determines aggregate savings. Though interest rate differentials can be theoretically caused by both variations in the natural and in the market rate, Wicksell argues that differentials are predominantly caused by shocks to the natural rate. In case the natural rate is higher than the market rate, arising profit opportunities cause an expansion in bank credit, and a large rise in investment expenditures generating excess demand on goods markets (investment larger than savings) and inflation. However, an increasing price level forces banks to increase the interest rate on bank loans due to inflation-induced reserve (deposit) outflows, causing interest rate convergence and a tendency towards goods market equilibrium in the long-run. By way of contrast, in case the natural rate is lower than the market rate, declining profit opportunities lead to a decline in investment expenditures and to a contraction in bank credit causing deflation. Deflation-induced excess reserves with banks cause a reduction of the market rate towards the natural rate reducing excess supply in the goods market. Summing up, cumulative movements in the absolute price level induced by interest rate divergence guarantee a convergence of the natural and the market rate, and thereby a tendency towards goods market equilibrium, whereas the old and the new equilibrium differ by the absolute price level. As a result, relative prices are stable in the long-run, whereas the absolute price level is unstable, implying that the monetary equilibrium, i.e. the equality of the natural and the market rate, is also unstable since there is no mechanism guaranteeing a perfect adjustment of the market to the natural rate. For example, the market rate can over- or undershoot the natural rate inducing a new cumulative process in the reverse direction. Furthermore, there exists also the possibility of a changing natural rate during the adjustment process, inducing a new interest rate divergence. Regarding monetary policy conclusions, Wickell's theory states that if zero inflation is accepted to be the main goal of monetary policy, the prime rate has to be stabilized at the the level of the natural rate.

Hayek's (1933, 1939, (1935) 1967) theory of business cycles also explains fluctuations in investment and aggregate economic activity by the divergence of the natural and the market rate as Wicksell. However, as opposed to Wicksell, interest rate differentials are caused mainly by monetary disturbances, and long-run equilibrium is guaranteed by the price structure between investment and consumption goods. At below-equilibrium market rates, an expansion in bank credit creates overinvestment in capital goods industries and "forced saving" by inflation, which is mainly caused by an excess demand for consumption goods resulting from the shift of resources from consumption to capital goods industries.

Rising inflation causes banks to increase the market rate, leading to a declining interest rate differential and to a reduction in the supply of loans. Rising market rates, a reduction in credit, as well as rising consumption goods prices lead to an abrupt decline of capital goods' discounted present value causing losses and bankruptcies in the capital goods sector. Consequently, there is an abrupt stop in the capital goods production and a shift to consumption goods production. However, capital goods having been used in the capital goods sector cannot be used in the consumption goods sector due to lacking complementarities. As a result, the sudden stop of the traverse causes real capital shortages, a deflationary downturn, and an adjustment of the market rate to the natural rate. Summing up, monetary changes lead to distortions in the vertical structure of production, i.e. to imbalances between the production of consumption and capital goods, causing a "crisis" in order to return to the "old equilibrium" structure of production.[65] Unlike Wicksell's theory, distortions in the price structure, not cumulative movements of the price level, guarantee a return to the equilibrium.

Despite the fact that both authors explain the discrepancies between the natural and the market rate by exogenous shocks, both approaches can be classified as endogenous business cycle theories since they focus on the internal (price) mechanisms which guarantee a stable tendency towards equilibrium in the long-run. Hence, both Wicksell and Hayek viewed the role of exogenous factors as secondary, though they admit that exogenous shocks are the triggers for evolving disequilibria.[66]

Uncertain and Self-Fulfilling Expectations as the Source of Fluctuations in Investment, Bank Credit, and Aggregate Economic Activity. While early theories explain fluctuations in credit and investment by productivity and/or monetary shocks, there are other authors emphasizing that volatility in finance and investment results mainly from unstable expectations about the future. Keynes (1936, 1937) argues that aggregate instability is largely caused by fluctuations in investment, whereas volatility of investment is due to agents' expectations about an uncertain future being subject to large fluctuations which might be unrelated to changes in anything other than "market psychology" itself.[67] In a similar vein, Lavington (1921) attributes volatility of aggregate economic activity to the inherent instability of business confidence which can become self-fulfilling. For example, a rise in business confidence, which can be justified by fundamentals or not, leads to actions which are a real cause of increased confidence resulting in a boom. Consequently, a drop in confidence, which can be purely random, can lead to an economic downturn.

While Keynes and Lavington stress the interaction of expectations and investment neglecting more or less the question of investment finance, Hawtrey (1913, (1926) 1950) emphasizes the role of volatile expectations as the main source of fluctuations in bank credit determining the aggregate level of investment. He attributes the trade cycle to the inherent stability of credit which is mainly caused by unstable, self-fulfilling expectations of two sorts. Firstly, by volatile expectations of businessmen regarding the level of

[65] For business cycle theories caused by distortions in the vertical structure of production, see also Tugan-Baranovskii ((1894) 1913) and Spiethoff (1925).

[66] For details on Wicksell's and Hayek's business cycle theories, see e.g. Hagemann (1994, 2002), Hagemann and Trautwein (1996), and Trautwein (1998).

[67] See also section 4.4.1 for a detailed discussion of Keynes' theory of the formation of expectations.

aggregate demand which can be self-fulfilling, since banks are assumed to accommodate very passively changes in the demand for credit; as a result, an increase in expected demand causes an increasing demand for credit and investment goods, thereby validating the initial increase in expected demand. Secondly, by volatile expectations of bankers regarding the extent to which they can expand the supply of loans without causing a dangerous deterioration of reserves, depending upon the rate at which other banks expand their loan supply. In the same way, Leijonhufvud (1968, 1981) argues that serious macroeconomic instability occurs only if the exhaustion of "liquid buffer stocks" causes liquidity constraints to bind which causes instability, as revisions of expectations about future incomes become self-fulfilling.

In contrast to these early theories, which were not founded on quantitative analysis, recent research on expectations-driven endogenous business cycles, as e.g. models by Benhabib and Day (1982), Benhabib and Nishimura (1985), Grandmont (1985, 1986), and Grandmont and Laroque (1986), rely on an explicit formal modelling of intertemporal optimizing behaviour of agents in order to analyze precisely the influence of expectations on macroeconomic variables, giving rise to autonomous fluctuations without the occurrence of exogenous shocks. These models claim that even if the real fundamental characteristics of an economy do not change over time, prices and quantities are subject to cyclical fluctuations under laissez-faire in case agents expect them to fluctuate. Consequently, endogenous macroeconomic fluctuations caused by self-fulfilling expectations arise even in a world with individual intertemporal optimization, laissez-faire policy, and competitive market clearing. Formally, these models rely on the theory of deterministic nonlinear dynamical systems including bifurcation theory. A new similar formal approach, the so-called "stationary sunspot equilibrium" approach, to be discussed in the following section, working also under the assumptions of individual intertemporal optimization, laissez-faire policy, and competitive market clearing, explains aggregate fluctuations also by revisions of self-fulfilling expectations, which are however, caused by random shocks and not by internal mechanisms as described above. In contrast to models of endogenous business cycles, the "stationary sunspot equilibrium" approach models fluctuations by linear but stochastic dynamics.

Keynesian Multiplier-Accelerator Models. The Keynesian tradition of business cycle modelling started with Kalecki (1935, 1937), Harrod (1939, 1948) and Domar (1946, 1957) who emphasized the inherent dynamic instability of economic growth. Their work was followed by business cycle models by Samuelson (1939), Kaldor (1940), Metzler (1941), Hicks (1950), Goodwin (1951), and Rose (1967) who explain the emergence of endogenous fluctuations by an interaction of the consumption multiplier and of various versions of the investment accelerator. One branch of these models considers net investment as a positive function of changes in output so that fluctuations in consumption are transmitted with increasing amplitude to fluctuations in investment. Other models are based on the capital stock adjustment principle, the so-called "flexible accelerator" mechanism. According to this principle, current investment is determined by the difference between the desired and the actual capital stock where the desired capital stock is positively dependent on output. As a result, net investment depends positively on output and negatively on the initially available stock of capital. The distinguishing feature of these models is the explanation of income fluctuations on the basis of demand side factors. However, in contrast to all other endogenous theories on business cycles, these models ignore monetary, financial and expectational factors due to a restriction of the analysis to real factors.

4.6.2 Theories of Exogenous Shock-Driven Business Cycles

Exogenous Real and Monetary Shocks as the Main Source of Fluctuations. Common to all theories explaining business cycles as a result of exogenous events, whether originating from policy or from random external shocks, is the belief that economic systems are fundamentally stable at the stationary equilibrium, and that fluctuations in macro variables are the result of the economic system's reaction to frequent exogenous shocks to real or financial variables. The classification of a shock-driven business cycle theory as "real" or "monetary" is linked to the distinction between the impulses and the propagation mechanisms first introduced by Frisch (1933), since there are models with real shocks and monetary propagations, models with monetary shocks and real propagations, and combinations of both. The work on exogenous shock-driven business cycles, which goes back mainly to Slutsky (1927) and Frisch (1933), can be subdivided into two different approaches, namely the "Equilibrium Business Cycle" approach, which is of neoclassical derivation, and "New Keynesian" approach which moves within the Keynesian tradition.

"Equilibrium Business Cycle" theory, which is based on the intertemporal Walrasian general equilibrium setting, perfect markets, rational behaviour of agents and instantaneous market-clearing, assumes that the long-run equilibrium of a competitive monetary economy that does not experience any exogenous shocks is characterized by a state which is stationary, or growing at a constant rate. As a result, any departure from the long-run Walrasian equilibrium is viewed as purely transitory being caused either by monetary or real shocks. Monetary shock-driven models mainly go back to Lucas' (1972, 1975, 1977b, 1980, 1981) business cycle theory[68] stating that all persistent monetary changes, inasmuch as they are predictable, will be correctly anticipated and met directly by proportional changes in prices and related nominal variables having no influence on real variables as e.g. output. Only random monetary shocks can lead to price surprises and miscalculations by agents inducing false production decisions since agents are not able to distinguish relative price changes from changes in the aggregate price level due to incomplete information about economy-wide aggregates such as the money stock and the overall price level. For example, in case there is a random unanticipated monetary expansion leading to aggregate inflation, producers wrongly interpret the unanticipated increase in the aggregate price level as an increase in relative prices, i.e. in selling prices, boosting the real rate of return and causing an expansion in output; after some time, when outside price data has become available, producers suddenly realize that their interpretation of the price increase has been wrong and start to reduce production which involves time and costs. Real-shock driven business cycle models, as e.g. by Kydland and Prescott (1980, 1982) and by Long and Plosser (1983) which are also labelled as "Real Business Cycle Theory", state that disturbances from the intertemporal Walrasian equilibrium are mainly caused by exogenous random shocks to preferences and technology.

[68] Other similar approaches can be found in Sargent and Wallace (1975), McCallum (1980), and Barro (1981).

The "New Keynesian" approach on business cycles is built upon the criticism of "Equilibrium Business Cylce" theory[69], stating that markets are not perfect and do not clear permanently since the "real world" is characterized by imperfect competition and asymmetric information, resulting in nominal rigidities, i.e. in sticky prices. The "New Keynesian" view on business cycles, being reviewed and summarized e.g. in Mankiw (1989) and Mankiw and Romer (eds.), aims at providing a theoretical microfoundation of the different behaviour of goods, labour and financial markets under agents' intertemporal optimizing behaviour from the Walrasian theory. According to New Keynesians, business cycles are caused by exogenous shocks generating cycles due to the aforementioned nominal rigidities.

Stationary Sunspot Equilibria - Self-Fulfilling Rational Expectations as the Main Source of Aggregate Fluctuations. "Equilibrium Business Cycle" theory as well as the "New Keynesian" approach, both working under the assumption of rational expectations, explain aggregate fluctuations by shocks to the fundamentals of an economy, i.e. by shocks to preferences, technology, and monetary variables. By way of contrast, stationary sunspot models, e.g. by Azariadis (1981), Cass and Shell (1983, 1988), Azariadis and Guesnerie (1986), and Woodford (1986, 1987, 1988, 1989), which also work under the intertemporal Walrasian equilibrium setting, laissez-faire and rational expectations, explain macro fluctuations by unpredictable changes in so-called "sunspot" variables which are unrelated to fundamentals but which influence agents' rational expectations. Generally, sunspot variables are modelled as random variables being subject to a stationary stochastic process which agents observe, though sunspot variables do not contain information about fundamentals as e.g. preferences, resources and technology. For example, the unforecastable change in expectations of businessmen regarding income from production in a given period to which the desired level of investment expenditure is adjusted, could serve as a typical sunspot variable which does not influence fundamentals but agents' rational expectations. The introduction of sunspot variables in an explicit equilibrium setting generates under certain conditions so-called stationary rational expectations equilibria, or "sunspot equilibria" in which expectations vary in response to sunspot-state variables that do not provide, as aforementioned, any information about changes in fundamentals. These equilibria can be interpreted as representations of repetitive fluctuations in which sudden and random revisions of agents' expectations, due to sudden and random changes in the sunspot variable, become self-fulfilling. Changing expectations caused by random shocks to the sunspot variable cause a change in the outcome so that the initial change in expectations is validated ex post. As a result, the stationary sunspot equilibrium approach emphasizes the role of volatile expectations as an independent and causal factor of macro fluctuations, even if fundamentals are constant over time. These models postulate that even in an intertemporal Walrasian equilibrium setting under laissez-faire and rational expectations, there exists an inherent instability of market economies which has been already emphasized by early authors as Keynes, Lavington, Hawtrey who, however, did not explain changes in business confidence or animal spirits by individual rational behaviour which led, before the introduction of the sunspot equilibrium approach, to the conclusion by contemporary business cycle theory that self-fulfilling revisions of expectations were irrational and inconsistent with individual rational choice.

[69]For criticism on "Equilibrium Business Cycle" theory, see e.g. Summers (1986).

4.6.3 An Assessment

After having outlined the most important theories of business cycles, both in a historical and in a methodological perspective, the following discussion compares the present approach with standard theory of business cycles by elaborating the common grounds and differences, and by highlighting new elements of the present model which have not been considered yet by standard theories.

A Comparison with Theories of Endogenous Business Cycles. Regarding the common grounds of the present approach with standard theory of endogenous business cycles, there are seven striking similarities. Firstly, in the present model, fluctuations in bank credit, i.e. in the debt-asset ratio λ, as emphasized by Wicksell and Hayek, as well as uncertain and self-fulfilling (profit) expectations ρ as emphasized by Keynes, Lavington, and Hawtrey, being the main determinant of investment demand and bank credit, are the two "driving" forces of endogenous fluctuations in macro variables. Secondly, endogenous fluctuations are also driven by the investment accelerator as emphasized by Kaldor, Hicks, and Samuelson, i.e. by investment demand $\eta(q)$ steering the debt-asset ratio λ by equation 4.18, where Tobin's q depends on the profit rate r, and thereby indirectly on capacity utilization u. Thirdly, profit expectations ρ are driven by "mass psychology" or "animal spirits" as emphasized by Keynes, and allow for self-fulling revisions even though agents are assumed to be rational (at least in the long-run) as highlighted by modern authors as Benhabib, Day, Grandmont, Laroque, and Nishimura. Fourthly, endogenous fluctuations arise completely under laissez-faire as stressed by Benhabib, Day, Grandmont, Laroque, and Nishimura, since fiscal policy is excluded and monetary policy is passive by holding m and h constant over the business cycle; consequently, there are no policy shocks which could induce aggregate fluctuations. Fifthly, both recessions as well as financial crises are caused by overinvestment and overindebtedness as highlighted by Wicksell and Hayek. Sixthly, cycles are mainly driven by the profit rate differential $r^e - r = \rho$, and by the "fundamental" risk premium $\sigma = r - (i - \hat{p})$ which corresponds to Wicksell's and Hayek's interest rate differential. Seventhly, the model economy is only cyclically stable being guaranteed by correcting actions of ρ, λ, r, i and $\hat{p}$ as in Wicksell, and does not converge to a stationary steady state.

Concerning the differences of the present approach to standard endogenous business cycle theory, there are three important issues to be mentioned. Firstly, the present model does not contain a sophisticated production structure, as e.g. Hayek's vertical production structure which differentiates explicitly between the production of investment and consumption goods. Secondly, though the model contains an indirect form of the investment accelerator, there is no consumption multiplier with which the investment accelerator could interact to generate endogenous fluctuations as stressed by Kaldor, Hicks, and Samuelson. Thirdly, the present approach is not built upon an intertemporal Walrasian equilibrium setting as latest endogenous business cycle models by Benhabib, Day, Grandmont, Laroque, and Nishimura.

A Comparison with Theories of Exogenous Shock-Driven Business Cycles. Respecting the common grounds with standard theory of shock-driven business cycles, there arise three similarities. Firstly, though the present model exhibits endogenous fluctuations, business cycles are additionally driven by direct shocks to business confidence ρ, becoming self-fulfilling and leading to "jumps" in other macro variables. Secondly, shocks to expectations can be of a pure sunspot type as mentioned by Azariadis, Cass, Guesnerie Shell, and Woodford, or stem from real (productivity shock) or financial shocks (financial liberalization) as highlighted by "Equilibrium Business Cycle" theory and by the "New Keynesian" approach. Thirdly, the present model works under the assumption of (at least long-run) rationality as all exogenous shock-driven models.

Respecting the differences, there are three issues to be named. Firstly, in the present approach business cycles evolve endogenously, i.e. there is no need of exogenous shocks to generate aggregate fluctuations. Secondly, though there exists a stationary state in the present model as in all shock-driven models, it is dynamically unstable whereas global dynamics are cyclically stable. Thirdly, only direct shocks to the state of confidence ρ can alter the amplitude of the business cycle instantaneously, whereas other types of (indirect) real or monetary shocks only change the vector field and do not lead to "jumps" in macro variables.

New Elements. The present approach to business cycles and financial crises constitutes a further development in business cycle research both from a methodological-theoretical and from an empirical perspective. Regarding the methodological-theoretical perspective, there are three innovations. Firstly, the present approach provides a broad synthesis between endogenous and exogenous business cycle theories since it (a) contains a complex interaction between the real and the financial sector due to a sophisticated financial structure and a rich set of transmission mechanisms, (b) uses an innovative theory of expectations which are driven by mass psychology, fundamentals, as well as by rational behaviour, (c) highlights that business cycles can be caused both by endogenous and by exogenous mechanisms, and (d) contains almost all nonlinear time profiles mentioned in models of endogenous business cycles.[70] Secondly, the present model provides a new formal theory of the formation of expectations which postulates a weaker form of rationality to hold in reality than current rational expectations models do. Furthermore, the introduction of long-run rationality allows both for a stationary state to exist and for the emergence of endogenous cycles under rational behaviour. Thirdly, the model makes a clear distinction between "tranquil" business cycles and financial crises by the introduction of the degree of financial fragility, which has not been considered in other standard theories on business cycles, often speaking of crises and recessions synonymously, as e.g. Hayek.

Respecting the empirical perspective, the model provides two innovations. Firstly, in contrast to many business cycle models, the present approach contains major real and financial indicators as variables and parameters, which are used by empirical research to describe and to forecast business cycles, as e.g. business confidence, rate of capacity utilization, investment, bond and stock prices, total corporate profits, net cash flow, labour share in national income, total private borrowing, real money supply, short-term interest rates, bond yields, commercial and industrial loans outstanding, etc. Furthermore, the time patterns of these variables predicted by the model correspond in most cases to the

[70]For a summary of the main nonlinear relationships in endogenous business cycle models, see Zarnowitz (1992), p. 11-14.

stylized facts of business cycles.[71] Secondly, the predictions of the time patterns of the model's endogenous variables during episodes of financial crises and their close link to business cycles fits very closely the stylized facts as already outlined in section 4.5.6.[72]

[71] For an overview of major economic indicators used in empirical analysis' of business cycles and their stylized time patterns, see Moore (1983), chapter 6, and Zarnowitz (1992), pp. 23-28. For major indicators used for business cycle forecasting, see Zarnovitz (1992), chapter 9.

[72] See also Zarnowitz (1992), pp. 105-109 for the close link between business cycles and financial crises, as well as for the behaviour of macro variables during episodes of financial distress in the U.S. from 1818-1982.

4.7 Mathematical Supplements

All partial derivatives summarized qualitatively in table 4.1 are given explicitly below.

Response of Capacity Utilization u to Various Shocks.[73]

$$\frac{\partial u}{\partial \lambda} = \frac{1}{|\mathbf{J}|} d_{r+\rho}\, nx_{\hat{s}-\hat{p}}(\lambda + j\lambda^s_{j-\hat{p}} - j\lambda^s_q) \qquad < 0$$

$$\frac{\partial u}{\partial \rho} = \frac{1}{|\mathbf{J}|}(-nx_{\hat{s}-\hat{p}})\, d_{r+\rho}\,(\lambda^s_{j-\hat{p}} - \lambda^s_q) + d_{i-\hat{p}}\beta_\rho(\lambda^s_{j-\hat{p}} - (1+\lambda)\lambda^s_q)) \qquad > 0$$

$$\frac{\partial u}{\partial h} = \frac{1}{|\mathbf{J}|}(-m)\, nx_{\hat{s}-\hat{p}}\,(-\lambda^s_{j-\hat{p}} + \lambda d_{r+\rho}\lambda^s_{mh} + (1+\lambda)\lambda^s_q) \qquad > 0$$

$$\frac{\partial u}{\partial m} = \frac{1}{|\mathbf{J}|}(-h)\, nx_{\hat{s}-\hat{p}}\,(-\lambda^s_{j-\hat{p}} + \lambda d_{r+\rho}\lambda^s_{mh} + (1+\lambda)\lambda^s_q) \qquad > 0$$

$$\frac{\partial u}{\partial \alpha} = \frac{1}{|\mathbf{J}|}(-\lambda)\, d_{r+\rho}\, nx_{\hat{s}-\hat{p}}\, \lambda^s_\alpha \qquad < 0$$

$$\frac{\partial u}{\partial i^*} = \frac{1}{|\mathbf{J}|}(-d_{i-\hat{p}})\, nx_{\hat{s}-\hat{p}}\,(\lambda^s_{j-\hat{p}} - (1+\lambda)\lambda^s_q) \qquad > 0$$

$$\frac{\partial u}{\partial v} = \frac{1}{|\mathbf{J}|}\, u\, d_{r+\rho}\, nx_{\hat{s}-\hat{p}}\,(\lambda^s_{j-\hat{p}} - \lambda^s_q) \qquad < 0$$

$$\frac{\partial u}{\partial \delta} = \frac{1}{|\mathbf{J}|}\, d_{r+\rho}\, nx_{\hat{s}-\hat{p}}\,(\lambda^s_{j-\hat{p}} - \lambda^s_q) \qquad < 0$$

[73]For all following partial derivatives, it has been additionally assumed that economic agents' reaction of money demand with respect to the expected profit rate is larger in absolute terms than their reaction as to the real interest rate on government bonds, i.e. it holds that $|d_{r+\rho}| > |d_{i-\hat{p}}|$, respectively $|d_u| > |d_{r+\rho}| > |d_{i-\hat{p}}|$. Furthermore, it has been assumed that it holds that $d_{r+\rho} + d_{i-\hat{p}}\,\beta_\rho < 0$ (see e.g. $\partial u/\partial\rho$).

Response of the Profit Rate r to Various Shocks.

$$\frac{\partial r}{\partial \lambda} = \frac{1}{|\mathbf{J}|}(-nx_{\hat{s}-\hat{p}})(\lambda + j\lambda^s_{j-\hat{p}} - j\lambda^s_q)(d_u + d_{\hat{p}_a}\psi_u) \qquad < 0$$

$$\frac{\partial r}{\partial \rho} = \frac{1}{|\mathbf{J}|} nx_{\hat{s}-\hat{p}}(d_{r+\rho}(\lambda^s_{j-\hat{p}} - \lambda^s_q)(-1 + v + \lambda\psi_u)$$

$$+d_{i-\hat{p}}\beta_\rho(\lambda^s_{j-\hat{p}} - \lambda^s_q)(-1 + v + \lambda\psi_u) + \lambda\,\lambda^s_q(d_u + d_{\hat{p}_a}\psi_u)) \qquad > 0$$

$$\frac{\partial r}{\partial h} = \frac{1}{|\mathbf{J}|} m\,nx_{\hat{s}-\hat{p}}(\lambda\, d_u\, \lambda^s_{mh} - (-1 + v)(\lambda^s_{j-\hat{p}} - \lambda^s_q) + \lambda(-\lambda^s_{j-\hat{p}} + d_{\hat{p}_a}\, \lambda^s_{mh} + \lambda^s_q)\,\psi_u) \qquad > 0$$

$$\frac{\partial r}{\partial m} = \frac{1}{|\mathbf{J}|} h\,nx_{\hat{s}-\hat{p}}(\lambda\, d_u\, \lambda^s_{mh} - (-1 + v)(\lambda^s_{j-\hat{p}} - \lambda^s_q) + \lambda(-\lambda^s_{j-\hat{p}} + d_{\hat{p}_a}\, \lambda^s_{mh} + \lambda^s_q)\,\psi_u) \qquad > 0$$

$$\frac{\partial r}{\partial \alpha} = \frac{1}{|\mathbf{J}|} \lambda\, nx_{\hat{s}-\hat{p}}\lambda^s_\alpha(d_u + d_{\hat{p}_a}\psi_u) \qquad < 0$$

$$\frac{\partial r}{\partial i^*} = \frac{1}{|\mathbf{J}|} d_{i-\hat{p}}\, nx_{\hat{s}-\hat{p}}(\lambda^s_{j-\hat{p}} - \lambda^s_q)(-1 + v + \lambda\psi_u) \qquad > 0$$

$$\frac{\partial r}{\partial v} = \frac{1}{|\mathbf{J}|} (-u)\, nx_{\hat{s}-\hat{p}}(\lambda^s_{j-\hat{p}} - \lambda^s_q)(d_u + d_{\hat{p}_a}\psi_u) \qquad < 0$$

$$\frac{\partial r}{\partial \delta} = \frac{1}{|\mathbf{J}|}(-nx_{\hat{s}-\hat{p}})(\lambda^s_{j-\hat{p}} - \lambda^s_q)(d_u + d_{\hat{p}_a}\psi_u) \qquad < 0$$

Response of Price Level's Growth Rate $\hat{p}$ to Various Shocks.

$$\frac{\partial \hat{p}}{\partial \lambda} = \frac{1}{|\mathbf{J}|} d_{r+\rho}\, nx_{\hat{s}-\hat{p}}(\lambda + j\lambda^s_{j-\hat{p}} - j\lambda^s_q)\,\psi_u \qquad < 0$$

$$\frac{\partial \hat{p}}{\partial \rho} = \frac{1}{|\mathbf{J}|} nx_{\hat{s}-\hat{p}}\,(d_{r+\rho}(-\lambda^s_{j-\hat{p}} + \lambda^s_q) + d_{i-\hat{p}}\beta_\rho(-\lambda^s_{j-\hat{p}} + (1 + \lambda)\lambda^s_q))\,\psi_u \qquad > 0$$

$$\frac{\partial \hat{p}}{\partial h} = \frac{1}{|\mathbf{J}|} m\, nx_{\hat{s}-\hat{p}}(\lambda^s_{j-\hat{p}} - \lambda\, d_{r+\rho}\, \lambda^s_{mh} - (1 + \lambda)\lambda^s_q)\,\psi_u \qquad > 0$$

$$\frac{\partial \hat{p}}{\partial m} = \frac{1}{|\mathbf{J}|} h\, nx_{\hat{s}-\hat{p}}(\lambda^s_{j-\hat{p}} - \lambda\, d_{r+\rho}\, \lambda^s_{mh} - (1 + \lambda)\lambda^s_q)\,\psi_u \qquad > 0$$

$$\frac{\partial \hat{p}}{\partial \alpha} = \frac{1}{|\mathbf{J}|} (-\lambda)\, d_{r+\rho}\, nx_{\hat{s}-\hat{p}}\, \lambda^s_\alpha\, \psi_u \qquad < 0$$

$$\frac{\partial \hat{p}}{\partial i^*} = \frac{1}{|\mathbf{J}|} (-d_{i-\hat{p}})\, nx_{\hat{s}-\hat{p}}\,(\lambda^s_{j-\hat{p}} - (1 + \lambda)\lambda^s_q)\,\psi_u \qquad > 0$$

$$\frac{\partial \hat{p}}{\partial v} = \frac{1}{|\mathbf{J}|} u\, d_{r+\rho}\, nx_{\hat{s}-\hat{p}}(\lambda^s_{j-\hat{p}} - \lambda^s_q)\,\psi_u \qquad < 0$$

$$\frac{\partial \hat{p}}{\partial \delta} = \frac{1}{|\mathbf{J}|} d_{r+\rho}\, nx_{\hat{s}-\hat{p}}\,(\lambda^s_{j-\hat{p}} - \lambda^s_q)\,\psi_u \qquad < 0$$

Response of Tobin's q to Various Shocks.

$$\frac{\partial q}{\partial \lambda} = \frac{1}{|\mathbf{J}|} nx_{\hat{s}-\hat{p}} \left(d_{r+\rho}(-1+v+\lambda\psi_u) - (1+\lambda+j\,\lambda^s_{j-\hat{p}})(d_u + d_{\hat{p}_a}\,\psi_u)\right) \quad < 0$$

$$\frac{\partial q}{\partial \rho} = \frac{1}{|\mathbf{J}|} nx_{\hat{s}-\hat{p}}\,\lambda^s_{j-\hat{p}}(d_u + d_{\hat{p}_a}\,\psi_u + d_{i-\hat{p}}\beta_\rho(-1+v+\lambda\,\psi_u)) \quad > 0$$

$$\frac{\partial q}{\partial h} = \frac{1}{|\mathbf{J}|} m\,nx_{\hat{s}-\hat{p}}(-\lambda^s_{j-\hat{p}}(-1+v+\lambda\,\psi_u)$$
$$+\lambda^s_{mh}(-d_{r+\rho}(-1+v+\lambda\,\psi_u) + (1+\lambda)(d_u + d_{\hat{p}_a}\,\psi_u))) \quad > 0$$

$$\frac{\partial q}{\partial m} = \frac{1}{|\mathbf{J}|} h\,nx_{\hat{s}-\hat{p}}(-\lambda^s_{j-\hat{p}}(-1+v+\lambda\,\psi_u)$$
$$+\lambda^s_{mh}(-d_{r+\rho}(-1+v+\lambda\,\psi_u) + (1+\lambda)(d_u + d_{\hat{p}_a}\,\psi_u))) \quad > 0$$

$$\frac{\partial q}{\partial \alpha} = \frac{1}{|\mathbf{J}|} nx_{\hat{s}-\hat{p}}\,\lambda^s_\alpha\,(-d_{r+\rho}(-1+v+\lambda\,\psi_u) + (1+\lambda)(d_u + d_{\hat{p}_a}\psi_u)) \quad < 0$$

$$\frac{\partial q}{\partial i^*} = \frac{1}{|\mathbf{J}|} d_{i-\hat{p}}\,nx_{\hat{s}-\hat{p}}\,\lambda^s_{j-\hat{p}}(-1+v+\lambda\psi_u) \quad > 0$$

$$\frac{\partial q}{\partial v} = \frac{1}{|\mathbf{J}|} (-u)\,nx_{\hat{s}-\hat{p}}\,\lambda^s_{j-\hat{p}}(d_u + d_{\hat{p}_a}\psi_u) \quad < 0$$

$$\frac{\partial q}{\partial \delta} = \frac{1}{|\mathbf{J}|} (-nx_{\hat{s}-\hat{p}})\,\lambda^s_{j-\hat{p}}\,(d_u + d_{\hat{p}_a}\psi_u) \quad < 0$$

Response of the Interest Rate on Loans j to Various Shocks.

$$\frac{\partial j}{\partial \lambda} = \frac{1}{|\mathbf{J}|} nx_{\hat{s}-\hat{p}}((1+j\,\lambda^s_q)(d_u + d_{\hat{p}_a}\,\psi_u) - d_{r+\rho}(-1+v+j(-\lambda^s_{j-\hat{p}} + \lambda^s_q)\,\psi_u)) \quad > 0$$

$$\frac{\partial j}{\partial \rho} = \frac{1}{|\mathbf{J}|} nx_{\hat{s}-\hat{p}}(-d_u\,\lambda^s_q - (d_{r+\rho}(\lambda^s_{j-\hat{p}} - \lambda^s_q) + d_{\hat{p}_a}\,\lambda^s_q)\,\psi_u$$
$$+d_{i-\hat{p}}\,\beta_\rho(-\lambda^s_{j-\hat{p}}\,\psi_u + \lambda^s_q(1-v-\psi_u))) \quad < 0$$

$$\frac{\partial j}{\partial h} = \frac{1}{|\mathbf{J}|} (-m)\,nx_{\hat{s}-\hat{p}}\,((1-v)\,d_{r+\rho}\,\lambda^s_{mh}$$
$$+d_u\,\lambda^s_{mh} - (-1+v)\lambda^s_q + (-\lambda^s_{j-\hat{p}} + d_{\hat{p}_a}\,\lambda^s_{mh} + \lambda^s_q)\,\psi_u) \quad < 0$$

$$\frac{\partial j}{\partial m} = \frac{1}{|\mathbf{J}|} (-h)\,nx_{\hat{s}-\hat{p}}\,((1-v)\,d_{r+\rho}\,\lambda^s_{mh}$$
$$+d_u\,\lambda^s_{mh} - (-1+v)\lambda^s_q + (-\lambda^s_{j-\hat{p}} + d_{\hat{p}_a}\,\lambda^s_{mh} + \lambda^s_q)\,\psi_u) \quad < 0$$

$$\frac{\partial j}{\partial \alpha} = \frac{1}{|\mathbf{J}|} nx_{\hat{s}-\hat{p}}\,\lambda^s_\alpha\,((-1+v)\,d_{r+\rho} - d_u - d_{\hat{p}_a}\,\psi_u) \quad > 0$$

$$\frac{\partial j}{\partial i^*} = \frac{1}{|\mathbf{J}|} d_{i-\hat{p}}\,nx_{\hat{s}-\hat{p}}\,(-\lambda^s_{j-\hat{p}}\psi_u + \lambda^s_q\,(1-v+\psi_u)) \quad < 0$$

$$\frac{\partial j}{\partial v} = \frac{1}{|\mathbf{J}|} u\,nx_{\hat{s}-\hat{p}}(d_u\,\lambda^s_q + (d_{r+\rho}\,(\lambda^s_{j-\hat{p}} - \lambda^s_q) + d_{\hat{p}_a}\,\lambda^s_q)\,\psi_u) \quad > 0$$

$$\frac{\partial j}{\partial \delta} = \frac{1}{|\mathbf{J}|} nx_{\hat{s}-\hat{p}}(d_u\,\lambda^s_q + (d_{r+\rho}\,(\lambda^s_{j-\hat{p}} - \lambda^s_q) + d_{\hat{p}_a}\,\lambda^s_q)\,\psi_u) \quad > 0$$

Response of the Domestic Interest Rate on Bonds i to Various Shocks.

$$\frac{\partial i}{\partial \lambda} = 0$$

$$\frac{\partial i}{\partial \rho} = \beta_\rho < 0$$

$$\frac{\partial i}{\partial h} = 0$$

$$\frac{\partial i}{\partial m} = 0$$

$$\frac{\partial i}{\partial \alpha} = 0$$

$$\frac{\partial i}{\partial i^*} = 1$$

$$\frac{\partial i}{\partial v} = 0$$

$$\frac{\partial i}{\partial \delta} = 0$$

Response of the Exchange Rate's Growth Rate $\hat{s}$ to Various Shocks.[74]

$$\begin{aligned}
\frac{\partial \hat{s}}{\partial \lambda} &= \frac{1}{|\mathbf{J}|}\eta_q\,(1+\lambda+j\,\lambda^s_{j-\hat{p}})(d_u+d_{\hat{p}_a}\psi_u) \\
&\quad -d_{r+\rho}(\eta_q\,(-1+v+\lambda\psi_u)+(\lambda+j\,\lambda^s_{j-\hat{p}}-j\,\lambda^s_q)(-1+u_{\hat{p}_a}\psi_u)) && \lesseqgtr 0 \\
\frac{\partial \hat{s}}{\partial \rho} &= \frac{1}{|\mathbf{J}|}(-1)\,(\eta_q\lambda^s_{j-\hat{p}}+g_{i-\hat{p}}\beta_\rho(\lambda^s_{j-\hat{p}}-(1+\lambda)\lambda^s_q))(d_u+d_{\hat{p}_a}\psi_u) \\
&\quad +d_{r+\rho}(\lambda^s_{j-\hat{p}}-\lambda^s_q)(-1+u_{\hat{p}_a}\psi_u+g_{i-\hat{p}}\beta_\rho(-1+v+\lambda\psi_u)) \\
&\quad +d_{i-\hat{p}}\beta_\rho((1+\lambda)\lambda^s_q(-1+u_{\hat{p}_a}\psi_u)+\lambda^s_{j-\hat{p}}(-1+u_{\hat{p}_a}\psi_u-\eta_q(-1+v+\lambda\psi_u))) && \lesseqgtr 0 \\
\frac{\partial \hat{s}}{\partial h} &= \frac{1}{|\mathbf{J}|}m\,(-1-\lambda)(d_u\,\eta_q\,\lambda^s_{mh}+\lambda^s_q+d_{\hat{p}_a}\,\eta_q\,\lambda^s_{mh}\,\psi_u-u_{\hat{p}_a}\,\lambda^s_q\,\psi_u) \\
&\quad +\lambda^s_{j-\hat{p}}(1-u_{\hat{p}_a}\,\psi_u+\eta_q(-1+v+\lambda\,\psi_u)) \\
&\quad +d_{r+\rho}\,\lambda^s_{mh}(\eta_q(-1+v+\lambda\,\psi_u)+\lambda(-1+u_{\hat{p}_a}\,\psi_u))) && \lesseqgtr 0 \\
\frac{\partial \hat{s}}{\partial m} &= \frac{1}{|\mathbf{J}|}h\,(-1-\lambda)(d_u\,\eta_q\,\lambda^s_{mh}+\lambda^s_q+d_{\hat{p}_a}\,\eta_q\,\lambda^s_{mh}\,\psi_u-u_{\hat{p}_a}\,\lambda^s_q\,\psi_u) \\
&\quad +\lambda^s_{j-\hat{p}}(1-u_{\hat{p}_a}\,\psi_u+\eta_q(-1+v+\lambda\,\psi_u)) \\
&\quad +d_{r+\rho}\,\lambda^s_{mh}(\eta_q(-1+v+\lambda\,\psi_u)+\lambda(-1+u_{\hat{p}_a}\,\psi_u))) && \lesseqgtr 0 \\
\frac{\partial \hat{s}}{\partial \alpha} &= \frac{1}{|\mathbf{J}|}\lambda^s_\alpha\,((-1-\lambda)\,d_u\,\eta_q+d_{r+\rho}(\eta_q(-1+v+\lambda\psi_u)+\lambda(-1+u_{\hat{p}_a}\psi_u))) && <0 \\
\frac{\partial \hat{s}}{\partial i^*} &= \frac{1}{|\mathbf{J}|}g_{i-\hat{p}}(d_u(-\lambda^s_{j-\hat{p}}+(1+\lambda)\lambda^s_q)+d_{r+\rho}(\lambda^s_{j-\hat{p}}-\lambda^s_q)(-1+v+\lambda\psi_u)) \\
&\quad -d_{i-\hat{p}}((1+\lambda)\lambda^s_q(-1+u_{\hat{p}_a}\psi_u)+\lambda^s_{j-\hat{p}}(1-u_{\hat{p}_a}+\eta_q(-1+v+\lambda\,\psi_u))) && \lesseqgtr 0 \\
\frac{\partial \hat{s}}{\partial v} &= \frac{1}{|\mathbf{J}|}(-u)(-\eta_q\,\lambda^s_{j-\hat{p}}(d_u+d_{\hat{p}_a}\psi_u)+d_{r+\rho}(\lambda^s_{j-\hat{p}}-\lambda^s_q)(-1+u_{\hat{p}_a}\psi_u)) && <0 \\
\frac{\partial \hat{s}}{\partial \delta} &= \frac{1}{|\mathbf{J}|}\eta_q\,\lambda^s_{j-\hat{p}}(d_u+d_{\hat{p}_a}\psi_u)-d_{r+\rho}(\lambda^s_{j-\hat{p}}-\lambda^s_q)(-1+u_{\hat{p}_a}\psi_u) && <0
\end{aligned}$$

[74] For $\partial s/\partial \alpha$, it has been assumed that $((-1-\lambda)\,d_u\,\eta_q+d_{r+\rho}(\eta_q(-1+v+\lambda\psi_u)+\lambda(-1+u_{\hat{p}_a}\psi_u)))>0$. For $\partial s/\partial v$ and for $\partial s/\partial \delta$, it has been assumed that $(-\eta_q\,\lambda^s_{j-\hat{p}}(d_u+d_{\hat{p}_a}\psi_u)+d_{r+\rho}(\lambda^s_{j-\hat{p}}-\lambda^s_q)(-1+u_{\hat{p}_a}\psi_u))>0$.

Chapter 5

A Model of Financial Crises and Endogenous Fluctuations in Emerging Market Countries

The empirical analysis has demonstrated that financial crises both in industrial and in emerging market countries in the post Bretton-Woods era were characterized by extensive boom-bust cycles and exhibited similar time patterns of almost all macroeconomic variables which were investigated in chapter 3. Though lots of financial crises in emerging markets in the 1980s were caused by inconsistent macroeconomic policies (especially in some Latin American countries in the late 1970s, having triggered the international debt crisis in the 1980s), latest financial crises in the 1990s (Mexico, Asia, Brazil) happened without any severe macroeconomic mismanagement. As a result, boom-bust cycles and the subsequent and unavoidable financial collapse were not anymore caused by expansionary macroeconomic policy but by other factors.

In order to find an explanation of latest crises' episodes, economic theory started to analyze financial crises in emerging markets like crises in industrial countries by moral hazard and balance sheet models, having been already set out in sections 3.5, 4.5.3 and 4.5.4. The critical assessment of standard theories of financial crises in industrial countries however, has suggested the view that financial crises are not solely caused by self-fulfilling expectations or exogenous shocks, but can be also viewed as a part of an extensive business cycle which generates financial instability *endogenously*, especially after financial liberalization. Since particularly emerging markets have been subject to large-scale Washington Consensus liberalization policies both in the real and in the financial sector since the 1980s, it could be argued that financial crises in emerging markets can be explained as well by positive exogenous shocks to expectations, giving rise to an endogenous above-average build-up of financial fragility by overshooting expectations and overindebtedness, leading finally to systemic financial (twin) crises. This view of financial crises suggests that emerging market crises are comparable to financial crises in industrial countries with the only exception that overindebtedness in emerging markets is mainly caused by capital inflows in foreign currency, and not directly by overlending via the domestic banking system. It must be noted however, that in case of large-scale capital inflows, the domestic financial system also plays a central role for the generation of excessive cycles by transforming foreign capital into domestic credit, even if the financial system still suffers from past financial repression.

Following the cyclical approach to financial crises in industrial countries, this chapter develops a theoretical model of financial crises in emerging markets, being a modified version of the crisis model of industrial countries given in chapter 4. Since the model structure and assumptions are similar, the following description only highlights the differences and refers to the explanations given in chapter 4.

5.1 The Real Side

Consider a small emerging market economy having pegged its currency to an international reserve currency like the US-$ or the Euro in order to stabilize inflation, or to support an export-led growth strategy.

Output is assumed to be demand determined, and goods market equilibrium expressed in terms of the numéraire PK, where P denotes the domestic price level and K the capital stock, is given by

$$u = \frac{PY}{PK} = \frac{Y}{K} = \eta(\underset{+}{q}) + g(\underset{-}{i - \hat{p}}) + nx(\underset{+}{\hat{s} + \hat{p}^* - \hat{p}}), \tag{5.1}$$

stating that in equilibrium capacity utilization $u = Y/K$, where Y denotes real output, equals aggregate demand adjusted for the numéraire being composed of three components. The first demand component is the "warranted" growth rate of the capital stock $I/K = \eta(\cdot)$, being positively dependent on Tobin's q. The second demand component is normalized real government expenditure $G/K = g(\cdot)$, being negatively dependent on the real interest rate on government bonds $i - \hat{p}$, where i denotes the nominal interest rate on bonds, and $\hat{p} = \dot{P}/P$ the growth rate of the domestic price level P. The third demand component consists of normalized real net exports $NX/K = nx(\cdot)$, being positively dependent on the growth rate of the real exchange rate $\hat{s} + \hat{p}^* - \hat{p}$, i.e. the Robinson condition is assumed to be fulfilled, where $\hat{s} = \dot{s}/s$ denotes the growth rate of the nominal exchange rate, expressing the rate of change of the price of one unit foreign currency in domestic currency; $\hat{p}^* = \dot{P}^*/P^*$ denotes the growth rate of the foreign price level which is assumed to be zero throughout the analysis. In a fixed exchange rate system it holds that $\hat{s} = 0$, though the exchange rate can be either used as a macroeconomic policy instrument, or changes suddenly during exchange rate crises. Consequently, $\hat{s}$ will be treated as a parameter in the model.

The overall impact of the price level's growth rate $\hat{p}$ on capacity utilization u, being denoted by $\partial u/\partial \hat{p}_a$, is not clear since an increase in $\hat{p}$ lowers the real interest rate on government bonds leading to an expansion in $g(\cdot)$ and in u, but at the same time deteriorates the real exchange rate leading to a drop in $nx(\cdot)$ and in u. In the crisis model for industrial countries, the overall influence has been positive, i.e. $\partial u/\partial \hat{p}_a > 0$, because government expenditure has been assumed as having a greater influence on capacity utilization than net exports. In emerging market countries however, being much more dependent on trade, net exports have a much greater influence on capacity utilization than in industrial countries, though there are countries in which government expenditure represents a large fraction of aggregate demand as well. Consequently, since there is no clear answer on the sign of $\partial u/\partial \hat{p}_a$, it is assumed that the influence is zero, which is consistent with the fact that net exports have a much greater influence on u in emerging market countries than in industrial countries, i.e. in the following it holds that

$$\frac{\partial u}{\partial \hat{p}_a} = -\frac{\partial g}{\partial (i - \hat{p})} - \frac{\partial nx}{\partial (\hat{s} - \hat{p})} = 0.$$

Empirical data have shown that investment finance in emerging market countries depends heavily on foreign capital. There are two main forms of foreign debt finance in emerging markets which differ mainly with respect to the sectoral allocation, i.e. with respect to the question of which sector in the economy receives and allocates foreign capital in the domestic economy. On the one hand, there is a "direct" form of finance, according to which domestic business firms directly receive foreign capital from international financial institutions; as to this direct form of finance, firms have to book debt denominated in foreign currency in their balance sheets which exposes them directly to foreign exchange risk. On the other hand, there exists also an "indirect" form of finance, being characterized by domestic banks receiving foreign debt, and creating loans to domestic business firms in domestic currency; according to this indirect form of finance, banks, not firms, are directly exposed to foreign exchange risk, though in case of a sharp devaluation, banks are going to cut their credit lines to domestic firms because of a sharp reduction in their net worth and foreign loan withdrawals, exposing firms indirectly to foreign exchange rate risk.

The present model assumes a "direct" way of finance, assuming that the capital account is fully liberalized, i.e. that international transactions as to bonds, shares, and granting loans denominated in foreign currency to domestic agents no longer underly any restrictions, like e.g. capital controls. The domestic financial sector however, is modelled as still being underdeveloped and suffering from past financial repression, but being in transition to a fully liberalized scheme. Consequently, the domestic financial sector cannot attract sufficient financial means (deposits) to serve the financial needs of the private business sector in the form of loans, and in most cases offers much higher loan rates than international financial institutions.[1]

Owing to the transition process from financial repression to a fully liberalized scheme, domestic firms' debt side contains both loans in domestic currency L priced at the nominal domestic loan rate j, having been allocated by the domestic financial sector during the financial repression period, and loans in foreign currency L^* priced at a nominal international interest rate on loans j^*, having been allocated by international financial institutions after financial sector and capital account liberalization. As firms are exposed to exchange rate risk in case of sudden changes in $\hat{s}$, interest rate costs on foreign loans have to be adjusted for the growth rate of the exchange rate $\hat{s}$, resulting in an "actual" nominal interest rate on foreign loans $j^* + \hat{s}$. Business firms' net profits Q are then given formally as

$$Q = PY - wN - \delta PK - jL - (j^* + \hat{s})\, \bar{s}\, L^*,$$

that is, net profits are determined by earnings PY less labour costs wN, where w denotes the nominal wage rate and N labour input, less depreciation on capital δPK, where δ denotes the depreciation rate, less interest rate costs on the stock of domestic loans jL, less interest rate costs on the foreign stock of loans $(j^* + \hat{s})\bar{s}L^*$, where $\bar{s}$ denotes the initial

[1]By way of contrast, the financial crisis calibration model for emerging markets presented in chapter 6 assumes an indirect way of finance, according to which banks play the central role in allocating foreign capital to domestic firms.

fixed nominal exchange rate.[2] Dividing both sides of the profit equation by PK results in the net profit rate, given by

$$r = \frac{PY}{PK} - \frac{wN}{PK} - \frac{\delta PK}{PK} - \frac{jL}{PK} - \frac{(j^* + \hat{s})\bar{s}L^*}{PK} = u(1-v) - \delta - j\,\lambda - (j^* + \hat{s})\bar{s}\lambda^*,$$

where $v = wN/(PY)$ denotes the wage share with respect to gross nominal product[3] being treated as a parameter in the model, $\lambda = L/(PK)$ the "domestic" debt-asset ratio relating the stock of domestic loans outstanding to the capital stock valued at replacement costs, and $\lambda^* = L^*/(PK)$ the "foreign" debt-asset ratio in foreign currency relating the stock of foreign loans outstanding to the capital stock valued at replacement costs. In the following, it is assumed that the initial value of the fixed exchange rate amounts to $\bar{s} = 1$; therefore, the rate of change of the exchange rate $\hat{s}$ is always expressed for a given value of $\bar{s} = 1$. As a result, the profit rate on capital reads as

$$r = u(1-v) - \delta - j\,\lambda - (j^* + \hat{s})\lambda^*. \tag{5.2}$$

The supply side of the model is described by a simplified Phillips curve relationship, formally expressed as

$$\hat{p} = \psi(u \underset{+}{-} u^*), \tag{5.3}$$

stating that in case actual capacity utilization u exceeds the "natural full employment level of capacity utilization" $u^* > 0$ there is inflation, and in case $u < u^*$ the economy is in a state of deflation. As in the industrial crisis model, inflation and deflation expectations are incorporated in the state of confidence parameter ρ. Likewise, equation 5.3 neglects a direct influence of foreign prices and the nominal exchange on domestic prices, though emerging market countries are considered as being much more open economies than industrial countries. This assumption can be justified by assuming a very restrictive nominal wage setting behaviour as a part of domestic macroeconomic stabilization and liberalization policies, in order to prevent wage indexation from generating excessive wage-price spirals due to foreign price and exchange rate changes, counteracting the aims of stabilization and liberalization policies. Still, the model incorporates an indirect influence of $\hat{s}$ on $\hat{p}$ by the fact that an increase in $\hat{s}$ leads, via an expansion of net exports nx, to an increase in capacity utilization u, and thereby to a higher value of the growth rate of the price level $\hat{p}$.

[2]Note that after the foreign loan amount of L^* has been exchanged at a fixed nominal exchange rate $\bar{s}$ into domestic currency, a change in $\bar{s}$ influences the effective interest rate and thereby interest payments on foreign loans in *domestic* currency, but *not* in foreign currency. For example, given a loan in foreign currency $L^* = 100$ US-\$ at an international interest rate of $j^* = 5\%$ yields 5 US-\$ interest payments in foreign currency, and at a fixed nominal exchange rate of $\bar{s} = 1$ Peso/US-\$, 5 Pesos nominal interest rate payments in domestic currency. After a devaluation of 100% of the Peso, the new fixed nominal exchange rate is $\bar{s} = 2$ Peso/US-\$, resulting in interest payments of 5 US-\$ in foreign currency, but in 10 Pesos in domestic currency which increases the nominal effective interest rate on foreign loans in domestic currency to $j^* + \hat{s} = 5\% + \frac{10-5}{5} = 105\%$, whereas the nominal effective interest rate on foreign loans in foreign currency remains at $j^* = 5\%$. It is important to note that the profit equation only refers to *interest* payments on loans (foreign and domestic), but not to redemption payments of loans. Consequently, the adverse impact of increasing redemption payments of foreign loans on firms' profits in case of a devaluation of the home currency is excluded. Yet, an increase in the foreign debt burden due to a devaluation of the home currency, and its influence on investment and expectations is treated in the dynamic version of the model in section 5.4.

[3]Note that $\frac{wN}{PK} = \frac{wN}{PY}\frac{PY}{PK} = vu$.

5.2 The Financial Side

5.2.1 A Stylized Financial Structure

A highly simplified and stylized domestic financial structure of emerging market economies with an underdeveloped, but fully liberalized domestic financial sector is given in figure 5.1. There are seven types of agents in the economy: households, firms, domestic banks, government, central bank, foreign private agents and foreign banks. It is assumed that especially foreign banks dominate the domestic financial system with respect to the allocation of capital from international savers to domestic investors.

Households

Deposits	D	Net Worth	NW_{HH}
Domestic Government Bonds	$P_{BD} B_D$		
Foreign Government Bonds	$\bar{s} P_{BF} B_F$		
Equities	$P_E E$		

Firms

Capital Stock *(Valued at Demand Price of Capital)*	$P_K K$	Domestic Loans from Domestic Banks	L
		Foreign Loans from Foreign Banks	$\bar{s} L^*$
		Equities	$P_E E$

Banks

Deposits at Central Bank *(Required Reserves)*	$D_{BA}(=\tau D)$	Deposits	D
Loans to Firms	L	Net Worth	NW_{BA}

Central Bank

Domestic Credit Component	H	Deposits of Commercial Banks *(Required Reserves, Interest-Free Bank Reserves)*	D_{BA}
Foreign Reserves from Foreign Loans	R		
Foreign Reserves *(Exclusive Reserves from Foreign Loans)*	B		
			$=M$ *(High-Powered Money)*

Government

Net Worth *(Negative)*	NW_{Gov}	Domestic Government Bonds	$P_B B_D$

Figure 5.1: Stylized Financial Structure in Emerging Market Countries

There are eight sorts of assets which are prized at their current market or discounted present values, i.e. there is no distinction between book and market values. The terminology regarding the designation of nominal and real stocks, as well as market prices of bonds, equities and of the capital stock is based on the terminology introduced in section 4.2.1. The first sort of assets are deposits D, the second sort are domestic government bonds $P_{BD}B_D$, where B_D denotes the real stock of bonds, and P_{BD} the market price in domestic currency per real unit of domestic government bonds. Foreign government bonds which are denoted in domestic currency $\bar{s}P_{BF}B_F$, where B_F represents the real stock of foreign bonds, P_{BF} the market price per real unit in foreign currency, and $\bar{s}$ the fixed nominal exchange rate, constitute asset type three. Domestic and foreign government bonds are assumed as being imperfect substitutes since domestic bonds bear a risk premium reflecting the emerging market country's risk of default. Asset type four is the capital stock, where K denotes the real stock of capital, and P_K the demand price of capital implying a nominal market value of $P_K K$. The capital stock is partly financed by the issuance of equities representing asset type five whose nominal market value equals $P_E E$, where E denotes the real stock of equities which is assumed as being constant throughout the analysis, and whose market market price is represented by P_E denoting the price per real unit of equities in domestic currency. The remaining part of the capital stock is financed on the one hand by domestic loans from domestic banks to firms L constituting asset type six, and on the other hand by foreign loans from foreign banks to domestic firms L^* making up asset type seven, whose nominal value in domestic currency amounts to $\bar{s}L^*$. Asset type eight is high powered money M held by domestic banks as required reserves in the form of interest-free deposits $D_{BA} = \tau D = M$ at the central bank, where τ denotes the required reserve ratio. High-powered money M consists of the domestic credit component H being issued by the central bank to domestic commercial banks, foreign reserves stemming from exchanging foreign loans into domestic currency R, and foreign reserves exclusive foreign loans B. The explicit separation of foreign reserves into reserves stemming from foreign loans R, and reserves stemming from other international monetary transactions B is necessary to describe the indebtedness of the domestic firm sector in foreign currency, and to separate private capital flows for investment finance from other international financial transactions.

Regarding central bank reserves R, there are two possible ways of transforming foreign loans into high-powered money. The first "direct" way assumes that firms directly sell foreign loans in the foreign exchange market which is controlled by the central bank, and receive domestic high powered money which is immediately spent for new investment, and transformed into domestic deposits with banks since cash is excluded. The second "indirect" way assumes that firms act through domestic banks by selling their foreign loan amounts to banks, receiving deposits in domestic currency which are immediately spent for investment and transformed into households' deposits in the end; in order to pay firms in domestic currency, banks sell firms' loan amount in foreign currency in the foreign exchange market to the central bank and receive high powered money.

Changes in foreign reserves exclusive foreign loans B cover imbalances in the foreign exchange market arising from current or capital account disequilibria. It must be noted that there are cases in which B can take a negative value, meaning that overall foreign reserves do not suffice to cover all liabilities of the firm sector, i.e. in these cases it holds that $R + B < R$.

Households hold their nominal wealth NW_{HH} in the form of deposits D, domestic government bonds $P_{DB}B_D$, foreign government bonds $\bar{s}P_{BF}B_F$, and equities $P_E E$. Though domestic and foreign government bonds are assumed to be imperfect substitutes being traded internationally, equities are assumed to be not tradable internationally due to information asymmetries.

Firms finance the capital stock by issuing equities E, and by taking domestic L and foreign loans expressed in domestic currency as $\bar{s}L^*$. Since the real stock of equities E is assumed as being constant, new investment is financed by a combination of retained earnings and taking new (foreign) loans.[4] Assuming instantaneous adjustments to bring the stock market into equilibrium, which implies a zero net worth of firms,[5], results in the demand price of capital being determined by the equity market, the domestic loan market, the foreign loan market, and by the level of the fixed nominal exchange rate, formally

$$P_K = \frac{P_E E + L + \bar{s}L^*}{K}.$$

Domestic banks create deposits D as a multiple of high powered money M (monetary base) which is held by banks as required reserves in the form of deposits $D_{BA} = M$ at the central bank. Neglecting cash and excess reserves of banks[6], demand for high powered money stems only from the required reserve ratio τ controlled by the central bank, resulting in the exogenous money multiplier $m = 1/\tau$. Summing up, it holds that $M = D_{BA} = \tau D = \frac{1}{m}D$. Since the domestic banking sector is assumed as being underdeveloped and cannot invest in other assets than loans, banks' adding-up constraint is formally given as

$$(1-\tau)D + NW_{BA} = L, \qquad \text{where} \qquad \tau D = D_{BA} = M,$$

stating that banks' input for the creation of loans L consists of deposits adjusted for required reserves plus banks' net worth NW_{BA}. Though domestic firms are assumed to finance new investment by foreign loans, domestic banks are still vulnerable to adverse shocks hitting the firm sector due to an increase in the amount of non-performing domestic loans, resulting from the existing stock of domestic loans L. If, for example, there is an international real or financial shock reducing firms' collateral values and profits drastically, e.g. by a drop in the terms-of-trade or by a foreign interest rate increase, domestic firms' illiquidity and insolvency does not only lead to an increasing amount of foreign non-performing loans, but also to an augmenting stock of domestic non-performing loans, which in severe cases can lead to a systemic international *and* domestic banking crisis.

The domestic government issues bonds being held by domestic households and foreign agents in order to finance budget deficits. The market value of government bonds amounts to $P_{DD}B_D$, where the real stock of bonds B_D is assumed as being constant throughout the analysis.[7] There are no government assets, resulting in a negative government net worth NW_{Gov}. The foreign government also issues bonds for budget deficit finance, where market price of foreign government bonds in domestic currency amounts to $\bar{s}P_{BF}B_F$.

Monetary policy takes the form of controlling the required reserve ratio τ, the domestic credit component H, and foreign reserves B by interventions in the foreign exchange

[4]Though the comparative-static version of the model considers explicitly changes in the stock of domestic loans L in order to describe the overall macroeconomic effects of future domestic credit variations, the dynamic version assumes that new investment is exclusively financed by foreign loans L^*, which is consistent with the view of a current underdeveloped domestic banking sector.

[5]For details, see section 4.2.1.

[6]See e.g. Bernanke and Blinder (1988) for the explicit introduction of banks' excess reserves, resulting in an interest rate dependent money multiplier.

[7]The problem of a high and increasing level of government debt in domestic and in foreign currency due to past and current inconsistent expansionary fiscal and monetary policies (like e.g. in many Latin American countries as Argentina, Brazil or Mexico) is neglected in the model, since the present explanation of financial crises focuses more on inherent market mechanisms generating financial instability, than on inconsistent macroeconomic policies.

market. Furthermore, the central bank can engage in active exchange rate policy by official revaluations or devaluations of the exchange rate, i.e. by variations in $\bar{s}$ or $\hat{s}$.

Though the model is based on the assumptions of complete capital account liberalization and instantaneous portfolio adjustments, there is no perfect capital mobility since firstly, not all assets are traded internationally (e.g. equities), and secondly, because assets being traded internationally are viewed as being only imperfect substitutes, differing by a risk premium (e.g. government bonds). Furthermore, domestic assets are also considered as being only imperfect substitutes, like e.g. equities and domestic government bonds whose rate of returns do not have to be equal in equilibrium.

Private domestic wealth W_P (government and central bank excluded) is given as

$$W_P = NW_{HH} + NW_{BA} = P_K K + (H + B) + P_{DB} B_D + \bar{s} P_{BF} B_F,$$

that is, by the sum of the capital stock valued at the demand price of capital, required reserves of domestic banks at the central bank less reserves stemming from foreign loans[8], domestic government bonds and foreign government bonds; inside debt like deposits and domestic loans cancel out. Overall domestic wealth (government and central bank included) is given as

$$W = NW_{HH} + NW_{BA} + NW_{Gov} = P_K K + (H + B) + \bar{s} P_{BF} B_F,$$

stating that overall wealth consists of the capital stock valued at the demand price of capital, high powered money less foreign reserves from foreign loans, and foreign government bonds.

5.2.2 Financial Market Equilibria

All financial market equations refer to the portfolio structure given in figure 5.1, whereas financial market equilibria are not modelled as a standardized portfolio approach in order to keep the model formally tractable.[9]

Deposit market equilibrium being normalized by the numéraire PK is formally given as

$$m(h + b + \lambda^*) = d(\underset{+}{u}, \underset{-}{\hat{p}}, \underset{-}{i - \hat{p}}, \underset{-}{r + \rho}), \tag{5.4}$$

where $m = 1/\tau$ denotes the money multiplier treated as a parameter in the model, $h = H/(PK)$ the normalized domestic credit component, $b = B/PK$ normalized foreign reserves excluding reserves stemming from foreign loans, and $\lambda^* = \bar{s}\lambda^*$ (where $\bar{s} = 1$) the foreign debt-asset ratio in domestic currency being equivalent to normalized foreign reserves expressed in domestic currency R, i.e. $\lambda^* = \bar{s}\lambda^* = L^*/(PK) = R/(PK)$, stemming from foreign loans to domestic firms, and $d(\cdot) = D(\cdot)/(PK)$ normalized demand for deposits. The expression $1/(h + b + \lambda^*)$ stands for the "velocity" of high-powered money with respect to the value of the capital stock. Households' demand for deposits is positively dependent on capacity utilization u representing the transaction motive for money demand, and negatively dependent on the growth rate of the price level $\hat{p}$, i.e. households flee ceteris paribus from money in case of inflation, and go into money in case

[8]Foreign loans cancel out since it holds that $R = \bar{s}L^*$.

[9]For a discussion of the pros and cons of standardized portfolio approaches, see section 4.2.2.

of deflation. Since households divide their nominal wealth, apart from deposits, among domestic bonds, foreign bonds, and equities, deposit demand is negatively dependent on the real interest rate on domestic government bonds $i-\hat{p}$ (where the nominal interest rate on government bonds i is determined by uncovered interest rate parity adjusted for a risk premium being derived below), and positively dependent on the expected rate of return on capital $r+\rho$, where ρ represents the "state of confidence" expressing the difference between the expected and the actual profit rate.[10] Like in the financial crisis model for industrial countries, the overall influence of $\hat{p}$ on $d(\cdot)$, being indicated as $\partial d/\partial \hat{p}_a$, is not clear since e.g. a rise in $\hat{p}$ on the one hand reduces deposit demand, but on the other hand lowers the real interest rate on domestic government bonds $i-\hat{p}$, increasing the demand for deposits. In order to overcome this theoretical as well as empirical tradeoff, the following analysis assumes that the overall influence of $\hat{p}$ on $d(\cdot)$ is positive; formally it holds that

$$\frac{\partial d}{\partial \hat{p}_a} = \frac{\partial d}{\partial \hat{p}} + \frac{\partial d}{\partial (i-\hat{p})}\frac{\partial (i-\hat{p})}{\partial \hat{p}} = \frac{\partial d}{\partial \hat{p}} - \frac{\partial d}{\partial (i-\hat{p})} > 0,$$

implying that the indirect influence of the real interest rate on domestic bonds as to variations in $\hat{p}$ dominates the direct influence of $\hat{p}$ on deposit demand.

Owing to the assumption of imperfect capital mobility in the market for government bonds, UIP does not hold and has to be adjusted for the country's risk of default. As a result, the domestic nominal interest rate on bonds i is determined by the nominal interest rate on foreign bonds i^* adjusted for expected exchange rate changes $\hat{s}^e$, and for a country specific risk premium rp, formally

$$i = i^* + \hat{s}^e + rp.$$

As in the industrial country model, exchange rate expectations and the risk premium are assumed as being negatively dependent on the "state of confidence" parameter ρ, i.e. a rise in ρ increases overall credibility, leading to shrinking values of $\hat{s}^e$ and rp due to appreciation expectations of the home currency and due to a lower country default risk, whereas a fall in ρ leads to lower credibility and to increases in $\hat{s}^e$ and rp.[11] Summing up, equilibrium in the international market for bonds is given formally by

$$i = i^* + \underset{-}{\beta(\rho)}, \tag{5.5}$$

implying that in case $\rho > 0$, implying $\beta < 0$, it holds that $i < i^*$, in case $\rho < 0$, implying $\beta > 0$, it holds that $i > i^*$, and that in case $\rho = 0$, implying $\beta = 0$, it holds that $i = i^*$.

Equilibrium in the equity market is represented by the equilibrium condition in the market for real capital, because assuming a constant real stock of equities E, a constant capital stock K, a given fixed exchange rate value of $\bar{s} = 1$, and treating the domestic and the foreign loan stock L and L^* as parameters implies that the equity market can be subsumed, according to the definition of the demand price for capital $P_K = (P_E E + L + \bar{s}L^*)/K$, under the market for real capital.[12] Equilibrium in the market for real capital can be simplified by making use of a modified version of Tobin's q, given formally as

$$q = \frac{r+\rho}{j^* + \hat{s}^e + rp},$$

[10]For further details on the "state of confidence", see section 4.2.2.

[11]The arguments for assuming $\hat{s}^e + rp = \underset{-}{\beta(\rho)}$ are discussed in detail in section 4.2.2.

[12]For details of this procedure, see section 4.2.2.

stating that q is the ratio of expected net profits to a risk adjusted *expected* reference interest rate domestic investors demand for holding capital assets. Because investment is mainly financed by foreign loans, the reference interest rate is approximated by the risk-adjusted foreign loan rate in terms of domestic currency. Hence, the reference interest rate consist of the nominal interest rate on foreign loans j^* adjusted for expected exchange rate changes $\hat{s}^e$, and for the country specific risk premium rp representing default risk. Since Tobin's q incorporates expectations on future developments, the nominal foreign interest rate is adjusted for *expected* exchange rate changes, and not for the actual rate of change. In order to simplify the analysis it is assumed, like in equation 5.5 defining equilibrium in the international bond market, that expected exchange rate changes and the country specific risk premium can be expressed by the same function $\beta(\rho)$, being negatively dependent on the state of confidence, formally

$$q = \frac{r + \rho}{j^* + \underset{-}{\beta(\rho)}}.$$

This version of Tobin's q can be further simplified by linearization, being used in the model as

$$q = r + \rho - (j^* + \underset{-}{\beta(\rho)}). \tag{5.6}$$

Since Tobin's q is both and indicator for the liquidity and the solvency position of business firms, financial distress in the firm sector caused by real sector or financial sector shocks, being indicated by a fall in q, can be caused by shrinking values of r and ρ, or by an increase in j^*.

The domestic market for loans is neglected owing to the assumption of an underdeveloped banking sector; consequently, L and λ, respectively, as well as j are treated as parameters in the model. By way of contrast, the market for foreign loans is explicitly considered according to the "credit view" of macroeconomic activity. Since loans are longer term contracts which can be only adjusted with some time lags, it is assumed that the stock of foreign loans L^*, i.e. the "foreign" debt-asset ratio $\lambda^* = L^*/(PK)$, is predetermined in the short run, and that foreign banks fully satisfy firms' loan demand L^{*d} which is equivalent to the actual stock of loans, i.e. it holds that $L^{*d} = L^*$, or equivalently expressed in term of the numéraire PK, firms' "warranted" or demanded foreign debt-asset ratio λ^{*d} coincides with the actual foreign debt-asset ratio, i.e. it holds that $\lambda^{*d} = \lambda^*$. Consequently, the comparative static version of the model considers λ^* as a parameter, whereas the dynamic version treats λ^* as an endogenous variable which is adjusted over time. Since there arise situations in which foreign banks' supply of loans L^{*s} does not coincide with the actual stock or demanded stock of foreign loans, equilibrium is assumed to be reached by variations in the nominal interest rate on foreign loans j^* which adjusts foreign banks' loan supply to the actual stock of foreign loans. Accordingly, equilibrium in the foreign loan market can be expressed as

$$L^* = L^{*s}(\cdot)$$

where foreign banks' loan supply $L^{*s}(\cdot)$ depends, among j^*, on other variables being determined below. Dividing both sides by the numéraire transforms the equilibrium condition into debt-asset ratio terms

$$\lambda^* = \lambda^{*s}(\cdot),$$

where $\lambda^{*s} = L^{*s}/(PK)$ is banks' "warranted" supply of the foreign debt-asset ratio. Banks' loan supply, or warranted supply of the foreign debt-asset ratio, is assumed to depend on three determinants. Firstly, though the nominal interest rate on foreign loans j^* is assumed to equilibrate the foreign loan market, foreign banks' supply of loans depends on the real interest rate on foreign loans $j^* - \hat{p}^*$, which is however equivalent with the nominal rate because it has been assumed that $\hat{p}^* = 0$. As a result, the loan supply is positively dependent on j^* ,because, for a given stock of loans, a higher interest rate generates higher profits for banks. Secondly, foreign banks' loan supply depends positively on Tobin's q, reflecting the level of domestic firms' collateral varying positively with q, and thereby the risk of business firms' default. Moreover, Tobin's q is also an indicator for banks' net worth position since banks' profits, and thereby net worth is determined mainly by the amount of non-performing loans in the firm sector which is a negative function of q. Consequently, a higher value of q leads to higher profits and a higher level of banks' net worth and allows to expand the loan supply, since under international risk standards a bank's supply of loans has to be a positive function of its net worth.[13] As a result, an indicator for a banking crisis, both domestic and international, in the model is a sharp drop in the value of q, implying a drop in business firms' profits and net worth leading to an increase in non-performing domestic and foreign loans, generating a reduction in banks' profits and banks' net worth. The third determinant of banks' loan supply is the degree of domestic and international financial regulation indicated by the parameter α, where an increase in α means stronger financial regulation for foreign banks which reduces their supply of loans. For example, the establishment of capital controls by an emerging market economy would lead to an increase in α and thereby to a decline in the loan supply of international banks. Summing up, equilibrium in the foreign loan market is given by

$$\lambda^* = \lambda^{*s}(\underset{+}{j^*}, \underset{+}{q}, \underset{-}{\alpha}), \tag{5.7}$$

stating that, e.g. an increase in Tobin's q, or financial liberalization indicated by a fall in α, lead to an excess supply of loans, or equivalently to a higher supplied debt-asset ratio $\lambda^{*s}(\cdot)$ at a constant stock of λ^*, which reduces the price of foreign loans j^*, and thereby the supply of loans until loan market equilibrium is restored.

5.3 Short-Run Comparative-Static Analysis

5.3.1 General Results

The macromodel is described by equations 5.1 to 5.7, containing seven endogenous variables $b, q, j^*, \hat{p}, r, u$ and i, and eleven parameters $\lambda, j, \lambda^*, \rho, h, m, \hat{s}, v, \delta, \alpha$ and i^*. Assuming that the implicit function theorem is fulfilled, partial derivatives of all endogenous variables with respect to all parameter can be obtained by solving the linear system given as

$$\mathbf{J} \cdot \mathbf{v} = \mathbf{z}$$

for $\mathbf{v}$, where $\mathbf{J}$ denotes the Jacobian matrix containing all partial derivatives of system 5.1 to 5.7 with respect to all endogenous variables, $\mathbf{v}$ the vector of differentials of all

[13]For details, see section 4.2.2.

endogenous variables, and $\mathbf{z}$ the vector of differentials with respect all parameters of system 5.1 to 5.7. In explicit terms, the basic linear system to be solved reads as

$$\begin{bmatrix} 0 & -\eta_q & 0 & 0 & 0 & 1 & -g_{i-\hat{p}} \\ 0 & 0 & \lambda^* & 0 & 1 & v-1 & 0 \\ 0 & 0 & 0 & 1 & 0 & -\psi_u & 0 \\ m & 0 & 0 & -d_{\hat{p}_a} & -d_{r+\rho} & -d_u & -d_{i-\hat{p}} \\ 0 & 0 & 0 & 0 & 0 & 0 & 1 \\ 0 & 1 & 1 & 0 & -1 & 0 & 0 \\ 0 & -\lambda_q^{*s} & -\lambda_{j*}^{*s} & 0 & 0 & 0 & 0 \end{bmatrix} \cdot \begin{bmatrix} db \\ dq \\ dj \\ d\hat{p} \\ dr \\ du \\ di \end{bmatrix}$$

$$= \begin{bmatrix} d\hat{s}\; nx_{\hat{s}-\hat{p}} \\ -d\delta - d\lambda\, j - dv\, u - dj\; \lambda - d\lambda^*(\hat{s}+j^*) - d\hat{s}\,\lambda^* \\ 0 \\ -dh\, m - d\lambda^*\; m + d\rho\; d_{r+\rho} - dm\,(b+h+\lambda^*) \\ di^* + d\rho\; \beta_\rho \\ -d\rho\; (\beta_\rho - 1) \\ d\alpha\; \lambda_\alpha^{*s} - d\lambda^* \end{bmatrix}, \quad (5.8)$$

where partial derivatives are denoted by $x_i = \partial x/\partial i$; for example, $d_{r+\rho} = \partial d/\partial(r+\rho)$ denotes the partial derivative of deposits demand $d(\cdot)$ with respect to the expected profit rate $r+\rho$. The determinant of the Jacobian matrix of system 5.8 reads as

$$|\mathbf{J}| = m(((v-1)\,\eta_q + 1)\,\lambda_{j*}^{*s} - (\lambda^* + 1)\,\lambda_q^{*s}),$$

whose sign can be shown to be positive under three assumptions. Firstly, it is assumed that foreign banks' reaction to interest rate changes with respect to the warranted supply of the debt-asset ratio is much larger than their reaction to changes in Tobin's q with respect to the loan supply, i.e. it holds that $\lambda_{j*}^{*s} \gg \lambda_q^{*s}$.[14] Secondly, empirical estimates have shown that the reaction of the growth rate of the capital stock with respect to changes in Tobin's q is a number much smaller than one, i.e. it holds that $\eta_q \ll 1$.[15] Thirdly, a realistic range for the foreign debt-asset ratio is $0 < \lambda^* < 1$, though values of $\lambda^* > 1$ are possible; in this case however, the entire firm sector would be bankrupt which is a very unrealistic scenario. Note that a necessary and sufficient condition for the firm sector to be solvent is $\lambda + \lambda^* < 1$. A negative value of the foreign debt-asset ratio is excluded because in this case the firm sector would own claims against the foreign banking sector. Under these assumptions, and taking into consideration that $v < 1$ and $m > 0$, the signs of the different parts of the Jacobian's determinant are given by

$$((v-1)\,\eta_q + 1) > 0 \quad \text{and} \quad ((v-1)\,\eta_q + 1)\,\lambda_{j*}^{*s} - (\lambda^* + 1)\,\lambda_q^{*s} > 0,$$

implying a positive sign of the determinant of the Jacobian, i.e.

$$|\mathbf{J}| > 0.$$

[14]For further details and justification of this assumption, see section 4.3.1; the only difference compared with the industrial crisis model is that emerging markets rely on foreign loans by foreign banks.

[15]For example, an econometric estimation of the determinants of the capital stock's growth rate by the IMF has detected a value range for the influence of Tobin's q on I/K of $0.01 < \eta_q < 0.03$; see International Monetary Fund (2003b), pp. 26-28.

All partial derivatives are given explicitly in section 5.7, whereas table 5.1 summarizes the results as to the signs of qualitative impact effects. Since the signs of partial derivatives with respect to the exchange rate's growth rate $\hat{s}$ depend on the level of the foreign debt-asset ratio λ^*, there have been introduced two different rows in table 5.1 for $\hat{s}$, where $\hat{s}^\dagger$ represents the signs when the foreign debt-asset ratio is comparatively high, and $\hat{s}^\ddagger$ the signs when the foreign debt-asset ratio is comparatively low.

Table 5.1: Signs of Qualitative Impact Effects on Temporary Variables

Response in	u	r	$\hat{p}$	q	j^*	i	b
λ	-	-	-	-	+	0	-
j	-	-	-	-	+	0	-
λ^*	-	-	-	-	+	0	$-^\S$
ρ	+	+	+	+	-	-	+
h	0	0	0	0	0	0	-
m	0	0	0	0	0	0	-
$\hat{s}^\dagger$	-	-	-	-	+	0	-
$\hat{s}^\ddagger$	+	+	+	+	-	0	+
v	-	-	-	-	+	0	-
δ	-	-	-	-	+	0	-
α	-	-	-	-	+	0	-
i^*	-	-	-	-	+	+	-

§: Explicit sign ambiguous, i.e. $\gtreqless 0$ (see section 5.7). Sign in table chosen by assumption.

Except for one partial derivative, all signs are unambiguous. It must be noted however, that there are lots of counteracting interdependencies being incorporated in each derivative which are illustrated by the explicit forms given in section 5.7. Consequently, the following qualitative discussion of the signs highlights only the most important nexus between a parameter and an endogenous variable, and is definitely not complete.

A rise in the domestic debt-asset ratio λ leads to a decline in the profit rate on capital r according to equation 5.2, lowering Tobin's q, investment demand $\eta(q)$, and capacity utilization u according to equations 5.6 and 5.1, inducing a further decline in r, q and u. Due to the domestic economic contraction, the price level's growth rate $\hat{p}$ declines according to equation 5.3, leading in severe cases even to deflation. Since there is an overall decline in asset prices, firms' shrinking collateral values induce foreign banks to demand a higher loan rate j^* on foreign loans to compensate for higher risk of default according to equation 5.7. A fall in q also raises the amount of non-performing loans which reduces on the one hand foreign banks' profits, and on the other hand domestic banks' profits. As a result, a higher domestic indebtedness creates both liquidity and solvency problems for international, as well as for domestic banks. Since the domestic interest rate on government bonds i solely depends on the foreign interest rate on bonds i^* and on the state of confidence parameter ρ according to equation 5.5, the effect of λ on i is zero. However, a rise in λ creating a fall in u, causes ceteris paribus a decline in the demand for deposits according to equation 5.4, and a rising demand for domestic and international bonds, generating a downward pressure on i which induces capital outflows (capital flows from foreign loans are zero since the foreign debt-asset ratio λ^* is treated as a parameter in the comparative-static version of the model), i.e. a fall in b according to equation 5.4, in order to restore equilibrium in the market for international bonds according to equation 5.5.

A rise in the domestic interest rate on domestic loans to firms j, and a rise in the foreign debt-asset ratio λ^* operate in the same way like an increase in the domestic debt-asset ratio λ, inducing a reduction in r, q, u and $\hat{p}$ according to equations 5.2, 5.6, 5.1 and 5.3. Falling asset prices cause shrinking collateral values, an increasing number of non-performing loans, and a fall in domestic and foreign banks' profits, inducing foreign banks to demand a higher interest rate on loans j^* to compensate for a higher risk of default according to equation 5.7. There is no influence of j and λ^* on i according to equation 5.5, whereas the economic contraction puts a downward pressure on i by increasing domestic and international bond demand, generating capital outflows and shrinking central bank reserves b according to equation 5.4.[16]

An increase in the state of confidence ρ acts in the opposite direction in comparison with increases in λ, j and λ^*. A rising ρ leads to an increase in r, q, u and $\hat{p}$ according to equations 5.2, 5.6, 5.1 and 5.3. Increasing asset prices and collateral values reduce the risk of default of domestic firms inducing foreign banks to demand a lower interest rate j^* on foreign bank loans according to equation 5.7, leading to further increases in r, q, u and $\hat{p}$. A rising q lowers the amount of non-performing loans and increases profits of domestic and foreign banks. Due to the domestic economic expansion, the country risk premium decreases and economic agents expect a future appreciation or a lower devaluation of the home currency, leading to a decline in the interest rate on government bonds i according to equation 5.5. A rising value in u increases ceteris paribus the demand for deposits, and lowers the demand for domestic and international bonds according to equation 5.4, leading to an upward pressure on i which induces capital inflows and increasing central bank reserves b.

Monetary policy represented by variations in the domestic credit component h, and in the money multiplier m caused by variations in the required reserve ratio τ, do not have both any real sector and financial sector consequences, validating the Mundell-Fleming result that monetary policy under fixed exchange rates is ineffective. The reason for the ineffectiveness of monetary policy stems from the fact that there is no disturbance of the deposit market equilibrium according to equation 5.4, since changes in h and m are immediately offset by counteracting changes to the same amount in central bank reserves b, leading to a constant amount of high powered money which is reflected in partial derivative values $\partial b/\partial h = -1$, and $\partial b/\partial m = -(b + h + \lambda^*)/(m)$, causing a constant deposit supply $m(h+b+\lambda^*)$ (see section 5.7) and a constant interest rate on government bonds i. Since there is no influence of h and m on the interest rate on foreign loans to domestic firms j^*, there are no variations in r, u, q and $\hat{p}$.

Exchange rate policy being indicated by variations in the exchange rate's growth rate $\hat{s}$ depends crucially on the level of foreign debt of domestic firms, i.e. on the level of the

[16]Though the influence of λ^* on b is not clear (see section 5.7), it has been assumed that an increase in the foreign debt-asset ratio λ^* has the same effect on central bank reserves b like an increase in the domestic debt-asset ratio λ.

foreign debt-asset ratio λ^*. If there is a comparatively low level of foreign debt, i.e. in case domestic firms finance most of the capital stock by domestic loans, a devaluation of the exchange rate $\hat{s}^{\ddagger}$ is expansionary like in the standard Mundell-Fleming model, since the negative effect of rising interest rate payments on foreign loans on the profit rate according to equation 5.2, is overcompensated by an increase in capacity utilization u stemming from an increase in net exports $nx(\hat{s} - \hat{p})$ according to equation 5.1, rising r according to equation 5.2. Owing to rising values in r and u there is a rise in asset prices and Tobin's q according to equation 5.6, leading to higher collateral values and to a decrease in the interest rate on foreign loans j^*, inducing a further rise in u, r and q and in the price level's growth rate $\hat{p}$ according to equation 5.3. Since there is no influence of $\hat{s}$ on ρ, the domestic interest rate on government bonds i remains constant according to equation 5.5, though a rising value of u causes an upward pressure on i according to equation 5.4, inducing a rise in central bank reserves b. It must be noted however, that in spite of an economic expansion in case of a devaluation, the expansion is very small due to the limited ability of the domestic financial sector to provide sufficient financial means, and due to restricted commitment of foreign banks; i.e. an increase in q stimulating domestic investment, cannot be fully realized since investment demand is rationed by available credit λ and λ^*. Accordingly, financial liberalization, allowing domestic firms to take foreign debt, promotes domestic growth since investment is not rationed any more by available credit.

Yet, a higher level of foreign debt λ^* induced by financial liberalization makes the domestic economy much more vulnerable to exchange rate variations and to changes in available foreign credit. If the foreign debt-asset ratio has become comparatively high due to financial liberalization, a devaluation of the exchange rate is no longer expansionary, but contractionary since a rise in $\hat{s}^{\dagger}$ leads to a large increase in interest payments on foreign debt, and to a decline in the profit rate r according to equation 5.2, though a devaluation leads to an increase in net exports and to an increase in capacity utilization u according to equation 5.1. However, the negative effect of a lower r on Tobin's q and on u overcompensates the positive influence of nx on u, because there is a sharp drop in investment demand according to equation 5.1. Falling asset prices and collateral values induce foreign banks to demand a higher interest rate on foreign loans j^* according to equation 5.7, leading to further declines in r, q and u. Owing to the economic contraction, the domestic price level decreases, i.e. there is a fall in $\hat{p}$ according to equation 5.3, which in severe cases even leads to deflation worsening firms' profits, since among rising interest rate payments on foreign debts, real interest payments on domestic debt and the real stock of domestic debt increase, leading to a further decline in $r, u, q, \hat{p}$ and to a rising j^*. Because of the economic contraction, there is a downward pressure on i according to equation 5.4, leading to shrinking central bank reserves b, contradicting the standard view that devaluations stop reserve outflows, because devaluations cause a recession and not a recovery of the domestic economy.

A higher wage share with respect to gross nominal product v, being caused either by a negative shock to labour productivity Y/N or by a higher nominal wage w, and a negative technology shock indicated by a higher depreciation rate δ, both lead to the same qualitative results.[17] According to equations 5.2, 5.6, 5.1 and 5.3, a rise in v or δ leads to a

[17] All partial derivatives with respect to v and δ are almost identical, and differ only by multiplication with u; see section 5.7 for details.

decline in the profit rate r, in Tobin's q, in investment demand $\eta(q)$, in capacity utilization u, and in the price level's growth rate $\hat{p}$. Falling asset prices and collateral values cause a higher share of non-performing loans and lower profits for both domestic and foreign banks, inducing foreign banks to increase the interest rate on foreign loans j^* according to equation 5.7, generating further declines in r, q, u and $\hat{p}$. There is no influence of v and δ on i, though the economic contraction leads to a decline in deposit demand and to an increase in domestic and international bond demand, putting a downward pressure on i, and causing a decline in central bank reserves b according to equation 5.4.

Stronger international financial regulation (e.g. the establishment of quantitative restrictions on the amount of foreign loans, a (Tobin-) tax on international transactions, a tax on international interest rate payments or simply the introduction of capital controls) being indicated by a rising value in α, leads to a domestic economic contraction due to a higher loan rate on foreign loans j^* according to equation 5.7, inducing a fall in the profit rate r, in Tobin's q, in capacity utilization u and in the growth rate of the domestic price level $\hat{p}$ according to equations 5.2, 5.6, 5.1 and 5.3. Falling asset prices and shrinking collateral values induce an additional increase in the foreign interest rate on loans j^* according to equation 5.7, leading to a further contraction in r, q, u and $\hat{p}$. Because of the fall in u, there is fall in deposit demand according to equation 5.4, generating a downward pressure on i which induces capital outflows and shrinking central bank reserves b.

An increase in the foreign interest rate on government bonds i^* leads to capital outflows and to a loss in central bank reserves b which reduces the amount of high powered money, and induces a rise in the domestic interest rate on government bonds i until equilibrium in the international bond market is restored according to equation 5.5, where $\partial i^*/\partial i = 1$ (see section 5.7 for details). A rise in i reduces government expenditure $g(i - \hat{p})$, capacity utilization u, the profit rate r, Tobin's q and the price level's growth rate $\hat{p}$ according to equations 5.1, 5.2, 5.6 and 5.3. Reductions in collateral values induce an increase in the foreign interest rate on loans j^* according to equation 5.7, leading to further declines in r, q, u and $\hat{p}$.

5.3.2 A Comparative-Static View of Financial Crises

Empirical studies of financial crises in emerging market countries in the Post-Bretton Woods era confirm that emerging market crises are characterized by almost the same stylized facts as crises in industrial countries, as e.g. by the link between extensive boom-bust cycles in goods and financial markets, and the occurrence of financial crises on the cycle's upper turning point, having been outlined in chapter 3. Analyzing the dynamic behaviour of macroeconomic variables during business cycles containing financial crises results in the identification of a highly stylized boom-bust cycle being described in the following paragraphs, and being formally outlined by the comparative-static version of the model according to table 5.1. As mentioned in section 4.3.2, the following theoretical comparative-static description of financial crises is only a qualitative approach in order to describe the behaviour of the core "driving" forces of financial crises, serving a theoretical base for the dynamic analysis which is able to confirm the comparative-static results by endogenous model mechanisms.

The Boom Phase. Most boom periods in emerging markets culminating in a full-fledged financial crisis begin with extraordinary positive expectations as to future macroeconomic performance. In most cases, this increase in the overall "state of confidence" in the economy has its roots in "Washington Consensus" style macroeconomic programmes and/or in orthodox macroeconomic stabilization policies having been described in detail in chapter 3.3.2. The most important components of these macroeconomic policies making countries vulnerable to financial crises are firstly, the establishment of a fixed exchange rate regime to stabilize inflation or to support an export-led growth strategy by an undervalued currency, and secondly, domestic and international financial liberalization including deregulation of the domestic financial sector and the liberalization of international capital flows.

Due to past financial repression of the domestic financial sector, an economic expansion can be only financed by capital inflows which are in most cases "pulled" by high profit expectations due to far-reaching economic reforms and a stable exchange rate, and "pushed" by low interest rates and low growth in industrial capital exporting countries. Due to the "original sin" hypothesis, capital inflows are generally denominated in foreign currency. In most cases (see e.g. Latin America in the mid 1970s and in the 1990s, and Asia in the 1990s), macroeconomic reforms in emerging markets induce huge volumes of capital inflows which exhibit at first long-term maturities, but then become more short-term over time. The surge in capital inflows is mostly supported by implicit or explicit government guarantees to stabilize the exchange rate and/or to bail-out troubled banks in order to minimize the loss of foreign investors in case of a banking or currency crisis, leading in lots of cases to moral hazard and overborrowing being described in the next paragraph.

The transformation of capital inflows in foreign currency into domestic investment projects (or consumption) can take, as outlined above, either a direct form in which firms take loans from abroad, or an indirect form in which domestic banks take foreign loans and transform their liabilities into domestic loans in domestic currency to firms and households. Independently of the kind of capital inflow transformation, rising profit expectations and an increasing supply of foreign finance cause a credit boom by decreasing international and domestic interest rates which lead to a domestic economic expansion and increasing leverage of firms and financial institutions in foreign currency. Rising aggregate demand leads to higher profits increasing firms' and banks' net worth and stock market valuations, making their balance sheets look sounder and inducing further capital inflows due to higher collateral values and lower risk premiums.

Translating these empirical facts of boom phases, including increasing profits, rising stock market valuations, augmenting GDP growth, decreasing domestic and international interest rates, increasing domestic and foreign leverage by firms and banks, to the comparative-static version of the model, the initial "Washington Consensus" financial liberalization shock can be indicated by a fall in α representing the liberalization of international capital flows, and by an increase in m representing domestic financial liberalization by a much lower required reserve ratio than in financial repression times. Low international interest rates in capital exporting countries are indicated by a fall in i^*. Financial liberalization policies and favourable international financial market conditions cause an increase in ρ. Capital inflows and rising foreign leverage by taking directly loans from foreign financial institutions is represented by an increase in the foreign debt-asset ratio λ^*. Though the domestic banking sector does not receive foreign loans, the transformation of foreign financial means into aggregate demand, and thereby into deposits, enables domestic banks to supply an increasing amount of loans in domestic currency. Accordingly, there is also a rising domestic leverage of firms by taking loans from domestic financial institutions being indicated by an increase in the domestic debt-asset ratio λ. Though rising domestic and foreign leverage cause ceteris paribus a domestic macroeconomic contraction with decreasing capacity utilization u, a lower profit rate r, a decreasing Tobin's q, lower growth in the price level $\hat{p}$, and an increase in the interest rate on foreign loans j^*, the positive effects of changes in α, m, i^* and ρ, causing a macroeconomic expansion, dominate the boom phase. As a result, overall macroeconomic effects are an increase in capacity utilization u caused by a rising profit rate r and a rising Tobin's q, decreases in the foreign loan rate j^* and in the domestic bond rate i, a higher growth rate of the price level $\hat{p}$, and increasing international central bank reserves b.

The Overborrowing Symptom. The expansion phase of a business cycle is generally characterized by profit expectations growing much faster than actual profits, implying that domestic agents have to increase their fraction of external funds in domestic, and mainly in foreign currency to finance new investment projects. Since financial systems in emerging markets are more bank-based due to the absence of deep and well-developed capital markets, economic agents have to rely more on foreign loans than on equity placements, increasing business firms' and banks' leverage in foreign currency. This process of overborrowing, being defined as a situation in which an increase in indebtedness is mainly based on overly optimistic expectations which cannot be justified by the development of actual profits, is supported predominantly by foreign investors through a rising volume of capital inflows. The growth in profit expectations is driven by rising actual gross profits (profits before external financing costs) owing to boosting aggregate demand induced by the domestic credit boom, and by herding behaviour of investors. Overborrowing increases the overall financial fragility in the economy since both domestic agents and international creditors become more vulnerable to shocks in financial, as well as in goods markets. Domestic debtors depend increasingly on the willingness of international investors to roll over or to increase debt, whereas international investors become more and more dependent on the ability of domestic agents to fulfill their payment commitments hinging upon a further growth in aggregate demand.

In terms of the model, the overborrowing process can be described by an increase in the domestic and in the foreign debt-asset ratio λ and λ^*, and by an increase in the state of confidence parameter ρ, the growth in ρ being much larger than the growth in λ and λ^*. Macroeconomically, the net effect results in a general expansion in domestic activity, being described by an increase in capacity utilization u, an increase in Tobin's q mainly driven by an increasing ρ, a decrease in the foreign loan rate j^* owing to higher collateral values, a decrease in the domestic bond rate i, an increase in the growth rate of the domestic price level $\hat{p}$, and by an increase in central bank reserves b. During this stage of the business cycle, the (net) profit rate r cannot increase due to growing external financing costs, though capacity utilization u and thereby gross profits increase. In order to distinguish the overborrowing phase from a state of "irrational exuberance" being described in the following paragraph, it seems reasonable to assume a positive constant value of r.

The Upper Turning Point and "Irrational Exuberance". The upper turning point of the business cycle is characterized by a steady deterioration of cash flows and the profit rate, since the growth of external finance costs is larger than the growth of actual gross profits (profits less external financing costs), increasing overall financial fragility. However, profit expectations, asset prices, and the degree of indebtedness tend to grow further though their increase cannot be validated by the development of net actual profits, driving the economy into a state of "irrational exuberance" since profit expectations are no longer based on economic fundamentals. The "bubble" in financial markets is closely linked to a general overheating in the real sector, being characterized by excess demand and almost full capacity utilization causing domestic inflation to rise. Owing to an acceleration in inflation, the real exchange rate deteriorates generating or magnifying a current account deficit which is financed by capital inflows, making the economy more vulnerable to a reversal of international capital flows since the stock of international reserves is becoming smaller than the stock of foreign claims, though international reserves as a whole are still increasing in this stage of the business cycle. In case international investors lose confidence in the performance of the domestic economy and withdraw collectively their funds, the exchange rate collapses since the central bank has not sufficient foreign reserves to serve all claims by foreign investors. In order to stabilize the real exchange rate and the balance of payments by fighting domestic inflation, central banks generally sterilize capital inflows to prevent a further expansion in domestic credit and in capacity utilization. Sterilization of capital inflows however, has only a limited capacity to slow down the domestic boom since a rising supply of central bank assets (mostly bonds) causes domestic interest rates to rise inducing further capital inflows. Under fixed exchange rates there is no possibility for central banks to increase the discount rate in order to slow down the boom, since a rising level of domestic interest rates would cause a further increase in capital inflows at this stage of the business cycle.

In terms of the model, the upper turning point is characterized by the same conditions like the overborrowing phase, namely by an increase in the debt-asset ratios λ and λ^* and by an increase in the state of confidence parameter ρ. As in the state of overborrowing, all endogenous variables behave as in a macroeconomic expansion except for the profit rate r which is decreasing, distinguishing the conditions at the upper turning point from conditions during the overborrowing process. This "irrational" result stems from the fact that the negative effect of increasing values of λ and λ^* on r dominate the positive effect of ρ on r, resulting in a decline in the profit rate due to rising debt costs. However, as to the influence on Tobin's q, the positive influence of an increasing value of ρ dominates the negative effect of a decreasing r, leading to an overall rising value of Tobin's q and giving rise to an increase in capacity utilization u, an increase in the growth rate of the domestic price level $\hat{p}$, and to decreases in the foreign interest rate on loans j^* and in the domestic interest rate on bonds i. As to central bank reserves, overall normalized reserves $b+\lambda^*$ increase though the reserve component b is decreasing due to rising current account deficits. Sterilization of capital inflows, being the result of an increase in the foreign debt-asset ratio λ^*, by a decrease in the normalized domestic credit component h has no real sector and financial market effects since a decreasing h is offset by a rising b, limiting capital outflows generated by current account deficits.

The Burst of the Bubble. The exuberance in real, as well as in financial markets comes to halt when investors realize that profit expectations cannot be validated by the actual development of net profits. The triggering event of a collapse of profit expectations can be either a failure of an important corporate or financial business firm, or a foreign exogenous shock as e.g. an increase in foreign interest rates, or a negative terms of trade shock. It must be noted that especially foreign exogenous shocks *can* be the trigger of the bubble's burst, but can also only magnify the initial collapse of expectations. Consequently, exogenous shocks are *not* the main cause of a disruption in financial markets causing widespread illiquidity and insolvency; they can be better interpreted as a "wake-up" call for investors to realize that the existing financial structure has become fragile *endogenously* by overborrowing, and to revise expectations downwards on actual economic fundamentals. The reason why exogenous shocks are often viewed as main sources of financial crises is the fact that firstly, these shocks cause the beginning of financial crises, and secondly, aggravate already existing financial fragility by being the trigger for falling asset prices, and by deteriorating already fragile cash flow positions. Irrespective of the triggering event, the financial market bubble's burst leads to a sudden and large decline in asset prices, and to an increase in domestic as well as in foreign interest rates since the risk of default, being represented by largely dropping collateral values, increases. Regarding capital flows, the steady inflow of foreign capital comes to a *sudden stop*, and marks the beginning of an reversal of capital flows, i.e. the beginning of huge volumes of capital outflows.

In terms of the model, the drop in profit expectations is represented by a sharp fall in the state of confidence ρ, causing a reduction in Tobin's q, an increase in the foreign interest rate on loans j^* due to falling collateral values, an increase in the domestic interest rate on government bonds i due to depreciation expectations, and owing to an increase in the country risk premium. Regarding international capital flows, there are two mechanisms causing a reversal in capital flows. Firstly, the "sudden stop problem", i.e. the halt of inflows of foreign loans is represented by a fall of the growth rate of λ^* to zero. Secondly, depreciation expectations and an increasing country risk premium caused by a fall in ρ mark the beginning of capital outflows being indicated by a fall in b. In case an exogenous shock, as e.g. a foreign interest rate increase being indicated by a rise in i^*, triggers the collapse of expectations, the fall in asset prices, the rise in interest rates, and the reversal of capital flows are amplified because a rising value of i^* causes a rise in i, a fall in b, a decline in Tobin's q and thereby an increase in j^*.

The Bust Cycle, Financial and Twin Crisis, Debt Deflation and the Liquidity Trap. Whether a large drop in asset prices causes a systemic financial crisis, containing widespread bankruptcies among firms and financial institutions inducing a deep recession and deflationary spirals, or simply readjusts expectations to economic fundamentals without any negative repercussions on the real sector, depends upon the initial degree of financial fragility when an asset bubble bursts, as well as on the extent of the initial asset price decline. If firms and financial institutions have become highly leveraged both in domestic as well as in foreign currency during the boom phase, and if their collateral values react very sensitively to asset price fluctuations, an asset bubble's burst is likely going to cause a full-fledged financial crisis, being characterized by a domestic and perhaps a foreign banking crisis, a currency crisis (generating a twin crisis), and by a large contraction in the real sector.

Regarding systemic financial crises, the initial fall in expectations and the resulting decline in asset prices causes collateral values to drop sharply, initiating a large rise in domestic and international interest rates due to increasing default risk. Liquidity problems then emerge on the one hand through rising debt costs, and on the other hand by a sharp fall in earnings caused by a drop in aggregate demand. In order to meet due payment obligations business firms, as well as banks have to engage in widespread fire-sales of assets since liquidity in capital markets has dried up, and rolling over or increasing debt becomes impossible. Domestic and foreign financial institutions incur losses by an increasing amount of non-performing loans, causing a widespread domestic banking crisis and also failures among foreign financial institutions. Foreign investors start to withdraw their funds which are in most cases short-term, causing further liquidity needs in foreign currency for business firms and for banks, resulting in further fire-sales of assets since foreign exchange reserves cannot be obtained by debt-finance.

Owing to large current account deficits having been financed by capital inflows during the boom phase, central banks face a liquidity problem in foreign currency since the stock of existing reserves falls short of the stock of foreign claims. In order to cope with large capital outflows and a limited stock of foreign reserves, central banks generally have the choice between two alternatives which are both "bad" alike. In order to prevent a devaluation by reducing further capital outflows, central banks have to pursue contractionary monetary policy, leading to high domestic interest rates to compensate investors for increasing default risk. A monetary contraction however, increases banks' refinancing costs and leads quickly to an increase in loan rates, causing a further deterioration of corporate and bank balance sheets due to higher debt costs, and leading to a further drop in expectations and perhaps to further capital outflows. If, on the other hand, central banks do not want to act contractionary in order to prevent further bankruptcies among domestic business firms and banks, large-scale capital outflows and a limited stock of foreign reserves inevitably lead to a devaluation of the domestic currency and thereby to a twin crisis, engendering a "debt explosion" of foreign debt (valued in domestic currency) being equivalent to a Fisherian debt deflation process in domestic currency which is caused by deflation. Increasing foreign interest payments and an increasing stock of foreign debt in domestic currency terms causes further liquidity and solvency problems among banks and business firms, magnifying the real and the banking crisis, and inducing further capital outflows.

In case central banks abandon the fixed exchange rate system and establish a flexible post-crisis exchange rate regime, the gain in monetary independence can be possibly undermined either by the emergence of a liquidity trap situation, or by accelerating domestic inflation. Regarding the emergence of a liquidity trap, relaxing monetary conditions cannot turn the economy into a recovery since balance sheet conditions and credit shortages both in domestic and in international financial markets cannot be removed. In severe cases, a liquidity trap situation can turn the economy into a deep depression with deflationary spirals aggravating the debt-deflation process. If, on the other hand, the domestic economy depends heavily on imports which are denominated in most cases in foreign currency, the transition to a flexible exchange rate system including an initial large devaluation of the domestic currency, can cause high domestic inflation, compelling the central bank to raise domestic interest rates, inducing a further macroeconomic contraction in order to prevent accelerating inflation or even hyperinflation.

Comparing systemic financial crises in emerging market economies with full-fledged financial crises in industrial countries, it is obvious that the macroeconomic contraction in the real sector in emerging markets is much deeper than in industrialized economies which is caused by two factors. Firstly, the reversal of foreign capital flows, leading either to a sharp increase in interest rates and/or to devaluation, causes much larger and much quicker liquidity and solvency problems for firms and financial institutions than in industrialized countries. Secondly, due to the higher degree of openness of emerging market economies in goods markets and due to dependence on foreign capital, monetary authorities are forced to act more contractionary to stabilize domestic inflation or the exchange rate.

In terms of the model, a systemic financial crisis is caused by a further decline in the state of confidence ρ, leading to a decrease in Tobin's q, in the profit rate r, in capacity utilization u, in the price level's growth rate $\hat{p}$, and in foreign exchange reserves b, whereas the increase in the risk of default in the corporate sector leads to a higher foreign loan rate j^*. Depreciation expectations and increases in the country risk premium cause a higher domestic bond rate i and capital outflows b. Foreign financial institutions withdraw foreign loans to firms, thereby inducing further capital outflows being indicated by a fall in λ^*. Though generally, a reduction in λ^* leads ceteris paribus to a macroeconomic expansion, the deleveraging process cannot turn the economy into a recovery since the effect of a falling ρ dominates. Central banks' attempt to stop capital outflows, thereby preventing a devaluation, is represented by a reduction in m or h, however having only a compensating effect on b which increases, but having no effect on capital outflows caused by withdrawing foreign loans indicated by a fall in λ^*. As a result, if there is no possibility to stop the reduction in capital outflows stemming from a decline in λ^*, central banks have to devalue the domestic currency when foreign exchange reserves are used up. Since foreign reserves $b+\lambda^*$ tend to be smaller than λ^* since $b < 0$, at the time of devaluation the foreign debt-asset ratio is large enough to cause a contractionary devaluation indicated by a large rise in $\hat{s}^\dagger$, causing a sudden deterioration of r by increasing foreign interest rate costs, leading to declines in $q, u, \hat{p}$ and to a rise in j^*.[18] The emergence of a liquidity trap situation after the abolition of the fixed exchange rate regime cannot be shown by the model since the partial derivatives are only calculated for a fixed exchange rate and for given changes in $\hat{s}$. If, however, central banks only engage in a unique (contractionary) devaluation in order to stabilize the exchange rate, there is no possibility to turn the economy into recovery due to the ineffectiveness of monetary policy under fixed exchange rates, which is consistent with a liquidity trap situation.

The Recovery Phase. At the beginning of the bust cycle, firms and financial institutions start to consolidate their balance sheets and cash flows by reducing the level of domestic and foreign debt which requires investment spending to decline. A recovery, which in most cases has to be financed again by foreign capital inflows because of the domestic disintermediation process caused by the domestic banking crisis, can begin only

[18]An increase in domestic inflation caused by devaluation, i.e. by an increase in $\hat{s}^\dagger$, cannot be shown by the model since the Phillips curve equation 5.3 does not contain foreign prices and the exchange rate by assumption.

if balance sheets, cash flows, and profits are viewed as being strong enough to fulfill payment obligations resulting from new loans in foreign currency. Furthermore, new capital inflows will start only if exchange rate expectations have been stabilized which can be obtained in most cases only by a new fixed exchange rate system, or by a strictly managed floating regime.

In terms of the model, a macroeconomic expansion is going to start only if reductions in the debt-asset ratios λ and λ^* have led to a recovery in the state of confidence ρ, initiating a new expansion phase being indicated by a rise in $u, r, \hat{p}, q, b$ and declines in i and j^*.

5.4 Long-Run Dynamic Analysis

5.4.1 Finance, Investment and Long-Run Profit Expectations

The main limitation of the comparative-static analysis of financial crises by the static version of the model is the fact that it provides only a qualitative description of the stylized facts without giving an explanation of the causes of variations in parameters. This theoretical gap can be closed by endogenizing the two core parameters of the model, the state of confidence parameter ρ and the foreign debt-asset ratio λ^*, "driving" an emerging market economy, and being predominantly responsible for the emergence of financial crises. The dynamic version of the model describes, in a similar fashion as the financial crisis model for industrial countries, that financial fragility is an *endogenous* phenomenon being inherently linked to *each* business cycle, but that the degree of financial fragility deciding upon the occurrence of a financial crises is determined by exogenous events.

The Dynamic Behaviour of Long-Run Profit Expectations. Empirical studies of business cycles and financial crises have identified a stylized behaviour of profit expectations being characterized firstly, by cumulative upward and downward movements during the boom and bust cycle, and secondly, by reversals of cumulative processes at the upper and the lower turning point induced by a readjustment of expectations to fundamental data.

Translating these observations into a dynamic equation for the state of confidence parameter requires to take into account different expectation formation schemes. In order to describe cumulative upward and downward movements in expectations, the model refers to Keynes' beauty contest theory explaining the formation of a general market convention by "chartist-type" behaviour. Following general market sentiments, i.e. bulls and bears in financial markets, can be considered as being rational since speculating against general market conventions results in lower returns, even if actual market psychology cannot be justified by economic fundamentals. Formally, "chartist-type" behaviour can be expressed as

$$\dot{\rho} = \underset{+}{z(\rho)},$$

stating that the time derivative of ρ, being denoted as $\dot{\rho} = \partial\rho/\partial t$, is positively dependent on the actual state of confidence ρ. Accordingly, "chartist-type" dynamics generate a positive/negative feedback loop or a cumulative upward/downward movement, since positive/negative profit expectations ($\rho > 0, \rho < 0$) are going to increase/decrease further.

The reversal of expectations at the upper and the lower turning point of the business cycle can be explained by "fundamentalist-type" behaviour, and/or by a kind of long-run "rationality" of investors. Regarding fundamentalist behaviour, a reversal in expectations at the end of the boom and the bust phase is likely going to occur since an increasing divergence of expectations and economic fundamentals cannot be maintained forever. An increasing trade-off between expectations and actual data reduces the share of "chartist-type" investors, and increases the weight of "fundamentalist-type" investors emphasizing that expectations cannot be justified any longer. When a critical mass of investors relying on fundamental data, and recognizing that expectations have been overly optimistic or pessimistic is reached general market sentiment shifts into the reverse direction.

There are various variables which could serve as economic fundamental data investors refer to. Potential fundamentals reach from macrodata like interest rates, terms of trade etc., up to microdata as sales or profits. Since the present model concentrates on the explanation of endogenous financial fragility, suitable fundamentals should focus on the financial structure of the model economy. For present purposes, the two core fundamentals influencing the state of confidence parameter ρ are assumed as being on the one hand, current profitability being an indicator for liquidity, and on the other hand the debt-asset structure being an indicator for solvency.

Regarding the construction of an indicator for current profitability, the actual profit rate r could serve as a reliable variable. However, restricting current profitability to r would neglect the influence of general economic conditions on firms' profitability and would also not allow to make any assessment on the question of whether profits are comparatively "high" or "low". As a result, the current profit rate r has to be compared with a riskless (expected) domestic reference rate of return, being represented by the real interest rate on domestic government bonds $i - \hat{p}$ which, according to UIP given in equation 5.5, can be expressed alternatively as $i^* + \beta(\rho) - \hat{p}$. Thus, current profitability is measured as the difference between the profit and the real interest rate on domestic bonds denoted as σ^*, and formally given as

$$\sigma^* = r - (i^* + \beta(\rho) - \hat{p}). \tag{5.9}$$

The difference σ^* can be interpreted as a risk premium firms have to pay to equity holders in order to compensate for the risk of default. As regards the influence of σ^* on $\dot{\rho}$, it is assumed that an increasing σ^* caused by a rise in $r, \rho, \hat{p}$, or by a decline in i^* increases current profitability, and thereby leads to a rising value of $\dot{\rho}$, i.e. in mathematical terms it holds that $\partial\dot{\rho}/\partial\sigma^* > 0$. It has to be emphasized that despite the fact that only domestic investors are able to hold equities, foreign investors also use the difference between the domestic profit rate and the real interest rate on domestic government bonds as an indicator for current profitability and for the liquidity status of domestic firms when making their decisions on the supply of foreign loans, which emphasizes the fact that domestic as well as foreign agents' formation of expectations and actions are based on the same economic data.

Concerning an indicator for solvency risk, the degree of indebtedness is a reasonable economic fundamental. Since a large fraction of debt in emerging markets is denominated in foreign currency, the foreign debt-asset ratio λ^* could suit as a reliable indicator.

However, concentrating solely on λ^* would disregard the fact that insolvency can emerge very quickly and easily by a devaluation of the home currency. Consequently, in order to capture exchange rate risk the foreign debt-asset ratio has to be formulated in domestic currency, being defined as

$$\lambda_d^* = \lambda^* s.$$

Considering the influence of the foreign debt-asset ratio in domestic currency terms λ_d^* on $\dot{\rho}$, it is assumed that an increasing value of λ_d^*, caused either by a higher foreign debt-asset ratio λ^* or by a devaluation of the home currency $\hat{s} > 0$, leads to higher risk of insolvency, and thereby to a fall in $\dot{\rho}$, i.e. formally it holds that $\partial\dot{\rho}/\partial\lambda_d^* < 0$.[19]

Summing up, the influence of chartist-type and fundamentalist-type behaviour on the change of the confidence parameter results formally in

$$\dot{\rho} = z(\underset{+}{\rho}, \underset{+}{\sigma^*}, \underset{-}{\lambda_d^*}),$$

stating that in boom and bust phases, when expectations are largely driven by mass psychology, the influence of ρ on $\dot{\rho}$ dominates, i.e. $\dot{\rho} > 0$, whereas at the upper and lower turning points, when the difference between actual and expected profitability and solvency reach extreme values, the influence of σ^* and λ_d^* dominates inducing a reversal in expectations, i.e. $\dot{\rho} < 0$.

As outlined in section 4.4.1, the use of "chartist-fundamentalist" expectation formation schemes has been criticized by the rational expectations school, arguing that assuming a chartist-fundamentalist behaviour excludes rationality by investors. According to the rational expectations school, using chartist techniques and forecasts which are at some points revised by a coming out of "new" fundamental data which could not be foreseen or observed, neglects the fact that agents are rational in the sense that market participants are able to develop a "correct" model of the economy processing all available information on which expectations are based. By way of contrast, the rational expectations hypothesis loses its validity under complete and irreducible uncertainty, making a chartist-fundamentalist-type expectations scheme a more realistic concept.

Regarding the dynamic version of the model, both schools of thought are applicable since equations 5.1 up to 5.7 set up a model on which profit expectations can be based, but the model also assumes explicitly long-run incomplete and irreducible uncertainty making it necessary for investors to rely, next to a rational evaluation of the model, additionally on market sentiments and on economic fundamentals. Accordingly, the model structure unifies both concepts regarding profit expectations, by assuming at least some long-run rationality by investors in the sense that investors believe in the long-run rational expectations equilibrium $r^e = r$, implying a long-run steady state value $\rho_E = 0$. As to the formation of current profit expectations, the assumption of long-run rationality implies that investors believe in the state of confidence ρ, irrespective of fundamentals and chartist forecasts, to move in some *"corridor"* or *"normal range"* which cannot be left. In reality this corridor can be very large and is going to vary among different business cycles, since a positive technology shock or financial liberalization, which are believed to break past long-run growth trends in an upward direction, generate more optimistic profit expectations

[19] Note that changes in the exchange rate by depreciation or appreciation, and their influence on λ_d^* are always expressed for the initial value of the fixed exchange rate $\bar{s} = 1$, i.e. if there is no change in s ($d\hat{s} = 0$), it holds that $\lambda_d^* = \lambda^*$.

than a "normal" business cycle without being induced by extraordinary and large positive external shocks.

Long-run rationality, or short-run corridor behaviour of ρ are implemented formally in a similar way as in equation 4.16 in the industrial country model by a modified function for $\dot{\rho}$, which reads as

$$\dot{\rho} = z(\underset{-,0,+}{\rho}, \underset{+}{\sigma^*}, \underset{-}{\lambda_d^*}), \tag{5.10}$$

stating that irrespective of σ^* and λ_d^*, there exist values for ρ which induce investors to rely on mass psychology, i.e. $\partial\dot{\rho}/\partial\rho > 0$, but there exist also values for ρ causing investors not to change their expectations, i.e. $\partial\dot{\rho}/\partial\rho = 0$, or even to speculate against the trend of mass psychology, i.e. $\partial\dot{\rho}/\partial\rho < 0$.[20] Regarding the corridor concept, being represented in figure 5.2 which is a slightly modified version of figure 4.2 depicting equation 5.10 for constant values $\bar{\sigma^*}$ and $\bar{\lambda}_d^*$, it is assumed that there exists a "realistic" or "normal" range for the state of confidence $\rho_l < \rho < \rho_u$, where ρ_l and ρ_u denote the negative lower and the positive upper limit, in which it is reasonable to rely on general market sentiments, i.e. to expect ρ to continue the past upward or downward trend since speculating against the market trend would result in losses. In formal terms, within the range $\rho_l < \rho < \rho_u$ it holds that $\partial\dot{\rho}/\partial\rho > 0$. However, the closer ρ moves to the lower and the upper bounds, the more investors doubt ρ to be consistent with its long-run level $\rho_E = 0$; formally, slope $\partial\dot{\rho}/\partial\rho > 0$ is decreasing both in range $0 < \rho < \rho_u$ for increasing values in ρ, and in range $0 > \rho > \rho_l$ for decreasing values in ρ. At the corridor's "corner points" ρ_l and ρ_u, investors stop believing in a further decline or rise in ρ since the state of confidence has reached its minimum or maximum level which can be justified rationally; formally, at $\rho = \rho_l$ and $\rho = \rho_u$, it holds that $\partial\dot{\rho}/\partial\rho = 0$. In case the state of confidence exceeds ρ_u, or falls short of ρ_l, investors start to speculate against the past development of ρ, since the actual level of ρ cannot be justified rationally any longer; formally, in ranges $\rho > \rho_u$ and $\rho < \rho_l$, it holds that $\partial\dot{\rho}/\partial\rho < 0$.

Figure 5.2 indicates that there arise three possible dynamic equilibria A, B and C from equation 5.10, where the rational expectations equilibrium $\rho_E = 0$ represented by point C is unstable, and the two outer "irrational" equilibria at points A and B are dynamically stable. Points A and B are denoted as "irrational" equilibria because settling down dynamically in A or B would mean a steady long-run under- or overestimation of profits outside the "realistic" corridor. Figure 5.2 highlights the fact that the dynamic system tends to instability in case rational investors follow general market sentiments, and to stability in case investors rely on the believe in a long-run rational expectations equilibrium $\rho_E = 0$ which however, results in an "irrational" long-run steady state which is stable. As a result, since stylized facts indicate that there is no long-run irrationality of investors, the dynamics of other economic variables, as e.g. the foreign debt-asset ratio, have to guarantee either the existence of a dynamically stable rational expectations equilibrium, or stable cyclical motions around the unstable rational expectations equilibrium.

[20] Though equation 5.10 and equation 4.16 in the industrial country model seem to be identical, there are two important differences. Firstly, in the industrial country model σ^* refers to the domestic real bond rate, and secondly, since industrial countries are mainly indebted in domestic currency, the financial structure in equation 4.16 is represented by the domestic debt-asset ratio λ neglecting exchange rate variations.

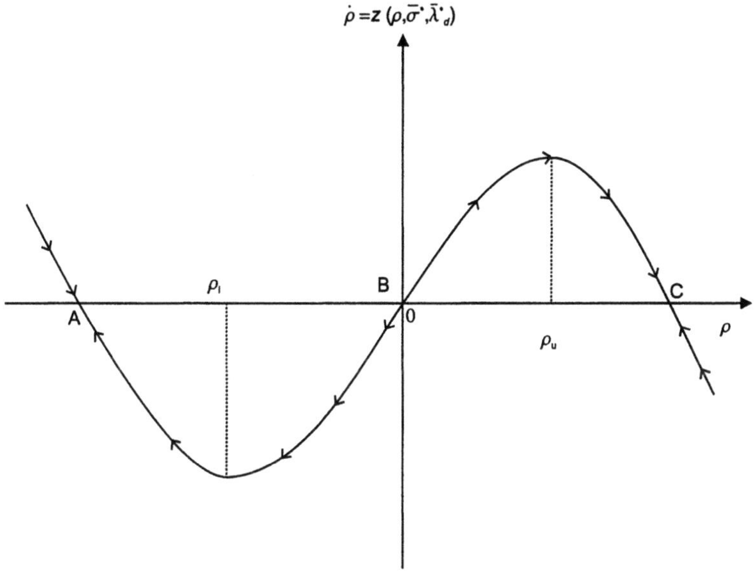

Figure 5.2: Graphical Representation of Function $\dot{\rho} = z(\rho, \bar{\sigma^*}, \bar{\lambda^*_d})$.

The Dynamic Behaviour of the Foreign Debt-Asset Ratio in Domestic Currency Terms. Since the domestic financial system is assumed to suffer from past financial repression, new investment is financed either by retained earnings or by taking new foreign loans $\dot{L}^*$. Accordingly, the financing condition for new investment reads as

$$P\,I = s_r\,r\,P\,K + \dot{L}^*\,s$$

where s_r denotes the retention ratio. Dividing both sides by the numéraire PK and using the fact that $1/(PK) = \lambda^*/L^*$, the financing condition can be transformed into

$$\eta(q) = s_r\,r + \frac{\dot{L}^*}{L^*}\,\lambda^*_d.$$

The financing condition contains no explicit financial constraint which could serve to describe how credit rationing, i.e. a binding constraint on L^*, leads to a drop in real investment spending. However, the financing condition comprehends an implicit form of credit rationing by the investment function $\eta(q)$. In case there is a drop in Tobin's q, which is caused by deteriorating fundamentals or by a sudden decline in the state of confidence, both factors leading generally to a reduction in lending activity by financial institutions, investment spending and thereby an increase in indebtedness is going to be cut. To get a differential equation in λ^*_d, the growth rate of the foreign debt-asset ratio expressed in domestic currency, given formally as

$$\frac{\dot{\lambda}^*_d}{\lambda^*_d} = \frac{\dot{L}^*}{L^*} + \frac{\dot{s}}{s} - \frac{\dot{P}}{P} - \frac{\dot{K}}{K} = \frac{\dot{L}^*}{L^*} + \hat{s} - \hat{p} - \eta(q),$$

has to be solved for $\dot{\lambda}_d^*$, and combined with the modified nominal financing condition, resulting after some algebra in the second dynamic equation of the system, reading as

$$\dot{\lambda}_d^* = \eta(q)\,(1-\lambda_d^*) - s_r\, r + (\hat{s} - \hat{p})\,\lambda_d^*. \tag{5.11}$$

Since the initial fixed exchange rate level has been defined as $\bar{s} = 1$, equation 5.11 expresses $\dot{\lambda}_d^*$ and $\hat{s}$ on the basis of the initial value $\bar{s} = 1$.[21] Regarding equation 5.11, possible causes of an increase in foreign indebtedness for a given stock of λ_d^*, are ceteris paribus an increase in the capital stock's growth rate $\eta(q)$, drops in s_r and r, and an increase in the real exchange rate $\hat{s} - \hat{p}$. The negative impact of an increase in $\hat{s} - \hat{p}$ on indebtedness in domestic currency captures both the effect of a domestic Fisherian debt deflation process, and the effect of a foreign "debt" deflation process by a devaluation of the home currency.

5.4.2 The Local Dynamics of the System

Equations 5.10 and 5.11 set up a nonlinear dynamic system in the two variables λ_d^* and ρ reading as

$$\dot{\lambda}_d^* = G_1(\lambda_d^*, \rho) = \eta(q)\,(1-\lambda_d^*) - s_r\, r + (\hat{s} - \hat{p})\,\lambda_d^* \tag{5.12}$$

$$\dot{\rho} = G_2(\lambda_d^*, \rho) = z(\rho, \sigma^*, \lambda_d^*). \tag{5.13}$$

For local stability analysis purposes, the nonlinear system is going to be linearized by a linear Taylor expansion around the local intertemporal equilibrium point $\lambda_{d_E}^*, \rho_E$ resulting in

$$\begin{bmatrix} \dot{\lambda}_d^* \\ \dot{\rho} \end{bmatrix} = \begin{bmatrix} \frac{\partial G_1}{\partial \lambda_d^*} & \frac{\partial G_1}{\partial \rho} \\ \frac{\partial G_2}{\partial \lambda_d^*} & \frac{\partial G_2}{\partial \rho} \end{bmatrix}_{(\lambda_{d_E}^*, \rho_E)} \cdot \begin{bmatrix} \lambda_d^* - \lambda_{d_E}^* \\ \rho - \rho_E \end{bmatrix} = \mathbf{J_E} \cdot \begin{bmatrix} \lambda_d^* - \lambda_{d_E}^* \\ \rho - \rho_E \end{bmatrix},$$

where $\mathbf{J_E}$ denotes the Jacobian matrix evaluated at the local dynamic equilibrium $\lambda_{d_E}^*, \rho_E$. In order to derive the local stability properties of the system, the signs of the partial derivatives of the Jacobian matrix $\mathbf{J_E}$ have to be evaluated by making use of the comparative static results given explicitly in section 5.7. The derivative of function G_1 with respect to λ_d^* reads as

$$\frac{\partial G_1}{\partial \lambda_d^*} = -\eta(q) + (\hat{s} - \hat{p}) + (1-\lambda_d^*)\frac{d\eta}{dq}\frac{\partial q}{\partial \lambda_d^*} + (-s_r)\frac{\partial r}{\partial \lambda_d^*} + (-\lambda_d^*)\frac{\partial \hat{p}}{\partial \lambda_d^*} \qquad < 0$$

which is assumed as being negative because firstly, s_r and $\partial \hat{p}/\partial \lambda_d^*$ are relatively small in comparison with the other terms, and secondly, because in case the fixed exchange rate prevails it holds that $\hat{s} = 0$.[22] The derivative of function G_1 with respect to ρ is given by

$$\frac{\partial G_1}{\partial \rho} = (1-\lambda_d^*)\frac{d\eta}{dq}\frac{\partial q}{\partial \rho} + (-s_r)\frac{\partial r}{\partial \rho} + (-\lambda_d^*)\frac{\partial \hat{p}}{\partial \rho} \qquad > 0,$$

[21]Note that since $\bar{s} = 1$, it holds that equation 5.11 can be converted into $\dot{\lambda}_d^* = \eta(q)\,(1-\lambda^*) - s_r\, r + (\hat{s} - \hat{p})\,\lambda^*$.

[22]The effects of a devaluation on the dynamic stability, and possible changes in the relevant functions are discussed in detail in section 5.4.5.

which is assumed as being positive, because s_r and $\partial\hat{p}/\partial\rho$ are relatively small in comparison to the other terms being positive. The derivative of function G_2 with respect to λ_d^* is formally given by

$$\frac{\partial G_2}{\partial \lambda_d^*} = \frac{\partial z}{\partial \lambda_d^*} + \frac{\partial z}{\partial \sigma^*}\frac{\partial \sigma^*}{\partial \lambda_d^*} \qquad < 0,$$

which is unequivocally negative, and for which it holds that

$$\frac{\partial \sigma^*}{\partial \lambda_d^*} = \frac{\partial \sigma^*}{\partial r}\frac{\partial r}{\partial \lambda_d^*} + \frac{\partial \sigma^*}{\partial \hat{p}}\frac{\partial \hat{p}}{\partial \lambda_d^*} \qquad < 0.$$ [23]

The derivative of G_2 with respect to ρ reads as

$$\frac{\partial G_2}{\partial \rho} = \frac{\partial z}{\partial \rho} + \frac{\partial z}{\partial \sigma^*}\frac{\partial \sigma^*}{\partial \rho} \qquad \gtreqless 0,$$

where

$$\frac{\partial z}{\partial \rho} \gtreqless 0, \quad \frac{\partial \sigma^*}{\partial \rho} = \frac{\partial r}{\partial \rho} + \frac{\partial \sigma^*}{\partial \beta}\frac{\partial \beta}{\partial \rho} + \frac{\partial \hat{p}}{\partial \rho} > 0 \quad \text{and} \quad \frac{\partial z}{\partial \sigma^*}\frac{\partial \sigma^*}{\partial \rho} > 0,$$

leading to an equivocal sign of the partial derivative $\partial G_2/\partial\rho$. The sign of $\partial G_2/\partial\rho$ depends on the derivative of function z with respect to ρ, i.e. on the actual level of the actual state of confidence ρ and its position relative to the "normal" range $\rho_l < \rho < \rho_u$. Consequently, the signs of the Jacobian matrix for all relevant subcases as to local dynamic stability can be summarized as

$$\mathbf{J} = \begin{bmatrix} \frac{\partial G_1}{\partial \lambda_d^*} & \frac{\partial G_1}{\partial \rho} \\ \frac{\partial G_2}{\partial \lambda_d^*} & \frac{\partial G_2}{\partial \rho} \end{bmatrix} = \begin{bmatrix} - & + \\ - & -,0,+ \end{bmatrix},$$

where local dynamic stability or instability of a fixed point is determined by investors' behaviour as to further changes in ρ, depending on the current position of ρ relative to the "normal" corridor $\rho_l < \rho < \rho_u$, i.e. by the signs of derivatives $\partial z/\partial\rho$ and $\partial G_2/\partial\rho$.

Regarding the local stability of fixed points, there arise three relevant and possible cases as in the financial crisis model for industrial countries. *Case 1* refers to the situation when the state of confidence at the fixed point ρ_E is around the two corner points ρ_l and ρ_u, i.e. when investors stop to rely on general market sentiments, or when ρ_E is generally outside the normal range $\rho_l < \rho < \rho_u$, i.e. when investors assess the actual value of ρ as being irrationally exaggerated or understated. In these cases, it holds that

$$\frac{\partial z}{\partial \rho} \leqslant 0, \quad \text{or} \quad \frac{\partial z}{\partial \rho} > 0 \quad \text{but very small},$$

causing $\partial G_2/\partial\rho$ to exhibit a negative, zero or slightly positive sign since

$$\frac{\partial G_2}{\partial \rho} = \underset{-,0,+\text{small}}{\frac{\partial z}{\partial \rho}} + \underset{+}{\frac{\partial z}{\partial \sigma^*}}\underset{+}{\frac{\partial \sigma^*}{\partial \rho}},$$

[23]Note that functions $r = r(\lambda^*)$ and $\hat{p} = \hat{p}(\lambda^*)$ can be simply transformed into $r = r(\lambda_d^*/s)$ and $\hat{p} = \hat{p}(\lambda_d^*/s)$; for a given fixed exchange rate $\bar{s} = 1$ it holds that $r(\lambda^*) = r(\lambda_d^*)$ and $\hat{p}(\lambda^*) = \hat{p}(\lambda_d^*)$.

and accordingly,

$$\frac{\partial G_2}{\partial \rho} \leqslant 0, \quad \text{or} \quad \frac{\partial G_2}{\partial \rho} > 0 \quad \text{but very small.}$$

Respecting local dynamic stability properties being evaluated by the trace and the determinant of the Jacobian matrix, a local fixed point being characterized by the conditions of case 1 exhibits local asymptotic stability, i.e. the fixed points is either a stable node or a stable focus since the trace's sign is negative and the determinant's sign positive, formally it holds that

$$tr\,\mathbf{J_E} = \underset{-}{\frac{\partial G_1}{\partial \lambda_d^*}} + \underset{-,0,+\text{small}}{\frac{\partial G_2}{\partial \rho}} < 0,$$

and

$$|\mathbf{J_E}| = \underset{-}{\frac{\partial G_1}{\partial \lambda_d^*}}\;\underset{-,0,+\text{small}}{\frac{\partial G_2}{\partial \rho}} - \underset{+}{\frac{\partial G_1}{\partial \rho}}\;\underset{-}{\frac{\partial G_2}{\partial \lambda_d^*}} > 0.$$

Case 2 refers to the situation when the state of confidence at the fixed point ρ_E is located around the rational expectations equilibrium $\rho_E = 0$, i.e. when investors largely rely on general market sentiments. This case however, has to be distinguished by investors' sensitivity as to changes in ρ because it can be assumed that investors either react hypersensibly, i.e. $\partial z/\partial \rho \gg 0$, or "normally" around the rational expectations equilibrium ρ_E, i.e. $\partial z/\partial \rho > 0$. Case 2 refers to a situation in which investors are assumed to react hypersensitively, i.e. it holds that

$$\frac{\partial z}{\partial \rho} \gg 0,$$

leading to a largely positive sign of $\partial G_2/\partial \rho$, formally given by

$$\frac{\partial G_2}{\partial \rho} = \underset{+\text{large}}{\frac{\partial z}{\partial \rho}} + \underset{+}{\frac{\partial z}{\partial \sigma^*}}\;\underset{+}{\frac{\partial \sigma^*}{\partial \rho}} \gg 0.$$

Regarding local dynamic stability, such a fixed point exhibits the characteristics of a saddle point, i.e. the fixed point is locally unstable since the sign of the Jacobian's trace is largely positive and the sign of the Jacobian's determinant is negative, which are both formally given as

$$tr\,\mathbf{J_E} = \underset{-}{\frac{\partial G_1}{\partial \lambda_d^*}} + \underset{+\text{large}}{\frac{\partial G_2}{\partial \rho}} \gg 0,$$

and

$$|\mathbf{J_E}| = \underset{-}{\frac{\partial G_1}{\partial \lambda_d^*}}\;\underset{+\text{large}}{\frac{\partial G_2}{\partial \rho}} - \underset{+}{\frac{\partial G_1}{\partial \rho}}\;\underset{-}{\frac{\partial G_2}{\partial \lambda_d^*}} < 0.$$

Case 3 refers to the same situation as case 2, however, investors are assumed as reacting "normally" near the rational expectations equilibrium $\rho_E = 0$. In this case, it holds that

$$\frac{\partial z}{\partial \rho} > 0,$$

leading to a positive sign of $\partial G_2/\partial\rho$, but being smaller than the positive sign of $\partial G_2/\partial\rho$ in case 2; formally,

$$\frac{\partial G_2}{\partial\rho} = \underset{+}{\frac{\partial z}{\partial\rho}} + \underset{+}{\frac{\partial z}{\partial\sigma^*}}\,\underset{+}{\frac{\partial\sigma^*}{\partial\rho}} > 0.$$

With respect to dynamic stability properties, such a fixed point is dynamically unstable, i.e. it exhibits either characteristics of an unstable node or of an unstable focus, since both the trace and the determinant of the Jacobian have a positive sign. The Jacobian's trace is given by

$$tr\,\mathbf{J_E} = \underset{-}{\frac{\partial G_1}{\partial\lambda_d^*}} + \underset{+}{\frac{\partial G_2}{\partial\rho}} > 0,$$

exhibiting a positive sign, since condition $|\partial G_1/\partial\lambda_d^*| < |\partial G_2/\partial\rho|$ is fulfilled which is consistent with the assumptions under case 1 and 2. The sign of the Jacobian's determinant given by

$$|\mathbf{J_E}| = \underset{-}{\frac{\partial G_1}{\partial\lambda_d^*}}\,\underset{+}{\frac{\partial G_2}{\partial\rho}} - \underset{+}{\frac{\partial G_1}{\partial\rho}}\,\underset{-}{\frac{\partial G_2}{\partial\lambda_d^*}} > 0,$$

can be only assumed to be positive in case it holds that

$$\left|\underset{-}{\frac{\partial G_1}{\partial\lambda_d^*}}\,\underset{+}{\frac{\partial G_2}{\partial\rho}}\right| < \left|\underset{+}{\frac{\partial G_1}{\partial\rho}}\,\underset{-}{\frac{\partial G_2}{\partial\lambda_d^*}}\right|,$$

which is going to be proved in the ensuing phase diagram analysis.

5.4.3 Phase Diagram Analysis

Demarcation curve $\dot{\lambda}_d^* = G_1(\lambda_d^*, \rho) = 0$ has a positive slope over the entire range in the (λ_d^*, ρ) space since it holds that

$$\left(\frac{d\lambda_d^*}{d\rho}\right)_{G_1} = -\frac{\frac{\partial G_1}{\partial\rho}}{\frac{\partial G_1}{\partial\lambda_d^*}} > 0. \tag{5.14}$$

The course of demarcation curve $\dot{\rho} = G_2(\lambda_d^*, \rho) = 0$ is mainly influenced by the course of the function $\dot{\rho} = z(\rho, \bar{\sigma}^*, \lambda_d^*)$ being depicted in figure 5.2. Formally, the slope of demarcation curve $\dot{\rho} = G_2(\lambda_d^*, \rho) = 0$, being denoted as $(d\lambda_d^*/d\rho)_{G_2}$, is given by

$$\left(\frac{d\lambda_d^*}{d\rho}\right)_{G_2} = -\frac{\overset{-,0,+}{\frac{\partial G_2}{\partial\rho}}}{\underset{-}{\frac{\partial G_2}{\partial\lambda}}} \lesseqgtr 0, \tag{5.15}$$

whose sign depends on derivative $\partial G_2/\partial\rho$ being predominantly determined by derivative $\partial z/\partial\rho$. Formally, in case $\partial z/\partial\rho < 0$ for which it holds that $|\partial z/\partial\rho| > |(\partial z/\partial\sigma^*)(\partial\sigma^*/d\rho)|$, derivative $\partial G_2/\partial\rho$ becomes negative, i.e. $\partial G_2/\partial\rho < 0$, leading to a negative slope of the demarcation curve $\dot{\rho} = 0$, i.e. $(\partial\lambda_d^*/\partial\rho)_{G_2} < 0$. In case derivative $\partial z/\partial\rho$ takes a value of $\partial z/\partial\rho = (-\partial z/\partial\sigma^*)(\partial\sigma^*/d\rho)$, derivative $\partial G_2/\partial\rho$ becomes zero, i.e. $\partial G_2/\partial\rho = 0$, leading to a zero slope of demarcation curve $\dot{\rho} = 0$, i.e. to $(\partial\lambda_d^*/\partial\rho)_{G_2} = 0$. In case derivative $\partial z/\partial\rho$ takes negative values for which it holds $|\partial z/\partial\rho| < |(\partial z/\partial\sigma^*)(\partial\sigma^*/d\rho)|$, a zero value, or positive values, the sign of derivative $\partial G_2/\partial\rho$ becomes positive, i.e. $\partial G_2/\partial\rho > 0$, leading to a positive slope of demarcation curve $\dot{\rho} = 0$, i.e. $(\partial\lambda_d^*/\partial\rho)_{G_2} > 0$. Though the turning points of demarcation curve $\dot{\rho} = 0$, for which it holds that $(\partial\lambda_d^*/\partial\rho)_{G_2} = 0$, do not correspond exactly to the boundary points of the normal range ρ_l and ρ_u, the course of demarcation curve $\dot{\rho} = 0$ can be equivalently described as the course of function $\dot{\rho} = z(\rho, \bar{\sigma}^*, \bar{\lambda}_d^*)$. Consequently, demarcation curve $\dot{\rho} = G_2(\lambda_d^*, \rho) = 0$ is going to exhibit a positive slope for values of ρ lying around the normal range, becoming less and shrinking to zero if ρ reaches the area of the corner points ρ_l and ρ_u, and becoming negative if ρ lies in the area outside the normal range.

Since the local stability analysis has distinguished between the two cases, investors reacting hypersensibly in the "normal" range of ρ (case 2), i.e. $\partial z/\partial\rho \gg 0$, and investors reacting "normally" in the "normal" range (case 3), i.e. $\partial z/\partial\rho > 0$, there arise also two possible kinds of demarcation curves $\dot{\rho} = 0$, differing with respect to the positive steepness of their slope near the "normal" range of ρ. In case investors react hypersensibly, the positive slope around the corridor $\rho_l < \rho < \rho_u$ is steeper than in case investors react "normally". These two different cases are illustrated in figure 5.3, where the dotted demarcation curve $\dot{\rho} = 0$ represents the case of hypersensitive investors in the "normal" range, and the solid demarcation curve the case of normally reacting investors in the "normal" range. It has to be noted that the distinction between normally and hypersensitively reacting investors does not apply to the area outside the normal range, since there is no influence on the local and global dynamics of the system. Consequently, the parts with negative slope of the dotted demarcation curve in figure 4.3 could alternatively run flatter than the negatively sloped parts of the solid demarcation curve without changing the local and global dynamics of the system.

The explicit consideration of different degrees of investors' sensitivity measured by different values of $\partial z/\partial\rho$ is necessary from a formal point of view, since different values of $\partial z/\partial\rho$ decide whether the dynamic system exhibits multiple dynamic equilibria, or a single dynamic equilibrium point. Regarding the case when investors react very sensitively as to changes in ρ in the normal range, there arise three fixed points being depicted in figure 5.4. Points A and C are locally asymptotically stable since demarcation curve $\dot{\rho} = 0$ is negatively locally sloped because $\partial z/\partial\rho < 0$ and $\partial G_2/\partial\rho < 0$, whereas demarcation curve $\dot{\lambda}_d^* = 0$ is positively locally sloped, i.e. it holds that

$$\underset{+}{\left(\frac{\partial\lambda_d^*}{\partial\rho}\right)_{G_1}} > \underset{-}{\left(\frac{\partial\lambda_d^*}{\partial\rho}\right)_{G_2}}$$

$$-\frac{\frac{\partial G_1}{\partial\rho}}{\frac{\partial G_1}{\partial\lambda_d^*}} > -\frac{\frac{\partial G_2}{\partial\rho}}{\frac{\partial G_2}{\partial\lambda_d^*}},$$

which after rearranging can be transformed into the determinant of the Jacobian at the fixed points A and C, being denoted as $|\mathbf{J}|_{(A,C)}$, having a positive sign since

$$|\mathbf{J}|_{(A,C)} = \underset{-}{\frac{\partial G_1}{\partial\lambda_d^*}}\,\underset{-}{\frac{\partial G_2}{\partial\rho}} - \underset{+}{\frac{\partial G_1}{\partial\rho}}\,\underset{-}{\frac{\partial G_2}{\partial\lambda_d^*}} > 0.$$

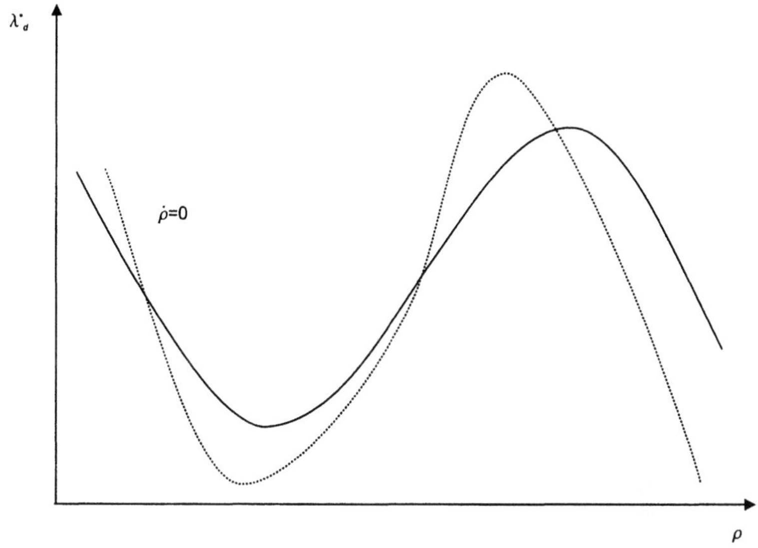

Figure 5.3: Different Demarcation Curves for $\dot{\rho} = 0$ Depending on Investors' Sensitivity as to Changes in ρ

The Jacobian's trace at A and C, being denoted as $tr\,\mathbf{J}_{(A,C)}$, has got a negative sign because

$$tr\,\mathbf{J}_{(A,C)} = \underset{-}{\frac{\partial G_1}{\partial \lambda^*_d}} + \underset{-}{\frac{\partial F_2}{\partial \rho}} < 0,$$

classifying points A and C according to case 1 of the local stability analysis as locally stable fixed points.

Fixed point B exhibits the characteristics of a saddle point since both demarcation curves have a positive slope, where demarcation curve $\dot{\rho} = 0$, being subject to $\partial z/\partial \rho \gg 0$ and $\partial G_2/\partial \rho \gg 0$, is steeper than demarcation curve $\dot{\lambda}^*_d = 0$ at point B, formally

$$\underset{+}{\left(\frac{\partial \lambda^*_d}{\partial \rho}\right)_{G_1}} < \underset{+}{\left(\frac{\partial \lambda^*_d}{\partial \rho}\right)_{G_2}}$$

$$-\frac{\frac{\partial G_1}{\partial \rho}}{\frac{\partial G_1}{\partial \lambda^*_d}} < -\frac{\frac{\partial G_2}{\partial \rho}}{\frac{\partial G_2}{\partial \lambda^*_d}},$$

which after rearranging terms yields the Jacobian's determinant at fixed point B, being denoted as $|\mathbf{J}|_{(B)}$, whose sign is negative since

$$|\mathbf{J}|_{(B)} = \underset{-}{\frac{\partial G_1}{\partial \lambda^*_d}}\,\underset{+\,\text{large}}{\frac{\partial G_2}{\partial \rho}} - \underset{+}{\frac{\partial G_1}{\partial \rho}}\,\underset{-}{\frac{\partial G_2}{\partial \lambda^*_d}} < 0.$$

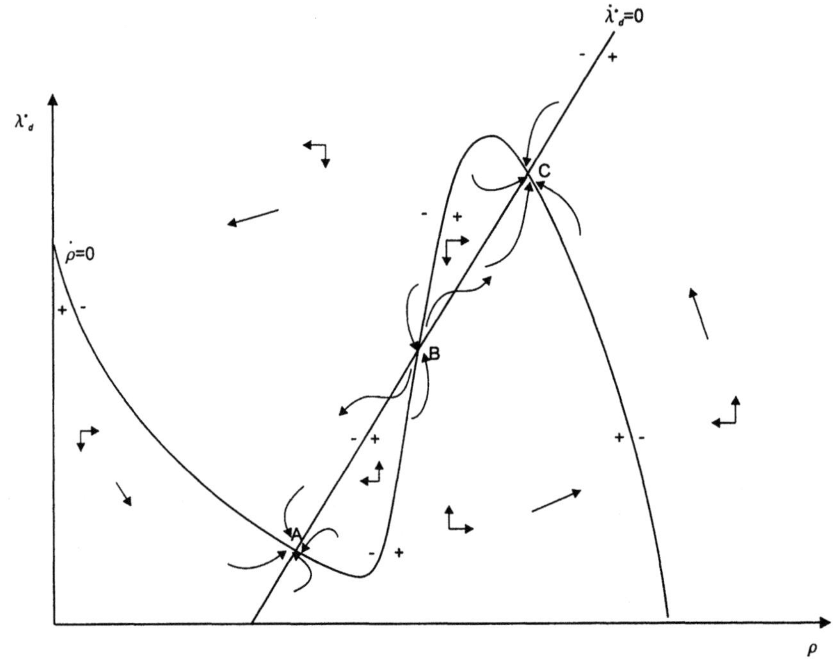

Figure 5.4: Phase Diagram in Case of Hypersensitively Reacting Investors within the Normal Range of ρ

The Jacobian's trace at B, being denoted as $tr\,\mathbf{J}_{(B)}$, has a positive sign according to

$$tr\,\mathbf{J}_{(B)} = \underbrace{\frac{\partial G_1}{\partial \lambda_d^*}}_{-} + \underbrace{\frac{\partial G_2}{\partial \rho}}_{+\,\text{large}} > 0,$$

classifying fixed point B as a saddle point according to case 2 of the local stability analysis.

As in the industrial country model, the case of long-run dynamics under hypersensitively reacting investors has no empirical relevance since coming to a long-run halt in points A or C would mean a steady under- or overestimation of profits since $\rho_E \neq 0$ in A and C, being located near the boundary points of the normal range of ρ. Furthermore, the dynamics of the economy would be subject to path dependent behaviour since reaching point A or C would be solely dependent on the initial starting point of the economy which can be located everywhere in the (λ_d^*, ρ) space. Imposing stability by assuming that rational investors can generally jump to the stable arm of the saddle point trajectories, and thereby moving smoothly into point B is not possible since ρ does not exhibit the characteristics of a *pure* forward looking or jump variable, firstly due to its dependence on the backward looking variables σ^* and λ_d^*, and secondly due to the absence of (short-run) rational expectations.

Though there is no internal mechanism which guarantees a jump of ρ on the stable branches of the saddle point equilibrium, it is important to note that "jumps" in ρ are generally possible in case of direct exogenous shocks, solely having an influence on the state of confidence to ρ. As opposed to direct shocks to ρ, both direct exogenous shocks to economic fundamentals λ_d^* and σ^*, and indirect shocks to λ_d^* and σ^* via exogenous shocks to other variables influencing λ_d^* and σ^*, do not cause a jump in ρ. A very prominent example of a direct exogenous shock to ρ in emerging market countries, leaving economic fundamentals λ_d^* and σ^* unchanged at the moment of the shock, is the introduction of a "new growth regime" including liberalization of goods and financial markets and stabilization of output and inflation via orthodox stabilization programmes. A direct exogenous shock to ρ causes a discontinuous jump in the ρ-coordinate within the (λ_d^*, ρ)-space, but leaves both demarcation curves and the vector field unchanged, giving rise to a new dynamic process initiated by a new initial condition. By way of contrast, a direct exogenous shock to σ^*, or any shock to variables influencing σ^*, leave the current position within the (λ_d^*, ρ)-space unchanged, whereas both demarcation curves and the vector field are subject to changes. An exogenous shock to the foreign-debt asset ratio λ_d^* caused by a change in the exchange rate's growth rate $\hat{s}$, leads both to a jump in the λ_d^*-coordinate, and to a change of both demarcation curves, as well as to a change in the vector field. By way of contrast, a change in λ_d^* caused by an exogenous shock in λ^*, causes, as a direct shock to ρ, only a jump in λ_d^*, but leaves both demarcation curves and the vector field unchanged.[24]

In spite of the existence of jumps in ρ, there is no mechanism guaranteeing, as in rational expectations model, a jump on the stable branch of saddle point equilibrium B. Thus, the dynamic system is likely to settle down in stable fixed points A and C. Yet, coming to a long-run halt in points A and C, being characterized by long-run expectation errors, is an unrealistic scenario both from an empirical perspective and from a theoretical perspective, since it is not consistent with the assumption of long-run rational behaviour. Consequently, it seems plausible that in case investors, coming to a halt in points A or C, are going to adjust their profit expectations subsequently after having realized that current expectations cannot be fulfilled, leading to a readjustment of function $\dot{\rho} = z(\rho, \sigma^*, \lambda_d^*)$, and thereby to a shift of the demarcation curve $\dot{\rho} = 0$ until in the long-run profit expectations are fulfilled by the actual development of profits. Accordingly, to get an empirically meaningful result, it seems reasonable to assume firstly, that the state of confidence's long-run steady state value settles down in the rational expectations equilibrium $\rho_E = 0$ since every long-run divergence $r^e \neq r$ leads to a readjustment of functions $\dot{\rho} = z(\rho, \sigma^*, \lambda_d^*)$ and $\dot{\rho} = 0$, and secondly, that there exists only a single intertemporal equilibrium point $(\lambda_{d_E}^*, \rho_E)$, where $\rho_E = 0$ and $\lambda_{d_E}^* > 0$ since demarcation curve $\dot{\lambda} = 0$ is a strictly monotone increasing function in the (λ_d^*, ρ)-space. However, imposing these assumptions requires to assume investors to behave "normally" in the "normal" range of ρ, i.e. $\partial z/\partial \rho > 0$, leading to a less steeper demarcation curve $\dot{\rho} = 0$, as having been represented by the solid

[24]These results were drawn from analyzing the impacts of various forms of exogenous shocks on both demarcation curves, and on the integral curves of system 5.12 and 5.13, given by

$$\frac{d\lambda_d^*}{d\rho} = \frac{G_1(\lambda_d^*, \rho)}{G_2(\lambda_d^*, \rho)} = \frac{\eta(q)\,(1-\lambda_d^*) - s_r\, r + (\hat{s} - \hat{p})\,\lambda_d^*}{z(\rho, \sigma^*, \lambda_d^*)},$$

and derived from system 5.12 and 5.13 by the elimination of dt.

line in figure 5.3, in order to get only one intersection of the two demarcation curves being depicted in figure 5.5.

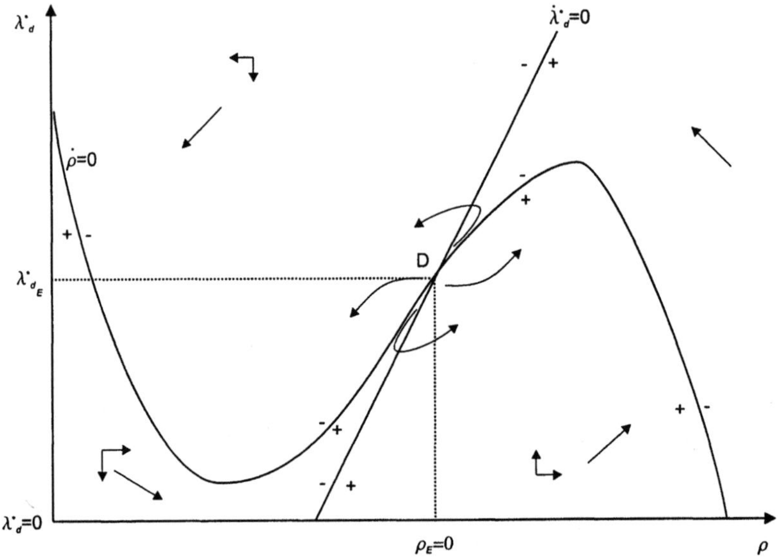

Figure 5.5: Phase Diagram for "Normally" Reacting Investors Within the Normal Range of ρ.

Regarding the dynamics when investors behave normally in the normal range for ρ in figure 5.5, there arise two important properties. Firstly, the local fixed point D is locally unstable (unstable node or unstable focus) since both demarcation curves have a positive slope, where demarcation curve $\dot{\lambda}_d^* = 0$ is steeper than demarcation curve $\dot{\rho} = 0$ because $\partial z/\partial\rho > 0$ and $\partial G_2/\partial\rho > 0$, formally given by

$$\underset{+}{\left(\frac{\partial\lambda_d^*}{\partial\rho}\right)_{G_1}} > \underset{+}{\left(\frac{\partial\lambda_d^*}{\partial\rho}\right)_{G_2}}$$

$$-\frac{\frac{\partial G_1}{\partial\rho}}{\frac{\partial G_1}{\partial\lambda_d^*}} > -\frac{\frac{\partial G_2}{\partial\rho}}{\frac{\partial G_2}{\partial\lambda_d^*}},$$

which, after rearranging terms, can be transformed into the determinant of the Jacobian at the local equilibrium D which is denoted as $|\mathbf{J}|_{(D)}$, having a positive sign since

$$|\mathbf{J}|_{(D)} = \underset{-}{\frac{\partial G_1}{\partial\lambda_d^*}}\underset{+\,\text{normal}}{\frac{\partial G_2}{\partial\rho}} - \underset{+}{\frac{\partial G_1}{\partial\rho}}\underset{-}{\frac{\partial G_2}{\partial\lambda_d^*}} > 0.$$

The Jacobian's trace at point D, being denoted as $tr\,\mathbf{J}_{(D)}$, has a positive sign because

$$tr\,\mathbf{J}_{(D)} = \underbrace{\frac{\partial G_1}{\partial \lambda_d^*}}_{-} + \underbrace{\frac{\partial G_2}{\partial \rho}}_{+\,\text{normal}} > 0,$$

classifying fixed point D according to case 3 of the local stability analysis as an unstable fixed point. The second property of the dynamic system under normally reacting investors is the fact that the system exhibits cyclical motions in a counterclockwise direction. Accordingly, a first ad-hoc interpretation would suggest that this result cannot be empirically meaningful since the dynamic system is going to explode. However, as the following section is going to outline, the global dynamics exhibit some form of bounded cyclical fluctuations leading to a cyclically stable dynamic system.

5.4.4 The Global Dynamics of the System

The Emergence of a Globally Stable Closed Orbit. As in the financial crisis model for industrial countries, it can be shown that the dynamic system in figure 5.5 contains at least one closed orbit which is an attractor, i.e. a limit cycle, by applying the Poincaré-Bendixon theorem.[25] One prerequisite for the emergence of a limit cycle is the existence of a compact set $\mathcal{D}$ from which trajectories once having entered cannot escape. However, constructing a compact set requires some definitions as to the global boundedness of variables λ_d^* and ρ. Regarding λ_d^*, values $\lambda_d^* < 0$ are not possible since in this case the firm sector would possess claims on the banking sector, making $\lambda_d^* = 0$ a reasonable lower bound. Realistic values for λ_d^* move inside the range $0 < \lambda_d^* < 1$, whereas when dealing with systemic financial crises values $\lambda_d^* > 1$ have also to be considered as possible scenarios, indicating that the entire firm sector is bankrupt, which is however a very rare case. Though considering values $\lambda_d^* > 1$, it seems reasonable that there exists an upper bound for the foreign-debt asset ratio, since in case all borrowers are bankrupt international negotiations regarding debt restructuring, debt relief, etc., will follow. Accordingly, there exists a lower bound $\lambda_d^* = 0$ and an upper bound $\lambda_d^* > 1$. Considering the state of confidence, ρ is allowed to take values largely outside the normal range $\rho_l < \rho < \rho_u$, but ρ is also considered as not being able to take infinite positive or negative values. As a result, ρ can also be viewed as a variable with a negative lower and a positive upper bound.

Taking into consideration the upper and lower bounds of λ_d^* and ρ, figure 5.5 can be modified by adding an invariant set which is represented by the simply connected set $\mathcal{D}$ in figure 5.6 as rectangle $OPQR$. Regarding the trajectories on the boundaries of set $\mathcal{D}$, there arise situations in which trajectories may hit the boundaries, making it necessary to modify them in a natural way according to the assumptions made on the boundary values of λ_d^* and ρ in order to guarantee that trajectories once having entered the set cannot leave the set any more.

The second condition for applying the Poincaré-Bendixon theorem requires that the fixed point has to be dynamically unstable. Since figure 5.6 contains only one unstable fixed point D, the global dynamics contain at least one closed orbit which is an attractor, i.e. the system possess at least one limit cycle to which all trajectories converge as

[25]For details see section 4.4.4.

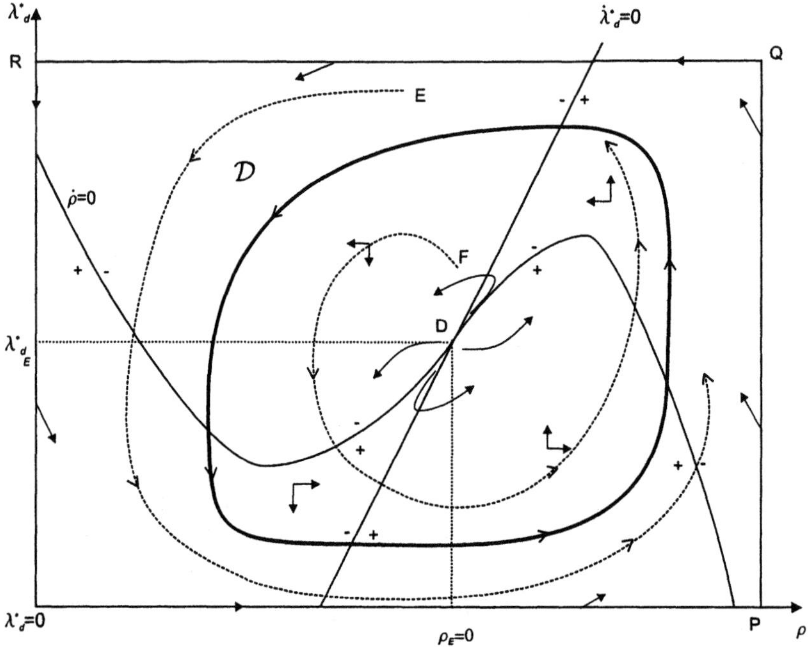

Figure 5.6: The Existence of a Limit Cycle

$t \to \infty$, being represented by the solid circle in figure 5.6. Each trajectory starting within the compact set $\mathcal{D}$, being indicated by the two sample trajectories starting in points E and F, or starting outside set $\mathcal{D}$ but after some time entering the set $\mathcal{D}$, converges to the limit cycle by either spiraling inward (trajectory starting in E) or spiraling outward (trajectory starting in F). There is no possibility for the emergence of separatrices being an alternative form of limit sets due to the absence of at least one further fixed point being characterized by saddle point properties.

The Emergence of a Supercritical Hopf Bifurcation. As the Poincaré-Bendixon theorem only provides sufficient conditions for the existence of at least one limit cycle, the dynamics described by equations 5.12 and 5.13 being represented in figure 5.6 could engender multiple closed orbits, with the inner- and the outermost orbits being stable, and the remaining closed orbits alternating between stability and instability with increasing amplitude. As to the emergence of endogenous financial fragility and financial crises, the existence of multiple limit cycles would suggest that there exist "small" limit cycles near the fixed point D where no severe disruptions in financial markets occur next to "large" limit cycles causing a financial crisis on each business cycle whose duration is much longer than those of "small" limit cycles. Accordingly, the question of whether the economy converges to a virtuous or to a vicious cycle depends on the initial condition in the (λ_d^*, ρ)-space, being influenced predominantly by exogenous shocks. This view on long-run dynamics would justify permanent market interventions by a social planner in order to guarantee a long-run "virtuous" cyclical behaviour with low business cycle amplitudes and financial stability. In case of an adverse exogenous shock, the social planner would have to catapult the system back by choosing of a favourable initial condition to the basins of attraction of the limit cycle with the lowest amplitude near the unstable fixed point. However, since both the foreign-debt asset ratio λ_d^*, and the state of confidence ρ show backward looking characteristics, an instantaneous jump induced by the social planner to the most favourable initial condition is almost impossible.

It must be noted however, that the foreign debt-asset ratio λ_d^* can be "steered" by a social planner to a certain degree, i.e. to move within a well-defined range, by strict financial market regulation in order to prevent the foreign-debt asset ratio from "tipping" into the basins of attraction of a business cycle giving rise to financial crises. Furthermore, the foreign-debt asset ratio can be subject to social planner induced jumps in case of negotiations regarding debt relief and debt restructuring. Yet, in most cases negotiations on debt relief or restructuring only take place when the economy has already experienced a systemic financial crises followed by a deep depression. As a result, even if there exists the possibility of social planner-induced jumps in λ_d^*, there is no possibility to prevent negative repercussions by social planner-induced instantaneous jumps in order to neutralize adverse exogenous shocks. The only possibility to protect the economy against negative exogenous shocks to the foreign debt-asset ratio is to impose strict financial market regulation minimizing negative impacts, e.g. by imposing a debt ceiling on foreign debt, so that possible devaluations do not lead to widespread illiquidity and insolvency.

Summing up, the existence of multiple limit cycles implies firstly, that capitalist systems are inherently unstable, secondly, that long-run financial stability or instability is determined by random shocks, thirdly, that in case the economy is subject to business cycles with high amplitudes, each long-run business cycle generates a systemic financial crisis, and fourthly, that in case the economy has converged to a long-run excessive boom-bust cycle, a business cycle with modest amplitudes can be only reached by exogenous events as e.g. debt relief or debt restructuring programmes.

Reality however shows firstly, that capitalist systems tend to be stable in the long-run, secondly, that financial fragility is not a purely exogenous phenomenon, thirdly, that not each business cycle is subject to a excessive boom-bust cycle including financial crises, and fourthly, that economies having been hit by financial crises in lots of cases tend to converge back *endogenously* to a financially stable equilibrium situation though recovery periods can be very long. As a result, the emergence of multiple limit cycles, some subject to ever lasting financial stability, and some subject to recurrent financial crises which can be both only left by random exogenous events, is a very unrealistic scenario. As a result, to provide empirically meaningful results, the dynamics of equations 5.12 and 5.13 should engender an "equilibrium" business cycle, i.e. a single limit cycle, on which no systemic financial crisis can occur, and on which economies operate during "tranquil" times. The emergence of extraordinary financial fragility in comparison with tranquil times, as well as the occurrence of financial crises on the upper turning point can be explained by a large external shock, like e.g. a technology or liberalization shock, catapulting the economy from its position on the "equilibrium" cycle outside the limit cycle, implying a convergence process back to the "equilibrium" cycle with a much larger amplitude including financial fragility and perhaps a financial crisis.

The existence of a single limit cycle can be proved by applying the existence and the stability part of the Hopf bifurcation theorem having been outlined in section 4.4.4. Since the stability of the fixed point, and thereby the dynamic properties of the system depend on investors' feedback sensitivity regarding the state of confidence, derivative $\partial z/\partial \rho = \partial \dot{\rho}/\partial \rho = \mu$ is used as the relevant parameter μ in order to study the nature of bifurcation when μ is varied.

The existence part of the Hopf bifurcation theorem states that in case the parameter μ is increased from $\mu < \mu_0$ to $\mu > \mu_0$, where $\mu = \mu_0$ denotes the critical value when the characteristic roots become pure imaginary, the fixed point changes its stability properties from being locally stable into being locally unstable, as the real parts of the characteristic roots $Re\,\theta(\mu)$ change their sign from being negative for $\mu < \mu_0$ to being positive for $\mu > \mu_0$. Accordingly, the first step to show the reversal of signs of the real parts of the characteristic roots is the emergence of pure imaginary roots at the critical parameter value $\mu = \mu_0$ according to condition *H.1*[26] of the Hopf bifurcation existence theorem. The characteristic equation of the nonlinear dynamic system 5.12 and 5.13 reads as

$$\theta^2 + \underbrace{\left(-\frac{\partial G_1}{\partial \lambda_d^*} - \frac{\partial G_2}{\partial \rho}\right)}_{a_1 = -tr\,\mathbf{J}} \theta + \underbrace{\left(\frac{\partial G_1}{\partial \lambda_d^*}\frac{\partial G_2}{\partial \rho} - \frac{\partial G_1}{\partial \rho}\frac{\partial G_2}{\partial \lambda_d^*}\right)}_{a_2 = |\mathbf{J}|} = 0,$$

defining the characteristic roots as

$$\theta_{1,2} = \underbrace{\frac{-a_1}{2}}_{Re\,\theta} \pm \frac{\sqrt{4a_2 - a_1^2}}{2}\,i.$$

In order to get a pair of pure imaginary roots two conditions have to be fulfilled. Firstly, the determinant of the Jacobian $|\mathbf{J}|$ has to be positive, i.e. it must hold that

$$a_2 > 0.$$

Secondly, the trace of the Jacobian $tr\,\mathbf{J} = -a_1$ has to vanish, causing the real part $Re\,\theta$ to become zero, i.e.

$$Re\,\theta = \frac{-a_1}{2} = 0, \quad \text{implying} \quad a_1 = 0.$$

The first condition $a_2 > 0$ is fulfilled, since both demarcation curves in figure 5.6 have a positive slope, the $\dot{\lambda}_d^* = 0$ demarcation curve being steeper than the $\dot{\rho} = 0$ demarcation curve, resulting in a positive sign of the Jacobian's determinant. Generally, condition $a_2 > 0$ is fulfilled for values $\mu = \partial z/\partial \rho \leq 0$ and for $\mu = \partial z/\partial \rho > 0$ (see cases 1 and 3 of the local stability analysis), but not for values $\mu = \partial z/\partial \rho \gg 0$ (see case 2 of the local stability analysis). As a result, condition $a_2 > 0$ holds for all possible values of function 5.13 when investors are assumed as behaving "normally" in the normal range.

The second condition $a_1 = 0$ determines the Hopf bifurcation point $\mu = \mu_0$ when the real parts of the characteristic roots become zero and closed orbits emerge. Since

[26]See section 4.4.4.

$\partial G_2/\partial \rho = \partial z/\partial \rho + (\partial z/\partial \sigma^*)(\partial \sigma^*/\partial \rho)$, condition $a_1 = 0$ can be transformed into

$$-\frac{\partial G_1}{\partial \lambda_d^*} - \left(\frac{\partial z}{\partial \rho} + \frac{\partial z}{\partial \sigma^*}\frac{\partial \sigma^*}{\partial \rho}\right) = 0,$$

and solved for $\partial z/\partial \rho$ determining the critical value $\mu_0 = (\partial z/\partial \rho)_0$ as

$$\mu_0 = \left(\frac{\partial z}{\partial \rho}\right)_0 = -\frac{\partial G_1}{\partial \lambda_d^*} - \frac{\partial z}{\partial \sigma^*}\frac{\partial \sigma^*}{\partial \rho}.$$

In order to determine the sign of the real parts of the characteristic roots for values $\mu > \mu_0$ and $\mu < \mu_0$, it can be shown that

$$Re\,\theta = \frac{-a_1}{2} \lesseqqgtr 0$$

implies

$$a_1 \gtreqqless 0$$

and

$$-\frac{\partial G_1}{\partial \lambda_d^*} - \frac{\partial z}{\partial \sigma^*}\frac{\partial \sigma^*}{\partial \rho} \gtreqqless \frac{\partial z}{\partial \rho},$$

leading to

$$\mu_0 \gtreqqless \mu.$$

Summarizing the results leads to the conclusion that

$$Re\,\theta \lesseqqgtr 0 \quad \Leftrightarrow \quad a_1 \gtreqqless 0 \quad \Leftrightarrow \quad \mu \lesseqqgtr \mu_0,$$

stating that in case $\mu < \mu_0$ there arise no closed orbits and the real parts are negative implying local stability of the fixed point. In case $\mu > \mu_0$, there exist closed orbits and the real parts become positive implying local instability of the fixed point. For $\mu = \mu_0$, the real parts vanish implying the existence of a pair of pure imaginary roots $\theta = \pm\sqrt{a_2}i$ leading to the emergence of closed orbits.

Considering the second part *H.2*[27] of the Hopf bifurcation existence theorem, it holds that

$$\left.\frac{d\,Re\,\theta(\mu)}{d\,\mu}\right|_{\mu=\mu_0} = \left.\frac{d(-\frac{1}{2}\,a_1)}{d\left(\frac{\partial z}{\partial \rho}\right)}\right|_{\mu=\mu_0} = -\frac{1}{2}\left(-\frac{\partial G_1}{\partial \lambda} - \left(\frac{\partial z}{\partial \rho} + \frac{\partial z}{\partial \sigma^*}\frac{\partial \sigma^*}{\partial \rho}\right)\right) = \frac{1}{2} \quad > 0,$$

stating that condition *H.2* is fulfilled, and implying that there exist closed orbits according to the Hopf bifurcation existence theorem.

Regarding stability properties of the closed orbits emerging from variations in μ, it can be shown that the present case illustrated in figure 5.6 is subject to a *supercritical Hopf bifurcation*[28], being characterized firstly, by the absence of closed orbits and local stability of the fixed point in case $\mu < \mu_0$, and secondly, by the emergence of closed orbits

[27] See section 4.4.4.

[28] For details, see 4.4.4.

being attractors, i.e. limit cycles, and local instability of the fixed point in case $\mu > \mu_0$. Though stability properties of local bifurcations generally can only be investigated by the use of normal forms, there are special cases in which general forms of demarcation curves, being described by parameterized functions and their relative position to other demarcation curves, can be used for analyzing the emergence of supercritical or subcritical Hopf bifurcations. It can be shown for example, that a supercritical Hopf bifurcation in $\mathbb{R}^2$, here in an (x_1, x_2) space, emerges if firstly, one of the demarcation curves, here $\dot{x}_1 = 0$, takes the form of a cubic polynomial of type

$$x_2(x_1) = -b_0 x_1^3 + b_1 x_1^2 \pm b_2 x_1 \pm b_3 \quad \text{where} \quad b_i > 0,$$

and parameter b_1 is chosen sufficiently small, and secondly, if the second demarcation curve, here $\dot{x}_2 = 0$, is steeper at the fixed point than demarcation curve $\dot{x}_1 = 0$ engendering only one fixed point.[29] Applying these conditions to the present case illustrated in figure 5.6, it can be seen that the $\dot{\rho} = 0$ demarcation curve can be described by a cubic polynomial of type

$$\lambda(\rho) = -b_0 \rho^3 + b_1 \rho^2 - b_2 \rho + b_3 \quad \text{where} \quad b_i > 0,$$

and that demarcation curve $\dot{\lambda} = 0$ is steeper at the fixed point D than the non-linear demarcation curve $\dot{\rho} = 0$.[30] Accordingly, the Hopf bifurcation emerging from the dynamic system 5.12 and 5.13 is supercritical, implying that for each parameter value $\mu > \mu_0$ there exists only one closed orbit around the unstable fixed point which is an attractor, i.e. for each $\mu > \mu_0$ there exists only one limit cycle to which all trajectories converge for $t \to \infty$, being illustrated in figure 5.6.

5.4.5 A Dynamic View of Financial Crises and Macroeconomic Fluctuations

The comparative static description of financial crises in section 5.3.2 has shown that the two "driving" forces during boom-bust cycles including financial crises are the foreign debt-asset ratio λ_d^*, i.e. capital flows, and the state of confidence parameter ρ. The static version however, has been only in a position to provide a qualitative description of financial crises by the use of the signs of partial derivatives, since there has been no possibility to determine formally the net effect of the two counteracting forces λ_d^* and ρ due to the absence of a formal description of why λ_d^* and ρ grow or decline by different rates during different stages of the business cycle. By way of contrast, the dynamic version of the model has been able to close this formal gap by deriving *endogenous* time paths for λ_d^* and ρ during different stages of business cycles.

Regarding the evolution of endogenous financial fragility and subsequently following financial crises in emerging markets, the dynamic analysis has to distinguish on the one hand, as the industrial country model, between "tranquil equilibrium business cycles" and cycles involving financial crises, and on the other hand, as opposed to the financial crisis model for industrialized countries, among different types of financial crises. Since

[29]For these conditions, see Wiggins (1990) chapter 3.1B, pp. 270-278, Lux (1992), p. 189, and Flaschel, Franke and Semmler (1997), chapter 3, pp. 33-60.

[30]The condition choosing b_1 sufficiently small is assumed as being fulfilled.

emerging markets' financial structure is characterized by a large stock of external debt and fixed exchange rate systems, it is possible that a domestic financial crisis including a domestic and perhaps international banking crisis can cause a currency crisis (twin crisis) in case foreign exchange reserves do not suffice to meet capital outflows, thereby deteriorating the original crisis due to increases in foreign interest payments and in the stock of foreign debt, reducing net worth. Accordingly, the following analysis distinguishes firstly, between cycles involving no financial crises and cycles generating financial distress, and secondly, between domestic financial crises without currency crises and twin crises.

5.4.5.1 The Emergence of Endogenous Long-Run Equilibrium Business Cycles

The dynamic version of the model being illustrated in figure 5.6 indicates that economies, after having been hit by an external shock, tend to converge in counterclockwise motions to a kind of "equilibrium business cycle" in the long-run with a constant amplitude indicated by the limit cycle. There are different possibilities of converging to the long-run equilibrium cycle depending on the initial condition, which hinges upon the size and the sign of the exogenous shock having catapulted the economy away from the limit cycle. If a shock catapults the dynamic system from a point on the limit cycle to the inner area of the limit cycle, e.g. to point F in figure 5.6, the system is going to converge with growing amplitudes to the limit cycle, where all amplitudes during the convergence process are smaller than the equilibrium amplitude on the limit cycle. If, by way of contrast, an exogenous shocks catapults the economy to the outer area of the limit cycle, e.g. to point E in figure 5.6, the economy converges with declining amplitudes to the limit cycle, where all amplitudes during the convergence process are larger than the limit cycle's amplitude. As a result, there are three possible ways of dynamic behaviour of economies predicted by the model (on the limit cycle, converging from the outer region, converging from the inner region), which have to be compared with the stylized facts of financial crises and business cycles in order to determine the feasible regions of the dynamic model.

Empirical studies of financial crises state that firstly, systemic financial crises are commonly linked to extensive boom-bust cycles being subject to much larger amplitudes in goods and financial markets than in "tranquil times", secondly, that not each business cycle generates a financial crisis, thirdly, that financial crises are often preceded by a large exogenous shock, as e.g. a liberalization shock or technology shock, and fourthly, that crisis frequency in emerging market countries is higher than in industrial countries which could be explained by the first stylized fact since empirical studies of business cycles have shown that business cycles in emerging market countries are subject to higher amplitudes regarding goods and financial market fluctuations than business cycles in industrial countries. Summing up, there exist periods of "tranquil" business cycles without any disruptions in financial markets in which goods and financial market variables fluctuate "normally", but there arise also periods with business cycles being characterized by large fluctuations in goods and financial markets, and by the emergence of financial crises. In most cases, after the occurrence of a severe financial crisis, economies tend to recover to tranquil period business cycle fluctuations, whereas the recovery period can be very long.

Applying these empirical observations to the dynamic version of the model illustrated in figure 5.7, which is a modified version of figure 5.6, it is obvious that the dynamically stable limit cycle indicated by points A, B, C, D and E describes business fluctuations

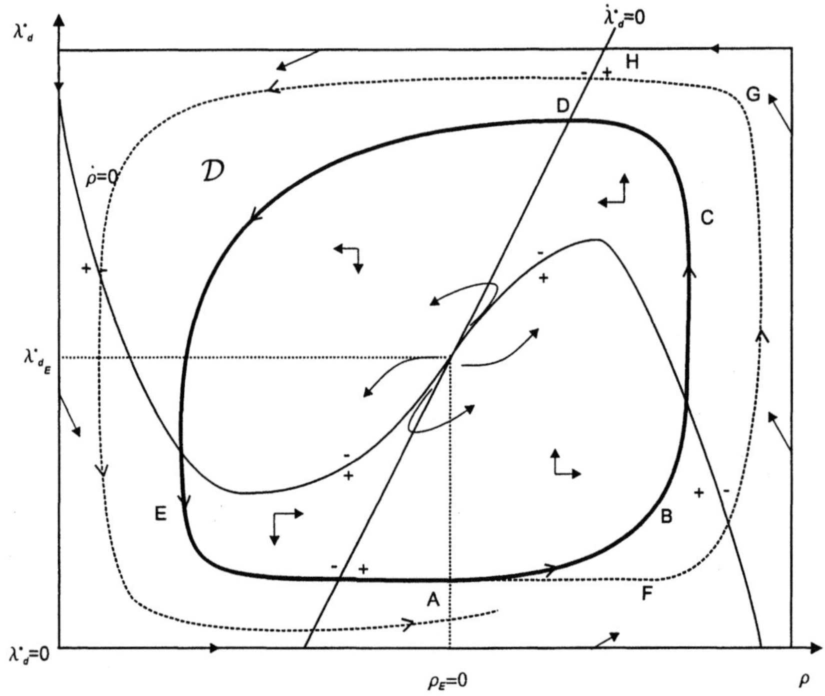

Figure 5.7: Financial Crisis I: Domestic Financial Crisis without Currency Crisis

during tranquil periods which do not lead to systemic financial crises. Therefore, the limit cycle in figure 5.7 can be viewed as an equilibrium business cycle to which economies converge in the long run. It must be noted however, that this equilibrium cycle also contains overborrowing and financial strains on the upper turning point, yet to a much lesser extent than cycles including financial crises.

The inner area of the limit cycle, which is characterized by increasing fluctuations whose amplitudes are however smaller than those of the equilibrium business cycle, has to be excluded from the feasible region, since there is no correspondence with the stylized facts displaying a change between tranquil equilibrium cycles with modest and constant amplitudes and extensive boom-bust cycles with much larger amplitudes leading to financial crises. By way of contrast, the area between the limit cycle and the outer bounds of the invariant set $\mathcal{D}$ contains business cycles with much larger amplitudes than equilibrium fluctuations. These cycles are characterized by much heavier overborrowing during the upswing, leading to high financial fragility and possibly to systemic financial crises during the bust phase. However, even in case an extensive business cycle has caused a systemic financial crisis, economies tend to converge back to the equilibrium business cycle.

Summing up, there arise three important dynamic properties out of the model. Firstly, the feasible region of the model is defined by the invariant set $\mathcal{D}$ without the inner area of the limit cycle. Secondly, economies tend to converge to an equilibrium business cycle being characterized by a normal functioning of goods and financial markets. Thirdly, extensive boom-bust cycles including systemic financial crises can only be induced by a large external shock, i.e. economies tend to be dynamically or cyclically stable in the long run.

In order to elaborate the differences between cycles involving financial crises and tranquil time business cycles, the dynamic analysis begins with an explanation of the different stages of the stylized equilibrium business cycle serving as a reference path for non-equilibrium cycles. The equilibrium business cycle starts in point A after the last downturn has ended. The boom phase begins with domestic and foreign agents realizing that economic fundamentals (λ_d^* and σ^*) have returned to historical positive levels, causing profit expectations to rise which leads to higher investment demand and slowly rising capital inflows for investment finance. During this early stage of the boom phase, new investment is mainly financed by profits since profit expectations and investment demand have not gained speed yet which would require to rely mainly on external finance. By making use of the comparative static results according to table 5.1, the early boom phase is marked by an increase in $u, r, \hat{p}, q$ and b, and by a decline in j^* and i due to the much faster and larger increase in ρ than in λ_d^*. A prosperous economic development causes profit expectations to rise very quickly, which can be justified by positive fundamental data (low λ_d^* and high σ^*), but which is also the consequence of an increased reliance on general market sentiments since chartist behaviour starts to dominate the expectation formation scheme. Though the growth rate of capital inflows during the boom phase, being described by the path from A to B, is less than profit expectations' growth rate, the growth of capital inflows accelerates.

Point B marks the beginning of the overborrowing process, which is however, characterized by much lower foreign debt-asset ratios than business cycles generating systemic financial crises. During the early stage of the overborrowing phase, profit expectations grow much faster than actual profits, implying that the large rise in investment demand has to be financed by an extensive increase in the fraction of external finance. The rise in external finance leads to a decrease in the growth rate or even to a stagnation of actual profits owing to rising debt costs. Despite the fact that the growth rate of r is decreasing, or even becoming zero, the state of confidence increases further, since on the one hand, the expectation formation scheme is dominated by chartist type behaviour, and on the other hand, economic fundamentals provide a neutral picture with both λ_d^* and σ^* increasing[31], leading not to a unequivocal deterioration of fundamental data. According to the comparative-static results in table 5.1, the overborrowing phase is marked by increases in $u, \hat{p}, q$ and b, declines in j^* and i, and by a constant value in r.

The latter stage of the overborrowing phase leading to the upper upper turning point being indicated by point C, is characterized by an accelerating increase in the foreign debt-asset ratio and by a slow down in the growth rate of profit expectations, driving the economy in a state of "irrational" behaviour since the actual profit rate declines due to rising debt costs, causing σ^* to shrink considerably, whereas profit expectations are going to rise further since the expectation formation scheme is dominated by chartist type behaviour. In terms of the comparative-static version of the model, the path to the upper turning point C is described by augmentations in $u, \hat{p}, q$, and declines in r, j^* and

[31] An increase in σ^* results from r remaining constant, $\hat{p}$ increasing and $\beta(\rho)$ decreasing.

i. Overall normalized foreign reserves $\lambda_d^* + b$ increase due to a sharp rise in λ_d^*, whereas b declines due to rising current account deficits caused by a real overvaluation of the domestic currency due to accelerating domestic inflation.

At the upper turning point C, the growth in profit expectations comes to halt at the maximum level of ρ when investors realize on the one hand, that ρ has approached or even exceeded the upper bound of the normal range, and on the other hand that there has been a growing trade-off between r^e and r which cannot be maintained further. Consequently, there follows a sudden switch in the expectation formation scheme from market sentiment-based to fundamental data-based causing a decline in ρ, which leads to a drop in asset prices being indicated by a fall in q, and to rises in j^* and i according to table 5.1 since collateral and net worth positions have deteriorated. The switch of expectations, as well as the drop in asset prices at C can be caused by very small but *endogenous* triggering events, like e.g. a downgrading of an important business firm or bank by international rating agencies, or by bankruptcies or illiquidity among some firms or financial institutions. Shrinking collateral values and increasing default risk lead to a sharp decline in capital inflows, and to a much lower, but still positive, growth rate of the foreign debt asset ratio. The rise in the foreign debt-asset ratio on the path from point C to D results mainly from a decline in the profit rate leading, according to equation 5.12, to a liquidity squeeze which is financed by increasing (short-term) foreign debt. By way of contrast, if creditors are not willing to increase debt to finance due payment commitments, banks and business firms are going to become illiquid or even insolvent. Yet, in comparison with systemic financial crises, there are no widespread bankruptcies following the decline in asset prices on path C to D, since the extent of the decline is much smaller and financial intermediaries, as well as business firms are much less indebted, and therefore much less exposed to asset price volatility.

The downswing starts in point D being characterized firstly, by expectations being dominated again by pessimistic chartist type behaviour, and secondly, by firms and foreign financial institutions beginning to deleverage their balance sheets, causing capital outflows, i.e. a reduction in λ_d^*. The viability of the fixed exchange rate system during this stage depends on the level of overall normalized foreign reserves $\lambda_d^* + b$. If large current account deficits during the boom phase have led to $b < 0$, i.e. in case imports were financed by capital inflows, a sharp and sufficient reduction in foreign loans could give rise to a currency crisis since the central bank could possibly not be able to meet the demand for foreign reserves. However, since equilibrium business cycles do not lead to excessive real sector expansion and inflation during the boom phase, the real exchange rate's deterioration does not cause historical high current account deficits and massive losses of international reserves. Furthermore, since the drop in asset prices and the increase in default risk is moderate in comparison with systemic financial crises, there will be no withdrawal of foreign loans to a large extent. Consequently, during the bust phase of an equilibrium business cycle, the central bank is able to meet all capital outflows, thereby maintaining the fixed exchange rate system. Though the reduction of the foreign debt-asset ratio would lead ceteris paribus to a macroeconomic expansion, there is an economic contraction since the chartist-dominated decline in ρ is larger than the decline in λ_d^*, causing according to table 5.1 a reduction in $u, r, \hat{p}, q$ and b, and a further rise in j^* and i. The duration of the bust cycle depends on how fast balance sheets can be restructured, and thereby on the downward amplitude of profit expectations.

The recovery phase is going to begin in case foreign and domestic investors consider firms' balance sheets as having returned to a sustainable level. The expectation formation scheme again switches from pessimistic chartist type behaviour having led to an underestimation of the actual profit rate, i.e. $r^e < r$, to fundamental data-based, since on the one hand, ρ has moved to the lower bound of the normal range, and on the other hand, economic fundamentals (λ_d^* and σ^*) have returned to "sound" levels according to investors' perception. The time path to the starting point of a new business cycle, i.e. path E to A, is marked by an almost constant foreign debt-asset ratio and fast increasing expectations which again are increasingly based on general market sentiments.

5.4.5.2 Domestic Financial Crisis without Currency Crisis

In contrast to equilibrium business cycles, excessive boom-bust cycles leading to systemic financial crises generally start with a positive exogenous shock, increasing profit expectations substantially after the last business cycle has ended, catapulting the economy from point A in figure 5.7 to point F. Examples for such positive shocks in the post Bretton-Woods era in emerging market countries have been large-scale populistic, orthodox and heterodox stabilization and liberalization programs in the 1970s, followed by Washington Consensus-based liberalization programs in the late 1980s and early 1990s in order to overcome the negative repercussions of the international debt crisis in 1982-1983 which had led to liberalization reversals, e.g. by reimposing capital controls.[32] Liberalization policies have been generally believed to improve economic efficiency by a better allocation of resources leading to an acceleration in growth, productivity and profitability. Thus, liberalization policies generally cause a sharp rise in profit expectations and in (international and domestic) investors' willingness to provide sufficient external financial means to finance the expansion process. Positive shocks in the form of the introduction of a new technology regime represent another source of rising profit expectations.

The boom phase of an extensive boom-bust cycle being induced by a shift from point A to point F in figure 5.7 is characterized by the same development of variables as during the equilibrium cycle's boom period. However, the initial change of all variables ,and thereby their amplitude during the dynamic adjustment process is much larger, being indicated by the dotted trajectory starting in point A and moving through point F. Since profit expectations have risen substantially, which is expressed in a large rise in ρ combined with a very low λ_d^* and a sustainable σ^*, there is a much greater expansion in investment, and consequently in actual profits than during an equilibrium business cycle, validating the initial increase in profit expectations. The expectation formation scheme tends to switch very fast from fundamental-based to general market sentiment-based. As most of investment is financed by profits, capital inflows tend to be very modest at the outset of the boom phase. As a result, a large increase in ρ and a moderate increase in λ_d^* lead to sharp increases in $u, r, \hat{p}, q$ and b, leading to very favourable financial market conditions, i.e. to large declines in j^* and i.

The overborrowing phase starts much earlier and to a much larger extent than on the equilibrium cycle, requiring to finance investment, though there is an large rise in actual profits, by an increasing amount of external debt since profit expectations grow much

[32]An excellent overview of different kinds of stabilization programs in the 1970s and 1980s can be found in Agénor and Montiel (1999), chapter 10.

faster than actual profits. The early stage of the overborrowing phase is characterized firstly, by capital inflow's growth rate accelerating which slows down the increase in the profit rate, and secondly, by profit expectations growing much faster than the degree of indebtedness due to the predominance of chartist type behaviour. Accordingly, there is a further large rise in $u, r, \hat{p}, q$ and b, and a decline in j^* and i.

During the latter overborrowing phase leading to the upper turning point, debt-asset ratios reach historical high levels which are mainly caused by "mania" expectations, driving the economy in a state of "irrational excuberance" since the profit rate declines substantially due to rising debt costs, whereas indebtedness and profit expectations keep on growing though economic fundamentals (large λ_d^* and low σ^*) would indicate a downward revision of profit expectations. Due to the fact that the increase ρ dominates the increase in λ_d^*, there is a further rise in $u, \hat{p}, q$ and another decline in j^* and i, whereas r deteriorates substantially. Normalized international reserves $\lambda_d^* + b$ tend to increase due to the large rise in λ_d^* albeit b decreases considerably owing to historical high current account deficits which are caused by a large real overvaluation of the domestic currency hinging upon a large increase in domestic inflation.

The upper turning point G is reached when domestic and international investors realize that profit expectations cannot be validated by actual profits since ρ has moved significantly out of the normal range, and σ^* and λ_d^* have reached historical poor levels. Accordingly, there is a quick switch from chartist type to fundamental data type behaviour as to the formation of expectations, leading to the burst of the asset price bubble. As during tranquil cycles, the triggering events of the wake-up call may be *endogenous* failures of important banks or firms, as well as a downgrading by international rating agencies. A rise in international interest rates leading to a further decline in r and σ^* may be also a trigger for the sudden fall in ρ. The rise in international interest rates can be viewed either as an exogenous shock, or as an endogenous reaction on deteriorating liquidity and solvency positions. However, even if the rise in international interest rates is considered as being an exogenous event, the endogenous collapse of expectations would have occurred as well without this kind of exogenous shock. Consequently, the rise in international interest rates only accelerates the unavoidable *endogenous* collapse of ρ, and is *not* in a position to cause a widespread financial crisis alone. The burst of the asset price bubble leads to a sudden decline in q and to sharp rises in j^* and i, leading to a sharp fall in r which causes widespread and sudden bankruptcy and illiquidity among firms. The large increase in nonperforming loans triggers a domestic and possibly an international banking crisis since banks' net worth and cash flow deteriorate significantly. Accordingly, capital inflows come to a sudden stop since default risk has increased and international investors start to withdraw their funds, causing liquidity and solvency problems for domestic firms due to the fact that meeting due payment obligations requires a fire-sale of assets since rolling-over or increasing debt has become impossible due to a sharp reduction in credit markets' liquidity. The sudden stop in capital inflows is indicated by a sharp reduction of the growth rate of λ_d^* on path GH, leading to widespread illiquidity and insolvency since due payment commitments cannot be rolled-over. By way of contrast, a drop in profit expectations on the upper turning point of an equilibrium business cycle allows for an increase in λ_d^* to meet due payment obligations which is indicated by path CD.

The bust phase beginning at point H in figure 5.7 is marked by pessimistic chartist type behaviour gaining momentum, and by large capital outflows causing widespread illiquidity and bankruptcy. Since the fall in λ_d^* is much smaller than the drop in ρ, there is a widespread economic contraction, i.e. according to table 5.1, there is a large decline in $u, r, \hat{p}, q$ and b, and a sharp rise in j^* and i reflecting tight financial market conditions. The viability of the fixed exchange rate systems depends on the level of b, hinging upon the amount of accumulated current account deficits during the boom and the overborrowing process. If large current account deficits have led to $b < 0$, i.e. in case current account deficits have been financed by capital inflows in the form of foreign loans, and foreign investors withdraw an amount which is larger than $\lambda_d^* + b$ where $b < 0$, the central bank is forced to abandon the fixed parity since it is not able to meet the demand for foreign currency. Since the model is not given in explicit form, there is no possibility to determine the time of the currency collapse, as well as the critical amount of reserves like e.g. in first generation currency crisis models.[33] Yet, in order to elaborate the differences between a financial crisis without a currency crises and a twin crises, it is assumed in the present case that though there arose current account deficits in the past, the central bank is able to meet all capital outflows even if there is no monetary contraction at point H which would cushion the fall in reserves.

In case the central bank tries to limit capital outflows by a monetary contraction, a decline in h or m could only slow down the decrease in b, since under fixed exchange rates there is no possibility to influence any other real or financial market variable according to table 5.1, thereby having no effect on ρ and λ_d^*. As a result, there is no possibility to induce a downward jump from point H to a trajectory lying nearer to the equilibrium cycle by contractionary monetary policy. Likewise, a domestic monetary expansion is not able to induce a downward movement from point H since there is no possibility to influence the foreign debt burden by domestic monetary policy. In graphical terms, the only effects of changes in h and m are a change of the current trajectory's slope in point H, as well as a change of both demarcation curves which are still not going to be analyzed.

Though there is no debt increase induced by a forced devaluation in the present case, the economy enters a severe recession or even a depression accompanied by deflationary spirals, leading to an increase in the real debt burden. Even if the central bank abandoned the fixed parity in order to regain monetary independence, a recovery induced by a monetary expansion would be very unlikely due to a liquidity trap situation which would be additionally amplified by an increase in the foreign debt burden due to a devaluation of the domestic currency. In this case, overindebted balance sheets prevent an economic upswing since there is no sufficient supply of credit to finance new investment projects due to an absence of financial markets' willingness, or due to disintermediation caused by large-scale bankruptcies among domestic and international banks.

The duration of the bust phase in the present case is much longer than on the equilibrium cycle, since on the one hand, foreign indebtedness is much higher which requires a longer period of balance sheet restructuring, and on the other hand, profit expectations are far more depressed by pessimistic chartist behaviour. The recovery phase begins if λ_d^* and σ^* have returned to sustainable levels from investors' perspective who realize that their expectations had been too pessimistic in the past. After having conceived that there has been a steady underestimation of actual profits, i.e. $r^e < r$, the expectation formation

[33]By way of contrast, the linear calibration model for emerging markets, being an explicit example of the present model, which is going to be analyzed in chapter 6, is able to determine the time of the collapse as well as the critical stock of foreign exchange reserves.

scheme switches quickly from pessimistic chartist behaviour to fundamental data-based behaviour and a new cycle can begin which however, is subject to a lower amplitude than the financial crisis cycle in case there are no exogenous shocks.

5.4.5.3 The Occurrence of a Twin Crisis

This paragraph examines the long-run dynamics in case the central bank is not able to maintain the fixed exchange rate at the upper turning point due to lacking foreign exchange reserves which is depicted in figure 5.8 being a modified version of figure 5.7. The boom and the overborrowing phase of the twin crisis case correspond to the domestic financial crisis case as to the behaviour of λ_d^* and ρ, and consequently, as to the development of all other endogenous variables according to table 5.1. Likewise, it is assumed that large current account deficits having been financed by capital inflows have led to a large depletion of reserves, i.e. it holds that $b < 0$ when the system reaches the end of the overborrowing phase. At the upper turning point however, when the asset bubble bursts and capital flight begins, it is assumed that foreign investors' withdrawals exceed the stock of normalized reserves $\lambda_d^* + b$ where $b < 0$, leading to a suspension of the fixed parity. Lacking international reserves can stem firstly, from larger capital outflows at the upper turning point due to a higher risk aversion of investors, secondly, from larger current deficits during the upswing, and thirdly, from a smaller initial stock of international reserves b at the outset of the cycle.

Regarding currency crises, there are several alternative post-collapse regimes, like e.g. a unique devaluation or a flexible exchange rate regime following the speculative attack. For the present case, it is assumed that in case a currency crisis occurs, the central bank carries out a unique devaluation, which can be justified by the fact that the transition to a fully flexible regime would make the economy more susceptible to fluctuations in the stock of foreign debt valued in domestic currency. A unique devaluation corresponds to a permanent increase in parameter $\hat{s}$ from $\hat{s} = 0$ to $\hat{s} > 0$ in the model. It must be noted that a permanent value of $\hat{s} > 0$ over more than one period does not correspond to a devaluation in each period following the speculative attack since the growth rate of s is related to an initial value of $\bar{s} = 1$. Accordingly, a constant devaluation rate in each period would correspond to increasing values in $\hat{s}$ for each period.

In order to elaborate the global dynamics of the system in case of a devaluation, the influence of changes in $\hat{s}$ on the slopes of the two demarcation curves $\dot{\lambda}_d^* = G_1(\lambda_d^*, \rho) = 0$ and $\dot{\rho} = G_2(\lambda_d^*, \rho) = 0$ has to be investigated firstly. According to equation 5.14, and by table 5.1, the change of the slope of demarcation curve $\dot{\lambda}_d^* = G_1(\lambda_d^*, \rho) = 0$ is given by

$$\frac{d\left(\frac{d\lambda_d^*}{d\rho}\right)_{G_1}}{d\hat{s}} = -\frac{\partial\left(\frac{\partial G_1}{\partial \rho}\right)}{\partial \hat{s}} \cdot \frac{1}{\left(\frac{\partial G_1}{\partial \lambda_d^*}\right)} + \frac{\left(\frac{\partial G_1}{\partial \rho}\right)}{\left(\frac{\partial G_1}{\partial \lambda_d^*}\right)^2} \cdot \frac{\partial\left(\frac{\partial G_1}{\partial \lambda_d^*}\right)}{\partial \hat{s}} \gtreqless 0,$$

because

$$\frac{\partial\left(\frac{\partial G_1}{\partial \rho}\right)}{\partial \hat{s}} = -\frac{\partial \lambda_d^*}{\partial \hat{s}} \frac{d\eta}{dq} \frac{\partial q}{\partial \rho} < 0,$$

and

$$\frac{\partial\left(\frac{\partial G_1}{\partial \lambda_d^*}\right)}{\partial \hat{s}} = -\frac{d\eta}{dq}\frac{\partial q}{\partial \hat{s}} + 1 - \frac{\partial \hat{p}}{\partial \hat{s}} - \frac{\partial \lambda_d^*}{\partial \hat{s}}\frac{d\eta}{dq}\frac{\partial q}{\partial \lambda_d^*} + (1-\lambda_d^*)\frac{d\eta}{dq}\frac{\partial\left(\frac{\partial q}{\partial \lambda_d^*}\right)}{\partial \hat{s}}$$
$$- s_r \frac{\partial\left(\frac{\partial r}{\partial \lambda_d^*}\right)}{\partial \hat{s}} - \frac{\partial \lambda_d^*}{\partial \hat{s}}\frac{\partial \hat{p}}{\partial \lambda_d^*} - \lambda_d^* \frac{\partial\left(\frac{\partial \hat{p}}{\partial \lambda_d^*}\right)}{\partial \hat{s}} \gtreqless 0,$$

being positive if it holds that

$$-\frac{d\eta}{dq}\frac{\partial q}{\partial \hat{s}} + 1 - \frac{\partial \hat{p}}{\partial \hat{s}} - \frac{\partial \lambda_d^*}{\partial \hat{s}}\frac{d\eta}{dq}\frac{\partial q}{\partial \lambda_d^*} - s_r \frac{\partial\left(\frac{\partial r}{\partial \lambda_d^*}\right)}{\partial \hat{s}} - \frac{\partial \lambda_d^*}{\partial \hat{s}}\frac{\partial \hat{p}}{\partial \lambda_d^*} - \lambda_d^* \frac{\partial\left(\frac{\partial \hat{p}}{\partial \lambda_d^*}\right)}{\partial \hat{s}} > \left|(1-\lambda_d^*)\frac{d\eta}{dq}\frac{\partial\left(\frac{\partial q}{\partial \lambda_d^*}\right)}{\partial \hat{s}}\right|,$$ [34]

which is assumed to be fulfilled in the present case. As a result, there is no possibility to determine an unequivocal sign for the change of the slope of demarcation curve $\dot{\lambda}_d^* = G_1(\lambda_d^*, \rho) = 0$, so that the change of dynamics cannot be analyzed without making use of assumptions.

It seems reasonable to assume that the slope of demarcation curve $\dot{\lambda}_d^* = G_1(\lambda_d^*, \rho) = 0$ cannot become negative, which would imply a change of the local dynamics from instability to stability, provided that the slope of demarcation curve $\dot{\rho} = G_2(\lambda_d^*, \rho) = 0$ remains positive which is going to be proved later on, since empirical evidence shows that economies hit by twin crisis do not converge to a stable long-run fixed point equilibrium. Consequently, demarcation curve $\dot{\lambda}_d^* = G_1(\lambda_d^*, \rho) = 0$ can only take values from zero to plus infinity. However, for reasons of simplicity it is assumed that the slope of demarcation curve $\dot{\lambda}_d^* = G_1(\lambda_d^*, \rho) = 0$ does not change in case of changes in $\hat{s}$, i.e. formally it holds that

$$\frac{d\left(\frac{d\lambda_d^*}{d\rho}\right)_{G_1}}{d\hat{s}} = -\frac{\partial\left(\frac{\partial G_1}{\partial \rho}\right)}{\partial \hat{s}}\frac{1}{\left(\frac{\partial G_1}{\partial \lambda_d^*}\right)} + \frac{\left(\frac{\partial G_1}{\partial \rho}\right)}{\left(\frac{\partial G_1}{\partial \lambda_d^*}\right)^2}\frac{\partial\left(\frac{\partial G_1}{\partial \lambda_d^*}\right)}{\partial \hat{s}} = 0,$$

which is indicated in figure 5.8 by demarcation curve $\dot{\lambda}_d^* = G_1(\lambda_d^*, \rho) = 0$ being valid for $\hat{s} = 0$ and $\hat{s} > 0$.

According to equation 5.15, and by table 5.1, the change of the slope of demarcation curve $\dot{\rho} = G_2(\lambda_d^*, \rho) = 0$ for variations in $\hat{s}$ is given formally by

$$\frac{d\left(\frac{d\lambda_d^*}{d\rho}\right)_{G_2}}{d\hat{s}} = -\frac{\partial\left(\frac{\partial G_2}{\partial \rho}\right)}{\partial \hat{s}}\frac{1}{\left(\frac{\partial G_2}{\partial \lambda_d^*}\right)} + \frac{\left(\frac{\partial G_2}{\partial \rho}\right)}{\left(\frac{\partial G_2}{\partial \lambda_d^*}\right)^2}\frac{\partial\left(\frac{\partial G_2}{\partial \lambda_d^*}\right)}{\partial \hat{s}},$$

[34]Note that it holds that

$$\frac{\partial\left(\frac{\partial q}{\partial \lambda_d^*}\right)}{\partial \hat{s}} = -m\,\lambda_{j\cdot}^{*S} < 0, \qquad \frac{\partial\left(\frac{\partial r}{\partial \lambda_d^*}\right)}{\partial \hat{s}} = m\,(-\lambda_{j\cdot}^{*S} + \lambda_q^{*S}) < 0, \qquad \frac{\partial\left(\frac{\partial \hat{p}}{\partial \lambda_d^*}\right)}{\partial \hat{s}} = -m\,\eta_q\,\lambda_{j\cdot}^{*S}\,\psi_u < 0,$$

which can be derived by differentiating the relevant partial derivatives given in section 5.7 with respect to $\hat{s}$.

which, by taking into consideration that

$$\frac{\partial\left(\frac{\partial G_2}{\partial \rho}\right)}{\partial \hat{s}} = \frac{\partial\left(\frac{\partial z}{\partial \rho}\right)}{\partial \hat{s}} + \frac{\partial\left(\frac{\partial z}{\partial \sigma^*}\right)}{\partial \hat{s}}\frac{\partial \sigma^*}{\partial \rho} + \frac{\partial\left(\frac{\partial \sigma^*}{\partial \rho}\right)}{\partial \hat{s}}\frac{\partial z}{\partial \rho} = 0, \text{ [35]}$$

and

$$\frac{\partial\left(\frac{\partial G_2}{\partial \lambda_d^*}\right)}{\partial \hat{s}} = \frac{\partial\left(\frac{\partial z}{\partial \lambda_d^*}\right)}{\partial \hat{s}} + \frac{\partial z}{\partial \sigma^*}\frac{\partial\left(\frac{\partial \sigma^*}{\partial \lambda_d^*}\right)}{\partial \hat{s}} < 0, \text{ [36]}$$

can be simplified into the expression

$$\frac{d\left(\frac{d\lambda_d^*}{d\rho}\right)_{G_2}}{d\hat{s}} = \frac{\overbrace{\left(\frac{\partial G_2}{\partial \rho}\right)}^{-,0,+}}{\underbrace{\left(\frac{\partial G_2}{\partial \lambda_d^*}\right)^2}_{+}} \cdot \underbrace{\frac{\partial\left(\frac{\partial G_2}{\partial \lambda_d^*}\right)}{\partial \hat{s}}}_{-} \gtreqless 0,$$

whose sign is dependent on the position of ρ, i.e. whether ρ lies inside or outside the normal range, which is represented by the sign of derivative $\partial G_2/\partial \rho$. Accordingly, in case of a devaluation, i.e. $\hat{s} > 0$, the demarcation curve becomes flatter over the entire range being depicted in figure 5.8, where the dotted line represents the demarcation curve before the devaluation $\dot{\rho}_1 = 0\,(\hat{s} = 0)$, and the solid line the demarcation curve after the devaluation has taken place $\dot{\rho}_2 = 0\,(\hat{s} > 0)$.

The global dynamics in case of a devaluation occurring at the upper turning point are depicted in figure 5.8 which is an extended version of figure 5.7. Since the boom and the overborrowing phase of the twin crisis case coincide with the domestic financial crisis case, figure 5.8 contains both types of global dynamics where the solid lines refer to the twin crisis case and the dotted lines refer to the domestic financial crisis case. In case there is no devaluation at the upper turning point, the boom-bust cycle containing a systemic domestic financial crisis follows time path A, F, G, K converging in the long-run to the equilibrium business cycle A, B, C as it was depicted in figure 5.7.

The first stage of the twin crisis case (boom and overborrowing phase) follows the same time path to the upper turning point A, F, G as the domestic financial crisis case. At the upper turning point G however, withdrawals of foreign investors exceed the stock of normalized international reserves $\lambda_d^* + b$ where $b < 0$, compelling monetary authorities to devalue the domestic currency, which is indicated by the jump from point G to H since the domestic value of foreign debt increases discontinuously by $\hat{s}$ per cent. This kind of "foreign debt explosion" emerging from a devaluation of the home currency is equivalent to the Fisherian debt deflation process stemming from deflation of the domestic price level. At the moment of devaluation, there is also a switch from demarcation curve

[35]Note that it holds that $\frac{\partial\left(\frac{\partial z}{\partial \rho}\right)}{\partial \hat{s}} = 0$, $\frac{\partial\left(\frac{\partial z}{\partial \sigma^*}\right)}{\partial \hat{s}} = 0$, and $\frac{\partial\left(\frac{\partial \sigma^*}{\partial \rho}\right)}{\partial \hat{s}} = 0$, which can be derived from equations 5.9 and 5.10.

[36]Note that it holds that $\frac{\partial \frac{\partial z}{\partial \lambda_d^*}}{\partial \hat{s}} < 0$, and $\frac{\partial \frac{\partial \sigma^*}{\partial \lambda_d^*}}{\partial \hat{s}} = \frac{\partial \sigma^*}{\partial r}\frac{\frac{\partial r}{\partial \lambda_d^*}}{\partial \hat{s}} + \frac{\partial \sigma^*}{\partial \hat{p}}\frac{\partial \frac{\partial \hat{p}}{\partial \lambda_d^*}}{\partial \hat{s}} < 0$, which can be derived from equations 5.9 and 5.10.

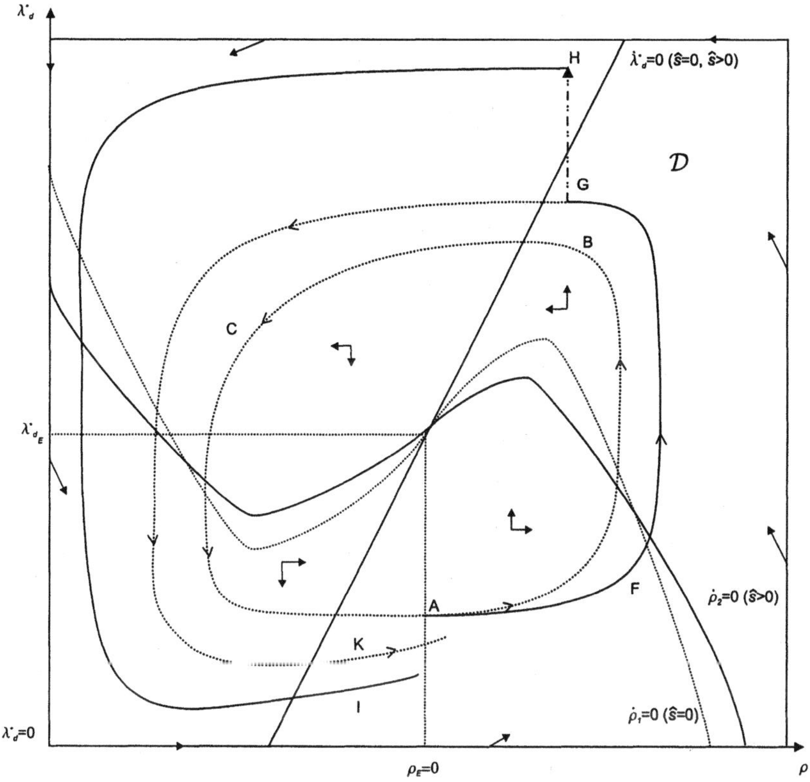

Figure 5.8: Financial Crisis II: Twin Crisis

$\dot{\rho}_1 = 0\,(\hat{s} = 0)$ to $\dot{\rho}_2 = 0\,(\hat{s} > 0)$. The post-devaluation dynamics (bust and recovery phase) are described by time path H, I, converging to a "new" equilibrium business cycle in the long-run which emerges from the change of demarcation curve $\dot{\rho} = G_2(\lambda_d^*, \rho) = 0$. However, regarding the characteristics of the new equilibrium business cycle, there is no analytical possibility to determine whether the new limit cycle being relevant for the post-devaluation phase of the twin crisis case becomes greater or smaller.

Comparing the post-devaluation bust and recovery phase with the domestic financial crisis case leads to the observation that, according to figure 5.8, after the occurrence of a currency crisis, the subsequent financial and real sector crisis is much more severe than a financial crisis without a speculative attack owing to a further and sudden devaluation-led squeeze in net worth and cash flow positions. Accordingly, restructuring of unsound balance sheets during the recovery phase lasts much longer than in the domestic financial crisis case since net worth positions are more depressed.

Regarding empirical examples, there arose two large boom-bust cycles having generated systemic financial crises in the post Bretton-Woods era in emerging market countries. The first one started in the mid 1970s and ended in the international debt crisis in the early 1980s. The recovery period lasted almost one decade due to long lasting negotiations regarding debt relief and debt restructuring. The second cycle began in the early and mid 1990s when emerging markets were again subject to huge capital inflows which led as well to systemic financial crises in Mexico (1994), Asia (1997/1998), Russia/Brazil (1998/1999) and in Argentina (1995 and 2000). The recovery phase of the second cycle has not been completed yet. Both cycles were preceded by large liberalization and stabilization efforts. In several countries, as e.g. in Mexico, there were no equilibrium cycles between the two boom-bust cycles indicating that after the economies had recovered from the first liberalization and stabilization shock in the late 1970s, there were hit by the Washington Consensus liberalization and stabilization shock in the late 1980s which gave rise to a new extensive cycle and systemic financial crises.

5.4.6 A Keynesian Perspective on Global Dynamics

After having studied the global dynamics under the combination of chartist-fundamentalist and long-run rational behaviour, there arises the important question of how global dynamics are going to change if the assumption of long-run rationality is given up. In such a pure chartist-fundamentalist or pure Keynesian world, investors' expectations are driven mainly by general market sentiments during the upswing and the downswing, and by fundamental data at the turning points. Hence, there exists no "rational" mechanism, as well as no "normal" corridor for the state of confidence ρ guaranteeing a reversal of expectations irrespective of fundamental data in case it can be observed that ρ has left the normal range.

In terms of the model, a pure Keynesian expectation formation scheme can be represented by a modified non-linear differential equation in the state of confidence ρ, given formally as

$$\dot{\rho} = G_2(\lambda_d^*, \rho) = z(\underset{+}{\rho}, \underset{+}{\sigma^*}, \underset{-}{\lambda_d^*}), \tag{5.16}$$

for which it holds that $\partial z/\partial \rho > 0$ over the entire range for ρ, but which becomes less positive the more ρ departs from its long-run equilibrium level $\rho_E = 0$ whose existence will be proved and outlined below. It still holds that $\partial z/\partial \sigma^* > 0$ and $\partial z/\partial \lambda_d^* < 0$ as in equation 5.13. Equation 5.16 results in an S-shaped demarcation curve $\dot{\rho} = G_2(\lambda_d^*, \rho) = 0$ having the largest positive slope near the intertemporal equilibrium $\rho_E = 0$, and becoming less positive for $\rho > 0$ and $\rho < 0$. The assumption that $\partial z/\partial \rho > 0$ declines with increasing difference $|\rho - \rho_E|$ represents investors' belief that the state of confidence ρ can increase or decrease infinitely, but is subject to changes $\dot{\rho}$ becoming smaller in absolute terms the more ρ departs from its equilibrium level $\rho_E = 0$. Regarding foreign debt dynamics, it is assumed that equation 5.12 still holds.

The dynamic system consisting of equations 5.16 and 5.12 generates two different types of global dynamics hinging upon the strength of the influence of the current state of confidence ρ on investors' change in profit expectations $\partial z/\partial \rho$. As in the Keynesian case for industrial countries discussed in section 4.4.6, the assumption of hypersensitive investors near the intertemporal equilibrium level, i.e. $\partial z/\partial \rho \gg 0$ near $\rho_E = 0$, generates multiple equilibria giving rise a limit set in the form of a saddle loop having being illustrated in figure 4.8. It has been argued that this form of global dynamics does not explain the stylized facts due to the existence of multiple equilibria.

Hence, to rule out multiple intertemporal equilibria it is necessary to assume that investor behave "normally" near the intertemporal equilibrium $\rho_E = 0$, i.e. it holds that $\partial z/\partial \rho > 0$ near $\rho_E = 0$. The assumption that the intertemporal equilibrium in a pure Keynesian world corresponds to the long-run rational expectations equilbrium $\rho_E = 0$ seems as a contradiction in terms at first sight. However, in a long-run state of $\rho_E \neq 0$, investors are going to revise their expectations leading to a shift in function $\dot{\rho} = z(\lambda_d^*, \sigma, \rho)$ and in demarcation curve $\dot{\rho} = G_2(\lambda_d^*, \rho) = 0$ even in a pure Keynesian world, since expectations have not been fulfilled by the actual development setting up a new dynamic process. Readjustments of expectations and thereby shifts in function $\dot{\rho} = z(\lambda_d^*, \sigma, \rho)$ and in demarcation curve $\dot{\rho} = G_2(\lambda_d^*, \rho) = 0$ are going to continue as long as profit expectations coincide with actual profits, justifying $\rho_E = 0$ as a reasonable assumption even in a Keynesian world.

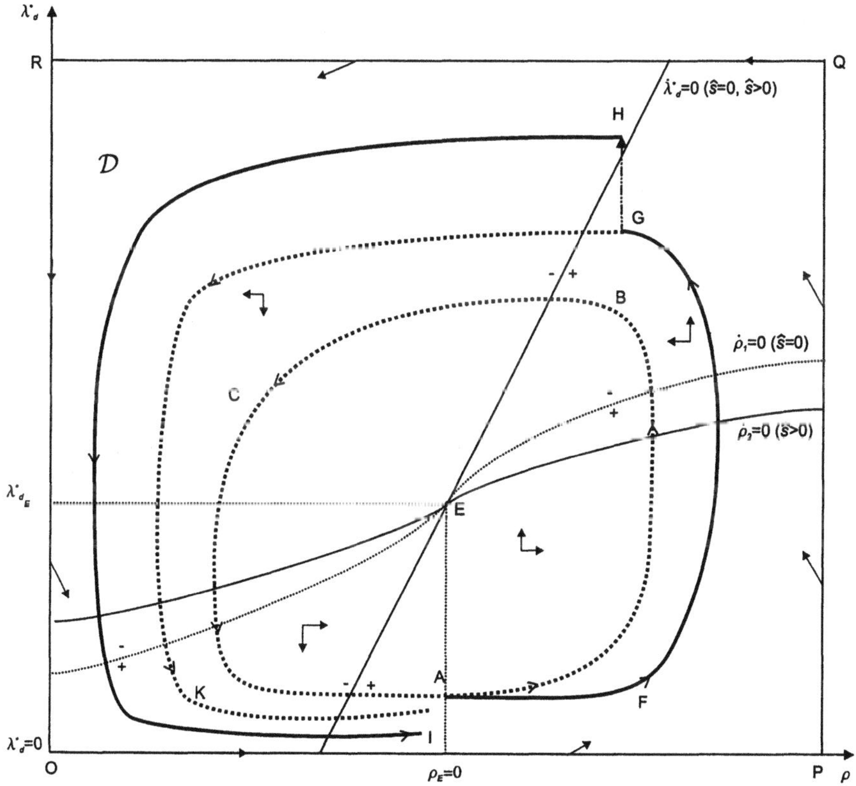

Figure 5.9: Financial Crises in a Pure Keynesian World with Normally Reacting Investors

The global dynamics under normally reacting investors for the emerging market case are depicted in figure 5.9. The dynamic system gives rise to the emergence of closed orbits by the Poincaré-Bendixon theorem because the local fixed point E is unstable, and rectangle $OPQR$ describes an invariant set $\mathcal{D}$ from which trajectories once having entered cannot escape; the boundary values of $\mathcal{D}$ can be justified economically as in section 5.4.4. As opposed to the case involving long-run rational behaviour, there is no possibility to determine the number of cycles without transforming the dynamical system into e.g. a Liénard equation. In case there evolve multiple closed orbits, the economy is cyclically unstable, as in the industrial country case in section 4.4.6, due to the existence of multiple equilibrium cycles with different amplitudes. As a result, there exist equilibrium cycles near equilibrium E with low amplitudes, as well as equilibrium cycles near the boundaries of compact set $\mathcal{D}$ engendering a financial crisis on each business cycle. Which of these equilibrium cycles is going to be realized is a matter of the initial condition of the system, so that exogenous shocks are able to catapult a cyclically stable economy with low amplitudes to an equilibrium cycle with high amplitudes and financial crises.

Though the case of multiple equilibrium cycles can arise theoretically from system 5.16 and 5.12, it is an unrealistic scenario from an empirical viewpoint since economies tend to be cyclically stable in the long-run, a fact which requires the existence of only one limit cycle being subject to low amplitudes and financial stability. However, even if there exists only one closed orbit as assumed and illustrated by the dotted limit cycle moving through points A, B and C in figure 5.9, there arise important differences to the case involving long-run rational behaviour. Firstly, it is obvious that an equilibrium business cycle in a Keynesian world has a greater amplitude regarding financial and real variables than in a world with long-run rationality. Secondly, at the upper turning point B, tensions in financial markets generating bankruptcies among firms and banks are much stronger, causing much deeper recessions or even depressions. Thus, it is not clear whether there exist equilibrium business cycles in the Keynesian case without systemic financial crises. Thirdly, if there arise no financial crises on the equilibrium cycle, economies are cyclically and financially stable in the long-run, so that financial crises can be only caused by exogenous shocks as in the case with long-run rational behaviour. However, in case the economy is hit by an exogenous shock giving rise to a financial crisis, the resulting boom-bust cycle is subject to a much larger amplitude, generates a much deeper financial crisis, and a much longer bust period than under long-run rational behaviour which is is illustrated in figure 5.9. The boom-bust cycle giving rise to a full-fledged financial crisis starts with a positive shock to the state of confidence ρ, catapulting the system from point A to point F. As there is no long-run rational behaviour, the boom and overborrowing phase last much longer and generate a much higher degree of financial fragility. Whether the economy enters a domestic financial crisis or a twin crisis depends, as in the case involving long-run rational behaviour, on the stock of foreign reserves at the upper turning point G. If withdrawals of foreign investors do not exceed the central bank's stock of foreign reserves, the fixed parity can be maintained, leading to a systemic domestic and possibly international banking crises, and to large-scale bankruptcies among domestic firms. This case is portrayed by the dotted semicircle starting in point G moving through point K and converging in the long-run to the limit cycle.

In case capital outflows exceed the stock of foreign exchange reserves at the upper turning point G, the fixed parity cannot be maintained any longer, leading to a twin crisis which induces several changes of the global dynamics. Firstly, in case $\hat{s} > 0$, demarcation curve $\dot{\rho}_1 = 0\,(\hat{s} = 0)$ becomes flatter, being indicated by demarcation curve $\dot{\rho}_2 = 0\,(\hat{s} > 0)$, whereas demarcation curve $\dot{\lambda}_d^* = 0$ is assumed not to change its slope according to the formal results in section 5.4.5. However, as outlined before, there is no possibility to derive any formal results regarding the characteristics of the "new" limit cycle stemming from the change of demarcation curve $\dot{\rho} = 0$. Secondly, there is a sudden increase in foreign debt in domestic currency terms being represented by the jump from point G to point H in figure 5.9. Thirdly, the bust phase being described by the solid semicircle starting in point H and moving through point I leads to a very deep depression having a much larger contractionary effect on the economy than a domestic financial crisis.

Summing up, a pure chartist-fundamentalist approach requires very restrictive assumptions in order to be consistent with the stylized facts of financial crises. Otherwise, there arise forms of aggregate instability which do not meet empirical regularities. Moreover, it cannot be proved formally whether the ad-hoc assumptions imposed, as e.g. the existence of a unique closed orbit, actually arise from dynamic system 5.16 and 5.12. By way of contrast, the assumption of long-run rational behaviour generates much stronger model results without making use of restrictive assumptions. However, a strict rational expectations approach cannot explain the emergence of endogenous cycles and endogenous financial fragility in the absence of exogenous shocks. Thus, only the combination of chartist-fundamentalist and rational behaviour is able to produce model results which are consistent with the stylized facts.

5.5 A Comparison with Standard Theory of Financial Crises

The advantages of the present model framework over standard theory of financial crises have been already outlined in detail in section 4.5 containing a formal description of standard models of the explanation of financial crises in industrial countries. This section enlarges the discussion of standard theory of financial crises on the one hand, by applying crisis models which were developed for industrial countries to emerging market economies, and on the other hand, by focusing on standard theory which has been especially elaborated for emerging market countries.

The formal description of standard models of financial crises is carried out by the application of the comparative-static results according to table 5.1 though lots of standard approaches are modelled dynamically. However, a dynamic application of the present model to standard theory would not result in deeper basic insights as to the causes of financial crises, and would only complicate the formal analysis. It is obvious that the present model structure cannot reflect exactly the model structures of all standard approaches. Hence, if necessary, the following analysis falls back on other variables or parameters than in the original models to understand the basic logic. Models which have been already discussed in section 4.5 are only going to be outlined by the comparative-static version of the emerging market model without any further explanation of the basic model structure.

5.5.1 Inconsistent Macroeconomic Policy Models

The Absence of Financial Crises in Case of Deflationary Monetary Policy Under Fixed Exchange Rates. The application of Flood and Garber's (1981b) closed economy bank run model under deflationary monetary policy, having set out in section 4.5.1, to the emerging market country model shows that contractionary, or deflationary monetary policy engenders no financial crisis in an open economy under fixed exchange rates, as a reduction in high-powered money h leads to a compensating increase in foreign reserves b to the same amount because of $\partial b/\partial h = -1$, improving the stability of the fixed exchange rate system.[37] As there is no further impact of h on other real and financial sector variables in the model, validating the Mundell-Fleming result that monetary policy under fixed exchange rates is ineffective, there arises no possibility of bank runs which are induced by declining asset values of banks.

Currency Crises Triggering Bank Runs Due to Inflationary Monetary Policies Under Fixed Exchange Rates. The application of Flood and Garber's (1981a) closed economy bank run model under inflationary monetary policy, discussed in section 4.5.1, to the emerging market country model results in no banking crisis if expansionary monetary policies are moderate and do not lead to a breakdown of the the fixed exchange rate system, validating also the Mundell-Fleming result of the ineffectiveness of monetary policy under fixed exchange rates. If there is no currency crisis going to occur, an increase in h does only induce a decline in foreign exchange reserves b to the same amount as it holds that $\partial b/\partial h = -1$, leaving the money supply and all other real and financial market variables unchanged.

However, in case of overly excessive expansionary monetary policies, the fixed exchange rate system is going to collapse, inducing a twin crisis. Following the model results, a steady rise in h causes an enduring decline in b, which leads to a speculative attack and to a devaluation of the home currency, i.e. to a rise in $\hat{s}$, when, according the results of first-generation currency crises models, the flexible shadow exchange rate has increased to the level of the fixed exchange, or equivalently, when the stock of foreign exchange reserves $b + \lambda_d^*$ falls below a certain minimum threshold value. If the stock of foreign debt λ^* is comparatively high, the devaluation of the home currency is contractionary, leading to a domestic macroeconomic contraction, being associated with a decline in $u, r, \hat{p}, q$, and an increase in j^* due to shrinking collateral values and deteriorating liquidity positions. Furthermore, rising failures of firms possibly cause a domestic and international banking crisis. If there are widespread bankruptcies among firms and domestic banks, foreign investors are going to withdraw foreign loans, i.e. λ^* declines, which partly offsets the negative effects of the rise in $\hat{s}$. However, since investment is constrained by available credit, investment activity and the state of confidence ρ will decline, leading to a further macroeconomic contraction. A bank run can be a possible outcome even if there is a deposit insurance system in case accumulated losses by banks undermine the credibility of a bail out.

If, by way of contrast, the stock of foreign debt λ^* at the time of the breakdown of the fixed exchange rate system is comparatively low, a devaluation of the home currency leads to a macroeconomic expansion, improving collateral values and liquidity positions of

[37]For this result, see section 5.7.

firms and banks. Consequently, a devaluation can strengthen the stability of the financial system if balance sheets are not financially fragile.

First Generation Currency Crises Models. The application of Krugman's (1979) and Flood and Garber's (1984a) first generation currency crises models, having set out in section 4.5.1, to the emerging market country model leads to the same result as the application of Flood and Garber's (1981a) closed economy bank run model under inflationary monetary policy to open economy considerations, as in both cases financial crises are caused by overly excessive expansionary monetary policy.

Twin Crises Emerging From First Generation Currency Crises. In order to overcome the inability of first generation currency crises models to explain the occurrence of twin crises, latest models of inconsistent macroeconomic policies have started to consider explicitly the influence of the domestic banking sector on the transmission of financial crises. A prominent example is Buch and Heinrich's (1999) model, which enlarges Flood and Garber's first generation currency crisis approach (1984a) by the introduction of a domestic banking sector which grants loans to domestic firms in domestic currency, and finances itself mainly by taking foreign loans in foreign currency in international credit markets. The interest rate on foreign loans consists of a risk free international interest rate, plus the exchange rate's expected rate of change, plus a risk premium, depending negatively on banks' net worth. Banks' net worth position is determined by banks' profits which are negatively dependent on the interest rate on foreign loans. Accordingly, a rise/fall in banks' profits induces a rise/fall in net worth, leading to a fall/rise in the risk premium, and to a fall/rise in the interest rate on foreign loans, causing a further rise/fall in banks' profits.

A banking crisis, i.e. a sharp reduction in banks' net worth induced by a sharp fall in banks' profits, can be caused, firstly, by an exogenous increase in the international risk free interest rate, secondly, by depreciation expectations of the domestic currency, and thirdly, by a rise in the risk premium. Though the model considers explicitly exogenous foreign interest rate shocks as a cause of financial crises, Buch and Heinrich emphasize the role of overly expansionary monetary policies as the main source of twin crises. Following the logic of first-generation currency crises models, an excessive and persistent increase in high-powered money causes firstly, large capital outflows leading to a depletion of foreign exchange reserves, and secondly, increasing devaluation expectations which induce a rise in the risk premium and in the interest rate on foreign loans. The rise in interest rate costs leads to a reduction in banks' profits and in banks' net worth, triggering a banking crisis. The domestic banking crisis leads to massive capital outflows and triggers a currency crisis deteriorating the initial banking crisis.

In terms of the emerging market model, expansionary monetary policy, being represented by an increase in h, leads, as in the extended Krugman (1979) and Flood and Garber (1981a) models having been described above, to shrinking reserves b, causing a banking crisis *after* a contractionary devaluation has taken place. However, according to Buch and Heinrich's model, the logic is vice versa, i.e. the logic runs from a banking crisis, being triggered by devaluation expectations, to a speculative attack. In terms of the emerging market model, devaluation expectations caused by expansionary monetary policy are represented by a fall in the state of confidence ρ, leading to a domestic macroeconomic contraction and to a banking crisis by a fall in $u, r, \hat{p}, q$, and by an increase in j^* and i. Apart from the increase in h, the fall in ρ leads to additional capital outflows, i.e. to a further reduction in b, which, in case the normalized stock of foreign exchange reserves $b + \lambda^*$ falls short of a certain minimum level, leads to a currency crisis (and to a twin crisis), i.e. to a rise in $\hat{s}$, deteriorating the macroeconomic contraction in case the foreign debt-asset ratio λ^* has been comparatively high. Capital outflows lead to a decline in λ^* which offsets partly the contractionary effects on the economy, but which cannot overcompensate the negative effects of the fall in ρ and the rise in $\hat{s}$.

5.5.2 Self-Fulfilling Expectations Models

Unpredictable Bank Runs Due to Random Withdrawals Without Foreign Borrowing. Diamond and Dybvig's bank run model (1983) studies the effects of random shifts in expectations of depositors in a closed economy, i.e. banks and depositors have no possibility to get into foreign debt. As a result, the application of the Diamond-Dybvig story to the emerging market model requires that the foreign debt-asset ratio λ^* takes a zero value. Shifts in expectations are represented, as in section 4.5.2, by changes in the state of confidence parameter ρ, where $\rho > 0$ marks the "no-run" equilibrium, and $\rho < 0$ the "bank-run" equilibrium.

In terms of the emerging market country model, the no-run equilibrium, i.e. $\rho > 0$, is characterized by comparatively large values in $u, r, \hat{p}, q$ and b, and by comparatively low values in j^* and i, indicating a high degree of financial stability and a stable fixed exchange rate regime. By way of contrast, the bank run equilibrium, i.e. $\rho < 0$, is characterized by comparatively low values in $u, r, \hat{p}, q$ and comparatively high values in j^* and i, indicating a high degree of financial fragility among domestic banks and firms, as well as depreciation expectations of the home currency leading to large capital outflows and possibly to a breakdown of the fixed exchange rate system, i.e. to a sharp decline in b.

Though the open-economy extension of the Diamond-Dybvig model is able to illustrate the occurrence of banking, currency and twin crises, the model provides no clearness with respect to the chronological order of events in case of the bank-run equilibrium, since there arise three possible forms of financial crises. Firstly, if the fall in ρ does not lead to large capital outflows, the fixed exchange rate system will prevail despite a bank run. Secondly, if the fall in ρ leads to a very quick speculative attack, the devaluation of the home currency can stabilize the economy since there is an expansionary devaluation due to $\lambda^* = 0$. Hence, a domestic banking crisis and a subsequent run can be avoided by a macroeconomic expansion, stabilizing liquidity and solvency positions of the banking and the firm sector. Thirdly, the fall in ρ can lead to a twin crisis if the currency crisis following the domestic banking crisis cannot restore financial stability by an expansionary devaluation.

Unpredictable Bank Runs Due to Random Withdrawals With Foreign Borrowing. Chang and Velaso's models (1998a, 1998b, 1998c, 1999) extend Diamond and Dybvig's closed economy bank run model (1983) to an open economy framework with emerging market features in which domestic banks can take foreign debt at a fixed exchange rate. Chang and Velasco differentiate among two forms of financial crises, one emerging from a domestic creditor panic, having discussed briefly in section 4.5.2, and one originating from a foreign depositor panic.

Regarding the domestic creditor panic case, Chang and Velasco assume explicitly that domestic banks definitely pay back all foreign debt, and that due foreign debt can be rolled-over at the same conditions as before in order to abstract from a foreign creditor panic, and to elaborate the differences between financial crises being triggered by domestic depositors and by foreign creditors. As in the Diamond-Dybvig model, there arise two possible equilibria. The "no run" equilibrium is characterized by only a small fraction of domestic depositors withdrawing their funds from banks, which can meet all payments obligations. The "bank-run" equilibrium is characterized by all depositors withdrawing their funds because each domestic depositor expects all others to do the same. Banks are going to fail in case of a bank run as the face value of deposits is larger than the liquidation value of banks' long-term assets. As in the Diamond-Dybvig model, Chang and Velasco's framework does not explain why expectations can shift from the no-run to the run equilibrium. As a result, a domestic creditor panic can simply arise from sudden and inexplicable random events. As there are no runs by foreign depositors by assumption, a domestic creditor panic cannot induce a currency, and thereby a twin crisis.

In terms of the emerging market model, the switch between the no-run and the bank run equilibrium in Chang and Velasco's model can be explained, as in the Diamond-Dybvig case, by a sudden change in the state of confidence parameter ρ, where $\rho > 0$ is associated with the no-run equilibrium, and $\rho < 0$ with the bank run equilibrium. As foreign exchange reserves stem only from foreign loans, implying that normalized reserves amount to $\lambda^* > 0$ where it holds that $b = 0$, a collapse of the fixed exchange system is not possible because, even in case of foreign depositor run, all payment commitments in foreign currency can be met.

In order to study the effects of a foreign creditor panic, Chang and Velasco's assumption that banks always repay foreign debt even in case of a bank run because of foreign creditors' willingness to roll-over debt on the same conditions as before, is given up. Accordingly, there arises now the possibility that in case of a domestic depositor panic, banks' liquidation value does not suffice to meet all foreign payments commitments, making banks susceptible to self-fulfilling bank runs by domestic depositors, which are induced by shifts in expectations of foreign creditors. Chang and Velasco show that a run of domestic depositors is possible if and only if foreign creditors refuse to grant new loans or refuse to roll-over short-term debt, giving rise to a self-fulfilling banking panic. If foreign creditors fear the possibility of a domestic bank run they will refuse to grant new loans or to roll-over short term debt, which makes banks susceptible to a bank run since banks' liquidity and the stock of assets to meet depositors withdrawals has declined. If a run then actually occurs, foreign lenders' pessimistic expectations, as well as their decision not to grant new loans and/or to roll-over existing loans are validated, i.e. expectations are self-fulfilling. If on the other hand, foreign creditors do not believe in the possibility of a domestic bank run, they are not going to refuse to extend new loans and/or to roll-over short-term debt, implying that a bank run is not going to occur, which validates also foreign creditors' expectations ex post. However, Chang and Velasco's model does also not explain why expectations can shift, i.e. the long-run equilibrium is determined by random events and independent of economic fundamentals.

According to Chang and Velasco, an important implication of foreign debt effects described above is the fact that the amount of foreign loans has no influence on banks' fragility, but only the maturity structure, i.e. the more debt contracts are short-term, the higher the probability that foreign investors are not willing to roll-over debt because of the fear of a bank run. However, this implication only results from the assumption that banks do not have to pay interest on foreign loans, which is given up later on when exogenous shocks are studied as potential triggering events of bank runs.

In terms of the emerging market model, a domestic bank run induced by foreign creditors can be also explained by a shift of the state of confidence from $\rho > 0$ to $\rho < 0$, since domestic and foreign agents have been assumed to be subject to the same expectational climate. Chang and Velasco's claim that the amount of foreign debt has no influence on the probability of a bank run can also be validated by the current model if interest payments on foreign debt are excluded, i.e. if an increase in λ^*, indicating an increase in increase banks' financial fragility, has no effects on r and q, and thereby no effects on $u, \hat{p}, j^*, i$ and b, which implies that the balance sheet structure does not matter, but only the maturity. Consequently, as long as there are no interest payments on foreign debt, and as long as the maturity of debt and investment projects are synchronized there arises no possibility of a banking crisis, i.e. the financial structure does not matter according to the Modigliani-Miller theorem.

Concerning the link between bank runs and currency crises, Chang and Velasco show that monetary authorities can either save banks in case of a bank run or preserve the fixed exchange rate, but cannot do both, where the decision on whether to protect domestic banks or the fixed exchange rate, depends on the exchange rate regime. In case the monetary authority operates under a currency board, it cannot act as a lender of last resort in case of a bank run since liquidity supports to troubled banks, i.e. issuing new high powered money, are only possible if there is an equivalent increase in foreign exchange reserves. Consequently, under a currency board, a domestic bank run leads to disintermediation effects among the banking system but does not lead to a currency collapse since there are sufficient foreign reserves to meet the entire demand for foreign currency. By way of contrast, if the central bank acts as a lender of last resort under a "normal" fixed exchange rate system, a bank run can be prevented by providing sufficient liquidity to banks, but there arises the possibility of a currency crisis since the amount of domestic high powered money falls short of foreign exchange reserves. In case of a speculative attack, a currency crisis can only be avoided if the the central bank can acquire sufficient foreign assets from international lending organizations or foreign governments. One important implication of the model results is the fact that there arises no possibility of a twin crisis, as there is only a choice between a bank run or a currency crisis, being determined by the choice of the fixed exchange rate regime.

In terms of the emerging market model, a currency board regime is characterized by the condition $h = \lambda^* + b$, whereas according to Chang and Velasco, it holds that $h = \lambda^*$ at the outset, since it has been assumed that $b = 0$ at the beginning. As a result, in case foreign agents withdraw their funds due to a sudden drop in ρ, leading to a domestic banking crisis and to a macroeconomic contraction, the fixed exchange rate can survive, since the entire demand for foreign currency can be met, and since the reduction of h and λ^* is compensated by an increase in b leaving the money supply unchanged. In case the central bank acts as lender of last resort under a "normal" fixed exchange rate regime, the increase in h due to the liquidity support is compensated by a fall in b and does not stop further capital outflows stemming from a reduction in λ^* and in ρ, leading to a currency crisis which, in case λ^* is comparatively high at the moment of devaluation, causes a contractionary devaluation.

Apart from the Diamond-Dybvig mechanism of self-fulfilling bank runs, Chang and Velasco study other causes of bank runs within their model framework, like e.g. financial liberalization, moral hazard and overinvestment, exogenous shocks and inconsistent macroeconomic policies. Though these causes of bank runs do not stem originally from self-fulfilling expectations, Chang and Velasco show that negative macroeconomic effects following these kinds of bank runs can be amplified by self-fulfilling expectations. Yet, these model extensions are not going to be discussed here, since they are applications of models which are going to be described in sections 5.5.1, 5.5.3 and 5.5.4.

Self-Fulfilling Currency Crises. Similar to Diamond-Dybvig's model bank run model, second-generation currency crises models by Flood and Garber (1984b) and Obstfeld (1986, 1994, 1997), generally abstracting from banking sectors, emphasize the role of self-fulfilling expectations as the trigger of currency crises.[38] In contrast to first generation currency crises models, highlighting the inconsistency between the fixed exchange rate system and the course of macroeconomic policy, second generation models explain currency crises, following the closed-economy models by Barro and Gordon (1983a, 1983b)[39], by governments facing a trade-off between price stability, being supported by a fixed exchange rate system, and other macroeconomic objectives, like e.g. high employment and low interest rates. As long as the benefits of the fixed exchange rate system, i.e. the benefits of price stability, outweigh the costs, like e.g. high domestic interest rates, low employment and a loss of reputation in case of a devaluation, the fixed parity is maintained. Second generation models explicitly assume, in contrast to first generation models, that the costs of a peg do not depend on the level of foreign exchange reserves by assuming that governments can lend reserves without any restrictions from international organizations. By way of contrast, the cost-benefit relation of the fixed exchange rate system depends on private agents' expectations. Accordingly, a sudden shift of expectations towards a devaluation of the home currency can induce governments to abandon the peg, since costs in the form of higher interest rates or lower employment induced by higher inflation expectations and wages outweigh the benefits. Since governments follow the shift in market sentiments, expectations become self fulfilling. If, on the contrary, market participants expect the peg to be credible, there arise no higher costs, leading actually to a stable exchange rate validating also expectations. Still, second generation models provide no explanation, as the entire bank run literature, for the shift in expectations, i.e. for the switch from a "no-attack-equilibrium" to an "attack equilibrium".

Obstfeld (1994) develops two models highlighting different transmission channels for the occurrence of self-fulfilling currency crises. In his first model, the domestic government maintaining a fixed exchange rate in order to stabilize the domestic price level (PPP is assumed to hold) is indebted in domestic currency at a floating interest rate. Further-

[38]For a detailed discussion of second generation currency crises models, see Radke (2000b) and (2000c). An overview of first and second generation currency crises models can also be found in Flood and Marion (1998).

[39]For open economy extensions of the Barro-Gordon model, see e.g. Spahn (1996, 1997).

more, uncovered interest parity is assumed to hold leading to higher debt costs of the domestic government if foreign interest rates increase and/or devaluation expectations arise. The government faces a trade-off between maintaining the peg and benefiting from price stability, and comparatively high debt costs which could be minimized by abandoning the peg in order to pursue an independent low interest rate policy. As a long as the benefits outweigh the costs, the peg will be maintained, where costs depend crucially on private agents' expectations regarding the sustainability of government debt. According to Obstfeld, there arise two possible self-fulfilling equilibria depending on the state of expectations, one leaving the exchange rate unchanged, and the other one leading to a breakdown of the fixed parity. The "no-attack equilibrium" prevails if private agents believe in government debt to be sustainable at current interest rates, i.e. if agents do not expect the government to devalue the domestic currency in order to lower interest rates, and thereby debt costs. As a result, there arise no devaluation expectations, and domestic interest rates remain at foreign levels, not forcing the government to devalue. Private agents' expectations are self-fulfilling since expecting the exchange rate to remain unchanged leads to sustainable debt costs, and thereby to a maintenance of the peg. If, on the contrary, private agents expect the government debt not to be sustainable at current interest rates, they expect the government to devalue in order to lower interest rates by expansionary monetary policy. Emerging devaluation expectations lead to higher domestic interest rates according to UIP, increasing debt costs and forcing the government to devalue actually if interest rates have risen to a level on which costs of the peg outweigh the benefits. Expectations in the "attack equilibrium" are also self-fulfilling, since expecting the government to devalue creates conditions, here rising interest rates, which actually force the government to devalue.

Obstfeld's second model emphasizes the government's trade-off between maintaining price stability by a credible fixed exchange rate regime, and a high level of employment, as the fixed parity does not allow to react on adverse output shocks reducing employment, by realignments of the fixed exchange rate. Output and employment are assumed to depend negatively on real wages, where the domestic price level is fixed due to a fixed exchange rate system (PPP is assumed to hold). Nominal wages are positively dependent on inflation expectations which coincide with devaluation expectations of the home currency. Output and employment are also assumed to be influenced stochastically by positive or negative shocks. As a discretionary fixed exchange rate system induces, following the model results by Kydland and Prescott (1977), and Barro and Gordon (1983a, 1983b), an inflation bias by steady devaluations, the government is assumed to follow a rule of maintaining a fixed parity, but is allowed to abandon the rule when disturbances to the economy are too large and too costly. In order to avoid that such "escape clauses"[40] also induce an inflation bias by steady devaluations, governments have to bear additional fixed costs, as e.g. in the form of a penalty fee, in case of a realignment. As a result, the fixed exchange rate prevails as long as costs in the form of deviations from price and output targets are lower than costs of using the "escape clause" leading to a devaluation of the home currency. However, costs arising from deviations of prices and output from their target levels depend heavily on private agents' expectations, generating multiple outcomes for a given shock. If private agents believe in stability of the fixed exchange rate in case

[40] "Escape-clause" models were originally developed by Flood and Isard (1989), and Persson and Tabellini (1990).

of a given negative shock, nominal wage demands are moderate and deviations from the output target are only caused by a stochastic shock leaving the fixed parity unchanged. Expectations are self-fulfilling since agents believe in the stability of the fixed exchange rate in case of a given shock, which does not increase the costs of maintaining the fixed parity, and thereby does not lead to a devaluation. If, by way of contrast, private agents expect the government to devalue in case of the occurrence of the same given negative shock, wage demands increase and output is reduced, on the one hand by rising real wages, and on the other hand by the negative shock. As a result, in case the economy is actually hit by a negative shock, the government is forced to devalue since costs have increased due to deteriorating expectations. Expectations are again self-fulfilling since arising devaluation expectations increase the costs of maintaining the peg in case of a shock, leading to a devaluation of the home currency in case the shock actually hits the economy.

In order to describe second generation currency crises models by means of the emerging market crisis model assume firstly, that the stock of normalized foreign exchange reserves $\lambda^* + b$ is irrelevant for the maintenance of the fixed exchange rate since reserves can be lent from international organizations, and secondly, that the foreign debt-asset ratio λ^* is comparatively small triggering a macroeconomic expansion in case of a devaluation. In order to show how rising interest rates due to devaluation expectations can trigger a currency crisis assume that i denotes the interest rate on domestic government bonds, and that the government abandons the peg in case i reaches a certain threshold level. In case there arise no devaluation expectations, it holds that $d\rho = 0$ leaving i unchanged and implying the maintenance of the peg. If, on the other hand, agents expect a devaluation, ρ declines leading to a rise in i and, if a certain threshold level is exceeded, to a suspension of the peg.

In order to show how a shift in expectation can trigger a crisis in case of stochastic real sector shocks, assume that the wage share v depends negatively on ρ, stating that in case of devaluation expectations wage pressure increases, where negative real sector shocks are represented by a rise in the depreciation rate δ. The government is assumed to maintain the peg as long as cost evolving from capacity utilization, being negatively influenced by increases in v and δ, and from the inflation rate deviation from their target levels is smaller than costs which are imposed in case of a devaluation. In case agents do not expect the government to devalue in case of a negative technology shock of size $d\delta = x$, costs in the form of reduced capacity utilization only emerge from a rise in δ, leaving the peg unchanged. If, on the contrary, agents expect the government to devalue in case of a negative technology shock of the same size $d\delta = x$, ρ declines, leading to a rise in v, and inducing a reduction in u. In case the negative technology shock actually hits the economy, the shock-induced reduction in u leads to a suspension of the peg.

5.5.3 Asymmetric Information Models

Unpredictable Bank Runs Due to Asymmetric Information and Exogenous Shocks Without Foreign Borrowing. Models by Calomiris, Gorton, Chari and Jagannathan[41] have stressed that widespread bank runs can be triggered by exogenous shocks, not by self-fulfilling expectations, since depositors cannot find out, after a neg-

[41]See section 4.5.3 for references.

ative shock has hit the banking systems, which banks are still solvent and which banks have gone bankrupt due to information asymmetries, and therefore are going to run all banks. Bank runs remain an unpredictable event since there is no possibility to determine the probability of the negative shock's occurrence. These closed-economy models abstract from foreign borrowing by banks.

Rendering this approach into the emerging market model requires that the foreign debt-asset ratio takes a value of zero, i.e. $\lambda^* = 0$, in order to exclude foreign borrowing. A widespread bank run occurs if a negative shock leads to liquidity and solvency problems among firms and banks via a deterioration of Tobin's q, which causes a widespread disbelief in the healthiness of the banking system, being indicated by a fall in the state of confidence parameter from $\rho > 0$ to $\rho < 0$. According to the emerging market model, shocks leading a drop in q and ρ, and triggering a bank run, can be a tightening up of financial market regulation, i.e. an increase in α, negative productivity shocks like an increase in the wage share v and in the depreciation rate δ, or a foreign interest rate shock being represented by a sharp increase in i^*. In case a bank run occurs, there is a sharp macroeconomic contraction indicated by comparatively low values in $u, r, \hat{p}, q$ and b, and by comparatively high levels of interest rates j^* and i, causing possibly a twin crisis if $b = 0$.

The Likelihood of Bank Runs and Twin Crises Due to Exogenous Shocks in Open Economies With Foreign Borrowing. The above-cited closed-economy bank run models by Calomiris, Gorton, Chari and Jagannathan state that bank runs generally occur if the banking system is hit by an adverse shock, but do not specify explicitly the extent, or threshold values of a shock being necessary to trigger a run. That is, these models do not distinguish among small shocks causing no bank runs, and large shocks causing widespread bank runs. Goldfajn and Valdés (1997b) try to overcome this drawback by introducing a known probability distribution of a domestic productivity shock, making it possible to calculate the likelihood of financial crises. Their model is based on an open economy version of Diamond-Dybvig's bank run model similar to Chang and Velasco's approach[42], in which domestic banks offer short-term deposits only to foreign agents and invest the funds into a long-run domestic risky technology, needing time to mature, and whose return is a random variable, being dependent on random productivity shocks for which a probability distribution is known. Foreign investors can choose to invest their funds either in a secure, short-term international asset or into deposits of the domestic banking system. As in the Diamond-Dybvig model, bank runs have devastating effects on the domestic economy, since early deposit withdrawals by foreign investors make banks liquidate their investments in the long-term technology, leading to bank failures, as the short-run liquidation value of banks' long-term assets is less than the nominal value of deposits.

In contrast to Diamond-Dybvig's and Chang and Velasco's models, bank runs are caused by large adverse random productivity shocks, and cannot arise from self-fulfilling expectations. Hence, foreign investors are going to engage in massive early withdrawals if an adverse productivity shock hits the economy, leading to a fall of the domestic technology's return to a value which is lower than the return of the international short-term asset. Since the probability distribution of the productivity shock is known, Goldfajn and Valdés' model is able to determine the probability of a bank run, as well as the thresh-

[42]See section 5.5.2 for references.

old value of the productivity shock leading to a lower return of the domestic technology. In case the central bank does not own sufficient reserves to meet all capital outflows, a currency crisis is going to follow the domestic bank run whose probability also can be determined.

However, the logic of twin crises can also run from devaluation expectations to domestic bank runs which are followed by a currency crash. If the central bank is forced to devalue the domestic currency in case of a lack of sufficient foreign exchange reserves, foreign investors' return of holding domestic deposits is going to be reduced, i.e. devaluation expectations depend on the one hand on the extent of the productivity shock inducing investors to withdraw possibly funds early, and on the other hand, on the level of foreign exchange reserves like in first-generation currency crises models, since a higher stock of foreign reserves reduces the probability of a devaluation, thereby reducing the probability of a fall in the return of the domestic technology. As a result, if there is a low stock of foreign reserves, the probability of a bank run and a subsequent currency crisis increases. Among domestic productivity shocks, Goldfajn and Valdés also demonstrate the occurrence of twin crises in case of a foreign interest rate shock, increasing the return of the safe short-term international asset.

Rendering Goldfajn and Valdés' approach into the emerging market model requires that the occurrence of a bank run is defined by Tobin's q falling short of a lower threshold value q_l. An exogenous productivity shock leading to such a fall in Tobin's q can be caused by an increase in the wage share v, by a fall in the depreciation rate δ, and by an increase in the foreign interest rate i^*. If one assumes probability distributions for different realizations of v, δ and i^*, probabilities for realizations values being lower than q_l triggering a bank run can be calculated. A bank run causes a macroeconomic contraction, being represented by a declining values of $u, r, \hat{p}$, and by rising values of j^* and i. Capital outflows are represented by a fall in λ^* and b, leading to a currency crisis in case $b + \lambda^*$ do not suffice to meet all outflows.

In order to describe the twin crisis logic which runs from devaluation expectations to bank runs, consider that the state of confidence ρ, also representing expected changes of the exchange rate, depends positively on realizations of Tobin's q like in the long-run dynamic analysis, and on normalized foreign exchange reserves $b + \lambda^*$. The lower foreign exchange reserves are, the lower ρ becomes, leading to a fall in Tobin's q, and, if q falls short of q_l, to a banking crisis, which is followed by a speculative attack in case $b + \lambda^*$ do not suffice to meet all outflows. This case is also subject to a severe macroeconomic contraction which is deteriorated in case of a contractionary devaluation.

Moral-Hazard-Driven Financial Crises in Emerging Markets Caused by Exogenous Shocks or Self-Fulfilling Expectations. The analysis of moral hazard driven financial crisis models without foreign borrowing in section 4.5.3 has shown that the combination of government guarantees to bail out troubled banks, and the existence of an exogenous upper bound of governments' financial support, can generate financial crises by distorting incentives of banks, engaging in much riskier investment projects than it would be optimal under a regime without government guarantees. When it becomes obvious that government rescue packages necessary to bail out troubled banks exceed the limit of governments' financial support, caused either by exogenous shocks or by self-fulfilling expectations, and the government is forced to suspend its guarantees, bank runs will be the inevitable consequence.

Moral hazard driven financial crises in emerging markets differ from crises in industrial countries, as governments not only guarantee financial claims of domestic investors, but also financial claims of foreign investors in case of lenders', mostly domestic banks', default. As a result, the promise to bail-out domestic *and* foreign investors implies on the one hand, a guarantee to bail-out the domestic banking system, and on the other hand, a guarantee to maintain a fixed exchange rate level by the use of foreign exchange reserves, which makes domestic borrowers, as well as foreign lenders not to hedge against exchange rate risk, leading to further overinvestment due to overborrowing in *foreign* currency. Hence, financial support policies in emerging market countries are not only limited by an exogenous bound to support troubled banks by generating extra fiscal deficits, but additionally by the stock of foreign exchange reserves. According to emerging market crises models, triggering events causing the suspension of fixed exchange rate regimes and/or financial support policies for domestic banks, can be either exogenous shocks or self-fulfilling expectations.

Burnside, Eichenbaum and Rebelo (1998) emphasize the self-fulfilling nature of twin crises emerging from government guarantees. In their model, banks take deposits from foreign investors in foreign currency and lend to domestic agents in domestic currency, whereas foreign creditors' claims are protected by government guarantees. The protection of foreign investors' claims by the government causes domestic banks not to hedge against exchange rate risk, leading to overborrowing and excessive capital inflows, since the stock of foreign debt would be much smaller if there was no guarantee to hedge domestic banks against exchange rate risk. Domestic banks are assumed to declare bankruptcy in case of a devaluation and renege on their foreign debt. Consequently, a devaluation transforms contingent government liabilities into actual government liabilities. Furthermore, the government is assumed either to be unwilling, or to be unable to bail out foreign investors in case of a default of domestic banks by a fiscal reform, i.e. by tax finance to maintain a balanced fiscal budget, but engages in seignorage finance. Foreign investors however, do not know in advance that there will be an actual seignorage finance in case of default, but can only expect the government either to carry out a fiscal reform, or to bail out foreign investors by seignorage finance.

These model assumptions generate multiple equilibria giving rise to self-fulfilling financial crises. In case foreign investors believe in the commitment of the domestic government to bail out domestic banks without making use of seignorage finance, but by a fiscal reform (increasing taxes), there arise no devaluation expectations and no capital outflows leaving the exchange rate unchanged. As a result, there are no bankruptcies among banks which would call for government intervention, validating foreign investors' optimistic expectations. If, by way of contrast, foreign investors believe that, in case of default, the domestic government finances banks' foreign debt by seignorage, there arise devaluation expectations, leading to large capital outflows, and after some time, to an actual devaluation of the domestic currency, causing bankruptcy among banks. Since the government is actually not willing or not able to bail out foreign investors by a fiscal reform, bankruptcy among domestic banks leads to seignorage finance thereby validating investors' shift towards pessimistic expectations. According to the model, the shift in expectations is random and not explained, as in other self-fulfilling expectations models.

In contrast to the self-fulfilling nature of moral hazard driven financial crises, there are various authors emphasizing the role of adverse real shocks leading to a suspension of government guarantees, and thereby triggering a twin crisis. According to Velasco (1987) and Corsetti, Pesenti and Roubini (1998), an exogenous decline in output or productivity leads to negative cash flows by firms and banks which can be compensated by borrowing from abroad at a risk-free international interest rate. Foreign borrowers are willing to lend to potentially illiquid domestic banks and firms due to the existence of government guarantees. When foreign borrowing has reached an upper bound, and foreign investors are not longer willing to increase their lending, e.g. due to an exogenously given debt ceiling by international financial markets, then firms and banks become illiquid, inducing a domestic banking crisis, and implying that banks' liabilities are transformed into government liabilities. Depending on the nature of foreign debt's repayment, and on the initial stock of foreign exchange reserves, a currency crisis can follow in case foreign exchange reserves do not suffice to meet foreign debt repayments.

According to Dooley's (1997, 2000) approach, a decline in international interest rates leads to an increase in the stock of the domestic government's net foreign exchange reserves due to a reduction in foreign government debt. This increase in government reserves is used to set up a domestic deposit insurance system which guarantees banks' liabilities. These credible government guarantees lead to capital inflows increasing domestic banks' stock of foreign debt. Banks are assumed not to plan to repay the full amount of their insured liabilities due to government guarantees, enabling them to engage in much riskier investment projects, leading to overborrowing in foreign currency. Foreign investors are willing to increase lending until banks' total liabilities equal the size of government's net foreign exchange reserves. Eventually, owing to steady overborrowing by domestic banks, foreign investors are going to run on domestic banks when foreign debt has reached the amount guaranteed by the government. As the government is assumed to cover fully banks liabilities, there are no foreign exchange reserves left to stabilize the fixed exchange rate, leading to a currency and to a twin crisis.

McKinnon and Pill (1996, 1997, 1998, 1999) emphasize the role of positive exogenous shocks, like financial liberalization or other economic reforms, in combination with deposit insurance systems to bail out domestic, as well as foreign creditors of banks, leading to overinvestment and overborrowing in domestic, as well as in foreign currency. In their model, liberalization policies allow for the use of a new investment technology financed by the domestic banking system whose return is subject to a probability distribution. Due to the existence of government guarantees, banks and firms do not rely on the "true" expected value of profits of the new investment technology, but on a distorted expected value which is much higher, since in case of default, losses are covered by the government. As a result, distorted incentives lead to overinvestment and overborrowing, which is additionally accelerated by foreign borrowing by domestic banks, allowing them to grant more loans. Twin crises are triggered by an exogenous "bad" realization of the investment technology, leading to an unexpected large drop in firms' earnings and causing huge losses among firms and banks which the government is not able, or unwilling to finance. Thus, a domestic banking crisis is going to occur, being followed by a currency crisis in case foreign exchange reserve do not suffice to meet all capital outflows.

In terms of the emerging market financial crisis model, the overinvestment and overborrowing phase can be explained by an increase in the state of confidence ρ, caused by distortions in risk perception by firms and banks due to the existence of government guarantees as already outlined in section 4.5.3. Accordingly, overestimation of profits and underestimation of potential risk leads to a macroeconomic expansion being represented by an increase in $u, r, \hat{p}, q$, and by a decline in j^* and i. Due to the favourable economic environment, there are large capital inflows represented by an increase in b, and by an increase in the foreign-debt asset ratio λ^* which slows down the macroeconomic expansion but is not able to compensate the positive effect of ρ.

A self-fulfilling financial crises can emanate from a shift towards pessimistic expectations regarding the maintenance of government guarantees without any fundamental cause. If the government is expected not to be willing, or to be unable to maintain the guarantees at all, or is believed to use seignorage finance to bail-out banks as outlined by Burnside, Eichenbaum and Rebelo (1998), there is a drop in the state of confidence parameter ρ, representing on the one hand, the "real" expected profit rate in case guarantees are absent, and on the other hand, devaluation expectations caused by inflation expectations stemming from expected seignorage finance. If the drop in ρ is large enough, the macroeconomic contraction, being represented by a decline in $u, r, \hat{p}, q$, and a rise in j^* and i, causes widespread losses among firms and banks whose accumulated value exceeds the upper bound of the government's financial support policy. If the government simply abandons guarantees, banks and firms go bankrupt, leading to a bank run by foreign investors which is followed by a currency crisis, since foreign exchange reserves do not suffice to meet all capital outflows, leading to a further macroeconomic contraction due to a contractionary devaluation. If, on the other hand, the government bails out foreign investors, but relies partly on seignorage finance in order to prevent a bank run, being represented by a large increase in h, this policy has also its natural bound since it leads to a decline of foreign exchange reserves b, causing a currency crisis which leads to a contractionary devaluation and bankruptcies among banks and firms, inducing eventually a bank run of foreign investors. In both cases, the occurrence of twin crises stemming from an ex ante shift towards pessimistic expectations validates ex post investors' expectations. If, by way of contrast, agents believe either in the maintenance of government guarantees, or in the absence of seignorage finance in case of default, there is no drop in ρ, implying stability of the financial system which validates investors' optimistic expectations.

A shock-triggered financial crisis is represented by an actual fall in the profit rate r, caused e.g. by negative productivity shocks like increases in v and δ, or by international financial market shocks like increases in α or i^*, leading to a decline in $q, u, \hat{p}, b$, and to an increase in j^* and i. In case the exogenous shock is large enough, and government guarantees cannot be maintained, there are widespread bankruptcies among firms and banks, causing a fall in ρ to its "true" value, and leading to a full-fledged twin crisis by the mechanisms outlined above.

5.5.4 Credit Constraint and Balance Sheet Models

Fourth-Generation Crises Due to Exogenous Shocks. As described in section 4.5.4, fourth-generation models define a financial crisis as a credit crunch, leading to a drop in investment and output via a reduction in banks' and/or firms' collateral values which can be caused either by exogenous shocks or by self-fulfilling expectations. Fourth-generation financial crisis models referring to emerging markets differ from models of industrial countries by emphasizing that emerging market countries face, in contrast to industrial countries, an international credit constraint in foreign currency, stemming from the "original sin" hypothesis. Hence, a financial crisis in emerging markets is defined as a situation in which the international credit constraint becomes binding, leading to reductions in investment and output.

Regarding exogenous shock-driven financial crisis models by Mishkin (1991, 1997, 1996, 1998a, 1998b, 1999a, 1999b), Céspedes, Chang and Velasco (2001a, 2001b), Velasco (2001, 2002), and Caballero and Krishnamurthy (2002), adverse shocks like reductions in net exports, sudden declines in productivity, and increases in foreign interest rates reduce firms' profits and collateral values, thereby leading to systemic financial crises which are associated with large capital outflows, reductions in available credit, and collapses in investment and output.

In terms of the emerging market country model, negative productivity shocks like an increase in v or δ, or international financial market shocks as an increase in α or i^*, lead to a reduction in $r, q, u, \hat{p}, b$ and to an increase in j^* and i, being amplified by a fall in ρ, triggering banking and currency crises. In case the foreign debt-asset ratio is comparatively high, the devaluation of the home currency, i.e. $\hat{s} > 0$, is contractionary.

Fourth-Generation Crises Due to Self-Fulfilling Expectations. Fourth-generation financial crises driven by self-fulfilling expectations have been discussed mainly by theoretical models by Krugman (1999a, 1999b, 2001) and by Aghion, Bacchetta and Banerjee (2000, 2001, 2003). In order to explain the basic logic of these approaches, this paragraph refers to Krugman's modified Mundell-Fleming open-economy emerging market version of fourth-generation crisis models outlined in Krugman (1999a, 2001), which analyzes the interdependence of exchange rate variations, net worth and output fluctuations when firms' balance sheets are characterized by a considerable stock of debt denominated in foreign currency, and when investment activities are balance sheet constrained, i.e. when the availability of external investment finance depends positively on firms' net worth. Accordingly, for favourable levels of the exchange rate, the nominal value foreign debt in domestic currency is comparatively low, leading to a comparatively high level of net worth, stimulating investment demand. By way of contrast, adverse exchange rate levels lead to comparatively low net worth positions which dampen investment demand.

The aggregate effect of exchange rate variations on aggregate demand and output however, depends on the relative strength of the indirect balance sheet effect on investment in comparison with the direct effect on export competitiveness. Krugman assumes that for very low and for very high levels of the exchange rate, the export competitiveness effect dominates. If, for a given level of foreign indebtedness, the exchange rate is very low, firms' leverage is comparatively low, implying that a devaluation of the home currency does only increase firms' leverage to a small extent, whereas net exports' positive reaction is comparatively high. By way of contrast, if, for a given level of foreign debt, the exchange rate level is very high, firms are highly leveraged, implying that investment demand is almost zero, and that a devaluation of the home currency does only lead to a tiny contraction in investment demand, whereas net exports increase significantly. In the medium, and in the relevant range for exchange rate variations however, the balance sheet effect is assumed to dominate the export competitiveness effect, i.e. devaluations of the home currency are assumed to be contractionary. Furthermore, UIP is assumed to hold, and monetary authorities are modelled as "leaning against the exchange rate" due to the general "fear of floating" argument when foreign debt is high.

The model dynamics generate two stable equilibria, where one equilibrium is associated with a stable macroeconomic environment, and the other one with the occurrence of financial crises. The "no-crisis" equilibrium is characterized by a favourable exchange rate, leading to a comparatively low value of foreign debt in domestic currency, high net worth, high investment demand and high output. On the contrary, the "crisis" equilibrium is subject to a comparatively high level of the exchange rate, a high foreign debt stock in domestic currency, low net worth, low investment demand and low output. Krugman argues that there is no mechanism guaranteeing the prevalence of the "no-crisis" equilibrium, i.e. whether an economy faces a full-fledged financial crisis or not depends solely on the state of expectations. If international investor confidence is strong in domestic business firms, there will be no withdrawal of funds, leaving the exchange rate unchanged, and leading to the "no-crisis" equilibrium which validates international investors' expectations. If, on the contrary, international investors lose confidence in the firm sector and start to withdraw their funds, the exchange rate appreciates, leading to an increase in foreign debt and to a drop in net worth, investment and output, inducing a systemic financial crisis which validates investors' pessimistic expectations. Krugman argues that the triggering event catapulting an economy from the "no-crisis" to the "crisis" equilibrium may be a small random incident, or simply a shift of expectations without any cause.

The application of the Krugman model to the emerging market model requires that the foreign debt-asset ratio λ^* takes comparatively high values to allow for contractionary devaluations. Furthermore, since the Krugman model operates under a flexible exchange rate regime, the "no-crisis" equilibrium has to be consistent with the prevalent fixed exchange rate, i.e. it holds that $\hat{s} = 0$, whereas the "crisis" equilibrium has to be subject to a currency crisis, i.e. the central bank runs out of foreign exchange reserves leading to a devaluation of the home currency, i.e. to $\hat{s} > 0$. Generally, the "no-crisis" equilibrium is characterized by a favourable state of confidence, i.e. by $\rho > 0$, thereby leading to comparatively high levels of $u, r, \hat{p}, q$ and b, and to very low values of j^* and i, validating investors' optimistic expectations. If, on the contrary, investors expect a downturn of the economy, the state of confidence drops to $\rho < 0$, leading to a macroeconomic contraction, and thereby validating investors' pessimistic expectations. The "crisis" equilibrium is characterized by comparatively low levels of $u, r, \hat{p}, q$ and b, and by comparatively high levels of j^* and i which are going to deteriorate when the domestic currency devalues, i.e. when $\hat{s} > 0$, and a twin crisis is going to occur.

5.5.5 Endogenous Financial Crisis Models

Minsky's Financial Instability Hypothesis in the Open Economy. This paragraph extends Minsky's closed economy model to financial crises in open economies, and especially to financial crises in emerging markets being characterized by a large swings in short-term foreign debt. The following analysis only set outs open economy modifications of the closed economy version having been discussed in section 4.5.5.

The Minskian open economy approach also consists of the five theoretical components as discussed in section 4.5.5, where only the first component, Minsky's theory of financial stability, has to be enlarged by open economy considerations as set out in sections 2.3.2.3

and 2.3.2.4 by the introduction of foreign hedge, speculative, and Ponzi finance units. A typical Minsky cycle in emerging market countries begins with liberalization and/or macroeconomic stabilization policies (predominantly exchange rate based stabilization programmes) which are established to boost economic growth, or to stabilize macroeconomic aggregates due to past unsound policies which led to high inflation, low growth and to financial crises. The introduction of liberalization and stabilization policies generally causes a sharp increase in domestic interest rates due to the abolition of interest rate caps, disinflationary monetary policies, and due to a limited supply of credit stemming from underdeveloped domestic financial systems still suffering from past financial repression. As both liberalization policies and exchange rate based stabilization programmes are commonly associated with liberalized capital accounts, the most important source of finance is foreign debt, predominantly stemming from industrialized countries. As foreign creditors want to minimize uncertainties regarding future inflation, future exchange rates, future financial stability, etc., foreign debt-contracts are generally short-term. Moreover, foreign interest rates (in industrial countries) tend to be much lower than domestic ones due to higher exchange rate credibility, lower inflation, lower financial risk, etc. By way of contrast, domestic expected profit rates are generally much higher than foreign ones, as capacity utilization in emerging markets tends to be low and markets are not saturated, implying that a rise in investment and output leads to a quick and large rise in actual profits.

Low foreign interest rates, credible liberalization and stabilization programmes, and a comparatively high expected profit rate in emerging markets induce an *endogenous* build-up of financial fragility in emerging markets as profits can be realized by expanding investment which is financed by large short-term capital inflows. Accordingly, the introduction of liberalization and stabilization policies in emerging market countries is followed by a cumulative upward process by the interaction of actual profits, expected profits, and investment, which is financed by an increase in short-term debt. The foreign debt-led investment boom causes a substantial increase in financial fragility firstly, by a decline in the ratio of foreign hedge finance units to foreign (super) speculative and Ponzi finance units, and secondly, by an increase in the overall debt-asset ratio as investment expenditures and expected profits commonly grow faster than investment due to chartist-type behaviour of agents.

The boom phase comes to an end by endogenously rising labour and material costs which lead to a fall in the actual profit rate. Declining profits induce large capital outflows and rising short-term foreign interest rates due to endogenously increasing risk premia, leading to present value reversals, and financial posture downgrading. Rising capital outflows and rising foreign interest rates end up in a domestic banking crisis which is deepened by a subsequent currency crisis when foreign exchange reserves do not longer suffice to meet capital outflows. The twin crisis leads to a severe recession or even depression with deflationary spirals. In contrast to industrial countries, lender of last resort interventions by emerging market authorities to prevent a full-fledged systemic twin crisis are not possible. Following the results of Minsky's closed economy model, only an expansionary fiscal policy and increasing government budget deficits can induce a recovery.

In terms of the model, Minsky's open economy approach can be illustrated by the dynamic Keynesian version, being depicted in figure 5.9, and possibly giving rise to recurrent endogenous financial crises due to pure chartist-type behaviour of agents.

Other Approaches. There are similar approaches to financial crises in emerging markets which are associated with excessive boom-bust cycles in goods and financial markets, and large swings in capital flows, as e.g. works of Borio and Lowe (2002), Borio, Furfine and Lowe (2001), which however, as argued in section 4.5.5, provide only an empirical and descriptive analysis, and no theoretical foundation.

5.5.6 An Assessment

The results of the analysis of the differences, common grounds and new elements of the industrial country model in comparison with standard approaches to financial crises, outlined in section 4.5.6, are also valid for the comparison of the emerging market country model with standard models of financial crises and can be completely applied.

5.6 A Comparison with Standard Business Cycle Theory

The discussion of common grounds, differences and new elements of the present approach to financial crises and endogenous fluctuations in industrial countries in comparison with standard theory of business cycles, outlined in section 4.6, can be fully applied to the model results regarding financial crises and business cycles in emerging markets except for the difference that in emerging markets business cycles are mainly driven by capital flows in foreign currency, and not by domestic financial flows in domestic currency.

5.7 Mathematical Supplements

All partial derivatives summarized qualitatively in table 5.1 are given explicitly below. The signs of partial derivatives with respect to the exchange rate's growth rate $\hat{s}$ depend on the level of foreign debt; for a comparatively high foreign debt-asset ratio λ^* the signs are marked by †, and for a relatively low foreign debt-asset ratio by ‡. For all partial derivatives, except for derivatives with respect to $\hat{s}$, it has been assumed that $\hat{s} = 0$ because of the fixed exchange rate regime.

Response of Capacity Utilization u to Various Shocks.

$$
\begin{aligned}
\frac{\partial u}{\partial \lambda} &= \frac{1}{|\mathbf{J}|}(-j\, m\, \eta_q\, \lambda_{j^*}^{*s}) && < 0 \\
\frac{\partial u}{\partial j} &= \frac{1}{|\mathbf{J}|}(-m\, \lambda\, \eta_q\, \lambda_{j^*}^{*s}) && < 0 \\
\frac{\partial u}{\partial \lambda^*} &= \frac{1}{|\mathbf{J}|}(-m\, \eta_q\, (1 + \lambda^* + j^*\, \lambda_{j^*}^{*s})) && < 0 \\
\frac{\partial u}{\partial \rho} &= \frac{1}{|\mathbf{J}|}(-m((-1 + \beta_\rho)\eta_q\, \lambda_{j^*}^{*s} + g_{i-\hat{p}}\, \beta_\rho(-\lambda_{j^*}^{*s} + (1 + \lambda^*)\lambda_q^{*s}))) && > 0 \\
\frac{\partial u}{\partial h} &= 0 && \\
\frac{\partial u}{\partial m} &= 0 && \\
\frac{\partial u}{\partial \hat{s}} &= \frac{1}{|\mathbf{J}|} m(nx_{\hat{s}-\hat{p}} - \eta_q\, \lambda^*)\lambda_{j^*}^{*s} + m\, nx_{\hat{s}-\hat{p}}(-1 - \lambda^*)\lambda_q^{*s} && < 0^\dagger, > 0^\ddagger \\
\frac{\partial u}{\partial v} &= \frac{1}{|\mathbf{J}|}(-m\, u\, \eta_q\, \lambda_{j^*}^{*s}) && < 0 \\
\frac{\partial u}{\partial \delta} &= \frac{1}{|\mathbf{J}|}(-m\, \eta_q\, \lambda_{j^*}^{*s}) && < 0 \\
\frac{\partial u}{\partial \alpha} &= \frac{1}{|\mathbf{J}|} m\, \eta_q\, (1 + \lambda^*)\, \lambda_\alpha^{*s} && < 0 \\
\frac{\partial u}{\partial i^*} &= \frac{1}{|\mathbf{J}|}(-m\, g_{i-\hat{p}}(-\lambda_{j^*}^{*s} + (1 + \lambda^*)\, \lambda_q^{*s})) && < 0
\end{aligned}
$$

Response of the Profit Rate r to Various Shocks.

$$\frac{\partial r}{\partial \lambda} = \frac{1}{|\mathbf{J}|}(-j\, m(\lambda_{j^*}^{*s} - \lambda_q^{*s})) \qquad < 0$$

$$\frac{\partial r}{\partial j} = \frac{1}{|\mathbf{J}|}(-m\, \lambda(\lambda_{j^*}^{*s} - \lambda_q^{*s})) \qquad < 0$$

$$\frac{\partial r}{\partial \lambda^*} = \frac{1}{|\mathbf{J}|} m((-1+v)\eta_q - \lambda^* + j^*(-\lambda_{j^*}^{*s} + \lambda_q^{*s})) \qquad < 0$$

$$\frac{\partial r}{\partial \rho} = \frac{1}{|\mathbf{J}|} m((-1+v)g_{i-\hat{p}}\, \beta_q(-\lambda_{j^*}^{*s} + \lambda_q^{*s}) + (-1+\beta_\rho)((-1+v)\eta_q\, \lambda_{j^*}^{*s} - \lambda^*\, \lambda_q^{*s})) \qquad > 0$$

$$\frac{\partial r}{\partial h} = 0$$

$$\frac{\partial r}{\partial m} = 0$$

$$\frac{\partial r}{\partial \hat{s}} = \frac{1}{|\mathbf{J}|}(-m((-1+v)nx_{\hat{s}-\hat{p}} + \lambda^*)(\lambda_{j^*}^{*s} - \lambda_q^{*s})) \qquad < 0^{\dagger}, > 0^{\ddagger}$$

$$\frac{\partial r}{\partial v} = \frac{1}{|\mathbf{J}|}(-m\, u(\lambda_{j^*}^{*s} - \lambda_q^{*s})) \qquad < 0$$

$$\frac{\partial r}{\partial \delta} = \frac{1}{|\mathbf{J}|}(-m\, (\lambda_{j^*}^{*s} - \lambda_q^{*s})) \qquad < 0$$

$$\frac{\partial r}{\partial \alpha} = \frac{1}{|\mathbf{J}|} m((1-v)\eta_q + \lambda^*)\, \lambda_\alpha^{*s} \qquad < 0$$

$$\frac{\partial r}{\partial i^*} = \frac{1}{|\mathbf{J}|} m(-1+v)g_{i-\hat{p}}(-\lambda_{j^*}^{*s} + \lambda_q^{*s}) \qquad < 0$$

Response of the Growth Rate of the Price Level $\hat{p}$ to Various Shocks.[43]

$$\frac{\partial \hat{p}}{\partial \lambda} = \frac{1}{|\mathbf{J}|}(-j\, m\, \eta_q\, \lambda_{j^*}^{*s}\, \psi_u) \qquad < 0$$

$$\frac{\partial \hat{p}}{\partial j} = \frac{1}{|\mathbf{J}|}(-m\, \lambda\, \eta_q\, \lambda_{j^*}^{*s}\, \psi_u) \qquad < 0$$

$$\frac{\partial \hat{p}}{\partial \lambda^*} = \frac{1}{|\mathbf{J}|}(-m\, \eta_q(1+\lambda^*+j^*\, \lambda_{j^*}^{*s})\psi_u) \qquad < 0$$

$$\frac{\partial \hat{p}}{\partial \rho} = \frac{1}{|\mathbf{J}|}m((1-\beta_\rho)\eta_q\, \lambda^* + g_{i-\hat{p}}\, \beta_\rho(\lambda^* - (1+\lambda^*)\lambda_q^{*s}))\psi_u \qquad > 0$$

$$\frac{\partial \hat{p}}{\partial h} = 0$$

$$\frac{\partial \hat{p}}{\partial m} = 0$$

$$\frac{\partial \hat{p}}{\partial \hat{s}} = \frac{1}{|\mathbf{J}|}m(-\eta_q\, \lambda^*\, \lambda_{j^*}^{*s} + nx_{\hat{s}-\hat{p}}(\lambda_{j^*}^{*s} - (1+\lambda^*)\lambda_q^{*s}))\psi_u \qquad < 0^{\dagger}, > 0^{\ddagger}$$

$$\frac{\partial \hat{p}}{\partial v} = \frac{1}{|\mathbf{J}|}(-m\, u\, \eta_q\, \lambda_{j^*}^{*s}\, \psi_u) \qquad < 0$$

$$\frac{\partial \hat{p}}{\partial \delta} = \frac{1}{|\mathbf{J}|}(-m\, \eta_q \lambda_{j^*}^{*s} \psi_u) \qquad < 0$$

$$\frac{\partial \hat{p}}{\partial \alpha} = \frac{1}{|\mathbf{J}|}m\, \eta_q(1+\lambda^*)\lambda_\alpha^{*s}\, \psi_u \qquad < 0$$

$$\frac{\partial \hat{p}}{\partial i^*} = \frac{1}{|\mathbf{J}|}m\, g_{i-\hat{p}}(\lambda_{j^*}^{*s} - (1+\lambda^*)\lambda_q^{*s})\psi_u \qquad < 0$$

[43] As in the financial crisis model for industrial countries, it has been assumed that ψ_u is a positive, but very small number. For details, see section 4.3.1.

Response of Tobin's q to Various Shocks.

$$\frac{\partial q}{\partial \lambda} = \frac{1}{|\mathbf{J}|}(-j\,m\,\lambda^{*s}_{j^*}) \qquad < 0$$
$$\frac{\partial q}{\partial j} = \frac{1}{|\mathbf{J}|}(-m\,\lambda\,\lambda^{*s}_{j^*}) \qquad < 0$$
$$\frac{\partial q}{\partial \lambda^*} = \frac{1}{|\mathbf{J}|}(-m\,(1+\lambda^* + j^*\,\lambda^{*s}_{j^*})) \qquad < 0$$
$$\frac{\partial q}{\partial \rho} = \frac{1}{|\mathbf{J}|}(-m(-1+(1+(-1+v)g_{i-\hat{p}})\beta_\rho)\lambda^{*s}_{j^*}) \qquad > 0$$
$$\frac{\partial q}{\partial h} = 0$$
$$\frac{\partial q}{\partial m} = 0$$
$$\frac{\partial q}{\partial \hat{s}} = \frac{1}{|\mathbf{J}|}(-m((-1+v)nx_{\hat{s}-\hat{p}} + \lambda^*)\lambda^{*s}_{j^*}) \qquad < 0^\dagger, > 0^\ddagger$$
$$\frac{\partial q}{\partial v} = \frac{1}{|\mathbf{J}|}(-m\,u\,\lambda^{*s}_{j^*}) \qquad < 0$$
$$\frac{\partial q}{\partial \delta} = \frac{1}{|\mathbf{J}|}(-m\,\lambda^{*s}_{j^*}) \qquad < 0$$
$$\frac{\partial q}{\partial \alpha} = \frac{1}{|\mathbf{J}|}m(1+\lambda^*)\lambda^{*s}_{\alpha} \qquad < 0$$
$$\frac{\partial q}{\partial i^*} = \frac{1}{|\mathbf{J}|}(-m(-1+v)g_{i-\hat{p}}\,\lambda^{*s}_{j^*}) \qquad < 0$$

Response of the Foreign Loan Rate j^* to Various Shocks.

$$\frac{\partial j^*}{\partial \lambda} = \frac{1}{|\mathbf{J}|} j\, m\, \lambda_q^{*s} \qquad > 0$$

$$\frac{\partial j^*}{\partial j} = \frac{1}{|\mathbf{J}|} m\, \lambda\, \lambda_q^{*s} \qquad > 0$$

$$\frac{\partial j^*}{\partial \lambda^*} = \frac{1}{|\mathbf{J}|} m\, (1 + (-1+v)\eta_q + j^*\, \lambda_q^{*s}) \qquad > 0$$

$$\frac{\partial j^*}{\partial \rho} = \frac{1}{|\mathbf{J}|} m(-1 + (1 + (-1+v)g_{i-\hat{p}})\beta_\rho)\lambda_q^{*s} \qquad < 0$$

$$\frac{\partial j^*}{\partial h} = 0$$

$$\frac{\partial j^*}{\partial m} = 0$$

$$\frac{\partial j^*}{\partial \hat{s}} = \frac{1}{|\mathbf{J}|} m((-1+v)nx_{\hat{s}-\hat{p}} + \lambda^*)\lambda_q^{*s} \qquad > 0^{\dagger},\ < 0^{\ddagger}$$

$$\frac{\partial j^*}{\partial v} = \frac{1}{|\mathbf{J}|} m\, u\, \lambda_q^{*s} \qquad > 0$$

$$\frac{\partial j^*}{\partial \delta} = \frac{1}{|\mathbf{J}|} m\, \lambda_q^{*s} \qquad > 0$$

$$\frac{\partial j^*}{\partial \alpha} = \frac{1}{|\mathbf{J}|} m(-1 - (-1+v)\eta_q)\lambda_\alpha^{*s} \qquad > 0$$

$$\frac{\partial j^*}{\partial i^*} = \frac{1}{|\mathbf{J}|} m(-1+v)g_{i-\hat{p}}\, \lambda_q^{*s} \qquad > 0$$

Response of the Domestic Interest Rate on Government Bonds i to Various Shocks.

$$\frac{\partial i}{\partial \lambda} = 0$$
$$\frac{\partial i}{\partial j} = 0$$
$$\frac{\partial i}{\partial \lambda^*} = 0$$
$$\frac{\partial i}{\partial \rho} = \beta_\rho < 0$$
$$\frac{\partial i}{\partial h} = 0$$
$$\frac{\partial i}{\partial m} = 0$$
$$\frac{\partial i}{\partial \hat{s}} = 0$$
$$\frac{\partial i}{\partial v} = 0$$
$$\frac{\partial i}{\partial \delta} = 0$$
$$\frac{\partial i}{\partial \alpha} = 0$$
$$\frac{\partial i}{\partial i^*} = 1$$

Response of Central Bank Reserves b to Various Shocks.[44]

$$\frac{\partial b}{\partial \lambda} = \frac{1}{|\mathbf{J}|}\left(-j(d_{r+\rho}(\lambda_{j^*}^{*s} - \lambda_q^{*s}) + \eta_q\,\lambda_{j^*}^{*s}(d_u + d_{\hat{p}_a}))\right) \qquad < 0$$

$$\frac{\partial b}{\partial j} = \frac{1}{|\mathbf{J}|}\left(-\lambda(d_{r+\rho}(\lambda_{j^*}^{*s} - \lambda_q^{*s}) + \eta_q\,\lambda_{j^*}^{*s}(d_u + d_{\hat{p}_a}))\right) \qquad < 0$$

$$\begin{aligned}\frac{\partial b}{\partial \lambda^*} = \frac{1}{|\mathbf{J}|}&(-m(1+(-1+v)\eta_q)\lambda_{j^*}^{*s} - d_u\,\eta_q(1+\lambda^*+j^*\,\lambda_{j^*}^{*s}) + m(1+\lambda^*)\lambda_q^{*s}\\ &+d_{r+\rho}((-1+v)\eta_q - \lambda^* + j^*(-\lambda_{j^*}^{*s}+\lambda_q^{*s})) - d_{\hat{p}_a}\,\eta_q(1+\lambda^*+j^*\,\lambda_{j^*}^{*s})\psi_u) \qquad \gtreqless 0\end{aligned}$$

$$\begin{aligned}\frac{\partial b}{\partial \rho} = \frac{1}{|\mathbf{J}|}&\,d_{r+\rho}\,((1+(-1+v)\beta_\rho\,(-g_{i-\hat{p}}+\eta_q))\lambda_{j^*}^{*}\\ &+(-1+\beta_\rho((-1+v)g_{i-\hat{p}} - \lambda^*))\lambda_q^{*s})\\ &+d_{i-\hat{p}}\,\beta_\rho\,((1+(-1+v)\eta_q)\lambda_{j^*}^{*} - (1+\lambda^*)\lambda_q^{*s})\\ &+(-(-1+\beta_\rho)\eta_q\,\lambda_{j^*}^{*} + g_{i-\hat{p}}\,\beta_\rho(\lambda_{j^*}^{*} - (1+\lambda^*)\lambda_q^{*s}))(d_u + d_{\hat{p}_a}) \qquad > 0\end{aligned}$$

$$\frac{\partial b}{\partial h} = -1 \qquad < 0$$

$$\frac{\partial b}{\partial m} = -\frac{b+h+\lambda^*}{m} \qquad < 0$$

$$\begin{aligned}\frac{\partial b}{\partial \hat{s}} = \frac{1}{|\mathbf{J}|}&\,d_{r+\rho}((-1+v)nx_{\hat{s}-\hat{p}} + \lambda^*)(-\lambda_{j^*}^{*} + \lambda_q^{*s})\\ &+(-\eta_q\,\lambda^*\,\lambda_{j^*}^{*} + nx_{\hat{s}-\hat{p}}(\lambda_{j^*}^{*} - (1+\lambda^*)\lambda_q^{*s}))(d_u + d_{\hat{p}_a}\,\psi_u) \qquad < 0^{\dagger},\ > 0^{\ddagger}\end{aligned}$$

$$\frac{\partial b}{\partial v} = \frac{1}{|\mathbf{J}|}\left(-u\,(d_{r+\rho}(\lambda_{j^*}^{*} - \lambda_q^{*s}) + \eta_q\,\lambda_{j^*}^{*}(d_u + d_{\hat{p}_a}\,\psi_u)\right) \qquad < 0$$

$$\frac{\partial b}{\partial \delta} = \frac{1}{|\mathbf{J}|}\left(-(d_{r+\rho}(\lambda_{j^*}^{*} - \lambda_q^{*s}) + \eta_q\,\lambda_{j^*}^{*}(d_u + d_{\hat{p}_a}\,\psi_u)\right) \qquad < 0$$

$$\frac{\partial b}{\partial \alpha} = \frac{1}{|\mathbf{J}|}\,\lambda_\alpha^{*s}(d_{r+\rho}((1-v)\eta_q + \lambda^*) + \eta_q(1+\lambda^*)(d_u + d_{\hat{p}_a}\,\psi_u)) \qquad < 0$$

$$\begin{aligned}\frac{\partial b}{\partial i^*} = \frac{1}{|\mathbf{J}|}&\,d_{i-\hat{p}}((1+(-1+v)\eta_q)\lambda_{j^*}^{*} - (1+\lambda^*)\lambda_q^{*s}\\ &-g_{i-\hat{p}}((-1+v)d_{r+\rho}(\lambda_{j^*}^{*} - \lambda_q^{*s}) - (\lambda_{j^*}^{*} - (1+\lambda^*)\lambda_q^{*s})(d_u + d_{\hat{p}_a}\,\psi_u)) \qquad < 0\end{aligned}$$

[44] For $\partial b/\partial\lambda$ and $\partial b/\partial j^*$ it has been assumed that $d_{r+\rho}(\lambda_{j^*}^{*s} - \lambda_q^{*s}) + \eta_q\,\lambda_{j^*}^{*s}(d_u + d_{\hat{p}_a}) > 0$ which is can be justified, as in the crisis model for industrial countries, by assuming a larger reaction of households' deposit demand as to changes in capacity utilization than as to changes in the expected profit rate $r+\rho$, i.e. it has been assumed that $|d_u| > |d_{r+\rho}|$ which holds for all partial derivatives for b.

Chapter 6

A Calibration Model of Financial Crises in Emerging Markets

6.1 The Nature of Calibration Models

6.1.1 Solution Procedures to Dynamic General Function Models, Limitations, and Simulation Methods

The method of solving dynamic portfolio balance macro models of the type given in chapters 4 and 5 is generally carried out in three steps. Firstly, the instantaneous short-run equilibrium is determined without considering dynamic adjustment equations, being followed by conventional comparative static techniques to examine the short-run effects of changes in parameters. Secondly, the long-run steady-state equilibrium is determined by substituting the steady-state values of dynamic adjustment equations into the original model equations, being as well followed by comparative statics in order to study the long-run effects of changes in parameters. Thirdly, if analytically possible, the dynamic stability conditions of the model are going to be analyzed in order to determine whether the system, after having been hit by a shock, is able to converge to a steady-state or not.[1]

Though these solution procedures are standard fundamental methods of macroeconomic analysis they are subject to limitations. Firstly, even models with a small number of equations and limited complexity regarding the interdependence of variables, give rise to indeterminacy as to the comparative static effects both in the short-run and in the long-run. Accordingly, general function models lose very fast their ability to provide general results which is often overcome by introducing restrictive assumptions as to the class of functions being used, parameter value ranges, etc. Secondly, even if it is possible to determine the signs of the comparative static effects, the partial derivatives cannot provide any information about the absolute or relative size regarding the changes in endogenous variables caused by changes of parameters. Thirdly, respecting dynamic stability analysis, even with small models it is often impossible to determine stability conditions without making restrictive assumptions, though stability conditions can be derived analytically. Fourthly, even if the dynamics of the system are comparatively simple, as e.g. the dynamics of a linear 2×2 system, it is not possible to derive any information regarding the

[1]This kind of procedure can be found e.g. in Tobin (1969), Blinder and Solow (1973), Tobin and Buiter (1976, 1980), Turnovsky (1977), Turnovsky and Miller (1984), and Taylor (1991).

time profile of the transitional dynamics or adjustment paths to the steady-state. Fifthly, both the short-run and the long-run equilibrium can be considered as not being of relevant economic interest since on the one hand, the short-run equilibrium is too short with respect to time in order to allow for relevant feedback effects, and on the other hand, the long-run equilibrium is too long regarding time since it takes an infinite time until the system settles on the steady-state. Accordingly, the transitional dynamics, the traverse, or the adjustment path of a system from an initial steady-state to another one, after it has been hit by an exogenous disturbance, is the actual field of interest for economists and policymakers.

In order derive information about the transitional dynamics of an economic system, the original general function model has to be transformed into a model structure in which each equation is specifically determined, e.g. as a linear or non-linear function being "well-behaved" or not, and in which every parameter has to take a specific value. As a result, the transitional dynamics depends heavily on the specific form of functions, and on the choice of parameter values, since assuming only a different functional form of a model equation, or only modifying slightly one parameter value, can change results considerably. Though these simulation techniques can provide important insights into the transitional dynamics of an economic system, a simulation result is only valid for a specific set of functions and parameters. As a result, one important objective of simulation approaches is to formulate simulation models which are valid for a wide range of functional forms and parameters whose validity is generally tested by performing a large number of simulations with different combinations of function and parameter sets. However, validity tests analyzing different combinations of functions and parameters can lead very quickly to a huge potential number of possible combinations even in small models which cannot be all simulated. Furthermore, lots of simulation models cannot be solved analytically, implying a restriction to certain numerical solutions calculated by computer programmes. As a result, the specific form of functions, as well as the range of parameter values have also to be restricted to a "feasible" function and parameter set which limits the general validity of the model. However, simulation techniques can be still useful in pointing out where clear time patterns exists.

The numerical specification of both static and dynamic general equilibrium models regarding the choice of parameters can be carried out either by using stochastic estimation procedures through single-equation or multi-equation methods, or by applying deterministic calibration techniques. Regarding stochastic estimation procedures, maximum likelihood methods are a commonly used technique to estimate parameters of economic models. Though this approach is viewed as most satisfactory from a statistical viewpoint, maximum likelihood procedures are subject to various limitations as to the applicability for general equilibrium models. Firstly, for lots of classes of general equilibrium models depending on the functional forms of the model equations, the likelihood function is not well defined since error terms are not distributed independently. Secondly, the number of parameters which have to be estimated increases very fast with the number of model equations. Accordingly, with a "normal" sample size, the number of parameters to be estimated exceeds very fast the number of available data points, intensifying the degrees of freedom problem. For example, the number of parameters to be estimated in larger models can take values in the thousands. Though these limitations can be partly overcome by subdividing economic models into subsystems, stochastic estimation procedures seem to be infeasible for simulation procedures.

An alternative simulation approach ,which can be used to overcome at least partly the limitations of stochastic estimation procedures, is to "calibrate" an economic model. The term "calibration", which can be described as "theoretical simulation", refers to the fact that the numerical specification of the model is adjusted to a base year observation. That is, the model has to be able to reproduce a base year data set as model solution, which is assumed to represent an equilibrium of the economy, by an appropriate choice of the parameter set. If possible, the "key" parameters of the model are generally determined by literature search basing on econometric estimation before calibration can be carried out. However, owing to the widespread use of CES production and utility functions in general equilibrium models, key parameters are mainly elasticities for which either only limited, contradictory, or no information is available in the literature. If there are no key parameter values to be obtained by literature research or empirical estimation, key parameters are simply "chosen" at will in order to generate a base year observation as model solution. In this case, sensitivity analysis is employed to prove at least some robustness of the results by trying alternative parameter values with respect to the robustness of the model findings. Though being better analytically tractable than stochastic estimation procedures, calibration techniques are also subject to various limitations. Firstly, the "selection" of parameters in order to adjust the model solution to the base year observation is arbitrary. Secondly, calibration does not provide any basis for a statistical test because it fits perfectly the data set which has been used for numerical specification. Thirdly, if key parameters are chosen arbitrarily, sensitivity analysis can neither "prove" that the parameters used in the model are "true", nor that the model results are generally valid.[2]

6.1.2 Simulation of Financial Crises with Calibration Techniques

The financial crisis models discussed in chapters 4 and 5 are consistent with the solution procedure of dynamic general function models outlined above, firstly, with respect to the determination of the instantaneous equilibrium and the subsequent short-run comparative-static analysis carried out in sections 4.3 and 5.3, and secondly, with respect to the local stability analysis according to sections 4.4.3 and 5.4.3, but do not correspond as to the steady-state analysis. Though several possible steady-state values for the two state variables have been analyzed, there has been no determination of the steady-values of the remaining variables, as well as no long-run comparative static analysis for three reasons. Firstly, since the dynamic system does not converge to a fixed point attractor, but converges to a dynamically stable closed orbit whose time path can only be proven to be existent, there is no possibility to determine analytically the "steady-state" cycle values of the two state variables in the form of explicit solutions. As a result, there is no possibility to substitute the "equilibrium cycle values" of the two state variables into the equation system to derive long-run cyclical steady-state solutions for the remaining endogenous variables. Secondly, though the dynamic system possesses a steady-state value, this intertemporal equilibrium is of limited economic interest since it is locally unstable, i.e. the economic system will never settle at that point. Likewise, the long-run value for

[2]The pros and cons of calibration techniques vs. stochastic estimation procedures of economic models are discussed e.g. in Mansur and Whalley (1984).

the state of confidence has been assumed to be $\rho_E = 0$, i.e. only the steady-state value of the debt-asset ratio will change, being also irrelevant for the remaining endogenous variables since the steady-state will not be reached. Thirdly, regarding long-run comparative statics, mathematical tools applicable for the analysis of 2×2 nonlinear systems are not able to provide any information regarding the nature of different limit cycles in case parameters are changed. There exist no possibilities, even graphically, to determine how a cycle changes if a certain parameter is varied, having been discussed in figure 5.8 in chapter 5.4.5, when the dynamic system was hit by a devaluation which changed the nature of the adjustment path and resulted in a "new" limit cycle whose graphical form with respect to the "old" limit cycle could not be determined.

Albeit the solution procedure of the crisis models in chapters 4 and 5 provides deep insights into the dynamics of financial cycles, it underlies some limitations especially with respect to the dynamics of financial crises' episodes. Firstly, in order to obtain unambiguous results in the short-run comparative static analysis, restrictions were imposed. Secondly, the comparative static description of financial crises outlined in sections 4.3.2 and 5.3.2 was only in a position to describe the stylized facts by the use of ad-hoc assumptions regarding the relative strength of counteracting forces during a financial cycle, i.e. the short-run partial derivatives given in sections 4.7 and 5.7 contain no information as to their absolute and relative magnitude. Thirdly, the cyclical dynamic stability of the system could be only proved by assumptions and by imposing restrictions. Fourthly, phase diagram analysis used in sections 4.4.4 and 5.4.4 is not able to provide any insights as to the time profile of the adjustment process to the limit cycle. Fifthly, the short-run, as well as the long-run cyclical equilibrium of the models do not provide any insights into the origin and into the dynamics of financial crises, since crises episodes are *transitional* dynamic phenomena. According to the crisis models, a financial crisis is a dynamic process occurring due to an exogenous shock between two cyclical steady-states representing "tranquil" times. Thus, financial crises are abnormal or extraordinary events in historical time which are not part of a steady-state, even if the steady-state is subject to cyclical fluctuations involving some financial distress at business cycle peaks as outlined in sections 4.4.5 and 5.4.5. Thereupon, in order to obtain an explicit description of financial crises' dynamics, the general function models given in chapters 4 and 5 have to be numerically specified and simulated. This chapter concentrates on the simulation of a modified emerging market crisis model since the model structure is richer and more complex than the industrial country case. Furthermore, the simulation results of the emerging market case can be simply applied to crisis periods in industrial countries.

Regarding the choice of simulation techniques, the following simulation is based on calibration techniques as stochastic estimation procedures are very difficult to carry out due to the reasons mentioned above, and actually do not exist. However, a calibration of financial crises calls for a modification of general calibration procedures since episodes of financial crises differ considerably from other economic phenomena being simulated. Firstly, the econometric literature provides only limited information regarding key parameters of financial crisis models, since general economic theory works with different model structures which are based on a "normal" functioning of economies, and which generally abstract from balance sheet positions of different sectors, or from "irrational" expectations. Secondly, it is impossible to find a long-run steady-state base year observation data set to which model parameters can be adjusted for a model aiming at providing a "general" theory of financial crises, being applicable to a wide range of countries, and not only to a specific country at a specific historical time. Furthermore, even if it was possible to determine key parameters for a steady-state solution, there is no guarantee that these parameter values remain constant in times of financial distress, representing extraordinary dynamic disequilibria. As a result, working with parameters being relevant in tranquil times can become impossible, which necessitates finding parameter values being applicable to times of financial distress, which is however also almost impossible since there exists no "steady-state crisis situation" from which parameters can be obtained. Summing up, a calibration of financial crises can only be carried out by a numerical specification of model equations for which parameters have to be varied arbitrarily as long as the calibration model generates a "stylized facts solution" of financial crises. Subsequently, this model solution has to be tested as to its robustness by sensitivity analysis for the key parameters of the model. To the reader, such a procedure may seem to be arbitrary but there are no better options due to the lack of relevant empirical data. However, such a kind of calibration can provide important theoretical insights with respect to transmission mechanisms during crises periods which can be used as a basis for future empirical research and improved calibrations.

The application of this kind of calibration technique to the emerging market crisis model given in chapter 5 can be carried out in several ways. If research interest lies especially on the global and transitional dynamics of the two state variables ρ and λ_d^*, ad-hoc assumptions as to the numerical specification of the 2×2 nonlinear system given by equations 5.12 and 5.13 can be made, being followed by a computer simulation procedure within a phase diagram analysis.[3] However, such an ad-hoc calibration is of limited interest since parameter values of the two basic differential equations are not derived from the entire model structure. In order to obtain "consistent" parameter values for the 2×2 nonlinear differential equation system, general functions given by equations 5.1 to 5.7 would have to be formally and parametrically specified in order to substitute the solutions of $r, \eta(q), q, \hat{p}$ and σ in terms of ρ and λ_d^* into the two differential equations 5.12 and 5.13.

Nevertheless, such a "consistent" approach can turn out to be infeasible for five reasons. Firstly, reducing the basic equation system, for which specific functional and parametric forms have been assumed, means that the two differential equations 5.12 and 5.13 contain all parameters having been employed in equations 5.1 to 5.7. Owing to existing nonlinearities and a large number of parameters, it is possible that an analytical solution of the "consistent" 2×2 nonlinear system is not to be found even by computer programmes, requiring to rely on specific parameter values and to solve the model numerically, which limits the general validity of the model results. Secondly, even if the model can be solved analytically, it is difficult to "find" a parameter combination which fits the stylized facts due to the lack of empirical data. Assuming e.g. only two parameters for each equation in system 5.1 to 5.7 amounts to 14 parameters. If each parameter is allowed to take only 10 specific values, being a very low number, there arise 10^{14} parameter combinations which lead to different dynamic outcomes. As a result, it can turn out to be very difficult to determine the parameter set fitting the stylized facts. Thirdly, owing to the large number of parameters, analytical stability analysis in nonlinear systems becomes almost impossible

[3]Such ad-hoc calibrations can be found e.g. in Flaschel, Franke and Semmler (1997), pp. 41-43 concentrating on price and quantity adjustments over time.

which requires to rely again on a numerical stability analysis by "searching" for parameter sets which generate a dynamically stable solution. Numerical solutions however, limit the general validity of the calibration model. Fourthly, among the search for a consistent parameter set, the choice of initial conditions of the state variables influences the dynamic properties of the system. As a result, some sets of initial conditions can generate stable dynamics fitting the stylized facts, whereas other sets engender chaotic dynamics. Fifthly, a calibration of emerging market crises has to be able to show the occurrence of twin crises, i.e. the model equations have to determine the time of the speculative attack in order to differentiate between the dynamics before and after the devaluation, which requires to make use of the concept of the shadow exchange rate firstly introduced by Flood and Garber (1984a). Since the exchange rate's growth rate has been treated as exogenous in the general function model, the calibration model has to be modified with respect to exchange rate and international reserve dynamics in order to solve the model for a flexible and for a fixed exchange rate regime.

Summing up, given the nonlinear dynamic character, the large number of equations and parameters, the need for modification of model equations, as well as the complexity of interdependencies between financial markets and the real sector, a calibration of the emerging market crisis model can be only carried out under very restrictive assumptions. Firstly, the system's dynamics have to be modified in order to determine the pre- and past-devaluation dynamics, which requires to use another basic differential system whose properties however, are not known. If the new system is supposed to generate nonlinear dynamics and to be analytically soluble, then either the dynamics of ρ or λ_d^* have to be abandoned in favour of the introduction of exchange rate and reserve dynamics, since it is not possible to analyze analytically the characteristics of nonlinear systems being higher than of second order. Secondly, given the complex dynamics of the model, a solution can be possibly only obtained by numerical methods, which implies the imposition of very restrictive assumptions as to the set of parameters and initial conditions. As a result, the advantage of having a very sophisticated model structure generating nonlinear dynamics would not offset the disadvantages of limiting the general validity of the model.

This trade-off is partly overcome in the present case by the introduction of a log-linear approximation of the nonlinear crisis model of chapter 5 which can be solved analytically, and which distinguishes between the pre- and post-devaluation period by explicitly considering exchange rate and international reserves dynamics. However, making use of linear dynamics means that the system is not longer able to generate endogenous steady state cycles, as well as cyclical adjustment paths. This implies that for every stage of an excessive business cycle generating financial crises, i.e. for the boom, the overborrowing and for the bust phase, a separate calibration has to be carried out. As a result, the endogenous character of expectations and indebtedness is lost since ρ and λ_d^* have to be used as the *exogenous* "driving forces" of the dynamic system. However, the dynamics of all other variables, as well the dynamics before and after a devaluation can be derived, being not feasible with sophisticated nonlinear model structures as given in chapters 4 and 5. Accordingly, the log-linear calibration model is supposed to be viewed as a complementary model and *not* as a substitute.

In contrast to the theory of financial crises presented in chapters 4 and 5, almost all standard theories, except for moral hazard models and Minsky's financial fragility approach, claim that financial crises are caused by negative shocks whose magnitude is sufficient to generate a high degree of financial fragility and to trigger financial crises. As a result, standard theory does not explain the fact that, in most cases, the build-up of financial fragility is caused by a positive shock to expectations, and that a subsequent financial crisis can be triggered by a very small negative shock whose impact on overall financial fragility can be almost neglected. However, in accordance with standard theory, there arise also situations in reality in which financial crises have their origin in large negative shocks. Yet, these cases occur less frequently in reality than financial crises caused by excessive business cycles. In order to be consistent with the stylized facts, to demonstrate the general validity of the model, and to point out the logic of standard exogenous shock-driven financial crisis models, a separate simulation in addition to the three boom-bust simulations (boom phase, overborrowing phase, bust phase) is carried out for a negative foreign interest rate shock for which the influence of changing profit expectations has been eliminated.

6.2 The Real Side

All variables except for interest rates, risk premia, the profit rate, and the state of confidence, are expressed as natural logs due to the log-linear structure of the model, where natural logs are labelled simply as "logs" in the following. Parameters attached to interest rates, risk premia, the profit rate and the state of confidence in equations defining the natural log of an endogenous variable represent semi-elasticities, whereas parameters attached to the remaining variables represent pure elasticities. Parameters used in equations defining interest rates, the risk premium, and the profit rate represent derivatives.

Consider a small emerging market economy following a "Washington Consensus" style policy and/or an IMF orthodox stabilization programme with open trade, deregulation of domestic industries, domestic financial market liberalization and capital account liberalization. The economy is assumed to peg its exchange rate to an anchor currency like the U.S.-$, the Yen or the Euro. Reasons for a fixed exchange rate regime can reach from inflation stabilization programmes (see e.g. Latin America) to export-led growth strategies (see e.g. Asia). Domestic prices are assumed to be determined by the (natural) log of PPP, reading formally as

$$\ln P(t) = \ln s(t) + \ln P^*(t), \tag{6.1}$$

where $\ln P(t)$ denotes the log of the domestic price level, $\ln P^*(t)$ the log of the foreign price level, and $\ln s(t)$ the log of the exchange rate expressing the price of one unit foreign currency in domestic currency. The foreign price level is assumed to remain constant throughout the analysis.

Output is assumed to be determined by the demand side of the economy. The resulting goods market equilibrium in natural log-form is given formally by

$$\begin{aligned}\ln Y(t) = y_0 + y_1 (\ln s(t) + \ln P^*(t) - \ln P(t)) \\ + y_2 (\ln P_K(t) - \ln P(t)) - y_3(f(t) - \zeta \ln P(t)),\end{aligned} \tag{6.2}$$

$$y_0, y_1, y_2, y_3 > 0, \qquad \text{and} \qquad \zeta > 0,$$

where $\ln Y(t)$ denotes the log of real output and the right hand side of equation 6.2 the log of real demand for goods consisting of four components.[4] The first demand component y_0 represents autonomous demand for domestic goods. The second demand component are net exports being positively dependent on the log of the real exchange rate $\ln s(t)+\ln P^*(t)-\ln P(t)$. Investment demand which is positively dependent on the log of Tobin's q, being defined as $\ln q(t) = \ln P_K(t) - \ln P(t)$ and determined below, constitutes demand component three. Demand component four is government expenditure, being negatively dependent on the nominal long-term interest rate on domestic government bonds $f(t)$, and positively dependent on the log of domestic price level $\ln P(t)$, where ζ is a positive parameter. It is assumed that government expenditures are reduced when nominal long-term interest rates increase, leading to a rise in the overall nominal debt burden, but expand if there is a rise in the price level which reduces the real value of public debt, and the real value of interest payments; y_0, y_1, y_2, y_3 are positive parameters which are going to be specified in the calibration process.

Profits of the business firm sector are represented by the profit rate on capital which is formally given by

$$r(t) = r_0 + r_1 \ln Y(t) - r_2\, j(t) - r_3\, \delta(t) \\ -r_4 (\ln s(t) + \ln P^*(t)) - (\ln P(t) + \ln K(t)), \tag{6.3}$$

$$r_0, r_1, r_3, r_4 > 0, \qquad \text{and} \qquad r_2 \gtreqless 0,$$

stating that the profit rate $r(t)$ is determined by firms' cash flow (earnings less costs) which is deflated by the log of the capital stock valued at replacement costs $\ln P(t) + \ln K(t)$. Earnings are assumed to be positively dependent on the log of real output $\ln Y(t)$. Costs can be subdivided into three components. The first cost component emerges from external debt in the form of interest rate costs on bank loans which are approximated, for reasons of simplicity which are discussed in detail in section 6.3.2, by the loan rate $j(t)$, implying a neglect of the direct influence of the total stock of loans $L(t)$ on interest rate costs $j(t)L(t)$, and thereby on the profit rate $r(t)$. The influence of interest rate costs on the profit rate however, is not unambiguous and varies considerably over the business cycle, i.e. there arise situations in which a decreasing loan rate leads to decreasing total interest rate costs increasing the profit rate, but there are also situations in which a decreasing loan rate increases total interest rate costs leading to decline in the profit rate. In order to take these effects into account, parameter r_2 is allowed to take positive as well as negative values in different phases of the business cycle which are discussed in section 6.3.2 and specified in the calibration process. The second cost component stems from depreciation on the capital stock, where $\delta(t)$ denotes the depreciation rate. The costs for imported intermediate goods, whose price in domestic currency in log-form is $\ln s(t) + \ln P^*(t)$, constitute cost component three. For reasons of simplicity, imported intermediate goods and imported final goods are valued by the same price, i.e. by the log of the foreign price level $\ln P^*(t)$; r_0, r_1, r_3, r_4 are positive parameters which are going to be specified for the calibration procedure.

[4]The non-log version of equation 6.2 reads as $Y(t) = e^{y_0} \left(\frac{s(t)P^*(t)}{P(t)}\right)^{y_1} \left(\frac{P_K(t)}{P(t)}\right)^{y_2} \left(\frac{e^{f(t)}}{P(t)^{\zeta}}\right)^{-y_3}$.

6.3 The Financial Side

6.3.1 A Stylized Financial Structure

Figure 6.1 depicts a simplified and stylized financial structure of small open emerging market economies being characterized, in contrast to chapter 5, by a "developed" domestic financial sector, i.e. the banking sector is fully liberalized and does not suffer any more from past financial repression. Accordingly, the domestic banking sector plays a key role for the allocation of national and international funds into domestic investment opportunities since information asymmetries between foreign savers and domestic investors can be best reduced by banks' intermediation.

Assets and debts are priced at their current market or discounted present values, i.e. there is no distinction between book and market values. In order to distinguish between real stocks, market prices and nominal market values of bonds, equities, and the capital stock, the real stock of equities is denoted as E, the real capital stock as K, and the real stock of bonds as B_{xx}, where the first subscript denotes whether bonds are Short-term or Long-term, and the second one whether they are Domestic or Foreign. As bonds and equities, i.e. real capital, are traded in financial markets, they are valued at their market price P_{xxx}, denoting the price in domestic or foreign currency per real unit, where the first subscript describes whether it concerns the price of Bonds, the (demand) price of the capital stock K, or the price of Equities; the second and third subscript only refer to bond prices and distinguish whether bond prices relate to Short-term or Long-term bonds, and whether they are Domestic or Foreign. Bond prices are inversely related to their interest rates. Nominal market values of equity and bond holdings are $P_E E$ and $P_{Bxx}B_{xx}$. Since foreign short-term bonds $P_{SFB}B_{SF}$ and foreign loans to banks, denoted as L_F, are denominated in foreign currency, nominal stocks are multiplied by the exchange rate s expressing the price of one unit foreign currency in domestic currency. In contrast to figure 5.1, the exchange rate does not appear with its pegged value $\bar{s}$ in balance sheets, since the calibration model solves the equation system both for a fixed and for a flexible exchange rate, whereas the theoretical emerging market crisis model in chapter 5 only considered different pegged exchange rate values.

There are six types of agents in the economy, households, firms, the government, domestic banks, the central bank and foreign investors holding nine sorts of assets. The first sort are deposits D, the second sort domestic short-term government bonds $P_{SDB}B_{SD}$ being traded internationally, and being imperfect substitutes for foreign short-term government bonds $sP_{SFB}B_{SF}$ which constitute asset sort three. Though the international financial market for short-term government bonds underlies no restrictions, yields differ due to the existence of a risk premium on domestic short-term bonds reflecting the domestic government's and the country's risk of default. Asset type four takes the form of domestic long-term bonds $P_{LDB}B_{LD}$ which are not traded internationally since there are no foreign substitutes. Asset type five is the capital stock K being valued at the demand price of capital P_K. Firms' capital stock is partly financed by the issuance of equities, being asset sort six, whose nominal value amounts to $P_E E$, where the real stock of equities E is assumed to remain constant throughout the analysis. The remaining part of the capital stock is financed by bank loans L constituting asset type seven and being denominated in domestic currency. It is assumed that new investment is financed

Households

Deposits	D		
Short-Term Domestic Bonds	$P_{SDB} B_{SD}$		
Long-Term Domestic Bonds	$P_{LDB} B_{LD}$	Net Worth	NW_{HH}
Short-Term Foreign Bonds	$s P_{SFB} B_{SF}$		
Equities	$P_E E$		

Firms

Capital Stock *(Valued at Demand Price of Capital)*	$P_K K$	Domestic Loans From Domestic Banks	L
		Equities	$P_E E$

Banks

Deposits at Central Bank *(Required Reserves)*	$D_{BA}(=\tau D)$	Deposits	D
Loans to Firms	L	Loans from Central Bank	L_{BA}
		Foreign Loans	sL^*
		Net Worth	NW_{BA}

Central Bank

Loans to Banks *(Domestic Credit Component)*	$L_{BA}=H$	Deposits of Commercial Banks *(Required Reserves)*	D_{BA}
Foreign Reserves	$Z=(sL^*+B)$		$=M$ *(High-Powered Money)*

Government

		Short-Term Domestic Bonds	$P_{SDB} B_{SD}$
		Long-Term Domestic Bonds	$P_{LDB} B_{LD}$
		Net Worth *(Negative)*	NW_{Gov}

Figure 6.1: Stylized Financial Structure in Emerging Markets with a "Developed" Domestic Banking System

by taking new bank loans and by retained earnings, and not by issuing equities, being consistent with the credit view on macroeconomic activity. Asset type eight takes the form of foreign loans denominated in foreign currency L^* from foreigners to domestic banks whose nominal value in domestic currency amounts to sL^*. Asset type nine is high powered money M which is held by domestic banks as required reserves (cash and excess reserves are excluded) in the form of deposits with the central bank $D_{BA} = \tau D = M$, where τ denotes the required reserve ratio.

High powered money is generated on the one hand by granting interest bearing loans to banks L_{BA} constituting the domestic credit component $H = L_{BA}$, and on the other hand by buying foreign reserves Z. Regarding the domestic credit component H, the present model explicitly considers, in contrast to the financial crisis models in chapters 4 and 5, the existence of a domestic money market in which banks' demand for the domestic credit component is inversely related to the central banks' official discount rate i_C. Accordingly, monetary policy in the present model is carried out by variations in the official discount rate and not by variations in the money supply. Regarding foreign exchange reserves, the model assumes that Z develops from two main sources. Firstly, Z comes into being by banks selling their stock of foreign loans L^* to the central bank at the exchange rate s, which can be used e.g. for reducing $L_{BA} = H$ with D_{BA} remaining constant, or for increasing D_{BA} and thereby D and L, leaving $L_{BA} = H$ unchanged. Secondly, in a fixed exchange rate regime Z develops also from imbalances of current and capital account transactions of other sectors which are offset by variations in international reserves being denoted as B and expressed in domestic currency terms, i.e. it holds that $sL^* + B = Z$. Regarding B, it is assumed firstly, that all international monetary transactions stemming from capital account or current account transaction are carried out via the domestic banking sector due to information asymmetries, which sells or buys foreign high powered money to or from the central bank in the foreign exchange market, and secondly, that no other sector than the central bank possesses foreign high powered money.[5] It is important to note that it is possible for situations to arise in which B takes a negative value (e.g. due to large accumulated current account deficits) implying $Z < sL^*$, i.e. foreign exchange reserves would not suffice to pay back all foreign loans in case of a sudden and complete withdrawal of foreign investors. Such a situation also implies that foreign loans can be only paid back completely without any further external financing by capital inflows, if the economy is able to generate sufficient current account surpluses in the future.

Despite the fact that domestic financial markets and the capital account are fully liberalized, and portfolio adjustments are assumed to be instantaneous, there exists no perfect capital mobility in the model arising from three assumptions. Firstly, only short-term bonds are assumed to be traded internationally due to the lack of suitable substitutes (domestic long-term bonds) or due to insurmountable information asymmetries (equities). Secondly, short-term bonds are assumed only to be imperfect substitutes owing to the existence of a risk premium. Thirdly, domestic assets are assumed to be only imperfect substitutes, i.e. there is no condition requiring e.g. the equality of equities' and long-term bonds' rate of returns.

Households' nominal net worth NW_{HH} consists of deposits D, domestic short-term bonds $P_{BSD}B_{SD}$, domestic long-term bonds $P_{BLD}B_{LD}$, foreign short-term bonds $sP_{BSF}B_{SF}$, and equities $P_E E$.

Firms' capital stock is financed by bank loans L and by issuing equities E whose real stock is assumed to be constant. The equity price P_E is assumed to bring the stock market instantaneously into equilibrium, resulting in a zero net worth of firms.[6] Accordingly, the demand price of capital P_K is determined via the equity and the domestic loan market, being derived from firms' balance sheet identity as

$$P_K = \frac{L + P_E E}{K}.$$

[5]For example, if households want to sell a fraction of short-term foreign bonds, they sell their bonds to banks and receive deposits in domestic currency valued at the prevailing exchange rate. Then, banks sell these bonds in the international market for short-term government bonds receiving foreign reserves which are immediately sold to the central bank increasing either D_{BA}, or reducing H where D_{BA} remains unchanged.

[6]For details, see section 4.2.1.

Banks create deposits as a multiple of the monetary base M. Demand for high-powered money stems exclusively from the required reserve ratio τ since cash and excess reserves are excluded. Accordingly, the money multiplier amounts to $m = 1/\tau$[7], i.e. it holds that $M = D_{BA} = \tau D = \frac{1}{m}D$. Required reserves D_{BA} are "financed" on the one hand by borrowing domestic credit $H = L_{BA}$ at the central bank's official discount rate i_C, and on the other hand by selling foreign exchange reserves Z to the central bank, where Z stems from the exchange of foreign loans L^* at the exchange rate s, and from selling reserves B arising from imbalances of current and capital account transactions. Accordingly, in an environment of financial liberalization and deregulation in which banks are allowed to tap international capital markets, the capacity to create deposits, and thereby loans, is influenced on the one hand by domestic monetary conditions, but also by international monetary conditions which can be illustrated by solving banks' adding-up constraint for the stock of loans L, formally given by

$$L = (1 - \tau)D + H + sL_F + NW_{BA} \qquad \text{where} \qquad \tau D = D_{BA} = H + Z = M.$$

As a result, the capacity of creating loans is positively dependent on D, H, L_F and NW_{BA}, and negatively dependent on τ.

The domestic government issues bonds, both short-term $P_{SDB}B_{SD}$ and long-term $P_{LDB}B_{LD}$ to finance its budget deficits. Since the government is assumed not to own any assets, government's net worth NW_{Gov} is negative. The stock of government debt is assumed to remain constant throughout the analysis since the model focuses on financial crises being endogenously driven by market forces, and not by inconsistent macroeconomic policies.

General monetary policy tools are the required reserve ratio τ, and the official discount rate i_C steering the domestic credit component H. In the case of a fixed exchange rate regime, the central bank tries to stabilize the exchange rate via interest rate policy and changes in foreign reserves Z, whereas in the case of a flexible exchange rate it holds that $Z = 0$ since the central bank does not intervene in the foreign exchange market and follows an independent interest rate policy. The central bank is not assumed to engage in official revaluations of the exchange rate, i.e. in case of a currency crisis there is a transition from a fixed exchange rate regime to a fully flexible exchange rate regime.

Private domestic wealth (excluding government and central bank) is given by

$$W_P = NW_{HH} + NW_{BA} = P_K K + P_{SDB}P_{SD} + P_{LDB}B_{LD} + sP_{SFB}B_{SF} + Z - sL^*,$$

i.e. by the capital stock, by domestic short-term and long-term bonds, by short-term foreign bonds, by foreign exchange reserves less foreign loans.

Overall domestic wealth (including government and central bank) is given by

$$W = NW_{HH} + NW_{BA} + NW_{Gov} = P_K K + sP_{SFB}B_{SF} + Z - sL^*,$$

i.e. by the capital stock, by foreign short-term bonds, by international reserves less foreign loans.

[7]For this simplifying assumption, see section 4.2.1.

6.3.2 Financial Market Equilibria

All financial market equations are derived by approximations of the portfolio structure given in figure 6.1, following the simplified portfolio approach having been introduced in chapters 4 and 5.[8] The equilibrium condition in the market for deposits in log-form reads as

$$\ln m(t) + \gamma \ln H(t) + (1-\gamma)\ln Z(t) - \ln P(t) = d_1 \ln Y(t) - d_2 i(t) - d_3 f(t), \tag{6.4}$$

$$0 < \gamma < 1, \qquad \text{and} \qquad d_1, d_2, d_3 > 0.$$

The left hand side of equation 6.4 represents the log of real supply of deposits by banks and the right hand side the log of households' real demand for deposits. The log of real deposit supply consists of the log of high powered money $\ln H(t)$ and of foreign reserves $\ln Z(t)$, where γ denotes a weighting factor[9], $\ln m(t)$ the log of the money multiplier which is assumed to be constant[10], and $\ln P(t)$ the log of the domestic price level.[11] It is assumed that banks do not pay interest on deposits. The log of real deposit demand by households depends positively on the log of real output $\ln Y(t)$, negatively on the interest rate on domestic short-term bonds $i(t)$, and negatively on the interest rate on domestic long-term bonds $f(t)$. For reasons of simplicity, there is no direct negative dependence of deposit demand on the expected profit rate $r(t) + \rho(t)$, where $r(t)$ denotes the actual profit rate and $\rho(t)$ the state of confidence. However, in order to capture the influence of equities on other asset holdings by households, equation 6.9 defining Tobin's q establishes an inverse relationship between the interest rate on short-term bonds $i(t)$ and the expected profit rate $r(t) + \rho(t)$; γ, d_1, d_2, d_3 are positive parameters to be specified for the calibration of the model.

Equilibrium in the domestic money market in which domestic banks can borrow high powered money from the central bank at the official discount or prime rate $i_C(t)$ is described by banks' demand for domestic credit component in log-form $\ln H(t)$, given formally as

$$\ln H(t) = h_0 - h_1 i_C(t), \qquad h_0, h_1 > 0, \tag{6.5}$$

stating firstly, that banks' demand for domestic credit is negatively dependent on the prime rate $i_C(t)$ which is used as the main monetary policy instrument in the model, and secondly, that the central bank provides each amount of domestic credit demanded by banks at the prevailing discount rate; h_0 and h_1 are positive parameters to be specified in the calibration process.

Foreign loans to domestic banks $L^*(t)$ denominated in foreign currency are represented by the log of their net loan inflow version $\ln LF^*(t)$, being defined as the log of the sum of foreign loan inflows less the sum of foreign loan outflows, i.e. it holds that $\ln LF^*(t) = \ln \dot{L}^*(t)$.[12] Net foreign loan inflows to domestic banks are assumed to be determined

[8] For a discussion of the pros and cons of a standardized portfolio approach, see section 4.2.2.

[9] Accordingly, the log of high powered money $\ln M(t)$ is defined as $\ln M(t) = \gamma \ln H(t) + (1-\gamma)Z(t)$.

[10] In log-terms the relation between the money multiplier and the required reserve ratio is given by $\ln m(t) = -\ln \tau(t)$.

[11] The non-log version of the deposit market equilibrium reads as $m\, H(t)^{\gamma}\, Z(t)^{1-\gamma} P(t)^{-1} = Y(t)^{d_1}\, e^{-i(t)\, d_2}\, e^{-f(t)\, d_3}$.

[12] Note that $\ln LF^*(t) = \ln \dot{L}^*(t)$ is an approximation of the log of net loan inflows' growth rate due to

firstly by domestic banks' collateral, and secondly by the difference between lending costs in domestic and in foreign currency. Regarding the dependence of net capital inflows on banks' collateral, the model assumes that an increase in collateral leads to higher net capital inflows, where banks' collateral is approximated by banks' net worth $NW_{BA}(t)$, being an indicator both for the liquidity or profit position, and for the solvency position. Respecting the difference in lending costs, domestic banks are assumed to decide upon the amount of foreign borrowing by comparing the cost of borrowing domestic credit $i_C(t)$ in the domestic money market with the cost of borrowing foreign funds. The cost of borrowing foreign funds, being expressed by the foreign loan rate on foreign funds $j^*(t)$, consists of three components, formally given by

$$j^*(t) = i_C^*(t) + rp(t) + E_t[\ln \dot{s}(t)],$$

where $i_C^*(t)$ denotes the foreign official discount rate representing refinancing costs of foreign lenders, $rp(t)$ the risk premium reflecting domestic banks' risk of default to be determined below, and $E_t[\ln \dot{s}(t)]$ the exchange rate's expected rate of change reflecting currency risk, where $s(t)$ denotes the price of one unit foreign currency in domestic currency, and $E_t[x]$ the expectations operator expressing the expected value of a variable x conditional on all information available up to date t. Regarding the formation of exchange rate expectations, the model assumes that agents behave rationally, i.e. it holds that $E_t[\ln \dot{s}(t)] = \ln \dot{s}(t)$. The assumption of rational expectations contradicts the expectation formation scheme employed in chapters 4 and 5, having claimed that exchange rate expectations depend on the state of confidence, implying that agents are only rational in the long-run. However, imposing short-run rationality as to exchange rate expectations and long-run rationality as to profit rate expectations can be justified by the fact that the exchange rate is a "forward-looking" variable whose value typically incorporates all information as it becomes available, whereas an economy's profit rate depending on technology, the quality of the capital stock, balance sheet structures, business cycle phases etc., as defined by equations 4.16 and 5.10, is a "backward-looking" or "sluggish" variable whose evolution is tied to the past.[13] Furthermore, imposing short-run rationality as to exchange rate expectations is consistent with current financial crisis models in order to derive the time path of the flexible shadow exchange rate, as well as the time of speculative attack. Summing up, net foreign loan inflows to domestic banks in log-terms are formally given as

$$\begin{aligned} \ln LF^*(t) &= lf_1 \ln NW_{BA}(t) + lf_2 \left(i_C(t) - j^*(t)\right) \\ &= lf_1 \ln NW_{BA}(t) + lf_2 \left(i_C(t) - (i_C^*(t) + rp(t) + E_t[\ln \dot{s}(t)]\right), \end{aligned} \tag{6.6}$$

$$lf_1, lf_2 > 0, \qquad \text{and} \qquad E_t[\ln \dot{s}(t)] = \ln \dot{s}(t),$$

where lf_1 and lf_2 are positive parameters to be specified in the calibration procedure. It holds that $\ln LF^*(t) \gtreqless 0$, where $\ln LF^*(t) > 0$ is assumed to determine a net inflow, and

the fact that a variable's $x(t)$ growth rate, being defined in continuous form as $\hat{x}(t) = \dot{x}(t)/x(t)$, can be approximated in log-terms as $\ln \hat{x}(t) = \ln(\dot{x}(t)/x(t)) = \ln \dot{x}(t) - \ln x(t) \approx \ln \dot{x}(t)$.

[13] The distinction between rational forward-looking and sluggish variables, as well as their influence on the dynamic stability of theoretical models are discussed in appendix D.

$\ln LF^{*}(t) < 0$ a net capital outflow. International capital flow reversals can be caused according to equation 6.6 by a drop in the log of banks' net worth $\ln NW_{BA}(t)$, by an increase in the foreign prime rate $i_C^*(t)$, by an increase in the risk premium $rp(t)$, or by depreciation expectations of the exchange rate, i.e. by $E_t[\ln \dot{s}(t)] > 0$.

Banks' net worth position $NW_{BA}(t)$ depends on banks' profits which are assumed to hinge predominantly upon the amount of non-performing loans of firms. The amount of non-performing loans itself, depends on the liquidity and on the solvency status of firms which are approximated by firms' profit rate on capital $r(t)$. Hence, the log of banks' net worth $\ln NW_{BA}(t)$ is formally given by

$$\ln NW_{BA}(t) = nw_0 + nw_1\, r(t), \qquad nw_0, nw_1 > 0, \tag{6.7}$$

stating that a fall in the profit rate worsens firms' cash flow position to meet their payment obligations on loans, leading to an increase in non-performing loans, and reducing banks' profits and net worth; nw_0 and nw_1 are positive parameters to be specified in the calibration process. As a result, a banking crisis can be defined, according to equation 6.7, as a situation in which banks' net worth falls short of a certain minimum level (e.g. $\ln NW(t) = 0$) set up by regulation authorities.

The risk premium $rp(t)$ in equation 6.6, being an indicator for banks' default risk, is assumed to depend negatively on banks' collateral which is approximated by the log of banks' net worth $\ln NW_{BA}(t)$, formally

$$rp(t) = rp_0 - rp_1 \ln NW_{BA}(t), \qquad rp_0, rp_1 > 0, \tag{6.8}$$

stating that the risk premium increases if banks' net worth decreases, where rp_0 and rp_1 are positive parameters to be specified in the calibration process.

Equity market equilibrium is represented by the equilibrium condition in the market for real capital. Assuming that equity demand and supply can be subsumed under real capital demand and supply as in sections 4.2.2 and 5.2.2, equilibrium in the market for real capital in log-form is formally given by

$$\ln K(t) + \ln P_K(t) - \ln P(t) = -k_1 i(t) + k_2(r(t) + \rho(t)), \qquad k_1, k_2 > 0, \tag{6.9}$$

the left hand side representing the log of the supply of capital in real terms, i.e. the capital stock valued at Tobin's q whose value in log-terms corresponds to $\ln q = \ln P_K(t) - \ln P(t)$, and the right hand side representing the log of real demand for capital by households; k_1 and k_2 are positive parameters to be specified in the calibration process. Real demand for capital by households is, according to the portfolio framework depicted in figure 6.1, negatively dependent on the interest rate on short-term bonds $i(t)$, and positively dependent on the expected profit rate $r(t) + \rho(t)$ on real capital, where $r(t)$ represents the current rate of profit, and $\rho(t)$ state of confidence, i.e. the difference between the expected and the actual rate of profit on real capital. Though the domestic loan rate $j(t)$ would be a suitable reference interest rate for the determination of Tobin's q, the model emphasizes the influence of short-term portfolio shifts by households on the demand price of capital being represented by $i(t)$. However, the the domestic loan rate $j(t)$ is implicitly included in equation 6.9 via its influence on firms' profit rate $r(t)$, being specified in greater detail below.

The international market for short-term government bonds cannot be described by UIP due to the assumption of imperfect capital mobility, i.e. the domestic and the foreign interest rate differ by a risk premium. Since the model emphasizes the evolution of financial fragility induced by the private sector, and not by the government in the form of inconsistent macroeconomic policy, the risk premium domestic short-term government bonds bear is assumed to be exogenous. Accordingly, equilibrium in the international market for short-term government bonds reads as

$$i(t) = i_C^*(t) + \alpha + E_t[\ln \dot{s}(t)], \qquad \text{and} \qquad E_t[\ln \dot{s}(t)] = \ln \dot{s}(t), \tag{6.10}$$

where $i(t)$ denotes the domestic interest rate on short-term bonds, $i_C^*(t)$ the foreign prime rate which is assumed to be a proxy for the foreign interest rate on short-term government bonds, α the exogenous given risk premia domestic bonds bear, and $E[\ln \dot{s}(t)]$ the exchange rate's expected rate of change.

The market for domestic loans and its changing demand and supply conditions over the business cycle is, among the state of confidence, one of the most important determinants of the calibration process. As having demonstrated in chapters 4 and 5, each phase of tranquil and financial crisis cycles is characterized by a specific debt-asset ratio/state of confidence constellation. However, as outlined in section 6.1.2, the log-linear calibration model does not engender endogenous nonlinear debt and expectations dynamics due to the need to solve the model for a flexible and for a fixed exchange rate regime. This constraint requires firstly, a linear dynamic system in the log of the exchange rate $\ln s(t)$ and in the log of foreign reserves $\ln Z(t)$, and, as a result, secondly, separate linear calibrations of each business cycle phase (boom, overborrowing, and bust) which are characterized by different assumptions as to the state of confidence, loan market reactions with respect to loan rate changes, and as to the influence of interest rate costs on firms' profit rate and on the real sector.

The changing influence of the state of confidence $\rho(t)$ over the business cycle is captured by assuming a steady and exogenously increasing value of $\rho(t)$ during the boom and during the overborrowing phase, and an exogenously decreasing value of $\rho(t)$ during the bust phase. As it will be discussed later, the exogenous character of the state of confidence could have been endogenized by some variables of the calibration model which, however, has been omitted for reasons of mathematical tractability.

Changing loan market reactions and their changing influence on firms' profit rate over the business cycle are taken into consideration by using different assumptions, firstly, as to the loan rate semi-elasticity with respect to the stock of loans, and secondly, as to the derivative of firms' profit rate with respect to the loan rate representing the influence of total debt costs on the profit rate. In order to derive these specific conditions formally, a general loan market equilibrium condition has to be specified in a first step. To keep the model formally tractable, it is assumed firstly, that banks behave as monopolists in the market for loans by setting the interest rate on loans $j(t)$, and secondly, that firms act as price takers whose demand for loans is negatively dependent on the loan rate. Regarding the loan rate determination, banks' are assumed firstly, to use markup pricing with regard to their refinancing costs, and secondly, to vary the loan rate according to the level of firms' capital stock valued at the stock market which serves as collateral. Formally, the loan rate set by banks is given by

$$j(t) = j_0 - j_1 (\gamma \ln H(t) + (1 - \gamma) \ln Z(t)) - j_2 \ln P_K(t), \qquad j_0, j_1, j_2 > 0 \tag{6.11}$$

where j_0, j_1 and j_2 are positive parameters to be specified in the calibration process. The $j_1(\cdot)$ term indicates that the loan rate depends negatively on the log of banks' input factors to create deposits and loans, setting up a positive relationship between the loan rate and refinancing costs. If, for example, there is an increase in the domestic prime rate $i_C(t)$ increasing the cost for domestic credit $\ln H(t)$, banks reduce $\ln H(t)$ implying a reduction in deposits and in banks' capacity to create loans which increases the loan rate. The same effect works through (the log of) foreign exchange reserves $\ln Z(t)$. If there is a sudden net capital outflow reducing $\ln Z(t)$, being induced by foreign investors withdrawing loans $L^*(t)$ from banks, and/or by domestic residents fleeing to quality by reducing domestic asset holdings and buying foreign assets reducing B in figure 6.1, there is a decline in domestic high powered money, reducing the ability to create deposits and loans which is reflected in a higher loan rate. The $j_2(\cdot)$ term indicates that the loan rate incorporates a risk premium firms have to pay in order to compensate for the risk of default. This risk premium is dependent on the market valuation of firms' capital stock serving as collateral. Since the log of the real capital stock $\ln K(t)$ is assumed constant throughout the analysis, firms' collateral value can be approximated by the log of the demand price of capital $\ln P_K(t)$, to be determined below, being both an useful indicator for firms' liquidity and solvency. Equation 6.11 suggest that the higher the demand price of capital, being caused by a higher market valuation of equities, the lower the loan rate. Consequently, banks amplify the amplitude of business cycles by relaxing credit market conditions in boom phases and by tightening them in downswings according to the financial accelerator effect. The parameter j_0 can be considered as a theoretical maximum loan rate if high powered money is zero and firms are bankrupt, i.e. the log of the demand price of capital reaches a lower bound $\ln P_K(t) = 0$.

In order to determine the influence of total interest rate costs $j(t)L(t)$ on firms' profit rate, the equilibrium stock of loans $L(t)$ has to be specified as a function of the loan rate $j(t)$. Since banks have been assumed to behave as monopolists in the market for bank loans setting the loan rate according to equation 6.11, the equilibrium stock of loans can be determined by firms' loan demand which is depicted in figure 6.2 for different stages of the business cycle. However, the insertion of an additional loan demand function by firms would have magnified the complexity of the model by increasing the number of parameters to be specified in the calibration process. Therefore, the influence of the loan rate on the stock of loans, and thereby on total interest rate costs $j(t)L(t)$, has been specified by the loan rate semi-elasticity with respect to the stock of loans $\varepsilon_{L,j} = (dL/dj)(1/L)$ determining whether total interest rate costs rise or fall in case $j(t)$ varies. As a result, the loan rate semi-elasticity $\varepsilon_{L,j}$ determines the influence of loan rate changes on firms' profit rate $r(t)$ which is specified by the derivative of firms' profit rate with respect to the loan rate, i.e. by (dr/dj) which is equivalent to parameter r_2 in the profit rate equation 6.3, i.e. it holds that $r_2 = dr/dj$.

According to figure 6.2, the boom phase is characterized by a very inelastic loan demand schedule, which can be justified by firms acting conservatively as to the increase in indebtedness since profit expectations are still moderate during that stage, being represented by a positive but small state of confidence value $\rho_B(t)$. As a result, a reduction in the loan rate from j_1 to j_2, being caused by capital inflows and/or by increasing stock prices according to equation 6.11, leads to an increase in the stock of loans being indicated by the move from L_1 to L_2, but to a decrease in interest rate payments $j(t)L(t)$ since $\varepsilon_{L,j_B} > -1$, implying that a reduction in the loan rate $j(t)$ leads to an increase in firms' profit rate $r(t)$ which is represented by the derivative condition $r_{2_B} = -dr/dj > 0$. The

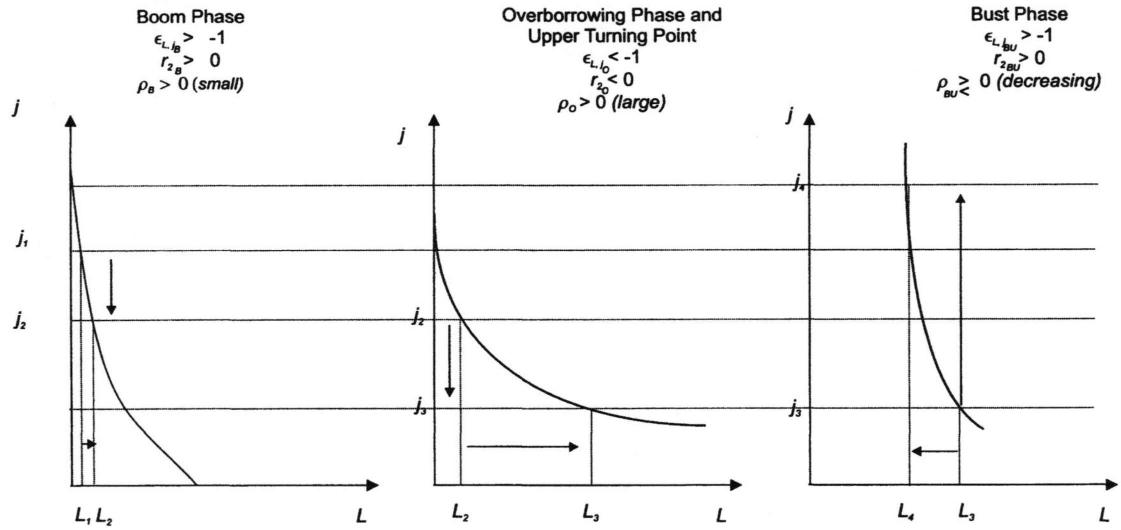

Figure 6.2: Loan Demand, Elasticities and the State of Confidence During Different Stages of the Boom-Bust Cycle

overborrowing phase and the situation at the upper turning point of the business cycle are characterized by a very elastic loan demand since profit expectations have grown rapidly, being represented by a large positive state of confidence value $\rho_O(t)$. Loan rate reductions, as indicated by the fall from j_2 to j_3 being caused by huge capital inflows, relaxing domestic monetary conditions, and by large increases in stock market valuations, lead to an enormous increase in the stock of loans being represented by the move from L_2 to L_3. Accordingly, loan rate reductions lead to an increase in total interest costs $j(t)L(t)$ since $\varepsilon_{L,j\,O} < -1$, implying that a reduction in the loan rate $j(t)$ leads to a decrease in firms' profit rate $r(t)$ due to the overborrowing effect, which is represented by the derivative condition $r_{2_O} = -dr/dj < 0$. When the asset price bubble bursts, making international investors withdraw foreign loans, and causing domestic investors to flee from domestic assets, leading to huge capital outflows, the bust phase is about to begin being characterized by a sudden change from a very elastic loan demand to a very inelastic loan demand, since profit expectations drop sharply, implying an initial high positive value of the state of confidence $\rho_{BU}(t)$ which is however, decreasing very fast leading to negative values. Comparing the semi-elasticity value $\varepsilon_{L,j}$ and the derivative value r_2 of the boom and the bust phase, having both the same sign in each phase, the bust phase's semi-elasticity is larger, implying also a larger value of r_2, since loans cannot be reduced as quickly as expanded in the boom phase due to the fact that a repayment of loans requires either higher cash flows, which is however, not possible during the bust phase, or a liquidation of parts of the capital stock which is often impossible in downswings due to the lack of demand for existing capital goods. As a result, sharp loan rate increases during the bust phase, being indicated in figure 6.2 by a rise from j_3 to j_4, which arise from large capital outflows, domestic monetary tightening, and from large declines in firms' market value of collateral due to collapses in equity prices according to equation 6.11, lead only to a small reduction in the stock of loans from L_3 to L_4 owing to firms' inability to liquidate parts of the capital stock. As a result, the increase in the loan rate leads to a rise in total interest costs $j(t)L(t)$ since $\varepsilon_{L,j\,BU} > -1$, implying that a rise in $j(t)$ leads to a fall in $r(t)$ which is represented by the derivative condition $r_{2_{BU}} = -dr/dj > 0$.

6.4 The Balance of Payments

The current account is represented approximately by the log of the trade balance, formally given as

$$\ln T(t) = tr_1(\ln s(t) + \ln P^*(t) - \ln P(t)) - tr_2 \ln Y(t), \qquad tr_1, tr_2 > 0, \qquad (6.12)$$

stating that the log of the trade balance denominated in domestic currency $\ln T(t)$ depends positively on the log of the real exchange rate $\ln s(t) + \ln P^*(t) - \ln P(t)$ implying a "normal" reaction, i.e. net exports increase if the real exchange rate increases and vice versa[14], and negatively on the log of real domestic income $\ln Y(t)$. Though international interest payments can amount to a substantial fraction of the current account, they are neglected for reasons of simplicity.

[14]A "normal" reaction of the trade balance with respect to real exchange rate movements implies that the Marshall-Lerner and Robinson condition are fulfilled.

The capital account in domestic currency is composed of foreign loans to banks being determined by equation 6.6, and of international short-term government bond transactions. Regarding private capital flows stemming from international bond transactions, the model assumes that net capital inflows are determined positively by the difference between the domestic risk adjusted and the foreign interest rate on short-term government bonds $i(t) - \alpha - i^*(t)$ which is however, according to equation 6.10, always zero. Accordingly, the log of the capital account in domestic currency is formally given by

$$\ln CA(t) = \ln s(t) + \ln LF^*(t),$$

stating that the log of the capital account $\ln CA(t)$ in domestic currency consist only of capital inflows in the form of the log of foreign loans to banks $\ln s(t) + \ln LF^*(t)$.

In a regime of fixed exchange rates, the log of the change in international reserves of the central bank $\ln \dot{Z}(t)$, or the balance of payments in log-form is given by

$$\ln \dot{Z}(t) = \phi \ln T(t) + (1 - \phi)(\ln s(t) + \ln LF^*(t)), \qquad 0 < \phi < 1, \qquad (6.13)$$

i.e. by the sum of the current and of the capital account in domestic currency, where ϕ is a weighting factor.[15] A regime of flexible exchange rates is characterized by the central bank not intervening in the foreign exchange market and owning no foreign exchange reserves, i.e. under flexible exchange rates it holds that $\ln Z(t) = \ln \dot{Z}(t) = 0$. Accordingly, the balance of payments in log-form is defined as

$$\ln T(t) = -\frac{1-\phi}{\phi}(\ln s(t) + \ln LF^*(t)),$$

stating that e.g. a current account deficit must be offset by a capital account surplus, i.e. by new capital inflows in the form of foreign loans, or leads alternatively to a depreciation of the exchange rate in order to equalize the current account in case private capital flows are zero.

6.5 Monetary and Exchange Rate Policy

Standard macroeconomic models generally assume that monetary policy is exercised by money supply policy, i.e. by variations in high-powered money arising from changes in the domestic credit component, and/or from interventions in the foreign exchange market. However, real world monetary policy to control goal variables as inflation, output or the exchange rate, is exercised by (prime) interest rate policy, having a direct influence on the liquidity status of financial intermediaries, and only an indirect influence on endogenous monetary aggregates which cannot be controlled perfectly, and whose influence on output and inflation has become very weak in the last decade due to velocity instability. It must be noted however, that interest rate policy is supplemented by money supply policy especially in periods of financial distress. A common strategy to avoid a collapse of domestic financial systems is to lower prime rates, and to inject large short-term amounts of liquidity into the financial system by increasing base money in order to avoid illiquidity among financial intermediaries. Regarding the prevention of a breakdown of fixed exchange rate regimes

[15]The non-log version of equation 6.13 reads as $\dot{Z}(t) = T(t)^{\phi}(s(t)LF^*(t))^{1-\phi}$.

whose viability depends on the overall level of foreign exchange reserves, central banks' common strategy is to increase domestic prime rates in order to stop capital outflows, and to intervene in the foreign exchange market by selling foreign reserves. If, however, a central bank faces a collapse of the domestic financial system, as well as a breakdown of the fixed exchange rate regime, being typical of twin crises' periods, there is no possibility to support both the domestic financial system and the exchange rate, i.e. one goal has to be abandoned.

Monetary policy in the form of interest rate policy can take various forms, depending on the one hand on central banks' preferences as to the relative importance of output and inflation targets, and on the other hand on the exchange rate regime.[16] Monetary policy in large industrialized countries with flexible exchange rate regimes, as e.g. in the U.S., is often designed according to Taylor's rule stating that optimal monetary policy should use the nominal prime rate to stabilize inflation and output on some chosen target levels.[17] Other industrialized countries having committed themselves exclusively and officially to price stability irrespective of output targets, as e.g. the United Kingdom, New Zealand or Canada, follow an inflation targeting strategy by adjusting the nominal prime rate to stabilize inflation on its target level. However, inflation targeting can be also interpreted as a special form of the Taylor rule which does not consider output gaps, but solely inflation gaps. Pure monetary targeting strategies, having been applied by the German Bundesbank until the start of EMU, and by the Swiss National Bank, trying to control money supply via the prime rate, have become very rare due to the breakdown of the relationship between monetary aggregates and the goal variables inflation and output.

An alternative form of monetary policy predominantly used by emerging market and small industrial countries to stabilize inflation without concerning output goals is exchange-rate targeting, either in the form of fixed exchange rate regimes, or in the form of crawling peg arrangements. In exchange-rate targeting regimes, only the key currency country with lowest inflation and most credible monetary policy can exercise an independent monetary policy. Other members of the system have to follow monetary policy of the key currency country, being carried out by adjusting the domestic prime rate to movements in the foreign prime rate, and to movements in foreign exchange reserves whose level determines the stability of the fixed exchange rate system. As a result, in a world of globalized financial markets in which capital account transactions are much larger in volume than current account transactions, exchange rate targeting is mainly achieved by stabilizing movements in capital account transactions via interest rate targeting. A stylized interest rate rule for an exchange rate targeting "follower" country could therefore read as

$$\Delta i_C(t) = \Delta i_C^*(t) - \Delta Z(t),$$

stating that the domestic prime rate $i_C(t)$ is adjusted positively to changes in the foreign prime rate $i_C^*(t)$, and inversely regarding changes in foreign exchange reserves $Z(t)$. If, for example, agents expect the exchange rate to depreciate without any change in the foreign prime rate, i.e. $\Delta i_C^*(t) = 0$, for example due to an unsustainable real exchange rate level, arising private capital outflows, causing a reduction in international reserves, i.e. $\Delta Z(t) < 0$, make monetary authorities increase the domestic prime rate to stabilize the exchange rate. If, on the other hand, there is an increase in the foreign prime rate, i.e.

[16]For details on various forms of monetary policy rules, see Sveriges Riksbank (1999).

[17]For details on the Taylor rule, see e.g. Taylor (1993).

$\Delta i^*_C(t) > 0$, the domestic prime rate has to be increased as well, since otherwise, arising capital outflows leading to a reduction in foreign exchange reserves would undermine the stability of the fixed exchange rate system.

In order to be consistent with the stylized facts regarding monetary policy under fixed exchange rate regimes, the present model assumes that exchange rate targeting by interest rate targeting is carried out by the domestic central bank stabilizing the capital account via variations of the domestic prime rate $i_C(t)$.[18] The capital account, being equivalent to net capital flows in the form of foreign loans to banks, is determined, according to equation 6.6, by domestic banks' net worth and by the risk adjusted interest rate differential between the domestic and the foreign money market rate. Accordingly, an appropriate monetary policy rule is to maintain a risk adjusted interest rate parity between the domestic and the foreign money market rate. This rule however, does not lead to zero net capital flows since it does not consider the effect of banks' net worth on capital flows, fitting the stylized fact that central banks are not able to control capital flows perfectly by prime rate adjustments. Thereupon, monetary policy in the model is assumed to follow the rule

$$i_C(t) = i^*_C(t) + rp(t) + E_t[\ln \dot{s}(t)], \qquad \text{where} \qquad E_t[\ln \dot{s}(t)] = \ln \dot{s}(t), \tag{6.14}$$

i.e. the domestic prime rate $i_C(t)$ is adjusted to guarantee a risk adjusted interest rate parity between the domestic and the foreign money market rate in order to stabilize foreign exchange reserves.[19]

After having defined monetary policy for a fixed exchange rate regime, the model has to specify as well a monetary policy rule for a flexible exchange rate regime, since the model equations have to be solved both for a fixed and for a flexible system in order to show the effects of a speculative attack on key macroeconomic variables. After the occurrence of a currency crisis there arise various policy alternatives. The feasible spectrum reaches from independent monetary policy up to exchange rate targeting on a devalued post-crisis level. The empirical analysis in chapter 3 has shown that especially emerging market countries operating officially under flexible exchange rate regimes often pursue actually a kind of exchange rate targeting due to the "fear of floating". Accordingly, post-collapse exchange rate regimes are often designed as fixed exchange rate regimes on a devalued post-crisis level, since a further devaluation of the domestic currency could cause on the one hand, high inflation undermining e.g. the achievements of inflation stabilization programmes, and on the other hand, a further deterioration of business firms' and intermediaries' balance sheets in case foreign debt is high. Thereupon, the present model assumes that monetary policy under a flexible exchange rate regime also follows the fixed exchange rate rule given in equation 6.14 to stabilize the exchange rate via prime rate adjustments.

[18] By way of contrast, the financial crisis models in chapters 4 and 5 do not consider the prime rate as the main monetary policy tool and assume that monetary policy is exercised via changes in the domestic credit component and/or in foreign exchange reserves.

[19] An alternative interest rate rule, which is obtained by transforming the differential rule $\Delta i_C(t) = \Delta i^*_C(t) - \Delta Z(t)$ in absolute terms, could have read $i_C(t) = i^*_C(t) + \beta(Z_E - Z(t))$, where Z_E stands for a warranted or equilibrium stock of international reserves. However, this kind of interest rate rule would have required to define and to model the determinants of the equilibrium stock of foreign reserves Z_E for which no general theory exists. In order to avoid such difficulties, monetary policy is assumed to follow equation 6.14.

6.6 Analytical Solution of the Model

The model structure regarding the number of equations, parameters, endogenous, and exogenous variables can be summarized as follows:

- *Model Equations.* The model is defined by equations 6.1 to 6.14, i.e. by 14 equations which are summarized in table 6.1.
- *Endogenous Variables.* The model contains 17 endogenous variables, i.e. $r(t)$, $i(t)$, $f(t)$, $j(t)$, $i_C(t)$, $rp(t)$, $\ln P(t)$, $\ln Y(t)$, $\ln H(t)$, $\ln LF^*(t)$, $\ln NW_{BA}(t)$, $\ln P_K(t)$, $\ln T(t)$, $\ln Z(t)$, $\ln \dot{Z}(t)$, $\ln s(t)$, $\ln \dot{s}(t)$.
- *Exogenous Variables.* The model contains 7 exogenous variables, i.e. $\ln P^*(t)$, $\delta(t)$, $\ln K(t)$, $\ln m(t)$, $\ln \bar{s}$, $\rho(t)$, $i_C^*(t)$, where $\rho(t)$ and $i_C^*(t)$ are used as the "forcing functions" for which exogenous linear time paths are going to be specified.
- *Parameters.* The model contains 31 parameters, i.e. y_0, y_1, y_2, y_3, ζ, r_0, r_1, r_2, r_3, r_4, d_1, d_2, d_3, γ, h_0, h_1, lf_1, lf_2, nw_0, nw_1, rp_0, rp_1, k_1, k_2, α, j_0, j_1, j_2, tr_1, tr_2, ϕ for which specific values are going to be assumed.

Solving the dynamic model for all endogenous variables requires firstly to eliminate the 13 endogenous variables $r(t)$, $i(t)$, $f(t)$, $j(t)$, $i_C(t)$, $rp(t)$, $\ln P(t)$, $\ln Y(t)$, $\ln H(t)$, $\ln LF^*(t)$, $\ln NW_{BA}(t)$, $\ln P_K(t)$, $\ln T(t)$ to obtain one basic differential equation in $\ln Z(t)$ and $\ln s(t)$ which has to be solved both for a flexible and for a fixed exchange rate system. In case of a fixed exchange rate system, the basic differential equation reduces to a first-order linear differential equation in $\ln Z(t)$ since it holds that $\ln s(t) = \ln \bar{s}$, and $\ln \dot{s}(t) = 0$. In case of a flexible exchange rate system, the basic differential equation reduces to a first-order linear differential equation in $\ln s(t)$ since the central bank is assumed to hold no foreign exchange reserves under flexible exchange rates, i.e. it holds that $\ln Z(t) = \ln \dot{Z}(t) = 0$.

The differential equation in $\ln s(t)$, as well as the differential equation in $\ln Z(t)$ are both functions of all parameters and all exogenous variables, where exogenous variables can be assumed as remaining constant or as being an exogenous function of time. As a result, both differential equations reduce to a linear first-order differential equation in the form of

$$\dot{x}(t) - \vartheta\, x(t) = \kappa a(t),$$

where ϑ and κ are constants containing all parameters of the model, and $a(t)$ is the forcing function, being a function of time t in case one ore more exogenous variables are assumed to be exogenous functions of time, but which reduces to a constant $a(t) = \bar{a}$ in case all exogenous variables are assumed to remain constant. Since the exchange rate is a pure forward looking variable being subject to rational expectations, the differential equation in $\ln s(t)$ is unstable, i.e. it holds that $\vartheta > 0$. As a result, in order to guarantee dynamic stability and to rule out bubbles, the general solution has to exclude the homogenous part, and the particular integral has to be solved forward looking being a function of exogenous variables $a(t)$.[20] Furthermore, in case of shocks, the exchange rate is allowed to "jump" on

[20]This solution method can be found almost in every model of currency crises, having been firstly introduced by Flood and Garber (1984a).

its new long-run equilibrium path in order to rule divergent dynamic behaviour. By way of contrast, foreign exchange reserves are a backward looking variable whose evolution is tied to the past, leading to a stable differential equation which is characterized by $\vartheta < 0$. Thus, the particular integral which is a function of exogenous variables $a(t)$ has to be solved backward looking, and the general solution including the solution of the homogenous equation is convergent.[21] However, in order to avoid difficulties regarding the selection of the initial condition for foreign exchange reserves, i.e. $\ln Z(0)$, it is assumed for every simulation that foreign exchange reserves' initial value equals its long-run steady state value, i.e. the general solution of foreign exchange reserves is generally given by the particular integral.[22] After having solved the basic differential equation for both the fixed and the flexible exchange rate system, the time paths of the remaining endogenous variables are obtained by backward substitution of the solutions for $\ln Z(t)$ and $\ln s(t)$.

6.7 Simulation Classifications and Assumptions

The calibration model is going to be simulated in different ways regarding the kind of "shocks" causing financial fragility in order to describe financial crises both as a positive shock-induced cyclical phenomenon, and as the result of a large adverse and exogenous shock without causing a cyclical dynamic behaviour. The simulation procedure consists of four different model simulations portraying the behaviour of all 14 endogenous variables and combinations of these variables. The first three model simulations, outlined in section 6.7.1, refer to the explanation of financial crises as the result of a positive exogenous shock to expectations generating an endogenous boom-bust cycle according to the theories outlined in chapters 4 and 5. The fourth model simulation, outlined in section 6.7.2, portrays the occurrence of financial crises caused by a large negative foreign interest rate shock.

6.7.1 Financial Crises as a Cyclical Phenomenon

Since there is no possibility to portray an endogenous cycle by the use of linear dynamic systems for the reasons outlined in section 6.1.2, each phase of the business cycle, i.e. the boom phase, the overborrowing phase and upper turning point, and the bust phase, is simulated separately. According to the dynamic analysis in chapters 4.4 and 5.4, the "driving" forces of an endogenous financial crisis cycle are the state of confidence $\rho(t)$ and the debt-asset ratio which is represented by parameter r_2 describing the influence of total debt costs on firms' profit rate $r(t)$. Since both the exogenous variable $\rho(t)$, and parameter r_2 take different values during different stages of the business cycle, the three business cycle phases being simulated can be classified according to specific constellations of $\rho(t)$ and r_2 as follows:

[21] For details regarding the solution of unstable and stable differential equations, the distinction among forward and backward looking variables, and solutions to general rational expectations models, see appendix D.

[22] The assumption that the initial values of endogenous variables coincide with their steady-state solution is a common procedure of simulation models which can be found e.g. in Montiel, Agénor and Ul Haque (1993).

Table 6.1: Summary Equations of the Calibration Model

6.1	$\ln P(t) = \ln s(t) + \ln P^*(t)$	Domestic Price Level (PPP)
6.2	$\ln Y(t) = y_0 + y_1 (\ln s(t) + \ln P^*(t) - \ln P(t)) + y_2 (\ln P_K(t) - \ln P(t)) - y_3(f(t) - \zeta \ln P(t))$	Goods Market Equilibrium
6.3	$r(t) = r_0 + r_1 \ln Y(t) - r_2 j(t) - r_3 \delta(t) - r_4 (\ln s(t) + \ln P^*(t)) - (\ln P(t) + \ln K(t))$	Profit Rate
6.4	$\ln m(t) + \gamma \ln H(t) + (1-\gamma) \ln Z(t) - \ln P(t) = d_1 \ln Y(t) - d_2 i(t) - d_3 f(t)$	Deposit Market Equilibrium
6.5	$\ln H(t) = h_0 - h_1 i_C(t)$	Money Market Equilibrium
6.6	$\ln LF^*(t) = lf_1 \ln NW_{BA}(t) + lf_2 (i_C(t) - (i_C^*(t) + rp(t) + E_t[\ln \dot{s}(t)])$	Net Foreign Loan Inflow
6.7	$\ln NW_{BA}(t) = nw_0 + nw_1 r(t)$	Banks' Net Worth
6.8	$rp(t) = rp_0 - rp_1 \ln NW_{BA}(t)$	Risk Premium
6.9	$\ln K(t) + \ln P_K(t) - \ln P(t) = -k_1 i(t) + k_2(r(t) + \rho(t))$	Stock Market Equilibrium
6.10	$i(t) = i_C^*(t) - \alpha + E_t[\ln \dot{s}(t)]$	Bond Market Equilibrium
6.11	$j(t) = j_0 - j_1 (\gamma \ln H(t) + (1-\gamma) \ln Z(t)) - j_2 \ln P_K(t)$	Domestic Loan Rate
6.12	$\ln T(t) = tr_1 (\ln s(t) + \ln P^*(t) - \ln P(t)) - tr_2 \ln Y(t)$	Current Account
6.13	$\ln \dot{Z}(t) = \phi \ln T(t) + (1-\phi) (\ln s(t) + \ln LF^*(t))$	Balance of Payments
6.14	$i_C(t) = i_C^*(t) + rp(t) - E_t[\ln \dot{s}(t)]$	Monetary Policy Rule

It holds that

1. $E_t[\ln \dot{s}(t)] = \ln \dot{s}(t)$,
2. $\ln s(t) = \ln \bar{s}$ and $\ln \dot{s}(t) = 0$ for a fixed exchange rate system,
3. $\ln Z(t) = \ln \dot{Z}(t) = 0$ for a flexible exchange rate system.

- *The Boom Phase.* Increasing profit expectations are represented by a linearly increasing state of confidence $\rho(t)$ with respect to time t, given formally as

$$\rho_B(t) = \rho_B(0) + \psi_B\, t, \qquad \psi_B > 0, \tag{6.15}$$

  where $\rho_B(0)$ denotes the initial value of ρ at the beginning of the boom phase at time $t = 0$, and ψ_B the strength of the increase in the state of confidence. The influence of a rising debt stock on total interest rate costs is assumed to be negative owing to figure 6.2, i.e. rising debt leads to an increase in the profit rate according to a loan rate semi-elasticity value with respect to the stock of loans of $\varepsilon_{L,j_B} > -1$, being reflected by a positive derivative of firms' profit rate with respect to the loan rate

$$r_{2_B} > 0. \tag{6.16}$$

  Given the forcing function 6.15 for the boom phase, both the time path of foreign exchange reserves $\ln Z(t)$, and the time path of the exchange rate $\ln s(t)$, are linear functions of time t, leading to linear time paths of all endogenous variables.

- *The Overborrowing Phase and the Upper Turning Point.* This stage of the business cycle is characterized by a steady increase in the state of confidence due to the dominance of the "chartist" effect on expectations, being described by the same type of linear function 6.15, formally given as

$$\rho_O(t) = \rho_O(0) + \psi_O\, t, \qquad \psi_O = \psi_B > 0, \qquad \rho_O(0) > \rho_B(0), \tag{6.17}$$

  where $\rho_O(0)$ denotes the initial value of ρ at the beginning of the overborrowing phase at time $t = 0$[23], being greater than $\rho_B(0)$, since $\rho(t)$ has grown during the boom phase; ψ_O denotes the strength of the increase in the state of confidence which is assumed to be equal to the value in the boom phase. In order to model the "irrational exuberance" effect of rising profit expectations, and a simultaneously declining actual profit rate due to an overproportional increase in total debt costs, the semi-loan rate elasticity with respect to the stock of loans is assumed to take a value of $\varepsilon_{L,j_O} < -1$ according to figure 6.2, being reflected in a negative derivative of firms' profit rate with respect to the loan rate, i.e. it holds that

$$r_{2_O} < 0, \tag{6.18}$$

  stating that an increase in the loan rate leads to a reduction in the actual profit rate. According to the linear forcing function 6.17, all endogenous variables are linear functions of time t.

- *The Bust Phase.* This phase is characterized by a sharp declining state of confidence, being described by an analogous linear function which is however a decreasing function of time t, formally given by

$$\begin{gathered} \rho_{BU}(t) = \rho_{BU}(0) + \psi_{BU}\, t, \qquad \psi_{BU} < 0, \\ |\psi_O| = |\psi_B| < |\psi_{BU}|, \qquad \rho_{BU}(0) > \rho_O(0) > \rho_B(0), \end{gathered} \tag{6.19}$$

[23]For reasons of simplicity, the time index t has been set to zero for the beginning of each business cycle phase.

where ψ_{BU}, being negative, denotes the strength of the decline in the state of confidence which is stronger than the positive effect in the boom and in the overborrowing phase; $\rho_{BU}(0)$ denotes the initial value of ρ at the beginning of the bust phase at time $t = 0$, being greater than $\rho_O(0)$ which is obviously greater than $\rho_B(0)$. The influence of a declining debt stock on total debt costs and on firms' profit rate is assumed to be inverse due to a loan rate semi-elasticity value with respect to the stock of loans of $\varepsilon_{L,j\,BU} > -1$ according to figure 6.2, i.e. though the stock of loans is decreasing, total debt costs increase due to an overproportional rise in the loan rate, leading to a decline in the profit rate which is represented by a positive derivative of the profit rate with respect to the loan rate, i.e. by

$$r_{2_{BU}} > 0. \tag{6.20}$$

Comparing the elasticity values $\varepsilon_{L,j}$ and derivative values r_2 in the boom and in the bust phase, having all the same sign, it holds that

$$\varepsilon_{L,j\,BU} > \varepsilon_{L,j\,B} \quad \text{and} \quad r_{2_{BU}} > r_{2_B} \tag{6.21}$$

since loan demand in the bust phase is less elastic than in the boom phase according to figure 6.2.

The simplifying assumption of an exogenously increasing or decreasing state of confidence in the model simulations, for reasons discussed in section 6.1.2, is very restrictive since the endogenous character of financial crises according to chapters 4 and 5 is lost. However, as the simulation results are going to show, the state of confidence $\rho(t)$ could have been endogenized theoretically by the difference between the actual profit rate and the real loan rate, i.e. by $r(t) - (j(t) - p(t))$, where $p(t) = d(\ln P(t))/dt = \dot{P}(t)/P(t)$ denotes the price level's growth rate. The difference $r(t) - (j(t) - p(t))$ can be interpreted as a risk premium firms have to pay to investors for holding capital assets, where the real loan rate serves as reference interest rate. This risk premium is similar to the risk premia σ and σ^* having been used in chapters 4 and 5 in equations 4.16 and 5.10 as a determinant of the state of confidence. As a result, the change of the state of confidence $\dot{\rho}(t)$ could have been determined by economic fundamentals, but not by "chartist" behaviour, given formally by

$$\dot{\rho}(t) = r(t) - (l(t) - p(t)), \tag{6.22}$$

which however has been omitted for reasons of simplicity with respect to the dynamic structure of the model.

6.7.2 Financial Crises as an Adverse Exogenous Shock Phenomenon

The fourth model simulation considers the effect of a permanent negative foreign interest rate shock by assuming a steady and linear increase in the foreign prime rate with respect to time t, being formally given as

$$i_C^*(t) = i_C^*(0) + \chi\, t, \qquad \chi > 0, \tag{6.23}$$

where $i_C^*(0)$ denotes the initial value of the foreign prime rate at time $t = 0$, and χ the strength of the foreign prime rate effect being positive. This simulation explicitly excludes the influence of the state of confidence on the macroeconomy, being denoted as $\rho_F(t)$ in the interest rate shock simulation, by the assumption

$$\rho_F(t) = 0 \tag{6.24}$$

throughout the analysis. In order to be consistent and comparable with the other simulations, the loan rate semi-elasticity $\varepsilon_{L,j\,F}$ value and the derivative value r_{2_F} are assumed to be equal to the bust phase simulation according to figure 6.2, i.e. it holds that

$$\varepsilon_{L,j\,F} = \varepsilon_{L,j\,BU} > -1 \qquad \text{and} \qquad r_{2_F} = r_{2_{BU}} > 0, \tag{6.25}$$

i.e. a rising loan rate leads to a rise in total debt costs by an underproportional reduction of the stock of loans, and, as a result, to decline in the profit rate $r(t)$. The assumption of an inelastic loan demand function in periods of rising domestic interest rates in order to support a fixed exchange rate regime fits the stylized facts, since domestic interest rates have to follow foreign interest rates instantaneously, whereas long-term loan finance of investment cannot be reduced instantaneously, and adjusts only gradually.

6.8 Sensitivity Analysis and Method of Graphical Representation

In order to guarantee consistency and general validity of the parameter sets, most parameter values, except for the "driving forces" ρ, r_2, i_C^*, and some few other parameters, are assumed to remain constant throughout all model simulations. The parameter values chosen in the simulation process do not apply to any real-world economy. In lieu, they are assumed to reflect conditions which are applicable to a large variety of possible systems, which calls for performing a sensitivity analysis with respect to "key" parameters of the model in order to test their robustness regarding the observed dynamic patterns of the simulation results. The "key" parameters which are going to be tested in each of the four simulations are

$$h_1, rp_1, nw_1, lf_1, j_2, k_2, r_1, r_2, y_2, y_3,$$

which have been selected according to their relative importance in comparison with the remaining parameters regarding the transmission of shocks into the real, and into the financial system of the economy. It must be stressed that sensitivity analysis cannot "prove" that the parameters used are "true", nor that the observed dynamic patterns are generally valid.

As the charts of the simulation procedure are going to portray, there arise situations in which some endogenous variables, as e.g. nominal and real interest rates, take unrealistic absolute numerical values, stemming on the one hand from the choice of unrealistic, but mathematically tractable values of exogenous variables and parameters, and on the other hand from the semi-logarithmic nature of the model distorting the general scale and the ratios of non-log and log variables. For example, regarding the simulation of financial crises as a cyclical phenomenon, during the boom and the overborrowing phase, being characterized by a declining risk premium and by a depreciating exchange rate, both the nominal prime interest rate and the nominal short-term interest rate on government bonds become negative according to equations 6.10 and 6.14, emanating from the fact that foreign prime interest rate has be assumed to be zero. Accordingly, unrealistic numerical values must not be interpreted as an indicator for the invalidity of calibration model, but result from a mathematically tractable choice of parameter and exogenous variable values.

Regarding the avoidance of unrealistic numerical values in calibration models, there are two generally adopted strategies, having however, both not been applied to the present model in order not to distort the general solution by adjusting the model results to reasonable numerical values. The first strategy is to plot the time paths of the endogenous variables only qualitatively without defining a parameter set and accordingly, without declaring numerical values on the axes of the plot.[24] The second strategy is to calculate in a first step for a given parameter set a baseline solution of the model without any forcing functions representing the steady-state solution of the model.[25] In a second step, a shock is introduced by an exogenously determined time path of an exogenous variable, and the model is going to be simulated numerically for the shock scenario without changing the initial parameter set. Finally, in a third step, the numerical differences between the steady-state and the shock scenario solution are calculated and portrayed in charts, often in the form of percentage deviations from the steady-state baseline result, eliminating the absolute numerical values of all endogenous variables and providing only information about the "direction" of the shock's influence on endogenous variables.[26] Accordingly, calibration models do *not* intend to generate relevant real-world numerical values like econometric simulation models based on estimation, but to provide information about the "direction" endogenous variables are going to follow in case the system is hit by a shock. Applying this kind of procedure to the present model means that the most important information provided by the simulations is the question of whether a variable is increasing or decreasing in the face of a shock, and not which numerical value an endogenous variable is going to take at a specific moment in time.

Regarding the graphical distinction in the charts between the fixed and the flexible exchange rate solution of the model, the fixed exchange rate solution is generally plotted by solid lines, and the flexible exchange rate solution by dotted lines. In case of the occurrence of a currency crisis, the pre-crisis phase plot is restricted to the fixed exchange rate solution, and the post-crisis phase plot is restricted to the flexible exchange rate solution. The time of a speculative attack is graphically determined by the intersection of the fixed exchange rate path and of the flexible or shadow exchange rate path in case the pre-crisis state is characterized by the shadow exchange rate being smaller than the fixed rate, making it unprofitable to attack the currency.[27] In case of a speculative attack, the log of the stock of foreign reserves $\ln Z(t)$ is reduced discontinuously to zero.

[24]This procedure can be found for example in Willman (1988), and in Calvo and Végh (1993).

[25]In terms of the present model, the steady-state solution could have been calculated by assuming the state of confidence to be zero which would have resulted in constant steady-state values for $\ln s(t)$ and $\ln Z(t)$ and, as a result, in constant steady-state values for all other endogenous variables.

[26]For this procedure, see e.g. Montiel, Agénor and Ul Haque (1993), chapter 5.

[27]For this procedure, see e.g. Willman (1988), Flood and Garber (1984a), and Agénor, Bhandari and Flood (1992).

6.9 Simulation of Financial Crises as a Cyclical Phenomenon

6.9.1 The Boom Phase

Following the simulation classification given in section 6.7, the first three model simulations refer to the emergence of financial crises as a part of an excessive business cycle which is going to be subdivided into the boom, the overborrowing and into the bust phase. The relevant parameter and exogenous variable set, as well as the specific form of the forcing function for the boom phase simulation are summarized in table 6.2. The time paths of all 14 endogenous variables as well as the time paths of additional 9 endogenous variables being combinations of the 14 basic endogenous variables are depicted in 23 panels in figures 6.3(a), 6.3(b), and 6.3(c). Though there exist various interdependencies among the endogenous variables of the model, the following qualitative description of the plots only highlights the most important causal relationships. Since there is no currency crisis during the boom phase, i.e. the shadow exchange rate value (dotted line in the uppermost right panel of figure 6.3(a)) is always smaller than the fixed exchange rate value (solid line) and even decreasing over time, all plots show the behaviour both for a flexible (dotted plots), and for a fixed exchange rate system (solid plots). The qualitative description starts with the fixed exchange rate case and discusses adjacently the differences to a flexible exchange rate system in order to highlight the effect of the choice of the exchange rate system regarding the generation of financial fragility during the boom phase.

The Boom Phase Under a Fixed Exchange Rate Regime. The boom phase is driven by an exogenously increasing state of confidence ρ according to equation 6.15 (forcing function), and by a positive r_{2_B} value according to condition 6.16. The increase in the state of confidence can be justified (and could have been endogenized) by an increasing positive difference between the profit and the real lending rate $r - (j - p)$ (figure 6.3(a)), serving as a fundamental indicator for actual profitability. A rising state of confidence causes, according to equation 6.9, a rise in the log of the demand price of capital $\ln P_K$ (figure 6.3(a)) and a rise in the log of Tobin's q, $\ln q$ (figure 6.3(a)), at a constant log of the domestic price level $\ln P$ (figure 6.3(a)) causing zero domestic inflation p (figure 6.3(a)). As a result, nominal and real interest rates (figure 6.3(b)) coincide under fixed exchange rates. The constant log of the domestic price level is caused, according to equation 6.1, by a constant log of the foreign price level $\ln P^*$ and by a fixed exchange rate value $\ln \bar{s}$. The rise in the log of Tobin's q stimulates investment demand and thereby the log of output $\ln Y$ (figure 6.3(c)) according to equation 6.2, causing an increase in the actual profit rate r (figure 6.3(a)) according to equation 6.3, leading to a further rise in $\ln P_K$, $\ln q$, $\ln Y$ and again in r. Accordingly, rising profit expectations and rising actual profits cause a cumulative expansion process in the real sector being subject to rising output, profits and share prices.

The dynamics on international financial markets amplify and accelerate the expansion process by a relaxation of external financing conditions, allowing banks to increase the stock of foreign loans being used to finance domestic firms' increasing external financing needs due to the expansion in the real sector. Banks' rise in foreign debt finance is caused

Table 6.2: Parameters, Exogenous Variables, and Forcing Function During the Boom Phase

		Parameters			
$y_0 = 0$	$y_1 = 0.35$	$y_2 = 0.8$	$y_3 = 0.8$	$\zeta = 0.01$	$r_0 = 2$
$r_1 = 0.0001$	$r_{2_B} = 0.75$	$r_3 = 0$	$r_4 = 0$	$\gamma = 0.5$	$d_1 = 0.03$
$d_2 = 0.05$	$d_3 = 0.02$	$h_0 = 40$	$h_1 = 4$	$lf_1 = 0.3$	$lf_2 = 0$
$nw_0 = 300$	$nw_1 = 8$	$rp_0 = 1$	$rp_1 = 0.005$	$k_1 = 2$	$k_2 = 8$
$\alpha = 0.01$	$j_0 = 2$	$j_1 = 1.4$	$j_2 = 0.105$	$tr_1 = 0.1$	$tr_2 = 0.9$
$\phi = 0.3$					
		Exogenous Variables			
$\ln P^*(t) = 0$	$\delta(t) = 0$	$\ln K(t) = 0$	$\ln m(t) = 2$	$\ln \bar{s} = 20$	$i_C^*(t) = 0$
		Forcing Function			
	$\rho_B(t) = \rho_B(0) + \psi_B t$		$\rho_B(0) = 0$	$\psi_B = 3.5$	

by an increase in firms' profit rate r which reduces the amount of nonperforming loans, leading to increasing bank profits and to an augmenting log of banks' net worth $\ln NW_{BA}$ (figure 6.3(c)) according to equation 6.7. This increase in banks' net worth lowers on the one hand the interest rate on foreign loans by a reduction of the risk premium rp (figure 6.3(c)) according to equation 6.8, and increases on the other hand foreign loan inflows $\ln LF^*$ (figure 6.3(c)) according to equation 6.6 due to an improved collateral position of domestic banks.

Increasing capital inflows make monetary authorities decrease the nominal domestic prime rate i_C (figure 6.3(b)), being equal to the real domestic prime rate $i_C - p$, according to equation 6.14 in order to stabilize the fixed exchange rate by reducing foreign loan inflows. However, since capital inflows cannot be controlled perfectly by monetary authorities according to equations 6.6 and 6.14, lowering the domestic prime rate is only able to weaken, but not to stop capital inflows $\ln LF^*$ since the influence of banks' net worth $\ln NW_{BA}$ dominates international capital movements. There arise no international capital flows from short-term bond transactions since the capital flow determining difference between the domestic nominal short-term interest rate on bonds i, being equal to the real short-term interest rate $i - p$, and the constant foreign prime rate i_C^*, adjusted by the constant risk factor α, is always zero according to equation 6.10. Thus, the domestic nominal and real domestic short-term bond rate, i and $i - p$ (figure 6.3(b)), remain constant at an α per cent higher level than the foreign prime rate.

The balance of payments and the level of the log of international reserves $\ln Z$ is dominated by the capital account surplus leading to an increasing stock of foreign reserves $\ln Z$ (figure 6.3(a)) according to equation 6.13, though the log of the current account $\ln T$ is deteriorating inducing a current account deficit. The deteriorating current account position $\ln T$ (figure 6.3(c)) is caused, according to equation 6.12, by an increase in the log of domestic output $\ln Y$ stimulating import demand, whereas there is no influence of the real exchange rate on the trade balance due to the validity of PPP.

Increasing foreign exchange reserves $\ln Z$ and a decreasing domestic prime interest rate i_C, causing a rise in the log of the domestic credit component $\ln H$ (figure 6.3(c)) due to a reduction of banks' lending costs according to equation 6.5, lead to an increase in the amount of high powered money $\ln M = \gamma \ln H + (1 - \gamma) \ln Z$ (figure 6.3(c)) and thereby to an increase in the supply of deposit according to equation 6.4. Though there is an increase in deposit supply, the nominal interest rate on domestic long-term bonds f, being equal to the real domestic long-term bond rate $f - p$, rises (figure 6.3(c)) due to an increase in deposits demand caused by a rise in the log of output $\ln Y$, being larger than the increase in deposit supply, inducing agents to sell long-term bonds owing to liquidity needs which lowers market prices on long-term bonds according to equation 6.4. The rise in the nominal interest rate on long-term government bonds f reduces government expenditure due to increasing government debt costs, and weakens partly the expansion of the log of output $\ln Y$ according to equation 6.2.

A rising stock of deposits induced by declining refinancing costs enables domestic banks to expand loans to domestic firms by lowering the loan interest rate j, being equal to real loan rate $j - p$, (figure 6.3(b)) according to equation 6.11. The expansion of domestic loans is additionally reinforced by improving collateral values of firms by a rising demand price of capital $\ln P_K$, leading to a further decline in the loan rate according to equation 6.11. As there is a total decline in total interest rate costs due to the decline in the loan rate being larger than the increase in the stock of loans, a falling loan rate j leads to an increase in firms' profit rate r according to equation 6.3, leading to cumulative repetitions of the expansion process described above.

The Boom Phase Under a Flexible Exchange Rate Regime. Though the simulation of financial crises as a cyclical phenomenon assumes a fixed exchange rate system to prevail until the occurrence of a speculative attack, it is important to study the effects of the exchange rate system on the build-up of financial fragility during the boom phase by comparing the dynamic patterns under fixed and flexible exchange rates. The dotted lines in figures 6.3(a), 6.3(b), and 6.3(c) illustrate that the boom phase under flexible exchange rates is characterized by less expansionary effects than under fixed exchange rates, being caused by the absence of central bank intervention in the foreign exchange market, weakening high-powered money expansion. Instead of leading to a rise in the log of the stock of foreign exchange reserves $\ln Z$, increasing capital inflows $\ln LF^*$, which are induced by the same expansionary mechanism as under fixed exchange rates[28], lead to an appreciation of the domestic currency, i.e. to a decline in $\ln s$ causing domestic deflation via PPP, as the rise in capital inflows is larger in absolute terms than the rise in the current account deficit $\ln T$ in domestic currency, which is induced by the expansion of import demand. Accordingly, due to the absence of the expansionary effect of increasing foreign exchange reserves $\ln Z$ on high-powered money $\ln M$, the reduction in the nominal j and in the real loan rate $j - p$ is less than under fixed exchange rates, leading to a smaller increase in firms' profit rate r, weakening the increase in the log of the demand price of capital $\ln P_K$, in the log of Tobin's q, $\ln q$, and in the log of output $\ln Y$. A smaller

[28] The expansion process is induced by a rise in ρ, leading to increasing values in $\ln P_K$, $\ln q$, $\ln Y$ and in r, inducing an increase in $\ln NW_{BA}$, and causing $\ln LF^*$ to rise.

increase in firms' profits leads to a less pronounced increase in banks' net worth $\ln NW_{BA}$, to lower capital inflows $\ln LF^*$, and to a smaller reduction in the risk premium rp, which requires a smaller reduction in the domestic prime rate i_C having a dampening effect on the increase in the log of the domestic credit component $\ln H$. Rising output $\ln Y$ and a less increasing deposit supply requires a larger increase in the long-term bond rate f than under a fixed exchange rate system. The nominal short-term bond rate i is lower than under fixed rates owing to exchange rate depreciation, whereas the real short-term bond rate $i - p$ is identical with the fixed exchange rate case since the deflation and the depreciation rate coincide. Summing up, a flexible exchange rate system creates a less pronounced increase in indebtedness of banks and firms under an identical time path of profit expectations, thereby creating a lesser degree of financial fragility than under fixed exchange rates.

Sensitivity Analysis. The dynamic solution depicted in figures 6.3(a), 6.3(b), and 6.3(c) is stable for a $\pm 10\%$ variation of all key parameters h_1, rp_1, nw_1, lf_1, j_2, k_2, r_1, r_2, y_2, and y_3, i.e. the dynamic patterns of all variables do not change. The solution is also stable for a $+20\%$ variation of all key parameters and, except for parameters nw_1, lf_1, l_2, r_2, in case of a -20% variation. A -20% variation of parameters nw_1, lf_1, l_2, and r_2 generates a boom which ends up in a currency crisis, but not in a banking crisis, due to a very fast increasing current account deficit leading to a depletion of foreign exchange reserves $\ln Z$, and to a speculative attack.

6.9.2 The Overborrowing Phase and the Upper Turning Point

The set of parameters, exogenous variables, as well as the specific form of the forcing function for the overborrowing process simulation are summarized in table 6.3. In comparison with the boom phase parameter set given in table 6.2, only the initial value of the state of confidence $\rho_O(0)$, being larger than the initial value of the boom phase $\rho_B(0)$ according to equation 6.17, and parameter r_{2_O}, having now a negative sign according to condition 6.18, have different values; all other parameters have the same values as in table 6.2.

The overborrowing process is driven, as the boom phase, by an exogenous increase in the state of confidence ρ according to equation 6.17, which could be justified by an increasing difference between the profit and the real lending rate $r-(j-p)$ (figure 6.4(a)), though the actual profit rate r is decreasing, or even becoming negative (figure 6.4(a)). Accordingly, the rise in difference $r - (j - p)$, i.e. the reduction of the negative value of $r - (j - p)$ according to figure 6.4(a), results from the real lending rate $j - p$ (figure 6.4(b)) declining more than the profit rate r. Such a situation in which the actual profit rate declines or even becomes negative, but profit expectations rise and induce a further increase in indebtedness by a further relaxation of financial market conditions, is a typical state of "irrational exuberance". In a state of irrational exuberance, agents' expectations are mainly driven by chartist behaviour, expecting the past trend to be continued in the future without any reasonable consideration of fundamental data which indicate a downward revision of expectations. In the present case, the rising state of confidence ρ can be explained by chartist behaviour either without any consideration of fundamental data, or partly according to a misinterpretation of a decline of the negative difference $r-(j-p)$ as an indicator of rising future profitability though actual profitability declines.

By figures 6.4(a), 6.4(b), and 6.4(c), the simulation of the overborrowing process is subject to a currency crisis taking place at time $t = 15.04$ when the flexible shadow exchange rate $\ln s$ (uppermost right panel in figure 6.4(a)) hits the fixed exchange rate $\ln \bar{s}$, inducing agents to sell domestic currency in huge volumes, and leading to a complete depletion of foreign exchange reserves $\ln Z$ (uppermost left panel in figure 6.4(a)) and to an abolition of the exchange rate peg. Yet, empirical evidence, as well theory of financial crises according to chapters 4 and 5 argue that the overborrowing phase of an excessive business cycle generally is not subject to a currency crisis, occurring only when profit expectations collapse, or already have collapsed. Furthermore, the post-currency crisis period is characterized, according to figures 6.4(a), 6.4(b), and 6.4(c), by unrealistic behaviour of some macrovariables, as e.g. by increasing share prices $\ln P_K$ and $\ln q$ (figure 6.4(a)) and declining nominal and real lending rates j and $j-p$, though the actual profit rate r (figure 6.4(a)) declines, though the log of banks' net worth $\ln NW_{BA}$ (figure 6.4(c)) is subject to a further decline and becomes even negative indicating a severe banking crisis, and though there are increasing foreign capital outflows $\ln LF^*$ (figure 6.4(c)) inducing a sharp increase in the domestic prime rate i_C (figure 6.4(b)). These results mainly stem from the assumption of a further exogenous increase in the state of confidence ρ after the occurrence of a speculative attack, being an unrealistic scenario, even according to the model since the difference $r-(j-p)$ (figure 6.4(a)) is declining, indicating a downward revision of profit expectations. However, these unrealistic post-currency crisis simulation results must not be misinterpreted as an indicator for the invalidity of the calibration model since firstly, the pre-currency crisis results match with the stylized facts described below, secondly, the simulation highlights the fact that a situation of irrational exuberance leads to a financial collapse (twin crisis) even if expectations have not yet collapsed, and thirdly, the simulation indicates that expectations are going to be reversed according to the difference between the profit and the real lending rate $r-(j-p)$ (figure 6.4(a)). Summing up, though the simulation of the overborrowing process generates a currency crisis, it is reasonable to analyze only the pre-currency crisis phase, since the build-up of financial fragility, being completely ignored by investors, takes place predominantly in the overborrowing phase being characterized by the absence of any financial distress in the economy. The collapse of a fixed exchange rate regime follows in most cases a domestic financial crisis (banking crisis and widespread bankruptcies among firms), being analyzed in the bust phase simulation, which has been caused by a crash in expectations when agents have realized that expectations cannot be fulfilled by actual developments.

In the pre-currency crisis phase of the overborrowing process when the economy approaches the upper turning point of the business cycle, the rise in the state of confidence ρ causes, according to equation 6.9, a rise in the log of the demand price of capital $\ln P_K$ (figure 6.4(a)), and a rise in the log of Tobin's q, $\ln q$ (figure 6.4(a)), where the log of the domestic price level $\ln P$ (figure 6.4(a)) remains constant according to PPP, resulting in zero inflation p (figure 6.4(a)) according to equation 6.1, causing a correspondence of nominal and real interest rates in the overborrowing phase. However, by equation 6.9, the rise in the log of the demand price of capital $\ln P_K$ and in the log of Tobin's q, $\ln q$, requires that the increase in the state of confidence ρ is stronger than the fall in the profit rate r (figure 6.4(a)), having been explained above by a chartist type dominated expectation formation scheme. The rise in the log of Tobin's q, $\ln q$, stimulates investment demand and has an expansionary influence on the log of output $\ln Y$ though the log of output $\ln Y$

Table 6.3: Parameters, Exogenous Variables, and Forcing Function During the Overborrowing Phase and at the Upper Turning Point

		Parameters			
$y_0 = 0$	$y_1 = 0.35$	$y_2 = 0.8$	$y_3 = 0.8$	$\zeta = 0.01$	$r_0 = 2$
$r_1 = 0.0001$	$r_{2_O} = -0.9$	$r_3 = 0$	$r_4 = 0$	$\gamma = 0.5$	$d_1 = 0.03$
$d_2 = 0.05$	$d_3 = 0.02$	$h_0 = 40$	$h_1 = 4$	$lf_1 = 0.3$	$lf_2 = 0$
$nw_0 = 300$	$nw_1 = 8$	$rp_0 = 1$	$rp_1 = 0.005$	$k_1 = 2$	$k_2 = 8$
$\alpha = 0.01$	$j_0 = 2$	$j_1 = 1.4$	$j_2 = 0.105$	$tr_1 = 0.1$	$tr_2 = 0.9$
$\phi = 0.3$					
		Exogenous Variables			
$\ln P^*(t) = 0$	$\delta(t) = 0$	$\ln K(t) = 0$	$\ln m(t) = 2$	$\ln \bar{s} = 20$	$i^*_C(t) = 0$
		Forcing Function			
	$\rho_O(t) = \rho_O(0) + \psi_O t$		$\rho_O(0) = 5$	$\psi_O = 3.5$	

(figure 6.4(a)) is actually declining according to equation 6.2, due to a large reduction in government expenditure which is caused by a sharp increase in the long-term interest rate on government bonds f according to equation 6.4, being explained below. Thus, the profit rate r declines not only owing to the overborrowing effect represented by a negative r_{2_O} value according to equation 6.3, but also by declining output reducing sales revenues. Accordingly, though the status of the real sector is characterized by declining profits and sales, share prices continue to rise owing to an unbounded increase in profit expectations, being characteristic of a state of irrational exuberance.

The reversal of the expansion process in the real sector is reflected in increasing financial tensions among banks due to a rising number of nonperforming loans which are mainly caused by illiquidity in the firm sector, i.e. by a declining profit rate r, but not by insolvency since collateral values of firms, i.e. the log of the demand price of capital $\ln \Gamma_K$, are subject to further increases. This contradictory picture of firms' financial status, i.e. rising illiquidity on the one hand, but rising solvency on the other hand, causes banks in most cases roll-over loans, or even to expand credit lines for potentially illiquid firms since their rising collateral values reduce losses by banks in case of firms' default. As a result, though banks face increasing liquidity failures among firms lowering banks' profits and the log of their net worth $\ln NW_{BA}$ (figure 6.4(c)) according to equation 6.7, banks are willing to increase credit lines, being reflected in a declining nominal j and real interest rate $j - p$ on loans (figure 6.4(b)) due to the dominance of the rising collateral value effect according to equation 6.11, which overcompensates the negative influence of a declining log of high powered money $\ln M$ (figure 6.4(c)). However, this relaxation of loan market conditions leads to an increase in firms' total debt costs since the percentage increase in the stock of loans is larger than the decline of the loan rate, lowering additionally firms' profit rate r (figure 6.4(a)) owing to the overborrowing effect according to equation 6.3.

Foreign investors start to withdraw their funds, leading to rising capital outflows $\ln LF^*$ due to a deteriorating collateral position of banks $\ln NW_{BA}$ according to equation 6.6, leading to an increase in interest rate costs on foreign loans by a rise in the risk premium rp according to equation 6.8. Rising capital outflows $\ln LF^*$, and a rising risk premium rp cause monetary authorities to increase the nominal prime rate i_C, leading also to an increase in the real prime rate $i_C - p$ (figure 6.4(a)), in order to stabilize capital outflows according to equation 6.14. Yet, since capital outflows cannot be controlled perfectly due to the dominance of banks' collateral effect according to equations 6.6 and 6.14, a rising capital account deficit leads to a depletion of the log of foreign exchange reserves $\ln Z$, though the log of the current account $\ln T$ is improving and even changing into a current account surplus due to a declining import demand, being caused by a shrinking log of output $\ln Y$. There arise no international capital flows from short-term bond transactions since the domestic nominal short-term bond rate i, being equal to the real short-term bond rate $i - p$ (figure 6.4(b)), remains constant at an α per cent higher level than the foreign prime rate i_C^*, leading to a zero value of the capital flow determining interest rate differential $i - (i_C^* + \alpha)$ according to equation 6.10.

An increasing nominal domestic prime rate i_C, causing a decline in the log of the domestic credit component $\ln H$ (figure 6.4(c)) by an increase in banks' lending costs according to equation 6.5, and a shrinking log of foreign exchange reserves $\ln Z$, lead to a declining log of high powered money $\ln M$ (figure 6.4(c)), reducing deposit supply according to equation 6.4. Though deposit demand is reduced by a shrinking log of output $\ln Y$ according to equation 6.4, agents are forced to sell domestic long-term bonds due to an excess demand for deposits which is caused by the deposit supply being reduced to a larger extent than deposit demand via a reduction of $\ln Y$. As a result, the nominal and the real interest rate on long-term government bonds f and $f - p$ (figure 6.4(b)) rise by equation 6.4, leading to a reduction in government expenditure which is larger than the rise in investment demand due to an increase in $\ln q$, causing the log of output $\ln Y$ to shrink.

Summing up, the overborrowing phase and the upper turning point are characterized by a chartist expectation formation scheme, leading to increasing share prices and to an expansion of loans to domestic firms though fundamentals, as the profit rate, output, banks' net worth, as well as rising capital outflows indicate an unavoidable downturn of the economy being associated with severe financial distress.

Sensitivity Analysis. The solution is stable within a ±10% variation range of all key parameters h_1, rp_1, nw_1, lf_1, j_2, k_2, r_1, r_2, y_2, and y_3. Except for a −20% decrease in parameter r_{2_O}, the solution is even stable in a ±20% range. A −20% decrease in r_{2_O}, being equivalent to a stronger overborrowing effect, only causes the difference between the profit and the real lending rate $r - (j - p)$ to decline in the pre-currency crisis period leaving all other dynamic patterns unchanged. This result indicates that, in case the formation of profit expectations follows the fundamental $r - (j - p)$ in periods of weak chartist influence, a rising overborrowing effect causes expectations to switch from optimism to pessimism, determining the upper turning point and the beginning of the bust phase.

6.9.3 The Bust Phase

The overborrowing process comes to a halt at the upper turning point of the business cycle when investors conceive suddenly that profit expectations cannot be realized any more because of unsustainable high external debt among firms and banks, leading to a steady deterioration of the liquidity status, and eventually of the solvency status. In most cases, the downward revision of profit expectations is caused by a small shock, as e.g. the failure of an important business firm or bank, having the effect of a "wake up call" on investors. Since investors do not follow fundamental data when forming profit expectations in the overborrowing phase, the triggering event for collapsing expectations is generally interpreted as an exogenous shock, being however an *endogenous* phenomenon since steady increasing debt costs and declining revenues finally must lead to illiquidity and insolvency. Accordingly, the triggering event causing a downward revision of expectations is only a mechanism to reveal widespread financial fragility which has been ignored so far. In an environment with low financial fragility, the same triggering event would not have caused a widespread collapse of expectations, since the development of actual profits would have validated the existing financial structure, and would have indicated no overindebtedness and widespread potential illiquidity and insolvency. According to the sensitivity analysis of the overborrowing phase, increasing indebtedness in the model, causing a steady fall in the profit rate r and in the log of banks' net worth $\ln NW_{BA}$, engenders finally a downward revision of expectations in case the overborrowing process is reinforced when the economy reaches the upper turning point of the business cycle, being a realistic scenario in a nonlinear real-world dynamic environment as shown in chapters 4 and 5.[29]

When the growth in profit expectations comes to a halt, the bust phase is about to begin whose simulation follows the set of parameters, exogenous variables, as well as the forcing function summarized in table 6.4. The bust phase is driven by a sharply declining state of confidence ρ whose initial value $\rho_{BU}(0)$ is the maximum the state of confidence can reach, and whose negative growth rate is larger in absolute terms than the positive growth rate of ρ during the boom and the bust phase according to equation 6.19. Furthermore, the bust phase is characterized by a loan rate semi-elasticity value with respect to the stock of loans of $\varepsilon_{L,j_{BU}} > -1$, being reflected in a positive parameter $r_{2_{BU}}$ whose value is greater than in the boom phase r_{2_B}, reflecting a much less elastic loan demand in the bust phase according to condition 6.21.

The dynamic patterns of the endogenous model variables depicted in figures 6.5(a), 6.5(b), and 6.5(c) differ, by comparison with the boom and the overborrowing simulation, with respect to the occurrence of a speculative attack, and with respect to "jumps" of almost all variables at the moment of speculative attack, whereas the pre-currency crisis period is almost a mirror image of the boom phase simulation. The pre-currency crisis period from time $t = 0$ until the moment of speculative attack at time $t = 20.47$ is characterized by a fixed exchange rate at level $\ln \bar{s} = 20$ (solid line in uppermost right panel in figure 6.5(a) for $0 < t \leq 20.47$), while the post-currency crisis period is subject to a flexible exchange rate regime starting at $\ln s = 20$ at time $t = 20.47$ and following the flexible exchange rate path for $t > 20.47$ (dotted line in uppermost right panel in

[29] Sensitivity analysis of the overborrowing process has shown that a steady fall in r_{2_O}, i.e. a strengthening of overindebtedness, leads to a declining negative value of the difference between the profit and the real lending rate $r - (j - p)$, causing a sharp reduction in the state of confidence ρ in case expectations are influenced by the fundamental $r - (j - p)$.

Table 6.4: Parameters, Exogenous Variables, and Forcing Function During the Bust Phase

		Parameters			
$y_0 = 0$	$y_1 = 0.35$	$y_2 = 0.8$	$y_3 = 0.8$	$\zeta = 0.01$	$r_0 = 2$
$r_1 = 0.0001$	$r_{2_{BU}} = 0.8$	$r_3 = 0$	$r_4 = 0$	$\gamma = 0.5$	$d_1 = 0.2$
$d_2 = 0.8$	$d_3 = 0.02$	$h_0 = 40$	$h_1 = 4$	$lf_1 = 0.3$	$lf_2 = 0$
$nw_0 = 30$	$nw_1 = 8$	$rp_0 = 1$	$rp_1 = 0.005$	$k_1 = 2$	$k_2 = 0.8$
$\alpha = 0.01$	$j_0 = 2$	$j_1 = 0.45$	$j_2 = 0.105$	$tr_1 = 0.1$	$tr_2 = 0.9$
$\phi = 0.3$					
		Exogenous Variables			
$\ln P^*(t) = 0$	$\delta(t) = 0$	$\ln K(t) = 0$	$\ln m(t) = 2$	$\ln \bar{s} = 20$	$i_C^*(t) = 0$
		Forcing Function			
	$\rho_{BU}(t) = \rho_{BU}(0) + \psi_{BU}\, t$		$\rho_{BU}(0) = 100$	$\psi_{BU} = -5$	

figure 6.5(a) for $t > 20.47$). The time paths of the remaining variables under the fixed exchange rate regime until time $t = 20.47$ are represented by solid lines, whereas their post-currency crisis paths are represented by dotted lines. The "jumps" of almost all endogenous variables at the moment of speculative attack at time $t = 20.47$, except for the log of the exchange rate $\ln s$ and the log of the domestic price level $\ln P$ as to equation 6.1, are originally caused by a sudden and discontinuous decline in the log of foreign exchange reserves $\ln Z$ at time $t = 20.47$ from $\ln Z > 0$ to $\ln Z = 0$ (uppermost left panel in figure 6.5(a)) leading to a downward jump in the log of high powered money $\ln M = \gamma \ln H + (1-\gamma)\ln Z$ (figure 6.5(c)) causing the remaining variables to change discontinuously.[30] The following qualitative description of the bust phase depicted in figures 6.5(a), 6.5(b), and 6.5(c) discusses at first the pre-currency crisis situation, and afterwards the speculative attack's effects and the post-currency crisis phase.

The Pre-Currency Crisis Phase. The reduction in the state of confidence ρ by equation 6.19, which can be justified by a declining difference between the profit and the real lending rate $r - (j - p)$ (figure 6.5(a)), leads to a decline in log of the demand price of capital $\ln P_K$ (figure 6.5(c)) by equation 6.9, and to a decline in the log of Tobin's q, $\ln q$ (figure 6.5(a)), at a constant log of the price level $\ln P$ (figure 6.5(a)), resulting in zero inflation p (figure 6.5(a)) by equation 6.1. Hence, in the pre-currency crisis phase, nominal and real interest rate are identical. The fall in the log of Tobin's q, $\ln q$, causes a reduction of investment demand leading to a fall in the log of output $\ln Y$ (figure 6.5(c))

[30] Among the decline in the log of foreign exchange reserves $\ln Z$, the decline in the log of high powered money $\ln M$ is additionally caused by a discontinuous fall in the log of the domestic credit component $\ln H$ (figure 6.5(c)) due to an upward jump in the domestic prime rate i_C (figure 6.5(b)). However, both the jump in $\ln M$, and the jump in i_C, are originally caused by the discontinuous decline in the log of foreign reserves $\ln Z$.

by equation 6.2. This reduction in sales engenders ceteris paribus a reduction in firms' profit rate r (figure 6.5(a)) by equation 6.3, causing a further decline in the log of the demand price of capital $\ln P_K$ according to equation 6.9, in the log of Tobin's q, $\ln q$, in the log of output $\ln Y$, and thereby again in the profit rate r. Thus, the fall in the state of confidence ρ leads to a contractionary cumulative process being subject to declining share prices, declining output, declining profits and deteriorating liquidity positions of firms.

Rising liquidity problems among firms, indicated by a fall in the profit rate r, cause a banking crisis by an increasing amount of nonperforming loans, leading to a reduction in banks' profits and in the log of banks' net worth $\ln NW_{BA}$ (figure 6.5(c)) by equation 6.7. Rising solvency problems among banks lead on the one hand, to an increase in interest rate costs on foreign loans by an increase in the risk premium rp (figure 6.5(c)) as to equation 6.8, and on the other hand to a rising growth of capital outflows $\ln LF^*$ (figure 6.5(c)) according to equation 6.6. There are no international capital flows from short-term bond transactions since the domestic nominal short-term interest rate on bonds i (figure 6.5(b)), being equal to the real short-term bond rate $i-p$ (figure 6.5(b)), always adjusts instantaneously to guarantee the risk adjusted interest parity condition 6.10 by having a constant α percent higher value than the foreign prime rate i^*_C.

Rising foreign loan outflows make monetary authorities increase the domestic prime rate i_C (figure 6.5(b)), being equal to the real domestic prime rate $i_C - p$ (figure 6.5(b)), as to equation 6.14 in order to stabilize the capital account. Since international capital flows cannot be steered perfectly by monetary authorities owing to the dominance of banks' collateral effect as to equations 6.6 and 6.14, a rising capital account deficit causes the central bank to intervene in the foreign exchange market by selling foreign reserves $\ln Z$ (figure 6.5(a)) according to equation 6.13, though the current account deficit $\ln T$ (figure 6.5(c)) improves and reverses into a current account surplus due to the fall in the log of output $\ln Y$ by equation 6.12, which however, does not suffice to offset rising capital outflows.

Declining foreign exchange reserves $\ln Z$, and a rising domestic prime rate i_C leading to a reduction of the log of the domestic credit component $\ln H$ (figure 6.5(c)), cause a reduction in high powered money $\ln M$ (figure 6.5(c)). This reduction in high powered money reduces banks' deposit supply as their input factor to create loans, leading to a rise in the nominal loan rate j (figure 6.5(b)), being equal to the real loan rate $j - p$ (figure 6.5(b)) by equation 6.11. However, the increase in the nominal loan rate j is also driven by declining collateral values of firms represented by a fall in the log of the demand price of capital $\ln P_K$ as to equation 6.11. As a result, tightening financial market conditions, as well as declining collateral values among firms lead to a further cumulative reduction in firms' profit rate r according to equation 6.3, since the rise in the loan rate is larger than the percentage reduction in the stock of loans according to condition 6.21.

The reduction in the log of high powered money $\ln M$, and accordingly in deposit supply, leads to an increase in the domestic nominal long-term interest rate on government bonds f (figure 6.5(b)) by equation 6.4, since the decline in deposit supply is larger than the decline in deposit demand, being caused by the fall in the log of output $\ln Y$, leading to an excess supply of long-term bonds. This increase in the domestic nominal long-term bond rate f, being equal to the real long-term bond rate $f - p$ (figure 6.5(b)), causes a reduction in government expenditures, and thereby a further cumulative reduction in the log of output $\ln Y$ by equation 6.2.

Speculative Attack and Post-Currency Crisis Phase. An actual and expected rise in the flexible shadow exchange rate $\ln s$ (figure 6.5(b)), caused by the capital account deficit being larger in absolute terms than the current account surplus according to equation 6.13, makes foreign exchange market participants attack the domestic currency by buying the entire stock of foreign exchange reserves $\ln Z$ at time $t = 20.47$ when it holds that $\ln s = \ln \bar{s}$. Attacking the domestic currency is profitable from an investor's viewpoint as the acquired stock of foreign reserves $\ln Z$ can be sold later at a much higher exchange rate value $\ln s$. This discontinuous reduction in the log of foreign exchange reserves $\ln Z$ (figure 6.5(b)) leads to a downward jump in the log of high powered $\ln M$ (figure 6.5(c)) which induces a discontinuous rise in the nominal long-term interest rate on bonds f (figure 6.5(b)), causing a discontinuous reduction in government expenditures and in the log of output $\ln Y$ by equation 6.2. This downward jump in the log of output $\ln Y$ causes a discontinuous reduction in sales, and therefore in firms' profit rate r (figure 6.5(a)) by equation 6.3. Suddenly rising liquidity problems among firms induce a stock market "crash", being represented by downward jumps in the log of the demand price of capital $\ln P_K$ (figure 6.5(a)) by equation 6.9, and in the log of Tobin's q, $\ln q$ (figure 6.5(a)), which is however dampened by an increase in the log of the price level $\ln P$ (figure 6.5(a)) by equation 6.1, causing inflation $\ln p$ (figure 6.5(a)) to jump from zero to a positive value. Consequently, all increases in nominal interest rates are dampened by increasing inflation. The drop in the log of Tobin's q, $\ln q$, causes a further deterioration of the cumulative contractionary process by a sudden decline in investment demand, a further discontinuous drop in the log of output $\ln Y$, in the log of the demand price of capital $\ln P_K$, and in firms' profit rate r.

The decline in firms' profit rate r leads to a rise in the amount of nonperforming loans, being reflected in a downward jump in the log of banks' net worth $\ln NW_{BA}$ (figure 6.5(c)) as to equation 6.7, intensifying the banking crisis. It must be noted that banks' net worth also drops suddenly by the increase in foreign debt due to the devaluation, which is however not incorporated in the model. Declining net worth of banks leads to a discontinuous rise in capital outflows $\ln LF^*$ (figure 6.5(c)) by equation 6.6 and to a sudden rise in the risk premium rp (figure 6.5(c)) according to equation 6.8. Since the central bank cannot intervene any longer in the foreign exchange market and the flexible exchange rate moves continuously, the sudden increase in the capital account deficit requires a sudden increase in the current account surplus $\ln T$ (figure 6.5(c)) in order to equalize the balance of payments according to equation 6.13 for which it holds that $\ln \dot{Z} = 0$. In order to stabilize risk-adjusted international short-term bond interest rate parity, the domestic short-term bond rate i (figure 6.5(b)) has to increase discontinuously by the expected and constant depreciation rate $\ln \dot{s}$ by equation 6.10. As monetary authorities are assumed to stabilize capital flows by interest rate pegging under flexible exchange rates as well, the sudden rise in capital outflows $\ln LF^*$ and in the risk premium rp requires an upward jump in the domestic prime rate i_C (figure 6.5(b)) by equation 6.14, which however, does not stop capital outflows and a further depreciation of the home currency due to the dominance of banks' collateral effect by equations 6.6 and 6.14.

The drop in the domestic prime rate i_C, causing a drop in the log of domestic credit $\ln H$ (figure 6.5(c)), the drop in foreign exchange reserves $\ln Z$, as well as the drop in the log of the demand price of capital P_K make banks increase discontinuously the nominal loan rate j (figure 6.5(b)) by equation 6.11. This sudden increase in the nominal loan rate

j leads to a further drop in the profit rate r according to equation 6.3, and as described above, to a further deterioration of the cumulative contractionary process.

All real interest rates of the model, namely the real loan rate $j - p$, the real domestic prime rate $i_C - p$, the real short-term interest rate on bonds $i - p$, and the real long-term interest rate on bonds $f - p$ (all depicted in figure 6.5(b)), are also subject to a discontinuous upward jump since the increase in inflation p does not suffice to overcompensate the rising nominal interest rate effect in order to reduce real interest rates. The difference between the profit and the real lending rate $r - (j - p)$ (figure 6.5(a)) also drops discontinuously indicating a further drop in expectations.

The post-currency crisis period is characterized by a further deterioration of the macroeconomic situation due to a further declining state of confidence and due to a rising exchange rate. Accordingly, the dynamic patterns of all endogenous variables in the post-currency crisis period can be explained by the same mechanisms of the pre-currency crisis period and by the effects of a collapsing exchange rate having already outlined in detail above.

Sensitivity Analysis. The simulation results are stable within a $\pm 10\%$ variation of all key parameters h_1, rp_1, nw_1, lf_1, j_2, k_2, r_1, r_2, y_2, and y_3. Except for a $+20\%$ increase in parameters nw_1 and lf_1, the solution is even stable within a $\pm 20\%$ variation range. A $+20\%$ rise in parameters nw_1 and lf_1 leads to a twin crisis at first, but afterwards to a recovery of the economy despite a decrease in the state of confidence ρ. This result can be explained by an improving balance of payments situation due to a rising current account surplus after the speculative attack, leading to a depreciation of the exchange rate according to equation 6.13. The decline in the log of the exchange rate $\ln s$ leads to a decline in the log of the price level $\ln P$ by equation 6.1, thereby increasing Tobin's q, $\ln q$, by overcompensating the contractionary effect of a decline in the state of confidence ρ on the log of the demand price of capital $\ln P_K$. The rise in the log of Tobin's q, $\ln q$, leads to a rise in investment demand, output, share prices, profits, and capital inflows, leading to a relaxation of financial market conditions and thereby to a macroeconomic expansion. This result is a typical (but unrealistic) example of an expansionary devaluation though the economy is subject to a twin crisis.

6.10 Simulation of Financial Crises Caused by an Adverse Foreign Interest Rate Shock

The following simulation demonstrates the emergence of a systemic financial crisis caused by a negative foreign interest rate shock and excludes the build-up of endogenous financial fragility. The relevant parameter and exogenous variable set, as well as the forcing function of the exogenous shock simulation are summarized in table 6.5. The simulation is driven, following mainstream theory having been outlined in sections 4.5 and 5.5, by an exogenously increasing foreign prime rate i_C^* according to equation 6.23. In order to be comparable with the boom-bust simulations, the present simulation assumes an identical loan rate semi-elasticity with respect to the stock of loans as the bust phase simulation in section 6.9.3, i.e. it holds that $\varepsilon_{L,j_F} = \varepsilon_{L,j_{BU}} > -1$, implying $r_{2_F} = r_{2_{BU}} > 0$ according to condition 6.25. Assuming a very inelastic loan demand is consistent with the stylized facts in periods of sudden and large financial tightening, since external finance of long-term investment projects cannot be reduced instantaneously without causing immediate illiquidity, but adjusts only gradually. To rule out profit expectation effects, the state of confidence ρ_F is assumed to be zero throughout the analysis according to condition 6.24.

Table 6.5: Parameters, Exogenous Variables, and Forcing Function During an Adverse Exogenous Foreign Interest Rate Shock

Parameters					
$y_0 = 0$	$y_1 = 0.35$	$y_2 = 0.8$	$y_3 = 0.8$	$\zeta = 0.01$	$r_0 = 2$
$r_1 = 0.0001$	$r_{2_F} = 0.8$	$r_3 = 0$	$r_4 = 0$	$\gamma = 0.5$	$d_1 = 3$
$d_2 = 5$	$d_3 = 2$	$h_0 = 20$	$h_1 = 4$	$lf_1 = 0.3$	$lf_2 = 0$
$nw_0 = 30$	$nw_1 = 5$	$rp_0 = 1$	$rp_1 = 0.005$	$k_1 = 2$	$k_2 = 8$
$\alpha = 0.01$	$j_0 = 2$	$j_1 = 0.0012$	$j_2 = 0.105$	$tr_1 = 0.1$	$tr_2 = 0.9$
$\phi = 0.3$					
Exogenous Variables					
$\ln P^*(t) = 0$	$\delta(t) = 0$	$\ln K(t) = 0$	$\ln m(t) = 2$	$\ln \bar{s} = 20$	$\rho_F(t) = 0$
Forcing Function					
$i_C^*(t) = i_C^*(0) + \chi t$	$i_C^*(0) = 0$	$\chi = 5$			

The dynamic patterns of all endogenous variables depicted in figures 6.6(a), 6.6(b), and 6.6(c) are almost identical with those of the bust phase simulation. The pre-currency crisis period is characterized by a fixed exchange rate $\ln \bar{s} = 20$ from time $t = 0$ until the moment of speculative attack at time $t = 9.16$ (solid line in uppermost right panel in figure 6.6(a) for $0 < t \leq 9.16$), whereas the post-currency crisis phase is subject to a flexible exchange rate having an initial value of $\ln s = 20$ at time $t = 9.16$, and following the flexible exchange rate path for $t > 9.16$ (dotted line in uppermost right panel in figure 6.6(a) for $t > 9.16$). The time paths of the remaining variables are characterized by solid lines for the pre-currency crisis phase and by dotted lines for the post-currency crisis phase. At the moment of speculative attack at time $t = 9.16$, all variables, except for the log of the exchange rate $\ln s$ and the log of the price level $\ln P$, are subject to a jump which is caused originally by a discontinuous decline in the log of foreign exchange reserves from $\ln Z > 0$ for $t < 9.16$ to $\ln Z = 0$ at the moment of speculative attack at time $t = 9.16$, leading to a downward jump of the log of high powered money $\ln M$, and resulting in jumps of all other endogenous variables.[31] The qualitative description of the panels in figures 6.6(a), 6.6(b), and 6.6(c) starts with the pre-currency crisis phase and continues with the effects of the speculative attack and the post-currency crisis period.

[31]Though the discontinuous reduction in the log of high powered money $\ln M$ (figure 6.6(c)) is additionally caused by a downward jump in the log of the domestic credit component $\ln H$ (figure 6.6(c)), having its origin in an upward jump in the domestic prime rate i_C (figure 6.6(b)) by equation 6.5, all jumps, though mainly influenced by the downward jump of the log of high powered money $\ln M$, are originally caused by the discontinuous decline in the log of foreign exchange reserves $\ln Z$.

The Pre-Currency Crisis Phase. The increase in the foreign prime rate i_C^* according to equation 6.23, makes monetary authorities increase the domestic prime rate i_C (figure 6.6(b)) by equation 6.14, in order to prevent capital outflows and to support the fixed exchange rate. The steady rise in the foreign prime rate i_C^* causes also a steady increase in the domestic nominal short-term interest rate on government bonds i (figure 6.6(b)) in order to guarantee the risk adjusted interest rate parity given by equation 6.10. There arise no capital outflows from international short-term bond transactions since the nominal short-term bond rate i, being always α percent higher than the foreign prime rate i_C^*, adjusts instantaneously, leaving the capital flow determining interest rate differential $i - \alpha - i_C^* = 0$ unchanged.

The rise in the domestic prime rate i_C reduces the log of the domestic credit component $\ln H$ (figure 6.6(b)) as to equation 6.5, causing partially a reduction in the log of high powered money $\ln M$ (figure 6.6(c)) which is also reduced by a fall in the log of foreign exchange reserves $\ln Z$ being explained below. The drop in the log of high powered money $\ln M$ causes a reduction of deposit supply requiring either a fall in the log of output $\ln Y$, or a rise in the nominal short-term bond rate i, or a rise in the nominal long-term bond rate f, or some other combinations which reduce deposit demand. In the present case, deposit market equilibrium as to equation 6.4, is restored by a reduction in the log of output $\ln Y$ (figure 6.6(c)), by an increase in the nominal short-term interest rate on bonds i induced by the rise in the foreign prime rate i_C^* (figure 6.6(b)), and by a decrease in the nominal long-term bond rate f (figure 6.6(b)) running counter partly to deposit market equilibrium by increasing deposit demand and boosting output by increasing government expenditures as to equation 6.2. The rise in the short-term bond rate i leads to fall in the log of the demand price of capital $\ln P_K$ (figure 6.6(a)) according to equation 6.9, and to a decline in the log of Tobin's q, $\ln q$ (figure 6.6(a)) as to equation 6.9 at a constant log of the price level $\ln P$ (figure 6.6(a)) and zero inflation p (figure 6.6(a)), implying a correspondence of all nominal and real interest rates. The fall in the log of Tobin's q, $\ln q$, reduces investment demand and the log of output $\ln Y$ (figure 6.6(a)) by equation 6.2, though there is an expansionary effect on output by the fall in the nominal long-term bond rate f increasing government expenditure. However, in the present case, the decline in investment demand due to a reduction in Tobin's q dominates, resulting in an overall reduction in the log of output $\ln Y$.

The reduction in the log of output $\ln Y$ causes a decline in sales revenues, leading to a reduction in firms' profit rate r (figure 6.6(a)) and to a deterioration of firms' liquidity status by equation 6.3. Arising difficulties in fulfilling payment commitments causes a rising number of nonperforming loans, reducing banks' profits and the log of banks' net worth $\ln NW_{BA}$ by equation 6.7, and marking the beginning of an unavoidable banking crisis. Declining collateral values with banks increase on the one hand interest rate costs on foreign loans by an increasing risk premium rp (figure 6.6(a)) as to equation 6.8, and induce on the other hand a rising growth of capital outflows $\ln LF^*$ (figure 6.6(a)) by equation 6.6. Though domestic monetary authorities follow foreign monetary policy by maintaining the risk adjusted interest rate parity condition 6.14, they cannot avoid a rising growth of capital outflows due to the dominance of banks' collateral effect according to equations 6.6 and 6.14. Rising loan outflows and an increasing capital account deficit lead to a declining log of foreign exchange reserves $\ln Z$ (figure 6.6(a)) by equation 6.13, despite an increasing current account surplus $\ln T$ (figure 6.6(c)) induced by the fall in the log of output $\ln Y$ by equation 6.12, which however, cannot offset the widening capital account deficit.

A declining amount of the log of high powered money $\ln M$ and a declining log of the demand price of capital $\ln P_K$, indicating rising solvency problems among firms, make banks increase the domestic nominal loan rate j (figure 6.6(c)) by equation 6.11, which leads to a further reduction in firms' profit rate r and to a deterioration of firms' liquidity position. The decline in the profit rate r causes a further reduction in the log of Tobin's q, $\ln q$, in the log of output $\ln Y$, and again in the profit rate r. Rising bankruptcies among firms aggravate banks' solvency status and lead to further capital outflows and to further declining foreign exchange reserves.

Summing up, a rising foreign prime rate causes a cumulative contractionary macroeconomic process leading eventually to the occurrence of a twin crisis. Though state of confidence effects have been ruled out, a declining negative difference between the profit and the real lending rate $r - (j - p)$ (figure 6.6(c)) indicates that, in case profit expectations followed the fundamental $r - (j - p)$, the cumulative downward process would be deteriorated by collapsing profit expectations.

Speculative Attack and Post-Currency Crisis Phase. Foreign exchange market participants attack the domestic currency when the rising flexible shadow exchange rate, which is induced by the capital account deficit being larger in absolute terms than the current account surplus by equation 6.13, equals the fixed exchange rate value at time $t = 9.16$, and is expected to appreciate further. The discontinuous reduction in the log of foreign exchange reserves $\ln Z$ (figure 6.6(a)) at time $t = 9.16$ causes a downward jump in the log of high powered money $\ln M$ (figure 6.6(c)) and, as a result, in deposit supply. Deposit market equilibrium is restored partially by an upward jump in the nominal short-term bond rate i (figure 6.6(c)) to the amount of the constant expected depreciation rate of the domestic currency $E_t[\ln \dot{s}] = \ln \dot{s}$, in order to offset excess supply of short-term bonds. The constant depreciation rate of the domestic currency causes a smooth increase in the log of the domestic price level $\ln P$ (figure 6.6(c)) by equation 6.1, and an upward jump in the inflation rate p (figure 6.6(c)) from zero to a constant positive value. Thus, all jumps in nominal interest rates are larger than jumps in real interest rates. The upward jump in the nominal short-term domestic bond rate causes a downward jump in the log of the demand price of capital $\ln P_K$ (figure 6.6(a)) as to equation 6.9, and in the log of Tobin's q, $\ln q$ (figure 6.6(a)). The decline in Tobin's q leads to a sudden drop in investment demand, reducing the log of output $\ln Y$ (figure 6.6(c)), though the downward jump in the nominal long-term bond rate f (figure 6.6(b)) leads to a partly compensating discontinuous increase in government expenditures by equation 6.2. However, as already described in the pre-currency crisis phase, the decline in investment demand is larger in absolute terms than the increase in government expenditure, causing a drop in the log of output $\ln Y$. Summing up, though the downward jump in the nominal long-term bond rate f runs counter to a reduction in deposit demand, deposit market equilibrium is restored by a rising nominal short-term bond rate i and by a decline in the log of output $\ln Y$ according to equation 6.4.

The sudden drop in sales revenues causes a further drop in the profit rate r, aggravating firms' liquidity and solvency problems, and increasing the amount of nonperforming loans which reduces banks' profits and the log of banks' net worth $\ln NW_{BA}$ (figure 6.6(c)) by equation 6.7. This deterioration of banks' collateral induces on the one hand an upward jump in lending costs on foreign loans by a sudden increase in the risk premium rp (figure 6.6(c)) as to equation 6.8, and causes on the other hand a discontinuous increase in the growth of loan outflows $\ln LF^*$ (figure 6.6(c)) by equation 6.6. Though monetary authorities try to stabilize capital outflows by a discon rAmlFtincrease in the domestic prime rate i_C, leading also to a downward jump in the log of the domestic credit component $\ln H$ (figure 6.6(c)) as to equation 6.5, rising capital outflows cannot be avoided due to the dominance of banks' net worth effect according to equations 6.6 and 6.14. A largely rising capital account deficit causes a further appreciation of the log of the flexible exchange rate $\ln s$ (figure 6.6(a)) according to equation 6.13, in spite of a discontinuous increase in the current account surplus $\ln T$ (figure 6.6(c)) as to equation 6.12 induced by a downward jump in the log of output $\ln Y$, which however, cannot offset rising capital outflows.

The downward jump in the log of high powered money $\ln M$, as well as the downward jump in the log of the demand price of capital $\ln P_K$, makes banks increase discontinuously the nominal loan rate j (figure 6.6(c)) by equation 6.11. This increase in lending costs results in a further decline in firms' profit rate r, aggravating liquidity and solvency problems, leading to more nonperforming loans and to an amplification of the domestic banking crisis. This sudden deterioration of banks' solvency status leads to further capital outflows, further tightening of international and financial market conditions, and to a deterioration of the cumulative contractionary process.

All real interest rates in the model, i.e. the real loan rate $j-p$, the real domestic prime rate $i_C - p$, the real short-term bond rate $i - p$, as well as the real long-term bond rate $f - p$ (all depicted in figure 6.6(b)), are also subject to discontinuous jumps, which are however much smaller than the jumps in nominal rates due to a relatively large increase in domestic inflation p. If state of confidence effects were considered in the model, and profit expectations followed the difference between the profit and the real lending rate $r - (j - p)$, the macroeconomic contraction induced by the speculative attack would be aggravated additionally by a drop in profit expectations as indicated by the downward jump in $r - (j - p)$ (figure 6.6(a)). Summing up, a currency crisis generally magnifies the cumulative contractionary macroeconomic process induced by an exogenous rise in the foreign prime rate i_C^*.

The post-currency crisis period is subject to a further macroeconomic contraction due to a further rise in the foreign prime rate i_C^* and in the log of the exchange rate $\ln s$. All endogenous variables, except for the log of the exchange rate $\ln s$, the log of the price level $\ln P$, and the log of foreign exchange reserves $\ln Z$, are subject to the same time patterns as during the pre-currency crisis phase and can be explained by the proceedings during the pre-currency crisis phase, and by the effects of the speculative attack having been outlined above.

Sensitivity Analysis. The simulation results are stable within $\pm 10\%$ variation range for all key parameters h_1, rp_1, nw_1, lf_1, j_2, k_2, r_1, r_2, y_2, and y_3. Except for a $+20\%$ variation of parameters nw_1, lf_1, l_2, k_2, r_2, y_2, and y_3, the solution is even stable within a $\pm 20\%$ range. A $+20\%$ increase of parameters nw_1, lf_1, l_2, k_2, r_2, y_2, and y_3 leads at first to a twin crisis, i.e. the parameter results are stable for the pre-currency crisis period, but then to a macroeconomic expansion in the post-currency crisis phase. This recovery effect can be explained, like in the bust phase sensitivity analysis, by an improvement in the balance of payments leading to a depreciating log of the exchange rate $\ln s$ and to a declining log of the price level $\ln P$ by equation 6.1. The steady fall in the log of the price level $\ln P$ leads to a rise in Tobin's q which stimulates investment demand, output, firms' and banks' profits, capital inflows, and leads to a general relaxation of financial market conditions.

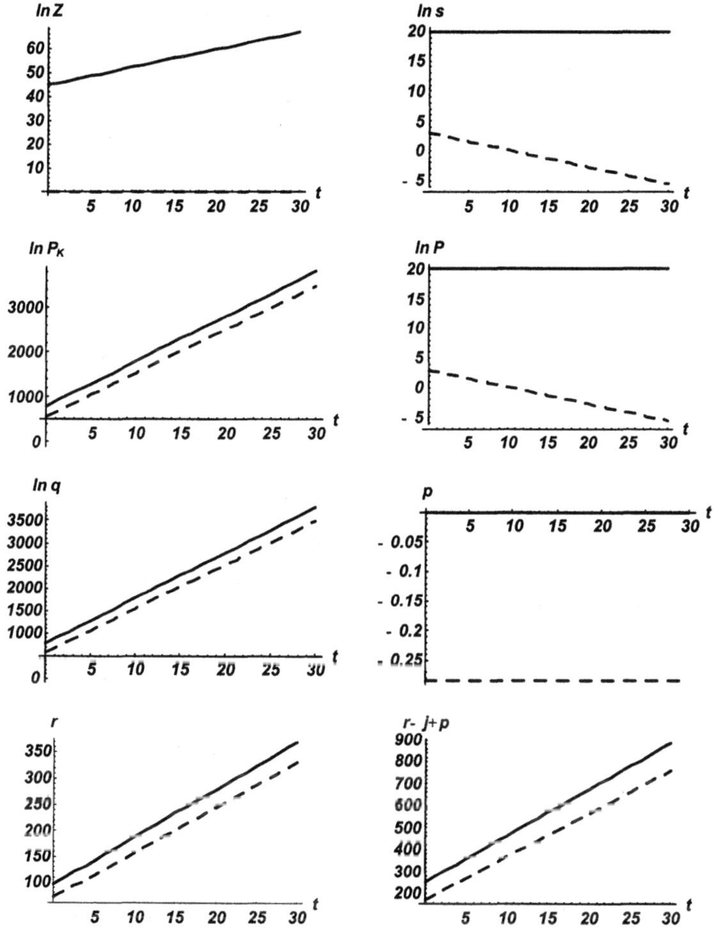

(a) Evolution of Endogenous Variables During the Boom Phase:

$\ln Z$: Log of Foreign Exchange Reserves, $\ln s$: Log of Nominal Exchange Rate, $\ln P_K$: Log of Demand Price of Capital, $\ln P$: Log of Price Level, $\ln q = \ln P_K - \ln P$: Log of Tobin's q, $p = \dot{P}/P$: Price Level's Growth Rate, r: Profit Rate, $r - j + p$: Difference Between Profit and Real Lending Rate.

Figure 6.3: Simulation of the Boom Phase

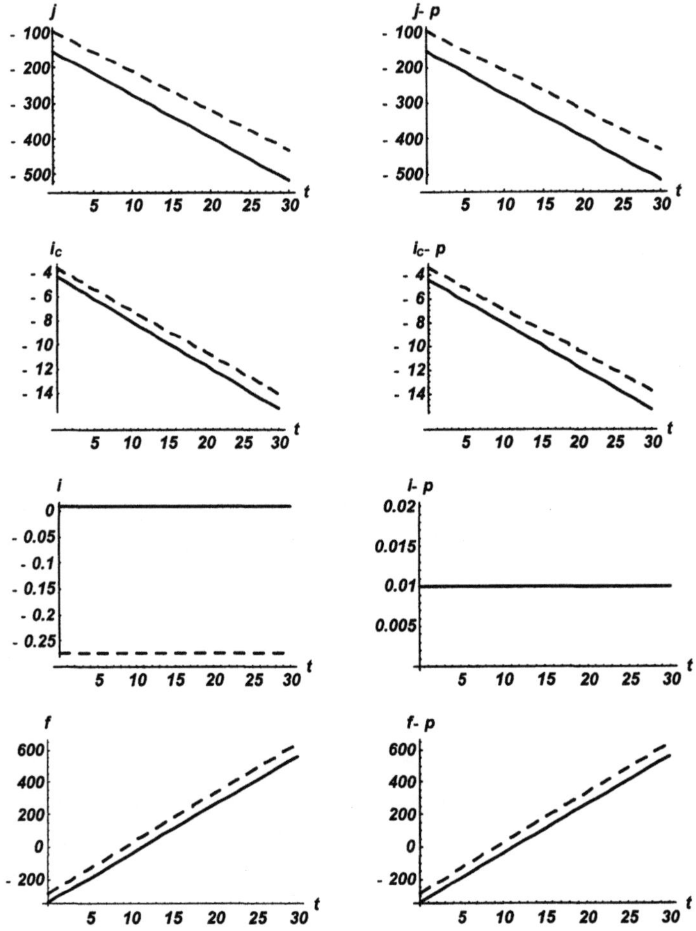

(b) Evolution of Endogenous Variables During the Boom Phase:

j: Nominal Lending Rate, $j-p$: Real Lending Rate, i_C: Domestic Prime Rate, $i_C - p$: Domestic Real Prime Rate, i: Domestic Short-Term Interest Rate, $i-p$: Domestic Short-Term Real Interest Rate, f: Domestic Long-Term Interest Rate, $f-p$: Domestic Long-Term Real Interest Rate.

Figure 6.3: Simulation of the Boom Phase (continued)

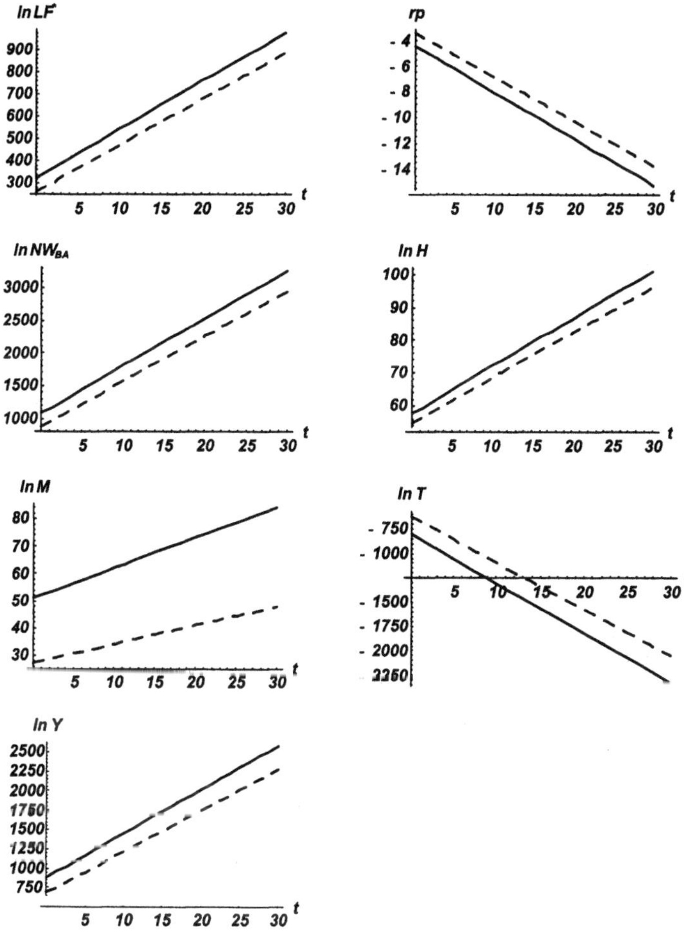

(c) Evolution of Endogenous Variables During the Boom Phase:

$\ln LF^* = \ln \dot{L}^*$: Log of Flows of Foreign Loans to Domestic Banks, rp: risk premium, $\ln NW_{BA}$: Log of Banks' Net Worth, $\ln H$: Log of Domestic Credit Component, $\ln M = \gamma \ln H(t) + (1-\gamma) \ln Z(t)$: Log of High Powered Money, $\ln T$: Log of Current Account (Trade Balance), $\ln Y$: Log of Domestic Output.

Figure 6.3: Simulation of the Boom Phase (continued)

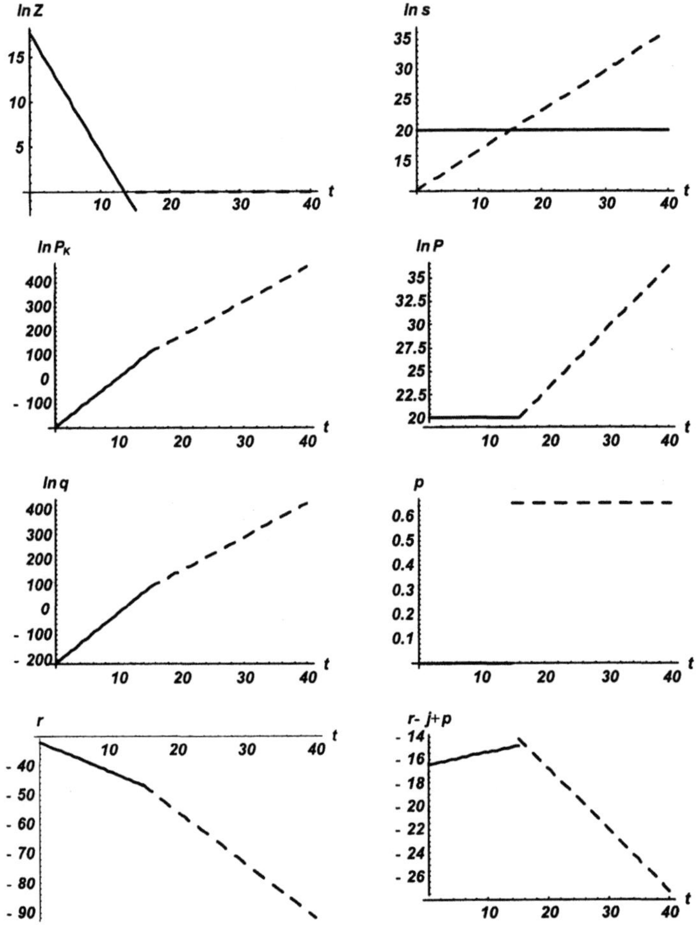

(a) Evolution of Endogenous Variables During the Overborrowing Phase and at the Upper Turning Point:

$\ln Z$: Log of Foreign Exchange Reserves, $\ln s$: Log of Nominal Exchange Rate, $\ln P_K$: Log of Demand Price of Capital, $\ln P$: Log of Price Level, $\ln q = \ln P_K - \ln P$: Log of Tobin's q, $p = \dot{P}/P$: Price Level's Growth Rate, r: Profit Rate, $r - j + p$: Difference Between Profit and Real Lending Rate.

Figure 6.4: Simulation of the Overborrowing Phase and the Upper Turning Point

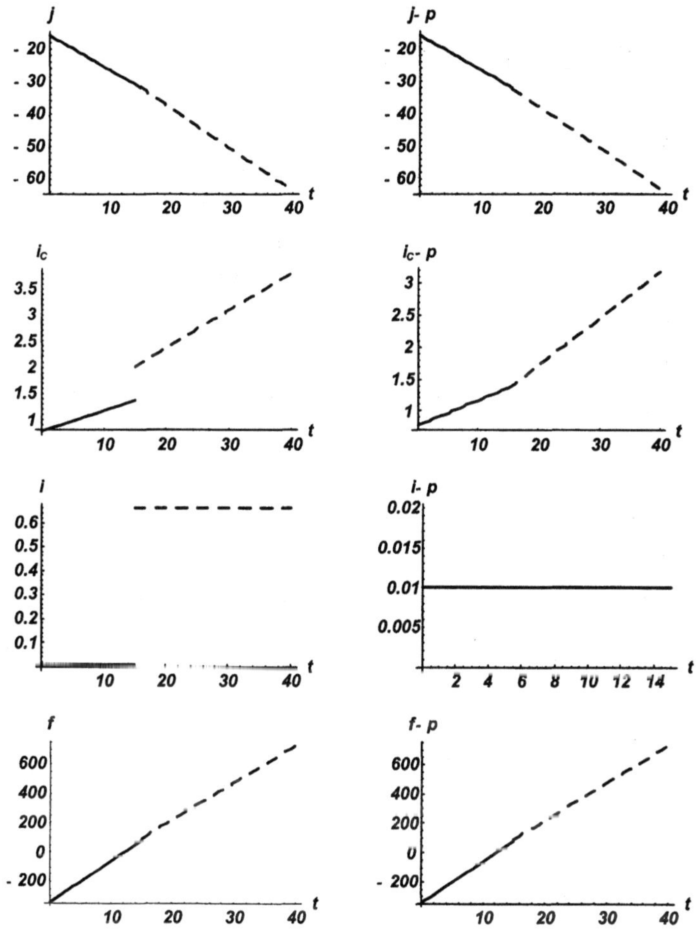

(b) Evolution of Endogenous Variables During the Overborrowing Phase and at the Upper Turning Point:

j: Nominal Lending Rate, $j - p$: Real Lending Rate, i_C: Domestic Prime Rate, $i_C - p$: Domestic Real Prime Rate, i: Domestic Short-Term Interest Rate, $i - p$: Domestic Short-Term Real Interest Rate, f: Domestic Long-Term Interest Rate, $f - p$: Domestic Long-Term Real Interest Rate.

Figure 6.4: Simulation of the Overborrowing Phase and the Upper Turning Point (continued)

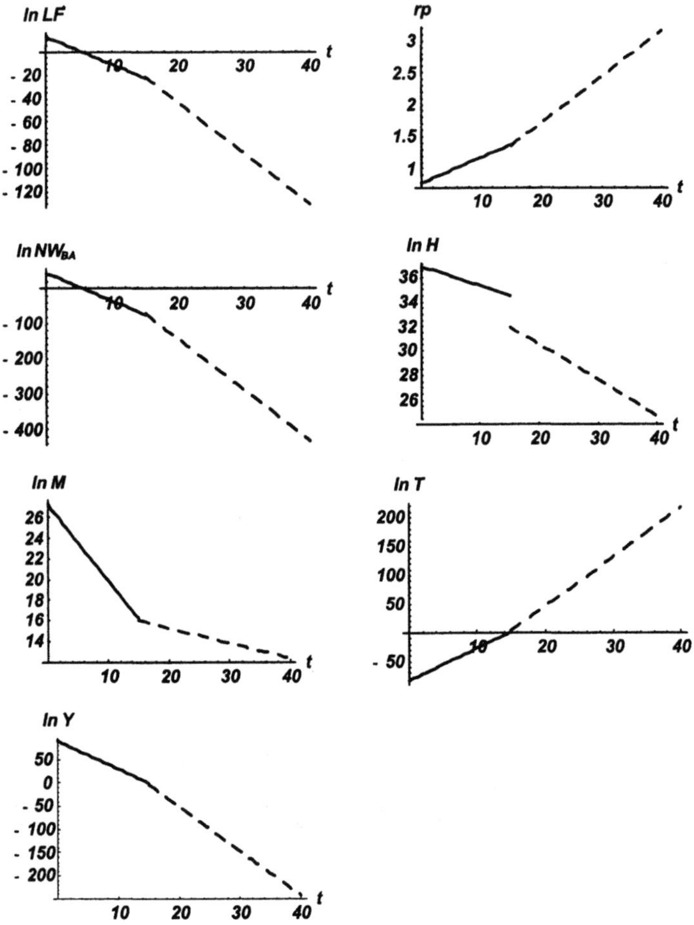

(c) Evolution of Endogenous Variables During the Overborrowing Phase and at the Upper Turning Point:

$\ln LF^* = \ln \dot{L}^*$: Log of Flows of Foreign Loans to Domestic Banks, rp: risk premium, $\ln NW_{BA}$: Log of Banks' Net Worth, $\ln H$: Log of Domestic Credit Component, $\ln M = \gamma \ln H(t) + (1-\gamma) \ln Z(t)$: Log of High Powered Money, $\ln T$: Log of Current Account (Trade Balance), $\ln Y$: Log of Domestic Output.

Figure 6.4: Simulation of the Overborrowing Phase and the Upper Turning Point (continued)

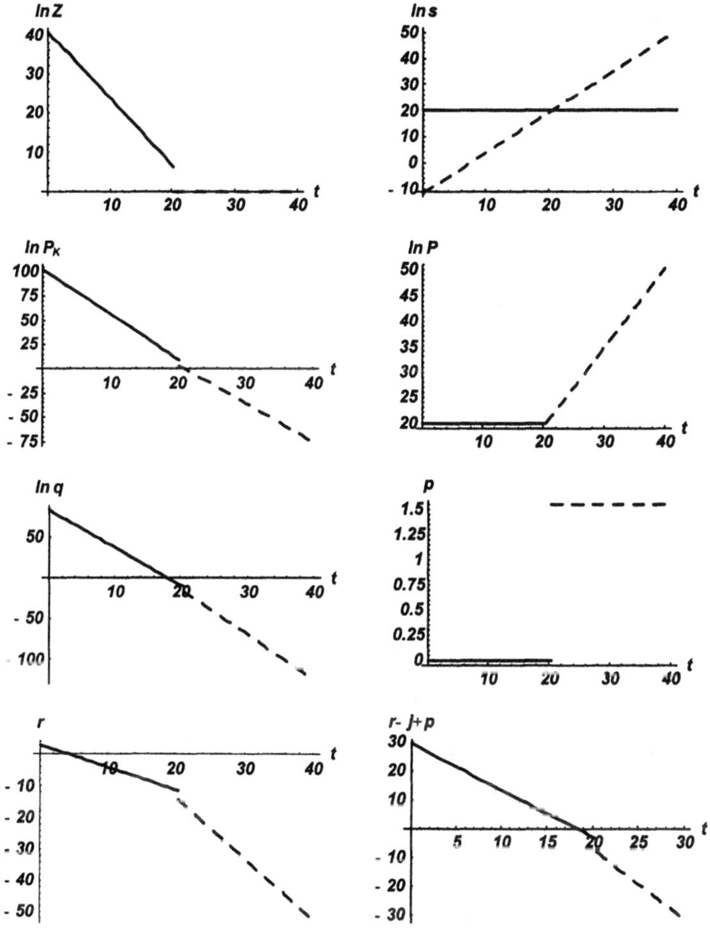

(a) Evolution of Endogenous Variables During the Bust Phase:

$\ln Z$: Log of Foreign Exchange Reserves, $\ln s$: Log of Nominal Exchange Rate, $\ln P_K$: Log of Demand Price of Capital, $\ln P$: Log of Price Level, $\ln q = \ln P_K - \ln P$: Log of Tobin's q, $p = \dot{P}/P$: Price Level's Growth Rate, r: Profit Rate, $r - j + p$: Difference Between Profit and Real Lending Rate.

Figure 6.5: Simulation of the Bust Phase

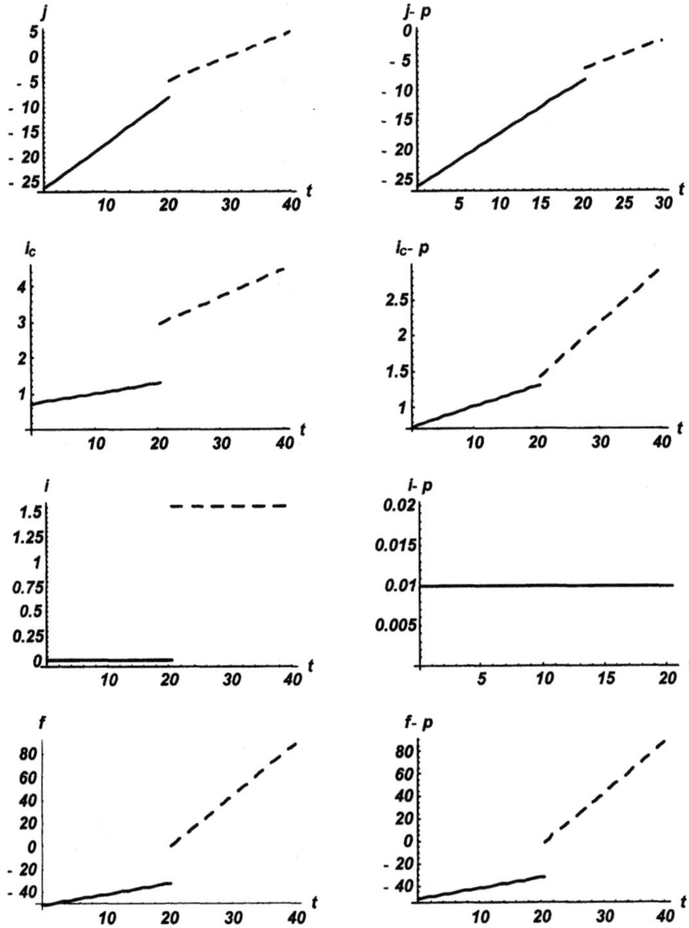

(b) Evolution of Endogenous Variables During the Bust Phase:

j: Nominal Lending Rate, $j - p$: Real Lending Rate, i_C: Domestic Prime Rate, $i_C - p$: Domestic Real Prime Rate, i: Domestic Short-Term Interest Rate, $i - p$: Domestic Short-Term Real Interest Rate, f: Domestic Long-Term Interest Rate, $f - p$: Domestic Long-Term Real Interest Rate.

Figure 6.5: Simulation of the Bust Phase (continued)

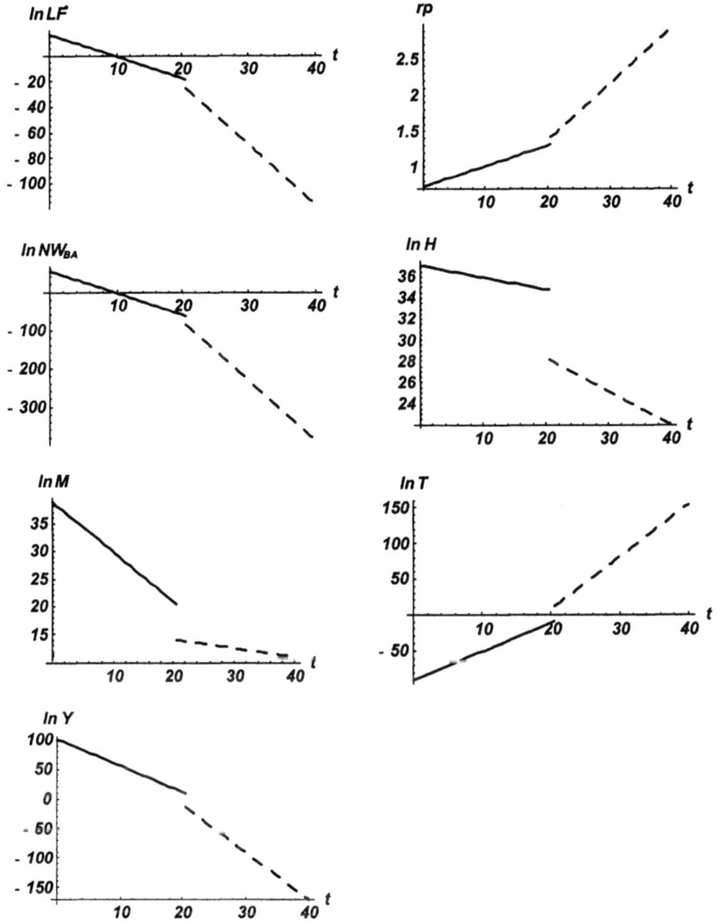

(c) Evolution of Endogenous Variables During the Bust Phase:

$\ln LF^* = \ln \dot{L}^*$: Log of Flows of Foreign Loans to Domestic Banks, rp: risk premium, $\ln NW_{BA}$: Log of Banks' Net Worth, $\ln H$: Log of Domestic Credit Component, $\ln M = \gamma \ln H(t) + (1-\gamma) \ln Z(t)$: Log of High Powered Money, $\ln T$: Log of Current Account (Trade Balance), $\ln Y$: Log of Domestic Output.

Figure 6.5: Simulation of the Bust Phase (continued)

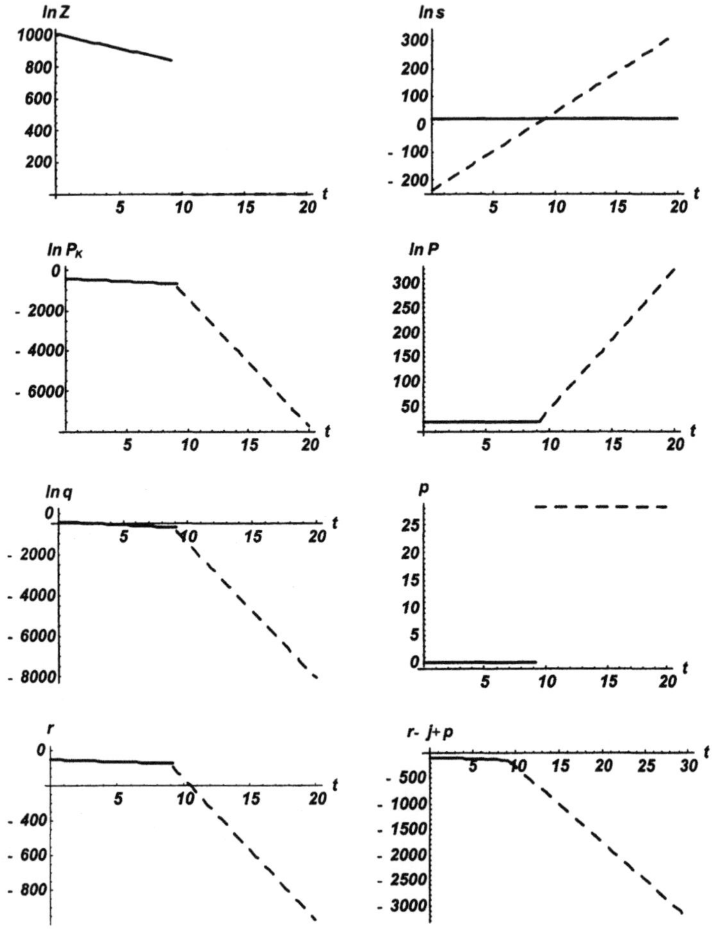

(a) Evolution of Endogenous Variables During Foreign Interest Rate Increase:

$\ln Z$: Log of Foreign Exchange Reserves, $\ln s$: Log of Nominal Exchange Rate, $\ln P_K$: Log of Demand Price of Capital, $\ln P$: Log of Price Level, $\ln q = \ln P_K - \ln P$: Log of Tobin's q, $p = \dot{P}/P$: Price Level's Growth Rate, r: Profit Rate, $r - j + p$: Difference Between Profit and Real Lending Rate.

Figure 6.6: Simulation of a Foreign Interest Rate Increase

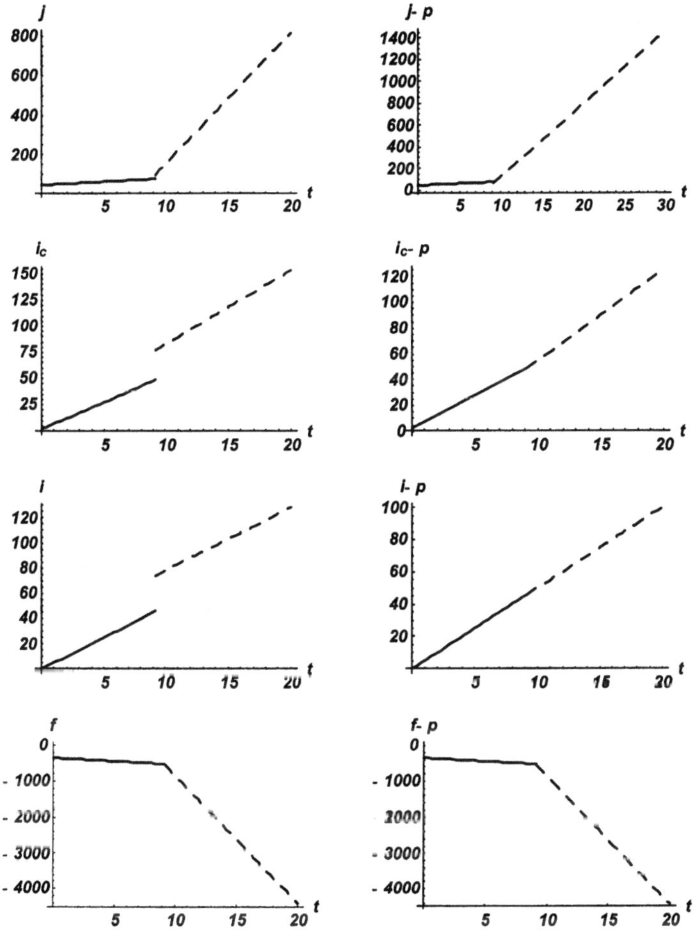

(b) Evolution of Endogenous Variables During Foreign Interest Rate Increase:

j: Nominal Lending Rate, $j - p$: Real Lending Rate, i_C: Domestic Prime Rate, $i_C - p$: Domestic Real Prime Rate, i: Domestic Short-Term Interest Rate, $i - p$: Domestic Short-Term Real Interest Rate, f: Domestic Long-Term Interest Rate, $f - p$: Domestic Long-Term Real Interest Rate.

Figure 6.6: Simulation of a Foreign Interest Rate Increase (continued)

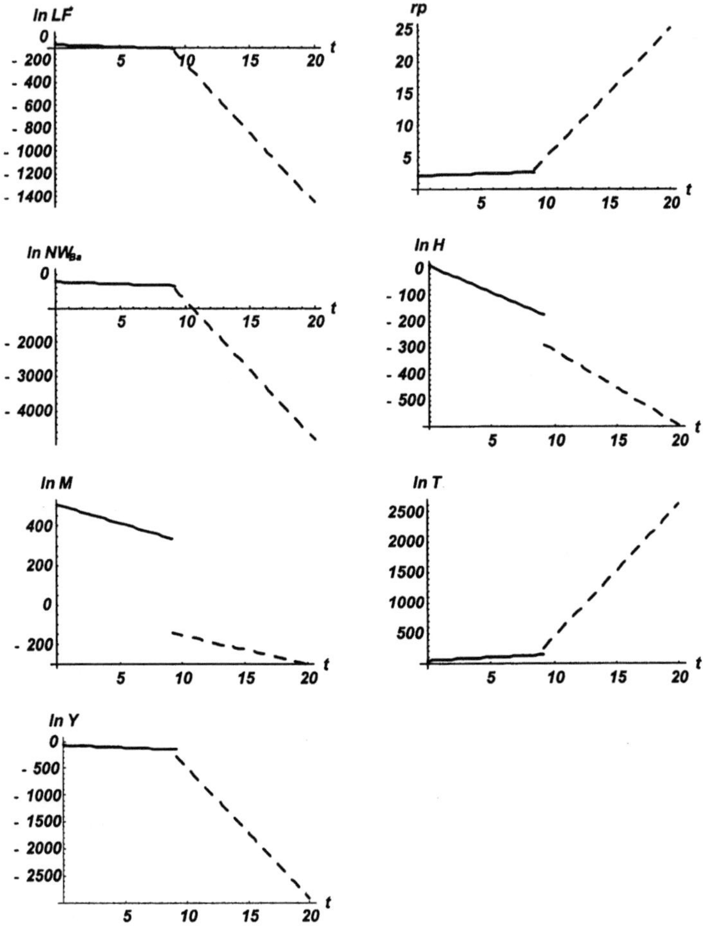

(c) Evolution of Endogenous Variables During Foreign Interest Rate Increase:

$\ln LF^* = \ln \dot{L}^*$: Log of Flows of Foreign Loans to Domestic Banks, rp: risk premium, $\ln NW_{BA}$: Log of Banks' Net Worth, $\ln H$: Log of Domestic Credit Component, $\ln M = \gamma \ln H(t) + (1 - \gamma) \ln Z(t)$: Log of High Powered Money, $\ln T$: Log of Current Account (Trade Balance), $\ln Y$: Log of Domestic Output.

Figure 6.6: Simulation of a Foreign Interest Rate Increase (continued)

Chapter 7

Conclusion

The present approach to financial crises offers both new perspectives for economic theory and alternative recommendations for economic policy which are discussed briefly in the following sections 7.1 and 7.2.

7.1 New Perspectives for Economic Theory

The comparison of the model results in chapters 4, 5, and 6 with the stylized facts of financial crises, having been set out in chapter 3, demonstrates clearly that the present approach to financial crises corresponds much better to the stylized facts than standard models having been reviewed in sections 4.5 and 5.5. This better performance is due to the introduction of innovative methods and concepts which have not been considered yet by most standard models. The following discussion highlights the most important innovations of the present approach in comparison with standard approaches, and ends with some proposals for further lines of research.

Regarding the major innovations of the present approach to financial crises, there are six issues to be highlighted. Firstly, the present approach does not follow the general polarization into models of exogenous financial crises on the one hand, and models of endogenous financial crises on the other hand, but provides a synthesis by demonstrating that financial fragility is an endogenous phenomenon which can be observed during each business cycle, but which can only induce a systemic financial crises if there is an exogenous positive shock to expectations. Thus, the present approach points out, in contrast to exogenous shock-driven models, that financial strains are not extraordinary exogenous events, and, in contrast to endogenous financial crisis models, that capitalist market economies are cyclically stable in spite of an endogenous build-up of financial fragility during the boom phase of business cycles.

Secondly, the present approach may possibly help both to prevent, and to predict financial crises much better than in the past, as it links general economic theory, i.e. economic analysis during tranquil times, with the theory of financial crises in a new way, by arguing that a certain degree of financial fragility is a part of "normal" economic life, and that financial crises have to be considered as a variant, or extreme form of general economic theory. By way of contrast, mainstream exogenous shock-driven models view the theory of financial crises as an isolated extra part, because financial crises are considered as pathologies which do not fit general economic theory. As a result, mainstream theory is built on two different theories, one for tranquil times and one for financial crises' periods, which are not compatible. Endogenous financial crisis models represent the other extreme by arguing that there is no distinction between tranquil periods and financial crises since capitalist systems are inherently financially unstable, implying that there is no theory for tranquil periods.

Thirdly, the present approach employs a promising kind of expectation formation scheme which overcomes the existing polarization into rational expectations on the one hand, and chartist-fundamentalist expectations on the other hand, by arguing that expectations are rational in the long-run, and that short-run expectations are driven both by an assessment of economic fundamentals and by general market sentiment. This synthetic approach to the formation of expectations provides a good theoretical explanation of fluctuations in profit expectations and asset prices over the business cycle, and stresses the empirical fact that macroeconomic activity is driven to a large extent by self-fulfilling expectations giving rise to cumulative upward and downward processes. Furthermore, this synthetic approach emphasizes that economic models should not be based completely on the rational expectations hypothesis, and that long-run rational expectations equilibria are only theoretical reference points which cannot be attained in the long-run, as expectations persistently fluctuate around these equilibria.

Fourthly, the present approach is based on a sophisticated financial structure with many assets and argues, in contrast to exogenous shock-driven and neoclassical mainstream models, that the financial structure is a crucial determinant of real economic activity and financial stability, as it determines aggregate liquidity, solvency, profits, and thereby whether financial constraints become binding or not, even in the long-run. Consequently, the general conclusion of neoclassical standard analysis that both money, and the financial structure are irrelevant in the long-run, has to be rejected. Furthermore, the present approach stresses the influence of financial intermediaries on aggregate economic activity and financial stability, not only in periods of financial distress, but also during tranquil periods, being neglected by standard neoclassical and Keynesian economic theory.

Fifthly, the present approach points out that both tranquil business cycles and financial crisis cycles are driven by an endogenous interaction of profit expectations and the financial structure of an economy. Moreover, the present approach highlights the fact that notwithstanding the existence of a stationary steady state, capitalist economies are only cyclically stable in the long-run, and do not converge to a stationary steady state. Consequently, long-run economic analysis should be based more on non-linear dynamic mathematical models than on linear ones.

Sixthly, the model structure of the present approach is much more complex than the model structures of standard approaches to financial crises, especially with respect to the number of parameters and endogenous variables, and with respect to the number of transmission mechanisms between the real and the financial sphere of an economy. Furthermore, the present approach contains major financial and real indicators as variables and parameters which are used in empirical business cycle analysis and in empirical financial crises' analysis. Consequently, in order to derive meaningful and useful results from theoretical models which can be applied to real-world phenomena, model structures have to be much more complex than models structures of standard approaches, as the explanation and the prediction of financial crises is a multidimensional phenomenon which influences almost all real sector and financial sector variables of an economy.

Though the present approach to financial crises represents an innovation in financial crisis modelling, it is subject to four major drawbacks which should be starting points for further research. Firstly, though the nonlinear dynamic general function models in chapters 4 and 5 are able to explain the emergence of endogenous business cycles and financial crises, they cannot provide exact information on the time paths of all endogenous variables, as well as on the transitional dynamics. One possible solution, as outlined in section 6.1, is to calibrate or to simulate general function models. However, simulations of complex models are often impossible due to the lack of relevant empirical data, and calibration techniques of nonlinear general function models have to be approximated by linear and exogenous shock-driven models in order to remain formally tractable. Accordingly, future research on business cycles and financial crises should concentrate on the development of quantitative methods to simulate, or to calibrate complex nonlinear dynamic systems.

Secondly, though the synthesis of the rational expectations hypothesis and market sentiment-driven expectations provides a good approximation to the formation of real-world expectations, it provides no formal conditions for the turning points of expectations. Such formal conditions could be empirically estimated and used to predict business cycle turning points, changes in asset price behaviour, and financial crises. Consequently, future research should focus more on formal methods to quantify the real-world formation of expectations.

Thirdly, notwithstanding the fact that the present approach emphasizes the endogenous character of indebtedness, as well as its influence on financial stability, there is no distinction between fluctuations in short-term and long-term indebtedness. In order to be consistent with the stylized facts, future models should be able to show the overproportional rise in short-term indebtedness during the upswing by the introduction of a term structure of interest rates.

Fourthly, the present approach neglects the phenomenon of contagion which could be investigated by multi-country models with interdependent expectation dynamics. Furthermore, future research should be able to distinguish between contagion induced by real factors, and by financial factors.

7.2 Policy Recommendations

This section elaborates policy recommendations which are based on the model results of chapters 4, 5, and 6. The following discussion is subdivided in three paragraphs, analyzing policy measures to prevent, to predict, and to manage financial crises.

Crisis Prevention. The present approach argues that financial crises are caused by exogenous positive shocks to expectations inducing an unsustainable build-up of financial fragility by excess volatility in asset prices, overborrowing and overinvestment. As a result, policy measures to prevent financial crises have to limit the increase in domestic and foreign indebtedness during the boom phase, as well as the overshooting process in profit expectations. As indebtedness and profit expectations are mutually dependent, policy measures which are designed to limit the increase in debt finance, e.g. by the imposition of additional external financial constraints, also limit the rise in profit expectations, as a lower degree of both domestic and foreign indebtedness implies lower investment, lower actual profits, lower net worth positions, lower asset prices, and thereby a less pronounced chartist-type behaviour of agents. In the same way, policy measures which are designed to limit the increase in profit expectations also limit the increase in indebtedness, as lower profit expectations imply lower asset prices, lower collateral values, and thereby a lower degree of indebtedness.

Respecting policy measures to limit the increase in domestic and foreign indebtedness during the boom phase, the present approach offers four recommendations. Firstly, the valuation of assets serving as collateral has to be based on international standardized valuation methods which determine the value of an asset by its underlying fundamentals and risks, and not by its current market price. This fundamental collateral value has to be equal to the maximum of level of indebtedness which however, has to be additionally positively dependent both on lenders' and borrowers' net worth. That is, if both the lender and borrower do not fulfill certain minimum net worth standards, the actual amount of debt finance has to be lower than the fundamental collateral value. To put it differently, higher indebtedness requires both a higher fundamental collateral value, and a higher net worth of the borrower and the lender. However, in order to be effective, these standardized asset valuation methods and minimum net worth standards have to refer not only to on-balance sheet items, but also to off-balance sheet assets and debts as the rapid growth of derivative markets in the past decades indicates an increase in the weight of off-balance assets and debts in balance sheets of the corporate and the financial sector.[1] Further prerequisites for the efficient functioning of standardized asset valuation methods and minimum net worth standards are the introduction of international accounting standards, rigorous disclosure requirements, effective international supervision and regulation of firms and financial institutions, and effective means of enforcement which could be achieved e.g. by the introduction of an international bankruptcy court. A first step to prevent an overvaluation of collateral values, excessive risk taking and overlending is the introduction of international minimum capital adequacy standards for the financial sector by the new Basel Capital Accord (Basel II), forcing financial institutions to evaluate risks in their portfolios, and limiting the amount of lending by the degree of collateral risk, as higher risk taking requires an increase in net worth. However, one main disadvantage of the Basel II accord, contradicting the recommendation made above, is the fact that financial institutions are allowed to evaluate their risk exposures by internal ratings, i.e. there are no general international rules for risk assessment being valid for all financial institutions. Consequently, the degree of financial stability is largely dependent on subjective risk perceptions of financial institutions.

Secondly, notwithstanding the fact that international financial market regulation in the form of asset valuation methods and minimum capital adequacy standards is an indispensable precondition for crisis prevention, it cannot replace domestic financial market regulation and supervision, since in a world of integrated financial markets, international

[1]The breakdown of LTCM in 1998, having almost led to a breakdown of the entire U.S. banking system which could be only prevented by effective lender of last resort interventions by the Federal Reserve, has demonstrated that unregulated trading in off-balance sheet assets and debts of a single financial institution can lead to an unsustainable build-up of financial instability, being able to induce a collapse of an entire domestic financial system which possibly spreads out to the international financial system. For the emergence of systemic risk due to off-balance sheet transactions, see also appendix C.

financial stability can be only achieved by domestic financial stability. Accordingly, excessive overborrowing and financial crises can be only prevented if there is an effective domestic supervision and regulation of domestic financial institutions, being based on international standards, and accounting for special features of domestic financial markets.

Thirdly, domestic and international financial market supervision and regulation have to be also a necessary ingredient of financial liberalization policies. Fast financial sector and capital account liberalization without standardized asset valuation methods, minimum net worth standards, safety nets, proper accounting standards, government supervision, etc., lead inevitably to excessive overborrowing and financial crises. By way of contrast, gradual and supervised liberalization processes are a robust basis for financial sector and economic development, and generate much higher welfare in the long-run than fast and unregulated financial liberalization policies. Furthermore, to limit large fluctuations in capital flows being associated with financial liberalization policies especially in emerging market countries, short-term portfolio flows should be limited in the early liberalization period, e.g. by the introduction of a Tobin tax, or even by temporary capital controls, whereas long-term foreign direct investments should be encouraged.

Fourthly, moral hazard has to be limited by transferring the risk associated with an investment project entirely back to the investor. In order to limit overborrowing in foreign currency, implicit or explicit government guarantees to support fixed exchange rate regimes have to be abandoned. Lacking guarantees and a higher degree of exchange rate flexibility make investors hedge against foreign exchange risk and reduce risky investment projects. Furthermore, the International Monetary Fund has to abandon its policy of bailing out private international investors by the provision of rescue packages in case of a crisis. However, a bailing-in policy of the private sector requires also that the International Monetary Fund refrains from promoting widespread and quick financial sector and capital account liberalization combined with stabilization policies which induce moral hazard. In order to prevent overborrowing and excessive risk taking by domestic financial systems, government guarantees for financial institutions regarded as too big to fail have to be abandoned. However, in order to be successful, this policy measure requires a restructuring of domestic financial markets transforming narrow oligopolies into competitive market structures. As long as this transformation is not completed, too-big-to-fail policies should not be abandoned since a failure of only one of the most important financial institutions can trigger a systemic financial crisis.[2]

Regarding policy measures to limit the overshooting of profit expectations during the boom phase, the present approach recommends a monetary policy approach which does not only stabilize inflation and output, but also profit expectations via a stabilization of the level of asset prices when they are too volatile, i.e. when there is excess volatility caused by unrealistic profit or unrealistic inflation expectations as outlined in sections

[2]Though government guarantees in the form of too-big-to-fail policies, as well as in the form of bail out policies by the International Monetary Fund have not been considered explicitly by general function models in chapters 4 and 5, their inclusion in the dynamic version of the models would induce both an additional rise in the state of confidence parameter ρ in the boom phase due to the government's promise to bear losses in case of default (inducing also an additional rise in the debt-asset ratios λ and λ^*), and an additional decline in the bust phase when government guarantees are going to be suspended (inducing also an additional decline in the debt-asset ratios λ and λ^*). In graphical terms, the introduction of government guarantees would give rise to financial crises' cycles with much larger amplitudes than those in figures 4.7, 5.7 and 5.8.

2.3.4 and 2.3.5. However, stabilizing asset prices when they are too volatile does not imply that monetary authorities should target specific levels of asset prices as there are also fundamentally justified movements in asset prices, which can be caused e.g. by general productivity shocks. Rather, central banks should prevent large misalignments in asset prices giving rise to an enormous increase in financial instability. It has to be emphasized that central banks should not only prevent asset prices from overshooting during boom phases, but also from undershooting during bust phases, being discussed in more detail below.

Crisis Prediction. The high incidence of financial crises in the post Bretton Woods era has led to the development of empirical early-warning systems of currency, banking, and twin crises by central banks, domestic and international regulation authorities, and research departments of private and official institutions to predict future crises, or even to prevent them by emergency measures.[3] However, past experience with these early-warning systems has shown that in most cases they are only useful to register financial crises, but not to predict future financial crises.

This poor record can be explained partly by the fact that the choice of leading indicators of early-warning systems is generally based on empirical studies of the stylized behaviour of macroeconomic variables during periods of financial distress which do not consider balance sheet indicators.[4] The present approach however, has demonstrated that especially balance sheet variables are very good leading indicators of financial distress, as profit expectations, asset prices and real economic activity generally tend to follow the actual behaviour of liquidity, and profit variables. As a result, the performance of early-warning systems could be improved considerably by the inclusion of balance sheet data of a large number of firms and financial institutions.

Another reason for the limited predictive power of early-warning systems may be the fact that they do not consider explicitly misalignments of asset prices, reflecting the misalignment of profit expectations. The present approach has pointed out that especially stock prices are a very good indicator for the state of profit expectations, which are also a leading indicator, as financial market and real sector variables tend to follow changes in expectations. Consequently, the predictive power of early-warning systems could be improved considerably by developing quantitative methods determining the degree of misalignment of asset prices, being a leading indicator of overborrowing and overinvestment.

Crisis Management. It should be a ground rule for crisis management that in case of a financial crisis, domestic and international authorities should avoid costs for those which did not cause the crisis, and to call those into account having contributed to the build-up of financial fragility by overborrowing and overlending. Consequently, crisis managers should generally minimize economic costs in the form of output losses, bankruptcies and unemployment, high inflation or deflation, and high interest rates, as these costs predominantly hit the entire population of a crisis country, while only a small fraction of the

[3]Examples of early-warning systems can be found in International Monetary Fund (1998a), chapter IV, Kaminsky and Reinhart (1998, 1999), and Glick and Hutchinson (1999).

[4]Following the terminology of section 3.4, these kinds of studies have been labelled as studies of the first class.

population and, especially in emerging market crises, foreign investors caused the crisis. This ground rule implies firstly, that domestic monetary and fiscal policies should prevent a crisis economy from slipping into a deep depression, and secondly, that international authorities, and especially the International Monetary Fund, should refrain from bailing out private investors generally, as well as from standing aside and letting nature run its course in case a country has been hit by a crisis.

Regarding the management of financial crises by domestic monetary policy, the present approach offers four recommendations which are consistent with the ground rule discussed above. Firstly, central banks should generally act as an efficient lender of last resort by short-run liquidity supports to still solvent financial institutions in order to prevent a breakdown of the domestic financial system. Secondly, monetary policy should guarantee the efficient functioning of domestic deposit insurance systems to prevent widespread banking panics. Thirdly, monetary policy should be expansionary to stabilize profits, liquidity, net worth positions, and thereby profit expectations, asset prices, output and the price level. By way of contrast, if monetary policy does not react quickly on collapses in asset prices by lowering interest rates, or even becomes contractionary, it reinforces the economic downturn, as there is no stabilization of the drop in liquidity positions, profits, net worth positions, asset prices, output and inflation, which validates investors pessimistic profit expectations and induces a further deterioration of the cumulative downward process. Fourthly, following the recommendation of expansionary monetary policy in case of a financial crisis, monetary policy under fixed exchange rates should not follow the generally adopted rule to increase interest rates sharply in case of a crisis in order to stabilize foreign and domestic investors' confidence, and thereby the fixed exchange rate by limiting capital outflows. Historical experience has demonstrated that contractionary monetary policy under fixed exchange rates in case of a crisis does not restore confidence, but undermines confidence as predicted by the present approach, as higher interest rates lead to further collapses in asset prices, liquidity positions, profits, net worth positions, leading to further capital outflows and deteriorating the economic downturn. Consequently, to prevent a collapse of fixed exchange rate regimes and a subsequent debt explosion due to a high stock of foreign debt, monetary authorities should make use of temporary capital controls, or a high short-run taxation of short-term portfolio outflows to stabilize domestic profits, asset prices, output and the exchange rate, which stabilizes foreign investors' confidence and reduces capital outflows.

Respecting the management of financial crises by domestic fiscal policy, the present approach provides two recommendations. Firstly, the main aim of fiscal policy in case of a crisis should be to stabilize profits, liquidity positions, net worth positions, asset prices and output by a large fiscal expansion, increasing aggregate demand, output and profits. However, a stabilization of profits by budget deficit financing can be only successful in case the size of the government sector is big enough to ensure that a drop in private investment can be completely offset by an increase in government expenditures, implying that policies which reduce the role of the state to minimum should be abandoned. Consequently, the generally adopted fiscal policy rule to cut government expenditures in case of a financial crisis to restore investors' confidence is as counterproductive as contractionary monetary policy, since it deteriorates the cumulative contraction following the collapse of asset prices. Secondly, budget deficits to stabilize profits should be offset by budget surpluses in expansionary phases which also serve to prevent crises as they constrain aggregate demand. Otherwise, rising deficits in case of a crisis may possibly undermine investors' confidence and deteriorate the economic downturn. Consequently, an efficient crisis management by fiscal policy requires a sound fiscal management during tranquil times aiming at a long-run balanced fiscal budget.

Respecting the management of financial crises by domestic and international financial market regulation authorities, the present approach recommends three policy measures. Firstly, in case of a crisis, insolvent financial institutions should be closed immediately to avoid widespread bank runs due to asymmetric information. However, this policy measure requires that insolvent financial institutions can be clearly distinguished from still solvent institutions which is only possible with international accounting standards and rigorous disclosure requirements. Secondly, regulation bodies should refrain from a strict enforcement of capital adequacy standards in case financial institutions do not fulfill minimum capital standards but are still solvent, in order to prevent further disintermediation effects which deteriorate the economic downturn. Thirdly, to dampen the adverse effects of currency crises in case of large foreign debt stocks, the International Monetary Fund should not offer general rescue packages to bail out private investors, but should use its funds as an international lender of last resort in cooperation with central banks to avoid bankruptcies of still solvent financial institutions by short-run liquidity supports in foreign currency.

Appendix A

Tobin's q-Theory of Investment

Tobin's q is defined as the ratio of the real market value of physical capital goods MV_r to the real reproduction or real replacement costs of those goods V_r, being equal to the ratio of the nominal market value of physical goods $MV = MV_r P$ to the nominal value of replacement costs of those goods $V = V_r P$, where P denotes the price level. Formally, Tobin's q is given as

$$q = \frac{MV_r}{V_r} = \frac{MV}{V}.$$

In case the market value of existing capital goods, which are traded e.g. in the stock exchange, is larger than replacement costs, i.e. if it holds that $q > 1$, then the *rate* of investment (Tobin 1969, p. 143), denoting the speed at which investors want to increase the capital stock, is positive, since buying new capital goods at replacement costs is cheaper than buying already existing capital goods at the stock exchange. By way of contrast, if the market value of capital goods is smaller than replacement costs, i.e. in case it holds that $q < 1$, the rate of investment is negative, because buying already existing capital goods at the stock exchange is cheaper than buying new capital goods at replacement costs. As a result, according to Tobin's q-theory of investment, the investment function, expressing the "desired" or "demanded" rate of investment $I/K = \dot{K}/K = \hat{K}$, being equal to the growth rate of the capital stock, where I denotes real investment and K the real capital stock, is positively dependent on q. Hence, one possible form of a q-investment function could be expressed formally as

$$\frac{I}{K}(\underset{+}{q}) = \pi\,(q-1),$$

where $\pi > 0$ is a positive constant. Thus, if $q < 1$ then $I/K < 0$, if $q > 1$ then $I/K > 0$, and if $q = 1$ then $I/K = 0$. This positive correlation between the rate of aggregate investment and the market value/replacement cost ratio has been also emphasized by Keynes who wrote,

> ... *The daily revaluations of the Stock Exchange, though they are primarily made to facilitate transfers of old investments between one individual and another, inevitably exert a decisive influence on the rate of current investment. For there is no sense in building up a new enterprise at a cost greater than that at which a similar existing enterprise can be purchased; whilst there is an inducement to spend on a new project what may seem an extravagant sum, if*

it can be floated off on the Stock Exchange at an immediate profit (Keynes, 1936 (1936), p. 151).

In order to specify a q-investment function, variables determining Tobin's q, i.e. variables determining the real market value MV_r and real replacement costs V_r of physical capital assets, have to be identified. The real market value of capital goods at time t, $MV_r(t)$, is determined by discounting expected real earnings at future times $s \geq t$, $X_r^e(s)$, by a real discount factor z_k representing investors' "required" real rate of return for holding physical assets, i.e. formally it holds that

$$MV_r(t) = \int_t^\infty X_r^e(s)\, e^{-z_K\,(s-t)} ds.$$

The discount rate z_K is *not* the long-term government bond rate, or the interest rate on long-term corporate bonds, but a rate which is appropriate for the valuation of future earnings, containing the risk and uncertainties of business firms' cash flows. Real replacement or real reproduction costs of physical capital assets at time t, $V_r(t)$, are determined by discounting expected real earnings at times $s \geq t$, $X_r^e(s)$, by the marginal efficiency of capital Z (internal rate of return, or real profit rate on physical assets), i.e. formally it holds that

$$V_r(t) = \int_t^\infty X_r^e(s)\, e^{-Z\,(s-t)} ds.$$

Assuming a constant value of expected real earnings for all periods $s \geq t$, i.e. $X_r^e(s) = X^e$, the real market value, real replacement costs and Tobin's q, all at time t, are defined as

$$MV_r(t) = \frac{X^e}{z_K}, \qquad V_r(t) = \frac{X_r^e}{Z}, \qquad q(t) = \frac{MV_r(t)}{V_r(t)} = \frac{\frac{X_r^e}{z_K}}{\frac{X_r^e}{Z}} = \frac{Z}{z_K}.$$

As a result, Tobin's q, and therefore the rate of aggregate investment is positively dependent on the ratio of the current profit rate to the risk-adjusted discount rate investors require to hold physical assets.

In order to obtain a relationship between the rate of return relation Z/z_K, and the relation of stock prices to the general price level, Tobin's q can be alternatively determined by defining the nominal market value at time t, $MV(t)$, of existing capital goods K as

$$MV(t) = P_K(t)\, K(t),$$

where $P_K(t)$ denotes the current market price of physical assets at time t, i.e. the so-called *demand price of capital*, which can be approximated by actual stock prices. By way of contrast, new capital goods are valued at their nominal replacement costs, i.e. by the so-called *supply price of capital* being equal to the current price level $P(t)$; as a result, the nominal value of new capital goods valued at replacement costs at time t, $V(t)$, is defined as

$$V(t) = P(t)\, K(t).$$

Consequently, Tobin's q can be alternatively expressed in nominal terms as

$$q(t) = \frac{MV(t)}{V(t)} = \frac{P_K(t)\, K(t)}{P(t)\, K(t)} = \frac{P_K(t)}{P(t)},$$

stating that q, and thereby the rate of investment, is positively influenced by the ratio of capital goods' market prices (stock prices) to the general price level. Putting all definitions together and neglecting time t, Tobin's q is given by

$$q = \frac{MV_r}{V_r} = \frac{MV}{V} = \frac{Z}{z_K} = \frac{P_K}{P}.$$

For the q-theory of investment and empirical investigations, see e.g. Brainard and Tobin (1968), Tobin (1969, 1975, 1978), Tobin and Buiter (1976, 1980), Tobin and Brainard (1977), Blanchard (1981), Blanchard, Rhee and Summers (1993).

Appendix B

Financial Constraints in Perfect Capital Markets

This section provides an example of financial constraints in perfect capital markets under Walrasian equilibrium theory to intertemporal decisions of economic agents. Despite the fact that the specific forms of financial constraints in intertemporal maximization models depend on assumptions, model structures, etc., they are all based on the concept of *intertemporal solvency* of agents which can be best illustrated by the following simple example[1] of an intertemporal maximization problem in an open economy with a free and perfect international capital market, reading as: Find a sequence of consumption levels $C_t, C_{t+1}, \ldots$ that maximizes utility U_t of a representative agent over an infinite planning horizon lasting from date t to $T \to \infty$, being specified by

$$U_t = \sum_{s=t}^{\infty} \beta^{s-t}\, u(C_s), \qquad 0 < \beta < 1, \tag{B.1}$$

subject to the two constraints

$$\sum_{s=t}^{\infty} \left(\frac{1}{1+i_r}\right)^{s-t} C_s + \lim_{T\to\infty} \left(\frac{1}{1+i_r}\right)^{T} F_{t+T+1} = (1+i_r)F_t + \sum_{s=t}^{\infty} \left(\frac{1}{1+i_r}\right)^{s-t} Y_s, \tag{B.2}$$

$$\lim_{T\to\infty} \left(\frac{1}{1+i_r}\right)^{T} F_{t+T+1} \geq 0, \tag{B.3}$$

where β denotes the subjective discount or time-preference factor being constant over time, i_r the real interest rate for borrowing or lending in the (perfect) international capital market being also assumed to be constant over time, Y_s income at the end of period s, C_s consumption at the end of period s, F_t the value of the economy's initial net foreign assets at time t, and $\lim_{T\to\infty}(1+i_r)^{-T}F_{t+T+1}$ the discounted present value of the economy's net foreign assets at the end of the (infinite) planning horizon. Note that net foreign assets in any period s, F_s, can also take a negative sign, i.e. $-F_s$, denoting net foreign debt in period s. The change in net foreign assets over period s, i.e. $F_{s+1} - F_s$, is equivalent to the current account over period s, CRA_s, being defined as

$$CRA_s = F_{s+1} - F_s = Y_s - C_s + i_r\, F_s, \tag{B.4}$$

[1]This example is a modified version of Obstfeld and Rogoff (1999), pp. 715-721.

i.e. as the difference between income and consumption in period s, plus interest income on net foreign assets in case $F_s > 0$, or less interest payments on foreign debt in case $F_s < 0$ in period s; note that constraint B.2 is obtained by rearranging the current account identity B.4.

The maximization problem B.1 is subject to the two intertemporal financial constraints B.2 and B.3, where constraint B.2 is the intertemporal budget constraint, having being derived, as aforementioned, from the current account identity B.4, and B.3, the inequality constraint, the no-Ponzi-game condition. Regarding constraint B.2, the expression $\sum_{s=t}^{\infty}(1+i_r)^{t-s}(Y_s - C_s)$ represents the present value of aggregate savings, being equivalent to the present value of the trade balance and thereby to the present value of net output the economy transfers to foreigners during the planning period from t to $T \to \infty$. As a result, the present value of net wealth of the domestic economy at time t, PNW_t, is composed of the initial value of foreign assets or debt $(1+i_r)F_t$ and the present value of aggregate savings during the planning period, i.e. formally it holds that

$$PNW_t = (1+i_r)F_t + \sum_{s=t}^{\infty}(Y_s - C_s). \tag{B.5}$$

Equation B.5 corresponds, according to constraint B.2, to the discounted present value of net foreign assets or debts at the end of the planning period in $T \to \infty$, i.e. it holds that

$$PNW_t = \lim_{T\to\infty}\left(\frac{1}{1+i_r}\right)^T F_{t+T+1} \tag{B.6}$$

where PNW_t and $\lim_{T\to\infty}(1+i_r)^{-T}F_{t+T+1}$ can be positive, zero or negative.

In case the present value of net wealth is positive or zero, i.e. in case there exist net foreign assets or no foreign assets at the end of the planning period ($F_{t+T+1} \geq 0$), being formally described by

$$PNW_t = \lim_{T\to\infty}\left(\frac{1}{1+i_r}\right)^T F_{t+T+1} \geq 0, \quad \text{implying} \quad -(1+i_r)F_t \leq \sum_{s=t}^{\infty}(Y_s - C_s), \tag{B.7}$$

then, the domestic economy is said to be *intertemporally solvent*. By way of contrast, if the present value of net wealth is negative, i.e. if there exists net foreign debt at the end of the planning period ($F_{t+T+1} < 0$), being formally described by

$$PNW_t = \lim_{T\to\infty}\left(\frac{1}{1+i_r}\right)^T F_{t+T+1} < 0, \quad \text{implying} \quad -(1+i_r)F_t > \sum_{s=t}^{\infty}(Y_s - C_s), \tag{B.8}$$

then, the domestic economy is said to be *intertemporally insolvent*.

The intertemporal solvency conditions B.7 and B.8, having been derived by wealth considerations above, are a combination of the two financial constraints B.2 and B.3 of the initial maximization problem. As a result, the intertemporal solvency condition B.7 can be alternatively derived by inserting the no-Ponzi-game condition B.3 into the intertemporal budget constraint B.2, which results in the *intertemporal solvency* condition

$$-(1+i_r)F_t \leq \sum_{s=t}^{\infty}\left(\frac{1}{1+i_r}\right)(Y_s - C_s), \tag{B.9}$$

implying $\lim_{T\to\infty}(1+i_r)^{-T}F_{t+T+1} \geq 0$. Intertemporal solvency arises, according to equation B.9, either by a positive present value of the trade balance which is greater than or equal to the initial value of foreign debt (where $F_t < 0$, implying that $-(1+i_r)\,F_t > 0$), or by a negative present value of the trade balance which is in absolute terms smaller than or equal to the initial value of net foreign assets (where $F_t > 0$, implying that $-(1+i_r)\,F_t < 0$).[2] Accordingly, intertemporal insolvency arises in case the present value of what the economy produces exceeds or is equal to the present value of its consumption, i.e. in case the present value of the trade balance is positive or zero.[3]

By way of contrast, the intertemporal insolvency condition B.8 can be obtained in case the no-Ponzi-game condition B.3 is violated, i.e. in case

$$\lim_{T\to\infty}\left(\frac{1}{1+i_r}\right)^T F_{t+T+1} < 0. \tag{B.10}$$

As a result, insertion of the violated no-Ponzi-game condition B.10 into the intertemporal budget constraint condition B.2 yields the *intertemporal insolvency* condition, being formally given by

$$-(1+i_r)F_t > \sum_{s=t}^{\infty}\left(\frac{1}{1+i_r}\right)(Y_s - C_s). \tag{B.11}$$

Accordingly, intertemporal insolvency can arise, according to inequalities B.11 and B.8, either from a positive present value of the trade balance which is smaller than the initial value of foreign debt (where $F_t < 0$, implying that $-(1+i_r)\,F_t > 0$), or from a negative present value of the trade balance which is smaller than initial value of net foreign assets (where $F_t > 0$, implying that $-(1+i_r)\,F_t < 0$).[4] Both cases imply that the domestic economy is intertemporally insolvent since the present value of net wealth PNW_t is negative, corresponding to a violation of the no-Ponzi-game condition B.3, i.e. formally in both cases it holds that

$$PNW_t = \lim_{T\to\infty}\left(\frac{1}{1+i_r}\right)^T F_{t+T+1} < 0$$

Accordingly, intertemporal insolvency arises in case the present value of what the economy consumes exceeds the present value of its output by a positive amount which never converges to zero, i.e. in case the present value of the trade balance is negative.[5] As a

[2]Another, but trivial condition for intertemporal insolvency arises in case of a positive present value of the trade balance being combined with initial net foreign assets, resulting in a steady increase in net foreign assets.

[3]This statement may be confusing because it has been stated that intertemporal solvency can also arise in case of a *negative* present value of the trade balance which is however smaller than the initial value of net foreign assets. However, the initial value of net foreign assets can be interpreted as an *initial trade balance surplus* which is larger than the present value of future trade balance deficits which results in an overall positive present value of the trade balance.

[4]As it was the case with intertemporal solvency, another, but also trivial condition for intertemporal insolvency arises in case of a negative present value of the trade balance which is combined with initial foreign debt.

[5]Note that an initial value of debt can be interpreted as an *initial trade balance deficit* which can be larger than the present value of future trade balances surpluses, resulting in an overall negative present value of the trade balance.

result, in case the domestic agents "play" a Ponzi-game, the domestic economy borrows continually to meet interest payments on foreign debt, which grows at least at the international interest rate i_r, and does not repay debt by reducing consumption below income, i.e. by trade balance surpluses. From the viewpoint of foreign creditors, the domestic economy is intertemporally "overindebted" or bankrupt due to the inability to repay debt which means a costless transfer of resources from foreigners to domestic agents.

The solution of the maximization problem B.1 requires, according to constraints B.2 and B.3, that the domestic economy has to remain intertemporally solvent either by a positive stock of net foreign assets or by zero net foreign assets at the end of the planning period. However, assuming a positive stock of net foreign assets at the end of the planning period would imply a costless transfer of resources of the domestic economy to foreigners, or, to put it differently, bankruptcy of the foreign economy. As a result, in order to rule out domestic as well as foreign bankruptcy, implying that all resources are used up at the end of the planning period, the no-Ponzi-game condition B.3 has to be modified into the transversality condition

$$\lim_{T\to\infty} (1+i_r)^{-T} F_{t+T+1} = 0, \tag{B.12}$$

which is one in four conditions which are necessary and sufficient for optimality. The transversality condition implies that only the equality version of the intertemporal solvency condition B.9, i.e.

$$-(1+i_r)F_t = \sum_{s=t}^{\infty} \left(\frac{1}{1+i_r}\right)(Y_s - C_s), \tag{B.13}$$

can guarantee an optimum. The necessary first-order condition for maximizing U_t with respect to consumption is given by the intertemporal Euler-equation

$$u'(C_s) = (1+i_r)\,\beta\, u'(C_{s+1}), \tag{B.14}$$

where $u'(C_s)$ denotes marginal utility from consumption in period s, and $(1+i_r)\beta u'(C_{s+1})$ marginal utility from future consumption in $s+1$ by reducing period s consumption and lending it for one period which is converted into $(1+i_r)$ units of period $s+1$ consumption raising utility in period s, U_s, by $(1+i_r)\,\beta\, u'(C_{s+1})$. The Euler equation states that at utility maximum, both quantities have to be equal, i.e. that the consumer cannot gain from feasible shifts of consumption between periods.[6] Thus, for the present maximization problem, conditions B.14, B.4 (or equivalently B.13), and B.12 are necessary and sufficient for optimality.

[6] A special cases arises if it holds that $\beta = (1+i_r)^{-1}$, i.e. in case the subjective discount factor equals the market discount factor, which leads to the modified Euler condition $u'(C_s) = u'(C_{s+1})$, stating that the consumption path is flat due to the wish to *smooth* consumption over the entire lifetime.

Appendix C

An Example of Off-Balance Sheet Transactions

There are numerous off-balance sheet transactions and investment strategies with a broad range of risk and return objectives. To illustrate the extremely high risk, but also the enormous profit opportunities associated with investments in contingent assets and claims, the following example refers to a very prominent off-balance sheet investment strategy used by banks, hedge funds[1] and other financial institutions, being called "short-selling strategy".

Financial institutions engaging in short-selling do not want to hedge against risk, but to take risk deliberately and to profit from market volatility. The term "short-selling" is a bit misleading since the short-selling strategy involves both a selling-position (short-positions) and a buying-position (long-positions). The aim of opening a short-position, being also labelled as baisse speculation, is to profit from future dropping asset prices. By way of contrast, the aim of opening a long-position, being labelled as hausse speculation, or to bull the market, is to profit from future rising asset prices.

The short-selling strategy involves the sale of an asset A (short-position) such as bonds, equities or foreign exchange, the vendor does not own, implying that asset A which is to be sold has to be borrowed firstly by another market participant with the promise of delivering it back at maturity date in the future at a given price. After having borrowed asset A at a given interest rate, the vendor sells asset A and receives funds which are used to buy another asset B (long-position) which is expected to raise in price, or which simply serves to earn a secure return to minimize potential losses, or to increase profits from the short-position. At maturity date when the investor has to deliver back asset A, the investor sells asset B and uses the funds to repurchase asset A in the market to deliver it back to the lender. The net earnings from the short-selling transaction are the selling price of asset A less the buying price of asset A, less borrowing costs for borrowing asset A, plus the selling price of asset B less the buying price of asset B, plus interest earnings from asset B. Neglecting asset A's borrowing costs and asset B's interest earnings, the

[1] There is no standard definition of hedge funds, but they can be described as pooled investment vehicles which are organized privately, administered by professional investment managers, not generally available to the public, and resident offshore for tax and regulatory purposes. Their legal status allows them, in contrast to mutual and pension funds, to engage in short-term, risky and leverage-based investment strategies. For an overview of hedge funds, see Eichengreen and Mathieson (1998), pp. 42-54, The President's Working Group on Financial Markets (1999), pp. 23-27, and de Brouwer (2001), pp. 18-31.

short-selling strategy generates profits if (1) the short-position asset A drops in price, if (2) the long-position asset B rises in price, or if (3) both situations coincide. Losses emerge if (1) the short-position asset A rises in price, if (2) the long-position asset B falls in price, or if (3) both situations coincide.

To illustrate the short-selling strategy by a concrete example[2], consider a hedge fund manager expecting a devaluation of the Thai bath in the next three months which is currently 30 bath per US-$. Suppose that bath can be borrowed in the three-month swap market at an annual interest rate of 10% which have to be repaid in three months at the current exchange rate of 30 bath per US-$. It is assumed that the hedge fund manager borrows 30 billion bath in the swap market for three months, i.e total borrowing costs in bath amount to $30 \cdot 10^9\,\text{bath} \cdot (10\%/4) = 750,000,000\,\text{bath}$. Afterwards, the hedge fund manager sells the 30 billion bath in the spot foreign-exchange market at 30 bath per US-$ and receives 1 billion US-$ and creates thereby a short-position of 1 billion US-$. In order to minimize losses, or to earn further profits, the hedge fund manager opens a long-position by buying a three-month US security with an annualized interest rate of 6% and with a fixed nominal value, i.e. total returns in three months from holding the US security amount to $1 \cdot 10^9\,\text{US-\$} \cdot (6\%/4) = 15,000,000\,\text{US-\$}$.

To illustrate both the risk and the profit opportunities, consider two different scenarios in three months at maturity date. Scenario 1 is characterized by an actual devaluation of the bath from 30 bath per US-$ to 40 bath per US-$, i.e. at maturity date the official exchange rate is 40 bath per US-$. Scenario 2 is characterized by a revaluation of the bath, e.g. to regain credibility of international investors, from 30 bath per US-$ to 20 bath per US-$, i.e. at maturity date the official exchange rate is 20 bath per US-$.

According to *scenario 1*, the hedge fund manager is going to sell at maturity date the US-security and receives 1 billion US-$ which are used to buy bath, but now at an exchange rate of 40 bath per US-$; that is, the manager receives 40 billion bath, where 30 billion bath are used to repay the debt and 10 billion bath are profits resulting from the bath's devaluation. The hedge fund manager's total earnings measured in US-$ consist of (1) the capital gain resulting from the bath devaluation which amounts to $10 \cdot 10^9\,\text{bath} \cdot 0.025\,\text{US-\$/bath} = 250,000,000\ \text{US-\$}$, (2) less bath borrowing costs which amount to $750,000,000\,\text{bath} \cdot 0.025\,\text{US-\$/bath} = 18,750,000\,\text{US-\$}$, (3) plus interest earnings from the US security which amount to $15,000,000\,\text{US-\$}$, resulting in total profits of $246,250,000\,\text{US-\$}$.

According to *scenario 2*, the hedge fund manager also sells at maturity date the US-security and receives 1 billion US-$ which are used to buy bath, but now at an exchange rate of 20 bath per US-$; that is, the manager receives only 20 billion bath, but has to repay 30 billion. Accordingly, the manager incurs a loss from the revaluation because she has to buy additionally 10 billion bath to repay debt. The hedge fund manager's total earnings measured in US-$ consist of (1) the capital loss resulting from the bath devaluation which amounts to $10 \cdot 10^9\,\text{bath} \cdot 0.05\ \text{US-\$/bath} = 500,000,000\ \text{US-\$}$, (2) less bath borrowing costs which amount to $750,000,000\,\text{bath} \cdot 0.05\,\text{US-\$/bath} = 37,500,000\,\text{US-\$}$, (3) plus interest earnings from the US security which amount to $15,000,000\,\text{US-\$}$, resulting in a total loss of $-522,500,000\,\text{US-\$}$ which can lead very quickly to bankruptcy since hedge funds generally work with low capital due to the fact that funds theoretically do not need any capital of their own to engage in short-selling transactions.

[2]This example is a modified version of de Brouwer (2001), p. 24.

Summing up, off-balance sheet transactions are subject to extremely high risk which generally cannot be observed by market participants and financial market regulators owing to two reasons. Firstly, off-balance sheet transactions are not reflected in on-balance sheet positions according to standard accounting rules, implying that there is no possibility to assess solvency and liquidity risk via changes in on-balance sheet positions. Regarding the short-selling example, the hedge fund's balance sheet does not contain an asset and a corresponding liability because the 30 billion bath are borrowed and immediately sold, though the fund is subject to a huge exposure. Secondly, companies engaging in off-balance sheet transactions generally do not reveal information about their off-balance sheet exposures, and usually publish only their on-balance sheet leverage. Accordingly, the lacking overview of risk associated with off-balance sheet transactions has the potential to adversely affect the stability of the entire financial system, as e.g. the LTCM debacle in the U.S. in 1999 which threatened the stability of the entire U.S. banking system, and which could be resolved only by massive lender of last resort interventions by the Federal Reserve.

Appendix D

Forward vs. Backward Looking Variables and Solutions of General Dynamic Rational Expectations Models

D.1 Forward and Backward Solutions of Linear Differential Equations

The dynamic behaviour of rational expectations models, as well as the uniqueness or nonuniqueness of rational expectations equilibria is dependent on the one hand, on the ratio of the number of unstable and stable roots, and on the other hand, on the ratio of the number of forward and backward looking variables. Forward and backward looking variables differ with respect to their dynamic behaviour and require distinct solution methods in order to obtain solutions which are consistent with real-world economic behaviour.[1] This section analyzes in a first step general solution procedures of stable and unstable differential equations which are applied in the following section to dynamic systems containing forward and backward looking variables.

In order to describe general solutions of dynamic systems, consider a first-order linear differential equation in the variable $x(t)$ in the form of

$$\dot{x}(t) = \delta x(t) + \gamma z(t), \tag{D.1}$$

where $z(t)$ is an exogenous function of time (which is also sometimes referred as a forcing function), and δ and γ are constants. To solve this differential equation is to express $x(t)$ as a function of current, future and past values of $z(t)$ (solution of the nonhomogeneous equation), *and* as a function of the initial value $x(0)$ when the system begins its evolution over time (solution of the homogenous equation).

The *particular integral*, or nonhomogeneous solution of a differential equation given by equation D.1 can be solved forward as well as backward. The *backward solution of the*

[1] See e.g. Blanchard (1979a) and (1979b).

particular integral of equation D.1 reads as

$$x(t) = \gamma \int_{-\infty}^{t} e^{(k-t)(-\delta)} z(k) dk, \tag{D.2}$$

whereas the *forward solution of the particular integral* of equation D.1 is given by

$$x(t) = -\gamma \int_{t}^{\infty} e^{(t-k)\delta} z(k) dk. \tag{D.3}$$

Accordingly, the particular integral of any differential equation can be theoretically solved forward as well as backward. However, in order to guarantee convergence of a differential equation, it is illustrated in a few moments that unstable systems are generally solved forward and stable systems backward.[2]

The Stable Case: $\delta < 0$. If parameter δ is assumed to be less than zero in equation D.1, the solution of the homogenous function is stable and reads as

$$x(t) = Ae^{\delta t}. \tag{D.4}$$

Accordingly, the general solution of equation D.1 solving the particular integral backward is represented by

$$x(t) = \gamma \int_{-\infty}^{t} e^{(k-t)(-\delta)} z(k) dk + Ae^{\delta t}, \tag{D.5}$$

whereas the general solution solving the particular integral forward is given as

$$x(t) = -\gamma \int_{t}^{\infty} e^{(t-k)\delta} z(k) dk + Ae^{\delta t}. \tag{D.6}$$

As the reader may verify, in case $\delta < 0$, the particular integral being solved backward is convergent, and the particular integral being solved forward is divergent. Yet, it is important to note that this statement is only valid if the forcing variable $z(t)$ is "well-behaved", that is, it does not change at too high or low an absolute rate. Pathological cases in which $z(t)$ is not well-behaved are ruled out throughout the further analysis. Since convergence of the particular integral is not reached by solving it forward, stable dynamic systems are solved backward. The definite or particular solution is obtained by solving first for the arbitrary constant A in equation D.5 by using an initial condition on variable $x(t)$, $x(0)$, at time $t = 0$, and afterwards by substituting A back in equation D.5.

The Unstable Case: $\delta > 0$. If parameter δ is assumed to be greater than zero in equation D.1, then, according to equations D.2 and D.3, the particular integral being solved backward is divergent, whereas the particular integral being solved forward is

[2]This general rule also applies to discrete dynamic systems containing difference equations, being discussed in Obstfeld and Rogoff (1999), pp. 726-731.

convergent. As a result, in order to guarantee dynamic stability of the long-run steady-state value, unstable systems are generally solved forward looking with respect to the particular integral. The general solution of equation D.1 for $\delta > 0$ reads as

$$x(t) = -\gamma \int_{t}^{\infty} e^{(t-k)\delta} z(k) dk + Ae^{\delta t}, \tag{D.7}$$

where the definite or particular solution is obtained again by solving for constant A by using an initial condition for variable $x(t)$, $x(0)$, at time $t = 0$, being followed by backwardsubstitution of A in equation D.7. Though the particular integral of equation D.7 is convergent, the time path of $x(t)$ is dynamically unstable for any value other than $A = 0$. Accordingly, in order to guarantee convergence of an inherent unstable system, the particular integral has to be solved forward, and the influence of the solution of the homogenous equation has to be ruled out by imposing the condition $A = 0$.

Most economic models containing forward looking variables, rational expectations and continuous market clearing lead to unstable differential equations and to general solutions as in equation D.7. However, though these models imply unstable dynamic behaviour, it is reasonable to assume the solution paths in most cases to be convergent, since time paths observed in practice are unlikely to lead to dynamic instability. As a result, economic models which would result in unstable time paths due to $\delta > 0$, are often restricted to the particular integral, being solved forward looking, by imposing the condition $A = 0$. Specifically economic models dealing with asset prices very often lead to dynamic instability by the emergence of self-fulfilling speculative asset-price bubbles which are caused by the divergence of the solution of the homogenous equation. These models generally rule out such self-fulfilling bubbles by imposing the condition $A = 0$, meaning that asset prices are assumed to be determined entirely by fundamentals, i.e. by the particular integral of the differential equation, which however, has to be solved forward looking. Yet, it is possible that there arise situations in which the particular integral may not converge leading to an infinite number of stable bubble solutions in case the forcing function is not well-behaved; however, as already mentioned, these cases are ruled out throughout the further analysis

D.2 The Leibnitz Rule: Differentiating a Definite Integral

In order to study forward and backward looking variables and their differential equation versions, it is necessary to understand the link between an ordinary linear differential equation and its integral solution of the non-homogenous function (particular integral). The particular integral solution can be transformed into its ordinary differential equation form by differentiating the particular integral with respect to time according to the Leibnitz rule being discussed in the following.

Consider a function $K(x)$ which is described by

$$K(x) = \int_{a}^{b(x)} F(t,x) dt, \tag{D.8}$$

where $K(x)$ depends on the integral of function $F(t, x)$ which is dependent on x and t, where t takes values from a to $b(x)$ so that t is also a function of x. The derivative dK/dx is obtained by using Leibnitz rule stating that

$$\frac{dK}{dx} = \int_{a}^{b(x)} F_x(t, x)dt + F[b(x), x]b'(x).^3 \tag{D.9}$$

When lower and upper limits are exchanged so that $K(x)$ is described by

$$K(x) = \int_{b(x)}^{a} F(t, x)dt, \tag{D.10}$$

then applying Leibnitz rule in order to obtain dK/dx results in

$$\frac{dK}{dx} = \int_{b(x)}^{a} F_x(t, x)dt - F[b(x), x]b'(x).^4 \tag{D.11}$$

D.3 Backward and Forward Looking Variables

From a mathematical perspective, the time path of a backward looking, predetermined, or sluggish variable is a continuous function of time at all points, i.e. its initial value is predetermined by its past evolution. By way of contrast, the time path of a forward looking, nonpredetermined, or "jump" variable is free to move discontinuously at appropriate points, i.e. its initial value is not predetermined by the past and can jump discontinuously if new information becomes available. To put it differently, the influence of past forcing-variable levels is relevant for backward looking variables, whereas it is not for forward looking variables. Generally, backward looking variables are subject to stable roots, whereas forward looking variables are subject to unstable roots[5].

The characterization of variables as backward or forward looking is dependent on the structure of an economic model. For example, the capital stock which needs time to accumulate, is a typical backward looking variable, whereas financial variables, as e.g. exchange rates, equity prices or interest rates, are typical forward looking variables whose values incorporate all information as it becomes available, i.e. "new" information can lead to a sudden and discontinuous jump in their values. The price level, as well as nominal wages can be backward looking, as well as forward looking variables. In case wages and prices are determined by contracts, it is obvious to treat them as backward looking variables. If, on the other hand, wages and prices are not determined by contracts and can be varied instantaneously, they are treated as forward looking variables.

The dynamic patters of backward and forward looking variables, as well as the link between their representation as differential equations and as general solutions of differential equations in integral form, can be best analyzed by the following examples of different

[3]For an interpretation of Leibnitz rule, see Chiang (1992), pp. 29-31.

[4]Leibnitz rule is also a necessary tool in continuous time dynamic optimization when applying Euler's calculus of variations technique. For applications, see Chiang (1992).

[5]See e.g. Obstfeld and Rogoff (1999), p. 728.

wage formation patterns which can be modelled both as backward looking and forward looking. A *backward looking* wage formation scheme can be described formally as

$$w(t) = \int_{-\infty}^{t} \mu e^{\mu(\tau - t)} P(\tau)\, d\tau \qquad \mu > 0, \tag{D.12}$$

stating that the current wage rate $w(t)$ in period t is the integral, or the sum of discounted past price levels $P(\tau)$ from $-\infty$ to time t, where μ represents both the discount factor and the adjustment speed of wages to prices. Differentiating equation D.12 with respect to time by applying Leibnitz rule[6] yields the backward looking wage adjustment mechanism in general differential equation form, given formally as

$$\dot{w}(t) = \mu(P(t) - w(t)), \tag{D.13}$$

being dynamically stable since $\mu > 0$. Equation D.13 states that workers have a fixed real wage steady-state target being equal to 1 (from $\dot{w}(t) = 0$ it follows that $P(t) = w(t)$), which however cannot be reached instantaneously due to lags in indexation of wages to price level changes[7]. The general solution of the stable differential equation D.13 is given by

$$w(t) = \int_{-\infty}^{t} \mu e^{\mu(\tau - t)} P(\tau)\, d\tau + A\, e^{-\mu t}, \tag{D.14}$$

where, in order to guarantee convergence of the nonhomogenous part of the general solution, the particular integral, being equivalent to equation D.12, is solved backward looking as discussed in section D.1.[8] The homogenous part of the general solution, which has been excluded in equation D.12 by restricting the solution for $w(t)$ to the nonhomogenous component by imposing $A = 0$, is convergent owing to $\mu > 0$. The general solution given in equation D.14 validates the fact that backward looking variables are usually subject to dynamic stability, provided that the particular integral is solved backward.[9]

[6]Applying Leibnitz rule to equation D.12 yields

$$\frac{dw}{dt} = \int_{-\infty}^{t} -e^{\mu(-t+\tau)} \mu^2 P(\tau)\, d\tau + (\mu e^{\mu(t-t)} P(t)) \cdot 1 = -\mu \int_{-\infty}^{t} \mu e^{\mu(\tau - t)} P(\tau)\, d\tau + \mu P(t) = \mu(P(t) - w(t)).$$

[7]For this kind of wage formation scheme, see also Sachs (1980).

[8]Note that the particular integral of differential equation D.13 can be solved also forward, given formally as

$$w(t) = -\mu \int_{t}^{\infty} e^{(t-\tau)(-\mu)}\, P(\tau)\, d\tau,$$

being however divergent.

[9]Another example of a backward looking variable generating dynamic stability is the time path of the capital stock being dependent on past accumulation. The change of the capital stock $\dot{K}(t)$ is formally given by

$$\dot{K}(t) = I(t) - \delta K(t),$$

i.e. by the difference between gross investment $I(t)$ and depreciation on the capital stock, where δ denotes

A *forward looking* wage formation scheme can be represented formally by

$$w(t) = \int_{t}^{\infty} \mu e^{\mu(t-\tau)} P(\tau)\, d\tau \qquad \mu > 0, \tag{D.15}$$

stating the the current wage rate $w(t)$ is the integral, or the sum, of discounted future prices from time t until ∞, where μ represents both the discount factor and the adjustment speed of wages to prices.[10] Differentiating equation D.15 with respect to time by applying Leibnitz rule, results in the general wage adjustment mechanism under forward looking behaviour in differential equation form, given by

$$\dot{w}(t) = \mu(w(t) - P(t)), \tag{D.16}$$

being dynamically unstable due to $\mu > 0$. Equation D.16 states that workers also have a fixed long-run real wage target being equal to 1. The general solution of the unstable differential equation D.16 is given by

$$w(t) = \int_{t}^{\infty} \mu e^{\mu(t-\tau)} P(\tau)\, d\tau + A\, e^{\mu t}, \tag{D.17}$$

where, in order to guarantee convergence of nonhomogenous component of the general solution, the particular integral, being equivalent to equation D.15, has been solved forward looking. The homogenous part of the general solution, which has been excluded in equation D.15 by restricting the solution for $w(t)$ to the nonhomogenous component by imposing $A = 0$, is divergent owing to $\mu > 0$. The general solution given in equation D.17 validates the fact that forward looking variables are usually subject to dynamic instability if the constant A of the homogenous part takes a value $A \neq 0$[11]. Since the time path for wages observed in reality generally tends to be bounded, except for periods of hyperinflation, stability in case of forward looking wage formation is reached by imposing the condition $A = 0$ (and by solving the particular integral forward). As a result, equation D.15 is the general bounded solution of the unstable differential equation D.16.[12]

Implicit in the forward looking wage formation scheme given in equation D.15 is the (unrealistic) assumption that economic agents know the future time path of the price level

---

the depreciation rate. This differential equation is stable since $\delta > 0$ and its general solution reads as

$$K(t) = \int_{-\infty}^{t} e^{(\tau-t)\delta}\, I(\tau) d\tau + A\, e^{-\delta t},$$

where the particular integral is solved backward looking being convergent.

[10]This wage formation scheme is a version of Calvo's (1983) overlapping contract model.

[11]The general solution would be also divergent if the particular integral had been solved backward.

[12]Another example of a forward looking variable generating dynamic instability is the time path of the exchange rate being determined by interest rate parity condition, reading as

$$\dot{s}(t) = s(t) + i(t) - i^{*}(t),$$

where $s(t)$ denotes the natural log of the exchange rate, $\dot{s}(t)$ the natural log of the exchange rate's change, $i(t)$ the domestic interest rate, and $i^{*}(t)$ the foreign interest rate. This differential equation is dynamically

$p(t)$. In world of uncertainty however, agents can only form expectations of the future *typifying*, forward looking equations. In that case, the stochastic counterpart to equation D.15 is given by

$$w(t) = \int_t^{\infty} \mu e^{\mu(t-\tau)} \, E_t[P(\tau, t)] \, d\tau, \tag{D.18}$$

stating that the current wage rate is the discounted present value of expected price levels $E_t[P(t)]$ from t to ∞, where $E_t[\cdot]$ denotes the expectations operator expressing the expected value of the price level conditional on all information available up to time t. Equation D.18 is the nonhomogenous part of the general solution of the stochastic unstable differential equation

$$E_t[\dot{w}(t)] = \mu(w(t) - P(t)), \qquad \mu > 0, \tag{D.19}$$

whose general solution reads as

$$w(t) = \int_t^{\infty} \mu e^{\mu(t-\tau)} \, E_t[P(\tau, t)] \, d\tau, + A \, e^{\mu t}.$$

In order to guarantee dynamic stability of the general solution, the unstable homogenous part has been eliminated by assuming $A = 0$.[13]

D.4 Forward Looking Variables, Rational Expectations and Dynamic Stability

The previous section has emphasized that expectations of a variable's future generally typify a forward looking variable, which, as outlined above, is usually subject to dynamic instability. Regarding the formation of expectations, many macroeconomic models assume that forward looking variables are subject to rational expectations. The rational

unstable, and its general solution reads as

$$s(t) = -\int_t^{\infty} e^{(t-k)} \, [i(k) - i^*(k)] dk + A \, e^t,$$

where the particular integral has been solved forward to guarantee convergence. Imposing stability of the exchange rate solution therefore requires to assume $A = 0$.

[13]The stochastic counterpart of the exchange rate solution determined by interest rate parity under uncertainty reading as

$$\dot{s}^e(t) = s(t) + i(t) - i^*(t),$$

where $\dot{s}^e(t)$ denotes the expected natural log of the exchange rate's change, is given by

$$s(t) = -\int_t^{\infty} e^{(t-k)} \, E_t[i(k,t) - i^*(k,t)] dk + A \, e^t.$$

expectation hypothesis can be stated formally for the case of one period ahead price expectations as

$$P_{t+1} = E_t[P_{t+1}] + \varepsilon_{t+1}, \tag{D.20}$$

where $E_t[P_{t+1}]$ is the prediction of the price level for time $t+1$ formed at time t, P_{t+1} the actual price level at time $t+1$, and ε_{t+1} a purely random error with zero mean which comes into being at time $t+1$. Equation D.20 states that the price fluctuates about its forecast level with a random error having an expected value of zero, i.e. except for the random term, individuals are able to predict future prices correctly. This assumption requires that the prediction being made by individuals is consistent with the prediction made by the model, conditional on all relevant information at that time. As a result, the "real" economy has to work exactly according to the model and each individual knows the model. The assumption of rational expectations is said to characterize an efficient market where prices reflect all available information, making it impossible to earn supernormal profits due to special information. In continuous time, assuming rational expectations with respect to the price level can be formulated as

$$E_t[P(t)] = P(t),$$

stating that the expected price level $E_t[P_t]$ in t equals the actual price level $P(t)$ in t.[14]

Using rational expectations in the stochastic forward looking wage formation scheme of the previous section leads to the dynamic system

$$\begin{aligned} E_t[\dot{w}(t)] &= \mu(w(t) - P(t)) \\ E_t[\dot{w}(t)] &= \dot{w}(t), \end{aligned}$$

whose general solution is given by

$$w(t) = \int_t^\infty \mu e^{\mu(t-\tau)}\, P(\tau)\, d\tau, + A\, e^{\mu t},$$

being dynamically unstable unless $A = 0$.[15] This result however, may *not* lead to the conclusion that every dynamic system containing a rational expectations scheme for forward looking variables generally leads to dynamic instability, though most macroeconomic models using rational expectations generate unstable roots. Rather, it is the combination of rational expectations *and* continuous market clearance that gives rise to dynamic instability. If, for example, a forward looking variable, following rational expectations and generating unstable roots, is tied to backward looking variable, then the system involves a negative eigenvalue leading to dynamic stability.

The influence of varying combinations of backward and forward looking variables on dynamic stability of macroeconomic models under rational expectations can be best outlined by the well-known Cagan (1956) model of hyperinflation.[16] The original model is

[14]For critical assessments of rational expectations, see any modern textbook on macroeconomics.

[15]In order to guarantee convergence of the nonhomogenous part of the general solution, the particular integral has been solved forward.

[16]The following description of the Cagan models follows Turnovsky (2000), chapters 3.3 to 3.5.

described by the following two equations

$$m(t) - p(t) = -\alpha\, \dot{p}^e(t) \tag{D.21}$$

$$\ddot{p}^e(t) = \gamma(\dot{p}(t) - \dot{p}^e(t)), \tag{D.22}$$

where $m(t)$ denotes the natural log of the nominal money stock, $p(t)$ the natural log of the price level, $\dot{p}(t)$ the actual inflation rate, and $\dot{p}^e(t)$ the expected rate of inflation. Accordingly, in this model the price level can be treated as a forward looking variable. Equation D.21 defines money market equilibrium, where the left hand side denotes the real money stock, and the right hand side money demand which is inversely related to expected inflation. Equation D.22 states that inflation expectations follow an adaptive expectation formation scheme, i.e. current inflation expectations are tied to past behaviour of the price level. As a result, the forward looking price level is tied to backward looking adjustment mechanism. Eliminating $\dot{p}^e(t)$ and $\ddot{p}^e(t)$ from equations D.21 and D.22 results in the following differential equation for the price level

$$\dot{p}(t) = \frac{\gamma}{1-\alpha\gamma}\,(m(t) - p(t)), \tag{D.23}$$

whose general solution, under the assumption that the nominal money stock is independent of time, i.e. it holds that $m(t) = \bar{m}$, is given by

$$p(t) = \bar{m} + A\, e^{-\frac{\gamma}{1-\alpha\gamma}}. \tag{D.24}$$

Accordingly, dynamic stability of the price level is guaranteed if it holds that $\alpha\gamma < 1$, known as the Cagan stability condition. To put it differently, as long as it holds that $\alpha\gamma < 1$, the divergent effect of the forward looking price level is eliminated by the backward looking expectation formation scheme.

The dynamic pattern of the model changes significantly if one assumes rational expectations, as in Sargent and Wallace's (1973) version of Cagan's model, by letting $\gamma \to \infty$ in equation D.22, resulting in

$$\dot{p}^e(t) = \dot{p}(t). \tag{D.25}$$

Combining the money market equilibrium given in equation D.21 with rational inflation expectations by equation D.25, results in the following unstable differential equation for the price level

$$\dot{p}(t) = -\frac{1}{\alpha}\, m(t) + \frac{1}{\alpha}\, p(t), \tag{D.26}$$

whose general solution, under the assumption $m(t) = \bar{m}$, reads as

$$p(t) = \frac{1}{\alpha}\, e^{\frac{t}{\alpha}} \int_t^{\infty} \bar{m}\, e^{-\frac{k}{\alpha}}\, dk + A\, e^{\frac{t}{\alpha}} = \bar{m} + A\, e^{\frac{t}{\alpha}\, t}.^{17} \tag{D.27}$$

The particular solution is obtained by using the initial condition $p(0) = p_0$ resulting in

$$p(t) = \bar{m} + (p_0 - \bar{m})\, e^{\frac{1}{\alpha}\, t}. \tag{D.28}$$

[17]Note that it holds that $\int_t^{\infty} \bar{m}\, e^{-\frac{k}{\alpha}}\, dk = \bar{m}\, \alpha\, e^{-\frac{t}{\alpha}}$ and therefore $\frac{1}{\alpha}\, e^{\frac{t}{\alpha}} \int_t^{\infty} \bar{m}\, e^{-\frac{k}{\alpha}}\, dk = \bar{m}$.

Both the general and the particular solution are dynamically unstable unless it holds that $A = 0$, implying that $p_0 = \bar{m}$, and validating the result that a pure forward looking variable under rational expectations and permanent market clearing leads to dynamic instability.

Stability of the Cagan model under rational expectations can be restored again by linking rational inflation expectations with a sluggish, or backward adjustment mechanism in the money market, i.e by ruling out permanent market clearing. The dynamic system is described by

$$m^d(t) - p(t) = -\alpha \dot{p}^e(t) \tag{D.29}$$

$$\dot{p}^e(t) = \dot{p}(t) \tag{D.30}$$

$$\dot{p}(t) = \theta(m(t) - m^d(t)), \tag{D.31}$$

where equation D.29 defines real money demand $m^d(t) - p(t)$, equation D.30 rational expectations, and equation D.31 the sluggish adjustment of actual inflation to discrepancies between the money stock $m(t)$, for which it holds that $m(t) = \bar{m}$, and nominal money demand $m^d(t)$. Eliminating $\dot{p}^e(t)$ and $m^d(t)$ yields the following differential equation of the price level

$$\dot{p}(t) = \frac{\theta}{1-\theta\alpha}(\bar{m} - p(t)), \tag{D.32}$$

whose general solution is given by

$$p(t) = \bar{m} + A\, e^{-\frac{\theta}{1-\theta\alpha}\, t}. \tag{D.33}$$

This solution is dynamically stable if $\theta\alpha < 1$, being analogous to the Cagan stability condition under adaptive expectations. As a result, the combination of a forward looking variable being subject to rational expectations, generating dynamic instability, and no complete market clearing due to a backward looking adjustment mechanism restores dynamic stability for $\theta\alpha < 1$. However, this method of achieving dynamic stability is only a theoretical possibility which is not used in rational expectations models.

Another method being generally used for achieving dynamic stability in models with forward looking variables being subject to rational expectations, uses the fact that forward looking variables can "jump" instantaneously to their new steady-state levels in case of a shock, i.e. there arise no transitional dynamics from the old to the new steady-state which anyway would be unstable. Since forward looking variables are determined by future expected values which may change suddenly in a *discrete* and not in continuous manner (e.g. by an unanticipated or even by an anticipated shock), they are free to take any value in time, i.e. they can jump. For example, an unanticipated once-and-for-all increase in the money supply from $m(0) = 0$ in $t = 0$ to $\bar{m}(0) > 0$ in Cagan model under rational expectations described by equations D.21 and D.25, whose general stable solution for a variable stock of money reads as

$$p(t) = \frac{1}{\alpha}\, e^{\frac{t}{\alpha}} \int_t^{\infty} m(k)\, e^{-\frac{k}{\alpha}}\, dk, \tag{D.34}$$

leads to an instantaneous jump of the price level from $p = 0$ to $p = \bar{m}$ at time $t = 0$, since

$$p(t) = \frac{1}{\alpha}\, e^{\frac{t}{\alpha}}\, \bar{m} \int\limits_{t}^{\infty} e^{-\frac{k}{\alpha}}\, dk = \bar{m}. \tag{D.35}$$

Summing up, forward looking or nonpredetermined variables usually lead to unstable roots, whereas backward looking or predetermined variables usually lead to stable roots. A general dynamic macroeconomic model contains both forward and backward looking variables, where forward looking variables are often subject to rational expectations, causing usually dynamic instability if there is no imposition of restrictions ruling out divergent behaviour of forward looking variables. As outlined above, divergent behaviour can be ruled out if forward looking variables are defined as jump variables, or in case forward looking variables are tied to backward looking variables. As a result, the relationship between the number of forward and backward looking variables, as well as the number of jump variables determines the stability and the uniqueness and nonuniqueness of rational expectations models, being analyzed in the following section.

D.5 Solutions to General Dynamic Rational Expectations Models

Consider a continuous-time linear rational expectations model of the form

$$\begin{pmatrix} \dot{\mathbf{X}}(t) \\ \dot{\mathbf{Y}}^{\mathbf{e}}(t) \end{pmatrix} = \mathbf{A} \begin{pmatrix} \mathbf{X}(t) \\ \mathbf{Y}(t) \end{pmatrix} + \mathbf{B}\,\mathbf{Z}(t) \tag{D.36}$$

where
$\mathbf{X}(t)$ is a $(n \times 1)$ vector of predetermined (backward looking) variables at time t,
$\mathbf{Y}(t)$ is a $(m \times 1)$ vector of nonpredetermined (forward looking, jump) variables at time t,
$\mathbf{Z}(t)$ is a $(k \times 1)$ vector of exogenous variables at time t,
$\mathbf{A}$ is a $(n+m) \times (n+m)$ matrix,
$\mathbf{B}$ is a $(n+m) \times k$ matrix,
$\mathbf{Y}^{\mathbf{e}}(t)$ is the expectation of $\mathbf{Y}(t)$ at time t.
Expectations are formed rationally, i.e. it holds that

$$\mathbf{Y}^{\mathbf{e}}(t) = \mathbf{Y}(t).$$

Furthermore, the growth rates of the exogenous variables are assumed to be bounded in order to guarantee the forcing functions to be well-behaved.

The general system D.36 is a system of order $(n+m)$, where $\bar{m}$ roots are unstable, and $n+m-\bar{m}$ roots are stable or have zero real parts. It is important to note that the number of unstable roots $\bar{m}$ need not be equal to the number of nonpredetermined variables m, since the dynamic structure can involve nonpredetermined variables which are tied to backward looking variables. According to Buiter (1984), the dynamic stability of the system, as well as the uniqueness or nonuniqueness of rational expectations equilibria depend on the relative numbers of jump variables m and unstable real roots $\bar{m}$ giving rise to three cases[18]:

1. If the number of unstable roots $\bar{m}$ equals the number of jump variables m, then there exists a unique stable (nonexplosive) solution of a general linear dynamic system.

2. If the number of unstable roots $\bar{m}$ is less than the number of jump variables m, there are an infinite number of stable solutions of a general linear dynamic system. These equilibria are often based on extraneous sources of uncertainty and therefore denoted as "sunspot" equilibria.

3. If the number of unstable roots $\bar{m}$ exceeds the number of jump variables m, there is no solution of the general linear dynamic system that is nonexplosive.

Lots of linear continuous dynamic rational expectations models are applicable to case 1. These models combine a sluggish, and a forward looking variable being subject to rational expectations in a 2×2 linear system of differential equations which give rise to a unique dynamic equilibrium being saddlepoint stable, stemming from the fact that the forward looking variable generates a positive and the backward looking variable a negative root. In order to guarantee dynamic stability, the forward looking variable is assumed to jump always on the stable adjustment paths of the system.[19] A very famous example is Dornbusch's exchange rate overshooting model (1976) where prices are backward looking and adjust slowly, and exchange rates are forward looking being subject to rational expectations. Accordingly, the linear system is characterized by one stable and one unstable root giving rise to saddlepoint behaviour, i.e. if the initial price and exchange rate combination is not located on one of the stable branches, the system is going to explode or implode. In order to guarantee dynamic stability, it is assumed that the exchange rate adjusts always by jumping on the stable adjustment paths since bubbles are ruled. For example, if an exogenous shock catapults the system out of the former steady state, the exchange rate jumps instantaneously on the new stable branch of the new saddle point system, ruling out divergent future behaviour. Since prices adjust slowly, the system cannot jump instantly to the new steady state but moves continuously on the stable arm towards the new long-run equilibrium.

[18]An analogous characterization of solutions in linear discrete-time rational expectations models can be found in Blanchard and Kahn (1980). Examples of all three cases in an open economy continuous time model can be found in Buiter and Miller (1981, 1982, 1984).

[19]Likewise, each linear dynamic optimization model generates saddlepoint behaviour whose stability is guaranteed by choosing the correct initial condition on a stable adjustment path.

Appendix E

Kalecki's Theory of Profits

This section sets out briefly Kalecki's theory of the determinants of profits, being an important ingredient of Minsky's financial instability hypothesis which is discussed in sections 4.5.5 and 5.5.5.[1]

Kalecki's simplest closed economy model, abstracting from government sector activities, consists of two production sectors, where one sector produces consumption goods (subscript C), and the other one investment goods (subscipt I). Aggregate real income is distributed among workers who receive wages, and capitalists who earn profits, where the neoclassical savings hypothesis is assumed to be valid, stating that there are no savings out of wages, and that there is no consumption out of profits. That is, workers spend all their wage income on consumption goods, and capital owners spend all their profit income on investment. Accordingly, the nominal amount of consumption expenditures C^n is equal to the sum of wage income in the consumption goods sector and wage income in the investment goods sector, i.e. formally, it holds that

$$C^n = P_C Y_C = w_C N_C + w_I N_I, \tag{E.1}$$

where P_C denotes the price of consumption goods, Y_C real output of consumption goods, w_C wages per unit of employment in the consumption goods sector, w_I wages per unit of employment in the investment goods sector, N_C the volume of employment in the consumption goods sector, and N_I the volume of employment in the investment goods sector.

Nominal profits in the consumption goods sector PR_C are determined by nominal sales revenues of consumption goods $P_C Y_C$ less wages in the consumption goods sector $w_C N_C$, i.e. formally it holds that

$$PR_C = P_C Y_C - w_C N_C. \tag{E.2}$$

Inserting equation E.1 in equation E.2, and solving for PR_C yields

$$PR_C = w_I N_I, \tag{E.3}$$

stating that profits in the consumption goods sector are determined by consumption demand of workers being employed in the investment goods sector.

[1]For references to this section, see Kalecki (1971), chapter 7, pp. 78-92, and Minsky (1982b), chapter 4, pp. 71-89.

Nominal profits in the investment goods sector PR_I are determined by nominal sales of investment goods $I^n = P_I Y_I$, where P_I and Y_I denote the price and real output of investment goods, less wages in the investment goods sector $w_I N_I$. Formally, nominal profits in the investment goods sector are given by

$$PR_I = P_I Y_I - w_I N_I. \tag{E.4}$$

Total nominal profits PR in the economy are determined by the sum of profits in the consumption goods sector and profits in the investment goods sector. Formally, total nominal profits are given as

$$PR = PR_C + PR_I. \tag{E.5}$$

The determinants of total profits are derived by inserting equations E.3 and E.4 into equation E.5, which yields

$$PR = P_I Y_I = I^n, \tag{E.6}$$

stating that the total level of nominal profits is determined by the nominal amount of investment. Consequently, a rise/fall in investment expenditures causes a rise/fall in total profits.

In the open economy version of the Kalecki model, which additionally considers government expenditures and taxation, as well as consumption out of profits and savings out of wages, the nominal amount of consumption C^n is given by

$$C^n = P_C Y_C = (1 - s^{'})(w_C N_C + w_I N_I) + c^{'} PR + G - T_W + Ex - Im, \tag{E.7}$$

that is, by consumption out of wages less savings out of wages $(1 - s^{'})(w_C N_C + w_I N_I)$, where s' denotes the marginal propensity of saving out of wages, plus consumption out of total nominal profits net of taxes $c^{'} PR$, where $c^{'}$ denotes the marginal propensity of consumption out of profits, plus government expenditures G, less taxes on total wage income T_W, plus exports Ex, less imports Im.

Nominal profits net of taxes in the consumption goods sector PR_C are formally determined by

$$PR_C = P_C Y_C - w_C N_C - T_{PR,C}, \tag{E.8}$$

i.e. by nominal earnings $P_C Y_C$, less labour costs $w_C N_C$, less taxes on profits in the consumption goods sector $T_{PR,C}$. Nominal profits net of taxes in the investment goods sector PR_I are formally given by

$$PR_I = P_I Y_I - w_I N_I - T_{PR,I}, \tag{E.9}$$

that is, by nominal earnings $P_I Y_I$, less labour costs $w_I N_I$, less taxes on profits in the investment goods sector $T_{PR,I}$.

Total nominal profits net of taxes PR are determined firstly, by inserting equation E.7 into equation E.8, resulting in a modified version of nominal profits net of taxes in the consumption goods sector, reading as

$$PR_C = w_I N_I - s' w(N_C + N_I) + c^{'} PR + G - T_W - T_{PR,C} + Ex - Im, \tag{E.10}$$

and secondly, by summing up equations E.9 and E.10, which yields

$$PR = (P_I Y_I + c^{'} PR - s'(w_C N_C + w_I N_I) + (G - T_W - T_{PR,C} - T_{PR,I}) + (Ex - Im)), \tag{E.11}$$

where $(G - T_W - T_{PR,C} - T_{PR,I})$ denotes the government budget deficit. Accordingly, profits increase/decrease if nominal investment $I^n = P_I Y_I$ increases/decreases, if consumption out of profits rises/falls, if savings out of wages decreases/increases, if there is a rise/fall in the government budget deficit, and if there is a rise/fall in net exports.

Symbol Glossary

Generally, the discussion of variables and parameters within each chapter is self-contained. Below, recurrent variables and parameters are listed. Departures from these conventions are clearly mentioned in the text.

A:	real stock of domestic assets
A^*:	real stock of foreign assets
B:	foreign exchange reserves exclusive reserves from foreign loans R
B_D:	real stock of domestic government bonds
B_{DB}:	real stock of domestic government bonds held by banks
B_{DH}:	real stock of domestic government bonds held by households
B_F:	real stock of foreign government bonds
B_{FH}:	real stock of foreign government bonds held by households
C:	real consumption
CA:	nominal value of capital account in domestic currency
CRA:	current account
CF:	cash flow (being defined differently)
CF^e:	expected cash flow (being defined differently)
D:	nominal stock of deposits
D_{BA}:	nominal deposits of commercial banks or required reserves $D_{BA} = \tau D$
DD:	nominal value of domestic debt in domestic currency
DB^*:	nominal value of foreign debt in foreign currency
E:	real stock of equities
E_B:	real stock of equities held by banks
E_H:	real stock of equities held by households
EA:	nominal earnings in domestic currency; $EA = P \cdot Y$
F:	net foreign assets
G:	real government demand
GPR:	nominal gross profits
H:	domestic credit component
I:	real net investment of fixed capital
K:	real stock of fixed capital
$\hat{K}$:	growth rate of the real stock of fixed capital; $\hat{K} = \dot{K}/K = I/K$
L:	nominal stock of domestic loans in domestic currency
L_{BA}:	loans from central bank to domestic banks
L^*:	nominal stock of foreign loans in foreign currency

LMA: liquid monetary assets
LF^*: net foreign loan inflows to domestic banks
M: nominal stock of money supply
N: volume of employment (working hours)
NFP: net foreign position
NW_x: net worth of sector x
NX: real net exports (exports less imports)
P: domestic price level or supply price of capital, respectively
P^*: foreign price level
P_A: market price of domestic assets
P_A^*: market price of foreign assets
P_{BD}: market price of domestic government bonds
P_E: market price of equities
P_{BF}: market price of foreign government bonds in foreign currency
P_K: demand price of fixed capital
P_{LBD}: market price of long-term domestic government bonds
P_{SBD}: market price of short-term domestic government bonds
P_{SFB}: market price of short-term foreign government bonds in foreign currency
PC: payment commitments
PR: nominal profits
PNW: present value of net wealth
Q_g: gross nominal profits
Q: net nominal profits (gross profits less external financing costs)
R: foreign exchange reserves from foreign loan inflows
T: nominal value of trade balance in domestic currency
U: lifetime utility
W: wealth
Y: domestic real output or total income, respectively
Z: foreign exchange reserves $Z = L^* + B$
d: real deposits relative to capital stock; $d = D/PK$
f: domestic nominal interest rate on long-term government bonds
g: real government expenditures per unit of capital; $g = G/K$
h: real domestic credit component relative to capital stock; $h = H/PK$
i: domestic nominal interest rate on short-term government bonds
i^*: foreign nominal interest rate on short-term government bonds
i_C: domestic prime rate (domestic central bank's discount rate)
i_C^*: foreign prime rate (foreign central bank's discount rate)
i_{DB}: domestic nominal interest rate on domestic debt
i_{DB}^*: foreign nominal interest rate on foreign debt
i_r: real interest rate
i_{RF}: risk-free reference interest rate
j: domestic nominal interest rate on domestic bank loans in domestic currency
j^*: foreign nominal interest rate on foreign bank loans in foreign currency
m: money multiplier; $m = 1/\tau$
nx: net exports per unit of capital; $nx = NX/K$

$\hat{p}$: domestic price level's growth rate; $\hat{p} = \dot{P}/P$

$\hat{p}^*$: foreign price level's growth rate; $\hat{p}^* = \dot{P}^*/P^*$

q: Tobin's q

r^e: expected (net) profit rate

r_g: gross profit rate on capital

r: (net) profit rate on capital (gross profit rate less external financing costs)

rp: risk premium (reflecting domestic banks' default risk)

s: nominal exchange rate (price of one unit of foreign currency in domestic currency)

$\hat{s}$: growth rate of the the nominal exchange rate; $\hat{s} = \dot{s}/s$

u: capacity utilization; $u = Y/K$

u^*: full employment level of capacity utilization

v: nominal wage share (in gross product); $v = wN/PY$

w: nominal wage rate

α: exogenous risk premium on domestic government bonds

β: subjective discount or preference factor

δ: rate of capital depreciation

η: "desired" or "demanded" growth rate of the capital stock; $\eta = I/K = \hat{K}$

λ: debt-asset ratio; $\lambda = L/(PK)$

λ^*: foreign debt-asset ratio in foreign currency; $\lambda = L^*/(PK)$

λ^*_d: foreign debt-asset ratio in domestic currency; $\lambda = s\,L^*/(PK)$

ρ: state of confidence, difference between expected and actual profit rate; $\rho = r^e - r$

σ: risk premium; $\sigma = r - (i - \hat{p})$

σ^*: risk premium; $\sigma^* = r - (i^* + \beta(\rho) - \hat{p})$

τ: required reserve ratio

Bibliography

Agénor, P.-R. *The Economics of Adjustment and Growth.* Havard University Press, Cambridge, Massachusetts, 2nd edition, 2004.

Agénor, P.-R., J. S. Bhandari, and R. Flood. Speculative Attacks and Models of Balance of Payments Crises. *IMF Staff Papers, International Monetary Fund*, 39(2), 1992.

Agénor, P.-R., and P. J. Montiel. *Development Macroeconomics.* Princeton University Press, Princeton, New Jersey, 2nd edition, 1999.

Aghion, P., P. Bacchetta, and A. Banerjee. A Simple Model of Monetary Policy and Currency Crises. *European Economic Review*, 44:728–738, 2000.

Aghion, P., P. Bacchetta, and A. Banerjee. Currency Crises and Monetary Policy in a Credit-Constrained Economy. *European Economic Review*, 45:1121–1150, 2001.

Aghion, P., P. Bacchetta, and A. Banerjee. A Corporate Balance-Sheet Approach to Currency Crises. *Journal of Economic Theory*, forthcoming 2003.

Akyüz, Y., and A. Cornford. Capital Flows to Developing Countries and the Reform of the International Financial System. UNU/WIDER Working Papers 190, The United Nations University UNU, World Institute for Development Economics Research, Helsinki, Finland, 2000.

Arrowsmith, D. K., and C. M. Place. *Ordinary Differential Equations.* Chapman and Hall, London, New York, 1990.

Arthur, B. W., J. H. Holland, B. Le Baron, R. Palmer, and P. Taylor. Asset Pricing Under Endogenous Expectations in an Artificial Stock Market. *Economic Notes, Banca Monte dei Paschi di Siena*, 26(2):297–330, 1997.

Asprem, M. Stock Prices, Asset Portfolios, and Macroeconomic Variables in Ten European Countries. *Journal of Banking and Finance*, 13:589–612, September 1989.

Azariadis, C. Self-Fulfilling Prophecies. *Journal of Economic Theory*, 15:380–396, 1981.

Azariadis, C., and R. Guesnerie. Sunspots and Cycles. *Review of Economic Studies*, 53: 725–738, 1986.

Bacchetta, P., and S. Gerlach. Consumption and Credit Constraints: Some International Evidence. *Journal of Monetary Economics*, 40:207–238, 1997.

Bakker, F. P., and B. Chapple. Advanced Country Experiences with Capital Account Liberalization. IMF Occasional Paper 214, International Monetary Fund, Washington, D.C., 2002.

Bank for International Settlements (BIS). *53th Annual Report.* Bank for International Settlements, Basle, Switzerland, 1983.

Bank for International Settlements (BIS). The Role of Asset Prices in the Formulation of Monetary Policy. *BIS Conference Papers*, 5, 1998.

Barro, R. *The Equilibrium Approach to Business Cycles*, chapter 2 in Money Expectations, and Business Cycles. Academic Press, New York, 1981.

Barro, R. The Stock Market and Investment. *Review of Financial Studies*, 3(1):115–131, 1990.

Barro, R., and D. Gordon. A Positive Theory of Monetary Policy in a Natural Rate Model. *Journal of Monetary Economics*, 17(1):589–610, 1983a.

Barro, R., and D. Gordon. Rules, Discretion, and Reputation in a Model of Monetary Policy. *Journal of Monetary Economis*, 12:101–121, 1983b.

Benhabib, J., and R. H. Day. A Characterization of Erratic Dynamics in the Overlapping Generations Model. *Journal of Economic Dynamics and Control*, 4:37–55, 1982.

Benhabib, J., and K. Nishimura. Competitive Equilibrium Cycles. *Journal of Economic Theory*, 35:284–306, 1985.

Berg, J., and L. Taylor. External Liberalization, Economic Performance, and Social Policy. CEPA Working Paper Series I, Globalization, Labour Markets, and Social Policy 1, Center for Economic Policy Analysis, February 2000.

Bernanke, B. Nonmonetary Effects of the Financial Crisis in the Propagation of the Great Depression. *American Economic Review*, 73:257–276, 1983.

Bernanke, B., and A. Blinder. Credit, Money and Aggregate Demand. *American Economic Review (AEA Papers and Proceedings)*, 78(2):291–295, May 1988.

Bernanke, B., and M. Gertler. Agency Costs, Net Worth and Business Fluctuations. *American Economic Review*, 79:14–31, 1989.

Bernanke, B., and M. Gertler. Financial Fragility and Economic Performance. *Quarterly Journal of Economics*, 105:87–114, February 1990.

Bernanke, B., and M. Gertler. The Financial Accelerator and the Flight to Quality. *Review of Economics and Statistics*, 78(1):1–15, 1994.

Bernanke, B., and M. Gertler. Inside the Black Box: The Credit Channel of Monetary Policy. *Journal of Economic Perspectives*, 9:27–48, 1995.

Bernanke, B., and M. Gertler. Monetary Policy and Asset Price Volatility. NBER Working Paper WP 7559, National Bureau of Economic Research, Cambridge, Massachusetts, February 2000.

Bernanke, B., M. Gertler, and S. Gilchrist. The Financial Accelerator and the Flight to Quality. *Review of Economics and Statistics*, 58:1–15, 1996.

Bernanke, B., M. Gertler, and S. Gilchrist. The Financial Accelerator in a Quantitative Business Cycle Framework. NBER Working Paper WP 6455, National Bureau of Economic Research, 1998.

Bernanke, B., M. Gertler, and S. Gilchrist. The Financial Accelerator in a Quantitative Business Cycle Framework. In J. Taylor and M. Woodford, editors, *Handbook of Macroeconomics*, volume 1C, pages 1341–1393, 1999.

Bernanke, B., and H. James. The Gold Standard, Deflation, and Financial Crises in the Great Depression: An International Comparison. In R. G. Hubbard, editor, *Financial Markets and Financial Crises*, Chicago, 1991. University of Chicago Press.

Bernanke, B., and C. Lown. The Credit Crunch. *Brookings Papers on Economic Activity*, (2):205–239, 1992.

Blanchard, O. Backward and Forward Solutions for Economies with Rational Expectations. *American Economic Review*, 69(2):114–118, 1979a.

Blanchard, O. Speculative Bubbles, Crashes, and Rational Expectations. *Economics Letters*, 3:387–389, 1979b.

Blanchard, O. Output, the Stock Market, and Interest Rate. *American Economic Review*, 71(1):132–143, 1981.

Blanchard, O., and S. Fischer. *Lectures on Macroeconomics.* The MIT Press, Cambridge, 1989.

Blanchard, O., and C. Kahn. The Solution of Linear Difference Models and Rational Expectations. *Econometrica*, 48:1305–1311, 1980.

Blanchard, O., C. Rhee, and L. Summers. The Stock Market, Profit, and Investment. *Quarterly Journal of Economics*, 108(1):113–136, 1993.

Blanchard, O., and J. Simon. The Long and Large Decline in U.S. Ouput Volatility. *Brookings Papers on Economic Activity, Brookings Institution*, 1:135–174, 2001.

Blejer, M. I., E. V. Feldman, and A. Feltenstein. Exogenous Shocks, Deposit Runs and Bank Soundedness: A Macroeconomic Framework. IMF Working Paper WP/97/91, International Monetary Fund, Washington, D.C., 1997.

Blinder, A., and R. Solow. Does Fiscal Policy Matter? *Journal of Public Economics*, 2: 319–337, 1973.

Bofinger, P., J. Reischle, and A. Schächter. *Geldpolitik: Ziele, Institutionen, Strategien und Instrumente.* Verlag Franz Vahlen, Munich, 1996.

Bordo, M., M. Ducker, and D. Wheelock. Aggregate Price Shocks and Financial Stability: An Historical Analysis. NBER Working Paper WP h0125, National Bureau of Economic Research, April 2000.

Bordo, M., M. Ducker, and D. Wheelock. Aggregate Price Shocks and Financial Stability, The United Kingdom 1796-1999. NBER Working Paper WP 8583, National Bureau of Economic Research, 2001a.

Bordo, M., and B. Eichengreen. Crises Now and Then: What Lessons from the Last Era of Financial Globalization? NBER Working Paper WP 8716, National Bureau of Economic Research, 2002.

Bordo, M., B. Eichengreen, D. Klingebiel, and M. Martinez-Peria. Is the Crisis Problem Growing More Severe? *Economic Policy*, 16(32):51–82, 2001b. Web Appedix available at http://www.economic-policy.org.

Bordo, M., and O. Jeanne. Boom-Busts in Asset Prices, Economic Instability, and Monetary Policy. NBER Working Paper WP 8966, National Bureau of Economic Research, 2002.

Bordo, M., and D. Wheelock. Price stability and financial stability: The historical record. *Federal Reserve Bank of St. Louis Review*, 80:41–62, September/October 1998.

Borio, C., C. Furfine, and P. Lowe. Procyclicality of the Financial System and Financial Stability: Issues and Policy Options. BIS Papers 1, Bank For International Settlements (BIS), Basle, Switzerland, 2001.

Borio, C., and P. Lowe. Asset Prices, Financial and Monetary Stability: Exploring the Nexus. BIS Working Papers 114, Bank For International Settlements (BIS), Basle, Switzerland, July 2002.

Boyce, W. E., and R. L. DiPrima. *Elementary Differential Equations and Boundary Value Problems.* Wiley, New York, 3rd edition, 1977.

Boyd, I., and J. M. Blatt. *Investment, Confidence and Business Cycles.* Springer, New York, 1988.

Brainard, W. C., and J. Tobin. Econometric Models: Their Problems and Usefulness, Pitfalls in Financial Model Building. *American Economic Review*, 58:99–122, May 1968.

Buch, C. M., and R. P. Heinrich. Twin Crises and the Intermediary Role of Banks. *International Journal of Finance and Economics*, 4:313–323, 1999.

Buiter, W. H. Saddlepoint Problems in Continuous Time Rational Expectations Models: A General Method and Some Macroeconomic Examples. *Econometrica*, 52:665–680, 1984.

Buiter, W. H., and M. Miller. Monetary Policy and International Competitiveness: The Problems of Adjustment. *Oxford Economic Papers*, pages 143–175, 1981.

Buiter, W. H., and M. Miller. Real Exchange Rate Overshooting and the Output Cost of Bringing Down Inflation. *European Economic Review*, 18:85–123, 1982.

Buiter, W. H., and M. Miller. Real Exchange Rate Overshooting and the Output Cost of Bringing Down Inflation: Some Further Results. In J. Frenkel, editor, *Exchange Rates and International Macroeconomics*, pages 317–368, Chicago, 1984. Chicago University Press.

Burnside, C., M. Eichenbaum, and S. Rebello. Prospective Deficits and the Asian Currency Crisis. NBER Working Paper WP 6758, National Bureau of Economic Research, October, 1998.

Caballero, R. Macroeconomic volatility in latin america: Facts and policy implications. *Economia, The Journal of the Latin American and Caribbean Economic Association*, 1 (1):31–108, 2000.

Caballero, R. J., and A. Krishnamurthy. A Dual Liquidity Model for Emerging Markets. *American Economic Review*, 92(2):33–37, 2002.

Cagan, P. The Monetary Dynamics of Hyperinflation. In M. Friedman, editor, *Studies in the Quantity Theory of Money*, Chicago, 1956. University of Chicago Press.

Cagan, P. *Determinants and Effects of Changes in the Stock of Money.* National Bureau of Economic Research, Cambridge, Massachusetts, 1965.

Calomiris, C., and G. Gorton. The Origins of Banking Panics: Models, Facts, and Bank Regulation. In R. G. Hubbard, editor, *Financial Markets and Financial Crises*, pages 109–173, Chicago, 1991. University of Chicago Press.

Calomiris, C., and C. Kahn. The Role of Demandable Debt in Structuring Optimal Banking Arrangements. *American Economic Review*, 1991.

Calvo, G. A. Staggered Contracts and Exchange Rate Policy. In J. A. Frenkel, editor, *Exchange Rates and International Macroeconomics*, pages 235–252, Chicago IL, 1983. University of Chicago Press.

Calvo, G. A., L. Leiderman, and C. M. Reinhart. Inflows of Capital to Developing Countries in the 1990s. *Journal of Economic Perspectives*, 10(2):123–139, 1996.

Calvo, G. A., and C. A. Végh. Credibility and the Dynamics of Stabilization Policy: A Basic Framework. In C. A. Sims, editor, *Advances in Econometrics*, Cambridge, 1993. Cambridge University Press.

Caprio Jr., G., and D. Klingebiel. *Bank Insolvency: Bad Luck, Bad Policy, or Bad Banking?* Paper presented to Annual World Bank Conference of Development Economics, http:// www.worldbank.org/ research/ interest/ prr stuff/ working papers/ abcde96.pdf, Download on January 11, 2000, April 1996.

Cashin, P., and C. J. McDermott. The Long Behaviour of Commodity Prices: Small Trends and Big Variability. IMF Working Paper 01/68, International Monetary Fund, Washington, D.C., 2002.

Cass, D., and K. Shell. Do Sunspots Matter? *Journal of Political Economy*, 91:193–227, 1983.

Cass, D., and K. Shell. Sunspot Equilibrium in an Overlapping Generations Economy with an Idealized Contingent-claims Manager. In J. Geweke W. Barnett and K. Shell, editors, *Economic Complexity: Chaos, Sunspots, Bubbles, and Nonlinearities*, Cambridge, 1988. Cambridge University Press.

Céspedes, L. F., R. Chang, and A. Velasco. Balance Sheets and Exchange Rate Policy. NBER Working Paper WP 7840, National Bureau of Economic Research, 2001a.

Céspedes, L. F., R. Chang, and A. Velasco. *Dollarization of Liabilities, Net Worth Effects, and Optimal Monetary Policy.* http://ksghome.harvard.edu/ .avelasco.academic.ksg/ research.html, Download on October 17, 2003, Februrary 2001b.

Chang, R., and A. Velasco. The Asian Liquidity Crisis. NBER Working Paper WP 6796, National Bureau of Economic Research, 1998a.

Chang, R., and A. Velasco. Financial Crises in Emerging Markets. Working Paper, Federal Reserve Bank of Atlanta, 1998b.

Chang, R., and A. Velasco. Financial Fragility and the Exchange Rate Regime. NBER Working Paper WP 6469, National Bureau of Economic Research, 1998c.

Chang, R., and A. Velasco. Liquidity Crises in Emerging Markets: Theory and Policy. NBER Working Paper WP 7272, National Bureau of Economic Research, 1999.

Chari, V. V., and R. Jagannathan. Banking Panics, Information, and Rational Expectations Equilibrium. *Journal of Finance*, 43:749–760, 1988.

Chiang, A. *Elements of Dynamic Optimization.* McGraw-Hill, New York, Singapore, 1992.

Corsetti, G., P. Pesenti, and N. Roubini. Paper Tigers? A Model of the Asian Crisis. NBER Working Paper WP 6783, National Bureau of Economic Research, 1998.

Crafts, N. Historical Perspectives on the Information Technology Revolution. Unpublished background paper for the october 2001 world economic outlook, International Monetary Fund, Washington, 2000.

Crockett, A. The Theory and Practice of Financial Stability. Essays in International Finance No. 203, International Finance Section, Princeton University, New Jersey, April 1997.

De Brouwer, G. *Hedge Funds in Emerging Markets.* Cambridge University Press, Cambridge, UK, 2001.

De Cecco, M. *Money and Empire: The Classical Gold Standard.* Blackwell, Oxford, 1974.

De Ferranti, D., G. E. Perry, I. S. Gill, and L. Serven. Securing Our Future in a Global Economy. Latin American and Caribbean Studies: Viewpoint Series, World Bank, Washington, 2000.

Deaton, A. *Understanding Consumption.* Clarendon Press, Oxford, 1992.

Debreu, G. *Theory of Value.* Yale University Press, New Haven, London, 1959.

Demirgüç-Kunt, A., and E. Detragiache. The Determinants of Banking Crises: Evidence from Developed and Developing Countries. IMF Working Paper WP/97/106, International Monetary Fund, Washington, D.C., 1997.

Diamond, D., and P. Dybvig. Bank Runs, Deposit Insurance and Liquidity. *Journal of Political Economy*, 91:401–419, June 1983.

Diaz-Alejandro, C. Good-Bye Financial Repression, Hello Financial Crash. *Journal of Development Economics*, 19, 1985.

Domar, E. D. Capital Expansion, Rate of Growth and Employment. *Econometrica*, 14: 137–142, 1946.

Domar, E. D. *Essays in the Theory of Economic Growth.* Oxford University Press, New York, 1957.

Dooley, M. P. A Model of Crises in Emerging Markets. NBER Working Paper WP 6300, National Bureau of Economic Research, 1997.

Dooley, M. P. A Model of Crises in Emerging Markets. *The Economic Journal*, 110: 256–272, 2000.

Dornbusch, R. Expectations and Exchange Rate Dynamics. *Journal of Political Economy*, 84:1161–1176, December 1976.

Dornbusch, R. *After Asia: New Directions for the International Financial System.* http:// www.mit.edu/ ~rudi, Download on May 15, 2000, July 1998a.

Dornbusch, R. *Asian Crisis Themes.* http:// www.mit.edu/ ~rudi, Download on May 15, 2000, February 1998b.

Dornbusch, R. *Emerging Market Crises: Origins and Remedies.* http:// www.mit.edu/ ~rudi, Download on May 15, 2000, July 1999.

Dornbusch, R. *A Primer on Emerging Market Crises.* http:// www.mit.edu/ ~rudi, Download on March 30, 2002, January 2001.

Dornbusch, R., I. Goldfajn, and R. O. Valdés. Currency Crises and Collapses. *Brookings Papers on Economic Activity*, 2:219–293, 1995.

Drees, B., and C. Pazarbasioglu. The Nordic Banking Crisis: Pitfalls in Financial Liberalization. IMF Occasional Paper 161, International Monetary Fund, Washington, D.C., April 1998.

Eatwell, J. International Capital Liberalization: The Impact on World Development. CEPA Working Paper Series I, Globalization, Labour Markets, and Social Policy 1, Center for Economic Policy Analysis, 1996.

Eatwell, J., and L. Taylor. *Global Finance at Risk.* The New Press, New York, 2000.

Eichengreen, B., and R. S. Grossman. Debt-Deflation and Financial Instability: Two Historical Explorations. In F. Capie and G.E. Wood, editors, *Asset Prices and the Real Economy.* St. Martin's Press, 1997.

Eichengreen, B., and R. Hausmann. Exchange Rates and Financial Fragility. NBER Working Paper WP 7418, National Bureau of Economic Research, November 1999.

Eichengreen, B., and D. Mathieson. Hedge Funds and Financial Market Dynamics. IMF Occasional Paper 166, International Monetary Fund, Washington, D.C., May 1998.

Eichengreen, B., and K. Mitchener. The Great Depression as a Credit Boom Gone Wrong. BIS Working Paper 137, Bank for International Settlements (BIS), Basle, Switzerland, September 2003.

Eichengreen, B., and A. Mody. Lending Booms, Reserves, and the Sustainability of Short-Term Debt: Inferences From the Pricing of Syndicated Bank Loans. *Journal of Development Economics*, 63:5–44, October 2000.

Eichengreen, B., M. Mussa, G. Dell'Ariccia, E. Detragiache, G. M. Milesi-Ferretti, and A. Tweedie. Capital Account Liberalization: Theoretical and Practical Aspects. IMF Occasional Paper 172, International Monetary Fund, Washington, D.C., 1998.

Eichengreen, B., and R. Portes. Anatomy of Financial Crises. In R. Portes and A. K. Swoboda, editors, *From Threats to International Financial Stability*, pages 10–58, Cambridge, 1987. Cambridge University Press.

Eichengreen, B., and A. Rose. Staying Afloat When the Wind Shifts: External Factors and Emerging-Market Banking Crises. NBER Working Paper WP 6370, National Bureau of Economic Research, 1998.

Eichengreen, B., and A. Rose. The Empirics of Currency and Banking Crises. *NBER Reporter*, 1999.

Eichengreen, B., A. Rose, and C. Wyplosz. Exchange Market Mayhem: The Antecedents and Aftermath of Speculative Attacks. *Economic Policy*, 21:249–312, October 1995.

Eichengreen, B., A. Rose, and C. Wyplosz. Contagious Currency Crises: First Tests. *Scandinavian Journal of Economics*, 98:463–484, 1996.

Fama, E. F. Stock Returns, Expected Returns, and Real Activity. *Journal of Finance*, 45(4):1089–1108, 1990.

Fazzari, S., R. G. Hubbard, and B. C. Petersen. Financing Constraints and Corporate Investment. *Brookings Papers of Economic Activity*, (1):141–195, 1988.

Fisher, I. *The Purchasing Power of Money: Its Determination and Relation to Credit, Interest and Crises.* Macmillan, New York, 1911.

Fisher, I. *Booms and Depressions.* Adelphi, New York, 1932.

Fisher, I. The Debt-Deflation Theory of Great Depressions. *Econometrica*, 1:337–357, 1933.

Flaschel, P., R. Franke, and W. Semmler. *Dynamic Macroeconomics.* The MIT Press, Cambridge, Massachusetts, London, England, 1997.

Flood, R., and P. Garber. The Lender of Last Resort and the Run on the Savings and Loans. NBER Working Paper WP 823, National Bureau of Economic Research, Cambridge, MA, 1981a.

Flood, R., and P. Garber. A Systematic Banking Collapse in a Perfect Foresight World. NBER Working Paper WP 691, National Bureau of Economic Research, Cambridge, MA, 1981b.

Flood, R., and P. Garber. Collapsing Exchange-Rate Regimes: Some Linear Examples. *Journal of International Economics*, 17:1–13, 1984a.

Flood, R., and P. Garber. Gold Monetization and Gold Discipline. *Journal of Political Economy*, 92:90–107, 1984b.

Flood, R., and P. Isard. Monetary Policy Strategies. *IMF Staff Papers, International Monetary Fund*, 36:612–632, 1989.

Flood, R., and N. Marion. Perspectives on the recent currency crisis literature. NBER Working Paper WP 6380, National Bureau of Economic Research, 1998.

Franke, R., and W. Semmler. A Model of the Financial Sector and its Reaction to Aggregate Fluctuations. In Willi Semmler, editor, *Business Cycles: Theory and Empirical Methods*, pages 231–267, Norwell, Massachusetts, 1994. Kluwer Academic Publishers.

Franke, R., and W. Semmler. Bond Rate, Loan Rate and Tobin's q in a Temporary Equilibrium Model of the Financial Sector. *Metroeconomica*, 50(3):351–385, 1999.

Frankel, J. *Financial Market and Monetary Policy.* MIT Press, Cambridge MA, 1995.

Friedman, M., and A. J. Schwartz. *A Monetary History of the United States 1867-1960.* Princeton University Press, Princeton, 1963.

Frisch, R. Propagation Problems and Impulse Problems in Dynamic Economics. In *Essays in Honour of Gustav Cassel*, pages 171–205, London, 1933. Allen & Unwin.

Frydl, E. J., and W. E. Alexander. The Length and Cost of Banking Crises. IMF Working Paper WP/99/30, International Monetary Fund, Washington, D.C., 1999.

Galbraith, J. K. *The Great Crash.* Houghton-Mifflin, Boston, 1972.

Gandolfo, G. *Economic Dynamics.* Springer Verlag, New York, Berlin, Heidelberg, 3rd edition, 1997.

Garber, P., and V. Grilli. Bank Runs in Open Economies and the International Transmission of Panics. *Journal of International Economics*, 27:165–175, 1989.

Garcia-Herrero, A., and T. J. Bali no. Monetary Impact of a Banking Crisis and the Conduct of Monetary Policy. IMF Working Paper WP/97/124, International Monetary Fund, Washington, D.C., 1997.

Gavin, M., and R. Hausmann. The Roots of Banking Crises: The Macroeconomic Context. In R. Hausmann and L. Rojas-Suarez, editors, *Banking Crises in Latin America*, Baltimore, 1996. The John Hopkins University Press.

George, H. *Progess and Poverty.* Reprint. Robert Schalkenbach Foundation, New York, 1879.

Gertler, M. Financial Structure and Aggregate Economic Activity: An Overview. *Journal of Money, Credit and Banking*, 20(3):559–588, 1988.

Gertler, M. Financial Capacity and Output Fluctuations in an Economy with Multiperiod Financial Relationships. *Review of Economic Studies*, 59:455–472, 1992.

Gertler, M., and S. Gilchrist. The Role of Credit Market Imperfections in the Monetary Transmission Mechanism: Arguments and Evidence. *Scandinavian Journal of Economics*, 95:43–64, 1993.

Gertler, M., and S. Gilchrist. Monetary Policy, Business Cycles, and the Behaviour of Small Manufacturing Firms. *Quarterly Journal of Economics*, 59:309–340, 1994.

Gertler, M., R. G. Hubbard, and A. Kashyap. Interest Rate Spread, Credit Constraints and Investment. In R.G. Hubbard, editor, *Financial Markets and Financial Crises*, Chicago, 1991. Chicago University Press.

Girton, L., and D. Roper. A Monetary Model of Exchange Market Pressure Applied to the Postwar Canadian Experience. *The American Economic Review*, 67(4):537–548, 1977.

Glick, R., and M. Hutchinson. Banking and Currency Crises: How Common Are Twins? Pacific Basin Working Paper Series PB99-07, Center for Pacific Basin Monetary and Economic Studies, Economic Research Department, Federal Reserve Bank of San Francisco, San Francisco, December 1999.

Goldfajn, I., and R. O. Valdés. Are Currency Crises Predictable? IMF Working Paper WP/97/159, International Monetary Fund, Washington, D.C., 1997a.

Goldfajn, I., and R. O. Valdés. Capital Flows and the Twin Crises: The Role of Liquidity. IMF Working Paper WP/97/87, International Monetary Fund, Washington, D.C., 1997b.

Goldstein, M. Coping with Too Much of a Good Thing. Policy Research Working Paper 1507, The World Bank, Washington, D.C., September 1995.

Goldstein, M., G. Kaminsky, and C. Reinhart. *Assessing Financial Vulnerability: An Early Warning System.* Institute for International Economics, 2000.

Goldstein, M., and P. Turner. Banking Crises in Emerging Economies: Origins and Policy Options. BIS Economic Papers 46, Bank For International Settlements (BIS), Monetary and Economic Department, Basle, Switzerland, October 1996.

Goodwin, R. M. The Non-Linear Accelerator and the Persistence of Business Cycles. *Econometrica*, 19:1–17, 1951.

Gordon, M. J. *The Investment, Financing and Valuation of the Corporation.* Irwing, Homewood, Illinois, 1962.

Gore, C. The Rise and Fall of the Washington Consensus as a Paradigm for Developing Countries. *World Development*, 28(5):789–804, 2000.

Gorton, G. Bank Suspension of Convertibility. *Journal of Monetary Economics*, 15(2): 177–193, 1985.

Gosh, A. R., T. Lane, M. Schulze-Ghattas, A. Bulir, J. Hamann and A. Mourmouras. IMF-Supported Programs in Capital Account Crises: Design and Experience. IMF Occasional Paper 210, International Monetary Fund, Washington, D.C., 2002.

Grandmont, J. M. On Endogenous Competitive Business Cycles. *Econometrica*, 53: 995–1045, 1985.

Grandmont, J. M. Stabilizing Competitive Business Cycles. *Journal of Economic Theory*, 40:57–76, 1986.

Grandmont, J. M., and G. Laroque. Stability of Cycles and Expectations. *Journal of Economic Theory*, pages 138–151, 1986.

Greenwald, B., and J. Stiglitz. Financial Markets, Imperfections and Business Cycles. *Quarterly Journal of Economics*, 108:77–114, 1993.

Greenwald, B., J. Stiglitz, and A. Weiss. Informational Imperfections in the Capital Market and Macroeconomic Fluctuations. *American Economic Review*, 74:194–200, 1984.

Grilli, V. Buying and Selling Attacks on Fixed Exchange Rate Systems. *Journal of International Economics*, 20:143–156, 1986.

Guckenheimer, J., and P. Holmes. *Nonlinear Oscillations, Dynamical Systems, and Bifurcation of Vector Fields.* Applied Mathematical Sciences Vol. 42. Springer Verlag, New York, Berlin, Heidelberg, 1986.

Hagemann, H. Hayek and the Kiel school: some reflections on the German debate on business cycles in the late 1920s and early 1930s. In H. Hagemann and M. Colonna, editors, *Money and Business Cycles: The Economics of F. A. Hayek (Volume I)*, pages 101–120, Aldershot, 1994. Edward Elgar.

Hagemann, H., editor. *Business Cycle Theory (Selected Texts 1860-1939).* Pickering & Chatto, London, 2002.

Hagemann, H., and H.-M. Trautwein. Cantillon and Ricardo Effects. Hayek's Contributions to Business Cycle Theory. *The European Journal of the History of Economic Thought*, 5, 1998.

Hardy, D. C., and C. Pazarbaşioğlu. Determinants and Leading Indicators of Banking Crises: Further Evidence. *IMF Staff Papers, International Monetary Fund*, 46(3): 247–258, December 1999.

Harrod, R. F. An Essay in Dynamic Theory. *Economic Journal*, 49:14–33, 1939.

Harrod, R. F. *Towards a Dynamic Economics.* Macmillan, London, 1948.

Hausmann, R., and L. Rojas-Suárez. *Banking Crises in Latin America.* Inter-American Development Bank and Johns Hopkins University Press, Washington, 1996.

Hawtrey, R. G. *Good and Bad Trade: An Inquiry into the Causes of Trade Fluctuations.* Constable & Co., London, 1913.

Hawtrey, R. G. The Trade Cycle. In American Economic Association, editor, *Readings in Business Cycle Theories*, London, (1926) 1950. Allen and Unwin.

Hayek, F. A. *Monetary Theory and the Trade Cycle.* Harcourt, Brace & Co., New York, 1933.

Hayek, F. A. *Prices and Production.* Kelley, New York, 2nd edition, (1935) 1967.

Hayek, F. A. *Profits, Interest and Investment.* George Routledge & Sons, London, 1939.

Hicks, J. R. *A Contribution to the Theory of the Trade Cycle.* Oxford University Press, Oxford, 1950.

Hirsch, M. W., and S. Smale. *Differential Equations, Dynamical Systems, and Linear Algebra.* Academic Press, New York, 1974.

Honohan, P., and D. Klingebiel. Controlling the fiscal costs of banking crises. World Bank Policy Research Paper 2441, World Bank, Washington, 2000.

Hopf, E. Abzweigung einer periodischen Loesung von einer stationaeren Loesung eines Differential-Systems. *Berichte der Mathematisch-Physikalischen Koeniglich-Saechsischen Academie der Wissenschaften Leipzig*, 94:1–22, 1942.

Hubbard, R. G. Is There a "Credit Channel" for Monetary Policy? *Federal Reserve Bank of St. Louis Review*, 77(3):63–77, May/June 1995.

International Moneary Fund (IMF). *World Economic Outlook. Financial Crises: Causes and Indicators.* International Monetary Fund, Washington, D.C., May 1998a.

International Moneary Fund (IMF). *World Economic Outlook. Financial Turbulence and the World Economy.* International Monetary Fund, Washington, D.C., October 1998b.

International Moneary Fund (IMF). *World Economic Outlook. Asset Prices and the Business Cycle.* International Monetary Fund, Washington, D.C., May 2000.

International Moneary Fund (IMF). *World Economic Outlook. Recessions and Recoveries.* International Monetary Fund, Washington, D.C., April 2002.

International Monetary Fund (IMF). *Global Financial Stability Report - Market Developments and Issues.* International Monetary Fund, Washington, D.C., September 2003a.

International Monetary Fund (IMF). *World Economic Outlook. Growth and Institutions.* International Monetary Fund, Washington, D.C., April 2003b.

Ishii, S., and K. Habermeier. Capital Account Liberalization and Financial Sector Stability. IMF Occasional Paper 211, International Monetary Fund, Washington, D.C., 2002.

Jaffee, D., and J. Stiglitz. Credit Rationing. In B.M. Friedman and F.H. Hahn, editor, *Handbook of Monetary Economics*, volume II, pages 837–888. Elsevier Science Publishers, 1990.

Jarchow, H.-J. *Theorie und Politik des Geldes 1.* UTB, Vandenhoeck and Ruprecht, Goettingen, Zurich, 10th edition, 1998.

Johansen, L. Substitution vs. Fixed Coefficients in the Theory of Economic Growth: A Synthesis. *Econometrica*, 27, 1959.

Jorgensen, D. Capital Theory and Investment Behaviour. *American Economic Review*, 53(2):247–259, 1963.

Kaldor, N. A Model of the Trade Cycle. *Economic Journal*, 50:78–92, 1940.

Kalecki, M. A Macroeconomic Theory of Business Cycles. *Econometrica*, 3:327–344, 1935.

Kalecki, M. A Theory of the Business Cycle. *Review of Economic Studies*, 4:77–97, 1937.

Kalecki, M. *Selected Essays on the Dynamics of the Capitalist Economy.* Cambridge University Press, Cambridge (GB), 1971.

Kamin, S. B. The Current International Financial Crisis: How Much is New? *Journal of International Money and Finance*, 18:501–514, 1999.

Kaminsky, G. L. Currrency and Banking Crises: The Early Warnings of Distress. International Finance Discussion Papers 629, Board of Governors of the Federal Reserve System, 1998.

Kaminsky, G. L., S. Lizondo, and C. M. Reinhart. Leading Indicators of Currency Crises. IMF Working Paper WP/97/79, International Monetary Fund, Washington, D.C., 1997.

Kaminsky, G. L., and C. M. Reinhart. Financial Crises in Asia and Latin America: Then and Now. *The American Economic Review (AEA Papers and Proceedings)*, 88 (2):444–448, May 1998.

Kaminsky, G. L., and C. M. Reinhart. The Twin Crises: The Causes of Banking and Balance-of-Payments Problems. *The American Economic Review*, 89(3):473–500, June 1999.

Kaminsky, G. L., and S. L. Schmukler. Short-Run Pain, Long-Run Gain: The Effects of Financial Liberalization. NBER Working Paper WP 9787, National Bureau of Economic Research, 2003.

Keynes, J. M. *The General Theory of Employment, Interest and Money.* Macmillan, London, 1936.

Keynes, J. M. The General Theory of Employment. *Quarterly Journal of Economics*, 51: 209–232, 1937.

Kindleberger, C. *Manias, Panics, and Crashes.* John Wiley & Sons, Inc., New York, 4th edition, 2000.

Kiyotaki, N., and J. Moore. Credit Cycles. *Journal of Political Economy*, 105(2):211–248, 1997.

Krugman, P. A Model of Balance-of-Payments Crises. *Journal of Money, Credit and Banking*, 11:311–325, 1979.

Krugman, P. *Peddling Prosperity.* W.W. Norton & Company, London, New York, 1994.

Krugman, P. *What Happened to Asia?* http://web.mit.edu/krugman/www/ DISINTER.html, Download on October 17, 2003, 1998.

Krugman, P. *Analytical Afterthoughts on the Asian Crisis.* http://web.mit.edu/krugman/www/MINICRIS.htm, Download on October 17, 2003, 1999a.

Krugman, P. *Balance Sheets, the Transfer Problem, and Financial Crises.* http://web.mit.edu/krugman/www/FLOOD.pdf, Download on October 17, 2003, 1999b.

Krugman, P. *Crises: The Next Generation.* Draft prepared for Razin Conference, Tel Aviv University, March 25-26, 2001, http://econ.tau.ac.il/research/sapir/Krugman.pdf, Download on October 17, 2003, 2001.

Krugman, P., and L. Taylor. Contractionary Effects of Devaluation. *Journal of International Economics*, 8:445–456, August 1978.

Kydland, F., and E. C. Prescott. A Competitive Theory of Fluctuations and the Feasibility and Desirability of Stabilization Policy. In S. Fischer, editor, *Rational Expectations and Economic Policy. A Conference Report*, pages 169–198, Chicago, 1980. University of Chicago Press for NBER.

Kydland, F., and E. C. Prescott. Time to Build Aggregate Fluctuations. *Econometrica*, 50(6):1345–1370, 1982.

Kydland, F. E., and E. C. Prescott. Rules rather than Discretion: The Inconsistency of Optimal Plans. *Journal of Political Economy*, 85(3):473–491, 1977.

Lamfalussy, A. *Financial Crises in Emerging Markets.* Yale University Press, New Haven, 2000.

Lavington, F. *The English Capital Market.* Methuen, London, 1921.

Leijonhufvud, A. *On Keynesian Economics and the Economics of Keynes: A Study in Monetary Theory.* Oxford University Press, New York, 1968.

Leijonhufvud, A. *Information and Coordination: Essays in Macroeconomic Theory.* Oxford University Press, New York, 1981.

Levine, R. Financial Development and Economic Growth. *Journal of Economic Literature*, 35:688–726, June 1997.

Lindgren, C.-J., G. Garcia, and M. I. Saal. *Bank Soundedness and Macroeconomic Policy.* International Monetary Fund (IMF), Washington, D.C., 1996.

Long, J. B., and C. I. Plosser. Real Business Cycles. *Journal of Political Economy*, 91 (1):39–69, 1983.
Lorenz, H.-W. *Nonlinear Dynamical Economics and Chaotic Motion.* Springer Verlag, New York, Berlin, Heidelberg, 2nd edition, 1993.
Lucas, R. E. Expectations and the Neutrality of Money. *Journal of Economic Theory*, 4: 103–124, 1972.
Lucas, R. E. An Equilibrium Model of the Business Cycle. *Journal of Political Economy*, 83:1113–1144, 1975.
Lucas, R. E. Understanding Business Cycles. In K. Brunner and A.M. Meltzer, editors, *Stabilization of the Domestic and International Economy*, pages 7–29, Amsterdam, 1977a. North Holland.
Lucas, R. E. Understanding Business Cycles. *Journal of Monetary Economics*, 3 (Supplement):7–30, 1977b.
Lucas, R. E. Methods and Problems in Business Cycle Theory. *Journal of Money, Credit and Banking*, 12:696–715, 1980.
Lucas, R. E. Tobin and Monetarism: A Review Article. *Journal of Economic Literature*, 19:558–567, 1981.
Lucas, R. E. Supply-Side Economics: An Analytical Review. *Oxford Economic Papers*, 42:293–316, 1990.
Lux, T. A Note on the Stability of Endogenous Cycles in Diamond's Model of Search and Barter. *Journal of Economics*, 56(2):185–196, 1992.
Mankiw, N. G. Real Business Cycles: A New Keynesian Perspective. *Journal of Economic Perspectives*, 3:79–90, 1989.
Mankiw, N. G., and D. Romer (eds.). *New Keynesian Economics*, volume I-II. The MIT Press, Cambridge, 1991.
Mansur, A., and J. Whalley. Numerical Specification of Applied General Equilibrium Models: Estimation, Calibration, and Data. In H. E. Scarf and J. B. Shoven, editors, *Applied General Equilibrium Analysis*, pages 69–127, New York, 1984. Cambridge University Press.
Marsden, J. E., and M. McCracken. *The Hopf Bifurcation and Its Applications.* Applied Mathematical Sciences Vol. 19. Springer, New York, Berlin, Heidelberg, 1976.
Mas-Colell, A. *Notes on Price and Quantity Tâtonnement Dynamics.* Springer, New York, Berlin, Heidelberg, 1986.
Mauro, P. Stock Returns and Output Growth in Emerging and Advanced Economies. IMF Working Paper WP/00/89, International Monetary Fund, Washington, D.C., May 2000.
Mayer, C. International Comparison of Financial Structures. In *Gertler et al.*, 1991.
McCallum, B. T. Rational Expectations and Macroeconomic Stabilization Policy. *Journal of Money, Credit and Banking*, 12:716–746, 1980.
McKinnon, R. I. *Money and Capital in Economic Development.* Brookings Institution, Washington, D.C., 1973.
McKinnon, R. I. *The Order of Economic Liberalisation: Financial Control in the Transition to a Market Economy.* John Hopkins University Press, Baltimore, MD, 2nd edition, 1993.
McKinnon, R. I., and D. J. Matthieson. How to Manage a Repressed Economy. Essays in International Finance No. 145, International Finance Section, Princeton University, New Jersey, December 1981.

McKinnon, R. I., and H. Pill. Credible Liberalizations and International Capital Flows: The Overborrowing Syndrome. In Ito, T. and A.O. Krueger, editor, *Financial Deregulation and Integration in East Asia*, pages 7–24. Chicago Universtiy Press, 1996.

McKinnon, R. I., and H. Pill. Credible economic liberalizations and overborrowing. *American Economic Review*, 87(2):189–203, 1997.

McKinnon, R. I., and H. Pill. International Overborrowing: A Decomposition of Credit and Currency Risk. Working Paper 98-004, Stanford University, Februray 1998.

McKinnon, R. I., and H. Pill. The Overborrowing Syndrome: Are East Asian Economies Different? In R. Glick, editor, *Managing Exchange Rates and Capital Flows: Lessons from the Pacific Basin*, New York, NY, 1999. Cambride University Press.

Meltzer, A. *Sustaining Safety and Soundness: Supervision, Regulation, and Financial Reform.* World Bank, Washington, 1995.

Metzler, L. A. The Nature and Stability of Inventory Cycles. *Review of Economics and Statistics*, 23:113–129, 1941.

Milesi-Ferretti, G. M., and A. Razin. Current Account Reversals and Currency Crises: Empirical Regularities. NBER Working Paper 6620, National Bureau of Economic Research, Cambridge, Massachusetts, 1998.

Miller, M., and J. Stiglitz. Bankruptcy Protection against Macroeconomic Shocks. mimeo, The World Bank, 1999.

Minsky, H. P. Financial Stability Revisited: The Economics of Desaster. In *Reappraisal of the Federal Reserve Discount Mechanism*, volume 3, pages 95–136, Washington, D.C., 1972. Board of Governors of the Federal Reserve System.

Minsky, H. P. *John Maynard Keynes.* Columbia University Press, New York, 1975.

Minsky, H. P. The Financial Instability Hypothesis: An Interpretation of Keynes and an Alternative to Standard Theory. *Nebraska Journal of Economics and Business*, 16(1), 1977.

Minsky, H. P. The Financial Instability Hypothesis: A Restatement. *Thames Papers in Political Economy*, Autumn 1978.

Minsky, H. P. *The Business Cycle and Public Policy, 1929-80, Joint Economic Committee.* Congress of the United States, U.S. Government Printing Office, Washington, D.C., 1980a.

Minsky, H. P. Capitalist Financial Processes and the Instability of Capitalism. *Journal of Economic Issues*, 14(2), 1980b.

Minsky, H. P. The Financial-Instability-Hypothesis: Capitalist Processes and the Behaviour of the Economy. In Charles P. Kindleberger and Jean-Pierre Laffargue, editors, *Financial Crises: Theory, history, and policiy*, pages 13–47, Cambridge (GB), New York, Sydney, 1982a. Cambridge University Press.

Minsky, H. P. *Inflation, Recesssion and Economic Policy.* Wheatsheaf Books Ltd, 1982b.

Minsky, H. P. *Stabilizing an Unstable Economy.* Yale University Press, New Haven, 1986.

Mishkin, F. S. Asymmetric Information and Financial Crises: A Historical Perspective. In R. G. Hubbard, editor, *Financial Markets and Financial Crises*, pages 69–108, Chicago, 1991. University of Chicago Press.

Mishkin, F. S. Symposium on the Monetary Transmission Mechanism. *Journal of Economic Perspectives*, 9(4):3–10, 1995.

Mishkin, F. S. Understanding Financial Crises: A Developing Country Perspective. In *Annual World Bank Conference on Development Economics*, pages 29–62. The World Bank, 1996.

Mishkin, F. S. The Causes and Propagation of Financial Instability: Lessons for Policymakers. In *Maintaining Financial Stability in a Global Economy - A Symposium Sponsored by the Federal Reserve Bank of Kansas City, Jackson Hole, Wyoming, August 28-30, 1997*, pages 55–96. Federal Reserve Bank of Kansas City, 1997.

Mishkin, F. S. The Dangers of Exchange-Rate Pegging in Emerging Market Countries. *International Finance*, 1(1):81–102, 1998a.

Mishkin, F. S. Promoting Japanese Recovery. In K. Ishigaki and H. Hino, editors, *Towards Restauration of Sound Banking Systems in Japan - the Global Implications*, pages 130–161, Kobe, 1998b. Kobe University Press.

Mishkin, F. S. Global Financial Instability: Framework, Events, Issues. *Journal of Economic Perspectives*, 13(4):3–20, 1999a.

Mishkin, F. S. Lessons from the Asian Crisis. *Journal of International Money and Finance*, 18:709–723, 1999b.

Mishkin, F. S., and S. G. Eakins. *Financial Markets and Institutions.* Addison-Wesley, New York, 3rd edition, 2000.

Mitchell, W. C. *Business Cycles and Their Causes.* University of California Press, Berkeley, California, 1941.

Modigliani, F., and M. H. Miller. The Cost of Capital, Corporate Finance, and the Theory of Investment. *American Economic Review*, 48:261–297, 1958.

Montiel, P., and C. M. Reinhart. The Dynamics of Capital Movements to Emerging Market Economies During the 1990s. In Montes Griffith-Jones, editor, *Short-term Capital Movements and Balance of Payments Crises*, Oxford, 1999. Oxford University Press.

Montiel, P. J., P.-R. Agénor, and N. Ul Haque. *Informal Financial Markets in Developing Countries.* Blackwell, Oxford (UK), Cambridge (USA), 1993.

Moore, G. H. *Business Cycles, Inflation and Forecasting.* Ballinger for NBER, Cambridge, Massachusetts, 2nd edition, 1983.

Morck, R., A. Schleifer, and R. W. Vishny. The Stock Market and Investment: Is the Market a Sideshow? *Brookings Papers on Economic Activity*, 2:157–202, 1990.

Mullins, M., and S. Wadhwani. The Effect of the Stock Market on Investment. *European Economic Review*, 33:939–961, May 1989.

Myers, S. The Capital Structure Puzzle. *The Journal of Financial Economics*, 52:261–297, 1984.

Nakaso, H. The Financial Crisis in Japan During the 1990s: How the Bank of Japan Responded and the Lessons Learnt. BIS Working Paper 6, Bank for International Settlements (BIS), Basle, Switzerland, October 2001.

Nasica, E. *Finance, Investment and Economic Fluctuations:.* Edward Elgar, Cheltenham (UK), Northhampton (US), 2000.

Nerlove, M. Expectations, Plans, and Realizations in Theory and Practice. *Econometrica*, 51:1251–1258, 1984.

Obstfeld, M. Rational and self-fulfilling balance of payments crises. *American Economic Review*, 76:72–81, 1986.

Obstfeld, M. The Logic of Currency Crises. Working Paper 4640, National Bureau of Economic Research (NBER), Cambridge (MA), February 1994.

Obstfeld, M. Destabilizing effects of exchange rate escape clauses. NBER Working Paper WP 2603, National Bureau of Economic Research, 1997.

Obstfeld, M., and K. Rogoff. *Foundations of International Macroeconomics.* The MIT Press, Cambridge (Massachusetts), London (England), 4th edition, 1999.

Palley, T. I. *Post Keynesian Economics: Debt, Distribution and the Macro Economy.* Macmillan Press, London, 1996.

Palma, G. The Three Routes to Financial Crises: The Need for Capital Controls. CEPA Working Paper Series III, International Capital Markets and the Future of Economic Policy Research 18, Center for Economic Policy Analysis, November 2000.

Persson, T., and G. Tabellini. *Macroeconomic Policy, Credibility and Politics.* Harwood Academic Publishers, 1990.

Phelps, E. S. Substitution, Fixed Proportions, Growth and Distribution. *International Economic Review*, 4, 1963.

Poterba, J. M., and A. A. Samwick. Stock Ownership Patters, Stock Market Fluctuations, and Consumption. *Brookings Paper on Economic Activity*, 2:295–357, 1995.

Prasad, E. S., K. Rogoff, S.-J. Jin, and A. Kose. Effects on financial globalization on developing countries: Some empirical evidence. IMF Occasional Paper 220, International Monetary Fund, Washington, D.C., 2003.

President's Working Group on Financial Markets. Hedge Funds, Leverage, and the Lessons of Long-Term Capital Management. Technical report, U.S. Government, Washington, D.C., April 1999.

Radke, M. P. *Währunskrisenmodelle der ersten Generation.* http:// www.uni-hohenheim.de/ wi-theorie/ 1generation.pdf, 2000a.

Radke, M. P. *Währunskrisenmodelle der zweiten Generation - Teil 1.* http:// www.uni-hohenheim.de/ wi-theorie/ 2generation.pdf, 2000b.

Radke, M. P. *Währunskrisenmodelle der zweiten Generation - Teil 2.* http:// www.uni-hohenheim.de/ wi-theorie/ 2generation2.pdf, 2000c.

Robbins, L. *The Great Depression.* Macmillan, New York, 1934.

Roberts, P. C. My Time with Supply-Side Economics. *The Independent Review*, 7(3): 393–397, winter 2003.

Rodrik, D. Who Needs Capital-Account Convertibility? Essays in International Finance No. 207, International Finance Section, Princeton University, New Jersey, May 1998.

Rojas-Suarez, L., and S. R. Weisbrod. Financial Market Fragilities in Latin America: The 1980s and 1990s. IMF Occasional Paper 132, International Monetary Fund, Washington, D.C., October 1995.

Rose, H. On the Non-Linear Theory of the Employment Cycle. *Review of Economic Studies*, 34:153–173, 1967.

Sachs, J. D. Wages, Flexible Exchange Rates, and Macroeconomic Policy. *The Quarterly Journal of Economics*, 94(4):731–747, June 1980.

Sachs, J. D., and F. Larrain. *Macroeconomics in the Global Economy.* Harvester Wheatsheaf, New York, 1993.

Sachs, J. D., A. Tornell, and A. Velasco. Financial Crises in Emerging Markets: The Lessons from 1995. *Brookings Papers on Economic Activity*, 1:147–215, 1996.

Samuelson, P. A. Interactions Between the Multiplier Analysis and the Principle of Acceleration. *Review of Economics and Statistics*, 21:75–78, 1939.

Sargent, T. J., and N. Wallace. Rational Expectations and the Dynamics of Hyperinflation. *International Economic Review*, 14:328–350, 1973.

Sargent, T. J., and N. Wallace. Rational Expectations, the Optimal Monetary Instrument, and the Optimal Money Supply Rule. *Journal of Political Economy*, 83:241–254, 1975.

Schwartz, A. J. Understanding 1929-1933. In K. Brunner, editor, *The Great Depression Revisited*, pages 5–48. Martinus Nijhoff, 1981.
Schwartz, A. J. Real and Pseudo-Financial Crises. In R. M. Kushmeider and W. S. Haraf, editors, *Restructuring Banking and Financial Services in America*, pages 34–62, Washington, D.C., 1986. American Enterprise Institute.
Schwartz, A. J. Why Financial Stability Depends on Price Stability. *Economic Affairs*, pages 21–25, Autumn 1995.
Schwartz, A. J. Comment on 'Debt-Deflation and Financial Instability: Two Historical Explorations' by B. Eichengreen and R. Grossman. In F. Capie and G.E. Wood, editors, *Asset Prices and the Real Economy*, pages 100–105. St. Martin's Press, 1997.
Semmler, W. *Asset Prices, Booms and Recessions.* Springer, Berlin, Heidelberg, New York, 2003.
Shaw, E. S. *Financial Deepening in Economic Development.* Oxford University Press, New York, 1973.
Sheng, A. *Bank Restructuring: Lessons for the 1980s.* World Bank, Washington, D.C., 1996.
Shiller, R. *Irrational Exuberance.* Princeton University Press, Princeton, 2000.
Shleifer, A., and L. Summers. The Noise Trader Approach to Finance. *Journal of Economic Perspectives*, 4(2):19–33, 1990.
Slutsky, E. *The Summation of Random Causes as the Source of Cyclic Processes*, volume 3. Conjuncture Institute, Moscow, 1927.
Solow, R. Technical Progress, Capital Formation and Economic Growth. *American Economic Review (Papers and Proceedings)*, 52, 1962.
Solow, R., J. Tobin, C.C. v. Weizsäcker, and M. Yaari. Neoclassical Growth with Fixed Factor Proportions. *Review of Economic Studies*, 33, 1966.
Spahn, H. P. Glaubwürdigkeit, Zeitinkonsistenz und Zinsdifferenzen in einem System fester Wechselkurse. *Kredit und Kapital*, 29:511–527, 1996.
Spahn, H. P. Credibility, Reputation, and the Instability of the EMS. In A. J. Cohen, editor, *Money, Financial Institutions, and Macroeconomics*, pages 235–251, Boston, 1997. Kluwer.
Spiethoff, A. Krisen. In *Handwörterbuch der Staatswissenschaften*, volume 6, pages 8–91, 1925.
Stiglitz, J. Capital Market Liberalization, Economic Growth, and Instability. *World Development*, 28(6):1075–1086, 2000.
Stiglitz, J., and A. Weiss. Credit Rationing in Markets with Imperfect Information. *American Economic Review*, 71:393–410, 1981.
Stiglitz, J., and A. Weiss. Asymmetric Information in Credit Markets and its Implications for Macro-Economics. *Oxford Economic Papers*, 44:694–724, 1992.
Stretton, H. Neoclassical Imagination and Financial Anarchy. *World Development*, 28 (6):1061–1073, 2000.
Summers, L. H. Some sceptical observations on real business cycle theory. *Quarterly Review Federal Reserve Bank of Minneapolis*, 10:23–27, 1986.
Summers, L. H. International Financial Crises: Causes, Prevention, and Cures. *American Economic Review (Papers and Proceedings)*, 90(2):1–16, 2000.
Sundararajan, V., and T. Baliño. Issues in Recent Banking Crises. In V. Sundararajan and T. Baliño, editors, *Banking Crises: Cases and Issues*, pages 1–57, Washington, 1991. International Monetary Fund.

Sveriges Riksbank (Bank of Sweden). Monetary Policy Rules. *Journal of Monetary Economics*, 43(3):521–704, June 1999.

Taylor, J. B. Discretion versus Policy Rules in Practice. *Carnegie-Rochester Conference Series on Public Policy*, 39:195–214, 1993.

Taylor, L. *Structuralist Macroeconomics.* Basic Books, New York, 1983.

Taylor, L. A Stagnationist Model of Economic Growth. *Cambridge Journal of Economics*, 9:383–403, 1985.

Taylor, L. *Income Distribution, Inflation, and Growth: Lectures on Structuralist Macroeconomic Theory.* The MIT Press, Cambridge (Massachusetts), London (England), 1991.

Taylor, L. External Liberalization, Economic Performance, and Distribution in Latin America and Elsewhere. UNU/WIDER Working Papers 215, The United Nations University UNU, World Institute for Development Economics Research, Helsinki, Finland, December 2000.

Taylor, L., and S. O'Connell. A Minsky Crisis. *Quarterly Journal of Economics*, 100: 871–886, 1985.

Tobin, J. A General Equilibrium Approach to Monetary Theory. *Journal of Money, Credit and Banking*, 1:15–29, 1969.

Tobin, J. Keynesian Models of Recession and Depression. *American Economic Review, Papers and Proceedings*, 65(2):195–202, 1975.

Tobin, J. Monetary Policies and the Economy: The Transmission Mechanism. *Southern Economic Journal*, 44(3):421–431, 1978.

Tobin, J., and W. C. Brainard. Asset Markets and the Cost of Capital. In R. Nelson and B. Balassa, editors, *Economic Progress: Private Values and Public Policy (Essays in Honor of William Fellner)*, pages 235–262, Amsterdam, 1977. North-Holland.

Tobin, J., and W. H. Buiter. Long-Run Effects of Fiscal and Monetary Policy on Aggregate Demand. In J. L. Stein, editor, *Monetarism*, Amsterdam, 1976. North-Holland.

Tobin, J., and W. H. Buiter. Fiscal and Monetary Policies, Capital Formation, and Economic Activity. In G. von Furstenberg, editor, *Government and Capital Formation*, volume II, pages 73–151, Ballinger, Cambridge MA, 1980.

Townsend, R. Optimal Contracts and Competitive Markets with Costly State Verification. *Journal of Economic Theory*, 21:265–293, 1979.

Trautwein, H.-M. Money, Equilibrium, and the Business Cycle: Hayek's Wicksellian Dichotomy. *History of Political Economy*, 28(1):27–55, 1996.

Trautwein, H.-M. The Credit View, Old and New. *Journal of Economic Surveys*, 14(2): 37–41, 2000.

Triffin, R. The Evolution of the International Monetary System: Historical Reappraisal and Future Perspectives. Princeton Studies in International Finance No. 12, International Finance Section, Princeton University, New Jersey, 1998.

Tugan-Baranowskii, M. *Les crises industrielle en Angleterre.* Giard & Brière, Paris, 2nd edition, (1894) 1913.

Turnovsky, S. J. *Macroeconomic Analysis and Stabilization Policy.* Cambridge University Press, Cambridge, 1977.

Turnovsky, S. J. *Methods of Macroeconomic Dynamics.* The MIT Press, 2nd edition, 2000.

Turnovsky, S. J., and M. H. Miller. The Effects of Government Expenditure on the Term Structure of Interest Rates. *Journal of Money, Credit and Banking*, 16:16–33, 1984.

U.S. Council of Economic Advisors. *Economic Report of the President and Annual Report of the Council of Economic Advisors.* Number 8. U.S. Government, Washington D.C., 1999.

van Wijnbergen, S. Credit Policy, Inflation and Growth in a Financially Repressed Economy. *Journal of Development Economics*, 13, 1983a.

van Wijnbergen, S. Interest Rate Management in LDCs. *Journal of Monetary Economics*, 12:433–452, 1983b.

Velasco, A. Financial crises and balance of payments crises. *Journal of Development Economics*, 27:263–283, 1987.

Velasco, A. *The Impossible Duo? Globalization and Monetary Independence in Emerging Markets.* http://ksghome.harvard.edu/~avelasco.academic.ksg/research.html, Download on October 17, 2003, May 2001.

Velasco, A. *IS-LM-BP in the Pampas.* http://ksghome.harvard.edu/~avelasco.academic.ksg/research.html, Download on October 17, 2003, November 2002.

Villa, A. *Asset Price Crises and Banking Crises: Some Empirical Evidence.* Bank of England, Bank for International Settlements, http://www.bis.org/pubs/confer08.pdf, Download on October 10, 2004, 2001.

Werner, R. A. *Princes of the Yen.* M. E. Sharpe, Armonk, London, 2003.

Wicksell, K. *Interest and Prices: A Study of the Causes Regulating the Value of Money.* Macmillan, London, (1898) 1936.

Wiggins, S. *Introduction to Applied Nonlinear Dynamical Systems and Chaos.* Springer, New York, Berlin, Heidelberg, 1990.

Williamson, J. What Washington Means by Policy Reform. In J. Williamson, editor, *Latin American Adjustment: How Much Has Happened?*, Washington, D.C., 1990. Institute for International Economics.

Williamson, J. What Should the World Bank Think about the Washington Consensus? *The World Bank Research Observer*, 15(2):251–264, August 2000.

Williamson, J., and M. Mahar. A Survey of Financial Liberalization. Essays in International Finance No. 211, International Finance Section, Princeton University, New Jersey, November 1998.

Willman, A. The Collapse of the Fixed Exchange Rate Regime with Sticky Wages and Imperfect Substitutability Between Domestic and Foreign Bonds. *European Econmomic Review*, 32:1817–1838, 1988.

Woodford, M. Stationary Sunspot Equilibria in a Finance Constrained Economy. *Journal of Economic Theory*, 40:128–137, 1986.

Woodford, M. Three Questions about Sunspot Equilibria as an Explanation of Economic Fluctuations. *American Economic Review, Papers and Proceedings*, 77:938, 1987.

Woodford, M. Imperfect financial intermediation and complex dynamics. In J. Geweke W. Barnett and K. Shell, editors, *Economic Complexity: Chaos, Sunspots, Bubbles, and Nonlinearities*, pages 309–334, Cambridge, 1988. Cambridge University Press.

Woodford, M. Finance, Instability, and Cycles. In W. Semmler, editor, *Financial Dynamics and Business Cycles: New Perspectives*, pages 18–37, New York, London, 1989. M. E. Sharpe, Inc.

Yan-Qian, Y. *Theory of Limit Cycles.* Translations of Mathematical Monographs 66. The American Mathematical Society, Providence, 1986.

Zarnowitz, V. *Business Cycles*, volume 27 of *NBER Studies in Business Cycles.* The University of Chicago Press, Chicago, London, 1992.

HOHENHEIMER VOLKSWIRTSCHAFTLICHE SCHRIFTEN

Band 1 Walter Deffaa: Anonymisierte Befragungen mit zufallsverschlüsselten Antworten. Die Randomized-Response-Technik (RRT). Methodische Grundlagen, Modelle und Anwendungen. 1982.

Band 2 Thomas Michael Baum: Staatsverschuldung und Stabilisierungspolitik in der Demokratie. Zur neoinstitutionalistischen Kritik der keynesianischen Fiskalpolitik. 1982.

Band 3 Klaus Schröter: Die wettbewerbspolitische Behandlung der leitungsgebundenen Energiewirtschaft. Dargestellt am Beispiel der Fernwärmewirtschaft der Bundesrepublik Deutschland. 1986.

Band 4 Hugo Mann: Theorie und Politik der Steuerreform in der Demokratie. 1987.

Band 5 Max Christoph Wewel: Intervallarithmetische Dependenzanalyse in der Ökonometrie. Ein konjekturaler Ansatz. 1987.

Band 6 Heinrich Pascher: Die U.S.-amerikanische Deregulation Policy im Luftverkehrs- und Bankenbereich. 1987.

Band 7 Harald Lob: Die Entwicklung der französischen Wettbewerbspolitik bis zur Verordnung Nr. 86-1243 vom 01. Dezember 1986. Eine exemplarische Untersuchung der Erfassung der Behinderungsstrategie auf der Grundlage des Konzepts eines wirksamen Wettbewerbs. 1988.

Band 8 Ulrich Kirschner: Die Erfassung der Nachfragemacht von Handelsunternehmen. Eine Analyse der ökonomischen Beurteilungskriterien und der wettbewerbsrechtlichen Instrumente im Bereich der Verhaltenskontrolle.1988.

Band 9 Friedhelm Herb: Marktwirtschaftliche Innovationspolitik. 1988.

Band 10 Claus Schnabel: Zur ökonomischen Analyse der Gewerkschaften in der Bundesrepublik Deutschland. Theoretische und empirische Untersuchungen von Mitgliederentwicklung, Verhalten und Einfluß auf wirtschaftliche Größen. 1989.

Band 11 Jan B. Rittaler: Industrial Concentration and the Chicago School of Antitrust Analysis. A Critical Evaluation on the Basis of Effective Competition. 1989.

Band 12 Thomas Märtz: Interessengruppen und Gruppeninteressen in der Demokratie. Zur Theorie des Rent-Seeking. 1990.

Band 13 Andreas Maurer: Statistische Verfahren zur Ermittlung von oligopolistischen Strukturen. 1990.

Band 14 Peter Mendler: Zur ökonomischen und politisch-institutionellen Analyse öffentlicher Kredithilfen. 1992.

Band 15 Heinrich J. Engelke: Die Interpretation der Rundfunkfreiheit des Grundgesetzes: Eine Analyse aus ökonomischer Sicht. 1992.

Band 16 Thomas Fischer: Staat, Recht und Verfassung im Denken von Walter Eucken. Zu den staats- und rechtstheoretischen Grundlagen einer wirtschaftsordnungspolitischen Konzeption. 1993.

Band 17 Stefan Elßer: Innovationswettbewerb. Determinanten und Unternehmensverhalten. 1993.

Band 18 Reinhard Scharff: Regionalpolitik und regionale Entwicklungspotentiale. Eine kritische Analyse. 1993.

Band 19 Karin Beckmann: Probleme der Regionalpolitik im Zuge der Vollendung des Europäischen Binnenmarktes. Eine ökonomische Analyse. 1995.

Band 20 Bernd Nolte: Engpaßfaktoren der Innovation und Innovationsinfrastruktur. Eine theoretische und empirische Analyse für ländliche Wirtschaftsräume in Baden-Württemberg. 1996.

Band 21 Klaus-Rainer Brintzinger: Die Nationalökonomie an den Universitäten Freiburg, Heidelberg und Tübingen 1918 - 1945. Eine institutionenhistorische, vergleichende Studie der wirtschaftswissenschaftlichen Fakultäten und Abteilungen südwestdeutscher Universitäten. 1996.

Band 22 Steffen Binder: Die Idee der Konsumentensouveränität in der Wettbewerbstheorie. Teleokratische vs. nomokratische Auffassung. 1996.

Band 23 Alexander Burger: Deregulierungspotentiale in der Gesetzlichen Rentenversicherung. Reformnotwendigkeiten versus Reformmöglichkeiten. 1996.

Band 24 Burkhard Scherer: Regionale Entwicklungspolitik. Konzeption einer dezentralisierten und integrierten Regionalpolitik. 1997.

Band 25 Frauke Wolf: Lorenzkurvendisparität. Neuere Entwicklungen, Erweiterungen und Anwendungen. 1997.

Band 26 Hans Pitlik: Politische Ökonomie des Föderalismus. Föderative Kompetenzverteilung im Lichte der konstitutionellen Ökonomik. 1997.

Band 27 Stephan Seiter: Der Beitrag Nicholas Kaldors zur Neuen Wachstumstheorie. Eine vergleichende Studie vor dem Hintergrund der Debatte über den Verdoorn-Zusammenhang. 1997.

Band 28 André Schmidt: Ordnungspolitische Perspektiven der europäischen Integration im Spannungsfeld von Wettbewerbs- und Industriepolitik. 1998.

Band 29 Bernd Blessin: Innovations- und Umweltmanagement in kleinen und mittleren Unternehmen. Eine theoretische und empirische Analyse. 1998.

Band 30 Oliver Letzgus: Die Ökonomie internationalen Umweltschutzes. 1999.

Band 31 Claudia Hafner: Systemwettbewerb versus Harmonisierung in Europa. Am Beispiel des Arbeitsmarktes. 1999.

Band 32 Jürgen Kulle: Ökonomie der Musikindustrie. Eine Analyse der körperlichen und unkörperlichen Musikverwertung mit Hilfe von Tonträgern und Netzen. 1998.

Band 33 Michael Ganske: Intertemporale Aspekte von Staatsverschuldung und Außenhandel. 1999.

Band 34 Margit Ströbele: Die Deregulierungswirkungen der europäischen Integration. Das Beispiel der Sondermärkte. 1999.

Band 35 Marion Benesch: Devisenmarktinterventionen in Theorie und Praxis. Eine umfassende Analyse ihrer Zielsetzungen, Wirkungsweisen und wirtschaftspolitischen Bedeutung. 1999.

Band 36 Torsten Gruber: Unterschiedliche geldpolitische Transmissionsmechanismen und Stabilitätskulturen als mögliche Ursachen geldpolitischer Spannungen in der Europäischen Währungsunion. 2000.

Band 37 Bertram Melzig-Thiel: Arbeit in der Informationsgesellschaft. Chancen und Risiken neuer Informations- und Kommunikationstechnologien für die Beschäftigung. 2000.

Band 38 Annette Fritz: Die Entsorgungswirtschaft im Spannungsfeld zwischen Abfallpolitik und Kartellrecht. Eine industrieökonomische Branchenstudie. 2001.

Band 39 Harald Strotmann: Arbeitsplatzdynamik in der baden-württembergischen Industrie. Eine Analyse mit amtlichen Betriebspaneldaten. 2002.

Band 40 Dietrich Benner: Qualitätsungewißheit bei Gütern mit Vertrauenseigenschaften. Entwicklung und Anwendung eines entscheidungstheoretisch fundierten Analyserahmens. 2002.

Band 41 Jürgen M. Schechler: Sozialkapital und Netzwerkökonomik. 2002.

Band 42 Kay-Uwe May: Haushaltskonsolidierung durch Ausgabekürzungen. Restriktionen und Strategien. 2002.

Band 43 Peter Kühnl: Der Wechselkurs als Zwischenziel der Geldpolitik im Aufholprozess. Die monetärkeynesianische Entwicklungsstrategie der Berliner Schule vor dem Hintergrund der makroökonomischen Entwicklung ausgewählter Länder Mittel- und Osteuropas. 2003.

Band 44 Steffen Wirth: Nichtparametrische Analyse von Bildungsertragsraten. Neuere Entwicklungen und Anwendungen. 2003.

Band 45 Bernhard Holwegler: Innovation, Diffusion und Beschäftigung. Die ökonomische Theorie der Technologiediffusion und ihr Beitrag zur Erklärung technologischer Arbeitslosigkeit. 2003.

Band 46 Guntram R. M. Hepperle: Zukunftsorientierte Industriepolitik. Möglichkeiten und Grenzen. 2004.

Band 47 Udo Vullhorst: Stabilisierungspolitik bei supranationaler Geldpolitik und nationaler Fiskalpolitik. Eine spieltheoretische Betrachung. 2004.

Band 48 Matthias Rösch: Die Bedeutung von Investivlöhnen und Gewinnbeteiligungen für Einkommensverteilung und Beschäftigung. 2004.

Band 49 Michael Bubik: Erfolgskriterien für Unternehmenszusammenschlüsse. Eine theoretische und exemplarische Analyse. 2005.

Band 50 Jörg Weltin: Internationale Unternehmensbesteuerung. Allokation der Besteuerungsrechte unter veränderten Rahmenbedingungen. 2005.

Band 51 Susanne Reichart: Zum Konvergenzprozess der mittel- und osteuropäischen EU-Beitrittsländer. 2005.

Band 52 Daniel Hartmann: Geldpolitik und Beschäftigung. Die geldpolitische Strategie der Federal Reserve: Vorbild oder Auslaufmodell? 2005.

Band 53 Marc Peter Radke: Explaining Financial Crises. A Cyclical Approach. 2005.

www.peterlang.de

Torsten Wezel

Determinants of Foreign Direct Investment in Emerging Markets

An Empirical Study of FDI Flows from Germany and its Banking Sector

Frankfurt am Main, Berlin, Bern, Bruxelles, New York, Oxford, Wien, 2005.
XII, 189 pp., num. fig. and tab.
Studien zu internationalen Wirtschaftsbeziehungen.
Edited by Michael Frenkel. Vol. 5
ISBN 3-631-53343-8 · pb. € 39.–* / US-$ 43.95 / £ 25.50
US-ISBN 0-8204-7658-7

Emerging markets frequently feature strong economic growth but also unique risks – political instability, legal uncertainty and corruption – which constitute barriers to foreign direct investment (FDI). This study analyzes empirically whether superior investment profiles of recipient countries matter for German FDI in addition to typical determinants such as labor costs, level of income and market openness. The specifics of banking FDI are also examined, notably the impact of incipient banking crises abroad and the risk-mitigating property of multilateral development banks acting as stakeholders in individual FDI projects. The concluding part highlights recent initiatives of international organizations to lower investment barriers, fight corruption and strengthen financial system stability.

Contents: Determinants of German Foreign Direct Investment in Latin America and Asia · Foreign Bank Entry into Emerging Economies: Determinants and Risks · Does Co-Financing by Multilateral Development Banks Increase "Risky" FDI?